Managing Technological Innovation

JOHN E. ETTLIE

Rochester Institute of Technology

John Wiley & Sons, Inc.

New York   Chichester   Weinheim   Brisbane   Singapore   Toronto

ACQUISITIONS EDITOR	Beth Lang Golub
ASSISTANT EDITOR	Samantha Alducin
MARKETING MANAGER	Jessica Garcia
SENIOR PRODUCTION EDITOR	Patricia McFadden
DESIGNER	Kevin Murphy
ILLUSTRATION EDITOR	Anna Melhorn
PRODUCTION MANAGEMENT	Hermitage Publishing Services

This book was set in 10/12 Garamond by Hermitage Publishing Services and printed and bound by Hamilton Printing. The cover was printed by Phoenix Color, Inc.

This book is printed on acid-free paper.

Library of Congress Cataloging in Publication Data

ISBN 0-471-31546-x

Printed in the United States of America

10 9 8 7 6 5 4 3 2

Preface

What's new? People ask that question but do they really want to know the answer? We are all attracted to what is new and different, some with fear and loathing. But change is here to stay and technological innovation is often at the heart of this novelty. Technological innovations can cause change in unanticipated and unintended ways. Park-Davis, the well-known drug division of Warner-Lambert, recently decided to change its production technology for the drug Nitrostat. Nitrostat is a heart medicine used to relieve the pains caused by angina. When the old technology to produce Nitrostat broke down and the new technology did not work, there was a Nitrostat shortage that caused a panic around the country. This is not the way you want to make the headlines of the *New York Times*.

Although technology can cause problems, it also can create enormous benefits for society. The computer, the airplane, and antibiotics are some examples of how technology benefits us. One cannot ignore our dependence on these breakthroughs as well as the minor improvements they make over the years to improve the quality of life. Developments literally push their way into our daily lives and they will do so forever.

This book is about technological change from the broad perspective of managers and professionals who must thrive and prosper in modern organizations. Most new products and services require at least some, sometimes extensive, changes in operations and information systems. Customers, distributors, and suppliers are affected by, if not the drivers of, change. Significant resources are expended every year on innovations all over the world. Dollars, yen, and pounds—you pick the currency. All this is done to launch new products, information systems, offices, plants, and equipment or for changes in methods in nearly every type of organization around the world. The intention is to impress customers, improve control, and reduce costs with as little pain as possible. Although things do not always work out as they are planned, as in the Parke-Davis case with Nitrostat, many of these problems can be avoided. The purpose of this book is to help eliminate the unnecessary and avoidable stresses caused by new technology.

The book is organized into four sections. These sections follow the typical life cycle of a technological innovation. Ideas for new technology are generated, grow, and are nurtured, commercialized, become successful or unsuccessful, and then mature. Then they are eventually replaced by the next generation of technologies. It may be somewhat comforting to remind ourselves that in spite of all these changes in technology, the problem or purpose of technology very rarely changes. It is only our way of dealing with the problem that changes. New technology does not replace or completely depose the existing modus operandi. Rather, the new technology takes its place right along side of the other technologies of earlier eras. Fax machines did not replace the telephone or mail service. The Internet has not replaced fax machines.

The first section of this book introduces the innovation process and raises the major issues and theories for managers (technological innovation, the innovation process, and the theory behind innovation). The second section is devoted to innovation planning (strategy, research and development management, and economic justification). The third section is devoted to the implementation of these plans (product innovation, operations strategy, and process innovation). The final section of the book discusses the management of future technologies (public policy, globalization, and management issues) and reinforces the central premise of this book—that integration issues must be confronted and managed in order to capture value from technological innovation in organizations.

Organizations are inherently complex and the addition of technological change increases the complexity to a level that would challenge any manager, professional, or concerned citizen. It is essential that we meet this fundamental fact head on. Technological change is not going to go away. There are ways of dealing with these changes and taking charge of the path to the future.

Integrating technology and change management within a firm and its environment (e.g., suppliers) is the key to understanding competitive capability. For example, product and process can not be separated. Managing the integration of these factors is an essential focus of the book. The linking of the appropriate organizational innovation with technological innovations is the secret to any successful change management process.

Managing Technological Innovation is designed for business students at all educational levels. It is also useful for change agents, engineering managers, project managers, program and brand managers, policy makers, and administrators in all professions. This book is helpful for anyone who encounters some form of technological change in their every day lives and for people who, in their careers and private life, will confront significant technological transitions.

The book can be used in different ways. It can be used as a primary text for an advanced undergraduate course. It can be used as required reading with little or no supplements. The text contains many exercises, cases for analyses, and several self-assessment tools. At the end of each chapter, longer cases are suggested for those who have the interest and the time to further explore the subject. Footnotes contain suggested readings.

If the book is used for a graduate course, such as an elective in technology management at a business or engineering college, then it serves well as a reader for the different segments of a typical course in this field. It can also be supplemented with other readings. If the text is used for a graduate business course, the book should be supplemented with an in-depth case on the subject being discussed. The materials that are chosen for this book are based on over 25 years of classroom testing. Finally, anyone interested in an introduction to the subject of innovation will find this book interesting and useful – especially reading chapters one and twelve.

This book can be many things to many different audiences. Some material might be viewed by some as strictly "academic." Kurt Lewin once said that there is nothing so practical as a good theory. The academic material in this book was purposely included to create a bridge between the academic and applied world of technological innovation.

However, you the reader chooses to use this book, it is a subject matter very pertinent to the world as it exists today. Technological change is at the heart of any cultural evolution in our society. Change may be inevitable, but the form and the outcomes of technological change are not predestined.

John E. Ettlie
January 2000

Acknowledgments

Unlike other book projects, this text was, and will no doubt be, a life's work. Therefore, my first humble thanks extend outside the scope of this book and the time period in which this book was written. When one thinks of the phrase "if it hadn't been for... this book would have never been written," the first person that comes to mind is Professor Albert H. Rubenstein. Al was my mentor at Northwestern University and his extraordinary patience with me eventually led to my thesis work in this field. I am always grateful to him.

I took my first "great books" course as independent study from Professor Gilbert Krulee, also during my years at Northwestern. It is unlikely that I would have chosen this profession if it had not been for Gil. As I have told him, when I find myself facing a difficult professional decision, I often ask myself what Gil would have done in this situation? Gil's style in the classroom left a lasting impression on me. Those were the best days, and even now, those hours in his courses are still fresh in my mind.

Over the years, I have been extremely fortunate to be blessed with many wonderful collaborators who rank with me as the best of the best colleagues. They never raised their voices, but they always made their point. Robert O'Keefe, William Bridges, Dave Vellenga, Steve Rosenthal, Jane Dutton, and Michael Johnson are among these cherished peers and friends. This book would not have been complete unless some of their ideas were in it. I thank them for their influence. Starting during the period of our first large innovation study, and more recently during my years at the University of Michigan, Karl Weick was a source of excellent advice and wisdom on a broad range of topics in this field and in the ethics of publishing. I also want to thank all of the graduate students I have worked with over the years who have significantly enriched my academic life. Among them Ernesto Reza, Joan Penner-Hahn, and Peter Swan have been the most tolerant.

This idea for this book was born at a professional conference in Chicago many years ago when Beth Golub and I had coffee and discussed the first "serious" proposal for this project. If I had been satisfied with the materials available for the technology management course I taught, there would have been no book. Beth agreed with me, and perhaps even more importantly, she convinced me to frame the project broadly, not just for the course I was teaching at the time but to take a wider scope. Of course, that advice came later when the project was well underway and Beth was the Wiley editor on the book. But without her persistence and encouragement, there would have been no book.

This book has gone through two rounds of formal reviews and insightful referees provided a tremendous service to the project with their comments and preferences. This is always one of the most difficult parts of the textbook writing process, but it is also one of the most important stages of the development of any work. I am in their debt. I would like to thank the following reviewers for their assistance in the development of the book: Daniel Berg, Rensselaer Polytechnic Institute, Michael B. Elmes, Worcester Polytechnic Institute, Mark Frohlich, London Business School, Kirk R. Karwan, University of South Carolina, Sara L. Keck, Pace University, D.N. Mallick, Boston College, John W. Medcof, McMaster University, Eric Munro, Keller Graduate School of Management, Karol I. Pelc, Michigan Technological University, Robert J. Schlesinger, San Diego State University, Gary Scudder, Vanderbilt University , and Hans Thamhain, Bentley College.

My colleagues and students who have persistently asked for the book to be finished so they could use it or recommend its use were the final source that sustained me professionally on this project. The opportunity to use drafts of the book in the classroom here and overseas was instrumental in developing this text. I thank Professor Arnd Huchzermeier and Horst Wildermann for the opportunity they gave me to globalize this project.

My MBA classes at the University of Michigan Business school led directly to the starting and finishing of this project. I thank each and every one of the students who took my course on technology management at Michigan over the years. I especially want to thank the MBA class of spring 1999 who used a draft version of this book as their text. These students made valuable suggestions on content and format. Professor Robert Haessler first suggested that I develop a new course and teach it as an operations elective. I want to thank him for that suggestion. Without Bob's instigation, there would have been no book because there would have been no course to teach.

Several of my family members were both directly and indirectly involved in this project. My daughter Gretchen had the most direct impact on the book with her help on permissions and other endless tasks with citations and details. My father Joseph Ettlie gave me the opportunity to learn on the job about technology or the absence of successful innovation, which was the inspiration for my first thesis topic in this field. And, of course, my wife Naza sustained me throughout this project and shares the "life" work aspect of this book.

My mentors and sources of inspiration have played no part in any flaws that appear in this book. They are mine alone to claim. I hope the value of other people's work that I have tried to capture here will shine through any shortcomings, and that others who follow will be encouraged by the book to carry on the traditions of the subject we all serve. If the text stimulates just one new and unique creative idea, I will have accomplished my purpose.

Contents

Section One

Getting Started with Innovation

Chapter 1

Technological Innovation

𝒞HAPTER OBJECTIVES

To introduce technological innovation and to illustrate the challenge of managing new technology using the cases of Webvan and the Denver International Airport (DIA) at the end of the chapter.

Technological innovations change our lives daily. Every new model car is different, every computer release challenges current knowledge, and every new medical finding opens the door to possible life-saving treatments. Technology-induced changes in the workplace profoundly affect organizational effectiveness, careers, and workplace comfort. Some companies leverage technology to sustain success; others do not. Either way, addressing the issue of technological change in the workplace is critical, for three primary reasons.

1. Technology-driven change is everywhere and always present.
2. Competitors use technology as part of major success strategies.
3. Value-capture from new technology is challenging and never guaranteed.

Most of the time, we hold technology as a constant, because it's convenient. This book assumes that change is the norm. As soon as the difference is forgotten, our jobs are at risk. March and Simon[1] were among the first to systematically address the issue of when innovation occurs in organizations. In 1958, they said that change is initiated in organizations primarily as a result of two forces—internal pressures, resulting from changes in the aspiration level of members, and external

---

[1] J. March and H. Simon, *Organizations* (New York, John Wiley & Sons, 1958).

pressures, which render existing performance levels inadequate. In extreme cases—when the environment changes abruptly or *jolts* the organization into reaction—the rate of innovation is likely to increase.

This book is about mastering technological change. Most of what has been written about this subject is either about the research and development (R&D) process or about the new products themselves. That is not surprising, since most R&D funds are spent on new-product introduction, and that is a considerable amount. In 1994, U.S. companies spent nearly $100 billion on R&D, according to a National Science Foundation report.[2] If all other R&D is included (e.g., government and university research), this figure doubles to more than $200 billion a year. These investments can have enormous impact on the life of a corporation. But R&D and new-product introduction are not the only factors in technological change. Take, for example, the "air war" between Honeywell and Litton, which raises nearly all the issues you need to begin understanding the nature of the technological innovation process.[3]

During the 1970s, Honeywell started intense development of a new type of gyroscope to make airplane navigation safer. After a series of critical events, Honeywell went from being a small player to being the dominant force in the market, controlling 90% of the orders. In the process, Honeywell left the former giant in the field, Litton, in its wake. Clever customer dealing, continuous improvement of the new technology, and leveraging this technology with the **attacker's advantage**[4] eventually forced Litton to resort to the last defense—the courtroom.

And there is yet another, equally important side to managing new technologies—integrating the three key functions of the firm (marketing, R&D, and operations). Nearly every new product or new service requires a new or modified process for implementation. U.S. companies spent more than $1 trillion for computer systems during the decade 1983–1993.[5] Are the benefits of these investments and others like it fully realized? Probably not.

DEFINING TECHNOLOGICAL INNOVATION

There are numerous ways to define technology, innovation, and change, and all of these definitions have merit for the purposes of this book. It is a matter of using the definition that best suits your purpose and approach to this subject. Several of these common definitions are summarized in Box 1-1.

The last definition from Professor Edward Roberts is adopted for this book and is reintroduced in Chapter 2. This definition is used because it is the most general; that is, it is not confined to just R&D, and it draws attention to the difference between an **idea** (invention) and the **commercialization** or **application** of this idea (an innovation).

---

[2] National Science Foundation, Division of Science Resources Studies, *Research and Development in Industry* (Washington, D.C.: U.S. Government Printing Office, 1994).

[3] W.M. Carely. "Air War: How Honeywell Beat Litton to Dominate Navigation-Gear Field." *Wall Street Journal* (September 20, 1996), p. A1.

[4] A. N. Foster, *Innovation: Attacker's Advantage* (New York: Summit Books, 1986).

[5] *Forbes* (March 29, 1993).

BOX 1-1

Definitions

Technology refers to "the theoretical and practical knowledge, skills, and artifacts that can be used to develop products and services as well as their production and delivery systems. Technology can be embodied in people, materials, cognitive and physical processes, plants, equipment, and tools."[6]

Invention versus innovation: "Invention is the creation of a new idea, but innovation is more encompassing and includes the process of developing and implementing a new idea."[7]

R&D/Innovation can be thought of as "another term for the process whereby new and improved products, processes, materials, and services are developed and transferred to a plant and/or market. Typically, this process is represented in the firm by a number of formally organized laboratories, departments, groups, teams and functions ... most easily recognized ... involve scientists and engineers."[8]

Managing for innovation in R&D is described in this way: "Employee perspectives and behaviors, and their subsequent effects on performance, can be significantly affected through systematic and creative use of staffing and career decisions ... (for example) regular placement of new members into project groups may perform an energizing and destabilizing function."[9]

Management of technology is defined as linking "engineering, science, and management disciplines to plan, develop, and implement technological capabilities to shape and accomplish the strategic and operational objectives of a organization."[10]

Innovation is defined as **invention + exploitation**.[11]

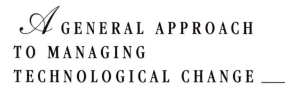

$\mathcal{A}$ GENERAL APPROACH TO MANAGING TECHNOLOGICAL CHANGE _____

In this book the spotlight is turned directly on the issue of how to capture the benefit called the **appropriation of rents**[12] from product and process innovation. In

---

[6] R. A. Burgelman, M. A. Madique, and S. C. Wheelwright (eds.), *Strategic Management of Technology and Innovation* (2nd ed.) (New York: McGraw-Hill, 1996), p. 2.

[7] A. H., Van de Van and Harold L Angle, "An Introduction to the Minnesota Innovation Research Program," in Van De Ven H. Angle, and M. Poole (eds.), *Research on the Management of Innovation* (New York: Ballinger Publishing Company, 1989), p. 12.

[8] A. H. Rubenstein, *Managing Technology in the Decentralized Firm* (New York: John Wiley & Sons, 1989), p. 1.

[9] R. Katz, "Managing Creative Performance in R&D Teams," in R. Katz (ed.), *The Human Side of Managing Technological Innovation* (New York: Oxford, 1997), 184.

[10] National Research Council Report, *Management of Technology: The Hidden Competitive Advantage,* (Washington, D.C.: U.S. Government Printing Office, 1987).

[11] E. B. Roberts. Managing invention and innovation, *Research-Technology Management,* (January–February 1988), pp. 11–29.

[12] D. J. Teece. "Capturing Value from Knowledge Assets: The New Economy, Markets for Know-how, and Intangible Assets," *California Management Review,* 40, no. 3 (Spring 1998), pp. 55–79.

most situations, process innovation is not developed within an organization but is at least partially purchased from the outside. Therefore, the unique challenge is to turn this investment to competitive advantage when much of this technology is also available to competitors. The theme is simple: To effectively manage product and process transitions, one must ultimately have intimate knowledge of the relationship between technological innovation processes and the administrative system of any enterprise.

Technological innovation and organizational innovation

The more change in the technology of products, services, and operations, the more changes in administrative procedures—new strategies, new organizational structures, and new operating procedures—will be required to successfully capture the potential benefits of the venture (see Figure 1-1). The failures of technological change typically occur when either too much technology is adopted too quickly (lower right of Figure 1-1) or not enough technology is adopted to stay ahead of competitors (upper left of Figure 1-1).

A recent case example might illustrate this challenge. A post-audit manager from a large durable goods manufacturing firm was requesting assistance in developing new policies for dealing with technology and machine tool suppliers. The company had decided to reorganize production from a traditional structure, in which machines and departments are grouped by function and technology, to cellular manufacturing. His company had just invested $200 million and a tremendous effort to upgrade its main facility. In the end, only a third of the anticipated and required capacity was attained. In other words, it was a very expensive failure in transition management. How could this failure have been prevented? One of the purposes of this book is to offer reasonable answers to this question. Part of the answer in the case of cellular manufacturing lies in how companies work with their technology suppliers.

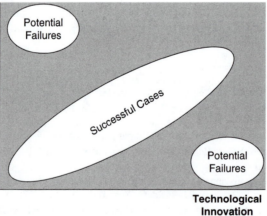

Figure 1-1   Successful Management of the Innovation Process

Source: Based on J. E. Ettlie, *Taking Charge of Manufacturing* (San Francisco: Jossey-Bass, 1988).

$\mathcal{T}$ECHNOLOGY MATTERS _____

Austrian economist Joseph Schumpeter was among the first to systematically argue that "individuals with vision gambling their own and investors' money on new products" is the engine that drives economic growth. A successful entrepreneur practices "creative destruction" of existing markets and competitors and fuels new economic growth. Competition between wired and cellular or wireless phones is a current example. Evidence for this theory includes the observation that protection of European markets stifles change and growth, while free markets in Asia, like Singapore, stimulate this process of creative destruction.[13]

Stanford economist Paul M. Romer carries on in the Schumpeter tradition by showing that technological discoveries are the driving engine of economic growth. More to the point, new ideas are what make the difference and are, at the same time, challenging. Land, machinery, and capital are scarce, but ideas and knowledge are abundant, and they don't follow the law of diminishing returns. Ideas build on each other and are reproduced cheaply. As you add more and more machinery, it delivers less and less additional output. Ideas, on the other hand, especially embodied in new technology, can continue to add value well beyond their cost. But the theory is not perfect. For example, critics of Professor Romer and his *new growth theory* point out that the United States has the most ideas and the greatest investments in generating new ideas, so why isn't it the fastest-growing economy? The answer is simple. The richest economies are never the fastest growing. This has important implications both for the amount of venture capital that might be made available by banks and for how much the U.S. government spends on big science projects such as magnetic levitation for trains.[14]

Productivity growth in the U.S. economy has, at least for the time being, returned to levels of the 1950s and 1960s—about 2 percent a year. Embedded in this figure are manufacturing productivity growth years of 3.2 percent in 1995, 3.7 percent in 1996, and 4 percent in 1997. These trends may have been previously hidden statistically by overstating the number of hours actually worked by employees. Since this "new economy" now appears to be real, it has to be explained. It has been argued that it has resulted from two primary factors: **trade** and **technology**. The reduction of the federal government's deficit has failed to remove America's chronic trade gap (about 1% of GDP), so this leaves only one explanation. Technology matters.[15]

A great deal of money is riding on that explanation. U.S. industry and government spent more than $150 billion on R&D in 1994 (industry's share was $132 billion; both numbers are rising). Another $250 billion is spent each year on new computer system technology. But does technology really make a difference?[16] Box 1-2 presents a summary of "technology matters" examples. Little of

---

[13] G. S. Becker, "Make the World Safe for 'Creative Destruction'," *Business Week* (February 23, 1998), p. 20.

[14] B. Wysocki, "Wealth of Notions: For this Economist, Long-term Prosperity Hangs on Good Ideas," *Wall Street Journal* (January 21, 1997), pp. A1, A8.

[15] "More Evidence of a New Economy," Editorials, *Business Week* (February 23, 1998), p. 138; and G. Koretz, "Is the Trade Gap a Ticking Bomb?" *Business Week* (February 23, 1998), p. 22.

[16] R. M. Wolfe, *Data Brief,* National Science Foundation, Directorate for Social, Behavioral and Economic Sciences, NSF 97-332 (December 16, 1997); See B. Wysocki, "Some Firms, Let Down by Costly Computers, Opt to 'De-Engineer," *Wall Street Journal* (April 30, 1998), pp. A-1, A-8.

BOX 1-2

Does Technology Matter?

1. U.S. durable goods manufacturers averaged 27 percent of new product revenues (introduced last five years), while the global average was 19 percent and new product firms averaged 49 percent.[17]

2. Introduction of catalytic cracking processes in the 1940s resulted in 98 percent labor cost savings, 80 percent savings in capital costs, and 50 percent savings in material inputs.[18]

3. U.S. manufacturing firms modernizing facilities in the late 1980s averaged a 32 percent reduction in scrap/rework; 54 percent through-put time reduction, and 59 percent reduction in service and warranty costs using new flexible automation.[19]

4. Successful business process reengineering (BPR) projects can achieve 75 percent or even 300 percent to 1000 percent improvements, but the "failure" rate is also high, at about 70 percent.[20]

5. Information system (IS) technology contributes 21 percent of the output of companies, and the average employee is six times more productive than the non-IS coworker.[21]

---

human endeavor or conditions is untouched by technology today. New products account for significant revenues,[22] new processes enhance productivity substantially, and business process reengineering (BPR) is a fact of life in many companies, in spite of the high failure rate of BPR (see Chapter 9).

---

[17] M. F. Wolf, "Meet Your Competition," Research Technology Management (Jan/Feb 1994), p. 18 ff. J. E. Ettlie, "Integrated Design and New Product Success," *Journal of Operations Management,* 40, no. 2 (April 1997), pp. 462–479; J. E. Ettlie and K. Sethuraman, "Resource-Based vs. Transactions-Cost Based Locus of Supply," working paper, 1997.

[18] Freeman C., *The Economics of Industrial Innovation* (2nd ed.) (Cambridge, Mass.: MIT Press, 1982).

[19] J. E. Ettlie and E. M. Reza, "Organizational Integration and Process Innovation," *Academy of Management Journal,* 35, no. 4 (1992), pp. 795–827.

[20] M. Hammer. "Reengineering Work: Don't Automate, Obliterate," *Harvard Business Review,* (July–August 1990), pp. 104–112; S. A. Thomas. "Re-engineering: The Hot New Managing Tool," *Fortune* (August 23, 1993), pp. 41–48; T. R. Rohleder and E. A. Silver. "A Tutorial on Business Process Improvement," *Journal of Operations Management,* 15 (1997), pp. 139–154.

[21] Gene Rovetz, "Computers May Really Be Paying Off," *Business Week* (February 14, 1994), p. 20.

[22] In one recent survey of 126 U.S. durable goods companies that had recently introduced at least one significant new product, the average percentage revenue from new products introduced during the last five years was 49 percent. In a random sample of 42 firms in these same industries (e.g., automobiles, machine tools, computers), taken at about the same time, the average percentage of revenues from new products was 27 percent. See, respectively, J. E. Ettlie, "Integrated Design and New Product Success," *Journal of Operations Management,* 15, no. 1 (February 1997), pp. 33–55; and J. E. Ettlie, "Product-process Development Integration in Manufacturing," *Management Science,* 41, no. 7 (July 1995).

TECHNOLOGY
AND LITERATURE _____

Literature has a rich tradition of exploring technology themes. Mark Twain had a churning, smoking steamboat bear down on Huck Finn in a raft on the Mississippi River. The irony is not lost on historians and history buffs, who know that Twain got his start as a riverboat captain (see Box 1-3).

Students of the history of technology also know that Mark Twain was the first writer to use a "type writing machine," the Remington No. 1, the first one ever made available to the general public. Obviously, there is more to technology and the human psyche, at least in American culture, than meets the eye.[23]

Mary Shelley spawned the **Frankenstein hypothesis** in her 1818 book *The Modern Prometheus,* later renamed *Frankenstein.* The Frankenstein hypothesis says that new technology will either immediately or eventually do more harm than good, no matter how honorable the intentions of the human creators. The unintended, negative consequences of technology are never balanced by the intended, positive outcomes.[24] Dr. Victor Frankenstein is, perhaps, the quintessential study of

---

BOX 1-3

Huck Finn Confronts the Steamboat

"…the night got gray and rather thick, which is the next meanest thing to fog. You can't tell the shape of the river, and you can't see no distance. It got to be very late and still, and then along comes a steamboat up the river. We lit the lantern, and judged she would see it … We could hear her pounding along, but we didn't see her good till she was close. She aimed right for us. Often they do that and try to see how close they can come without touching: sometimes the wheel bites off a sweep, and then the pilot sticks his head out and laughs, and thinks he's mighty smart … She was a big one, and she was coming in a hurry too, looking like a black cloud with rows of blow-worms round it; but all of a sudden she bulged out, big and scary, with a long row of wide open furnace doors shining like red-hot teeth, and her monstrous bows and guards hanging right over us. There was a yell at us, and jingling of bells to stop the engines, a powwow of cussing, and whistling of steam—and as Jim went overboard on one side and I on the other, she came smashing right through the raft."

SOURCE: Excerpt from *The Adventures of Huckleberry Finn,* Mark Twain (Samuel Langhorne Clemens), pp. 507, in *The Family Mark Twain* (New York: Harper & Brothers, 1935).

---

[23] The story of Samuel Clemens and the Remington No. 1 is retold in J. M. Utterback, *Mastering the Dynamics of Innovation* (Boston, Mass.: Harvard Business School Press, 1994), pp. 1–2.

[24] Ironically, the only U.S. federal agency ever charged specifically with the task of understanding and predicting the consequences of new technology was a branch of Congress, the Office of Technology Assessment (OTA). The OTA was discontinued after only 20 short years of service on September 30, 1995 in order to save money. The OMB (Office of Management and Budget), of the executive branch, does carry on some of OTA's mission, but only with a limp wrist. Cf., *Electricity Journal,* 8, no. 9 (November 1995), p. 3.

man unleashing forces that he only partially understands but plunging ahead nonetheless, in apparent arrogance.

A central theme of the book is that the *scale* of the human form that Dr. Frankenstein creates must be large to allow reanimation. The forces unleashed by the good doctor cannot be controlled or even predicted, and ultimately, he and his family are destroyed by the product of his genius. The "demon" is lost at the end of Shelley's book, his fate unknown. Society, as represented by other characters in the book, react violently to the monster. Immortality seems not only out of reach, but ultimately, undesirable.

The 1931 Universal Studios' movie *Frankenstein,* based on an 1823 play by Richard Brinsley Peake and a dramatization by Peggy Webling, captured on screen the frightening consequences of reaching for forbidden technology. Colin Clive's acting was superb as Dr. Frankenstein; his intense, maniacal stares at the power-generating equipment and test tubes are riveting. James Whale's direction creates an early climax in the film in the midst of a violent electrical storm, which gives life to the monster, played by Boris Karloff. The film is a blunt reminder that *not* all is well that ends well, as Shakespeare penned—great horrors can be inflicted along the way.

This theme is taken up in a different guise by Philip Dick in his 1968 book *Do Androids Dream of Electric Sheep?* which eventually became the movie *Bladerunner,* starring Harrison Ford as Rick Deckard. The Nexus-6 android is the focus of the book: a replicant of a human so perfect it can escape detection, even by the most expert of investigators. "Extra-clever andys," they are called in the book. Ultimately, the story is about manipulation of men and women—the Nexus-6 android "has evolved beyond a major—but inferior—segment of mankind. For better or worse," Deckard reflects early in the book. Now the Frankenstein monster does not stand out in a crowd as a deformed, caricature of a man, but can surpass a man or a woman, undetected to most. It lacks (the new hypothesis) only one human characteristic—empathy. Killing an android is referred to in the book as "retiring" it.

Kurt Vonnegut visits this theme in his first book, *Player Piano,* published in 1952. Vonnegut was a public relations agent for General Electric (GE) in New York in his early days, and was reacting to the company's attempt to automate the workplace with numerically controlled (NC) machine tools. The piano roll that calls the tune of the piano is like the roll of tape in the early NC machines of the 1950s, which encoded instructions for machine movement, theoretically replacing skilled operators. Like the modern chess player facing the IBM computer, Vonnegut's character, Paul Proteus, does battle with "Checker Charley," a computerized game player. Paul is winning and Charley's keeper, Fred Berringer, says: "...if Checker Charley was working right he couldn't lose."[25] Checker Charley proceeds to catch fire: "All the lights went on at once, a hum swelled louder and louder, until it sounded like a thunderous organ note, and suddenly died." Vonnegut's first book was prophetic: In reality, the perennial battle has been between chess-playing man and machine (see Box 1-4).

---

[25] K. Vonnegut Jr., *Player Piano* (New York: Delacorte Press, 1952), p. 50.

BOX 1-4

Machine Triumphs Over Man

IBM's Deep Blue Wins Chess Match

New York—In brisk and brutal fashion, IBM computer Deep Blue unseated humanity, at least temporarily, as the finest chess-playing entity on the planet yesterday, when Garry Kasparov, the world chess champion, resigned the sixth and final game of the match after only 19 moves, saying, "I lost my fighting spirit."

The unexpectedly swift dénouement to the bitterly fought contest came as a surprise, because until yesterday Mr. Kasparov had been able to match Deep Blue gambit for gambit.

The manner of the conclusion overshadowed the debate about the meaning of the computer's success. Grandmasters and computer experts alike went from praising the match as a great experiment, invaluable to both science and chess (if a temporary blow to the collective ego of the human race), to smacking their foreheads in amazement at the champion's abrupt crumpling.

SOURCE: B. Weber, *The Globe and Mail,* from *The New York Times* (May 12, 1997). Copyright © 1997 by the New York Times Co. Reprinted by permission.

Fact is always at least as amazing as fiction, and some would argue that it is more interesting because it really happened. But remember that Jules Verne predicted the use of nuclear-powered submarines and Isaac Asimov correctly predicted the use of earth-orbiting satellites for communications. It is not surprising that some technology forecasters use science fiction as their first stop in predicting the future.

$\mathcal{T}$RUTH IS STRANGER THAN FICTION

These examples of technological innovation and its consequences from well-known works of fiction often pale in the face of reality. Perhaps no disaster better illustrates the fallacy of technological invulnerability than the sinking of the *Titanic*.[26] The White Star Line's (Liverpool) famous "unsinkable" passenger ship was launched in Belfast by Harland and Wolff, Ltd., who were considered at the time to be the "highest priced and most painstaking shipbuilders in Europe." It sank early in the morning of April 15, 1912. Supposedly steaming fast on a quicker but more northern route, she struck an iceberg. Her lifeboats could accommodate only 1,178 people, or more than 1,000 short of the number aboard on the maiden

---

[26] What follows is drawn liberally from W. C. Wade, *The Titanic: End of a Dream* (rev. ed.) (New York: Penguin, 1986).

voyage. The *Titanic's* sister ship, *Olympic,* had sailed on its maiden voyage to New York on May 31, 1911, and it also carried fewer lifeboats than needed. But, *Shipbuilder* magazine had pronounced the ship "practically unsinkable," which eventually was shortened to just *unsinkable*. The vessels' airtight compartments did not allow for water overtaking the top of partition walls in the hull.

There were only a few detractors when the "twin monsters" first appeared. The *Economist* said the shipbuilders were trying to "lick creation," beyond underwriters' ability to insure them." The novelist, Joseph Conrad, opposed the "big ship movement," saying this was not progress—as if "elephantiasis, which causes a man's legs to become as large as tree trunks, would be a sort of progress, whereas it is nothing but a disease."

With nine steel decks, the *Titanic* was equivalent in height to an eleven-story building. Docked in a special birth in Southampton harbor on April 3, 1912, she rose out of the water "like the side of a cliff." Nearly 900 feet long, with four, 22-foot-diameter funnels, which rose 62 feet above the casing, the *Titanic* had everything. Suites, with spacious parlors and a private promenade deck, rented for $4,350 a day. The largest and most luxurious vessel on the water, the *Titanic* quickly acquired many nicknames besides "unsinkable." Included in the newspapers in England and the United States were accounts with names such as "the Wonder Ship," and "The Millionaires' Special." In fact, on the maiden voyage, first-class was at only 46 percent capacity, with 337 passengers. But most were captains of industry, with a combined worth of more than $500 million in 1912 dollars. These passengers included John Jacob Astor and Benjamin Guggenheim. J. P. Morgan missed the trip due to illness, although a cabin had been designated for him.

First-class passengers could use a gymnasium (which included a mechanical camel ride), the first swimming pool ever on a ship, a squash court, and a Turkish bath. There were elegant dining saloons, lounges, smoking rooms, libraries, and a grand saloon with concealed lighting behind a cathedral glass ceiling, giving the illusion of perpetual sunlight.

Second class was 40 percent booked with 271 passengers, and third class, or *steerage,* was booked to 70 percent capacity with 712 passengers, nearly all emigrants. Steerage was located forward and aft on the middle three decks and on the lowest passenger deck, and was named after an earlier practice in the 1860s when it was legal to transport people to one shore and then carry cattle back in the same quarters on the return trip. But accommodations on the *Titanic* for third class were nearly as good as the typical first- and second-class accommodations on other, smaller steamships of the day.

The crew and employees brought the total to 2,235 on board when the *Titanic* hit an iceberg at 10:25 on the evening of April 14, 1912; 1,522 were left in the water to perish when she sank.

When the *Titanic* sank, it ended the Victorian era, which began with the 1851 Great Exhibition in London's Hyde Park. Ironically, the exposition featured the equally huge yet appropriately elegant greenhouse called the Crystal Palace. When reports appeared that the band had played on the deck of the *Titanic* to the end (either "Autumn" or "Nearer, My God, to Thee"—it is disputed), Joseph Conrad objected to "such sentimentality," and was quoted as calling it "music to get drowned by."

In the aftermath, several uncanny, documented premonitions surfaced. Mayn Clew Garnet's story, "The White Ghost of Disaster," came off the presses at the same time the *Titanic* was preparing for its maiden voyage. Scheduled to appear in the May issue of *Popular Magazine,* the story told of an 800-foot liner that struck an iceberg and sunk, while only half the passengers on board could be saved because of insufficient lifeboats. Even more bizarre, Morgan Robertson's 1899 novel, *Futility,* featured an 800-foot liner named the *Titan* with a plot similar to the *Titanic* disaster.

With technology some tried to warn Captain Smith of iceberg danger—to no avail. A wireless message had arrived at 9 A.M. on April 12 from the *Caronia,* eastbound from New York to Liverpool, saying "West-bound steamers report bergs … in 42 degrees North from 49 degrees to 51 degrees West…"

With technology others aspired to raise the *Titanic,* when a consortium of wealthy families including the Guggenheims and Astors contracted with a wrecking company to attempt the job. They concluded in 1912 that their equipment was not up to the task, after six weeks of searching by four ships recovered only 328 bodies, including number 154, John Jacob Astor.

And, with new technology, still others would discover the wreck of the *Titanic* on September 1, 1985, when the U.S. Navy research vessel *Knorr* detected "unnatural forms" at 1:40 A.M. using the videocamera of the ARGO, a new robotic diver, operating 2.5 miles down. Technology for the mission was jointly developed by the French Institute for Research and Exploitation of the Sea, Woods Hole Oceanographic Institution, with funding from the National Geographic Society, and the U.S. Office of Naval Research. ARGO used sonar-guided videocameras, and a new French side-scanning sonar system on board the *Le Suroit* was capable of 3,000-foot-wide, highly detailed sweeps of the ocean floor. Closeups of the *Titanic* wreck were obtained from a second remote diver, the ANGUS. Technology had put the *Titanic* back in the headlines, but technology could not save the *Titanic* or her passengers on that night in April 1912.[27]

*H*ISTORY AND TECHNOLOGY

Historians have also taken a keen interest in technology, and classics on the subject like those of Lewis Mumford[28] and others are worthwhile reads. Burke's books[29] and his public television series have brought this subject to many who had never considered it interesting.

The history of the period of early modern automation in manufacturing takes on political overtones in books such as the *Forces of Production,* by David F. Noble,[30] beginning with the development of numerical control (NC) technology after World War II at MIT and funded by the U.S. Air Force. The central hypothesis of this well-written book is that NC was used by management in companies such as GE, to increase its control over the work force. The term **technological determinism** is

---

[27] J. P. Eaton and C. A. Haas, *Titanic: Destination Disaster—The Legends and Reality* (revised) (New York: W.W. Norton, 1996).

[28] L. Mumford, *Technics and Civilization* (New York: Harcourt, 1934).

[29] J. G. Burke and M. C. Eakin, *Technology and Change* (San Francisco: Boyd and Fraser, 1979).

[30] D. F. Noble, *Forces of Production* (New York: Oxford Press, 1984).

often used to describe this hypothesis—that technology is the force that shapes, irrevocably, the way we work. In sharp reaction to this hypothesis, technological determinism was the topic of early research and change process management methodologies such as the sociotechnical design school and workplace redesign efforts of later periods. The best examples of this work include Harvey Kolodny's work and the early work and foundations laid by Louis Davis and his associates, such as Jim Taylor,[31] which are discussed in Chapter 3.

Noble was quite aware of the fallacy of the technological determinism hypothesis. He shows how historically the development of NC programming and robotic programming took different technological development paths to the same end. NC programming eventually used a method of part and work fixture description encoded on tape (first paper, then milar), which modeled the metal removal process in mathematical space. Robotic programming used the "record–playback" method, in which you "teach" the robot to do the work by taking it through its paces manually and then recording the motion path on some memory device. During the early development period, both technologies were used, which may have been the inspiration, if unknowingly, for Vonnegut's *Player Piano*. How the tape is prepared does make a difference to Noble. The playback method clearly allows skilled labor to be part of the technology replacement process, not controlled completely by engineers or managers. In Kurt Vonnegut's recent book, *Time Quake* (1997), he says,

> Acculturated persons are those who find that they are no longer treated as the sort of people they thought they were, because the outside world has changed. An economic misfortune or a new technology, or being conquered by another country or political faction, can do that to people quicker than you can say Jack Robinson.

One of Noble's arguments, that management made a clear choice to use this technology to control the work force, is that there was no agreement at the time on how to economically justify the technology—that is, the technology could not be justified on purely economic grounds. Programming costs in early economic justification studies (1950s), in particular, were quite high, and did not endow the technology with great commercial potential.

As late as 1975, the U.S. Government Accounting Office (GAO) said, "There is no absolute method for predicting all costs associated with an N/C installation," and in 1983 Thomas Gunn from Arthur D. Little was quoted in a *Wall Street Journal* article as saying it took two to three times as much time and money to get the NC system working as opposed to existing technology.[32]

At the time, Harold Strickland, a representative of GE, said, "Our technical ability to automate exceeds our ability to prove economic feasibility."[33] This quote is typically echoed even by modern union representatives when they argue that management does not know what the outcomes will be when new technology is undertaken. Factory reorganization efforts such as those attempted "experiments" by GE—worker participation, quality circles, job enrichment, and job enlarge-

---

[31] J. C. Taylor and D. F. Felten *Performance by Design* (Englewood Cliffs, N.J.: Prentice-Hall, 1993).

[32] Both quoted in Noble, 1984, pp. 216 and 347, respectively.

[33] Noble, 1984, p. 216.

ment—were just further premeditated attempts by management to get more production out of the work force, according to Noble.

The Frankenstein hypothesis has now evolved into the idea that technology is dangerous because it is deskilling and dehumanizing. The implication is that this fate is worse than death. The empirical evidence to date, however, covering the thirty years of changing technology in manufacturing operations, fails to show any widespread deskilling, and in many situations, shows quite the opposite (c.f., Paul Adler's work).

Teams are in widespread use in the United States—82 percent of companies with more than 100 employees use teams.[34] Further, the use of teamwork typically has mixed results on productive outcomes, as well as on absenteeism and turnover. Most likely, this is because many other factors influence productivity (e.g., the size of the team) and personnel turnover. For example, unemployment rates affect the ability to get another job, and a *Wall Street Journal* article reports that 1.2 percent of the work force is leaving each month—a recent high in a booming economy.[35] However, teams consistently improve reported attitudes on the job.[36] These studies typically do not control for technology, and even in sociotechnical interventions, technology is considered a constant in the majority of settings.

$\mathscr{S}$CIENCE AND TECHNOLOGY

In sharp contrast to Noble's history of what he calls the "Second Industrial Revolution," J. Francis Reintjes focuses on the nature of university engineering research in *Numerical Control.* The nature of the work of bringing new technology to the marketplace is "long and unpredictable," and is likened to the "development" part of research and development (R&D). One of the decisions that has to be made is whether to seek a general solution to a problem or solve a specific subset of the problem.[37]

Indirectly, this account also shows how the ideal model of science being applied to guide engineering research is often not the case. In many situations, engineering research and solutions direct science to discover the physical principle or "law," rather than science guiding engineering. Reintjes tracks the history of NC beginning with William K. Linvill's 1949 dissertation in electrical engineering and John T. Parsons's visit to MIT in the same year in response to the call for a "power drive" or "power servomechanism." Parsons eventually secured Air Force funding for his project based on his experiments to produce airfoil shapes on machine tools driven automatically from data read from cards. He called his system the "Cardamatic milling machine."[38]

The first economic study on numerical control, described by Noble in *Forces of Production,* is also detailed by Reintjes. Was NC a commercially viable technology?

---

[34] S. G. Cohen, "What Makes Teams Work. Group Effectiveness Research From The Shop Floor to the Executive Suite," *Journal of Management*, 23, no. 3, (1997), p. 239.

[35] *Wall Street Journal,* October 7, 1997.

[36] J. E. Ettlie, *Taking Charge of Manufacturing* (San Francisco, Jossey-Bass, 1988).

[37] J. F. Reintjes, *Numerical Control* (New York: Oxford Press, 1991).

[38] Ibid., p. 18.

Only estimates of costs were possible, for a variety of reasons. Companies supplied parts for machining, and manual comparisons had to be supplied by these participating firms. Three years after inception, NC had per-part machining costs lower than outside estimates for manual production but "make-ready" costs (e.g., programming) were higher. Therefore, the overall costs in the MIT servo lab were higher than on the outside.

By 1958, data were available from other sources that confirmed this result. Machining costs and preparation, as well, were lower, but often programming costs were not included. In essence, programming was considered a development cost rather than a production cost, which allowed the development of NC to continue—especially since others were seeing benefits not normally included in cost estimates, like the machining of parts not normally attempted. The focus of development turned to programming to reduce its cost and increase its applicability, including the consideration of new programming languages.

Even when programming languages were developed, or refined, and systems for programming were simplified, including adaptations of the record–playback technique, a wide variance in performance of these NC technologies resulted. In one early, in-depth study conducted on site with plant personnel and nine different companies, NC utilization varied from 25 percent to 87 percent, based on two shifts of operation (see Table 1-1).[39] There was obviously more to performance outcomes with these technologies than the new system itself. This is taken up in great detail in subsequent chapters. But one has to ask the question: What accounts for this variance (see also Chapter 9)?

Next came the development of computer-aided design (CAD) and the linking of these two technologies. The automation of engineering work with CAD is a bit

$\mathcal{T}$ABLE 1-1   Historical NC Utilization Rates, Circa 1969

| Organization | Indicator/Score | | | | |
	Percent Time Utilized	Source	Precent Parts Done Wholly on NC	No. Shifts Operated	Final Ranking
A_1	25	time clock	*	$1/2$	9
A_2	65	chip time	*	1	4
A_3	54	chip time	*	1	5
A_4	30	time cards	*	> 1	8
B_1	*	*	75–80	2	3
B_2	75	time clock	*	2–3	2
B_3	40	chip time	50–75	2	6
C_1	*	*	10	1	7
C_2	87	spindle time	*	$2\,1/2$	1
C_3	Not included in this phase of data analysis				

* No records

---

[39] J. E. Ettlie, "Technology Transfer in the Machine Tool Industry," unpublished Masters Thesis, Northwestern University, 1971, p. 194g.

misleading, since computers were first applied to drafting and eliminated the need for the large wooden layout tables for pre-blueprint work. Much later, the computer was applied to engineering work and cathode-ray tubes (visual displays) were installed in engineering design offices as well as drafting studios.

$\mathcal{T}$ECHNOLOGY POLITICS

As illustrated by the two accounts (Noble and Reintjes) of the history of the development of NC technology, even when the facts agree, their interpretation differs. Reintjes rejoiced in the fact that some costs were lower with NC as early as three years after its birth in the lab. Noble saw this as the beginning of management tyranny. A more detailed comparison of this type is presented next. First, in Noble's camp, is another book by Beverly H. Burris, *Technocracy at Work*.[40] Burris defines technocracy as those forms of organizational control (technical control, bureaucracy, and professionalism) in the workplace—especially in computerized work settings, like telecommunications. Her history of technology emphasizes the control that structures being used to implement innovation have had over the work force, typical of the technological imperative—the idea that technology dictates all organizational forms and relationships.

Compare the Burris history with Jay Jaikumar's history of manufacturing in Table 1.2. Jaikumar was a Harvard Business School professor. In Burris's history, technocratic control begun in the 1960s has a deskilling force in the workplace. In Jaikumar's view shown in the last row entry under *skills required,* mechanical craft has evolved in many stages to experimentation in the numerical control era, roughly comparable to Burris's 1960s, and is succeeded by "learning, generalizing, abstracting" under computer-integrated manufacturing. The work philosophy of the last two epochs in Jaikumar's table are "control" and "develop." Note that Jaikumar's table also chronicles the exponential improvement in performance of manufacturing systems with each successive generation of production technology (e.g., rework progresses from 0.8 to 0.005 as a fraction of total work attempted).

Fast forward to 1998 and the United Auto Workers' strike of General Motors, and we have one of the most recent examples of technology and politics.[41] They used to say that what was good for GM was good for the country. They also used to say

---

[40] B. H. Burris, *Technocracy at Work* (Albany: State University of New York Press, 1993), especially page 6.

[41] Copyright by John E. Ettlie, June 1998, all rights reserved. Sources used for this case include, but are not limited to, the following: R. Blumenstein, R. L. Simison, and J. B. White, "Stepping on it: For GM, a Hard Line on Strike has Become a Matter of Necessity," *Wall Street Journal* (June 12, 1998), pp. A1, A4; F. S. Washington, "Smith Leads Revamping of GM Internal Education," *Automotive News* (June 22, 1998), p. 6; B. Vlasic, K. Naughton, and K. Kerwin. "If Ford Can Do It, Why Can't GM?" *Business Week* (June 29, 1998), pp. 36–38; R. Blumenstein and F. Warner, "GM Battles UAW More Aggressively Than Ever Before," *Wall Street Journal* (June 18, 1998), p. B12; F. Warner, "UAW Adopts Harder Stance in GM Fight," *Wall Street Journal* (June 24, 1998), p. A3; K. Jackson, "Strike Threatens Key Launches," *Automotive News* (June 22, 1998), pp. 1, 57; R. Blumenstein, "Hack-O-Gram Writer is Sent to Front Line of GM Strike," *Wall Street Journal* (June 29, 1998), pp. B1, B6; K. Kerwin, "The Shutdown GM Needs?" *Business Week* (July 13, 1998), pp. 34–36.

TABLE 1-2   Evolution of Manufacturing

| | 1800 | 1950 | 1900 1930 1940 1950 | 1970 | 1985 | 2000 |
	The English system of manufacture	The American system of manufacture	Scientific management (Taylorism)	Process improvement (statistical process control)	Numerical control	Computer-integrated manufacturing
Number of machines	3	50	150	150	50	30
Minimum efficient scale (number of people)	40	150	300	300	100	30
Indirect/direct labor ratio	0:40	20:130	60:240	100:200	50:50	20:10
Productivity increase over epoch	4:1	3:1	3:1	3:2	3:1	3:1
Rework as fraction of total work	0.8	0.5	0.25	0.08	0.02	0.005
Number of products	∞	3	10	15	100	∞
Engineering focus	Mechanical	Manufacturing	Industrial	Quality	Systems	Knowledge
Process focus	Accuracy	Repeatability	Reproducibility	Stability	Adaptability	Versatility
Control focus	Product functionality	Product conformance	Process conformance	Process capability	Product/ process integration	Process intelligence
Organizational change	Breakup of guilds	Staff/line separation	Functional specialization	Problem-solving teams	Cellular control	Functional integration
Work philosophy	"Perfect"	"Satisfy"	"Reproduce"	"Monitor"	"Control"	"Develop"
Skills required (machine operator)	Mechanical craft	Repetitive subskill	Repetitive subskill	Diagnostic ability	Experimentation	Learning, generalizing, abstracting

SOURCE: R. Jaikumar. "From filing and fitting to flexible manufacturing", Harvard Business School working paper, No. 88–045, Boston, 1988.

Reproduced in *IEEE Spectrum*, 30, no. 9 (1993), p. 27. © 1997 IEEE.

that the more union workers you had on your payroll, the more employees could afford to buy your cars.

Look at the issues that were contested in that strike and what was different this time. And let's focus on the single most important issue for the future, GM's failure to make good on a plan to invest all of a planned $300 million in the plant to upgrade production systems. GM balked at this investment when efficiency did not improve as forecast in the plant, and the UAW contended that the strike was set off by GM removing dies for a new product and shipping them to an Ohio plant, continuing its strategy to pit one local union against another. Not true. The strike was on, regardless. Blaming the strike on a few dies was not going to promote value capture from new technology. We return to this case in Chapter 9 and process innovation.

What has happened to all this technology and politics in the 1990s? See Box 1-5, "Where Have All The Robots Gone?" Ironically, the robots that revolutionized factories in the 1980s are now going into the "field" to save places like Three-Mile Island and Chernobyl. These are hostile-environment work-force

BOX 1-5

Where Have All the Robots Gone?

Where have all the robots gone? The answer, which is a modern symbol of Man's technology folly like the *Titanic,* is *Chernobyl.*

Robots were one of the major participating technology elements of the factory modernization revolution of the 1980s when countries would publish their annual new use and accumulated total of industrial robotics much like the space race of the 1960s and 1970s. Japan, the United States, and Germany were among the countries locked in serious competition to be the first to reach new levels of adoption and diffusion of robots in durable goods manufacturing like automotive body shops and paint systems. The incorporation of robots and other industrial automation technology allowing flexibility of operation through the use of programmable servomechanisms was an early step in a competitive strategy that elevated the manufacturing function to equal status with finance and marketing during that era.[42]

In the late 1980s U.S. robot sales slumped and bottomed out in 1987 at about $299 million. This was due, in part, to the fact that robots gradually became a decreasing proportion of the total investment and design of more integrated manufacturing systems being adopted in plant modernization programs. These systems included automated storage, retrieval, and materials handing technologies, large flexible manufacturing systems, and other hybrid manufacturing systems for mass customization and processing in a wide range of industries outside of durable goods such as the garment and clothing industries.[43]

During the next six years, the robot market hovered around $400 million a year and then began to take off again in 1993. In 1997, the market passed $1 billion. The market is still dominated by industrial buyers, but this category includes "field" robots. They were used first in places like Three-Mile Island to recover from that nuclear power plant disaster, and are now going to work at Chernobyl for cleanup. On April 26, 1986, the No. 4 nuclear reactor at Chernobyl, 75 miles north of Kiev, exploded. Chernobyl is one of the testing grounds for a new generation of robots that can withstand harsh conditions like maintaining offshore drilling platforms, disarming terrorist weapons, and exploring space, including space station construction, asteroid mining, and comet exploration.

The Chernobyl effort uses the Pioneer robot developed by a spin-off company from Carnegie Mellon University called RedZone Robotics, Inc. The development effort cost $2.7 million and was subsized by NASA and the U.S. Energy Department. The technology is being given to Ukraine, but some local officials—who continue to cope with Chernobyl's problems of deterioration and the aftermath of "nuclear lava" flows on a very limited budget—are skeptical. This budget has little slack for the experimentation with new robotic technology "toys," as one official refers to the

---

[42] R. Hayes and S. Wheelwright, *Restoring our Competitive Edge: Competing Through Manufacturing* (New York: John Wiley & Sons, 1984), pp. 192, 314, 351, 396–398.

[43] S. Baker and C. Matlack. "Chernobyl: If You Can Make It Here ... It's the Ultimate Proving Ground for Ultratough Robots," *Business Week* (March 30, 1998), pp. 168–169; J. Ettlie, *Taking Charge of Manufacturing,* 1988; L. M. Rausch, "International Patenting Trends in Manufacturing Technologies: Robots," National Science Foundation, Washington, U. S. Government Printing Office, Directorate for Social, Behavioral and Economic Sciences, NSF 99-343 (April 22, 1999). For more information see the NSF Web site: nsf.gov or call (301) 947-2722.

Pioneer. It is probably no coincidence that Ukrainian officials are somewhat resistant to providing the venue for this "rad-hard" robot (normal silicon chips could not withstand the radiation). The cost of the Pioneer robot is coming out of the U.S. $78 million contribution of the G-7, $758 million rehabilitation program. But the Pioneer, looking like a little bulldozer with a core borer and manipulator, hopes to make continued human exposure to radiation unnecessary and serve as a model for the next generation of robotics technology.

replacements. The market impact of this migration of robots to hazardous duty has been significant. After holding steady at about $400 million a year, the robot market took off in 1993. In 1997 the market passed $1 billion.

$\mathcal{T}$ECHNOLOGY AND ECONOMICS

Economists nominated numerical control as one of the major technologies of the era and studied it extensively. For example, in the cross-national study of the diffusion of new industrial processes, Nabseth and Ray included NC machine tools as their first chapter.[44] The advantages of using the technology were predicted to make significant improvements in manpower use, machining time, prolonged tool life, quality, and inventory savings.

The diffusion of NC machines is summarized in Figure 1-2. These diffusion curves clearly show the similarities and differences among countries in adoption of NC. In every country, larger firms (with more than 1,000 employees) adopt before smaller firms. On the other hand, Sweden and the United Kingdom were clearly ahead in adoption of this technology among sampled firms. The United States is not shown in Figure 1-3 but was slightly ahead of both Sweden and the United Kingdom, as would be expected, since the technology originated there.

Figure 1-3 shows the relationship between relative labor costs and diffusion; notice that the relationship between labor costs and adoption rates for NC is almost linear.[45] It is interesting to note that sociologists who studied diffusion originated the unique concept of **the strength of weak ties**[46] to explain how ideas spread through populations of disconnected groups.

The higher the labor cost rate, the greater the diffusion of NC, as of 1969. This finding was replicated in many subsequent studies, including several that are summarized later in this book, and the authors comment on how government intervention and batch size contribute to the diffusion rate.

---

[44] L. Nabseth and G. F. Ray, *Diffusion of New Industrial Processes,* (London: Cambridge Press, 1974). The first chapter is by Gebhardt and Hartzold.

[45] Ibid. As indicated by the regression equation in the footnote to the original table in Nabseth and Ray, 1974, p. 40.

[46] M. Granovetter, "The Strength of Weak Ties," *American Journal of Sociology,* 78 (1973), pp. 1360–1380. The strength of connections between unreacted groups predicts diffusion.

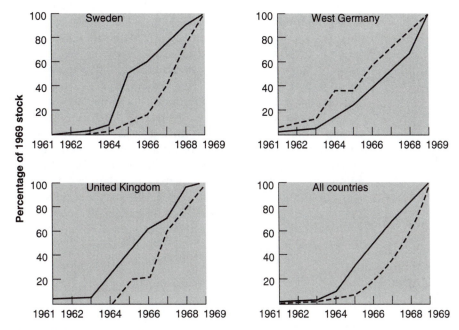

Figure 1-2   Growth of the Stock of Numerically Controlled Machines Used by the Sample Firms

NOTE: "All countries" includes Austria and Italy, but excludes the United States.

SOURCE: Table 3.9, Nasbeth and Ray, 1974, p. 36.

Several other process technologies, including special presses in paper making, tunnel kilns in brick making, basic oxygen steel making, float glass, gibberellic acid in malt making, continuous casting in steel, and shuttleless looms, are documented by Nabseth and Ray. But the lack of solid theory and clear comparative base was challenging in this project. What has emerged in the economics literature that is of

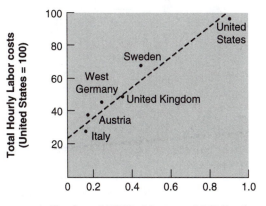

Number of NC Machines per 1,000 Employees

Figure 1-3   The Relation Between Labor Costs and the Diffusion of Numerical Control in 1969

NOTE: The regression equation is $y = -0.2775 + 0.0111x$, $R^2 = 0.927$, $SE = +0.0016$, where x is the labor cost indicator (Austria, 38; Italy, 27; Sweden, 69; United Kingdom, 50; United States, 100; West Germany, 46) and y is the level of diffusion.

SOURCE: Nasbeth and Ray, 1974, p. 40.

great value here is the theory of **appropriation of rents,**[47] or *models of how organizations can capture value from purchased technology when it is essentially available to anyone, including competitors*. This topic is taken up in Chapter 9.

It is not surprising that much of the subsequent applied research in economics and related fields turned to in-depth investigation of a few focus industries and in a few countries (e.g., see the Tushman and Anderson study discussed in Chapter 3). One of the early findings in Nabseth and Ray, however, was a bellwether for follow-up research: "the introduction of new technology often means big changes in structure and administrative practices."[48] The relationship between these organizational innovations and the technological innovations is the central theme throughout this book.

New products diffuse in patterns nearly identical to these new production technologies. These patterns can form the basis of making predictions about market penetration rates and investment returns on new technology projects. Actual and predicted sales of color televisions at the early stages of this product introduction are presented in Figure 1-4 from Urban and Hauser.[49] The difference between this sales curve and a typical diffusion curve is that a diffusion curve usually plots cumulative adoptions of a new good or service. In a sales forecast or plot of actual purchases, only the number of adoptions, as opposed to the proportion of some total possible adoptions, is included. A sales forecast for a new product will eventually taper off as the number of potential buyers declines (i.e., already have the product or are using the service).

$\mathscr{S}$ERVICE INNOVATIONS

We all use services but rarely think about how difficult they are to deliver well. Most services are co-produced by providers and clients, which changes all the

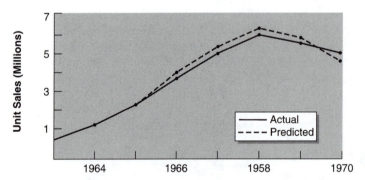

Figure 1-4   Color TV Sales vs. Projections
SOURCE: Adapted from Urban and Hauser, 1980, p. 104.

---

[47] D.J. Teece, "Capturing Value from Technological Innovation: Integration, Strategic Planning and Licensing Decisions," *Interfaces,* 18, no. 3 (1988), pp. 46–61.

[48] Nabseth and Ray, p. 310.

[49] G. Urban and J. R. Hauser, *Design and Marketing of New Products* (Englewood Cliffs, NJ: Prentice-Hall, 1980), p. 104.

rules for quality delivery. Services cannot be stocked into inventory, unless you count clients waiting in line to be served or patients in hospital beds, and other unique definitions of a warehouse such as airliner or hotel room space. Services have outcomes that are difficult to quantify and require close cooperation across functions.

Services are extremely difficult to standardize compared with products because services are often tailored for each unique customer.[50] It should come as no surprise that consumers generally tend to be more satisfied with products than with services, in not only the United States, but in Scandinavia and Europe as well.[51] Many service management courses grew out of a service marketing course that was combined with a service operations course, because the line that divides them is so fine.[52]

Although services are difficult to define and quantify, they have sometimes been called anything that can be bought or traded that cannot be dropped on your foot, and they have dominated the U.S. economy for over 150 years. In about 1960, services took off, and in 1996 constituted 75.6 percent of all value-added and 78.5 percent of all jobs in the United States. The trend is the same in Europe and all modern economies.

One recent study found that companies that lead their industries in financial performance obtained 49 percent of their revenues for new products from services.[53] Since the developed economies of the world are significantly invested in service industries, it is essential to understand the similarities and differences between new product and new service innovation.

James Brian Quinn and associates[54] argue that the producing power of any modern enterprise lies in its intellectual and systems capabilities rather than in hard assets such as materials and plants. This is especially true for large service industries: software, medical care, communications, education, entertainment, accounting, law, publishing (not printing, which is manufacturing), consulting, advertising, retailing, wholesaling, and transportation. Transportation alone is probably 10 to 15 percent of the GDP.

To keep these trends and statistics in perspective, it has been argued and demonstrated that about two out of three service-sector jobs depend on U.S. manu-

[50] F. Gallouj and O. Weinstein, "Innovation in Services," *Research Policy,* 26 (1997), pp. 537–556, especially page 540, where the authors use the behavioral term to describe service characteristics as "socially constructed," which is a result of the co-production between provider and user of a service. Even products, however, can be thought of, ultimately, as determined by the services they provide. For example, a car and driver provide transportation service. For a new treatment of co-production, see Rafael Ramirez, "Value Co-Production: Intellectual Origins and Implications for Practice and Research," *Strategic Management Journal,* 20 (1999), pp. 49–65.

[51] M. D. Johnson, *Customer Orientation and Market Action* (Upper Saddle River, NJ: Prentice-Hall, 1998), especially p. 63.

[52] W. E. Sasser, Jr., C. W. Hart, and J. L. Heskett, *The Service Management Course* (New York: The Free Press, 1991).

[53] B.T. Hudson, "Innovation Through Acquisition," *The Cornell HRA Quarterly,* 35, no. 3 (1994), pp. 82–87, cited in A. Chan, F. M. Go, and R. Pine, "Service Innovation in Hong Kong: Attitudes and Practice," *Service Industries Journal,* 18, no. 2 (April 1998), pp. 112–124.

[54] J. B. Quinn, J. J. Baruch, and K. A. Zien, *Innovation Explosion: Using Intellect and Software to Revolutionize Growth Strategies* (New York: The Free Press, 1997).

facturing.[55] However, it seems clear that most of the growth in modern economies will come from intellectually based services. Intellectual services, such as software, will be at the heart of service innovation in the foreseeable future.[56] Examples include Enterprise Resource Planning (ERP) systems, which are discussed later and are introduced for case analysis in Chapter 9. Companies worldwide are investing more than $10 billion every year in ERP systems, alone.

About 85 percent of all information technology is sold to the service sector in the United States, and about 75 percent of all capital investment goes into the service sector.[57] On the supply side, R&D in the service sector grew from 10 percent to 25 percent of all industrial research between 1988 and 1998. Consistent with these trends, the growth of service R&D is dominated by investment to improve information technologies.[58] Microsoft spends about 17 percent of sales on R&D, which is well above the traditional cutoff of 6 percent of sales spent on R&D by high-tech companies. Although manufacturing R&D still dominates the total research budget worldwide, in the United States, nonmanufacturing R&D accounted for about 25 percent of private research dollars in 1995.

Nonmanufacturing firms accounted for only 8 percent of industrial R&D in 1985 but grew to about 25 percent of the total in just ten years. Service-sector R&D rose to 26.5 percent of all R&D in 1998, passing manufacturing R&D, which was about 24 percent of company research in 1996.[59] Most of this growth was in computer software and biotechnology.

Small manufacturing firms benefit significantly from purchased, innovative services they would not otherwise be able to develop without outside help.[60] Programmable switching technology alone has had tremendous impact on the telecommunications industry.[61] Even larger manufacturing firms are tending to buy, rather than develop, their own services such as software.[62] The outsourced information-services sector of the economy is now estimated to be $32 billion worldwide.[63] Yet to capture the benefits of information services, companies often report the need to transform themselves.

Companies need internal service capability, no matter what business they are in. In addition to all the people employed in services business in the United States (almost 79 percent of all jobs in 1996), it has been estimated that another 12 percent of the work force in manufacturing perform services activities in information

---

[55] S. S. Cohen and J. Zysman, *Manufacturing Matters: The Myth of the Post-industrial Economy* (New York: Basic Books, 1987).

[56] Quinn, et al. (see footnote 54, p. 3) define technology as "knowledge systematically applied to useful purposes."

[57] J. B. Quinn, "Leveraging Intellect," *Executive Excellence,* 10, no. 10 (October 1993), pp. 7–8.

[58] J. E. Jankowski. "R&D: Foundation for Innovation," *Research-Technology Management,* 41, no. 2 (March–April 1998), pp. 14–20.

[59] P. Gwynne, "As R&D Penetrates the Service Sector, Researchers Must Fashion New Methods of Innovation Management," *Research-Technology Management,* 41, no. 5 (September-October 1998), pp. 2–4.

[60] A. MacPherson, "The Contribution of External Service Inputs to the Product Development Efforts of Small Manufacturing Firms," *R&D Management,* 27, no. 2 (April 1997), pp. 127–144.

[61] K. Mazovec, "Service Innovation for the 90s," *Telephony,* 235, no. 11 (September 14, 1998), pp. 78–82.

[62] J. E. Ettlie, "ERP: Corporate Root Canal?" Presented at Rochester Institute of Technology, Rochester, N.Y., January 25, 1999.

[63] R.-D. Kempis, and J. Ringbeck, "Manufacturing's Use and Abuse of IT," *McKinsey Quarterly,* no. 1 (1998), pp. 138–150.

services. These are the knowledge-based assets of the organization: people, data bases, and systems.[57] Perhaps only customer service is more important, and this quality function can also be significantly enhanced with information systems.[64]

A number of recent examples illustrates this shift in emphasis of the orientation of internal services, especially the information function, of the firm. Sun Life Assurance Company of Canada now measures the performance of information systems by their effect on external markets (e.g., the introduction of on-site quotation for agents using lap-top computers).[65] Other recent examples of customer-focused Information Services changes are ticketless or "E-ticket" for air travel,[66] and risk pooling at the Citywide Central Insurance Program of New York City.[67] There have also been widespread information technology applications to enhance the retail sector,[68] like the Trade Information Center of the U.S. Department of Commerce, which provides help primarily for small- and medium-sized exporters (1-800-USA-TRADE).[69] A counterexample is the apparent failure of hospitals to follow this trend of leveraging information services to enhance customer and patient satisfaction.[70]

Public Sector Management and Innovation Policy

Technological innovation in the public sector is introduced in Chapter 10, but a special category of service, state and local government, which accounts for a substantial portion of the GDP, is far too important to go unmentioned here. Landmark innovation research includes work done on state and local government more than twenty years ago, which still deserves attention. Two of these contributors, Robert Yin and Irwin Feller, warrant special mention because of their seminal contributions. Much of this research was motivated by the idea that local government's slow rate of productivity improvement was caused by the reluctance or inability to adopt technological innovations that could enhance government performance. These findings are reviewed in Chapters 9 and 10.

The challenge of making government more responsive and productive or the inability to integrate quality programs, information technology, and innovation

---

[64] This includes data mining and call center automation. See Bob Violino, "Defining IT Innovation," *Information Week,* No. 700 (September 14, 1998), pp. 58–70, which summarizes the tenth annual survey of 500 top information companies. Top priorities among respondents were year 2000 fixes, E-commerce, and customer service.

[65] J. Henderson, and C. M. Lentz, "Learning, Working and Innovation: A Case Study in the Insurance Industry," *Journal of Management Information Systems,* 12, no. 3 (Winter 1995/1996), pp. 43–65.

[66] C. Bickers, "Easy Come, Easy Go," *Far Eastern Economic Review,"* 161, no. 49 (December 3, 1998), p. 64.

[67] J. D. Harper. "Risk Pooling in New York City: The Anatomy of an Award Winning Innovation," *International Journal of Public Administration,* 19, no. 7 (1996), pp. 1193–1197.

[68] C. Wilder. "A Thousand Points of Services," *Information Week,* no. 700 (September 14, 1998), pp. 235–242.

[69] M. Zaineddin and M. B. Morgan, "A New Look: The Commerce Department's Trade Information Center Continues Its Tradition of Excellence with Expanded Services," *Business America,* 119, no. 5 (May 1998), pp. 16–17.

[70] T. D. West. "Comparing Change Readiness, Quality Improvement, and Cost Management Among Veterans Administration, For-Profit and Nonprofit Hospitals," *Journal of Health Care Finance,* 25, no. 1 (Fall 1998), pp. 46–58.

management remain significant challenges of the next decade in the service sector. Perhaps because so much can be done with just service-quality improvement interventions, technological innovation may be in the distant future or out of reach of many service firms or public agencies. With cost reductions of 30 percent or more in the typical service industry after quality and business process reengineering, and corresponding absence of administrative innovation adoption in some parts of the service sector,[71] the additional benefits of information and new technology and sustainable development[72] are far from being realized.

Perhaps the best current example of leveraging information systems for customer service is the dawning of the age of electronic commerce. Quinn and his colleagues call this "user-based innovation and virtual shopping," and argue that all innovation on the Internet is software.[73] Online trading,[74] electronic banking[75] and just plain surfing the Web for pleasure are part of this next generation of service innovation. E-commerce is the topic of the next section. Suffice it to say that the growth of the Internet, and its primary provider, America Online, has been so fast that fears of George Orwell's Big Brother and the thought police from his novel *1984* have quickly resurfaced.[76]

E-Commerce

No technology symbolizes our age better than the Internet. The resulting effect on business is known as electronic commerce, or e-commerce. This radical shift in our way of working and playing is essentially caused by the convergence of two technologies: *computers* and *telecommunications*. Akin to any other discontinuous historical example that merged more than one existing technology—like the creation of the factory system in the 1700s in England around spinning and weaving cotton technology—our century's version of the Industrial Revolution is at hand. The number of Americans using the Internet was approximately 5 million in 1993 and 62 million by 1997. In July 1993, there were approximately 1.8 million Internet

---

[71] K. Newman, "Re-engineering for Service Quality: The Case of the Leicester Royal Infirmary," *Total Quality Management,* 8, no. 5 (October 1997), pp. 255–264; also see G. Gianakis and C. P. McCue, "Administrative Innovation Among Ohio Local Government Finance Officers," *American Review of Public Administration,* 27, no. 3 (September 1997), pp. 20–286, where survey results indicated that in local government, less than 4 percent of respondents had adopted tools such as strategic planning, total quality management, and financial trend monitoring.

[72] D. F. Ball, "Management of Technology, Sustainable Development and Eco-Efficiency: The Seventh International Conference on Management of Technology," *R&D Management,* 28, no. 4 (1998), pp. 311–313.

[73] J. B. Quinn, J. Baruch, and K. A. Zien, "Software-based Innovation," *Sloan Management Review,* 37, no. 4 (Summer 1996), pp. 11–24.

[74] L. Edwards, "Innovation to Typify the Next Generation of Online Trading," *Wall Street & Technology* (November 1998), pp. 9, 12.

[75] R. T. Frambach, H. G. Barkema, B. Nooteboom, and M. Wedel, "Adoption of a Service Innovation in the Business Market: An Empirical Test of Supply-Side Variables," *Journal of Business Research,* 41, no. 2 (February 1998), pp. 161–174.

[76] A. Harmon, "As America Online Grows, Charges that Big Brother Is Watching," *New York Times* (January 31, 1999), p. 1, 20.

hosts; in 1997 there were more than 19.5 million. According to one estimate, Internet traffic doubles every 100 days in the United States.[77]

✖ What Is This Signature Technology of Our Age?[78]

The Internet is essentially a communication and transaction tool. Before the Internet, communication was analog—like a telephone—done through pictures and sound. The Internet is digital—it links the computer with telecommunications technology. A CD (compact disc) converts an analog signal (e.g., sound) into a long string of numbers (digital) to recreate an analog sound. These numbers are encoded on a CD so they can be "read" with light from a laser, and no physical contact is needed to replay the CD. It doesn't wear out from use (although some of my CDs have been abused).

Computer networks are essentially combinations of hardware and software systems—computers programmed with software languages connected to transmission lines by modems—short for *mo*dulator/*demo*dulator. If two computers are connected by a wire, one needs a device to send (modulate) and receive (demodulate) messages. Actually, two sets of wires are dedicated—one each—for this purpose. The wires could be telephone lines, and in that case, the modem can dial up another computer assigned a telephone number. Any kind of digital data can be sent, including a voice transmission. Naturally, telephone companies are a little nervous about the Internet. Character codes use a standard, such as Morse Code. One popular standard is the American Standard Code for Information Interchange (ASCII), which determines a bit sequence for each letter in English as well as other symbols used in communication, such as punctuation, digits, and upper- and lowercase letters. One of the improvements of digital over analog communication is that early research detected errors in analog encoding, transmission, and decoding, and added parity bits to strings to check for errors, producing less noise.

Local area networks (LANs) were the first to develop the Internet. They appeared in the late 1960s as computer systems began to decentralize away from exclusive dependence on mainframes. The first stage of this technology was the connecting of a circuit board in one computer by a cable to a circuit board in another computer. Then came three computers and finally a LAN, networking many computers together. This last stage required that computers have network interface hardware. We now have three elements in the system: circuit boards, cable, and connections to the LAN. Xerox's version of this LAN was called *Ethernet,* which became a leading technology of the day.

All this would have led rather quickly to the Internet if it hadn't been for one detail. Not all LANs were alike. Unless two organizations had the same LAN system, they couldn't network computers across town—or across the room, for that matter. Research on wide area networks (WANs), designed specifically to span large geographic areas, emerged about the same time as LANs. WANs do more than just link

---

[77] U.S. Department of Commerce, *The Emerging Digital Economy*, National Technical Information Service, PB98-137029, April 1998. However, the Internet cannot expand indefinitely—eventually, all computers will be linked and traffic will reach physical limits.

[78] Much of this section is based upon D. E. Comer, *The Internet Book* (Upper Saddle River, N.J.: Prentice-Hall, 1997).

two computers. They also use a dedicated computer to organize a set of transmissions at each site into a coordinated system while keeping individual computers separated and independent. At the time, just a few WAN projects were underway, but there were many LANs. It seemed hopeless that any type of standard would be adopted, let alone optimized.

About this time (late 1960s), the military became interested in using network communication, and projects began to be funded through ARPA, the Advanced Research Projects Agency (later called DARPA; the D was added for Defense). By the end of the 1970s, several WANs were operating, including ARPANET and others using satellites and radio transmission. Further work resulted in an integrated "internetwork," shortened to "internet," which linked WANs and LANs for the military. The prototype was capitalized: Internet. Two key innovations made all this happen: (1) Internet Protocol (IP) software for basic communication and (2) Transmission Control Protocol (TPC) software. The two were usually combined with the other systems needed and were called the TCP/IP Internet Protocol Suite. This system was adopted by the military in 1982.

From 1986 to 1996 the Internet grew from a few thousand networked computers, primarily at universities, to nearly 10 million linked computers. This growth was the result of merging two network research projects at Bell Labs and the University of California–Berkeley. The National Science Foundation saw this as a signal to adopt the goal of linking all scientists and engineers to promote U.S. competitiveness. The NSFNET was a project by IBM, MCI, and the University of Michigan's MERIT organization, which linked the university units, and became operational in 1988.

By 1991, the Internet was growing too fast for NSFNET's capacity, and the federal government could no longer afford to pay for the service, so a nonprofit company called Advanced Networks and Services (ANS) was formed out of the original three organizations (IBM, MCI, and MERIT). In 1992, ANSNET was running at thirty times the capacity of its predecessor. By 1995, MCI Corporation had a new, high-speed network, *vBNS,* and the Internet had been privatized.

There is, of course, much, much more to the story. There is the technology of routing messages, addresses for computers, the HTML (HyperText Markup Language) used for Web pages, and, naturally, the competition between network suppliers. Or is it competition? The antitrust case against Microsoft is taken up in Chapter 10. Here, limited space permits only a simple illustration given in Figure 1-5.[79]

Academicians have subsumed the Internet, along with other computer technology issues, under the general rubric of knowledge and knowledge management.[80] After Peter Drucker said that knowledge had become *the* major economic resource (after land, labor, and capital), it was OK to study it as a legitimate subject. This ignores the history of academic thought that has studied and classified knowledge for centuries. That knowledge has been the subject of dozens of applied academic fields, including R&D management, management information systems, cognition, computer science, and many others. One recent survey of 431 U.S. and European organizations found that actually changing behavior in the

---

[79] Ibid., p. 133.

[80] R.E. Cole, "Knowledge and the Firm," Special Issue of *California Management Review,* 40, no. 3, Spring, 1998.

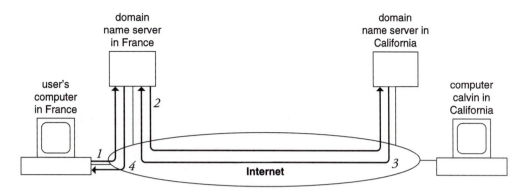

Figure 1-5   Example of Internet Usage: Network Users In France and California[80]

face of Internet expansion and cultural barriers to knowledge transfer was more important than general management and lack of strategy for adoption.[81] It is clear that information technologies are the key to supporting this knowledge revolution, but without theories and understanding of technology management, no innovation can be leveraged economically.[82] This issue is revisited in Chapter 9 with a discussion of enterprise integration and a short case on this topic.

E-commerce is the ultimate outcome of technology management for the Internet. More than half of all the computers in the United States are linked to LANs, and each month 2,000 businesses join the Internet and the 20,000 companies already there, doing business in cyberspace.[83] Nearly everyone has heard or read the story of Amazon.com,[84] which is a virtual bookstore, and one of the fastest growing companies in the history of business. Perhaps the most important development in e-commerce to date is the AT&T–TCI merger, which links telephones to cable and enables "digital convergence" on the most massive scale yet imagined in cyberspace. The Telecommunications Act of 1996 eliminated nearly every barrier between communication markets, and now that the Internet has become, prima facia, the platform for all digital transmission, there are almost no limits to what can accomplished by such an integrated company. It is the first U.S. nationwide communications firm to emerge since AT&T was broken up into its constituent companies.[85]

---

[81] R. Ruggles, "The State of the Nation: Knowledge Management in Practice," *California Management Review,* 40, no. 3 (Spring 1998), pp. 80–89.

[82] See, for example, M. Demarest, "Understanding Knowledge Management," *Long Range Planning,* 30, no. 3 (June 1997), pp. 374–384.

[83] H. E. Hudson, "Global Information Infrastructure: Eliminating the Distance Barrier," *Business Economics,* 33, no. 2 (April 1998), pp. 25–31.

[84] Amazom.com is a large, Internet-based book order house that grown from $28 million in sales in 1997 to $116 million in sales in 1998 (July); its stock price skyrocketed even though Amazom.com has yet to show a profit: the company lost $21.1 million during this same period, or 44 cents per share.

[85] P. Elstrom, C. Arnst, and R. Crockett, "At Last, Telecom-Unbound," *Business Week* (July 6, 1998), pp. 24–27.

$\mathcal{T}$ECHNOLOGY AND ORGANIZATIONS

Economists were not the only pioneers in studying the innovation process. Many organization theorists got started early on this subject and made seminal contributions to the field during this same period that diffusion research was getting underway. Among the first were James March and Herbert Simon who contended in 1958 that there would always be gentle pressure and a relentless tendency for gradual change in organizations due to goal succession and response to at least some change in the environment of every firm.[86]

Perhaps one of the best known, often cited, early empirical study on organizations and innovation was reported by Paul Lawrence and Jay Lorsch in 1967.[87] Their general model called for firms responding to uncertainty in their environments, causing more internal differentiation such as differences in time horizon and orientation. This increased differentiation precipitates the need for more coordinated action, which they called integration—the quality and state of collaboration—and techniques used to resolve conflicts. Their most important conclusion was based on the comparison of just six firms, so it is not surprising that their results have been difficult to replicate directly. However, their ideas have generally been verified indirectly by subsequent research.[88] Lawrence and Lorsch compared successful and unsuccessful (based on sales, profits, and rate of product changes) paired firms in plastics, food, and containers. In the competitive and uncertain plastics industry, more differentiation and integration were required, as would be expected by their "contingency" theory. Companies survive by "fitting" into their environment. That is, there are many successful ways to organize, depending on the environment of a firm or business unit.

$\mathcal{S}$URFING THE WEB FOR TECHNOLOGICAL INNOVATION

Here is a little experiment that might surprise you. Go to your favorite Web browser, such as aol.com, and surf for the term *technological innovation*. When I tried this, I expected the same number of "hits" on other Web sites as one would get entering this same term on a research database search of titles and abstracts in the business and economics literature. For example, ABI/Inform had 3,011 entries listed in February 1999. I was not prepared to find 248,840 "hits" on my search of cyberspace. Technological

---

[86] J. March and H. Simon, *Organizations* (New York: John Wiley & Sons, 1958).

[87] P. R. Lawrence and J. W. Lorsch, "Differentiation and Integration in Complex Organizations," *Administrative Science Quarterly,* 12 (June 1967), 1-47; J. H. Jackson and C. P. Morgan, *Organization Theory* (Englewood Cliffs, NJ: Prentice-Hall, 1978), especially pp. 236–238.

[88] Some of this research is introduced in Chapter 9 and includes J. Ettlie, R. O'Keefe, and W. Bridges, "Organizational Strategy and Structural Differences for Radical versus Incremental Innovation," *Management Science,* 30, no. 6 (1984), pp. 682–695; and J. Ettlie and E. Reza, "Organizational Integration and Process Innovation," *Academy of Management Journal,* 35, no. 4 (1992), pp. 795–827.

innovation is an extremely visible topic in our society. Let's hope this interest leads to the wisdom of managing our technologies.[89]

HAPTER SUMMARY _____

Technology is the fascination of all walks of life. Business organizations spend billions of dollars each year on new technology; authors of fiction marvel at its potential—good and bad. Historians, political scientists, economists, sociologists—all "ologists"—have taken a crack at sorting out what technology means, and all have a slightly different worldview of what the single most important thing technology might be. Innovation is defined as *invention + exploitation*. The management of technological innovation accounts for the relationship between technological innovation and organizational innovation.

One clear pattern emerges that is consistent with the treatment of technology here: There is great variation in the degree of success enjoyed by individuals and organizations attempting to produce economic value with new products, new services, and new operations systems. What accounts for this variation? We take up this question next, starting with the case of the Denver International Airport (circa 1994).

ISCUSSION QUESTIONS _____

1. Read the short case (attached), "Automation Off Course in Denver." What caused the failure of the new baggage system contributing significantly to the late opening of this new airport in 1994?

2. What could have been done to prevent the failure of this new technology introduction in luggage systems?

3. Detroit Metro Airport is building a new terminal with a new baggage-handling system. Advise the design team on how to proceed, based on what you have learned about DIA.

4. Read the short case "Webvan Group, Inc." at the end of the chapter. How does the concept of Webvan differ from other supermarket or gourmet food shopping options? What are the innovations behind the Webvan concept? What factors will determine the success or failure of this innovative new concept?

5. Go to the Internet and use a browser to search on "technological innovation" or comparable terms. What were your results? Now use an abstracting search engine such as ABI Inform or Social Science Citations Index and search on the same term(s). Compare your results with your Web search. Be prepared to share the results of your searches in class.

DDITIONAL
CASE SUGGESTIONS _____

There is an excellent, in-depth case on the Denver Airport project available from the Harvard Business School: BAE Automated Systems (A), HBS 9-396-311 (15 pages).

_____

[89] Many Web sites are available on this subject. However, because this part of our world changes so fast, only one is suggested here: the Web site and exchange system developed as part of the Technology and Innovation Management division of the Academy of Management, housed at McMaster University in Canada. To subscribe, send a message to Professor Christopher K. Bart. The homepage is http://irc.mcmaster.ca/home/bart.htm.

✕ CASE 1-1

Automation Off Course in Denver

If all BAE Automated Systems had to do was design a system to whiz luggage around a suburban warehouse here, with a whir and a clicketyclack, its record would be perfect. Or if it had to handle 100 bags a minute, as it does for United Airlines in San Francisco, it would have suffered no embarrassments.

But in Denver, BAE is now struggling to coax 4,000 automated baggage carts run by 100 computers and a web of motors and radio transponders into carrying 1,400 bags a minute. Several weeks ago, in a test of what will be the nation's largest baggage handling system, bags went flying, tumbling and bursting open, with some sliced in half—that is, when the system consented to run at all. Fortunately, the bags did not belong to anyone.

As a result, the new Denver airport failed last week to meet its planned opening, which had already been delayed from October because of several changes of plans among other reason. Airlines that have financed the $3.2 billion airport estimate their losses in the tens of millions of dollars.

Now comes the finger pointing, and executives of BAE, based in Carrollton, Tex., a Dallas suburb, are on the hot seat.

"I've become a media star, much against my wishes," said Gene Di Fonso, BAE's president and chief executive, who, though articulate, is no Dan Rather. "Talk shows, television interviews, you name it."

His point is simply that "it is not BAE's fault that the Denver airport has not opened on March 9." After all, Denver officials kept changing their plans, left too little time for testing, failed to fix electrical flaws and then, turned the whole system over to inexperienced managers—accusations city officials only partly deny. The company readily agrees that its system was not ready but says the airport was not ready either.

[Denver officials said on Thursday that they had been ready to open the airport on time. "The baggage system is the spine of the airport," Michael Dino, an assistant to the Denver Mayor, said in a telephone interview. "If the baggage system had been in place, we would have opened." He said that BAE and the city shared responsibility for the delays, adding that BAE failed to solve several software and mechanical problems by last week.]

In a brave new world of robots and computers, do gremlins still have dominion? Can a smudged bar code on a baggage tag or worker leaning on the wrong button actually scramble the whole baggage system, as in Denver, delaying flights from coast to coast?

"The answer is yes," said Peter G. Neumann, the founder and manager of Risks Digest, an Internet computer network forum on computer security and reliability. "You could, in fact, have a dramatic effect on air traffic around the country just by having an accidental screw-up." Technically speaking, though, Denver appears to be afflicted with glitches, which have known causes, not mysterious gremlins, he said.

New Target Date: May 15

The goal now is to open Denver International Airport on May 15, when the baggage system will be tested and proved, Mr. Di Fonso said, with backup systems and room for error. Tight computer security will prevent any accidental breakdowns and sabotage.

"The most complex and Draconian commands are permitted to a very, very few individuals, and those are only permitted in the master control center, and only a very, very few people have access," Mr. Di Fonso said.

As in a nuclear power plant? "Nah, not quite that complicated," he said, but the command center would be guarded and locked, behind a heavy steel door.

His company was known as Boeing Airport Equipment until the Boeing Company sold it in the early 1980's to private investors, who, in turn, sold it in 1985 to BTR P.L.C., the British industrial conglomerate that continues to own it. The $200 million Denver contract, stretching over several years, helped to doubled the BAE's annual sales to $100 million. There are 300 permanent employees, although hundreds more have worked in Denver.

Most of BAE's baggage systems, in many airports around the country, still rely on conventional conveyor belts, with each major airline at an airport having its own equipment. For United Airlines in San Francisco, BAE installed much faster technology, with carts running on steel tracks.

Monitoring Bags Via Computer

In Denver, agents will still dump bags on conveyor belts. But the conveyors will carry bags to a track, where a fiberglass cart will stop to receive each bag, then tilt

SOURCE: A. R. Myerson, *New York Times*, March 18, 1994, p. D1.

upward to hold it. Lasers will identify the bags by reading their bar code tags.

Through radio transponders, looking much like hockey pucks, mounted on the sides of each cart, the computers will process millions of messages a second, monitoring the locations of the carts and guiding them to the proper gates.

The Denver system represents a leap in scale, with 14 times the capacity of San Francisco's. It is the first such system to serve an entire airport. It is also the first where the carts will only slow down, not stop, to pick up and drop off bags, the first to be run by a network of desktop computers rather than a mainframe, the first to use radio links and the first with a system for oversized bags, which in Denver tend to be skis. It is even designed to reroute bags for sudden gate changes, or send them to special inspection stations, including one that is bomb-proof.

And, at 17 miles an hour, it is by far the fastest, about five times as fast as simple conveyor belts. The gates stretch more than a mile from the main terminal, or about two miles as the tracks go. But BAE promises to transport any bag from terminal to gate in 10 minutes, usually before the passengers get there.

Most of Denver's advanced features are on view at a sprawling warehouse here north of Dallas that BAE shares with the Giltspur Industrial exhibit company and a Fitz & Floyd china distribution center.

Telecarts, as BAE calls them, zip around narrow tracks on three levels, sometimes slowing to pick up or dump some battered bags from conveyor belts. After hundreds of cycles, said Jay Bouton, BAE's voluble sales manager, "They get kind of beaten up." Draped yellow caution tape keeps visitors from getting beaten up as well.

Mr. Bouton explained some of the technology—the software, the signaling—but after a while, begged off. "I'm not an engineer," he said. "But even the electrical engineers don't understand completely what's going on."

But Mr. Di Fonso, an aerospace engineer by training, did try to clarify what happened in Denver.

The Denver project had many counts against it from the start. When BAE began work in mid-1992, other work on the airport was well under way. The company agreed to what Mr. Di Fonso described as a crash schedule, provided that the airport did not tamper with the plans.

Not only did city officials repeatedly alter the system, he said, but they also rejected BAE's bid to operate and maintain it, saying the cost was too high.

"The city is leasing the baggage system to the airlines," Mr. Di Fonso said, his voice rising with exasperation. "The airlines are forming a consortium. The consortium then hires the maintenance company. And the maintenance company hires me."

Yet Another Bug

In September, BAE noticed another bug. Unexpected power surges were tripping circuits that shut the system's motors down. The city, BAE and United Airlines all hired their own consultants.

The solution required special filters to maintain an even power supply, which the city delayed ordering, Mr. Di Fonso said. Although the electrical glitches were the main reason given for having to postpone the airport's opening, Mr. Di Fonso said that too little testing had been done to establish the system's reliability.

The tests, to Mr. Di Fonso's discomfort, were open to reporters, photographers and television crews, who saw smashed baggage and airborne underwear. Smudged bar codes in one test meant that about two-thirds of the bags were shunted off to an area for sorting by hand.

The Denver experience, however, has apparently not caused the company to lose heart, or customers. A few doors down from Mr. Di Fonso's office sat a group of visitors from Heathrow Airport in London, poring over blueprints of a baggage system that will allow faster connections there.

Mr. Di Fonso, in other words, has few regrets about venturing into Denver. "Who would turn down a $193 million contract?" he said. "You'd expect to have a little trouble for that kind of money."

⚒ CASE 1-2

Webvan Group, Inc.

The concept is an Internet megastore. The location is Foster City, California. The aim is to sell $300 million in groceries over the Internet to discriminating shoppers the first year, delivered to your door. This is the dream of Mr. Louis Borders and his backers, who have given him $120 million in finding already, an enormous amount of money for a startup in a mature industry.

Behind the concept is a 330,000-square-foot high-tech warehousing system located in Oakland, California. It has five miles of conveyors, bar code readers, electric eye and scanner technology, and sixteen bins to collect shoppers' orders. The company's chief financial officer, Mr. Kevin Czinger, predicts that "the automated warehouse will give Webvan a 10-percentage point edge in profit margins over traditional supermarkets." These kind of results would make this new Internet-based company profitable in six to twelve months, not ten years like more typical Internet startups.

The challenge, of course, is that the typical supermarket may only have 3 percent margins to begin with. Worse, buyers in the "maximum selection and prestige" category of food companies can be extreme in their demands. One incorrectly packaged order of fish and the loss of a customer may be next. Earlier startups in the online supermarket category such as Peapod, Inc., lost $21 million in 1998. Albertson's, Inc. is testing an Internet store in Dallas with nonperishable goods only. A new competitor, HomGrocer.com in Bellevue, Washington, appears to be formidable, being started by former Netscape CEO, James L. Barksdale.[90] But Webvan thinks it can match and beat local supermarket prices, and says it won't charge membership fees and will waive delivery charges for orders over $50, because of its superior technology.

Shoppers and supermarket competitors are in for a jolt indeed if this concept is a success. Webvan already has plans to open another warehouse in Atlanta in a few months and then in twenty more cities that are large enough to have a major-league sports team. And if it works for groceries, it should work for ... almost anything else.

SOURCE: G. Anders, Co-founder of Borders to launch online megagrocer, *Wall Street Journal* (April 22, 1999), B1, B4.

[90] S. Hamm. Jim Barksdale, Internet angel, *Business Week* (May 10, 1999), pp. 60–65.

The Innovation Process

$\mathscr{C}$HAPTER OBJECTIVES

To review the basics of the innovation process—the history of technology, definitions, stage models, innovation types, research and development (R&D)—and to introduce technology strategy. Technology performance is reviewed. The case study of Gillette's Sensor Razor reveals many of the recurring issues of the innovation process.

The Industrial Revolution began in the early 1700s, primarily in England, with the automation of cotton cloth production. It is notable for its two important historical consequences:

1. In 1750, 80 to 90 percent of the world's population was engaged in agriculture; in 1950, this figure was 50 to 60 percent worldwide.
2. Between 1750 and 1850, the output per capita in England averaged 1 to 1.5 percent per annum—that is, output grew at a rate that doubled real output every fifty years and increased fourfold over the nineteenth century.[1]

Not only did the standard of living and population take off dramatically during this period, but subsequent technological innovations in other industries such as chemicals, electrical power, and steel had a dramatic impact in Europe and elsewhere. Some even referred to this as the *Second Industrial Revolution;* that is, the first revolution in textile production and factory organization spawned another discontinuous change in other industries.

---

[1] R. M. Hartwell (ed.), *The Causes of the Industrial Revolution in England* (London: Methuen & Company Ltd., 1967), pp. 1, 8.

Irony is sprinkled throughout the historical accounts of technology. This will not be the last irony to emerge in the history of the innovation process. England was primarily a country of sheep herders at the time of the first Industrial Revolution. The "natural" revolution should have occurred in automation of wool production. But wool is less amenable to automation, the markets for England's textile production were primarily in warmer climates, and the resistance of the entrenched system of wool production made it ripe for "invasion" by cotton automation. What is "natural" and what actually happens are not always obvious as technology histories unfold.

Sometimes called the "father of the factory system," Richard Arkwright patented a spinning machine and started a factory. Arkwright's spinning machine spun cotton into thread both faster and with stronger product. Pictured in Figure 2-1 Arkwright's spinning machine combined with many others to ultimately revolutionize production, work, and society.

The History of Technology

One of the great potential benefits of studying the history of technology is finding out that our particular era of technological change is not unique.[2] We would all like to think that our period of history is atypical, but a little thoughtful reading and reflection will easily convince most that this is simply not the case. Knowledge of this history is relevant to solving the technology management problems of today.

ARKWRIGHT'S SPINNING MACHINE
This 32-inch-high machine *(right)* patented by Arkwright could not only spin cotton thread much faster than the old spinning wheel, but it also spun a far stronger thread. It thereby made possible a cloth woven of cotton alone, rather than cotton mixed with flax as in the past.

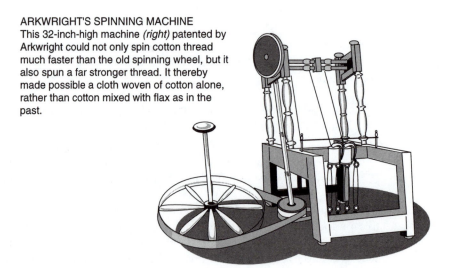

Figure 2-1   Arkwright's Spinning Machine
CORBIS/BETTMANN

[2] S. R. Barley, "What Can We Learn from the History of Technology?" *Journal of Engineering and Technology Management,* 15 (1998), pp. 237–255.

Another benefit is finding out that technology systems are much more complex than most imagine. The Industrial Revolution in England's 1700s, thought to be a unique epoch in technological history, was actually preceded and enabled by a Medieval Technical Revolution that began with the establishment of the Cistercian Order in 1098 in Clairvaux, France, as a reformation of the Benedictines. One of the two surviving branches is now called the Trappists (Cistercians of the Strict Observance).

The Cistercians established monasteries near rivers and streams to harness water power and solve a perplexing problem for the order, the reconciliation of two conflicting principles of devotion and self-sufficiency. Thomas Merton calls the resolution of this potential conflict "active contemplation," an exaggerated reverence for work in some monks, "doing things, suffering things, thinking things, making things tangible and concrete sacrifices for the love of God."[3] The Cistercians built elaborate abbeys that converted water power into all forms of productive activity to accomplish self-sufficiency, and there was still time left over for contemplation.[4] Are the conflicts we face today any more challenging?

Historical themes of the technological innovation process are repeated over and over. A final example of the introduction of continuous-aim firing in the U.S. Navy is illustrative.[5] The technology was first discovered, quite by accident, by an English officer, Percy Scott, in 1898, and was introduced in the U.S. Navy between 1900 and 1902. The example is selected because continuous aiming is based on a mechanical system—a technological innovation. How it was introduced into a well-ordered set of procedures typical of a military organization is instructive for modern managers with similar challenges.

The problem of aiming gunfire at sea is based on the context. Of course, range must be estimated. Worse, when the ship rolls, the gun and pointer or operator are off target. There is a lag in firing and delivery, and so the "art" of anticipating when to discharge has evolved. Gunfire at sea was uncertain and unreliable, but continuous aiming promised to make it more effective.

The continuous-aim firing system compensated for the roll of the ship by altering the gear ratio of the elevating gear. So the pointer and gun barrel stayed on the target throughout the roll of the ship. As soon as the aiming became more certain, the advantages of using a telescope site immediately became obvious. Soon after, the open site was replaced, but the telescope would recoil into the eye of the gunner. The telescope was then moved to the sleeve, which did not recoil, and the telescope did not move. With continuous aiming and telescopic siting, rapid, accurate firing at sea became a possibility. In six years, gunnery accuracy in the British and U.S. navies improved 3,000 percent during practice rounds.

---

[3] T. Merton, *Seven Story Mountain* (Fiftieth Anniversary Edition) (Orlando, Fla.: Harcourt, Brace & Company, 1998), p. 428.

[4] For example, see B. Gille, "Machines," in C. Singer, et al. (eds.), A History of Technology, Vol. 2, *The Mediterranean Civilizations and the Middle Ages* (New York: Oxford University Press, 1965), esp. pp. 650–651.

[5] E. E. Morison, "Gunfire at Sea," *Men, Machines, and Modern Times* (Cambridge, Mass.: MIT Press, 1966), pp. 17–44. Also see D. A. Schon, *Technology and Change* (New York: Dell Publishing, 1967), pp. 42–74, on corporate ambivalence toward innovation. Corporations attempt to maintain stability, but at the same time, they need to undertake technological innovation to survive.

Now the real story. How was this simple and wonderful technological innovation received by the Navy? The reaction to all of this was great resistance. Not until President Theodore Roosevelt intervened did the Navy reluctantly adopt the new system. The U.S. junior officer, William S. Sims, who installed the first system on a U.S. ship, was met with great resistance from Washington and the Navy establishment in the ordnance bureau, saying, among other things, that continuous-aim firing was impossible, even though it had been proven in China Station by Percy and Sims. U.S. Navy equipment was just as good as British Navy equipment, so the fault must be with the men who are to be trained by officers. Sims was persistent and eventually was championed by President Roosevelt.

After 1903, U.S. Navy gunnery officers became one of the most powerful members of a ship's crew, based on promotion lists, and Naval society did, indeed, change. This story is instructive because if the Navy can change, perhaps the most entrenched organization can also change. But the story also illustrates several characteristics of the innovation process.

▶ New technology is often discovered by chance.
▶ No matter how great the potential for solving a chronic problem, there is usually resistance to the adoption and spread or diffusion of a new product and the *changes in routine and organizational structure* needed to implement it.
▶ Authority has weight in the change process.

$\mathcal{D}$EFINITIONS REVISITED

For a subject so ubiquitous, one would think that there is universal agreement as to the definition of technological innovation, and related terms, but there is not. Most likely this disparity has occurred because writers have addressed the subject from different perspectives. Our purpose here is quite focused: What is important about technological innovation from the perspective of the manager?

✖ Innovation

The definition adopted here for technological innovation follows Roberts,[6] who says that **innovation** is composed of two parts, the generation of an idea or invention and the conversion of that invention into a business or other useful application:

$$Innovation = Invention + Exploitation$$

Roberts summarized what we know about managing the innovation process (Box 2-1).

This summary serves as a starting point in understanding the innovation process from the viewpoint of operations, but several of these summary points will be

---

[6] E. B. Roberts, "Managing Invention and Innovation," *Research-Technology Management* (January-February, 1988), pp. 11–29.

extrapolated later. For example, the distinction between *market pull* (i.e., "forces reflecting orientation to perceived need or demand," p. 18 in Roberts) and *technology push* (i.e., "undertaking projects for advancing the technical state-of-the art in an area without anticipation of the specific commercial benefits to be derived," Roberts, p. 19) innovations tends to be blurred by the need for integration and balance between functions during any successful innovating process.[7]

Some applied research has found that radical (new to the world) technology products and services usually result from technology push innovation, whereas incremental (improvements of existing) technology products usually result from market pull innovation. These two types of innovations appear to be quite different in the strategies and organizational structures they require. Initial findings suggest that this applies to new products, new processes, and even to technological innovations

---

BOX 2-1

What We Know About Innovation

▶ Highest product development success rates are produced when marketing and R&D organizations work in close collaboration.

▶ "Market pull" far more frequently leads to successful innovations than does "technology push," although both sources of initiating projects account for success and failure alike.

▶ Users not only furnish critical "market needs" input data to designers, but in some industries supply the actual innovations that manufacturers later adapt, improve, and commercialize.

▶ Downstream transfer to RD&E [research, development and engineering] results can be improved through use of multiple procedural, human, and organizational "bridges." Human bridges are the most effective transfer mechanism, and people movements, rotations, and face-to-face meetings should be used routinely and frequently.

▶ Most technologies move through evolutionary stages: an early one dominated by frequent product innovations; a transition characterized by increased process innovation and the emergence of a dominant product design; and a mature stage featuring much lower rate and more minor degree of both product and process innovation. A firm's innovation strategy and technological resource allocations should differ markedly, depending on the stage of its primary technology.

▶ "Competitive product profiling" is a useful method for initiating technical planning in a company, comparing the key technical performance characteristics of a product line with competitors' related products.

▶ Recent growth of venture capital and alliance methods reflects increasing recognition of the need to link external technologies with internal capabilities.

▶ Top management commitment is essential to assure success of broad-based programs aimed at institutionalizing the development of effective product and process innovations.

SOURCE: E. B. Roberts, "Managing Invention and Innovation," *Research Technology Management,* (January/February 1988), p. 11.

that are difficult to categorize, such as packaging innovations in the food industry.[8] But the general finding is worth noting now. *If the technological innovation involved—whether new product or process—is radical, then substantial changes in the organizations involved will be required for successful development and use of these innovations.* This basic theme is echoed throughout the book.

✳ Technology

The **great technology debate** among scholars is quite different from that of practitioners and philosophers. It is not whether technology hurts or harms society or some individuals in some societies (although that debate does emerge at times). Rather, there continues to be great confusion on what technology *is*. Before tackling the definition, consider the following simple technological innovation categories of the first dimension of innovation:

▶ New *products*

▶ New operations *processes*

▶ New *information systems* (hardware and software)

Each of these categories is considered separately in Section Three, but add two more categories to a second dimension of innovation and you have all you need to sort out the technology jungle:

▶ **Radical departures** from the past

▶ **Incremental departures** from the past

A third category of this dimension, **architectural innovation,**[9] exploits the notion that all innovations are really "systems" of parts. This category underscores the two types of knowledge needed to innovate: architectural knowledge about how the components go together and the knowledge of the components themselves.

Radial departures are extremely rare; perhaps only 6 to 10 percent of new products, for example, are truly new to the world.[10] New processing technology, such as a new way of making steel, uses a different science to convert ore to finished product and makes current knowledge obsolete. Incremental innovation is, of course, more typical. Since information technology is in the mainstream of technologies most people experience daily, an example of incremental IS technology software is presented in Box 2-2. Although the computer hardware industry continues to innovate at a blinding pace, innovation in software has slowed considerably.

---

[8] J. Ettlie, R. D. O'Keefe, and W. P. Bridges, "Organizational Strategy and Structural Differences for Radical versus Incremental Innovation," *Management Science,* 30, no. 6 (June 1984), pp. 682–695.

[9] R. Henderson and K. Clark, "Architectural Innovation: The Reconfiguration of Existing Product Technologies and the Failure of Established Firms," *Administrative Science Quarterly,* 35 (March 1990), pp. 9–30.

[10] Booz, Allen, & Hamilton, Inc., *New Products Management for the 1980s* (New York: Booz, Allen, and Hamilton, Inc, 1982). This percentage was 6 percent in 1997 of 25,261 new products introduced in the United States, 7 percent in 1996 (of 24,496 new products), and 19 percent in 1986 according to *Marketing News* (March 30, 1998).

BOX 2 - 2

Incremental Technology: Software Features Galore[11]

Microsoft argued in recent contention with the U.S. Department of Justice that any antitrust action against the company would hurt innovation (see the case at the end of Chapter 10). "What does the Justice Department know about software development?" representatives of Microsoft asked. But if Windows 98, recently released by Microsoft, is any indication, the Justice Department doesn't have to worry about disrupting innovation at the targeted company. There is little difference between Windows 95 and Windows 98 from the user's perspective. Contrast this with computer hardware, which has, and continues to be, faster and cheaper every time you turn around.

The software industry is beset with chronic incrementalism. The net result is that PCs cannot deal with the volumes of data and transactions needed in today's world of the Internet and electronic mail. Worse, much of today's software, loaded with features that most customers seldom use, is often beset with bugs and problems. PC sales are threatened by this slowdown in software development, because customers won't see the need to buy new systems if the old versions are doing just fine.

The history of Intuit, Inc. and its Quicken personal-finance software is a good case in point. Software programmers want to continue to add new features to the program, but consumers reject these add-ons and the disc space required. Customers want simpler ways to solve day-to-day problems such as figuring out how much they spend on utility bills. "What passes for innovation is more often than not, like Windows 98, simply an incremental improvement of an existing product." The Internet is where all the real innovative activity is happening today, where consumer interest is new and not dependent on investments in previous generations of technology. Only when a technology has a clear limitation is there an opportunity for a breakthrough, like the potential to improve e-mail. Microsoft's dominant position in the industry has probably contributed to this situation, as well, which may or may not be bad, depending on your viewpoint. But Microsoft has been ready to incorporate 3-D effects into its operating system for some time and can't seem to find a way to do it.

The PC could evolve into a major communications and control device. A PC could run the household, for example. As an alternative, innovation could take off in other directions. For example, as microchips continue to become more powerful and cheaper, they could be installed almost anywhere—in car tires, kitchen appliances, walls, or almost anything that has to work for a consumer. Intelligent machines may be just around the corner.

---

[11] This summary is based, in part, on Lee Gomes, "Bigger vs. Better: As Innovation Slows, Software Companies Pile on the Features," *Wall Street Journal* (June 25, 1998), A1, A5. Also see the case at the end of Chapter 10 by David Bank and John R. Wilke, "Browser Bruiser: Microsoft and Justice End a Skirmish, Yet War Could Escalate," *Wall Street Journal* (January 23, 1998), p. A1.

$\mathscr{S}$TAGE MODELS

As an organizing principle, the notion that an innovation evolves from the germ of an idea into a concept and eventually sees the light of day as a commercialized or applied idea is a convenient way to organize the entire subject of technology management. This idea is usually summarized in some form of stage model. An example of this type of stage model appears in Figure 2-2.

Not all of these stage models of the innovation process are the same, but most are similar. They vary a bit by perspective, as do the definitions of innovation. In this model, presumed to be derived from consulting, the process begins with conducting market research, which, in turn, leads to planning research, conducting research, applying know-how, and continually improving outcomes. If one compares this model with one that originates from the technological forecasting community, via Jospeh Martino (see Figure 2-3), there are some critical differences. For example, in the Martino version of the stages of the innovation process, scientific findings "kick-off" the process, and it ends with social and economic impact. The implication is that this process can be negative, as the last frame of the Martino model depicts dark smoke belching from a large truck's stack exhaust. Nevertheless, Martino implies that this process *does* represent a strange type of progress. Note that the original figure of a man appears to be right out of a cave. At the end, "modern" man prevails.

$\mathcal{T}$ECHNOLOGY STRATEGY

Technology strategy for an organization is covered in depth in Chapter 4, but it is helpful to introduce it here. Many readers will have already concluded that the R&D strategy of an organization (i.e., the portfolio of R&D project investments and long-range goals for research) is the same as its technology strategy (i.e., how a firm will acquire and use technologies for effective competition). In many cases, they overlap significantly; however, it is worth considering these two policies separately, at least at first, in a company. No organization can hope to independently develop all the technology usually required to sustain growth. Therefore, a technology strategy needs to consider technology acquisition issues in addition to investment choices.

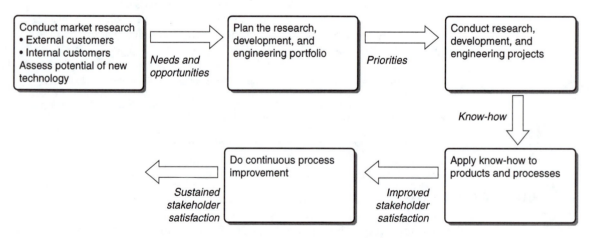

Figure 2-2   The Continuous Process of Technology Development
Source: P. R. Koyak. "Realizing the Power of Technology." *Prism* (1993), p. 6.

SCIENTIFIC FINDINGS... LABORATORY FEASIBILITY... OPERATING PROTOTYPE... COMMERCIAL INTRODUCTION...

WIDESPREAD ADOPTION... DIFFUSION TO OTHER AREAS... SOCIAL & ECONOMIC IMPACT...

Figure 2-3 Stages of Innovation

SOURCE: J. Martino, *The Futurist* (1993), p. 16. Used with permission from the World Future Society. Illustrated by Tom Chalkley.

One way to define **technology strategy** is by understanding the products and services a firm brings to market and the intersection of these outputs with their underlying technologies. A matrix can be used to array this corporate structure, with products or stages of the value-added chain along the top and technologies along the side of the matrix. This approach is summarized by Burgelman and his coauthors.[12] They emphasize that it is the degree of distinctive competence in these technologies—the firm's relative strength—that matters for strategic purposes. One can audit these capabilities, and the authors provide such an audit framework for both the business unit and the corporation with three essential questions:

1. How has the firm been innovative in areas of product and service offerings and/or production and delivery systems?
2. How good is the fit between the firm's current business and corporate strategies and its innovative capabilities?
3. What are the firm's needs in terms of innovative capabilities to support its long-term business and corporate competitive strategies?

Look carefully at the second point for a moment. The general consensus among strategists is that there ought to be consistency among strategies in a firm. There is even some empirical evidence supporting this notion. However, whenever a firm

---

[12] R. Burgelman, M. Maidique, and S. Wheelright. *Strategic Management of Technology 2nd Innovation,* (New York: Irwin/McGraw-Hill, 1996), pp. 5–8.

changes, it often changes part of what it does first, and then the other parts follow (see the platform approach to product development in Chapter 7). This means that sometimes in an innovating firm, strategies may not be consistent, so the term *fit* among strategies may need some subtle interpretation.

An example of technology strategy might illustrate these concepts. Caterpiller, Inc. recently shared a summary of its technology strategy, and its approach, which is outlined by Abraham Zadoks[13], Caterpillar's director of new technology, is quite reminiscent of the "House of Quality". The first house of quality arrays customers' wants and needs on the left against the hows on the top. In this summary from Caterpillar, customer *wants and needs* appear on the left side of the "house," as in QFD (Quality Function Deployment), and the *hows* are the various technology strategies. These strategies, in turn, lead into the second "house" for research programs, then to technologies, and then into products, which feed back into customer wants and needs all over again. The Caterpillar case is presented in Chapter 4. This renewal process also suggests a way of deciding when to refresh technology in products, which is described in Chapter 7, when the platform approach to product families is discussed.

Finally, and to be quite clear about terms, one must be careful not to confuse the terms *technology strategy,* which applies to corporations as a unit, and *technology policy,* which is the policy that governments pursue in their country's best interest for innovation. The two are often quite intimately related. If and how the government should support an individual firm's R&D, how these programs should be governed, and what should be proprietary and what should be public, might have significant implications for company's fortunes.[14] The issue of technology policy is taken up as a separate topic in Chapter 10. But the issue of technology strategy for firms and business units is of great importance to all managers, as we will see later. An illustration of these strategy issues appears in the case summary of Gillette's Sensor Razor launch, which is included at the end of the chapter. Note the interaction of product and process strategy in this introductory case.

$\mathscr{R}$&D MANAGEMENT

The first industrial research laboratory was begun by Thomas Edison. It is hard to evaluate what the effect of this management innovation has been, but the world has not been the same since. Edison started with a very careful study of the gas industry and patterned some of his practices on this older industry in introducing the incandescent lightbulb. But he is also said to have thought that the phonograph would be useful primarily as a means of recording old men's dying wishes.[15] So, the inventor who originated the industrial research laboratory did not have perfect vision.

It is not surprising that much of what is published on the innovation process is about R&D and its management. The organization of the creative function of an enterprise has always been considered challenging and different from managing the other functions of an organization. The management of technical professionals

---

[13] A. Zadoks, "Managing Technology at Caterpillar," *Research Technology Management,* 40, no. 1 (January/February, 1997), p. 49.

[14] R. Nelson, *National Innovation Systems* (New York: Oxford University Press, 1993), pp. 512–513.

[15] N. Rosenberg, *Perspectives on Technology* (Cambridge: Cambridge University Press, 1976), pp. 75, 197.

today is still very much reflective of issues introduced in early epochs of the innovation process. Ralph Katz characterizes this issue as the "challenges of 'dualism,' that is, operating effectively today while also innovating for tomorrow." His own research is focused on the socialization of new professionals and their careers in technical organizations.[16]

The fundamentals of R&D are straightforward. Industries vary by the extent to which firms participating in product groups invest in R&D. The measure most commonly adopted is **R&D intensity,** which is the investment in R&D as a percentage of sales on an annual basis. High-technology firms, among other things, spend more on R&D and have a higher R&D intensity ratio. But these same firms may not differ from their industry peers in this regard. About half the variance in R&D intensity can be explained by industry affiliation.[17] An example of this variation by industry appears in Table 2-1. The National Science Foundation has compiled R&D intensity by industry; the most recent data available are from 1994. The overall industry average (company and other, except federal, R&D) was 2.9 percent in 1994.

✖ Firm Size and R&D Expenditure

Table 2-1 summarizes R&D performance by firm size and illustrates the general trend supporting Schumpeter's original hypothesis that larger firms perform more R&D. Williamson modified this hypothesis slightly, suggesting that extreme size leads to diminished returns to R&D (see Figure 2-4a). "Assuming that R&D expenditures experience constant returns to scale, one could ... make a case for the proposition that the relative contribution to progressiveness is greatest among upper middle-sized firms."[18]

𝒯ABLE 2-1   Company and Other (Except Federal) R&D Funds as a Percentage of Net Sales in R&D (Performing Manufacturing Companies, by Industry and Size of Company: 1984–1994)

Distribution by Size of Company: (Number of Employees)	1984	1985	1986	1987	1988	1989	1990	1991	1992	1993	1994
Totals	2.6%	3.0%	3.2%	3.1%	3.1%	3.1%	3.1%	3.2%	3.3%	3.1%	2.9%
Fewer than 500	2.8	3.4	4.0	3.8	3.7	3.5	3.3	3.2	3.6	3.6	2.5
500 to 999	2.2	2.2	2.2	2.2	1.7	1.7	1.7	2.4	2.7	2.7	2.5
1,000 to 4,999	2.0	2.4	2.4	2.4	2.3	2.1	1.9	2.4	2.5	2.5	2.5
5,000 to 9,999	1.6	1.8	2.0	2.0	2.0	2.1	2.8	2.9	2.8	2.8	2.2
10,000 to 24,999	2.5	2.5	2.6	2.5	2.6	2.5	2.5	3.0	2.5	2.5	2.5
25,000 or more	3.2	3.5	3.7	3.8	3.7	3.7	3.6	3.8	3.7	3.7	3.6

NOTE: As a result of a new sample design, statistics for 1988–1991 have been revised since originally published. These statistics now better reflect R&D performance among firms in the nonmanufacturing industries and small firms in all industries.

SOURCE: National Science Foundation/SRS, *Survey of Industrial Research and Development* (Washington D. C.: U. S. Government Printing Office, 1994).

---

[16] R. Katz (ed.), *Managing Professionals in Innovative Organizations* (New York: Harper Business Division of HarperCollins Publishers, 1988), p. xi.

[17] W. Cohen, M. Levin, and D. Mowery, "Firm Size and R&D Intensity: A Re-examination," *Journal of Industrial Economics,* 35, no. 4 (1987), pp. 543–565.

This theory was supported by Ettlie and Rubenstein in study of new products. In Figure 2-4*b*, where new product radicalness was substituted for R&D intensity (intensiveness in Figure 2-4*a*).[19] The concept of size has always been problematical to research on innovation and in economics, as well. Size is often taken as a proxy for other firm characteristics such as access to resources, reputation, and political clout. Size has been argued to be both a cause and result of innovation. Size is considered by some as an asset in creating innovation potential by concentrating technical employees in a critical mass of thinkers working together on one problem from several perspectives. But larger firms also become sluggish, committed to the past, and invested heavily in status-quo maintenance.

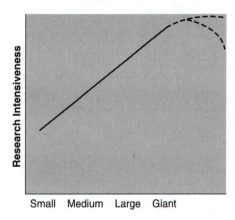

Figure 2-4*a*
Proposed Firm Size and R&D Intensity
Relationship

SOURCE: O. E. Williamson, "Markets and Hierarchies Analysis and Antitrust Implications", (New York: The Free Press, 1975), p. 182. Reprinted with the permission of The Free Press, a division of Simon & Schuster.

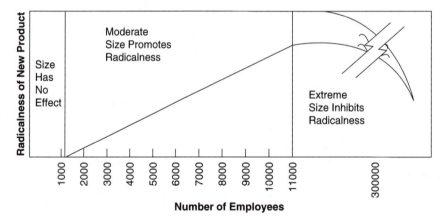

Figure 2-4*b*   Relationship Between Firm Size and New Product Radicalness (Based on 348 Manufacturing Cases)

SOURCE: J. E. Ettlie and A. H. Rubenstein, "Firm Size and Product Innovation," *Journal of Product Innovation Management,* 4 (1987), pp. 89–108. Figure 2, p. 99.

---

[18] O. E. Williamson, *Markets and Hierarchies Analysis and Antitrust Implications* (New York: The Free Press, 1975).

[19] J. E. Ettlie and A. H. Rubenstein, Firm size and product innovation, *Journal of Product Innovation Management,* 4 (1987), pp. 89–108.

Ettlie and Rubenstein attempted to sort out these issues by identifying truly radical innovations in the food, paper, chemical, rubber, machinery, and electrical equipment industries and noting their relation to company size. They sampled 348 new products introduced between 1979 and 1982. Industry experts and awards were used to qualify "radical" status and bestow this label on a sampled case. Nonresponse in the survey was unrelated to firm size—large and small firms responded equally. The simple correlation between size and radicaliness (on a 12-point scale) was $r = .11$, which is statistically significant ($p < .02$), but not a very large coefficient for this sample of new products. One cannot conclude that small or large size is either an asset or liability from this simple result.

The absence of simple relationship between size and innovative new product introduction occurs because the relationship is not linear. Small firms introduce radical and incremental new products at nearly the same rate. As size increases, fewer incremental and no innovation products appear in the distribution, until the "pure" case of innovation appears to peak at about 11,000 employees. Under 1,000 employees, which is well above what government archives typically use as the cutoff for a small firm (500 employees), there is no clear pattern of innovation. In companies with between 1,000 and 10,000 employees, innovation clearly builds, and size is an asset. But above 11,000 employees, the pattern is clear. Very large size corresponds significantly to a clear lack of innovation in product technology—large size is an innovating liability.

Are radical new products more likely to be successful? Ettlie and Rubenstein also investigated this question to determine whether having a radical new product, as opposed to other explanations, was significantly associated with commercial success (return a multiple of program investment). Statistically significant results were obtained: *Radical new products are significantly more likely to be commercially successful.*

The authors also found that commercial success was significantly correlated, controlling for other effects (including size), with the absence of over-budget requests and, to a lesser extent, the absence of continuing cost problems. This finding can be interpreted as an indication that, to the extent that size bestows resources on the innovation process, it can promote innovation. Size, per se, was not the determining factor of whether a firm was innovative, except in extremely large organizations, where it was a liability. Size was not significantly correlated with either over-budget requests or continuing cost problems. However, continuing cost problems *were* significantly associated with the introduction of new process technology. Small firms could be disadvantaged in this regard. These results are summarized in Table 2-2.

$\mathcal{T}$ABLE 2-2   New Product Success and Radical Technology

Predictor	Std. Regression Coefficient	Regression F	Cum. R^2
1. Over-budget (1=yes, 0=no)	−0.16*	11.2*	3%
2. Radical Product	0.14*	9.23*	4.5%
3. Continuing Cost (1=yes, 0=no)	−0.09	7.12*	5%

* $p < .01$ (For 348 new products introduced 1979–1982 in the food, paper, chemical, rubber, machinery, and electrical equipment industries.

SOURCE: J. E. Ettlie and A. H. Rubenstein, "Firm size and product innovation", *Journal of Product Innovation Management,* 4, (1987), Table 3, p. 100.

These results suggest that small firms need not be disadvantaged by size in becoming radically innovative. Many times, as we will see later, small companies need to have breakthrough products to crash down entry barriers in an industry. They can make up for resource shortages by cooperating with innovation partners, some of which are low cost, such as universities and federal laboratories—especially when new processing technology is required to introduce a new product. Customers and suppliers can also make good partners, and in research consortia, many such partners are available. In incubators, the proximity to other startup companies that apparently had the same problems seems to have helped significantly (see Chapter 10).

✳ R&D Allocation

For the average company, spending on R&D is the key resource allocation that determines whether innovative products will result. Refer to Table 2-3 again and note the industry differences. For example, the food industry (SIC, Standard Industrial Classification 20 and 21) with an R&D intensity of 0.5 percent in 1994 is substan-

𝒯ABLE 2-3   Company and Other (Except Federal) R&D Funds as a Percentage of Net Sales in R&D (Performing Manufacturing Companies, by Industry 1984–1994)

Industry and Size of Company	SIC Code	1984	1985	1986	1987	1988	1989	1990	1991	1992	1993	1994
Total		2.6%	3.0%	3.2%	3.1%	3.1%	3.1%	3.1%	3.2%	3.3%	3.1%	2.9%
Distribution by Industry:												
Food, kindred, and tobacco products	20, 21	0.4	0.6	0.6	0.6	0.5	0.5	0.5	0.5	0.5	0.5	0.5
Textiles and apparel	22, 23	0.5	0.5	0.5	0.4	0.4	0.5	0.6	0.6	0.6	0.6	0.6
Lumber, wood products, and furniture	24, 25	0.7	0.8	0.6	0.6	0.6	0.6	0.6	0.9	0.9	0.7	0.6
Paper and allied products	26	0.8	0.8	0.7	0.6	0.8	0.8	1.0	1.1	1.0	1.1	1.0
Chemicals and allied products	28	4.6	4.9	5.1	5.2	5.2	5.4	5.3	5.3	5.4	6.0	5.1
Industrial chemicals	281–82, 286	3.8	4.2	4.4	4.4	4.2	4.1	4.4	4.4	4.4	4.4	3.3
Drugs and medicines	283	8.2	8.0	8.4	8.7	8.8	8.9	8.8	8.9	9.6	12.5	10.2
Other chemicals	284–85, 287–89	2.9	3.1	3.3	3.3	3.4	3.9	3.4	3.0	2.7	2.7	2.5
Petroleum refining and extraction	13, 29	0.7	0.9	1.1	1.0	1.0	0.9	0.9	1.0	0.9	0.9	0.8
Rubber products	30	1.9	1.8	1.7	1.6	1.7	1.9	2.1	2.3	2.3	2.1	2.3
Stone, clay, and glass products	32	1.9	2.3	2.4	2.5	2.0	1.8	1.7	1.6	1.6	1.5	1.5
Primary metals	33	0.9	0.9	1.0	0.9	0.7	0.7	0.8	0.8	0.6	0.7	0.6
Ferrous metals and products	331–32, 398–99	0.6	0.5	0.7	0.6	0.5	0.5	0.5	0.5	0.4	0.4	0.3
Nonferrous metals and products	333–36	1.2	1.4	1.5	1.3	1.0	1.0	1.2	1.2	0.7	1.2	0.9

continues

$\mathcal{T}_{ABLE}$ 2-3   Continued

Industry and Size of Company	SIC Code	1984	1985	1986	1987	1988	1989	1990	1991	1992	1993	1994
Fabricated metal products	34	1.4	1.4	1.4	1.2	1.1	1.2	1.1	1.2	1.1	1.1	1.0
Machinery	35	5.8	6.7	7.3	7.1	6.8	7.3	7.2	7.5	7.3	4.5	3.8
Office, computing, and accounting machines	357	10.5	12.4	12.4	12.3	11.2	13.1	14.4	14.9	13.7	9.8	7.9
Other machinery, except electrical	351–56, 358–59	2.5	2.6	2.9	3.0	2.8	2.6	2.3	2.9	2.9	2.5	2.5
Electrical equipment	36	4.5	4.8	5.1	5.4	5.3	5.2	4.5	4.3	4.0	5.4	5.2
Radio and TV receiving equipment	365	3.7	4.3	3.6	3.2	2.4	1.8	1.6	1.0	0.6	4.0	1.0
Communication equipment	366	5.1	5.4	5.2	5.5	6.1	6.8	6.1	6.1	7.0	10.1	10.3
Electric components	367	6.6	8.2	9.2	8.5	8.0	7.7	7.4	7.2	7.0	7.8	7.3
Other electrical equipment	361–64, 369	2.2	2.0	2.2	2.6	2.3	2.3	2.2	2.2	2.1	2.3	2.1
Transportation equipment	37	3.3	3.4	3.6	3.4	3.5	3.5	3.4	4.0	4.2	3.9	3.7
Motor vehicles and motor vehicle equipment	371	3.0	3.1	3.3	3.4	3.4	3.7	3.7	4.1	4.0	3.7	3.4
Other transportation equipment	373–75, 379	2.0	2.3	2.7	2.5	2.6	2.5	2.1	2.1	2.1	1.9	1.2
Aircraft and missiles	372, 376	4.0	3.9	4.0	3.6	3.9	3.3	3.1	4.0	4.7	4.7	5.3
Professional and scientific instruments	38	7.6	8.3	8.2	7.5	7.1	6.8	7.1	7.1	7.2	7.2	6.5
Scientific and mechanical measuring instruments	381–82	8.3	8.4	8.4	8.1	7.6	6.9	6.9	6.3	6.2	6.4	5.8
Optical, surgical, photographic, and other instruments	384–87	7.3	8.1	8.0	7.2	7.1	7.1	7.5	8.0	8.2	7.9	7.2
Other manufacturing industries	27, 31, 39	1.1	1.0	1.2	1.1	1.0	0.9	0.9	0.8	1.3	1.3	1.1

SOURCE: National Science Foundation/SRS, 1994.

tially different from chemicals and allied products (SIC 28) at 5.1 percent and drugs and medicines (SIC 283) at 10.2 percent of sales spent on R&D in 1994. Anything more than 6 percent R&D intensity is usually considered a high-technology industry. And any firm within any industry spending more than 6 percent of sales on R&D would be considered working on high-technology products and services. These companies employ many technical professionals and generally serve products that are not mature (are growing quickly) and, in some cases, are changing more often.

How are R&D dollars spent? Mostly on new products. See Figure 2-5 from an annual R&D benchmarking survey. In 1994, companies that were members of the Industrial Research Institute spent about 41 percent of their R&D budgets on new products, up from 34 percent in 1988. Note that technical service spending was up slightly, which some believe is a consequence of bringing out more new products faster—they require more follow-up.

R&D spending is gradually globalizing. Although the majority of spending for all companies, regardless of their home of origin, is in the home country, the globalization of markets is forcing companies to outsource and localize more R&D

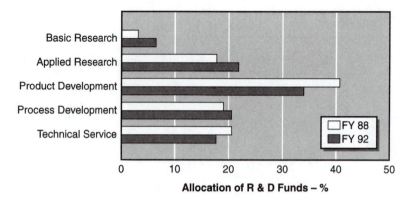

Figure 2-5 Allocation of R&D funds, FY 1988 and 1992

SOURCE: R. L. Whitely,. Cims Industrial Research Institute's Annual R&D Forecasting Trends, *Research Technology Management,* 37, no. 1 (1994), p. 22.

spending. U.S. corporate R&D spent overseas grew from $66.6 billion in 1987 to $85.6 billion in 1991 and is over $100 million today[20] (see Chapter 5).

Finally, the last basic issue, does R&D pay off? Most reports agree that R&D does add real value, but there are few rigorous empirical studies on this issue. Clearly, companies are not investing in R&D based on faith alone. And when profitability falls, R&D budgets are often the first easy target for cuts. One study, reported by Alden Bean, shows that the impact of basic and applied research was indirect but significant on total factor productivity for fifteen drug companies between 1971 and 1990 (see Figure 2-6).

Note that both new process development (see Figure 2-5) and new product development are significantly correlated with total factor productivity, based on regression coefficients (b = 1.76 and b = 3.38, respectively). (To test significance of a regression coefficient, double the standard error in parentheses. If it is less than the coefficient, the correlation is significant, controlling for other effects.[20]) Also note that basic and applied research have significant, but indirect, impacts on total factor productivity, operating through new product and process development (just new product development in the case of applied research).

Since Bean's findings controlled for firm size, it is interesting to note the results reported by Graves and Langowitz for the pharmaceutical industry.[21] They start with Schumpeter's hypothesis that innovative output increases with firm size but qualify this theory by finding that small firms may have an advantage in industries

---

[20] Regression coefficients are used here and in several other research studies summarized in this book as a way of estimating the strength of a causal relationship between at least two latent variables that have been measured using some operational definition. It is assumed that simple regression, which is one method of fitting a straight line to the relationship between two variables like height and weight of individuals (proposed to be a direct relationship with a line of positive slope), is easily within the grasp of the reader. Although multiple regression is slightly more complicated, it merely controls for the effects of other variables. LISREL models also include the estimates of latent variable indicators at the same time that "path" coefficients (here regression coefficients) are estimated. For an introduction to LISREL see Karl G. Joreskog and Dag Sorbom, *LISREL 7 User's Reference Guide,* Scientific Software International, Inc, Chicago, 1989.

[21] S. B. Graves and N. S. Langowitz, "Innovative Output and Firm Size in The Pharmaceutical Industry", *International Journal of Production Economics, Amsterdam,* 27, no. 1 (April 1992), p. 83.

Investments in: BR = Basic Research
                  AP = Applied Research
                  PCD = Process Development
                  PDD = Product Development
                  TFP = Total Factor Productivity (Fim)

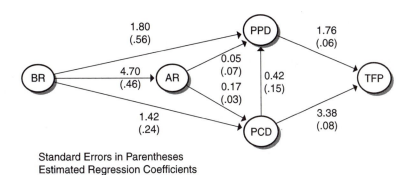

Standard Errors in Parentheses
Estimated Regression Coefficients

Figure 2-6   Basic Research Enhances the Contribution of Product and Process Development to Productivity Growth

SOURCE: A. S. Bean, Why some R&D organizations are more productive than others, *Research-Technology Management*, 38, no. 1 (Jan/Feb 1995), p. 38.

that are very innovative, require highly skilled personnel, and have a high concentration of large firms. Only modest increases in growth contribute significantly to shareholder value, and it is not surprising that the relationship between firm size and innovativeness continues to attract research effort.

This does not resolve the issue of differential investment of R&D resources. In firms that formalized research and development, and across countries that have firms investing in R&D, these investments pay off significantly in improved productivity. This return on private investment in R&D is substantially larger (seven times larger at the national level) than investment in capital equipment and structures.[22]

One other empirical study on the benefits from R&D is worth noting here. The study by Bernstein and Nadiri is often cited in the economics literature on cooperative versus competitive R&D.[23] They found that the social rates of return to R&D investment were approximately double that of private rates of return (the investing companies) in the chemical products and nonelectrical machinery industries. This social rate of return was roughly ten times the private rate of return in the scientific instruments industry.

Even with these impressive empirical results, the trend is toward more applied research with more immediate payoffs and in business units and divisions as opposed to corporate laboratories. For example, GE now spends the vast majority of R&D in its decentralized business groups, and this is the general trend among all U.S. R&D performers.[24]

---

[22] F. R. Lichtenberg, "Issues in Measuring Industrial R&D", Research Policy, 19, no. 2 (1992), pp 157–163.

[23] J. I. Bernstein and M. I. Nadiri, "Interindustry R&D Spillovers, Rates of Return, and Production in Industries," *American Economics Review*, 78 (May 1988, Papers and Proceedings 1987): pp. 429–34.

[24] See "Corporate Research: How Much Is It Worth?" *Wall Street Journal* (May 22, 1995).

Corporate research has gone the way of the telegraph and points to a critical recurring theme—scarce resources, especially in the age of globalization—become the rationale for more and more decisions, including innovation decisions. The case presented at the end of the chapter raises the practical issue of how much to spend on reinventing a company. R&D management is taken up later in Chapter 5.

✳ Manufacturing R&D

Since most U.S. R&D funds are spent on new products, where does new operations and manufacturing technology originate? How is it sourced? Most operations technology is purchased from suppliers. Banks and other service institutions buy hardware/software systems from computer companies and systems integrators. Manufacturing firms buy hardware/software systems from companies such as machine tool builders, materials handling equipment suppliers, and the like. Therefore, process technology adopters have the unique problem of appropriation of benefits from technological innovation.[25] That is, since suppliers are typically free to sell their hardware/software technology to anyone in a free-market economy, users of these technologies have to find unique ways of "appropriating," or capturing, the benefits of these nonexclusive technologies.

Of course, many companies, especially those in the process industries such as drugs and chemicals, spend a great deal on new processing technology. It is more difficult to decouple product and process in these industries. The more unusual case is to find product or service industry firms investing in manufacturing technology. Honda is the rare exception in the auto industry, for example, that supplies itself with much of its own process technology.

An alternative approach to this dilemma of capturing benefits from process innovation investments, which you don't want to sell to others, is to enter into collaborative R&D agreements to spread the risk and investment burden, which can be substantial. The Low Emissions Paint Consortium (LEPC) in the U.S. auto industry illustrates this broader trend toward collaborative R&D worldwide. This case presents the co-development of powder clear-coat painting systems by Ford Motor Company, General Motors Corporation, DaimlerChrysler Corporation, and key technology suppliers. This new system is being developed and designed to replace the current technology, which is a solvent-born clear-coat covering. When this system works, it will avoid regulatory constraints currently imposed on the auto industry painting process.

Most of the economic theory that predicts collaborative R&D behavior involves multistage game theory.[26] The economists are quite concerned generally with public versus private rates of return on R&D in these models, and they start by asking two basic questions: why do firms conduct R&D, and what are the incentives?[27] In theory, firms conduct R&D to generate knowledge to produce new products or to produce existing products at lower cost. A third reason for R&D is to sell knowledge to others.

[25] P. J. Teece. "Capturing Value from Technological Innovation: Integration, Strategic Planning, and Licensing Decisions, *Interfaces,* 18 (1988), pp. 46–61

[26] M. Momotta, "Cooperative R&D and Vertical Product Differentiation" *International Journal of Technology Management,* 10 (1992), pp. 643–661

[27] M. L. Katz, J. A. Ordover, F. Fischer, and R. Schmalensee, *R&D Cooperation and Competition: Comments and Discussion,* Brookings Papers on Economic Activity, Washington D. C. (1990), p. 137.

The source of divergence between public and private benefits (or the inability of private firms to appropriate all the benefits from R&D investments) results from several conditions. The most important theoretical reason is what economists call **technological spillover.** For example, firms cannot be sure that the knowledge generated is kept completely within the organization. A second reason comes from the condition frequently encountered in practice: New or cheaper products often require complementary technology or production assets. Government policies (such as antitrust laws) often block complete capture of benefits. Finally, the sale of R&D findings often results in benefits that are insufficient to justify the costs.

$\mathcal{T}$ECHNOLOGY AND SOCIETY

During the 1990s, the U.S. economy, generally, and manufacturing, in particular, experienced nearly unprecedented growth and high performance. Manufacturing productivity grew by a rate of 4.4 percent in 1996,[28] and 1998 industrial output was about 3 percent above 1997 levels.[29] Durable goods manufacturing, in particular, has been very strong, with increased output of 9.5 percent in 1997.[30] The Dow Jones Industrial Average soared from less than 6,000 in mid-1996 to 11,000 in mid-1999, before backing off that high.[31]

Unemployment levels are low[32] and since productivity is up, the hourly cost of U.S. production workers is still relatively low compared with the major developed regions of the world. In the United States, the 1996 hourly cost of a production worker was $17.70, up 3 percent from the previous year. In Europe, the 1996 cost per hour for a production worker was $22.37, but this was only 1.2 percent higher than 1995. In Japan, hourly production worker rates fell 12.4 percent in 1995 to $20.84 in 1996. If one uses the measure of cost per unit of output as the comparison base, the United States was enjoying a 5 to 10 percent labor advantage over Japan (using an exchange rate of 130 yen to the dollar) and a 25 percent labor advantage over Europe.

What accounts for this continuing vitality in U.S. economic statistics? One possible explanation of this high performance is the strategic drive for increasing effectiveness and efficiency with new products, new production technology, and improved methods in U.S. industry. Further, U.S. technology policy may also be instrumental in this success. We explore these hypotheses in the following pages. First, we analyze the data on the relationship between investment in R&D and performance of the largest U.S. companies. Then we confront the manufacturing technology and public policy question directly.

---

[28] "Data Bank," *National Productivity Review,* 17, no. 3 (Summer 1998), pp. 91–94.

[29] "Manufacturing Boom to Continue in 1998," *Graphic Arts Monthly,* 70, no. 3 (March 1998), p. 16.

[30] R. Raddock, "Industrial Production and Capacity Utilization: Annual Revision and 1997 Developments," *Federal Reserve Bulletin,* 84, no. 2 (February 1998), pp. 77–91.

[31] Dow Jones & Co. Web site: www.averages.dowjones.com.

[32] Unemployment among married men fell in June (1998) to 2.2% of the total civilian work force from 2.4% in May, based on data from the U.S. Department of Labor and joblessness among married women rose to 2.9% from 2.8% during the same period (*Wall Street Journal,* July 21, 1998), p. 41.

Technology and Economic Performance

Does technology have a positive impact on company performance, as so many have argued? R&D intensity has been shown to have a significant direct impact on market growth among 600 durable goods manufacturers in twenty countries,[33] as well as a significant indirect effect on total factor productivity by enhancing new product and new process development in the drug industry as we saw earlier.[34]

It seems clear from these results that technology makes a difference in economic outcomes. But *how* does technology matter? One theory is that new technology changes the knowledge base of organizations by enhancing the product or service capacity of units and underwrites the processing capability of operations.[35] Practically speaking, this comes down to how technical investments are made in a society. The majority of R&D dollars are currently allocated for the development of new products or new services, but this varies greatly by industrial sector.[36] As a consequence, processing technology, including information technology systems, are usually purchased rather than developed. There is an effort to tailor these information systems to support new product development and standardized operations (e.g., purchasing) in successful companies.[37] However, the reengineering of business processes has proven to be a risky business, with failure rates running as high as 70 percent.[38] Even though $250 billion is spent every year in the United States on new computer systems, appropriation of the benefits of these investments remains elusive.[39] On the other hand, about 60 percent of new products introduced in the United States are successful after they are commercialized.[40] Therefore, we concentrate here on investments in new plant, equipment, and information systems.

Manufacturing Technology

New processing technologies do not implement themselves. New systems are usually purchased outside and their development is episodic, especially for major modernization or new product and service launch. Therefore, appropriation or capture of benefits from these investments is problematic, primarily because the

---

[33] See, for example, J.E. Ettlie, "R&D and Global Manufacturing Performance," *Management Science,* 44, no. 1 (January 1998), pp. 1–11.

[34] Bean, 1995, p. 29.

[35] B. Wysocki, "Wealth of Notions: For this Economist, Long-Term Prosperity Hangs on Good Ideas." *Wall Street Journal* (January 21, 1997), pp. A1, A8.

[36] Wolfe (1994) reports that about 43% of R&D spending is for new products, but service R&D is also increasing, which suggests that this new product activity requires some "fixing" the field. Cohen et al. (1995) say that about half of the variance in R&D intensity is explained by the industry in which the firm operates.

[37] J. E. Ettlie, "Integrated Design and New Product Success," *Journal of Operations Management,* 15, no. 1 (February 1997), pp. 33–55.

[38] T. J. Crowe and J. D. Rolfes, "Selecting BPR Projects based on Strategic Objectives," *Business Process Management Journal,* 4, no. 2 (1998), pp. 114–136.

[39] B. Wysocki, "Pulling the Plug: Some Firms, Let Down by Costly Computers, Opt to 'Deengineer,'" *Wall Street Journal* (April 30, 1998), pp. A1, A8.

[40] J. E. Ettlie, "Integrated Design and New Product Success," *Journal of Operations Management Columbia,* 15, no. 1 (Feb 1997), p. 33.

technology is theoretically available to anyone who can pay for it, including competitors.[41] The extant literature on appropriation of manufacturing technology rents suggests two important conclusions.

1. Successful modernization hinges on the *extent* and *specific mosaic* of technologies adopted.

2. Performance of manufacturing technology depends on *which* (if any) *organizational innovations are adopted* in conjunction with deployment.

These two generalizations are quite far-reaching and complex, so they are discussed separately. To the extent that the resources of a firm determine how outcomes will be pursued, the role of government becomes more important.[42]

The Adoption of Manufacturing Technologies

During the last decade, the relative absence of rigorous applied research on the adoption of manufacturing technology has been replaced by a number of important contributions in both the academic and applied press. Much of this literature has been reviewed elsewhere,[43] so we focus here on just a few of the most relevant studies germane to the central questions of this inquiry. For the time being, we will set aside the limitations of this work and return to future research needs in Chapter 9.

Perhaps the most comprehensive data available on the investment in manufacturing technology, primarily in the durable goods and assembled products industries, resulted from collection in two panels by the U.S. Department of Commerce (DOC) in 1988 and 1993. Fortunately, comparative data were also collected in Canada at approximately the same time (1989). These data have been analyzed by several research teams, but we focus here on just a few. Efforts to duplicate this work in Europe are also relevant, but are mentioned only in passing here.

Seventeen specific manufacturing technologies used in durable goods manufacturing (SIC 34–38) were included in the DOC survey. These data have subsequently been augmented with statistics from the Census of Manufacturing and data from other sources to develop a comprehensive picture of technology impact for 7,000 plants.[44] Earlier results from nearly identical data showed that the more technology plants adopted ("technology intensity"), the higher the rates

---

[41] See, for example, D. Echevarria, "Capital Investment and Profitability of Fortune 500 Industrials: 1971–1990," *Studies in Economics and Finance,* 18, no. 1 (Fall 1997), pp. 3-35, who reports that "only 25% of the Fortune 500 … were able to obtain significantly increased profitability," p. 35.

[42] It is important to control for industry effects in these generalizations. Experience varies widely by economic sector. See R. S. M. Lau, "Operational Characteristics of Highly Competitive Firms," *Production and Inventory Management Journal,* 38, no. 4 (Fourth Quarter 1997), pp. 17–21.

[43] J. E. Ettlie and E. Reza, "Organizational Integration and Process Innovation," *Academy of Management Journal,* 34, no. 4 (October 1992), pp. 795–827; J.E. Ettlie and J. Penner-Hahn, "Flexibility Ratios and Manufacturing Strategy," *Management Science,* 40, no. 11 (November 1994), pp. 1444–1454; D. Upton, "What Really Makes Factories Flexible?" *Harvard Business Review* (July–August 1995).

[44] Much of this section is based on D. N. Beede and K. H. Young, "Patterns of Advanced Technology Adoption and Manufacturing Performance," *Business Economics,* 33, no. 2 (April 1998), pp. 43–48.

of employment growth and lower closure rates, controlling for other explanatory factors. Plants adopting six or more of these seventeen possible choices (e.g., numerically controlled machine tools) paid premiums of 16 percent for production workers and 8 percent for nonproduction workers. As much as 60 percent of the variance in wage premium paid by large plants can be explained by adoption of these manufacturing technologies. Between 1998 and 1993, increases in computer-aided design and local area networks were most prominent. Labor productivity, generally, was significantly enhanced by adoption of these technologies, which is typical of patterns established in earlier generations of research on this subject.

Analysis of the comparable Canadian data yielded similar results, with the added findings that manufacturing technology adoption was coincident with R&D spending by larger plants, with variance across industries. Adoption of inspection and programmable control technology appears to promote growth faster than other technologies, but it is not clear if controlling for other factors would sustain this result. Most important, Canadian data suggest that the mosaic of technologies adopted matters, as well as the number of technologies purchased. A comparable result for information technology has also emerged in one applied study introduced later (adoption of EDI or electronic data interchange).

There is considerable variance in the adoption mix of technologies in these data. In the United States, the most frequently used technologies, adopted stand-alone or in combinations, are computer-aided design (CAD) and numerical control (NC), even though this pattern is found in only 2 to 4 percent of cases. About 18 percent of these plants adopt unique combinations of technologies (e.g., common to only one or two plants), and adoption patterns generally do not follow industry groups.

The highest rate of job growth is associated with adoption of eleven of the seventeen technologies studied in the United States. In particular, local area networks (LAN) technologies, either combined with CAD or used exclusively for the factory, were associated with a 25 percent faster employment growth rate than plants that did not adopt any of the surveyed technologies from 1982 to 1987. CAD and NC were associated with a 15 percent higher job growth rate during the same period. Programmable logic (PLCs) and NC yielded a 10 percent higher employment growth rate. On the other hand, CAD and digital representation of CAD for procurement experienced a 20 percent slower job growth rate but very fast productivity growth.

Productivity levels were 50 percent higher (than nonadopters) among companies that used the following technologies: CAD, CAD output for procurement, LANs, inter-company networks, PLCs (programmable logic controllers), and shop floor control computers. Earnings for production workers versus nonproduction workers are more directly associated with adoption of these technologies. For example, production worker employment growth was 35 percent higher in plants that adopted LANs and shop floor control. But in 60 to 80 percent of the technology categories, there were higher earnings levels for both job categories.

Two general conclusions can be drawn from these results, in addition to the primary finding that the *pattern of adoption* determines performance, rather than simply the number of technologies used. First, outcomes vary by which technologies are adopted and the type of performance measured. This was called the **organizational effectiveness "paradox"** in earlier research.[45] Second, the combination of stand-alone technology such as CAD and integrating technologies such as LANs has the greatest impact on performance, regardless of outcome measure. Linking fabrication with assembly in successful plants suggests that functional coordination is essential to appropriation of adopted technology benefits. This integrating aspect of manufacturing technology is taken up in Chapter 3.

The literature and empirical findings on manufacturing technology adoption indicate the following:

1. The more technologies adopted by plants, the higher the rates of employment growth, the higher the wages, and the lower closure rates.

2. The mosaic of manufacturing technologies matters—not just the extent or number of technologies adopted (e.g., local area networks adopted with or without CAD account for 25 percent faster employment growth in adopters versus nonadopters).

CHAPTER SUMMARY

This chapter reviewed the basics of the innovation process—the history of technology, definitions, stage models, innovation types, research and development (R&D)—and its relationship to technology strategy and performance is reviewed.

New technology is often discovered by chance, and there is usually resistance to the adoption and spread or diffusion of a new product and the *changes in routine and organization structure* needed to implement it. Authority usually has weight in the change process.

Innovation is defined as invention + exploitation. There are two important types of innovations: those that depart radically from current practice and those that depart incrementally from the current method. Technology tends to unfold in stages, but the stages are often not in the prescribed order. Most R&D is spent on new products and new services.

R&D intensity is the investment in research, development, and engineering as a percentage of sales, usually on an annual basis, and this is the first "ratio" that needs to be calculated for any innovation case under study. More than 6 percent of sales spent on R&D generally qualifies the case as high tech, but there are no hard, fast rules. Organizational size or scale helps innovation, but only up to a point. A radically different product that differentiates the firm from competitors is just as important in new product success.

Technology promotes firm and society success, but investing in new products and services is different from trying to "appropriate" or capture the benefits of technology such as new information systems purchased from suppliers. Both are viable competitive options, and good companies excel at both types of innovating.

[45] R. E. Quinn and K. S. Cameron, "Organizational Effectiveness Life Cycles and Shifting Criteria of Effectiveness," *Management Science*, (1983), pp. 33–51.

CHAPTER 2
DISCUSSION QUESTIONS _____

1. Review Box 2-1, which presents Roberts's (1988) state-of-the-art summary of the innovation process. Choose a case of a problem encountered in the innovation process from your own experiences or in this book (such as the new process to produce a heart disease medication described in the preface) and indicate which of Roberts's suggestions could have helped solve this problem.

2. Look closely at the stage model in Figure 2-2. What's wrong with this model?

3. Read "How A $4 Razor Ends up Costing $300 Million" (Case 2-1) and answer the following questions:
- Why did Gillette decide to introduce the Sensor Razor?
- What are the technology transfer issues of the case?
- Did Gillette make the right decision on Sensor?
- What should Gillette do next?

ADDITIONAL
CASE SUGGESTIONS _____

1. Pilkington Float Glass, HBS 9-695-024 (15 pages) is a great history-of-technology case, with great relevance to today.

2. Beretta, HBS 9-687-044, is perhaps the best historical case of technology extant.

3. There is a Harvard case on the Sensor Razor: Gillette's Launch of Sensor, HBS 9-792-028.

CASE 2-1
How a $4 Razor Ends Up Costing $300 Million

There are 40 engineers, metallurgists, and physicists at Gillette Co.'s Reading (Britain) research facility who spend their days thinking about shaving and little else. In 1977, one of them had a bright idea. John Francis had already figured out how to create a thinner razor blade that would make Gillette's cartridges easier to clean. Then, the design engineer remembered a notion he had toyed with for years: He could set the thinner blades on springs so that they would follow the contours of a man's face. He built a simple prototype, gave it a test, and thought: "This is pretty good." He passed the idea to his boss, then went on to the next project.

As it turned out, Gillette thought John Francis's idea was pretty good, too. It took a while, but the innovation became the centerpiece of Sensor, the high-tech razor Gillette is introducing this month. Sensor is the single most expensive project Gillette has ever taken on: By the time the razor hits stores, the company will have spent an estimated $200 million in research, engineering, and tooling. Then, there's advertising. The company

may drop a total of $110 million on television and print campaigns this year alone, including a two-minute splash during the Super Bowl on Jan. 28.

Gillette is spending so heavily because Sensor may well be the most important product it has ever launched. It's the heart of the company's strategy to revitalize shaving systems, which have been losing market share in recent years to disposable razors from Bic Corp. and others. With some 67% of the market in North America and Europe, Gillette is still the leader in both types of shaver. But it clears only about 8¢ to 10¢ gross profit on each disposable razor, compared with 25¢ to 30¢ per cartridge refill for its Atra and Trac II system shavers.

If Sensor pays off, Gillette's management will also be vindicated in the take-over battles it fought from 1986 to 1988. Gillette first fended off Revlon Inc.'s Ronald O. Perelman, who offered $4.1 billion for the shaving company. It later won a fierce proxy fight with Coniston Partners, in part by convincing share-holders that a then-secret new technology—Sensor—would create greater long-term value than a breakup. But Gillette will need a huge win to justify its investment in Sensor. The new razor must add about four percentage points to Gillette's market share in the U.S. and Europe just to recoup its ad budget.

Those pressures also help explain why it took so long to get Sensor out the door. Gillette executives were reluctant to make the huge investment in manufacturing and marketing at a time when the company could still count on prodigious profits from its existing razors. In 1989, Gillette's net profit jumped an estimated 6%, to $285 million, on sales of $3.8 billion, up 7%. And fully 65% of operating profits and 32% of revenues came from razors and blades. Some analysts also believe Gillette's constant battles with corporate raiders and the resulting need to conserve cash may have delayed the project further.

The technical demands of building a razor with floating parts didn't make matters any easier. Take the springs themselves: Francis's original idea called for the blades to sit on tiny rubber tubes—filled, perhaps, with a compressible fluid. But that would have been too costly and complicated to manufacture by the millions. And Gillette wanted to mount the so-called skin guard, which stretches the skin before the blades shear the stubble, on slightly firmer springs—something it had trouble doing with rubber tubes.

ONE GOOD RESIN. Engineers in Boston decided instead to mold cantilevered plastic springs into the blade cartridge itself. But that presented another problem. Gillette used styrene plastic to mold blade cartridges for all its razors, because it's inexpensive and easy to work with. But a styrene spring, tests showed, lost some of its bounce over time. The engineers turned to a resin called Noryl, a stronger material that kept its bounce.

In 1983, Gillette tested a Sensor prototype with 500 men. They liked it—a lot more than they liked Atra and Trac II. Back at the company's South Boston development headquarters, engineers celebrated. Then, they wondered how they would ever mass-manufacture such a complicated gizmo. "We went to bed at night sometimes without the foggiest notion of how we were going to solve this one," recalls Donald L. Chaulk, director of Gillette's shaving technology laboratory.

The blades gave Gillette's scientists most of their sleepless nights. In the Atra razor, two blades simply slipped into slots in the plastic cartridge, separated by a steel spacer bar. Sensor's blades, though, were to "float" on the springs independently of each other. That meant the blades had to be rigid enough to hold their shape—though each is no thicker than a sheet of paper. Engineers decided to attach each blade to a thicker steel support bar.

The question was, how? For mass manufacturing, glue was too messy and too expensive. The answer was lasers. Engineers built a prototype laser that spot-welded each blade to a support without creating heat that would damage the blade edge, relying on a process more commonly used to make such things as heart pacemakers. The complex manufacturing process has one advantage: It makes the cartridge hard to copy. Competitors Wilkinson Sword North America Inc. and Schick, as well as private-label manufacturers, all make cheaper clone cartridges that fit Atra and Trac II handles.

In June, 1986, armed with its consumer test results and initial manufacturing success, Gillette's Safety Razor Div. won $10 million from the company's board to develop more substantial manufacturing equipment. A year later, the board granted another $10 million. That, executives say, was when it became clear that Sensor would become Gillette's next major product.

Yet even then, Sensor was caught in the middle of a factional struggle at Gillette. Boston-based executives in the razor division, recognizing the popularity of inexpensive disposables, wanted to produce both disposable and permanent versions of Sensor, with much of the marketing support going to the throwaway version. Another group, led by John W. Symons, who then headed European operations, believed Gillette was placing too much emphasis on the lower-profit disposables. Symons' European team was already playing down disposables by developing a heavy steel handle for the European Atra razor while halting ads and promotions for disposables.

At the same time its internal tussles were raging, Gillette was under siege—although executives deny that the take-over fight delayed Sensor's development. But analysts, who had expected a new shaving product in 1988, are still skeptical. "When you're trying to conserve cash, the last thing you do is roll out a multimillion-dollar new product," says Shearson Lehman Hutton Inc. analyst Andrew Shore.

TOUGH DEADLINE. The takeover wars may actually have determined the shape Sensor would take. As part of a reorganization accelerated by Perelman's bid, Gillette Chief Executive Colman M. Mockler Jr. brought Symons to Boston in January, 1988, as executive vice-president in charge of the shaving group—signaling, within the company, his decision to deemphasize disposables.

The shift "created a lot of difficulty within the company," Symons acknowledges now, especially among the Boston executives who were committed to disposables. He soon cleaned house, replacing most Safety Razor Group vice-presidents with his European team. He abruptly changed gears on Sensor, too. He canceled development of the disposable version and rejected the plastic handle that had been planned for the new system razor. Instead, he ordered development of a handsome steel version his team had tested in Europe. And he set a production deadline: January, 1990.

That was a tall order for the engineers in South Boston, who assembled a nine-member task force to work on the razor seven days a week for 15 months. "We told them: 'For the foreseeable future, Sensor is your life,'" Chaulk says. For the handle, the team built a plastic skeleton covered with a molded stainless steel shell, each half of which is formed in 22 separate stamping operations. "Clearly, it's a difficult bit of manufacturing," says Norman R. Proulx, president of Wilkinson Sword North America, a rival Gillette plans to acquire. "From a mass-production angle, they've done a lot of interesting stuff."

Now, Gillette has to convince men that all that technology makes for a better shave. It's pricing the basic razor at $3.75, well below Atra and Trac II, hoping to lure shavers from the older products. But at $3.79 per five-pack, cartridges will cost 25% more than those for Gillette's old systems, giving it about 8¢ more gross profit per cartridge.

Early returns are promising: Retailers have committed to buy Gillette's production capacity through the next year. In a few weeks, Gillette will see whether men actually pick Sensor off store shelves. Meantime, the engineers in South Boston are already cooking up more shaving innovations: There's a curved blade in the works, and perhaps a new ceramic blade. But don't expect to see them until the turn of the century.

SOURCE   K. H. Hammonds, *Business Week*, Jan. 29, 1990.

Chapter 3

Theories of Innovation

CHAPTER OBJECTIVES

To review theories of the innovation process. This chapter considers individuals, innovation, sociotechnical systems (STS) design, organizational innovation, and evolutionary theory. We will first introduce technological forecasting and then take it up again in Chapter 4. Specific examples explore the usefulness and accuracy of these theories. Exercises at the end of the chapter include a self-rating scale for individual innovation and firm-level performance data from a large sample of companies used to evaluate the Utterback–Abernathy model. The case study is the story of The Hewlett-Packard Inkjet Printer.

What makes one individual more creative than another? Why are some groups more innovative? Why are some organizations more innovative? There have been numerous attempts over the years to answer these questions, some based on critical analysis, and some on anecdotal evidence. In this chapter we explore the underlying models that inform answers to these questions about innovation variance and their implications.

INDIVIDUALS AND THE INNOVATION PROCESS

At Hewlett-Packard, management will do almost anything to keep a "tiny cadre" of their geniuses happy. Extra vacations are awarded to avoid burnout. It is the "brain power" of high technology, often manifested in software development, that companies such as HP and IBM nurture for competitive advantage. Other industries that thrive on creative genius include biotechnology, telecommunications, and computer chips. "Almost by definition, any genuinely high-tech product is the result of at least one idea that had never been thought before."[1]

High-tech companies—for example, Fujitsu Ltd. of Japan, Microsoft Corporation, AT&T's Bell Laboratories, and Sun Microsystems—seek creative people that will fit in. Fostering an environment where creativity flourishes and contributes to innovative firm behavior, however, is more difficult. Special recognition is one thing. Having R&D or engineering staff visit customers, with or without marketing staff, is another matter altogether. Many individuals and firms balk at these "extreme" practices.[2]

Finally, ideas may be born by individuals, but groups and teams mold new ideas into innovative products and services. Case histories of successful inventors such as Pieter Kramer, who originated the compact disk at Philips Electronics NV, or George Heilmeier, who invented the liquid crystal display at RCA Corporation's research laboratory in Princeton, New Jersey, are exceptions in this regard. For example, in the latter case of the liquid crystal, RCA could not see the commercial potential of this technology and Sharp in Japan eventually introduced it.

Stories of individual innovative genius, such as T. Edison, A. Bell, and others, are interesting, but are they useful? Can someone imitate genius? What does systematic theory and empirical research contribute to our understanding of individuals and innovation? We start with personality and demographics first, and then introduce other evidence on what Don Campbell called **acquired behavioral dispositions**—values, attitudes, and intentions to act—all focused on creativity and innovative tendencies of individuals.[3]

✶ Risk Taking and Age

In one of the little known but seminal empirical studies that provide insight into innovative behavior on the job, Victor Vroom and Bernd Pahl studied 1,484 male managers and their risk aversion. Vroom and Pahl used selected items from a choice-dilemma questionnaire that presented life situations to respondents, such as a married engineer deciding between a safe, secure job and startup company that offers more responsibility and advancement.[4] Results of average risk aversion scores plotted by age appear in Figure 3-1. Larger scores on the vertical axis represent more risk aversion, and smaller scores are for risk takers (they would accept the risky alternative at lower odds of payoff—say odds of success of 3 to 10 versus 9 to 10). Age is plotted on the horizontal axis. Vroom and Pahl hypothesized that older managers would be more risk averse.

Although the hypothesis is generally supported by the results—Figure 3-1 shows the straight line fitted to the data—the third-order polynominal curve (also in Figure 3-1) is a better fit with these data. To be precise, the cubic regression equation was:

$$R = 1.403 + .0406A - .0095A^2 + .00007A^3$$

[1] L. Hooper, "The Creative Edge," *Wall Street Journal,* (May 24, 1993), p. R6.

[2] Ibid, p. R8.

[3] D. T. Campbell, "Acquired Behavioral Dispositions," in S. Koch (ed.),: *Psychology The Study of Science,* 6 (1959).

[4] V. H. Vroom and B. Pahl, "Relationship Between Age and Risk Taking Among Managers", *Journal of Applied Psyschology,* 55, no. 5 (1971), pp. 399–405.

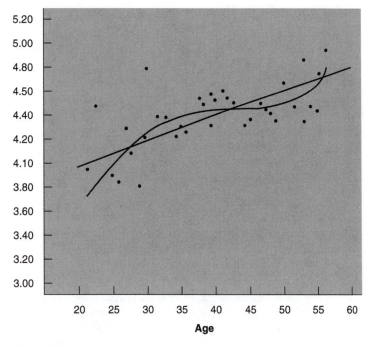

Figure 3-1 Age and Risk Taking Among Managers
SOURCE: Vroom and Pahl, 1971.

The implications are quite interesting. Risk taking decreases sharply until about age 35, then levels off until about age 50, when risk aversion sets in once again. This time often coincides with the most productive middle-management years of a person's career.

Data for women were not available in 1971, but it would be interesting to replicate this study today with both genders. A recent survey by *R&D Magazine* found much greater dissatisfaction among women with their technical careers than among male white managers. Only 27 percent of male respondents report discrimination, compared with 61 percent of women surveyed.[5]

Standardized measures of creativity show that people who are creative, regardless of the area of creativity—the arts, sciences, and so forth—do not have genius-level IQs. Their IQs are high, but not necessarily at the extreme of a typical population. These measures tend to be quite stable over time.[6] Joseph Anderson says that "creativity is nothing more than going beyond the current boundaries, whether these boundaries are technology, knowledge, social norms, or beliefs. So *Star Trek* (boldly going where no person has gone before) certainly qualifies. And so does Beethoven's Fifth Symphony."[7]

[5] Data from *R & D Magazine.*

[6] E. P. Torrance, "Giftedness in Solving Future Problems," *Journal of Creative Behavior* 12 (1978), p. 75. J. Khatena and E. P. Torrance, *Manual for Khatena-Torrance Creative Perception Inventory* (Chicago: Stoelting Company, 1976).

[7] J. Anderson, "Weirder than Fiction: The Reality and Myths of Creativity", *Academy of Management Executive,* 6, no. 4 (1992), p. 41.

Risk-taking propensity, innate intelligence, and creativity are assumed to be personality traits that change quite slowly, and age is something that cannot be influenced. What about other, less stable individual characteristics such as attitudes? We discuss this issue next.

Resistance to Change

The implied corollary to the hypothesis that people vary in risk taking is that new technology does not work because people irrationally resist change. They are not accustomed to change, so it is basic human nature to resist it.

No interpretation of the term *resistance to change* could be more unlike the real situation. This is one of those times that common sense is just wrong. The notion that people naturally resist change denies all human learning and knowledge development. A new view of organizational change is emerging in the academic[8] and practitioner world.[9] People resist loss of pay or loss of comfort or loss of control. People do not resist *change,* per se. In fact, some people benefit tremendously from change.

This new view of resistance to change is really the continuation in the literature of more insightful perspectives on resistance to change that ties it to lack of opportunity and loss of control as expressed in earlier literature. For example, Dr. W. Edwards Deming's notions of quality and change were reflected in his view that the "system" is at fault, which was the responsibility of management, not individuals embedded in the system.[10]

More recently, some authors are calling for a rethinking of change issues to the extent that people have been caught in

> the coils of a mental model called resistance to change that is failing to bring clarity to the issues they must face. Our primary prescription is to dispense entirely with this model and the term that captures it. By way of analogy, experts have recently called for an elimination of the term *child development...* They have discovered that the developmental patterns of boys and girls are different enough that little is gained by use of the aggregate term *child development*. We find the same to be true of resistance to change. *Change* is too broad a term for people to resist.[11]

So many people actively seek out change that the term *resistance to change* has lost its meaning. Newer terms and concepts may take its place, and several candidates are discussed next.

---

[8] E. Dent and S. Goldberg, "Challenging Resistance to Change," *The Journal of Applied Behavioral Science,* 35, no. 1 (March 1999), pp. 25–41.

[9] In our survey of 60 Enterprise Resource Planning cases (see Chapter 9), "resistance to change" was the number one lesson learned as a "new" view of change management. For example, how can people be expected to accommodate to a new ERP system if they are not trained? Companies typically underestimate their training and development budgets for ERP by 25 percent or more.

[10] For example: W. E. Deming, *The New Economics* (Cambridge, Mass.: MIT Press, 1993).

[11] E. B. Dent, and S. G. Goldberg, "Resistance to Change: A Limiting Perspective," *Journal of Applied Behavioral Science,* 35, no. 1 (March 1999), pp. 45–47.

✳ Innovative Attitudes

Program changes come more frequently in state agencies where key decision makers have more innovative values.[12] Other research has shown that innovative attitudes or values are often influenced by the situation.[13] How does one go about thinking and gauging innovative behavior on the job, since so few companies are high-tech and rely on just a few outstanding individuals? And how does one manage even the high-tech company when hundreds of people might be working on a project at the same time—not all of whom can be creative geniuses?

In an effort to search for a measure of occupation-free innovative tendency, Ettlie and O'Keefe developed and validated a questionnaire that draws on both the academic and practice literature on how to locate a creative person on the job.[14] This measure incorporates consideration of such tendencies and actions as combining several known ideas into a new combination to solve a problem, seeking out difficult problems to solve, placing value on being the first to try out a new use of an old method, and having a sense of humor. This last characteristic, "I am a wit," is worth remembering when the next section on playfulness is introduced. The questionnaire items from the Ettlie and O'Keefe scale to measure innovative intention attitude are reproduced in Box 3-1.

One of the surprises of this line of research, and something that goes against common sense, is that there is no consistent relationship between the risk taking climate of the organization or work group and the number of innovative people workers, regardless of their occupation. That is, one would expect that a work environment that supports calculated risk taking would have many innovative people employed there. This is not the case. Innovative people, regardless of their job—R&D scientist, software engineer, and so on—need to stand out in their workplace. A work climate that supports risk taking is only half the answer. It is the blend of people working together and meshing their innovative gears, so to speak, that converts good ideas into successful new products and services.

Take a moment now or "make an appointment with yourself" to fill out the self-assessment in Box 3-1. The scoring for the scale is included in Case 3-1.

✳ Playfulness

Mary Ann Glynn and Jane Webster have refined the concept of adult play and developed a measure of **playfulness.** They define adult playfulness as an "individual trait, a propensity to define (or redefine) an activity in an imaginative, nonserious or metaphoric manner so as to enhance intrinsic enjoyment, involvement, and satisfaction."[15] They have found scores on this scale to be significantly

---

[12] G. J. Hage and R. Dewar, "Elite Values versus Organizational Structure in Predicting Innovation," *Administrative Science Quarterly,* 18 (1973), pp. 279–290.

[13] See, for example, M. Rokeach and P. Klicjunas, "Behavior as a Function of Attitude-Toward Situation," *Journal of Personality and Social Psychology,* 22, no. 2 (1972), pp. 194–201.

[14] J. Ettlie and R. O'Keefe, *Journal of Management Studies,* 19, no. 2 (1982), pp. 163–182.

[15] M. A. Glynn and J. Webster, "Refining the Nomological Net of the Adult Playfulness Scale: Personality, Motivational, and Attitudinal Correlates for Highly Intelligent Adults. *Psychological Reports,* 72 (1993), pp. 1023–1026.

BOX 3-1

Innovative Intentions

Please indicate the extent to which each of the statements below is true of either your *actual* behavior or your *intentions* at work. That is, describe the way you are or the way you intend to be on the job. Use the following for your responses:

5—Almost always true

4—Often true

3—Not applicable

2—Seldom true

1—Almost never true

___ 1. I openly discuss with my boss how to get ahead.

___ 2. I try new ideas and approaches to problems.

___ 3. I take things or situations apart to find out how they work.

___ 4. I welcome uncertainty and unusual circumstances related to my tasks.

___ 5. I negotiate my salary openly with my supervisor.

___ 6. I can be counted on to find a new use for existing methods or equipment.

___ 7. Among my colleagues and co-workers, I will be the first or nearly the first to try out a new idea or method.

___ 8. I take the opportunity to translate communications from other departments for my work group.

___ 9. I demonstrate originality.

___ 10. I will work on a problem that has caused others great difficulty.

___ 11. I provide critical input toward a new solution.

___ 12. I provide written evaluations of proposed ideas.

___ 13. I develop contacts with experts outside my firm.

___ 14. I use personal contacts to maneuver myself into choice work assignments.

___ 15. I make time to pursue my own pet ideas or projects.

___ 16. I set aside resources for the pursuit of a risky project.

___ 17. I tolerate people who depart from organizational routine.

___ 18. I speak out in staff meetings.

___ 19. I work in teams to try to solve complex problems.

___ 20. If my co-workers are asked, they will say I am a wit.

SOURCE: J. Ettlie and R. O'Keefe, 1982. See Case 3-1 for scoring.

correlated with creativity and spontaneity, but the concept is not related to gender or age. Playfulness was related positively to work performance.

Scores on the adult playfulness scale have subsequently been found to be significantly correlated with innovative intention attitudes evaluated by Ettlie and

O'Keefe, as well as with intrinsic motivational orientation.[16] This suggests that this central playfulness characteristic of people can have substantial practical importance regardless of the job a person occupies. Eventually, it may be possible to organize departments or ad hoc teams with a variety of people who have different characteristics that are needed for innovative outcomes in organizations. Recent research on brainstorming suggests that individuals working both alone and in groups can be effective at stimulating idea generation.[17] It seems fairly safe to say that innovative tendencies of individuals can be predicted and even nurtured in organizations.

However, the stress of innovating on deadlines and with uncertain technologies can also create unusual management challenges. The case history of the development of the first version of the Apple Newton handheld computer is one example of such a situation. This case, as recounted in the *New York Times,* is included as Case 3-2 and is representative of what many companies have endured to innovate in a fast-moving, competitive market. The Apple Newton individuals and teams were obviously quite creative and innovative. Yet the outcomes of the first development effort were not as planned. The reasons for this partial success or partial failure, depending on your point of view, and the human cost of this development effort are detailed in this case for reflection and discussion.

✳ Mobility and the Innovation Process

Much of the discussion to this point assumes that people are creative in varying degrees, and they contribute accordingly in their respective organizational or institutional settings, where they are employed for life. The reality is quite different, of course. Creative and innovative individuals are usually quite mobile—they move from firm to firm seeking an organizational home that they are comfortable with and where the organization is comfortable with them. This process has been described by the simple sequence that if *voice* fails, agents will *exit* the firm if *loyalty* falters.[18]

Estimates vary, but about 25 percent of people in the U.S. work force change jobs (within or between organizations—excluding new entries) every year.[19] Besides individual attributes such as experience or organizational characteristics (e.g., firm size or internal labor markets), little research has been done on sociological factors in job shifting.

Two notable exceptions are among the refreshing alternatives to this state of affairs. The first is a book by Bridges and Villemez on employment practices and conditions, *The Employment Relationship.*[20] The study described in the book, which may be the most comprehensive research ever done on the subject, randomly sampled 2,000 employees and employers in Chicago. The findings bring

---

[16] J. Hage and R. Dewar, " Elite Values Versus Organizational Structure in Predicting Innovation," *Administrative Science Quarterly*, 18 (Sept 1973), pp. 279–290.

[17] R. I. Sutton and A. Hargadon, "Brainstorming Groups in Context: Effectiveness in a Product Design Firm," *Administrative Science Quarterly,* 41 (1996), pp. 685–718.

[18] A. O. Hirshman, *Exit, Voice and Loyalty* (Cambridge, Mass.: Harvard University Press, 1970).

[19] H. A. Haveman, and L. E. Cohen,"The ecological dynamics of careers: The impact of organizational founding, dissolution, and merger on job mobility," *American Journal of Sociology,* 100 (1994), pp. 104–152.

[20] W. P. Bridges and W. J. Villemez, *The Employment Relationship* (New York: Plenum, 1994).

into sharp focus the limitations of the internal labor markets. Not surprisingly, white women do not enjoy the same "built-in" mechanisms for promotion as white men. However, surprisingly Bridges and Villemez found that black workers are not disadvantaged in employment rights and actually seek out bureaucratically governed jobs, with formal promotion schemes. This may occur because their external opportunities for jobs are restricted by discrimination, the internal labor market in such organizations provides a favorable climate for their promotion, a combination of these. Thus, there is a negative relationship between internal and external labor market opportunities. Not surprisingly, government leads all organizational types in the use of bureaucratic control of internal labor markets. In the private sector there is a tradeoff between bureaucratic control and earnings.

The second exceptional study was by Haveman and Cohen[19] who tested the idea that founding, dissolution, and merger have predictable effects on employment opportunities. Dissolution and merger destroy jobs, while founding creates jobs. This ecological theory of career mobility was tested in the California Savings and Loan Industry from 1969 to 1988, where 5,816 thrift managers made 8,094 job shifts. This is about 1.4 moves per manager, who held 2.4 jobs over a typical five-year job history. About 23 percent of these moves were within the same firm, and 17 percent were moves between firms in the thrift industry. More than one sixth of savings and loan managers moved to newly founded organizations—about 10 percent of moves. More than 25 percent of entries into managerial positions were into newly founded savings and loan associations. One fourth of moves occurred when a thrift failed or merged.

Mobility and innovation are studied systematically even less often. However, there is some evidence from various cases that the more radical the new technology adopted by the firm, the more important "new blood" or interfirm mobility is to the innovation process. In a new-packaging study in the food industry, twenty-three of these food firms (41%) gained people that affected innovation decisions. More important, the adoption of one particular radically new packaging technology, the retort pouch ("flexible can"), was significantly correlated with positive flows of personnel to the team involved with the adoption decision.

Some data show that the more radical the new technology, the more important it is for the new (mobile) person to occupy a senior position (e.g., vice president) in the acquiring firm to stimulate adoption. In the food packaging study, about 27 percent of the cases (15 of 56 firms) involved managerial acquisitions during the previous three years that "had an important influence on the innovative decision-making" of the firms.[21] Cases from earlier studies also support this idea of senior mobility and radical operations technology adoption.[22]

Intrafirm mobility—movement of people across organizational boundaries within the company—is more important to the actual successful use of new technology once it is adopted. This type of mobility is also more likely to involve changes in personnel below general manager level. Ettlie studied 39 durable

---

[21] J. E. Ettlie, "The Impact of Interorganizational Manpower Flows on the Innovation Process," *Management Science,* 31, no. 9 (September 1985) pp. 1055–1071.

[22] J. E. Ettlie, "Manpower Flows and the Innovation Process," *Management Science,* 26, no. 11 (November 1980), pp. 1086–1095.

goods plants modernizing with flexible automation. In twenty-two (56%) cases, at least one personnel flow occurred during the post-adoption process.[23] Eleven of these involved at least one manufacturing engineers being promoted to manager, and four more involved manufacturing engineers being rotated into other positions (e.g., given team assignments) to accommodate the installation of the new production technology. This manufacturing engineering intrafirm mobility was significantly associated with greater uptime (better new system performance) and more inventory turns (less work-in-process inventory) achieved with the new production technology.

$\mathscr{S}$OCIOTECHNICAL SYSTEMS

Begun in the 1960s with the seminal work of pioneers such as Louis Davis and Albert Cherns,[24] Eric Trist and Hugh Murray and the Tavistock Institute,[25] among others, the sociotechnical systems (STS) model of organizational change was more than a theory. STS is a philosophy and a change methodology, as well as a movement to revolutionize thinking about joint design (social and technical) of work systems. Employee (not just blue-collar worker) attitudes in groups, self-regulating teams, and the quality of work life are at the heart of this approach. Identification of variances in work systems is central to STS design or redesign of work systems. A few authors have attempted to bridge the STS and total quality movements.[26]

However, the challenge to those wanting to incorporate STS philosophy to management of technology is that cases in which STS has been used in conjunction with the introduction of *new* technology have been rare.[27] There are refreshing exceptions to this general tendency, and they are introduced next.

The exceptions to mainstream STS intervention is well illustrated by the work of Harvey Kolodny and Moses Kiggundu. Starting with early work in new plants[28] and in woodlands harvesting, which showed that STS mechanical harvesting groups had double the productivity of lower performers,[29] they moved on to hypothesize how workplaces with microprocessors can be organized to regulate

---

[23] J. E. Ettlie, "Intrafirm Mobility and Manufacturing Modernization," *Journal of Engineering and Technology Management,* 6, nos. 3 & 4 (May 1990), pp. 281–302.

[24] L. E. Davis and A. B. Cherns (eds.), *The Quality of Working Life,* Vols. 1 and 2 (New York: The Free Press, 1975).

[25] E. Trist and H. Murray (eds.), *The Social Engagement of Social Science: A Tavistock Anthology* (Vol. II), (Philadelphia: University of Pennsylvania Press, 1993).

[26] J. Persico and G. N. McLean, "The Evolving Merger of Socio-Technical Systems and Quality Improvement Theories." *Human Systems Management,* 13, no. 1 (1994), pp. 11–18; C. C. Manz and G. L. Stewart, "Attaining Flexible Stability by Integrating Total Quality Management and Socio-Technical Systems Theory," *Organization Science* 8, no. 1 (January–February 1997), pp. 59–70.

[27] See J. Ettlie, *Taking Charge of Manufacturing* (San Francisco: Jossey-Bass, 1988) for a review of this issue.

[28] H. F. Kolodny and B. Drenser, "Linking Arrangements and New Work Designs," *Organizational Dynamics,* 14, no. 3 (Winter 1986), pp. 33–51.

[29] H. F. Kolodny and M. N. Kiggundu, "Towards the Development of a Sociotechnical Systems Model in Woodlands Mechanical Harvesting," *Human Relations,* 33, no. 9 (September 1980), pp. 623–645.

unpredictable variances.[30] Among their most recent contributions in this stream of STS with new technology is a cross-national study of computer-based, flexible manufacturing technology at twelve companies in Sweden, France, and Canada. Kolodny and Kiggundu *did not* support their first hypothesis, that work in new process technology settings will be organized to account for unpredictable variances, except in the food processing sector. Moderate or mixed support was obtained for hypotheses suggesting increasing concern for open processes, rules and procedures, and managing (versus reducing) complexity. Hypothesis four was strongly supported: Organizations installing new, computer-based process technologies will adopt integrative approaches (e.g., shared use of common databases, concurrent engineering, flatter organizational structures, self-regulating work teams, and new coordinating mechanisms). *This finding almost perfectly replicated earlier published work in similar settings.*[31] This convergence in findings from separate fields is extremely important and hard to overlook. Only moderate support was obtained for hypothesis five, which states that organizational designers will enlarge rationalities when applying STS to new process technologies. Nancy Hyer and co-workers found similar results with research on STS design for cellular manufacturing.[32]

Other exceptions to traditional STS applications include those by James Taylor, who worked directly with high-tech design teams in the startup of a semiconductor plant in Nampa, Idaho. The plant significantly changed the way microprocessors are manufactured.[33] Pan and Scarbrough have applied STS to knowledge management at Buckman Laboratories, which achieved dramatic improvements in customer response and product innovation rates.[34]

ORGANIZATIONS AND THE INNOVATION PROCESS

Why are some organizations more innovative? Why can some organizations sustain their innovative tendencies while others falter? Our starting point in exploring answers to these questions is the seductively simple notion of the S-curve.

✳ The Technology S-Curve

The **technology S-curve**, as Christensen calls it, theoretically captures the "potential for technological improvement ... resulting from a given amount of engineering

---

[30] M. Liu, H. Denis, H. Kolodny, and B. Stymne, "Organization Design for Technological Change," *Human Relations* 43, no. 1 (January 1990), pp. 7–22.

[31] J. Ettlie and E. Reza, "Organizational Integration and Process Innovation," *Academy of Management Journal,* 35, no. 4 (1992), pp. 795–827.

[32] N. Hyer, K. Brown, and S. Zimmerman, "A Socio-Technical Systems Approach to Cell Design: Case Study and Analysis," *Journal of Operations Management,* 17, no. 2 (January 1999), pp. 179–203.

[33] J. C. Taylor and R. A. Asadorian, "The Implementation of Excellence: STS Management," *Industrial Management,* 27, no. 4 (July–August 1985), pp. 5–15.

[34] S. Pan and H. Scarbrough, "A Socio-Technical View of Knowledge-Sharing at Buckman Laboratories," *Journal of Knowledge Management,* 2, no. 1 (September 1998), pp. 55–66.

effort," which varies over time.[35] The potential at the beginning of the technology life cycle is quite great, and then, at the end of the life cycle, increasing engineering effort has diminishing returns to performance of the technology. That is, the technology is approaching some "natural or physical limit" as it matures (see Figure 3-2). This graph schematically represents first gradual and then rapid improvement of a product's performance over time, which diminishes as returns to engineering effort (and time) progress and the technology becomes better understood.

This technological phenomenon has been expressed in various ways, all represented by this S-curve or *logistic curve,* as it is also known. For example, one can focus on the impact of better performance of a new technology product by tracking how much market is captured by that product.[36]

It is not difficult to see how this theory could be used to forecast technology. Much of the seminal work in this area was done by Dev Sahal and is published in his book *Patterns of Technological Innovation.*[37] Sahal was one of the first to not only propose, but also to show empirically, with detailed time-series data from cases, that there is a gradual improvement of understanding over time and a progressive exploitation of technology as its potential is understood. This general pattern is replicated for a variety of technology types, with subtle differences.

Further innovations often result from this cumulative learning process. This is shown as the dotted line in Figure 3-2. For example, the DC-3 airplane was introduced into service in 1936 and was the result of prior improvements in similar aircraft. It underwent a series of refinements throughout its lifetime, none of them breakthroughs. It then became the focus of development activity, and the DC-6 had many of the same features. (This will be taken up later in discussion of the Tushman–Anderson extension of this work.)

If one could understand the parametric differences between technology types, adjustments in technological forecasts could be made as a variation on the basic S-curve theme and equations. Sahal looked at aircraft, farm equipment, electrical power systems and other technologies. He found no support for the dichotomous

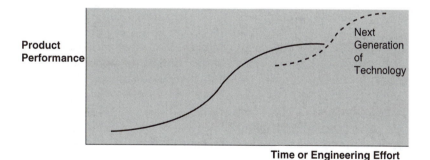

Figure 3-2   The Technology S-Curve
Source: Adapted from C. M. Christensen, 1992.

---

[35] C. M. Christensen, "Exploring the Limits of the Technology S-Curve, Part 1: Component Technologies," *Production and Operations Research,* 1, no. 4 (Fall, 1992), pp. 334 ff.

[36] Ibid. pp. 334–357.

[37] D. Sahal, *Patterns of Technological Innovation* (Reading, Mass.: Addison-Wesley, 1981).

idea of a "demand pull, technology push" difference among various technologies. Finally, these technologies "depend on the scale of the larger system designed to secure their effective utilization,"[38] which often explains many of the temporal variations between technologies that tend to be modified using local sources. For example, the Chinese failed in their attempt to develop smaller blast furnaces.

✳ Technological Forecasting

Technological forecasting is normally thought of as a set of tools that generate results as the raw material of technology strategies. But it is worth introducing the topic now because much of the underpinning of forecasting methodologies involves understanding the theory of technological innovation and the diffusion of innovation.

The classic work in this area is Joe Martino's book, *Technological Forecasting for Decision Making,* a must-read for anyone deeply involved in predicting innovation trends and trajectories. According to Martino, a technological forecast contains four elements:

▶ The technology that is being forecast
▶ The time of the forecast
▶ A statement of the characteristics of the technology
▶ A statement of the probability associated with the forecast[39]

It is rather easy to see how technology S-curves lend themselves directly to the forecasting of technology trends. For example, as data on the performance or diffusion of a technology become available, the rate of change in the progress of the technology can be predicted using a simple equation for the S-curve (Pearl or *logistic curve*):[40]

$$Y = \frac{L}{1 + ae^{-bt}}$$

where Y = rate of change in technological progress
L = value of the curve at the upper limit for the growth value,
e = base of the natural logarithms
t = time

If we know the shape of the curve, in this case the S-curve, then it is a matter of determining the a and b coefficients to fit the data to the curve. If the initial value of the curve is not zero, a constant can be added to the right-hand side of the equation. The advantage of the **Pearl curve** (Raymond Pearl was a demographer who studied population growth) is that shape (how steep) and location can be controlled independently to predict how quickly a technology will emerge and

---

[39] Ibid., p. 199.

[39] J. P. Martino, *Technological Forecasting for Decision Making* (New York: McGraw-Hill, 1993). The book comes with a CD to demonstrate the various forecasting techniques.

[40] Ibid., p. 61.

then gradually plateau. The place on the growth curve where two technologies intersect and substitution occurs is illustrated in the example of the speed of jet-powered aircraft and propeller-powered aircraft (see Figure 3-3). Normally, when data are actually fit to the Pearl curve, the curve can be straightened out by using a natural log transformation:

$$Y = \ln (y/L - y) = -\ln a + bt$$

The right-hand side of the equation is a straight line, with the normal a (intercept) and b (slope) parameters.

The emergence of the **dominant design** of a technology is the key to understanding these substitution curves and the characteristics of intergenerational survival of firms. Anderson and Tushman contend, based on research of three industries mentioned later, that the dominant design is the single basic architecture that becomes the accepted market standard. The dominant design is not necessarily the most innovative design. Rather, it is a combination of features, often pioneered elsewhere (e.g., the IBM 360 computer).[41]

Technological forecasting is discussed in greater depth in Chapter 4, where the various methods and approaches to forecasting innovation developments and diffusion are presented. Examples of actual forecasts used by companies are also included. Finally, it should be pointed out that the term *technological forecasting,* or predicting technology trends, is sometimes confused in the literature with the term *technological assessment,* or predicting the consequences of using a technology.[42] The theory behind *technological forecasting* is our focus here.

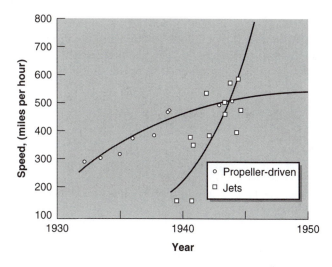

Figure 3-3

The Emergence of a New Dominant Design in Aircraft Power: Propellers vs. Jets

Source: J. P. Martino, *Technological Forecasting for Decision Making, 3rd edition* (New York: McGraw-Hill, 1993), p. 80. Figure 5-1. Reprinted with permission from The McGraw-Hill Companies.

---

[41] P. Anderson and M. L. Tushman, "Managing Through Cycles of Technological Change," *Research Technology Management* 34, no. 3 (May–June, 1991), pp. 26–31.

[42] See, for example, A. Henriksen, "A Technological Assessment Primer for Management of Technology," *International Journal of Technology Management,* 13, no. 5 (1997), pp. 615–638, where technology assessment is defined very broadly, including technological forecasting.

Evolution of the Productive Segment

Abernathy and Wayne, and then Utterback and Abernathy, studied the evolution of the productive segment of the firm and originally proposed that successful firms tend to invest heavily in product R&D early in the life cycle of an industry or product group.[43] As the dominant design of a new product emerges, investments shift to process technology and strategies switch to cost minimization, as opposed to product feature variety. The basis of competition varies with the stage of maturity of the product-process core of the industry. Although there are problems with this model (e.g., contingencies required for successful performance can be explained independently of an evolutionary process),[44] provides a framework to compare the results of investments in manufacturing innovation.

The dematuration of durable goods manufacturing and the emergence of economies of scope afforded by flexible manufacturing technologies[45] offer a significant alternative to scale economies, requiring a rethinking of earlier theories. Distinguishing between radical and incremental innovation[46] and punctuated equilibrium models[47] does not sufficiently account for this trend. This dematuration was originally addressed by Abernathy and Townsend[48] with the inclusion of the atavistic tendency of the productive segment to *backtrack* from the systemic or last stage of development to earlier stages when the environment becomes less stable. This atavistic tendency is depicted in Figure 3-4, adapted from the original Abernathy and Utterback.

Abernathy and Utterback say that at times the best choice may be to "slow or reverse evolutionary progress or to remain in that particular stage which offers the best trade-off between conflicting objectives (of adaptability and innovativeness vs. higher productivity rates)."[49]

The 1955 Chevrolet

If **backtracking** is caused by changes in the firm's environment (competitors, customers, and government), then it assumes that earlier strategies and structures were better. Is this a good assumption? Were the "good old days" really so good?

---

[43] W. J. Abernathy and K. Wayne "Limits of the Learning Curve" *Harvard Business Review,* 52, no. 5 (Sept–Oct, 1974), p. 209ff; J. M. Utterback and W. J. Abernathy, "A Dynamic Model of Process and Product Innovation." *Omega,* 3, no. 6 (1975), pp. 639–656.

[44] J. E. Ettlie, "Evolution of the Productive Segment and Transportation Innovations," *Decision Sciences,* 10, no. 3 (July 1979), pp. 399–411.

[45] J. E. Ettlie and J. Penner-Hahn, "Flexibility Ratios and Manufacturing Strategy," *Management Sciences,* 40, no. 11 (November, 1994), pp. 1444–1454.

[46] J. E. Ettlie, W. Bridges, and R. O'Keefe, "Organizational Strategy and Structural Differences for Radical versus Incremental Innovation," *Management Science,* 30, no. 6 (June 1984), pp. 682–695.

[47] P. Anderson and M. L. Tushman, "Managing Through Cycles of Technological Change," *Research Technology Management,* 34, no. 3 (May/June 1991), p. 26.

[48] W. J. Abernathy and P. L. Townsend, 1975, p. 397. "Technology, Productivity, and Process Change." *Technological Forecasting and Social Change,* 7 (1975), pp. 379–396.

[49] W. J. Abernathy and J. M. Utterback, "Patterns of Industrial Innovation," *Technology Review,* 80, no. 7 (June/July 1978), p. 40.

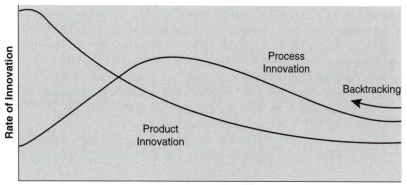

Competitive Emphasis	Fluid Pattern	Transitional Pattern	Specific Pattern
	Functional product performance	Product variation	Cost reduction
Innovation stimulated by	Information on users' needs and users' technical inputs	Opportunities created by expanding internal technical capability	Pressure to reduce cost and improve quality
Predominant type of innovation	Frequent major changes in products	Major process changes required by rising volume	Incremental for product and process, with cumulative improvement in productivity and quality
Product line	Diverse, often including custom designs	Includes at least one product design stable enough to have significant production volume	Mostly undifferentiated standard products
Production processes	Flexible and inefficient: major changes easily accommodated	Becoming more rigid, with changes occurring in major steps	Efficient, capital-intensive, and rigid, cost of change is high
Equipment	General purpose, requiring highly skilled labor	Some subprocesses automated, creating "islands of automation"	Special purpose, mostly automatic with labor tasks mainly monitoring and control
Materials	Inputs are limited to generally available materials	Specialized materials may be demanded from some suppliers	Specialized materials will be demanded; if they are not available, vertical integration will be extensive
Plant	Small-scale, located near user or source of technology	General purposes with specialized sections	Large-scale, highly specific to particular products
Organizational control	Informal and entrepreneurial	Through liaison relationships, project and task groups	Through emphasis on structure, goals, and rules

Figure 3-4   The Utterback-Abernathy Model

SOURCE: W. J. Abernathy and J. M. Utterback. Patterns of industrial innovation, *Technology Review,* 80 (1978), p. 40.

Take the case of the 1955 Chevrolet.[50] The car had a new body, a new V-8 engine (the first V-8 in a modern Chevy), and a new chassis and frame—what is commonly called a platform today. The car was launched from concept to pilot

---

[50] J. Ettlie and W. Stoll, *Managing the Design-Manufacturing Process* (New York: McGraw-Hill, 1990, pp. 8–11).

production in 24 months (summer of 1952 to summer of 1954), and dealers were stocked with cars by September 1954 for the 1955 model year launch.

The 1955 Chevy has become a classic, but few know that compared with today's launch periods, which range from 3 to 5 years, it has a classic development history. Based on reports from engineers who were actually involved in the development effort for the 1955 model year, the unique features of this case emerge. First, all design work was done in-house. Today, significant design decisions are sourced with first-tier suppliers in the auto industry.

Second, the drawing board acted like an engineering conference room, where many people could gather around to share in decision making. During the 1960s, computer-aided drafting and computer-aided design were introduced in the auto and aerospace industry, which decentralized the design process. This group decision making medium was lost forever (it would seem).

Third, all engineers at General Motors Corporation, including both design engineers and production engineers, as they were called then (we typically call them manufacturing engineers today) reported to a chief engineer during the 1950s. In most U.S. durable goods plants today, manufacturing engineers report to manufacturing managers.

Fourth, a new engine plant was under construction in Flint, Michigan, at the time of this launch program. Plant and car were designed together. Today, we rely on flexible manufacturing systems to absorb design changes, but many of these systems are not so flexible.

There are other differences, including simpler designs and smaller, less complicated organizations. The massive downsizing that occurred in the 1980s in manufacturing is just one indication that backtracking is underway. But can we return so easily to the past? Womak, Jones, and Roos[51] found that the "lean" Toyota Production System (TPS) principles account for the performance difference in the automotive industry. It took at least 30 years for Toyota to introduce and perfect this lean manufacturing system, and now the company applies these principles to its design process. But Toyota started with excellence in production systems and technology, not design and product technology. This seems to contradict—at least in the first analysis—the Utterback–Abernathy model. However, if one views Toyota which produced its first car in 1936 as "reinventing" the industry, there is less contradiction between the evidence and the theory. Toyota actually benchmarks Honda for product development.[52] Honda, which, according to Womak, Jones, and Roos, "manages" as opposed to "coordinates" product development for rapid product introduction, uses a matrix organization, since adopted by Ford Motor Company in their Ford 2000 program.[53]

EVOLUTIONARY THEORY

Nelson and Winter are considered by many to be at the beginning of the evolutionary theory-building movement, although it is clear that many published articles

---

[51] J. P. Womak, D. T. Jones, and D. Roos, (1990). *The Machine That Changed The World* (New York: Harper Perennial).

[52] John Shook, Personal Communication, 1995.

[53] See Fig 5–8, in Chapter 5.

presented technological evolutionary ideas before their book, *An Evolutionary Theory of Economic Change,* appeared. They introduced the term *routines* to describe "all regular and predictable behavioral patterns of firms,"[54] which form the elements of their evolutionary theory. What, then, is **evolutionary theory?** "The core concern of evolutionary theory is with the dynamic process by which firm behavior patterns and market outcomes are jointly determined over time."[55] Firms can be reduced to sets of capabilities, procedures, and decision rules under a given set of external conditions. Firms search for new ideas (i.e., technological innovations) to make changes; some grow, while others decline. R&D is generally directed to create something that did not exist before and is modeled as a probability distribution for coming up with new techniques. This distribution is considered to be a function of time, R&D policy (portfolio of investments), and local (near current solutions) versus all other searches. Imitation of other companies is possible in this model; primarily "best practice" and investment, market entry, and labor market conditions are modeled.

Nelson and Winter simulated their model of an economy and replicated earlier results for the U.S. economy, including rising labor rates and capital intensity. Then experiments with the model began using four variables: case of innovation, emphasis on imitation, cost of capital, and the labor savings basis of search. Natural trajectories were identified and included in more complex versions of the model, including "mechanization of processes previously done by hand."[56]. Industries differ considerably in their ability to exploit these "natural" types of trajectories. For example, as mentioned earlier, cotton production was easier than wool production to mechanize. In the United States, Texas cotton drove out southeastern cotton because the former was more amenable to mechanized picking.[57] Some firms track emerging technological opportunities better than others, and they tend to prosper, which leads to increasing concentration, but the exercise of market power by the dominant firm tends to lead to its decline. This was originally proposed by Williamson and supported by data from Ettlie and Rubenstein presented earlier—as size increases, innovation increases up to a point, and then declines sharply (Fig 2– 4a & b).

Further modeling indicates that firms with innovative R&D tend to lose out competitively to firms with "skillful and aggressive imitators,"[58] which is discussed in the section on collaborative R&D. Nelson and Winter also present simulation results that support a modified version of Schumpeter's basic notion of increasing innovation with size: this occurs only when innovation driven by R&D is profitable, which tends to eliminate small firms in an industry. When R&D is not profitable and market forces permit, R&D-intensive firms tend to be small. Technical progress and high R&D intensity go hand in hand, but as an industry matures and becomes more concentrated, technical progress is slower, as in the Utterback–Abernathy model.

---

[54] R. R. Nelson and S. G. Winter: *An Evolutionary Theory of Economic Change* (Cambridge, Mass.: Belknap Press, 1982, p. 14).

[55] Ibid., p. 18.

[56] R. R. Nelson and S. G. Winter, p. 260.

[57] Ibid., p. 261.

[58] Ibid., p. 350.

Evolutionary theory highlights one of the most salient features of the innovation process: It typically changes the measure of production very slowly over time and is rarely punctuated by rapid change. See Box 3-2 for an agriculture industry illustration.

BOX 3-2

Shake, Shake, Shake

Can the harvesting of grapes and other fruits and produce be mechanized? Does this destroy a "craft" tradition of manual harvesting, steal work from farm workers, and beg confrontation with their unions? Or does mechanical harvesting become inevitable with the gradual decline of the availability of a migrant work force in seasonally harvested agricultural goods and actually introduce a "humane" solution to backbreaking work?

The California wine industry first confronted these issues in mid-1960s when mechanical harvesting of grapes was under experimentation on the north coast.[59]

Several other agricultural industries have experienced and continue to experience periods of experimentation with mechanical harvesting and production methods. All these new technologies are variants on the common themes of a search for more productive methods to capture value from nature when the time window of opportunity for harvesting is quite narrow. But there are often long-term consequences of these experiments that are not obvious at the time of introduction of these technologies. For example, introduction of trunk shaking technologies in the pitted fruit industry in Michigan (e.g., cherry tree orchards in the Traverse City area) resulted in some trunk damage and shorter-lived orchards.

Many of these recent experiments in harvesting and crop maintenance are sustained by a curious three-way alliance between "tinkering" and inventive growers, agriculture engineers from land grant universities (e.g., Michigan State University), and agriculture equipment manufacturers. Representatives from these three camps often "cobble" together strange looking contraptions that do ingenious things in the fields and orchards, such as spraying infestations with far less chemical agent and much less damage to the environment using "vortex" methods, which is the first spraying innovation in this industry in 30 years.[60]

Now this same type of alliance between a U.S. Agriculture Department engineer and a manufacturer of berry-picking equipment has resulted in a machine that shakes the leaves of citrus leaves until fruit falls off. What's the result? A projected savings by cutting harvesting costs by two-thirds.[61] As in countless situations before, citrus fruit is now picked primarily by hand, which costs about $1.50 for a 90-pound box of fruit. Mechanical trunk shakers (mentioned above) required a chemical fruit loosener to be sprayed on the trees first, but no chemical has been approved for use in this industry. A "leaf shaker," developed by Blueberry Equipment, Inc. in South Haven, Michigan, and the

---

[59] D. Daryl Wykoff, Mirasson Vineyards (B), 1973 President and Fellows of Harvard College, Boston, MA.

[60] Personal Communication, Professor Gary Vanee, vanee@egr.msu.edu, 1999.

[61] C. Arnst, "Shake, Shake, Shake Your Fruit Tree," *Business Week* (March 30, 1998), p. 173.

Agriculture Research Service, looks like a "giant hairbrush." It has nylon bristles 12 feet long, which are designed to reach into the canopy to rotate and shake the tree until the fruit fall. During the past two growing seasons in Florida the shaker was tested on citrus product and harvested seven to nine trees a minute, which is up to fifteen times faster than manual harvesting. The cost was 50 cents for a 90-pound box of fruit. Turner Foods Corporation, which grows 18,000 acres of oranges, is now working with Blueberry Equipment to develop a commercial version of the shaking machine for next season.

Punctuated Equilibrium

Tushman and Anderson[62] argue, like Sahal and Nelson and Winter, that technologies evolve through periods of incremental change punctuated by breakthroughs that either enhance or destroy competencies of existing firms in an industry. They support this theory of **punctuated equilibrium** with evidence from the minicomputer, cement, and airline industries and find, among other things, the following:

1. Newcomers initiate competence-destroying technological changes, while existing firms use competence-enhancing technology.

2. Organizations that initiate major technological innovations have higher growth rates than other firms in that product class.

3. Until a dominant design emerges in the competition, there is considerable competitive turmoil, later reduced to relative calm when the current standard emerges in an industry and shake-out abates.

The data example they use from the commercial airplane industry is reproduced in Figure 3-5.

Note the punctuated pattern innovation in these data. First, there is the large performance impact of a major, radical technology breakthrough (e.g., the Boeing 247 and then the DC-2 and the DC-3, discussed earlier). This period is followed for a long time by only minor improvements in performance from incremental innovations (e.g., the DC-6 was similar to the DC-3, only larger). Then a breakthrough technology comes along, like the commercial jet engine, and there is another large spike in performance. Here it is the Boeing 707–120.

Refinement and application of the model appear later.[63] Comparisons between veterans and newcomers depend on whether one is discussing discontinuities (radical breakthroughs in technology) or dominant designs of actual products. Both are obviously important.

Newcomers have the advantage only for new products that undermine the competence of veterans. In all other cases, veterans have the edge, according to

---

[62] M. L. Tushman and P. Anderson, "Technological Discontinuities and Organizational Environments," *Administrative Science Quarterly,* 31(1986), pp. 439–465.

[63] P. Anderson and M. L. Tushman, " Managing Through Cycles of Technological Change", *Research-Technology Management,* 43, no. 3 (May/June, 1991), pp. 26–31.

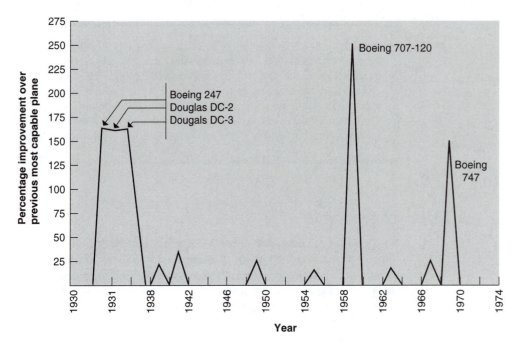

Figure 3-5   Seat-Miles-Per-Year Capacity of the Most Capable Plane Flown by U.S. Airlines, 1930–1978

SOURCE: M. L. Tushman and P. Anderson. "Technological Discontinuities and Organizational Environments." *Administrative Science Quarterly,* 31 (1986), pp. 439–465.

empirical findings in these three industries. It remains to be seen if these results hold up in other settings, but the model does make clear predictions for these other contexts. The results are also quite consistent with the notion introduced earlier, that managing for incremental innovation is quite different from managing for radical innovation. Therefore, it is not surprising that successful management styles for startup firms, especially in high-tech industries, are usually quite different from successful management styles in mature firms and industries.

Christoph Loch and Bernardo Huberman recently modeled punctuated equilibrium and found that the "expected time to adoption of the new technology [is affected by] the rate of incremental improvement, or learning, of the new technology, and the system's resistance to switching between equilibria."[64] Switching is inhibited if there is a large user population, as well as for other factors.

More Evolutionary Theories

The punctuated equilibrium model of the innovation process really represents a much larger class of evolutionary theories of the firm that have important implications for understanding new technology. Another example of this larger category of theories is described in David Audretsch's book *Innovation and Industry*

---

[64] Christoph Loch and Bernardo Huberman, "A Punctuated-Equilibrium Model of Technology Diffusion," *Management Science,* 45, no. 2 (February 1999), pp. 160–177.

$\mathcal{T}$ABLE 3-1   Summary of Growth Survival of U.S. Manufacturing Firms, 1976–1986

	New-firm Startups	Survival	Growth	Entrepreneurship	Compensating Factor Differentials	Revolving Door	Displacement
Scale economies	0	0	+	—	+	+	—
Capital intensity	+	+	—	—	NA	NA	NA
Market growth	+	+	+	0	—	—	0
Entrepreneurial regime	+	–	+	+	—	—	+
Routinized regime	–	+	+	—	+	+	—
Firm size	NA	+	+	NA	—	NA	NA

NOTE: + = the statistical findings of a positive relationship, — = the statistical findings of a negative relationship, 0 = the statistical findings of a nonsignificant relationship.

SOURCE: D. Audretsch, *Innovation and Industry Evolution* (Cambridge, Mass.: MIT Press, 1995, p. 169).

Evolution,[65] which attempts to capture the decentralization of most industries that took place worldwide during the last two decades. His study used a large manufacturing database of 20 million records over the period 1976 to 1986. Table 3-1 summarizes his results concerning firm entry, growth, and exit.

An interesting finding of Audretsch's analysis is that small firms, which are part of the "entrepreneurial technological regimes" are not deterred from entering industries in which scale economies dominate and the routinized technological regimes are used. However, small firms are more likely to exit under these conditions, which he calls the **revolving door model.** In industries in which scale economies do not dominate, small-firm entries gradually replace incumbents; this is called the **forest metaphor of exit and survival.**

Many other researchers have used evolutionary theory in their studies of the innovation process by examining various aspects of entry, performance, growth, and exit (sometimes called failure). Examples include Mitchell's study of the medial instruments industry[66] and Penner-Hahn's study of the globalization of the Japanese drug industry.[67] Both show how the use of strategy makes a difference in performance, growth, and survival of firms. Mitchell's study, in particular, shows how firms' new technology acquisitions, spinoffs, and old technology divestiture have a significant impact on long-term success.

✕ The Jolt Theory of Change

Perhaps one of the most interesting theories of change that has emerged during the last two decades is the **jolt theory** of organizational evolution (or revolution).[68] This explanation has the potential to be more encompassing than strategic

---

[65] David Audretsch, *Innovation and Industry Evolution* (Cambridge, Mass.: MIT Press, 1995).

[66] W. Mitchell, "The Dynamics of Evolving Markets: The Effects of Business Sales and Age on Dissolutions and Divestitures," *Administrative Science Quarterly,* 39, no. 4, p. 575.

[67] J. D. Penner-Hahn, "Firm and Environmental Influences on the Mode and Sequence of Foreign Research and Development Activities," *Strategic Management Journal,* 19, no. 2 (February 1998), p. 149.

[68] A. D. Meyer and J. B. Goes, "Organizational Assimilation of Innovations: A Multilevel Contextual Analysis," *Academy of Management Journal,* 31, no. 4 (December 1988), pp. 897–923.

response to technological threats (see Chapter 4). The premise is quite simple and yet extreme: Organizations change only when they are jolted from their environment. More specifically, "Abrupt alterations in environments are generally believed to jeopardize organizations; environmental jolts are found to be ambiguous events which offer propitious opportunities for organizational learning, administrative drama, and introducing unrelated changes."[69]

More recently, Meyer and his colleagues have refined this idea. "The organizational change literature contains diverse characterizations of change processes with contradictory implications for strategic managers," which can be resolved if change is classified as either continuous or discontinuous, the primary level at which change occurs is classified as organization or industry, and the primary mode of change is classified as adaptation, metamorphosis, evolution, and revolution."[70] This model is still developing, but has the potential to be incorporated into the other theoretical streams summarized in this chapter.

Emerging Theoretical Perspectives

The number of publications pertaining to innovating has escalated significantly during the last decade, so it is not possible to review all of the work here. Two recent attempts to consolidate the theory and empirical findings of the field are noteworthy. Both attempts appeared as special issues in the *Academy of Management, Review* and are summarized next.

The first summary is from Fiol's overview of collected special-issue articles, which appears in Figure 3-6.[71] In this model, the **absorptive capacity** of an organization is enhanced by both internal forces (individuals and organization culture) and external forces (diffusion of knowledge).[72] The capacity for innovation is then drawn on to enhance new product and process development and to speed up the development cycle. There is a constant tension in this model between the potential to absorb and the ability to generate innovation

The second summary of the field is in the introduction of a special issue of the *Academy of Management Journal* by Drazin and Schoonhoven.[73] They asserted that the theory used to explain innovation outcomes (increasing their number) has changed little in the last 30 years and has been guided by three basic assumptions:

1. Innovation is universally desirable for organizations.

---

[69] A. D. Meyer, "Adapting to Environmental Jolts," *Administrative Science Quarterly,* 27, no. 4 (December 1982), pp. 515–537.

[70] A. D. Meyer, G. R. Brooks, and J. B. Goes, "Environmental Jolts and Industry Revolutions: Organizational Responses to Discontinuous Change," *Strategic Management Journal* 11 (Summer 1990), pp. 93–110. (quote is from abstract)

[71] C. M. Fiol, "Squeezing Harder Doesn't Always Work: Continuing the Search for Consistency in Innovation Research," *Academy of Management Review,* 21, no. 4 (1996), p. 1012.

[72] The original seminar article on this topic was W. M. Cohen and D. A. Levinthal, "Absorptive Capacity: A New Perspective on Learning and Innovation," *Administrative Science Quarterly,* 35 (March 1990), pp. 128–152.

[73] R. Drazin and C. B. Schoonhoven, "Community, Population, and Organization Effects on Innovation: A Multilevel Perspective," *Academy of Management Journal,* 39, no. 5 (1996), p. 966.

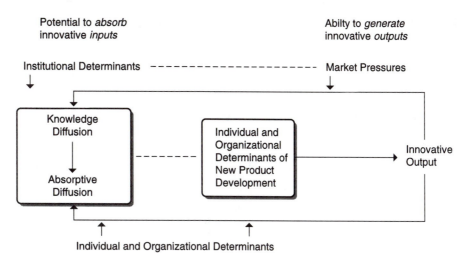

Figure 3-6 A Map of Innovation Research
SOURCE: C. F. Fiol, 1996, p. 1019.

2. Once an organization increases beyond a critical mass, it becomes more inert, less capable of meaningful organizational change, and only haltingly proficient at innovation.

3. Certain structures and practices can overcome inertia and increase the generation rate of innovation.

Contributions to their special issue relate to two research traditions in the field: the context of organizational innovation and the dynamics of industry-level effects on innovation (i.e., communities and populations). The Drazin and Schoonhoven summary of the first set of contributions on context is reproduced in Figure 3-7.

This theoretical summary indicates that context for innovating includes not just organizational level (e.g., corporate strategy) considerations but individual (e.g., creativity) and group (e.g., organization-project interaction) considerations. These concepts affect attention to innovation issues and availability of slack resources for innovating. One of the findings of this work is that top managers often become distracted from innovation agendas because of downsizing, acquisitions, mergers, cost reduction, and other strategic initiatives. This general tendency is repeated all too often in the cases relevant to this subject, and is much in evidence in the Gillette Sensor razor case (Case 2-1), where a hostile takeover distracted the top management team during the course of the development of this technology.

*S*UMMARY

The theories of innovation for organizations can be summarized with *three curves:*

1. The S-curve (also used in technological forecasting)

2. The two intersecting curves of product and process innovation from the Utterback–Abernathy model of evolution of the productive segment

3. The punctuated equilibrium curve, which has a "broken sawtooth" pattern

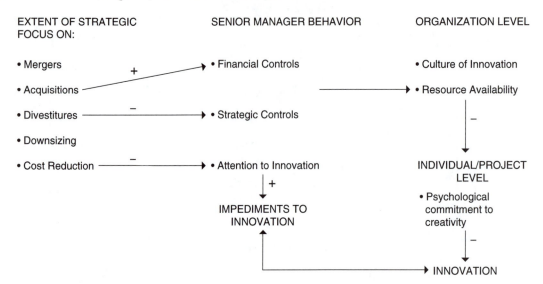

Figure 3-7   A Multilevel Model of the Effects of Context on Innovation
SOURCE: R. Drazin and C. B. Schoonhoven, 1996, p. 1070.

Other theoretical perspectives introduced in the chapter include prediction of individual innovation tendency, sociotechnical systems (STS) design, and more current, eclectic organizational models that draw on earlier theories (e.g., absorptive capacity) and research traditions that attempt to map capabilities and context onto innovation outputs. The causes of innovation are difficult to arrive at by applying common sense. For example, the dominant design that emerges during periods of *substitution* on the technology S-curve is rarely the most innovative available to the market. General managers have great influence over what these competing dominant designs will be. Strategy and innovation are taken up in the next chapter.

DISCUSSION QUESTIONS

1. Data on return on investment versus R&D and capital intensity from the PIMS[74] (ROI Performance Impact of Marketing Strategies) database are presented below. Examine these data carefully and decide whether they support the Utterback–Abernathy theory of evolution of the productive segment. Defend your answer.

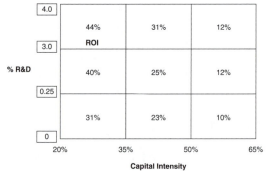

---

[74] See, for example, G. Labovitz, Y. S. Chang, and V. Rosansky, *Making Quality Work* (New York: HarperCollins, 1993). The authors use the PIMS database of more than 3,000 business units to show that companies that ranked in the top fifth on customer perceived quality had pretax return on investment (ROI) of more than 30 percent, while the bottom two-fifths had ROI of 16 percent.

2. Walk through one of the theoretical models of the innovation process (Figure 3-6 or 3-7) and explain what it means and what is missing.

3. Review Case 3-2 on Hewlett-Packand and answer the following questions:

- Is the ink jet printer a "technology push" product or a "market pull" product?

- What are the strengths and weaknesses of the H-P product development organization as described in this case?

- What is the likely competitive response to H-P's moves? Can a strategy to counteract these anticipated competitors' moves be developed now?

$\mathcal{A}$DDITIONAL CASE SUGGESTIONS _____

1. For services, the OTISLINE case is highly recommended: HBS 9-186-304 or the current revision. There is a good video with this case from HBS.

✼ CASE 3-1

Innovative Intentions and Behaviors in Organizations: Scoring Box[75]

1. Step one in the scoring of your innovative potential is to add your total score for all 20 statements, according to the directions in Box 3-1.

2. Next, you can compare yourself to the norms established by our samples of evening MBA students and managers.[76] *A total score of 70 is average.* Note that if you said "not applicable" to every question, your total score would have been 60. And if you had said "often true" to every question, your score would have been 80—the average is exactly halfway between these two response averages (or about 3 and 4 to every other question). A score *above 90 is truly remarkable,* and places you among the top 10 percent in our samples. If you scored at 90 or above, you have true innovative tendencies among the people in your job setting.

3. Our research also shows that some questions are better indicators than others of innovative intentions in organizations. In particular, question numbers 6 (new uses for existing methods), 7 (first to try new ideas), 12 (written evaluations of proposed ideas), 13 (develop contacts with experts outside the firm), and 18 (comments at staff meetings) are the best five questions indicating innovative tendencies. Go back to your individual statement scores and see how you responded to these five questions as a second check on the reliability of this paper-and-pencil measure of individual innovative tendency. If you scored 5 ("almost always true") to these five questions, and scored more than 90 total points, it is an even stronger indicator of your (or anyone else's) innovation tendencies. But remember, it takes all kinds of people in all types of roles (mentors, champions, managers, funds providers, etc.) to make an innovative system work. There is a role for *everyone* in an innovative, successful organization.

_____

[75] See J. Ettlie and R. D. O'Keefe, "Innovative Attitudes, Values, and Intentions in Organizations," *Journal of Management Studies* 19, no. 2 (1982), pp. 163–182.

[76] J. Ettlie, "A Note on the Relationship between Managerial Change Values, Innovative Intentions, and Innovative Technology Outcomes in Food Sector Firms," *R&D Management* 13, no. 4 (1983), pp. 231–244.

✼ CASE 3-2

How H-P Used Tactics of the Japanese to Beat Them at Their Game

It was such sweet revenge.

_____

SOURCE: S. Kreider Yoder, *Wall Street Journal,* Sept. 8, 1994, p. A1. Reprinted by permission of Wall Street Journal © 1994 Dow Jones and Company, Inc. All rights reserved.

Last year, Hewlett-Packard Co. faced a challenge from NEC Corp. The Japanese giant had plans to attack H-P's hegemony in the burgeoning computer-printer market in time-honored Japanese fashion: by undercutting prices with new, better designed models. Over a decade ago, the tactic helped other Japanese companies grab the lead from H-P in a business it had pioneered, hand-held calculators.

This time it didn't work. Months before NEC could introduce its inexpensive monochrome inkjet printer, H-P launched an improved color version and slashed prices on its bestselling black-and-white model by 40% over six months. NEC withdrew its entry, now over-priced and uncompetitive, after about four months on the market.

"We were too late," says John McIntyre, then a market-ing director at NEC's U.S. unit. "We just didn't have the economies of scale" to compete with H-P.

A few years ago, U.S. companies were ruing Japan's unbeatable speed to market and economies of scale in many industries, and printers were a prime example: Japan made four out personal of five computer printers that Americans bought in 1985. But now many American and Japanese companies are trading places, a shift con-firmed by an annual global survey that reported Tuesday that the U.S. has replaced Japan as the world's most com-petitive economy for the first time since 1985.

H-P is one of the most dramatic of an increasing num-ber of U.S. take-back stories, in technologies including disk drives, cellular phones, pagers and computer chips. H-P didn't even start making PC printers until 1984, but it is expected to have about $8 billion in printer revenue this year.

Among other things, the H-P story dispels common myths about the relative strengths of the U.S. and Japan, showing how big U.S. companies, under proper leader-ship, can exploit American creativity while using their huge resources to deploy "Japanese" tactics. H-P used its financial might to invest heavily in a laboratory break-through, then kept market share by enforcing rules that are gospel in Japan: Go for mass markets, cut costs, sus-tain a rapid fire of product variations and price cuts, and target the enemy.

Richard Hackborn, the H-P executive who led the charge, also succeeded because he could do what his Japanese counterparts couldn't: Buck the system. His printer-business teams were in out-posts like Boise, Idaho—far from H-P's increasingly bureaucratic Palo Alto, Calif., headquarters—where they were permitted, though sometimes reluctantly, to go their own way.

H-P's other top executives for the most part preached high-profit, high-cost products for niche markets—which is how H-P lost the calculator business. Mr. Hack-born's troops set profit margins below the corporate norm and went for the mass market themselves. They moved fast and defied corporate rules when it meant winning customers.

"If you're going to leverage American culture but com-pete globally you need a balance of entrepreneurship and central leverage," says Mr. Hackborn, who retired last year to become an H-P director. "The rugged individual-ism of cowboy culture alone doesn't work; but to be centrally directed doesn't either, because you lose the tremendous contribution of local innovation and accountability."

Japanese industrialists have often sermonized about U.S. complacency and myopia, but Japanese success, it turns out, can breed the same. H-P kept its huge lead because Japanese manufacturers, flush with success, spent too long squeezing profits out of old technologies and ignored signs that the American market—the bell-wether—was rapidly changing.

"H-P understood computers better, it understood American customers better, it got good products to mar-ket faster," says Takashi Saito, head of Canon Inc.'s inkjet-printer business. Japanese makers' culture hindered the kind of quick decision making needed in the fast-paced U.S. computer market, he says, and as a result, "The mar-ket is H-P's garden."

Hewlett-Packard's journey to the top of the printer market began with a laboratory accident in 1979 and culminated in a rout of the Japanese beginning in 1992.

When H-P started thinking of entering the printer mar-ket, it realized it couldn't unseat the dominant Japanese makers. such as Seiko Epson Corp. and Oki Electric Indus-try Co., without a technological advance. Japan had a lock on the mass market with low-cost, well-engineered "dot matrix" printers, which form relatively rough letters.

The seeds for the H-P breakthrough had been nur-tured by engineers in a converted janitor's closet at a Vancouver, Wash., plant since 1980. The year before, an H-P scientist noticed drops of liquid splattered over his lab bench. He had been testing a thin metal film by zap-ping it with electricity; when the metal grew hot, liquid trapped underneath began to boil and spurted out. The discovery evolved into the "thermal" inkjet.

Mr. Hackborn saw that inkjet technology had com-pelling advantages over laser printers for the mass mar-ket: It was cheaper, it was more easily adaptable for color printing and no one else had perfected it. The idea of using a jet to spit ink on paper had been around for years, but no one had found a good way to pump the ink through tiny holes. H-P's first inkjet printer in 1984 was hardly a knockout. It needed special paper, the ink tended to smear and it could print only 96 dots per inch, compared with today's 600 dots. "H-P's first inkjet was terrible quality," says Norio Niwa, president of Epson's U.S. unit. "Our engineers thought that if they announced such a product, they'd lose face."

H-P saw it differently. It had also introduced a success-ful line of expensive laser printers for corporate cus-tomers, but the company believed that ordinary com-puter users would soon demand higher-quality printouts of text, graphics and photographs. There was a mass market in the making—the kind that H-P had previously blown. To prevent a repeat, H-P had to invest heavily in its low-cost inkjet technology, Mr. Hackborn says, and "learn from the Japanese" by building it into a family of products.

Meanwhile, the Japanese were making mistakes. Canon, which had edged ahead of H-P in patenting early inkjet designs but had agreed to share the patents, chose a complex implementation that would set it years behind. And Epson, the king of dot-matrix printers, ignored warnings of changing consumer tastes.

Executives from Epson's U.S. unit began traveling to Japan around 1985 to tell headquarters that low-budget PC users would soon demand high-quality printers and that Epson should invest more in technologies such as inkjets, says Peter Bergman, a former Epson marketing executive. "Their approach was, 'Who are these Americans to come over and tell me how to build our products?'" he says.

Epson had an inkjet technology of its own, but it was an expensive variation. Besides, says Mr. Niwa, the Epson executive, "Every engineer was looking at dot matrix because we had a big market, big profits, big business, and the technology itself had a long history."

The same kind of mistake could have happened at H-P. Headquarters became increasingly bureaucratic, with product plans requiring many levels of approval. But business units are set up as fiefs, each having great autonomy. "We had the resources of a big company, but we were off on our own," says Richard Belluzzo, who has taken over from Mr. Hackborn. "There wasn't central planning…, so we could make decisions really fast."

Based on decisions made in the hinterlands, H-P engineers adopted two Japanese tactics: They filed a blizzard of patents to protect their design and frustrate rivals, and embarked on a process of continual improvement to solve the inkjet's problems. They developed print heads that could spit 300 dots an inch and made inks that would stay liquid in the cartridge but dry instantly on plain paper. One engineer tested all types of paper: bonded, construction, toilet—and, for good measure, added sandpaper, tortillas and socks.

In 1988, H-P introduced the Deskjet, the plain-paper printer that would evolve into the model now taking market share away from the Japanese. No rivals loomed, but the line still wasn't meeting sales goals in 1989. It was competing with H-P's own more-costly laser printers. Sales were too low to pay the high costs of research and factories. The inkjet division needed new markets to avert a financial crisis.

That autumn, a group of engineers and managers assembled for a two-day retreat at a lodge on Oregon's Mount Hood. They pored over market-share charts. That, says Richard Snyder, who now heads H-P's PC inkjet business, is "when the lights went on." H-P hadn't targeted the right enemy. Instead of positioning the inkjet as a low-cost alternative to H-P's fancy laser printers, the managers decided, they should go after the Japanese-dominated dot-matrix market.

Dot matrix, the biggest section of the market, had serious flaws—poor print quality and color. Epson, the No. 1 player, had a soft underbelly: No competitive inkjet and the distraction of an expensive and failing effort to sell a PC. "We said, 'Maybe this is a good time to attack,'" Mr. Snyder says.

H-P did so with the obsessive efficiency of a Japanese company. A week later, H-P teams were wearing "Beat Epson" football jerseys. The company began tracking Epson's market share, studying its marketing practices and public financial data, surveying loyal Epson customers and compiling profiles of Epson's top managers. Engineers tore apart Epson printers for ideas on design and manufacturing, a tactic the Japanese often use.

Among the findings: Epson's marketers got stores to put their printers in the most prominent spots; Epson used price cuts as tactical weapons to fend off challengers: consumers liked Epson machines for their reliability; Epson's printers were built to be manufactured easily. H-P responded, demanding that stores put its inkjet printers alongside Epson's. It tripled its warranty to three years and redesigned printers with manufacturing in mind.

Engineers learned Epson got huge mileage out of a product by creating a broad line consisting of slight variations of the same basic printer. By contrast, "we were taken with the notion at H-P that you had to come up with a whole new platform every time," Mr. Snyder says. Change came hard. In 1990, as H-P was developing a color printer, engineers were set on creating a completely new, full-featured mechanical marvel. Marketers suggested that a simpler, slightly clumsier approach, would be good enough for most consumers.

There was a near mutiny among the engineers until a product manager named Judy Thorpe forced them to do telephone polls of customers. It turned out people were eager for the product the engineers considered a "kludge." H-P learned that "you can tweak your not-so-latest thing and get the latest thing," Ms. Thorpe says. By sticking to the existing platform, H-P was able to get the jump on competitors in the now-booming color-printer market.

By 1992, it became clear to Japanese makers that dot-matrix printers were under assault, with sales falling for the first time as inkjet sales soared.

When the Computer City division of Tandy Corp., the Fort Worth, Texas, company, was preparing to open its first stores in the summer of 1991, it told printer makers that it expected inkjets to be a hot category, says Alan Bush, president of the chain. The Japanese responded that they didn't have anything ready. "We were very astounded," says Mr. Bush. "In the summer of '91, for an inkjet-product line you had your choice: H-P, H-P or H-P."

When Japanese printer makers that had been investing in inkjet research tried to move into the market, they ran into a brick wall: H-P had a lock on many important patents. Citizen Watch Co. found H-P had "covered the bases to make it very difficult for anyone else to get there," says Michael Del Vecchio, senior vice president of Citizen's U.S. unit. Citizen engineers trying to develop print heads learned H-P had some 50 patents covering how ink travels through the head. "It's like being in a maze: You go down this path and suddenly you're into an area that may infringe on their main patents and you have to back up and start over."

This barrier to entry meant competitors lost valuable time. "Every year that went by that we and other people were unsuccessful in reinventing the wheel, [H-P] got a greater and greater lead," says Mr. McIntyre, the former NEC executive.

Then there were H-P's economies of scale, which allowed it to undercut almost anyone else's prices; by the time Canon came out with the first credible competition, H-P had sold millions of printers and had thousands of outlets for its replacement cartridges. And H-P used its experience to make continual improvements in manufacturing. In constant dollars, for example, today's Deskjet costs half as much to make as the 1988 model.

This has allowed H-P to carry out a vital strategy: When a rival attacks, hit back quickly and hard. When Canon was about to introduce a color inkjet printer last year, H-P cut the price of its own version before its rival had even reached the market. The black and-white printer, priced at $995 in 1988, now lists for $365.

"They've been very good about eating their own young," Mr. McIntyre says.

And consuming the competition as well. H-P now holds 55% of the world market for inkjets. The success in printers, including lasers, has propelled enormous overall growth at H-P, making it one of the two fastest-growing major U.S. multinationals (the other is Motorola Inc.). H-P's other divisions have been transformed by the printer people's mass-market approach and now seek to make the lowest-cost personal and hand-held computers on the market.

H-P's lead in printers could bring even more profits because inkjet mechanisms are finding their way into facsimile machines and color copiers. Sales could explode if, as expected, inkjet becomes the technology of choice inside TV-top printers for interactive-TV services. Printers will "be like-toilets," says Mr. Hackborn. "They'll play a central role in the home."

Section Two

Planning Innovation

Chapter 4

Strategy and Innovation

CHAPTER OBJECTIVES

> To introduce the topic of innovating with strategic intent at all levels of aggregation—science and public policy, corporate and business unit strategies. This chapter focuses on technology competencies and forecasting, organizational strategies that include innovating, mergers and acquisitions, and the roles of leadership and ethics in managing innovation strategy. Emergent issues, including competitive response to innovation, are illustrated by examples from Bank of New York, ABB, Caterpillar, Inc., flexible packaging in the food industry, American Safety Razor Company, Maytag, automated vehicle identification in the rail industry, EDI (electronic data interchange), 3M, and the case of National Machinery.

As a general definition, an **innovation strategy** is a long-range plan for innovation and technology management. But how does that translate into corporate behavior? Is it innovation strategy when market pioneers capture and maintain larger shares than later entrants, often by investing more in R&D?[1] This is just one of the issues we will consider in this chapter. We start with an introduction of the Honda effect.

---

[1] T. S. Robertson and H. Gatignon, "How Innovators Thwart New Entrants into Their Market," *Planning Review,* 19, no. 5 (Sept/Oct 1991), pp. 4–11; M. J. Dowling and J. E. McGee, "Business and Technology Strategies and New Venture Performance: A Study of the Telecommunications Equipment Industry," *Management Science,* 40, no. 12 (December 1994), pp. 1663–1697.

$\mathscr{T}$HE HONDA EFFECT _____

The **Honda effect**—it's not what you think it is. Honda's rollout of the 1998 Accord has been widely celebrated in the trade press, which often includes reference to the speed of new product-line conversions. These conversions are measured in days (from 0 to 100% capacity, or 1,750 units per day, on two lines, in 20 days, it has been reported) rather than weeks or months, like other car companies. Toyota benchmarks Honda on new product development. All this is true and more, but that's not *the* Honda effect.

In February 1998, a team of managers and engineers from Honda presented the new Accord at the University of Michigan, College of Engineering. They outlined three Honda challenges that require new technology: (1) shaping the company to be both tough and agile; (2) worldwide self-reliance, growing in each region of the world, but working together at the same time; and (3) increasing commitment to the natural environment. Honda sales are up 38 percent in Japan and 20 percent in the United States compared with the last Accord launch, so Honda must be doing something right.

There are three versions of the Accord, all using the same platform, for the United States, Europe, and Japan. There is also considerable commonality in parts, tooling, welding equipment, and painting processes. The new model even includes a five-point suspension and accommodates the varying criteria of space, performance, and cost, using modular design driven by productivity demands. The Accord Coupe followed the sedan to market after only one month.

Is the Honda effect fast product introduction and launch? No, it's more. At the presentation, one of my colleagues asked the speakers if they used flexibility in their manufacturing operations in order to buy "options" on future design changes or to promote learning. But that wasn't the complete story either. Honda used flexibility to save money. So is that the Honda effect? No, that's not unique. GM, Ford, Chrysler, and the world wants to save money. Still not there.

How about the careful market positioning of the new Accord Coupe so as not to disturb Prelude sales? True, that was done, but no, that wasn't the Honda effect, either. How many prototypes did they need to launch the Coupe? That could be at least part of the Honda effect, since the answer was "more than one, but less than ten." How about the *increase* in the supply base from 384 to 408? No, that isn't it either.

The Honda effect is the unplanned, or **emergent strategies,** that companies use to respond to unforeseen circumstances, and they often arise from the autonomous actions of individuals deep within an organization rather than from some formal, top-down planning process. The Honda effect refers to the emergent strategy example that so aptly describes this phenomenon discussed by Richard Pascale, who documented the entry of Honda into the U.S. motorcycle market. That was 40 years and many yen ago.

---

[2] One of the not so obvious effects of a well-articulated intended strategy is the psychological effect of clear goals. See E. A. Locke, *A Theory of Goal Setting and Task Performance,* in E. A. Locke and G. P. Latham (eds.), with contributions by K. J. Smith and R. E. Wood (Englewood Cliffs, N.J.:Prentice Hall, 1990).

"When a number of Honda executives arrived in Los Angeles from Japan in 1959 to establish a U.S. subsidiary, their original aim **(intended strategy[2])** was to focus on selling 250-cc and 350-cc machines to confirmed motorcycle enthusiasts, rather than 50-cc Honda Cubs, which were a big hit in Japan." Honda managers just assumed that the Honda 50s were unsuitable for the U.S. market where everything was more luxurious than in Japan. "However, sales of the 250-cc and 350-cc bikes were sluggish ... and plagued by mechanical failure."

It didn't look good for Honda. But then something rather unusual happened. "Japanese executives were using the Honda 50s to run errands around Los Angeles and attracting a lot of attention... One day they got a call from a buyer at Sears, Roebuck..." And the rest is history. Honda executives were reluctant at first to give up on the bigger bikes, and switch to the smaller 50s, but they "stumbled onto a previously untouched market segment": Americans who had never owned a motorbike. Honda also found an untried channel of distribution: general retailers. By 1964, one of every two motorcycles sold in the United States was a Honda.[3]

"The conventional explanation for Honda's success is that the company redefined the U.S. motorcycle market with a brilliantly conceived intended strategy. The fact was that Honda's intended strategy was a near disaster."[4] The emergent strategy, on the other hand, that occurred as a result of unforeseen circumstances, should also attest to the open-minded and learning-oriented Honda managers in charge at the time. Bottom line: All strategies result from planned or emergent actions. Honda has been extremely good at both.

$\mathcal{B}$ACK TO BASICS: DEFINING STRATEGY

Let's review the basics of strategy. **Strategy making** is the process of matching an organization's *internal resources* with *environmental opportunities and risks* to *accomplish goals*. Most strategies have four elements: goals, strategies, action plans, and programs. Strategy in most companies is ordered in a hierarchy that begins with **corporate strategy** and answers this question: What business or businesses are we in? **Business strategy** is derived from corporate strategy: How should we compete in the business(es) we are in? Finally, **functional strategies**

---

[3] See C. W. L. Hill and G. R. Jones, *Strategic Management* (4th ed.) (Boston: Houghton Mifflin Company, 1998), especially pages 18–19. The original article on the Honda effect was by R. T. Pascale, "Perspectives on Strategy: The Real Story Behind Honda's Success," *California Management Review,* 26 (1986), pp. 47–72. The buzz over the Honda effect hardly ended with the original article: see H. Mintzberg, R. Pascale, M. Goold, and R. Rumelt, "The 'Honda Effect' Revisited," *California Management Review* 38, no. 4 (Summer 1996). That special issue continues the debate about whether deliberate planning or incremental learning constitute "strategy," but it hardly matters, if one adopts the view that both are important to strategic action. A recent report on Intel confirms this trend in high technology industries as well: R. A. Burgelman, "Fading Memories: A Process Theory of Strategic Business Exit in Dynamic Environments," *Administrative Science Quarterly,* 39 (1994), pp. 24–56. Burgelman found that inertial forces within Intel kept it committed to a technology (memory vs. microprocessors) long after resources had been reallocated. This is the way strategy emerges, sometimes as a result of the actions of middle managers.

[4] H. Mintzberg, R. Pascale, M. Goold, and R. Rumelt, "The 'Honda Effect' Revisited," *California Management Review,* 38, no. 4 (Summer 1996), p. 20.

follow. For example, part of operations strategy is to decide where to locate facilities—typically a long-term commitment is required for these decisions. Make-buy decisions are also long term, but probably easier to reverse.

Two extremely important contributions to the strategic management literature have deep relevance to innovation decision making. The first is the now classic **five forces model** and **generic strategy** framework by Michael Porter.[5] This is diagrammed Figure 4-1, and is the starting point of many strategic analyses. As we will see later, however, the importance of technology in this framework is probably underestimated.[6]

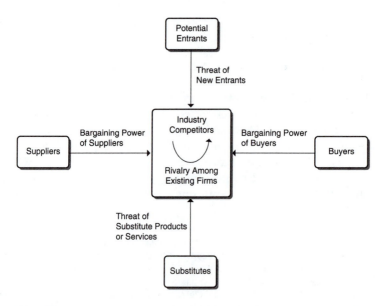

Figure 4-1   The Five Competitive Forces that Determine Industry Profitability

Adapted with the permission of The Free Press, a Division of Simon and Schuster, Inc., from Competitive Advantage: Creating and Sustaining Superior by Michael E. Porter. Copyright © 1985 by Michael E. Porter.

---

[5] M. E. Porter, *Competitive Advantage* (New York: The Free Press, 1985), esp. p. 5

[6] Also see J. Tidd, J. Bessant, and K. Pavitt, *Managing Innovation* (Chichester, UK: John Wiley & Sons, 1997), esp. pp. 66–67, for a critique of Porter's model.

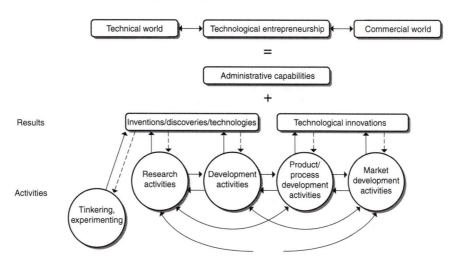

Figure 4-2   The Relationships Between Key Concepts Concerning Technological Innovation
SOURCE: Burgelman et al., 1996.

The second contribution is the most recent edition of a book on the strategic management of technology by Burgleman, Maidique, and Wheelwright.[7] A summary of the authors' approach is pictured in Figure 4-2. The key concept in this model is that results and activities + administrative capabilities = technological entrepreneurship in a technical and commercial context. This model makes the now-common assumption that whether the innovation process is initiated by markets or technical ideas, both will be required in an iterative process for successful innovation.

Although it is hard to underestimate the importance of these two contributions, it is also wise to keep these two models in perspective. They do not include all of the important, detailed concepts of this book, or the compilation of thousands of experienced managers and researchers whose work focused on new product, process, and information system deployment. That is not their intent. They are the sound footing on which to get started, not the end, by any means, of the innovative journey.

THE SCOPE OF INNOVATION STRATEGY _____

One way of dividing the strategy and innovation issue is by level of aggregation. Countries can have an innovation strategy, as can firms or consortia of companies,

---

[7] R. Burgelman, M. Maidique, and S. Wheelright, *Strategic Management of Technology and Innovation* (2nd ed.) (Chicago: Irwin, 1996).

business units within firms, and product or service divisions. One attempt to organize these perpectives is shown in Table 4-1.[8] Here the distinction is made between **science policy,** which includes concerns for scientific education and basic research funding (usually at the national level), **technology policy,** which focuses on creation of strategic or generic technologies (usually at the firm level), and **innovation policy,** which focuses on technology transfer (usually at the business unit level).

What is missing from these designations is a codification of ways to approach these issues or actual types of plans. For example, one science policy is not to try to pick winners in a technology race, but to foster only high-risk, basic research. For technology policy, a strategy might be to "make" all core technologies, and "outsource" all noncore technologies (e.g., information technology). For innovation policy, there are also many governance issues: there are different ways of competing such as through joint ventures, equity positions, R&D partnerships, or technology acquisitions. Should one form be encouraged over another?

*T*ABLE 4-1   Science, Technology, and Innovation Policy

Policy	Main Features	Recent Trends
Science policy	• Scientific education • Research in universities and government laboratories • Basic research • Focus on big issues (e.g., space, nuclear power)	• Selectivity ('foresight') Internationalization
Technology policy	• Support for creation of strategic or generic technologies (e.g., IT, biotechnology, and encouragement of new technology-based firms)	• Targeted research efforts • R&D collaboration • IPR protection • Regulation • Environmental issues • Favored procurement
Innovation policy	• Facilitating diffusion of technology • Encouraging transfer sciences, particularly AMT • SME focus	• Systematic approach to innovation • Network building • Intermediary development • Regionalization/decentralization • Building firm capabilities as well as resources

IT = information technology; AMT = advanced manufacturing technology; SME = small and medium enteprise.

SOURCE: Adapted from M. Dodgson and J. Bessant, *Effective Innovation Policy: A New Approach* (London: International Thomson Business Press, 1996), p. 5.

---

[8] M. Dodgson and J. Bessant, *Effective Innovation Policy: A New Approach* (London: International Thomson Business Press, 1996), p. 5.

TECHNOLOGICAL
COMPETENCIES _____

The ability of a firm, applying skill sets of employees, to perform activities on the value added chain is a competence.[9] Competencies unique to a firm might help explain how firms differ in capacity for change. What we are most concerned with here, of course, are the technological competencies that can be used as a basis for change strategy formulation. Pari Patel and Keith Pavitt studied more than 400 of the world's largest companies (47% in the United States, 29% from Europe, and 25% from Japan) and found that they stayed competitive because of three characteristics:

1. They were typically *multifield* and were becoming more so over time, with competencies extending beyond their product range in technical fields outside their *distinctive core.*

2. They were *highly stable* and *differentiated,* with both the *technology profile* and *directions* of localized search strongly influenced by firms' principal products.

3. The *rate* of search was influenced by both the firm's *principal products* and the conditions in its *home country.* However, considerable unexplained variance suggests scope for managerial choice.[10]

Patel and Pavitt used patent data as their measure of technological competency, and, although this method has limitations,[11] the findings are quite consistent with the extant wisdom on management of technology. They also found that these large firms, which tend to be diversified, are also quite diverse in their patenting activity; and their technologies are more diverse than their products. For example, 71 percent of chemical firms' patents are in chemical technologies, but they also have substantial competence outside their core fields. Another example is pharmaceutical companies, which have 10 percent of their patents concentrated in nonelectrical machinery. Firms seem to diversify for two primary reasons: the *technological interdependence between a firm's products and suppliers* of materials and equipment, and *emerging technological opportunities.*

---

[9] This definition is adapted from A. Afuah, *Innovation Management: Strategies, Implementation and Profits* (New York: Oxford, 1998), p. 52. This definition is similar to the idea of core competence used by C.K. Prahalad and G. Hammel, "The Core Competence of the Corporation," *Harvard Business Review,* 68, no. 3 (1990), pp. 79–91, who actually say that core competencies are embodied in the people of the organization.

[10] P. Patel and K. Pavitt, "The Technological Competencies of the World's Largest Firms: Complex and Path-Dependent, But Not Much Variety," *Research Policy,* 26 (1997), pp. 141–156.

[11] Ibid., p. 141, Patel and Pavitt list three limitations: (1) patents do not measure the extent of a firm's external linkages—but these links tend to be complementary; (2) patents measure codified knowledge and don't capture tacit knowledge—although, again, tacit knowledge tends to complement rather than substitute codified knowledge; and (3) patents do not measure software technology.

Although these profiles of technological competencies are very stable over time (1969–1984 versus 1985–1990), suggesting a constraint on direction of searches for new technology, the rate of search varies greatly. The greater the technological opportunity, the faster the accumulation of patents. Some industries and some countries promote more rapid search, and since about 90 percent of R&D is conducted in the home country, this has important implications for national policy. The Patel and Pavitt report is consistent with other studies. Jeffe studied 432 firms and found that R&D pays off as technological opportunity increases.[12] Cohen, Levin, and Mowery reported that industry explains half of the variance in R&D intensity.[13]

These findings are likely to apply primarily to product-related R&D, but Ettlie found that investments in computerization for manufacturing also varied by country and economic region. South America is currently behind the rest of the world on these investments, but this measure did not vary by industry for 600 durable goods companies in 20 countries.[14]

Patel and Pavitt found that their predictors accounted for less than 50 percent of the variance in patenting activity (56–80% of variance was unexplained), which leaves considerable room to explain these differences by factors that can be influenced at the firm level. This has been confirmed by others who have found that greater investments in R&D are positively associated with the presence of top managers with technical backgrounds.[15] This topic is taken up later (see Box 4-1).

Other research has attempted to verify Porter's contention that nations differ in their competitive strengths and weaknesses, including their ability to innovate.[16] Preliminary evidence supports this model. For example, Billings and Yaprak compared U.S. and Japanese firms in 14 industrial groups on inventive efficiency. R&D efficiency was measured in a number of ways, including sales, and value-added divided by R&D lagged by two to five years.[17] The United States is more R&D efficient in food, textiles, chemicals, rubber, metals, and fabricated metals, while Japan is more efficient in paper, petroleum, machinery, and scientific equipment. The two countries were equally R&D efficient in electrical equipment, transportation, and stone industries.

Mansfield found that U.S. firms adopted flexible manufacturing systems at lower rates than Japanese firms because projected returns were less. When one controls for average returns and adoption year, "there is no statistically significant

---

[12] A.B. Jeffe, "Technological Opportunity and Spillovers of R&D: Evidence from Firms' Patents, Profits, and Market Value," *American Economic Review,* 76, no. 5 (1986), pp. 984–1001.

[13] W. Cohen, M. Levin, and D. Mowery, "Firm Size and R&D Intensity: A Re-examination," *Journal of Industrial Economics,* 35, no. 4 (1987), pp. 543–565.

[14] J. Ettlie, "R&D and Global Manufacturing Performance," *Management Science,* 44, no. 1 (January 1998), pp. 1–11.

[15] Cited in P. Patel and K. Pavitt (1997): D. Bosworth and R. Wilson, *Technological Change: The Role of Scientists and Engineers* (Avebury, UK: Aldershot, 1992); F. Scherer and K. Hugh, "Top Management Education and R&D Investment," *Research Policy,* 21 (1992), p. 507.

[16] M. Porter, *The Competitive Advantage of Nations* (New York: MacMillan, 1990).

[17] B.A. Billings and A. Yaprak, "Inventive Efficiency, How the U.S. Compares with Japan," *R&D Management,* 25, no. 4 (1995), pp. 365–376.

tendency for the rate of imitation ... to be slower in the United States than in Japan or Western Europe." And, "users of flexible manufacturing systems tend to be much larger firms than nonusers" in all three regions of the world. Larger firms tended to install more flexible manufacturing systems.[18] This issue of payback on investments in new processing technology, when the appropriability regimen is weak (value capture difficult) because technology is outsourced, is revisited in Chapters 6, 8, and 9.

TECHNOLOGICAL FORECASTING

Strategies and plans are for the future. But if the future differs from the present, plans based on today's world will become obsolete. One way to avoid this problem is to forecast conditions that will be in place when plans are actually implemented. Market and sales forecasts are typical for any unit, but technology forecasting is different.

Technology forecasting was introduced in Chapter 3 with theories of innovation, and the method illustrated was an example of what Joe Martino calls *direct* forecasting.[19] That is, the technology S-curve represents actual behavior and measurements that can be made on the progress of a technology, usually of individual technical approaches to solving a technical problem. Technology S-curves of performance generally assume an upper limit based on physical capabilities determined by the underlying science of the area.

Diffusion of innovation can also be represented on an S-curve. The proportion of a population of potential adopters of a new technology can be plotted on the *y*-axis and time can be plotted on the *x*-axis of a graph. Here, the upper limit is the size of the population of potential adopters. For example, the proportion of the U.S. merchant marine using mechanical power began to escalate rapidly after 1820 and slowed down dramatically after 1900, approaching 100 percent in 1960. The S-curve can be approximated with what is often called the *growth* curve or *logistic* curve, which has several alternative mathematical functional formulae. The example in Chapter 3 was the Pearl curve.[20]

Although the relationship between the technology S-curve and technological forecasting with growth curves may be obvious, it may not be obvious why one

---

[18] E. Mansfield, "The Diffusion of Flexible Manufacturing Systems in Japan, Europe, and the United States," *Management Science,* 39, no. 2 (February, 1993), pp. 149–159.

[19] J. P. Martino, *Technological Forecasting for Decision Making* (New York: McGraw-Hill, 1993).

[20] There are many formulations of the technology S-curve. One, the Bass model, was recently tested in a curve-fitting exercise for five new medical equipment technologies (e.g., CT scan and MRI), and the model was found to be a good predictor of actual imitation in the diffusion process. See G. P. Sillup, "Forecasting the Adoption of New Medical Technology Using the Bass Model," *Journal of Health Care Marketing,* 12, no. 4 (December 1992). S-curves have also been used to track electrochemical technologies in the emerging electric vehicle industry. See R. N. McGrath, "Technological Discontinuities and Media Patterns: Assessing Electric Vehicle Batteries," *Technovation,* 18, no. 11 (November 1998), pp. 677–687.

would want to make the effort to forecast technology at all. One could ask the same question about sales forecasting. Although most companies do sales forecasting, many firms have more than one forecast in place. Marketing forecasts tend to be different from production or operations forecasts.

Operational plans often begin with forecasts of demand required, quite independently of why demand is growing, is on a plateau or is declining. Technology plans, then, ought to begin, at least in part, with forecasts about technological progress, quite independently of how or why these technological changes ought to occur. Dr. Martino says that anybody, any organization, or any nation that is affected by technology is, by default, entering into a forecasting exercise when resources are committed. By implication, the allocation of resources makes assumptions about the technology future. The alternatives to forecasting systematically are all used periodically: no forecast (or future same as past); window blind (linear) forecasting; panic or crisis forecasting, or waiting until something happens and reacting, and genius forecasting, or asking someone who has been successful in the past to forecast the future again.[21]

The virtues of using systematic technological forecasting is that these methods can be taught and mastered by people for cross-referencing, reviewed for soundness, and documented for learning when actual changes occur. If forecasts are precise, they can be checked for accuracy, and even if they are incorrect, they can still be helpful, because a measure of forecasting performance is possible when the prediction is explicit.

There are four basic methods of technological forecasting:

▶ **Extrapolation** (extension of a time-series pattern or trend, or incorporation of cycles) is very useful for long-term forecasting. An example is provided in Figure 4-3 using exponential conversion of the y-axis data for millions of kilowatt-hours of power generation.

▶ **Leading indicators** act as a barometer. Sometimes data are not directly available, so data on indicators like patents are often used.[22]

▶ **Causal models** predict outcomes based on cause and effect. For example, scientists know an eclipse will occur based on the laws of physics.

▶ **Probabilistic models** produce a probability distribution for various outcomes.

Developments in the field can be tracked by reading the well-established professional journal, *Technological Forecasting and Social Change.*

---

[21] J. P. Martino, "Technological Forecasting: An Introduction," *Futurist* 27, no. 4 (July–August 1993), pp. 13–16.

[22] Martino uses the example of Japanese applications for U.S. patents on cameras (p. 128 ff) in his book, *Technological Forecasting for Decision Making* (New York: McGraw-Hill, 1993). H. Ernst used patent data to show trends in computer-numerical control (CNC) for the machine tool industry, especially in the trade pattern between Japan and Germany; he found market activity followed quickly after patent activity. See H. Ernst, "The Use of Patent Data for Technological Forecasting: The Diffusion of CNC-Technology in the Machine Tool Industry," *Small Business Economics,* 9, no. 4 (August 1997), pp. 361–381.

✖ The Delphi Technique

One of the most commonly known technological forecasting methods, the **Delphi technique,** is also one of the most misunderstood.[23] Named after the Greek oracle and developed at the Rand Corporation in the 1960s, it is a method to systematically capture and use expert opinions on committees or panels. Delphi forecasting is appropriate only when no data on a technology exist. These special panels do not meet face-to-face; they are characterized by three important conditions: anonymity, iteration with controlled feedback, and statistical response. This is not an opinion survey, but rather, a way of systematically asking and summarizing expert judgment in successive "rounds" of Delphi forecasts.

An example of a Delphi forecast would be for auto experts to forecast when an electrically powered family sedan at inflation-adjusted average price will be generally available at dealerships or some other retail outlet. After the first round of estimates (the first round is often used to generate events), the panel is given feedback, in truncated fashion (quartile ranges), so it can see where it fell in the estimates. In later rounds, anonymous experts give reasons for estimates. One advantage of this method is that the training, discipline, and experience of experts do not overlap perfectly, so factors that could affect the forecast and actual unfolding of a technology that are external to the actual research and development process, such as political and social factors, often come into play.

Eventually (often four rounds is enough) a relative degree of stability (no changes in median forecast) or consensus is reached through an objective influ-

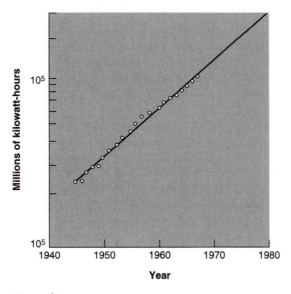

Figure 4-3 Example of Trend Extrapolation: U.S. Electric Power Production[24]

---

[23] See, for example, H. Lindstone and M. Turoff (eds.), *The Delphi Method: Techniques and Applications* (Reading, Mass.: Addison-Wesley, 1995).

[24] J. P. Martino, *Technological Forecasting for Decision Making* (New York: McGraw-Hill, 1993), p. 84. Figure 5-3.

ence process. A typical measure of consensus is the ratio of the interquartile range to the length of the forecast (span from current date to median forecast date). This ratio has been shown to be relatively constant across Delphi exercises, although the absolute uncertainty grows with length of forecast, as would be expected.[25]

✳ Technological Opportunities Analysis (TOA)

Alan Porter and his colleagues have made many contributions linking systematic technological forecasting with strategic planning, especially for emerging technologies.[26] They capture this link with a methodology called **TOA, or Technology Opportunities Analysis,** tested in their home organization, Georgia Institute of Technology. TOA blends monitoring, forecasting, and assessment. It focuses on research leaders and a survey in the *identification* phase of the methodology. A matrix was used to match important, emerging opportunities with Georgia Tech competitive advantages. A second matrix was added, which included risk (benefit/cost ratio) and growth potential (anticipated increase in R&D activities). When the survey by Porter and colleagues showed a high correlation between growth potential and risk, much of the information collected could be consolidated into one matrix. Phase two is devoted to *focus,* which is an in-depth analysis of areas identified; and phase three is the *analysis* of opportunities, requirements, and action options. In the analysis segment of TOA, benchmarking data from other institutions (e.g., MIT) were used. Advanced materials (e.g., composites) was one area identified with high priority, based on the survey results from 62 respondents.

Two important results were obtained from the analysis, in addition to a way of matching the strategic plan for the campus and the actual technology capability trends. First, relationships between the seven target (and other) areas were identified. More traditional departments and areas such as design benefit from this mapping. Second, management of technology issues surfaced:

1. Explosive *growth of centers* suggests opportunities for cross-university links.

2. *Industry participation* and collaboration could be coordinated.

3. *Faculty reward structure* could be evaluated for interdisciplinary collaboration as a distinct factor in promotion, tenure, and salary decision.

Essential to the success of a TOA is the use of *multiple technological forecasting methods* with quantitative and qualitative inputs (e.g., bibliometrics, analysis of funding levels, and survey of expert opinion).[27] Further, both bottom-up and top-

---

[25] Ibid., p. 21.

[26] See, for example, A. Porter, J. Xiao-Yin, J. Gilmour, S. Cunningham, et al., "Technological Opportunities Analysis: Integrating Technology Monitoring, Forecasting, and Assessment with Strategic Planning," *SRA Journal,* 26, no. 2 (Fall, 1994), pp. 21–31.

[27] This idea is consistent with an overarching of definition technology assessment, which departs from the early meaning of this term used almost exclusively to mean impact analysis, see A. Henricksen, "A Technological Assessment Primer for Management of Technology," *International Journal of Technology Management,* 13, no. 5, 6 (1997), pp. 615–638. Also, see C. W. Thomas, "Strategic Technology Assessment, Future Products and Competitive Advantage," *International Journal of Technology Management,* 11, no. 5/6 (1996), pp. 651–666; H. P. Tschirky, "The Role of Technology Forecasting and Assessment in Technology Management," *R&D Management,* 24, no. 2 (April 1994), pp. 121–129.

down actions become apparent in these analyses, as does the relationship to the research environment, including the national agenda.

✖ Technological Monitoring and Scenarios

One particular category of technological forecasting deserves special attention because of its popularity and ease of use—*monitoring*. For example, Xerox developed a method during the late 1980s to monitor the pace and quality of technology delivery systems, leading to at least two new products. The method leads to a checklist of technology mileposts, especially early in the product development cycle.[28] Some companies call this technology assessment,[29] not to be confused with the technology assessment formerly done by the U.S. Congress, which was essentially a technology impact program.

Technology scenarios often result from monitoring exercises.[30] Scenario analysis appears to be an appropriate planning tool for emerging technologies or emerging markets. Scenarios have been used for many years, generally in strategic planning, but the unique focus on technology for forecasting and planning is relatively new to most firms.

✖ Reducing Errors in Technological Forecasting

Although technological forecasts are rarely perfect, they are sometimes dead wrong. The AT&T picturephone is one such example: Developments were anticipated sooner than they took place, and alternative, cheaper technology became available. Now picture phone waits in the wings.[31] The competitive environment is a significant moderator of any technology–performance relationship in the history of a firm, as most everyone knows, but the magnitude of this relationship varies greatly.[32]

Examples of current developments influencing technology adoption curves include the infusion of open architecture in robotic controls,[33] and the collaboration among technology vendors and the growing importance of supply-chain management in ERP (Enterprise Resource Planning) systems.[34] The role of the Internet

[28] G. C. Hartmann and A. L. Lakatos, "Assessing Technology Risk—A Case Study," *Research-Technology Management,* 41, no. 2 (March/April 1998), pp. 32–38.

[29] A. D. Henriksen, "A Technology Assessment Primer for Management of Technology," *International Journal of Technology Management* 13, no. 5, 6 (1997). pp. 615–638.

[30] J. A. Bers, G. S. Lynn, and C. Spurling, "A Venerable Tool for a New Application: Using Scenario Analysis for Formulating Strategies for Emerging Technologies in Emerging Markets," *Engineering Management Journal: EMJ,* 9, no. 2 (June 1997), pp. 33–40.

[31] J. F. Coates, "What Picturephone Teaches About Forecasting," *Research-Technology Management* 41, no. 6 (November/December 1998), pp. 7–8.

[32] S. A. Zahra, "Technology Strategy and Financial Performance: Examining the Moderating Role of the Firm's Competitive Environment," *Journal of Business Venturing,* 11, no. 3 (May 1996), pp. 189–219.

[33] P. Miles, "Open Architecture: Forecasting the Adoption Wave," *Robotics World,* 16, no. 2 (Summer 1998), pp. 23–29.

[34] T. Stein, "ERP's Future Linked to E-Supply Chain," *Information Week,* 705 (October 19, 1998), pp. SS20.

in ERP development and diffusion is still very much a question in this forecasting exercise, and, therefore, it causes great uncertainty in current decision making for this information technology arena.

Using multiple forecasting methods and matching the appropriate method to the situation are both ways to avoid gross forecasting errors. For example, using patent data first as a leading indicator in predicting developments for two trajectories, light emitting diode (LED) material technology and thin film transistor (TFT) technology, can be used to illustrate both ideas. Trends in the patents for these two technologies can be taken as the first approximation for a road map. This road map can then be supplemented with academic journal findings and industrial information, the second sources of data, in order to modify technology planning.[35] There is also evidence that the errors in estimates of returns for adoption of new technology decrease as more firms use an innovation,[36] but this hardly helps innovators.

Choosing the right technological forecasting method depends on a few important factors:[37]

1. *Money* availability—money for development allows for relatively more effort in forecasting, but might also shorten the development cycle.

2. *Data availability*—Delphi requires little data; trend extrapolation requires more data.

3. *Data validity*—some methods require exacting standards; others are robust.

4. *Uncertainty of success*—some methods handle uncertainty better than others.

5. *Similarity of proposed and existing technologies*—the greater the likelihood of realizing the outcome.

6. *Number of variables affecting development*—some methods incorporate multiple factors better than others.

Levary and Han summarize the choice of technology forecasting methods depending on various circumstances (Table 4-2).[38]

In a recent review of the literature on technological forecasting and a review of 29 different models, Meade and Islam divided methods into three groups, depending on the timing point of inflexion in the innovation or substitution process. The authors concluded after simulation, "It is easier to identify a class of possible models rather than the 'best' model. This leads to *combining of model forecasts* [my emphasis] … with a tendency to outperform the individual component models,"[39] which endorses Porter's TOA.[40]

---

[35] S. Shang-Jyh Liu and J. Shyu, "Strategic Planning for Technology Development with Patent Analysis," *International Journal of Technology Management,* 13, no. 5/6 (1997), pp. 661–680.

[36] E. Mansfield, "A Note on Estimating the Returns from New Technology, How Much Learning," *International Journal of Technology Management,* 11, no. 7/8 (1996), pp. 814–820.

[37] See R. R. Levary and D. Han, "Choosing a Technological Forecasting Method," *Industrial Management,* 37, no. 1 (Jan/Feb, 1995), pp. 14–18.

[38] Ibid., p. 17.

[39] N. Meade and T. Islam, "Technological Forecasting—Model Selection, Model Stability, and Combining Models," *Management Science,* 44, no. 8 (August, 1998), pp. 1115–1130.

[40] Porter et al., 1994, pp. 21–31.

$\mathcal{T}_{\text{ABLE}}$ 4-2   Prerequisites for Use of Specific Technological Forecasting Methods

Forecasting method	Prerequisite
Delphi method	All participants should be experts in a given aspect of the proposed technology.
Nominal group process	(1) All participants should be experts in a given aspect of the proposed technology. (2) A group leader is necessary.
Case study method	Complex technology with only a small number of organizations involved can be studied.
Growth curve	(1) Available historical data that cover extended period of time. If historical data are not available from a long enough period, only limited information can be obtained from the data. (2) Technology's life cycle must be known.
Trend analysis	Each trend analysis model must have its own assumptions. Forecasting accuracy depends on the degree of satisfying the model assumptions.
Correlation analysis	The technology to be predicted must have similar characteristics to those of established technologies.
Analytic hierarchy process	Good-quality information must be available from a pair-wise comparison prior to technological forecasting.
System dynamics	The relationships among all variables affecting a technology development process must be known before a system dynamics model can be constructed.
Cross impact analysis	The interrelated future events affecting the likelihood of technology development must be known.
Relevance trees	The hierarchical structure of technology development must be known.
Scenario writing	Scenario developers must be experts in all aspects of the proposed technology.

SOURCE: R. R. Levary and D. Han, "Choosing Technological Forecasting Methods," 37, no. 1 (Jan/Feb 1995), pp. 14–18. © 1997 IEEE.

The way to evaluate a technological forecast, once you have one, is to consider several important issues. Don't believe any forecast that has the words "this will happen," in it. There are scenarios, yes, but rarely certainty. Make sure the forecast makes assumptions clear. Long-range forecasts (10 years) must be tentative and contingent, at best. If the forecast has quantitative use of data, what is the quality of the data and model used, and what factors could not be quantified?

Other issues arise. What should be monitored to validate the forecast? How does it relate to other forecasts? How does the forecast avoid the chronic problems of being optimistic about the pace of change and being too narrow in estimating the scope of the impact of change? Finally, in striking a balance between optimistic and pessimistic views, look for convergence in trends, for it is rare that a single factor will cause big changes.[41]

---

[41] Summarized from J. F. Coates, "How to Recognize a Sound Technology Forecast," *Research-Technology Management,* 38, no. 5 (September/October 1995), pp. 11–12.

$\mathscr{M}$ERGERS AND ACQUISITIONS (M&A'S)

Mergers and acquisitions, driven by cost pressures and globalization, are here to stay for a while, so this might be a good time to review what we know about this process.[42] There are three great myths about mergers and acquisitions:

1. A company can reduce risk through diversification.
2. A company can create value using a portfolio perspective.
3. Related mergers are easier than unrelated mergers to achieve.

Myth number one is that having more eggs in more baskets reduces the risk of firm failure. In fact, it is only through *focused* diversification that firms prosper and grow. Single business firms and conglomerates face the greatest risk, based on a study of 246 Fortune 500 firms by Michael Lubatkin and Sayan Chatterjee.[43] The lowest levels of unsystematic risk are encountered by firms with a midrange amount of diversification. As the authors put it, "Adding more legs to stand on" actually increases the possibility that the table will fall. Rather, a strategy of filling in the gaps to leverage key competencies is a better approach, especially through acquisition. Growing these gap components internally takes longer and is less likely to add "complementary" skills. 3M Corporation has done this well over the years.

Myth number two is that it is possible to create value using the portfolio approach to strategic management. The portfolio approach is similar to that of the Boston Consulting Group's 2 × 2 matrix of "cash cows," "stars," "dogs," and "question marks." Companies are often purchased because they have a technology that another company needs, and they agree to the purchase because they need resources to further nurture this unique technology. However, it is typical for the acquiring firm to treat this "star" as a "cash cow." The net result is failure. Sometimes, a firm does not actually use the 2 × 2 matrix itself, but the underlying "logic," which is actually flawed, is still operating. A good rule of thumb is that when you acquire a firm for technology reasons, set aside an additional 10 percent for continued investment in the technological development of that new partner. Further, labeling an existing business as a "cow" ignores potential development opportunities. The "don't forget how you got there" axiom when facing a big contest (competitor) applies here.

The third big myth is that related mergers are easier to manage than unrelated mergers. That is, synergy is its own reward. There are two barriers to making related mergers work easier than unrelated mergers. First, related mergers are often cast on paper and not in reality. Diligence can reduce surprises but cannot remove them. The escape of valued employees and the problem of incompatible cultures often get in the way of any successful merger implementation. The second problem in related mergers is "family feuds," typical of oil company mergers, which have not lived up to expectations.

---

[42] See, for example, an excellent practitioner article by M. Lubatkin and P. Lane, "Psst ... The Merger Mavens Still Have It Wrong!" *Academy of Management Executive,* 10, no. 1 (February 1996), pp. 21–37.

[43] M. Lubatkin and S. Chatterjee, "Extending Modern Portfolio Theory Into the Domain of Corporations," *Academy of Management Journal,* 37, no. 1 (February 1994), p. 109.

A corollary of this synergy myth is that one related acquisition leads to another when you have enough cash to afford the purchase. When Robert Eaton received an award for business leadership from the University of Michigan Business School (1999), he commented on the decision taken by the newly constituted management team of DaimlerChrysler not to pursue Nissan as an acquisition. In the end, the decision to drop out of the race for Nissan was made because adding a third partner to the assimilation process would have simply been too much, especially given the stretch of incorporating a Japanese partner with an American and a German partner, all at once. Nissan's debt notwithstanding, the timing and corporate culture issues dominated the decision.

What, then, is the preferred path for an acquisition? Again, Michael Lubatkin and Peter Lane have some suggestions, based on years of research and several decades of observing successful and unsuccessful mergers and acquisitions. The key, of course, its to make mergers truly strategic, because that is what they are—broad in scope and difficult to reverse, with long-term consequences for the firm.

First, make sure that a merger or acquisition is done for the right reasons. A company should not necessarily abandon a traditional, mature business and try to escape a hostile environment through a purchase. In fact, the most successful strategy in a mature industry might be a consolidation. Second, diversify close to home and keep eggs in similar baskets. Third, since a firm cannot invest enough R&D in all the areas likely to affect its performance, alliances and collaborations for innovation need to be considered as an alternative to acquisitions. Fourth, work for a while with a potential merger candidate before considering acquisition, which is a typical pattern we have observed in the formation of joint venture investments, including in the auto industry. Fifth, the fun begins after the merger, just as it was fun to consider and arrange a merger. Recall the typical pattern of failure for a technology acquisition: don't treat a star like a cash cow and never forget the value of a cash cow. If there is any doubt at all about a merger or acquisition, don't go ahead.

Buying or merging with a firm primarily for technological reasons is different from other motivations for M&A. There is a great temptation for the acquiring (or dominant partner) firm to treat a technology acquisition like a cash cow instead of an investment center in need of nurturing and growth. This is the single best way to defeat the purpose of a technology-motivated acquisition.[44]

If one adds information technology into this equation, the M&A game gets even more complicated. For example, in banking (see Box 4-1), there is the great temptation to add technology to the list of reasons for merger or purchase, but there can be hidden consequences and surprises in this type of strategic move. Be advised by this research and these examples not to treat technology acquisitions like cash cows, and be extremely cautious when information technology is involved to add additional time and budget into the plan to allow for continued evolution of these new systems (see Chapter 9 and Box 9-4).

---

[44] M. A. Hitt, R. E. Hoskisson, R. D. Ireland, and J. Harrison, "Are Acquisitions a Poison Pill for Innovation?" *Academy of Management Executive,* 5, no. 4 (November 1991), p. 22; A. Chakrabarti, J. Hauschildt, and C. Suverkrup, "Does It Pay to Acquire Technological Firms?" *R & D Management,* 24, no. 1 (January 1994), pp. 47–56.

BOX 4-1

Technology Drives Bank Mergers[45]

On April 22, 1998, Bank of New York Company offered $28 billion for Mellon Bank Corporation. Three reasons are typically given for this type of merger: customers, cost reduction, and computer and information systems technology. The goal is to achieve high-speed, integrated services that blanket a wide range of customers from checking accounts to mutual funds and insurance policies. All media would be covered: phones, home computers, and ATMs (automatic teller machines).

Bank mergers have also been encouraged by deregulation of size and geographic location. Decline in profitability of lending, primarily due to competition from other financial institutions, has also been an issue for banks. Operations costs have encouraged computerization: It costs 10.5 cents to process a paper check and 5.7 cents to process a check electronically. ATM transactions average 40 cents a customer, whereas tellers cost 90 cents to $2 per transaction.

IBM's integrated financial network is an electronic pipeline with the ability to offer home banking using either PCs (personal computers), telephone or interactive TV. Microsoft recently announced that it will allow its banking technology called OFX to work with IBM's standard called Gold.

Standards also figure into ATM technology. Customers with access to an ATM anywhere in the world should be able to obtain cash on networks such as Cirrus. Canadian Imperial Bank of Commerce is testing an ATM developed by Compaq computer's Tandem unit and NCR, which will dispense stock certificates, money orders, insurance forms, and savings bonds.

High-tech ATMs can also customize service, which is the key to customer satisfaction.[46] For example, if you prefer withdrawals in $50 bills, the system will comply every time. Customers can be prioritized by their profitability, as well. First Union Corporation in Charlotte, North Carolina, is using new software that helps predict customer bankruptcies at the Money Store. Banks with this type of information technology would make natural takeover targets.

Acquisitions made primarily for product and market reasons, however, can have the opposite effect on upgrading with ERP (enterprise resource planning) efforts. For example, Owens Corning's ERP efforts to standardize systems and remove legacy software, which began in 1994, have taken twice as long with twice the budget because of aggressive acquisition plans during this same period.[47] In some recent cases, and especially for smaller purchases, new members of the Owens family are keeping their legacy systems.

---

[45] M. Murrary and R. Narioetti, "Bank Merger's Major Engine Is Technology," *Wall Street Journal* (April 23, 1998), pp. B1, B9.

[46] M. D. Johnson, *Customer Orientation and Market Action* (Upper-Saddle River, N.J.: Prentice-Hall, 1998).

[47] See Chapter 9, Box 9-4.

ORGANIZATIONAL STRATEGIES THAT INCLUDE INNOVATING

How do technology initiatives and investments fit within the strategic plan of an organization? At ABB, business strategy and plans influence technology strategy development and are, in part, influenced by current performance results (Figure 4-4).[48]

ABB's approach is typical. Business strategy (*how* we will compete) flows from corporate strategy (*which businesses* do we want to be in—not shown in Figure 4-4) and, in turn, influences both the technology strategy development and evaluation. Technology strategy, in turn, influences technology planning, and so on. In addition to feedback of results into this process, note that the arrows between strategies for the business and technology strategy development indicate influence in both directions. This is critical in this type of business—the co-evolution of strategies and consistency between strategies.

Caterpillar, Inc., one of the world's best-known makers of construction equipment, takes a different approach.[49] More than 50 percent of Caterpillar's business is overseas, which has a negative impact on sales when any region of the world is in economic stress.[50] Figure 4-5 summarizes Caterpillar's "house of quality" approach

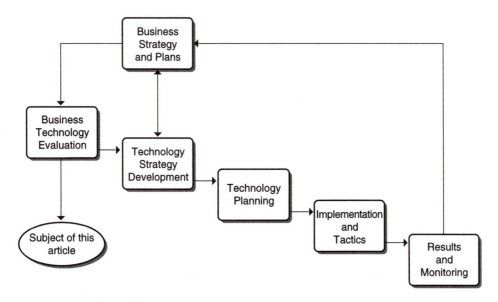

Figure 4-4 Business Technology Evaluation is Part of an Ongoing Technology Management Process Linking Business and Technology Strategy Development at ABB[48]

---

[48] H. M. Stillman, "How ABB Decides on the Right Technology Investments," *Research-Technology Management* (November-December 1997), pp. 14–34, Figure 1.

[49] Figure 1 from A. Zadoks, "Managing Technology at Caterpillar," *Research-Technology Management*, 40, no. 1 (Jan/Feb 1997), p. 49.

[50] See "In the Oasis: How Long Can the U.S. Stay Immune to What Ails World Economy?" *Wall Street Journal*, February 5, 1999.

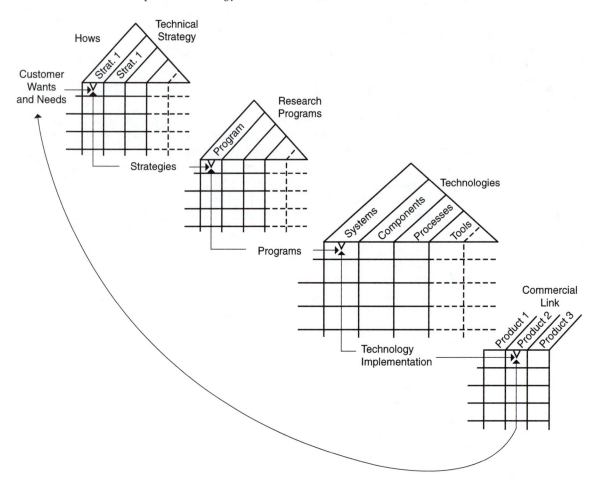

Figure 4-5   Managing Technology at Caterpillar

to managing technology.[51] Customer wants and needs feed into the first planning "house" and produces a series of technical strategies necessary to satisfy the market. These strategies, in turn, influence research programs, which, in turn, produce technologies, and then these feed into products.

What is missing from Caterpillar's summary is any mention of how customers are chosen, which apparently is part of corporate strategy. Caterpillar has engaged in some creative diversification, including the introduction of a "durable" line of boots and "rugged" footwear. Now the challenge to service these many new product introductions, as the trends in R&D investments indicated earlier (i.e., new product R&D as well as service R&D are on the rise in the United States).

[51] See, for example, J.R. Hauser and D. Clausing, "The House of Quality," *Harvard Business Review,* 1988, reprint No. 88307.

✺ Innovation Strategy Models

Numerous attempts have been made to characterize and codify innovation strategies. Several of these attempts are summarized in Table 4-3.

Most of these typologies make at least one primary distinction between innovation strategies, that is, whether the organization's intention is to be first or early in the innovating cycle.[52] This could apply to either the adoption or introduction of a new technology product or process. Secondary to this issue is whether an organization actually is able to make good on this intention.

Don Hambrick tested the Miles and Snow typology (see Table 4-3), which has prospectors in the position of first mover, and found support for the idea that this strategy works best in the volatile environment of an innovative industry. Hambrick also found that prospectors, or firms that introduce more new products, create "opportunities" for process innovation, and he reported a moderate, positive correlation between product R&D/sales and process R&D/sales.[53]

Freeman identified six categories of innovation strategy. Three are listed in Table 4-3 and are self-explanatory, being quite similar to the Miles and Snow categories. His other categories were *dependent, traditional,* and *opportunistic.* A dependent strategy is one in which a firm accepts a subordinate role to a stronger competitor, imitating product changes only as requested by customers. A traditional competitor continues on, more or less, with existing products and services and changes only (with cost-cutting) prices. Opportunistic competitors seek out market niches overlooked by others, usually first movers.

The Ettlie and Bridges study, also listed in Table 4-3, investigated the degree to which innovation strategies actually made a difference in adoption behavior among food companies considering the conversion from rigid to flexible packaging. They

𝒯ABLE 4-3   Innovation Strategies

Source	Categories
Miles and Snow (1978)	Defenders, prospectors, and analyzers
Freeman (1982)	Offensive, defensive, imitative, etc.
Ettlie and Bridges (1987)	Aggressive technology policy
Kerin, et al. (1992)	First movers

SOURCE: R.E. Miles and C.C. Snow, *Organizational Strategy, Structure and Process* (New York: McGraw-Hill, 1978); C. Freeman, *The Economics of Industrial Innovation* (2nd ed.) (Cambridge, Mass.: MIT Press, 1982); J.E. Ettlie and W.P. Bridges, "Technology Policy and Innovation in Organizations," J. Pennings and A. Buitendam (eds.), *Technology as Organizational Innovation* (Cambridge, Mass.: Ballanger Publishing, 1987), pp. 117–137; R.A. Kerin, P.R. Varadarajan, and R.A. Peterson, "First-Mover Advantage: A Synthesis, Conceptual Framework and Research Propositions," *Journal of Marketing* 56, no. 4 (1992), pp. 33–52.

---

[52] R.A. Kerin, P.R. Varadarajan, and R.A. Peterson, "First-Mover Advantage: A Synthesis, Conceptual Framework and Research Propositions," *Journal of Marketing,* 56, no. 4 (1992), pp. 33–52.

[53] D. C. Hambrick, "Some Tests of Effectiveness and Functional Attributes of Miles and Snow's Strategic Types," *Academy of Management Journal,* 26, no. 1 (1983), pp. 5–26.

used a measure of aggressive technology policy, which included careful consideration of the following distinguishing features:

1. Long-term investment in technological solutions to problems.
2. Planning human resources to implement strategic technological plan.
3. Openness to the environment using tracking and forecasting.
4. Structural adaptations (e.g., "tiger teams") for functional integration.

Results of the Ettlie–Bridges analysis are included in Table 4-4. They used a unique
scaling technique that detects partial ordering in a cumulative metric for the adoption
of one of the new flexible packaging technologies under study, the retortable pouch.

The retort is a cooker used to sterilize food normally put in a can. Here the food
is put in a flexible, multilaminated pouch instead. The pouch did not have to be
cooked as long, because distance to the center is less than in a can, so gourmet
food could be marketed with this packaging, and a "flat box" format enhanced
advertising possibilities, as well.

Ettlie and Bridges detected two types of firms (risk takers and nonrisk takers) in
their sample of 147 food-processing firms. The first type branched to the left at the
second decision point (Table 4-4). They (risk takers) knew whether a new product
was needed, but pursued active plans first. Others (nonrisk takers) determined

*T*ABLE 4-4   Decision Making for Radical Packaging Technology in the
Food Industry

Scale Score	Response Pattern
0	Fail all items (0000)
1	Know whether new product is needed (0001)
2	Know whether new product is needed + Active Plans (0011) Know whether new product is needed + Feasible to go ahead (0101)
3	Know whether new product is needed + Active plans + Feasible to go ahead (0111)
4	Know whether new product is needed + Active plans + Feasible to go ahead + Using retortable packaging technology (1111) (pass all items)

SOURCE: Figure 6-1. Scale of Innovation Adoption Response Patterns. J.E. Ettlie, and W.P. Bridges,
"Technology Policy and Innovation in Organizations," J. Pennings and A. Buitendam (eds.), *Technology
as Organizational Innovation* (Cambridge, Mass.: Ballanger Publishing, 1987), pp. 117–137.

feasibility first. The first type of firm was also significantly more likely to have an aggressive technology policy.

There are also high-tech examples of technology strategy. Christensen and Rosenbloom started with the punctuated equilibrium model introduced in the previous chapter and studied the disk-drive industry to investigate the attacker's advantage or first mover perspective on technology substitution.[54] However, instead of predicting whether incumbents or new entrants prosper with new technology based on the competence enhancing versus competence destroying hypotheses, they show that it is the value network the firm is participating in that determines outcomes in disk drives. They contrast their results to the Henderson and Clark study of photo-lithographic aligners, where new entrants always had the advantage and the pattern in components, but incumbents like IBM always seem to win (e.g., thin film heads).[55] Christensen and Rosenbloom found that new entrants led the disk-drive industry in technological discontinuity during three of the last five architectural changes, whereas established firms led only two.

The first transition in this industry was the switch between 1973 and 1980 from disk packs to Winchester drives (Figure 4-6). Incumbents led the industry by introducing 14-inch Winchester drives: IBM was first to introduce the 14-inch Winchester drive, followed by Control Data, and by Microdata in 1975. But all were serving the same established market with the same supply base: the mainframe computer builders. "As long as the technology addressed the customers' needs within the incumbents' networks," they led the way with changes. "Entrants led … when customers needs were in emerging networks …"[56] Later, in disk drives, new entrants led for the introduction of the smaller-sized Winchester drives, aimed at different customers, and represented by the open-circle dotted line plots in Figure 4-6. When 8-inch, 5.25-inch, 3.5-inch, and 2.5-inch drives were introduced, new entrants had the lead. New architectures shrank the drives and were purchased by a different market.

In 1989, Prairietek Corporation spun off from Miniscribe and introduced its first new product, the 2.5-inch Winchester drive, almost exclusively for notebook computer makers. New entrants ruled previous introductions of 3.5-inch drives for laptops, 5.25-inch drives for desktop computers, and 8-inch drives for minicomputers (later for mainframes). Incumbents were not involved in these valued-added networks and were preoccupied with the active previous generation of product and market customers. As long as their (incumbent) customers were happy, they had no reason to develop new-products architectures for new customers, which was attacked by new entrants. Further, the more removed the supply base from the ultimate system-of-use customer, the greater the mobility across networks. For example, firms supplying aluminum platters on which magnetic material is deposited were able to sell platters regardless of disk size—14- to 2.5-inch. Firms coating platters were more dedicated to drive makers and did not migrate as well across these transitions.

Figure 4-6, plots this pattern of discontinuity, where the solid dots are disk pack architecture and open circles the Winchester architecture. After 1973, when IBM

---

[54] C. M. Christensen and R. S. Rosenbloom, "Explaining the Attacker's Advantage: Technological Paradigms, Organizational Dynamics, and the Value Network," *Research Policy,* 24 (1995), pp. 233–257.

[55] R. M. Henderson and K. B. Clark "Architectural Innovation: The Reconfiguration of Existing Systems and the Failure of Established Firms," *Administrative Science Quarterly,* 35 (1990), pp. 9–30.

[56] C. M. Christensen and R. S. Rosenbloom, "Explaining the Attacker's Advantage: Technological Paradigms, Organizational Dynamics and the Value Network," *Research Policy,* 24 (1995), p. 253.

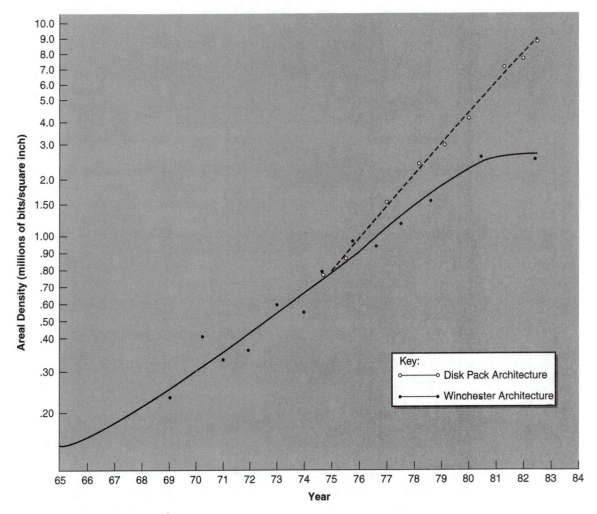

Figure 4-6   Discontinuous Innovation in Disk Drives

SOURCE: C. M. Christensen and R. S. Rosenbloom, "Explaining the Attacker's Advantage: Technological Paradigms, Organizational Dynamics, and the Value Network," *Research Policy,* 24 (1995), p. 251. Figure 5.

introduced the 14-inch Winchester drive, this technology was dominated by new entrants for other markets and value chains. This curve, represented by the open circles connected by a dotted line, diverges upward from the old technology performance curve. The implication for managing incumbents and discontinuous change is that without a substantial shift in the firm's orientation toward a new value chain, it is highly unlikely that the existing firm will be deflected, technology-wise, from its current course and current architecture.

Christensen recently published *Innovation and the General Manager,* a highly recommended book in which he significantly expands on this research (Figure 4-6) and includes many cases on new technology development and introduction.[57]

---

[57] C. M. Christensen, *Innovation and the General Manager* (New York: Irwin McGraw-Hill, 1999).

Technology Fusion

In their now-famous article on core competence, C. K. Prahalad and Gary Hammel[58] suggested that one of the essentials to strategic planning was knowing the trajectory of the core technologies so that the merging of these elements could be part of the firms, long-range agenda.

An example of this strategy is information (computer) and communication technologies, such as the Internet. Many times the merging of various technology elements results from the "evolution of a pattern of innovation based on technology fusion and the transition toward a knowledge-based economy," which supports trends toward a "transorganizational" hybrid product.[59] Other examples include the wireless ATM (automatic teller machine),[60] and AT&T's recent bid for Media One, which would allow the telecommunications company to enter the home on the Internet, the phone, and the TV all at once.[61] Telecommunications, in particular, is one of the best examples of technology fusion that has continued for nearly a decade.[62] All require new skill sets for the integrating firm to establish a new "core" competence.[63]

The author given credit for first documenting the concept of technology fusion was Fumio Kodama.[64] Mr. Kodama observed, quite rightly, that a company can either invest in R&D in breakthrough technology or focus on combining existing technologies into hybrid technologies, called **technology fusion.** Three principles are essential to technology fusion:

1. The market drives the R&D agenda.

2. Companies need intelligence-gathering *(monitoring)* capabilities.

3. Technology grows out of long-term associations with a wide variety of companies in many industries (and, one could add, universities and government laboratories).

One study found that accomplishing a strategy of technology fusion is not as easy as it sounds.[65] Although technological and economic maturity in the chemical

[58] C. K. Prahalad and G. Hammel, "The Core Competence of the Corporation," *Harvard Business Review* (May–June 1990), pp. 79–91.

[59] J. Millar, A. Demaid, and P. Quintas, "Trans-organizational Innovation: A Framework for Research," *Technology Analysis & Strategic Management,* 9, no. 4 (December 1997), pp. 399–418.

[60] T. Parker, "Wireless ATM Flexes Its Muscle," *Telephony,* 233, no. 20 (November 17, 1997), pp. 24–32.

[61] R. Siklos, A. Barrett, C. Yang, and R. Crockett, "The Net-Phone-TV-Cable Monster," *Business Week* (May 10, 1999), pp. 30–32.

[62] M. Kenward, "Telecom's Fusion Power," *International Management* 48, no. 5 (Europe Edition) (June 1993), pp. 38–43; L. Cauley, "Comcast Reaches Accord with AT&T on MediaOne," *Wall Street Journal* (May 5, 1999), pp. A3, A8.

[63] D. T. Lei, "Competence-building, Technology Fusion, and Competitive Advantage: The Key Roles of Organizational Learning and Strategic Alliances," *International Journal of Technology Management,* 14, nos. 2,3,4 (1997), pp. 208–237.

[64] F. Kodama, "Technology Fusion and the New R&D," *Harvard Business Review,* 70, no. 4 (July/August 1992), pp. 70–78.

[65] P. Hutcheson, A. W. Pearson, and D. F. Ball, "Sources of Technical Innovation in the Network of Companies Providing Chemical Process Plant and Equipment," *Research Policy,* 25, no. 1 (January 1996), pp. 25–41.

industry inhibits the research and development activities of plant contractors, little evidence was found of contractors adopting novel strategies to capture special advantage from technology developed by equipment manufacturing firms.

> Alliances between contractors and equipment manufacturers cannot only help to reduce plant design, procurement and erection costs, but also offer a means to counter the competitive threat from more specialist firms; in particular, the large equipment manufacturers that possess their own project contracting skills. Collaboration in niche and technology fusion type innovation offers a means of generating scope for technological competitive advantage while sharing cost and risk.[66]

✕ Competitive Response to Technological Threats

What is the likely response when a competitor introduces a new technology product or service? The literature on first-movers warns that *free rider* or *early Christian* risks are part of the potential penalty of departing from standard practice. Free riders are able to either benefit from the first-movers' changes without the costs (e.g., R&D) or take advantage of new markets that have opened and cannot be satisfied by just one innovator. Early Christians got the biggest, strongest lions in Roman times.[67] If one could predict competitive response, first-mover strategies might be more of a calculated risk and less dependent on luck, even if luck is always a factor in new ventures. The answer is not obvious.

When Gillette decided to reinvent the shaving industry with the introduction of the Sensor razor in 1990 (see Chapter 2), followed 8 years later by the Mach3,[68] what did rival companies do? Strong competitors like Wilkinson introduced new technology products to compete, but with limited success. Small competitors had their own reaction to this discontinuity. American Safety Razor (ASR) Company (with 6% of the U.S. market), for example, introduced a new cardboard box for blades with a modern looking navy blue container, and responded to new technology the only way possible with limited resources: *price.* ASR sells products at 40 percent below larger rivals such as Gillette (67% of the market) and Warner-Lambert's Schick unit (16% of the market).[69]

ASR is historically famous for its Burma-Shave advertising. It appeared on small roadside signs, presented in serial fashion, with rhymes like this one: "The Answer to a Maiden's Prayer/Is Not a Chin/Of Stubby Hair/Burma-Shave,"[70] The brand was

---

[66] Ibid., p. 25.

[67] Thanks to Bob Lund for this metaphor.

[68] K. H. Hammonds, "How a $4 Razor Ends Up Costing $300 Million," *Business Week* (January 29, 1990), pp. 62–63; W. C. Symonds, "Would You Spend $1.50 for a Razor Blade?" *Business Week* (April 27, 1998), p. 46; M. Maremont, "Gillette Finally Reveals Its Vision of the Future and It Has 3 Blades," *Wall Street Journal* (April 4, 1998), pp. A1, A10.

[69] J.R. Hagerty, "Concede Defeat to Gillette: Not Just Yet/Burma-Shave," *Wall Street Journal* (June 12, 1998), pp. B1, B8.

[70] A. C. Cooper and D. Schendel, "Strategic Responses to Technological Threats," *Business Horizons* (February 1976), pp. 61–69.

revived in 1996. Now the company is making blades to fit Gillette and Schick handles with slogans that ask consumers to compare prices. Sales are up 11 percent compared with an 8 percent increase at Gillette. Now ASR hopes customers will balk at the even higher price of Gillette's Mach3 razor, which is likely to retail for $6.50 to $7, nearly double ASR's high-end offerings.

One of the first studies to focus on strategic response to technological threat was published by Cooper and Schendel.[71] They studied 22 companies in seven industries, including the substitution of diesel-electric locomotives for steam, ball-point pens displacement of fountain pens, and jet engine for aircraft propellers. They found that:

1. Of the 22 firms, all but five made an effort to participate in the new technology.

2. Six of nine incumbents with R&D responded by participating in the new technology.

3. In every industry studied, the highest stage of development of existing technology occurred after the introduction of the new technology (e.g., vacuum tubes versus transistors).

4. Most incumbents divided technical efforts between the new and old technology.

5. Acquisition was not widely used as a competitive response—not because of constrained resources that prevented response, but because of the absence of a strategy.

Especially with respect to the last conclusion, Cooper and Schendel said that it was common for incumbent-firm spokespersons to emphasize the shortcomings of the new technology. This finding is only partially explained by the fact that in four of seven cases, the new technology was introduced by a firm outside the traditional industry. This same pattern occurred in three of four industries where capital requirements were not great. Consequently, the new technology did not always follow the traditional S-curve, which is typical of the substitution effect in generations of innovations. Sometimes the pattern is erratic and is affected by prevailing social and economic conditions (e.g., World War II in the case of the electric razor, propellers, and steam locomotives).

This pattern of competitive response appears to apply to many other situations. There is agreement in the literature with regard to competitive response. Companies generally compete with strengths and inertia is a powerful force, so when a firm is confronted with a new competitive threat, it is likely to continue doing what was done before, or more of it, before turning to other options. An example of this phenomenon is Epson's response to Hewlett-Packard's introduction of the ink jet printer (see Case 3-2). Epson, "the king of dot-matrix printers, ignored warnings of changing consumer tastes."[72] HP pioneered an alternative dominant design.

---

[71] Ibid., p. B1.

[72] R. McGrath, I. MacMillan, and M. L. Tushman, "The Role of Executive Team Actions in Shaping Dominant Designs: Towards the Strategic Shaping of Technological Progress," *Strategic Management Journal,* 13 (Winter 1992), pp. 137–161.

It seems the more radical the competitive first move, the more likely the response will be delayed, especially if the countermove is with a new product or new service, which is frequently the case. For example, it has taken decades for the major air carriers to respond to Southwest Airlines' unique brand of no-frills service, and along the way, there have been many new-entrant failures at imitation.[73] This strategic response pattern has not prevented new startups in the industry,[74] but there continue to be persistent questions about what innovative behaviors should be expected in a regulated industry. William Robinson found that new-entrant challengers typically use new technology to break entry barriers and delay incumbent response to competition. Robinson found that incumbents typically ignore new entrants, especially as a first response strategy.[75] When the challenge is a new product, the odds are about 50–50 that incumbents will respond eventually with their own new product. But price and advertising reactions are the most predictable.

When incumbents announce a new product and competitors see this as a hostile and committed (e.g., patents) move onto their turf, 75 percent will respond in at least one of the following ways:[76]

▶ 42 percent will introduce a new product

▶ 33 percent will use a market response (reduce price, advertise)

▶ 22 percent will issue a new product announcement

The greater the patent protection in an industry (typically higher tech) or the more concentrated, the more likely incumbents will react to new product announcements with a marketing mixed response rather than with a new product. That is, patents do seem to erect barriers to product initiatives. Other studies of multiple industries show that 60 percent of firms react to a new product with their own new product, regardless of the source of the threat—incumbent or new entrant.[77]

Strategic response or strategic first moves need not be confined to new products. New process technology options typically lurk in the wings of any industry. Many discontinuous changes have resulted from changes in operations technologies; float glass, continuous casting of steel, numerically controlled machine tools, and automated teller machines in banking are just a few. The introduction of fluid catalytic cracking processes in the 1940s resulted in a 98 percent savings in labor costs, 80 percent savings in capital costs, and 50 percent savings in material inputs per unit output.[78] It is also widely acknowledged in the diffusion literature that diffusion and successful application of process technology depend on

---

[73] W. Zellner, "Will This Short-Hauler Fly?" *Business Week* (June 8, 1998), p. 39.

[74] D. Leonhardt, "Small Airline, Tricky Flight Plan," *Business Week* (June 22, 1998), pp. 96–97.

[75] W. T. Robinson, "Sources of Market Pioneer Advantages: The Case of Industrial Goods Industries," *Journal of Marketing Research,* 25 (1998), pp. 31–52.

[76] T. S. Robertson, J. Eliashberg, and T. Rymon, (1995). "New Product Announcement Signals and Incumbent Reactions," *Journal of Marketing,* 59, no. 3 (July 1995), p. 1.

[77] D. Bowman and I. Gatignon, "Determinants of Competitor Response Time to a new product," *Journal of Marketing Research,* 32, no. 1 (February 1995), pp. 42–54.

[78] C. Freeman, *The Economics of Industrial Innovation* (2nd ed.) (Cambridge, Mass.: MIT Press, 1992), p. 27.

"big changes in structure and administrative practices."[79] Industrial applications of the steam engine, for example, required significant reorganization of factory production.

Cost pressures are often the stimulus for these process technology initiatives, and politics and unionism often enter into the equation. Huffy Corporation, the largest bicycle manufacturer in the United States, recently announced that it is closing its only remaining domestic operations in Celina, Ohio, because of Asian competition, which has driven bike prices down 25 percent in four years. Schwinn, another U.S. rival, now imports all of its products from foreign plants, and 60 percent of the bicycles sold in the United States last year were produced by foreign makers.[80] These cost-cutting pressures are not limited to small companies. Rockwell International Corporation, confronted with slow growth in the industrial automation business (especially in Asia) and changing technology in semiconductors (i.e., computer modems), recently announced that it will reduce its workforce of 48,000 by 10 percent. Rockwell had also sold its aerospace and automotive parts businesses.[81]

But there is an alternative to this cost-cutting, price warfare strategy. One of the many uncelebrated cases of the successful use of process technology as a strategic weapon is the history of National Machinery, summarized in Case 4-1. National teamed up with a few lead customers (see the case of Shamrock fasteners in Box 12-1) to reinvent the "nuts and bolts" industry. As you might expect, bolts have been made in much the same way for a long time. But National, having little choice but to reinvent itself during the 1980s, chose to consolidate and then redesign its bolt-forming equipment in a way that has become difficult to imitate. This new product introduction was followed quickly by the modernization of the plant in Tiffin, Ohio. A commodity industry was transformed by this strategy.

$\mathcal{L}$EADERSHIP AND INNOVATION

What drove Paul Aley, the president of National Machinery (Case 4-1) to create discontinuous change in a mature industry like nuts and bolts? What does it take to be an innovator? What is an innovative leader?

Earlier, the study of company leader background was introduced: greater investments in R&D are positively associated with the presence of top managers with technical background.[82] Box 4-2 discusses this topic in greater detail and reviews more data on process technology adoption, which also tends to follow the same pattern, with some interesting surprises.

---

[79] L. Nasbeth and G.F. Ray, *The Diffusion of New Industrial Processes* (London: Cambridge University Press, 1974), p. 310.

[80] C. Quintanilla, "Huffy to Close Its Largest U.S. Factory, Idle 950, to Combat Asian Competition," *Wall Street Journal* (May 29, 1998), p. A4.

[81] F. Rose, "Rockwell Plans Staff Cuts of Up to 10%," *Wall Street Journal* (June 26, 1998), p. A3.

[82] See note 15.

BOX 4-2

General Managers and Manufacturing Innovation

It has been nearly two decades since the classic article, "Managing Our Way to Economic Decline," by Robert Hayes and William Abernathy appeared in the *Harvard Business Review* (July-August, 1980). This trend gradually began to change in the 1980s. The *Wall Street Journal* (October 18, 1988), reported that CEOs from finance declined from 21.8 percent to 17.3 percent between 1984 and 1987, whereas CEOs from production and operations increased from 33.1 percent to 38.9 percent during the same period. What has been the impact of this changing profile of top management in manufacturing?

A study of more than three dozen companies that were in the process of modernizing their production processes and products showed that Hayes and Abernathy were only partially correct in their hypothesis that CEOs with nontechnical backgrounds caused decline in manufacturing firms. It is true that CEOs who have manufacturing experience do make an important difference in these North American manufacturing companies. In these companies, there was a significantly higher likelihood that the company would take calculated risks and adopt new processing technologies such as flexible manufacturing and flexible assembly. These companies were characterized by four important differences:

▶ A reputation of being first to try new methods and equipment

▶ An active campaign to recruit the best-qualified technical talent

▶ Commitment to technological forecasting

▶ Keen awareness of new technological capabilities

A company's commitment to training during modernization was much greater when senior vice-presidents and divisional managers had manufacturing experience. This commitment to training and development was reflected not only in plans and practices for training but in budgets as well. Training budgets for modernization that do not reach 10 percent of the total project cost might cast serious doubt on the company's commitment.

Surprisingly, manufacturing-experienced senior managers were significantly more likely to emphasize direct labor savings from modernization and automation of assembly operations. Divisional managers were the opposite and significantly more likely than other general managers in the study to support the adoption of administrative experiments (e.g., the use of technology agreements in union contracts, flatter organizational structures in plants, and adoption of charters for the future of the firm).

When divisional managers had manufacturing experience, the new system that was installed achieved significantly higher utilization than when the divisional manager did not have manufacturing experience. In divisions where the general manager had manufacturing experience, average utilization was 80 percent, as opposed to 61 percent in divisions headed by a manager with no manufacturing experence.

Source: J. E. Ettlie, "Why Some Manufacturing Firms Are More Innovative," *Academy of Management Executive,* 4, no. 4 (November 1990), pp. 7–20.

Although top managers with manufacturing experience were more likely to mount aggressive technology policies and adopt new flexible manufacturing systems, they were also more likely to emphasize direct labor savings as the rationale for change. The issue of economic justification for innovation is taken up in Chapter 6, but it is interesting to note this "generation" effect of top managers of the 1980s—they were more likely to emphasize the traditional evaluation methods for changing process technologies.

There is a fair amount of accumulated evidence to confirm the idea that management attitudes toward innovation and change are significantly correlated with policies and outcomes.[83] Pro-change managers are likely to launch innovative strategies and follow through on their implementation. Bank-rolling R&D is part of the necessary action required to make this happen, even in mature industries.[84] The way innovative strategy and structure interact has never been completely resolved, but concentrating technical talent clearly seems to be essential to implementing plans for new technology products. This is especially true in mature industries and for new products and incremental process innovations. Further, as firms diversify into less mature industries, managerial attitudes toward change become more important in predicting new product introduction and the adoption of radical processing technology.[85]

There is also evidence that the movement of senior managers across organizational boundaries is a trigger for change and is significantly correlated with the adoption of radical process technology.[86] Although these transitions are usually at the vice president level or higher in a company and usually come as a result of hiring an outsider, there are exceptions to the common wisdom that only outsiders can incite radical change in a firm. Take, for example, the story of Leonard A. Hadley, who recently became the chief executive officer of Maytag in Newton, Iowa. Mr. Hadley was known as a "loyal and unimaginative lieutenant of a less-than-dazzling chief executive," before he was voted in by the board of directors. But then something happened. He took bold moves, including making European operations profitable and selling them. And "at a company that had slighted inno-

[83] J. Hage and R. Dewar, "Elite Values versus Organizational Structure in Predicting Innovation," *Administrative Science Quarterly,* 18 (1973), pp. 279–290; D. Miller, M. F. R. Kets de Vries, and J. Toulouse, "Top Executive Locus of Control and its Relationship to Strategy-making Structure and Environment," *Academy of Management Journal,* 25, no. 2 (1982), pp. 237–253; S.G. Scott and R.A. Bruce, "Determinants of Innovative Behavior: A Path Model of Individual Innovation in the Workplace," *Academy of Management Journal,* 37, no. 3 (June 1994), pp. 580–607. These authors found that leadership, managerial role expectations, career state, and problem-solving style are significantly related to individual innovative behavior, which, in turn, has a positive impact on the supervisor-subordinate relationship.

[84] N. Myhrvold, "What's the Return on Research?" *Fortune,* 136, no. 11 (December 8, 1997), p. 88.

[85] J. E. Ettlie, "A Note on the Relationship Between Managerial Change Values, Innovative Intentions, and Innovative Technology Outcomes in Food Sector Firms," *R&D Management,* 13, no. 4 (1983), pp. 231–244. At the very minimum, support for innovation moderates the relationship between leadership style and unit performance. J. M. Howell and B. J. Avolio, "Transformational Leadership, Transactional Leadership, Locus of Control, and Support for Innovation: Key Predictors of Consolidated-Business-Unit Performance," *Journal of Applied Psychology,* 78, no. 6 (December 1993), pp. 891–902.

[86] J. E. Ettlie, "Manpower Flows and the Innovation Process," *Management Science,* 26, no. 11 (November, 1980), pp. 1086–1095; J.E. Ettlie, "The Impact of Interorganizational Manpower Flows on the Innovation Process," *Management Science,* 31, no. 9 (September 1985), pp. 1055–1071.

vation, he invested in new technology, pinning his hopes on the Maytag Neptune, an expensive front-loading washer." The gamble paid off: Maytag is now growing-faster than its arch rivals Whirlpool Corporation and GE's appliance group.[87] Whirlpool, in the meantime is designing a standard washer that will adapt to all cultural tastes. Hadley says that the appliance industry can't standardize globally and make money. "Gillette's new razor? Now there's a global product. But people think that every product fits into that category." After hearing this, it should come as no surprise that his approach to technology is called "contrarian."[88]

Maytag's policy for decades was *not* to be first to market. In 1993, Hadley set that rule aside and created the "Galaxy Initiative," which is a lineup of nine new, top-secret products, each with a code name after a different planet. The high-priced Neptune loads from the front, which is atypical of most American brands. It is gentler on clothes and uses less water, but is pricey at $1,100. Front-end loaders had been replaced in the 1950s by the industry because they had leaky doors and vibration problems. Without an agitator, consumers think them inferior, and initial market research was negative. Hadley went ahead, anyway. The Neptune has brought in explosive revenue, and the company has had to increase production three times. Sears which sold a third of all appliances in the United States in 1998, agreed to carry the Neptune.

Hadley intends to replace himself with an outsider, saying he made every effort to replace himself inside, but it didn't work. His successor? Lloyd Ward, age 49, Maytag's first black executive, newly arrived from Pepsi's Frito-Lay unit and a marketing expert. This is also contrary to the typical pattern of promotion from within for implementation of radical change.[89] The revolution and initiation of change must still be on at Maytag.

The pattern established at Maytag, although on the surface quite surprising, is typical of other leadership stories in the innovation literature. The reason Hadley surprised so many people, including his board, is that most of us go through life assuming technology will remain constant, are surprised at how long it takes us to change, and then wonder why we didn't do that sooner. Recently, a study of the adoption of Automatic Equipment Identification (AEI) software technology by the railroad industry confirmed this same pattern.[90] Again, we are focusing on a mature industry with a checkered history of new technology introduction, at best. AEI uses a radio frequency identification system scanning an electronic tag, on the move. It can be attached to railcar, locomotive, trailer, or container, which can then be used to update shipment and movement data files for carriers and shippers using fleet management systems. In the study, 92 respondents were interviewed in four Class I railroads. Understanding the benefits of using the technology are far more impor-

[87] C. Quintanilla, "So Who's Dull? Maytag's Top Officer Expected to Do Little, Surprises His Board," *Wall Street Journal* (June 23, 1998), pp. A1, A8.

[88] Ibid., p. A8.

[89] J. E. Ettlie, "Intrafirm Mobility and Manufacturing Modernization," *Journal of Engineering and Technology Management,* 6 (1990), pp. 281–302. Data in this article show that during the initiation phase of radical process innovation, interfirm movement of senior managers is typical, whereas during the implementation phase, engineers are promoted (intrafirm mobility).

[90] L. Williams and K. Roa, "Information Technology Adoption: Using Classical Adoption Models to Predict AEI Software Implementation," *Journal of Business Logistics,* 19, no. 1 (1998), pp. 5–16.

tant in predicting adoption than understanding the specifics about what technology is available and how it works. Calculated risk takers proceed with less information than those who are not risk takers.[91]

Many other firms and industries that once were noted for change came back with new change strategies as the result of leadership. Bank of America is another case in point. Known for pioneering introduction of the IMB 702 computer systems in the 1950s, Bank of America's leap of a decade ahead of the industry was lost and then regained by aggressive information technology management.[92] The pattern shows up in high-technology firms,[93] construction,[94] and the food industry, as indicated earlier. Only leadership can explain these kinds of changes. Leaders initiate with vision and follow up with policies, structures, and practices that will sustain change. For example, high-performance companies with innovative strategies often have innovative pay policies, and companies that emphasize cost leadership reward differently.[95]

Studies of the diffusion of technologies show how general managers translate policies into actions. For example, the diffusion of EDI (electronic data interchange) technology in the retail sector of Europe is significantly faster where competition is intense and where potential adopting firms have better knowledge of the effect of using EDI on the market. The context of diffusion is also important, of course. In countries where digital technology is generally available such as France, the United Kingdom, Holland, and Ireland, EDI adoption is more rapid than in Belgium, Luxembourg, and Germany, where the percentage of digital technology is relatively lower. Standardization of an exchange language for EDI (e.g., EANCOM in the retail sector) in a given country also tends to promote diffusion, as would be expected.[96]

Strategic alliances for innovation require general management leadership[97] in most cases because they commit the organization on a long-term basis and expose the core technology, at least in some instances, to outside influence and tampering, as well as potential leaks. Mergers apply, as well. After Percy Barnevik took over as CEO when Sweden's Asea joined with Switzerland's Brown Boveri, not only did new, difficult markets open up, but global presence was leveraged for local projects such as those in India and China. ABB's technology strategy was introduced

---

[91] See Table 4-3 and Figure 3-1.

[92] J.L. McKenney, R.O. Mason, and D.G. Copeland, "Bank of America: The Crest and Trough of Technological Leadership," *MIS Quarterly,* 21, no. 3 (September 1997), pp. 321–353.

[93] M. A. Madique and R. H. Hayes, "The Art of High-Technology Management," *Sloan Management Review,* 25 (Winter 1984), pp. 18–21. In this article, the authors argue that there are six "themes of success" for high technology management: (1) business focus, (2) adaptability, (3) organizational cohesion, (4) entrepreneurial culture, (5) sense of integrity, and (6) hands-on management.

[94] C. H. Nam and C. B. Tatum, "Leaders and Champions for Construction Innovation," *Construction Management and Economics,* 15, no. 3 (May 1997), pp. 259–270.

[95] E.F. Montemayor, "Congruence Between Pay Policy and Competitive Strategy in High-Performance Firms," *Journal of Management,* 22, no. 6 (1996), pp. 889–908.

[96] J. Jimenez-Martinex and Y. Polo-Rendondo," International Diffusion of a New Tool: The Case of Electronic Data Interchange (EDI) in the Retailing Sector," *Research Policy,* 26 (1998), pp. 811–827.

[97] R. F. Celeste, "Strategic Alliances of Innovation: Emerging Models of Technology-based Twenty-first Century Economic Development," *Economic Development Review,* 14, no. 1 (Winter 1996), pp. 4–8.

earlier (see Figure 4-4).[98] The recent merger of Chrysler Corporation and Daimler-Benz has clear technology mutual benefits for the two companies in their complementary product lines and platforms.[99] The challenge will be to overcome the obvious cultural differences in innovation style.[100]

Divestiture is also part of the strategic mosaic in technology leadership. For example, the Minnesota Mining and Manufacturing Company (3M), known for its product innovation, recently spun off its data storage and imaging businesses to operate at the pace of the digital storage industry.[98] By divesting a unit competing in a fast-paced industry, it is attempting to allow that company to compete with the autonomy it needs to be agile.

Leadership has been and will continue to be the single most important factor in strategy and innovation management. One illustrative study makes this clear. Hout and Carter reported on 550 American, European, and Japanese companies in a wide range of industries. None of the best-known programs, such as total quality management, reengineering, self-managed teams, or cross-functional task groups, are enough to distinguish the best performers from the worst. Only the senior executive group and their collective responsibility to rise above the details, making unexpected connections, can make the difference.[102] Progressive companies tend to have senior managers with pro-change values, who mount simple, aggressive strategies.[103]

$\mathscr{B}$USINESS ETHICS AND TECHNOLOGY

In every industry, managers struggle with the quest for profit and the responsibility to behave ethically. In many industries, technological innovations have also created new ethical dilemmas.[104] Cargill Inc.'s agreement to sell its North American seed business to Hoechst Schering AgrEvo GmbH for $650 million was recently cancelled, demonstrating the impact that litigation is having on the biotechnology industry. This case, in particular, raised problems concerning the ownership and use of plant genetic materials. "The proposed sale of Cargill Hybrid Seeds North

---

[98] J. Anderson, "Innovative Leadership," *Independent Energy,* 26, no. 1 (Jan/Feb 1996), pp. 42–44.

[99] A. Taylor III, "Gentlemen, Start Your Engines," *Fortune* 137, no. 11 (June 8, 1998), pp. 138–146.

[100] S. Shane, S. Venkataraman, and I. MacMillan, "Cultural Differences in Innovation Championing Strategies," *Journal of Management,* 21, no. 5 (1995), pp. 931–952.

[101] M. Ferelli, "3M Data Storage Spin-Off: Something Old, Something New," *Computer Technology Review* 15, no. 12 (December 1995), p. 38. For more information on 3M and innovation see R. A. Mitsch, "R&D at 3M; Continuing to Play a Big Role," *Research-Technology Management,* 35 (September/October 1992), pp. 22–26.

[102] T. M. Hout and J. C. Carter, "Getting It Done: New Roles for Senior Executives," *Harvard Business Review,* 73, no. 6 (November/December 1995), pp. 133–141.

[103] See for example: D. Miller and J.-M. Toulouse, "Quasi-rational Organizational Responses: Functional and Cognitive Sources of Strategic Simplicity," *Canadian Journal of Administrative Sciences,* 15, no. 3 (September 1998), pp. 230–244.

[104] L. T. Hosmer, *The Ethics of Management* (3rd ed.) (New York: McGraw-Hill, 1996).

America had been postponed for several months, pending the resolution of an intellectual property prediction lawsuit that Pioneer Hi-bred International filed against Cargill in October 1998, alleging inappropriate use of Pioneer's corn germplasm."[105] Could this situation have been avoided? What is the role of leadership in technology and business ethics?

An issue much closer to home in most organizations is the problem of employee privacy and ever-expanding computer monitoring technology.[106] The answer to questions regarding what is really meant by "privacy" in today's workplace may be surprising, given the current status of state and federal employee privacy protections, which seek to balance the employer's right to protecting organizational property[107] or evaluate performance with the employee's rights to privacy. Ironically, as employees are given more autonomy in computer environments that are becoming more user friendly, more unethical behavior is possible and, therefore, more occurs.[108]

The complexity of these issues is further illustrated by the recent case of The Body Shop, which prided itself on environmental ethical business practices[109] but, in fact, did not live up to all claims on "environmentally friendly" and "animal friendly testing" production and testing methodologies. Further, the push to advertise as an "ethical retailer" did not always sell with the public. Many leaders in the natural environmental movement have been heard to say that "green only sells if you have everything else right with your customer." Procter and Gamble (P&G) is another illustration of this ethic.

Some industries, such as pulp and paper, have always been plagued with environmental issues because of the nature of the technology used in conversion.[110] The choice of new technology in a resource-based industry has far-reaching implications for its ethical performance because the technological solutions usually give rise to new environmental challenges. Biodiversity issues continue to be a concern in the industry.

Most companies do not have a code of business ethics, but many models are available,[111] and technology can easily be used as the test case for these exercises. The most common issues of business ethics and technology, such as computer

---

[105] J. Papanikolaw, "Cargill, Monsanto Accused of Technology Misuse," *Chemical Market Reporter,* 255, no. 7 (February 15, 1999), pp. 3, 8.

[106] P. L. Hartman and G. Bucci, "The Economic and Ethical Implications of New Technology on Privacy in the Workplace," *Business & Society Review,* no. 102/103 (1998), pp. 1–24.

[107] K. Sibley, "Survey Ties High-tech to Unethical Practices," *Computing Canada,* 24, no. 20 (May 25, 1998), p. 4

[108] R. Cardinali, "Reinforcing Our Moral Vision: Examining the Relationship Between Unethical Behavior and Computer Crime," *Work Study,* 44, no. 8 (Nov/Dec 1995), pp. 11–17,

[109] M. Sillanpaa, "The Body Shop Values Report—Towards Integrated Stakeholder Auditing," *Journal of Business Ethics* 17, no. 13 (October 1998), pp. 1443–1456.

[110] J. Poesche, "Business Ethics in the Choice of New Technology in the Kraft Pulping Industry," *Journal of Business Ethics,* 17, no. 5 (Part 1). (April 1998), pp. 471–489.

[111] See the *Journal of Business Ethics* or other journals on the subject such as L. Hosmer, "Why Be Moral?: A reply to Shaw and Corvino," *Business Ethics Quarterly,* 7, no. 4 (October 1997), pp. 137–143, as well as textbooks on business ethics such as L. T. Hosmer, *The Ethics of Management* (3rd ed.) (Chicago: Irwin, 1996).

monitoring, are naturals for the top of the list for consideration. The general guideline to be followed is suggested by my emeritus colleague, Professor LaRue Hosmer: "Managers should act idealistically and energetically to increase justice or fairness or morality, following the ethical principles that generations of moral philosophers have devised to define those concepts."[112] Not only is this the "right" thing to do, but this type of behavior engenders *trust,* which is essential for creativity to flourish in organizations. Innovative ideas are shared in an environment of trust, and they are not shared when trust is not present.

UMMARY

Strategies are the outcomes of emergent and intended plans that organizations formalize in order to compete. Clear goals and vision are extremely motivating in a firm, and consistency between strategies at different levels and across units is a first principle of success. There are exceptions, and technology planning is often one. On occasion, parts of the organization will have to sprint ahead, spearheading change, making some strategies temporary inconsistent.

Technology strategies tend to be one of two types, broadly: first or early mover approaches, and follower strategies. It is possible for a company to have both strategies, depending on which service or product is under consideration. Technology forecasting can be of great help in guiding strategy intent selection. Part of this process is designed to identify technology trajectories and emerging dominant designs. This is the first step in establishing potential for technology fusion to enhance future core competence. Blending multiple technology forecasting methods is recommended. Mapping technology capabilities into products that satisfy customer needs is the goal. Technology monitoring and scenarios are becoming popular forecasting and planning techniques.

Merger and acquisition (M&A) activity increases unabated in North America and elsewhere in the world. However, *buying or merging with a firm, primarily for technology reasons, is different from other motivations for M&A.* There is a great temptation for the acquiring (or dominant partner) firm to treat a technology acquisition like a cash cow instead of an investment, in need of nurturing and growth. This is the most important strategic tendency to avoid in purchasing or working with a technology partner.

It is possible to predict competitor response to technology-intense moves such as new product introductions. Competitors will usually respond in kind to any action, but the bigger the change (e.g., a major new product introduction), the more delayed a competitor's response. Leadership is one of the keys that unlocks the innovative potential of an organization and sustains development and implementation of technological change. General managers and organizational leaders are the key to any technology strategy: the more aggressive the manager, the more aggressive the technology strategy; the more ethical the senior manager, the more ethical the firm.

---

[112] I. Hosmer, "What Is Moral? A Reply to Shaw and Corvino," *Business Ethics Quarterly,* (Oct 1997), pp. 137–144.

DISCUSSION QUESTIONS

Read Case 4-1 on National Machinery and answer the following questions.

1. Why was National Machinery so reluctant to change its product line and plant operations in the face of technological changes in the fastener industry?

2. Do you think National Machinery could have launched discontinuous change in this industry without the help of "lead users"?

3. Are lead users necessary for all discontinuous change in an industry?

4. Who benefits more in the case of discontinuous change—the first mover (e.g., National) or the early followers (Japanese and German competitors)?

ADDITIONAL CASE SUGGESTIONS

1. Highly recommended for the issues of corporate and technology strategy integration is the following case: Millipore New Product Commercialization: A Tale of Two New Products, HBS 9-594-010.

CASE 4-1

National Machinery

When Paul Aley took over as president of National Machinery in 1985, the company was in the dog days of its history. Adrift in calm waters, with an unforeseen storm heading in, technological competition was about to make life difficult. The "nuts and bolts" industry and the equipment used to form bolts, in particular, would not be considered high technology by most standards. And Tiffin, Ohio, is not Silicon Valley. But in this small heartland town during the last decade, technological comeback history was made. National was the industry leader, so why should managers worry about the competition? This is what happened.

National started in 1874, in the heyday of the U.S. equipment company epoch. It survived the Great Depression, expanded to Germany in 1958, and built a plant in Japan in 1975. Paul Aley's personal history with National Machinery begins after this era of global expansion. He started as one of thirty "trainees" in 1979, along with Tom Hay. At the time Aley ascended to the president's job, there were still no CNC (computer-numerical control) machine tools in the National home shop, and the company was building inventory in Japan, selling only ten machines a year, but running at full production.

Paul was hired to the job under the most unusual circumstances. The shop was in the throes of a UAW organizing movement, primarily driven by the issue of employee pensions. The local bank told the family owners and board members that it would not lend the company any more money until it got a new president. Paul convinced each member of the shop, primarily in small-group meetings and individually, that the worker would be better off with him than with the UAW. His "rainbow" strategy was simple and to the point. He said, "It's not us and them, it's us, unless I mess up." Everyone understood it. The union lost the election and Aley took over. Ironically, he would never have been given the chance if it hadn't been for that organizing movement. He told his staff, "Listen to our people and listen to our customers and we can do it," and it turned out he was right.

This case was written especially for this book. Copyright by John E. Ettlie, all rights reserved. The information for this case was obtained from interviews with Paul Aley and Tom Hay of National Machinery and Paul Morath of Shamrock Fastners on 10 June 1998. Other sources included *National Notes,* by Paul Aley, May 1998, a periodic publication of National Machinery, primarily designed for internal communication purposes. The author is responsible for all errors, but gratefully acknowledges help from Shamrock and National Machinery.

In a brilliant stroke of technology planning, Aley stepped up immediately and made three critical decisions:

1. Survive first: get better with the customer, one step at a time. He put his established engineers to work on incremental improvements of the product.

2. Tom Hays and a small group of engineers went to work on a radical new product.

3. Aley bought CNC equipment and modernized the plant, which was purchased by liquidating inventory.

In addition to these three technology decisions, Aley decided to change the philosophy of National Machine using all the same people—many of them "second stringers" who had never been given a chance to prove themselves. He hired only one new person—in sales. Everyone else was the same as before, but now doing different jobs. Before, craftsmen on the assembly floor had to make "one-of-a-kind" machines because components were so inconsistent. They prided themselves in being able to make up for mistakes upstream in the process. This was going to change. Instead of making one machine at a time, they were going to make 10, 20, 60, or 200 bolt-forming machines—all exactly the same, with zero defects, and they would take pride in the uniformity of the product. This was a radical change for most people in the shop. People began to get the message when the other five plants around the world were closed, and the company was down to just what they started with in 1957, the home shop in Tiffin. Only sales and service remained in Nurenberg, Germany, and Nagoya, Japan. But first and foremost, they had to have the right new product. They were going to get only one chance at this. The entire company became focused on just core customers, and with a common set of parts and a family of products—all in cold forming—the new strategy was struck.

The new line of products, called FORMAX, was introduced in 1989. Why did they choose this name? Does it stand for anything? Not really. Max was the director of sales. In a meeting one day when they were trying to figure out what to call the new line, someone said, "Well, this new product is for our core customers, or so Max tells, us, so it really is for Max…" The name stuck.

The product was sold to core and best collaborating customers with progress payments—sort of. Many customers were offered a 5 percent discount if they would pay for the machines before they were delivered. Several stepped up, and National could afford to build this new line of cold formers. Two machines were built. The first one was sold to Elco in Rockford, Illinois, the year National ran out of inventory. The second was kept in-house as the alpha version of the machine for R&D purposes. One part failed repeatedly, but was quickly redesigned and tested so Elco could be kept running. If the FORMAX line didn't work, it was curtains. But FORMAX was so radically different, potential customers could not ignore it, and competitors couldn't copy or innovate around National's patents.

With initial problems solved, demand for the FORMAX product began to build steadily. The word was out: If you wanted the best cold former, you had to have a FORMAX. Then management faced the toughest challenge yet. A large company—a good customer—wanted to buy out production for one whole year. A successor to FORMAX was in the works, and the offer was tempting. But Aley and his staff resisted. They would not become captive to one large customer. It didn't make sense. If people in the shop "owned" the product, how could you have only one customer? And 800 families in Tiffin, Ohio, depended on being right about this.

Paul Morath and others stepped up and alpha tested the FORMAX Plus machine, without a companion machine in Tiffin. The strategy was evolving—National could trust a few customers enough to do alpha testing outside the home plant, by temporarily moving some personnel to customer plants. Now the new machines would really be tested—under true customer conditions.

National quickly became constrained in engineering and manufacturing capacity. Some customers had to turn to National's competitors when delivery times got longer. So, National had to become more efficient in the shop and in the lab. Shipments were flat for four years, and National was missing opportunities to grow. The large-scale FORMAX machines, the latest in the platform of this discontinuous product, are considered to be the best way to overcome the Asian currency crisis and install growth as sustainable strategy.

Competitors? Why hasn't anyone stepped up to challenge the company that many had written off as dead and gone? According to Aley, they still haven't gotten it, for the most part. They still don't realize that the change has occurred. In the language of the innovation literature, the dominant design has changed. In particular, they don't know what kind of technical resources it takes to introduce and sustain a radical new platform of machine design. Two Japanese competitors are close, but not there. Paul monitors the size of the engineering staff of competitors as a precaution.

At the heart of the philosophy that changed National was what Tom Hay, now vice president of engineering, calls the genesis of the FORMAX line:

We wanted to do something for our customer and something for us." The only way to do that was to invent a new cold forming machine that leveraged the best ideas unique to the National engineering creativity but also made a leap in customer capability. The only way a machine could be reproduced that was a radical new concept was to use the "modular" approach to manufacturing and design. "When we fixed the transfer concept that didn't work on the original two machines in 1988, we were building on our knowledge of kinematics and working quickly to be successful. No competitor has put all the pieces together yet and nobody has over 50 engineers to design formers that can maintain 50 microns tolerance. We operate the plant on a zero defect plan and we meet the prints we produce."

Chapter 5

R&D Management

CHAPTER OBJECTIVES

> To introduce the topic of management of the technical function of an organization. To incorporate the concept of technology and innovation strategy in the R&D management discussion and to illustrate these concepts with the case of IBM. To emphasize the importance of the idea of R&D collaboration and illustrate some of the issues of joint R&D with the case of the Low Emissions Paint Consortium (LEPC) in the U.S. Automotive industry.

The purpose of the technical function of the firm is stated quite clearly by Roberts in the introduction to his book on generating technological innovation:[1]

1. Create new knowledge.
2. Generate technical ideas aimed at new and enhanced products, manufacturing processes, and services.
3. Develop those ideas into working prototypes.
4. Transfer these ideas as embodied in new products and services to manufacturing, distribution, and use.

It is often useful, at least at the outset, to characterize this process of innovation creation as quite orderly and manageable. For example, Steele[2] presents the **creation–application spectrum,** which is reproduced in Figure 5-1, as beginning with basic research and ending with product service. The distinction between basic

---

[1] E. B. Roberts, *Generating Technological Innovation* (New York: Oxford, 1987), p. 3.

[2] L. W. Steele, *Managing Technology: The Strategic View* (New York: McGraw-Hill, 1989), p. 10.

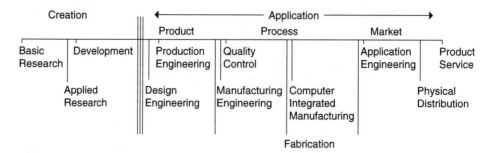

Figure 5-1   The Creation–Application Spectrum

Source: L. W. Steele, *Managing Technology: The Strategic View* (New York, McGraw-Hill, 1989), Figure 1.1, p. 10. Reproduced by permission of McGraw-Hill Companies.

(create new knowledge) and applied research (solve a problem) is usually quite clear. In the United States, most basic research is done in universities. But in practice, the distinction is often fuzzy. Furthermore, if customer voice is the only driving force behind innovation efforts, all gains tend to be incremental. Radical innovations—the ones that create new markets and real growth for the future of an organization—do not follow normal company routines. Preliminary findings from an ongoing IRI (Industrial Research Institute) study indicate that breakthroughs often result from a very "topsy-turvy process ... (and) generally evolve from projects that get repeatedly axed and restored.[3]

$\mathcal{W}$HY R&D?

Organizations meet specifications set by their customers. But the timely response to customer problems often requires considerable lead-time to come up with answers. Therefore, R&D and marketing are often working on the same issues, in parallel, not in series.

Stage models of the innovation process are, at best, an after-the-fact rationalization of what really happens during the innovation process. Not all customer problems can be solved and not all technology can be applied. But the basic idea holds: Incremental and radical innovation are different. Ultimately, only the combined efforts of all the key functions of the firm—marketing, R&D, and operations—must be integrated to satisfy customers.

$\mathcal{B}$ASIC VERSUS APPLIED R&D

The National Science Foundation (NSF)[4] divides research into three categories:

---

[3] O. Port and J. Carey, "Getting to Eureka!" *Business Week* (November 10, 1997), pp. 72–73.

[4] National Science Foundation, Science Indicators (1985, p. 221), reprinted in R. K. Jain and H. C. Triandis, *Management of R&D Organizations* (New York, John Wiley & Sons, 1990), pp. 6–7.

▶ *Basic research*. Basic research has as its objective "a fuller knowledge or understanding of the subject under study, rather than a practical application thereof." To take into account industrial goals, NSF modifies this definition for the industry sector to indicate that basic research advances scientific knowledge "not having specific commercial objectives, although such investigations may be in fields of present or potential interest to the reporting company."

▶ *Applied research*. Applied research is directed toward gaining "knowledge or understanding necessary for determining the means by which a recognized and specific need may be met." In industry, applied research includes investigations directed "to the discovery of new scientific knowledge having specific commercial objectives with respect to products or processes."

▶ *Development*. Development is the "systematic use of the knowledge or understanding gained from research, directed toward the production of useful materials, devices, systems or methods, including design and development of prototypes and processes."

$\mathcal{R}$&D METRICS

Managers and professionals have struggled for years with the issue of how to evaluate R&D—the outcomes of creative, intellectual work. The simple measure of R&D output, R&D intensity, or the ratio R&D spending to sales, is only a first-cut approximation of relative investment in research. Professionals involved in R&D benchmarking have, more recently, advocated using the "new sales ratio," which is the ratio of current annual sales of new products to total annual sales, without specifying how new is new (typically, it is 5 years).[5] As an alternative to the R&D ratio, some have advocated using a measure of R&D stock, rather than relative spending in a given year.[6]

In one recent survey of 10 international companies, John Hauser modeled the R&D/engineering metrics issue using the tier metaphor, starting with basic research, strategic research and engineering. This is summarized in Figure 5-2.[7] Hauser found that for applied research, market metrics can be used for project selection (the "tin cup analogy" funding from divisions). Strategic research relies on market and, especially, other metrics such as publications, patents, citations, and peer review, more typical of the internal R&D management process. Basic research metrics rely on *best people* approaches. John Hauser recommends that firms adopt *research tourism* metrics, encouraging researchers to take advantage of research spillovers from universities, other industries, and competitors to avoid

---

[5] R. Whiteley, T. Parish, R. Dressler, and G. Nicholson, "Evaluating R&D Performance Using the New Sales Ratio," *Research-Technology Management* 41, no. 5 (September/October, 1998), pp. 20–22. Also see A. Bean, et al., "Benchmarking your R&D," *Research-Technology Management* 42, no. 1 (January-February 1999), pp. 24–34.

[6] Personal communication with L. Lafebvre, 1999. See also footnote 22.

[7] J. Hauser, "Research, Development, and Engineering Metrics," *Management Science* 44, no. 12 (December 1998), pp. 1670–1689.

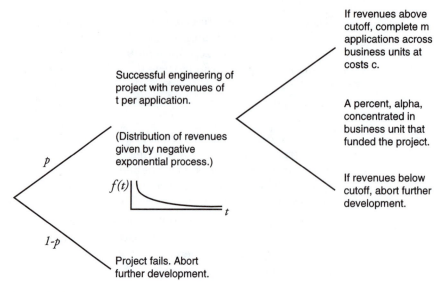

Successful engineering of project with revenues of t per application.

(Distribution of revenues given by negative exponential process.)

If revenues above cutoff, complete m applications across business units at costs c.

A percent, alpha, concentrated in business unit that funded the project.

If revenues below cutoff, abort further development.

p

$1-p$

Project fails. Abort further development.

Figure 5-2   Decision Tree Representing Project Outcomes

the NIH ("not invented here") factor. (Also see Figure 5-7 on information pattern as it varies by basic and applied research.)

PATENTS

An idea can be patented if it is new, useful, and nonobvious (and not abstract as with a scientific theory or law of nature). Article I, Section 8 of the United States Constitution says, "The Congress shall have Power To … promote the Progress of Science and useful Arts, by securing for limited Times to Authors and Inventors the exclusive Right to their respective Writings and Discoveries." In the Patent Act of 1790 and laws thereafter, Congress described how patents would be granted. George Washington's proposal, that entrepreneurs who imported new foreign inventions to the United States should have exclusive rights, in order to encourage industry in the new country, was dropped. The U.S. Patent Office was established in 1836. But laws are political compromises. The courts declared invalid almost two thirds of all U.S. patents that it ruled on between 1921 and 1973. Commercial success has gained wide acceptance as a measure of the nonobvious, and so it is emphasized and links inventions with innovations.[8]

Although there was great domestic concern about the ratio of foreign to domestic applications for patents during the last decade, recent indications are that this upset was not well founded. Patent applications are up (see Figure 5-3) and are

---

[8] S. Lauber, "New, Useful, and Nonobvious," *Invention & Technology* (Spring-Summer 1990), pp. 9–16. Comments on this section by Luke A Kilyk, patent attorney, are greatly appreciated. The following Web sites may be useful for following developments in patent law: www.abanet.org/intelprup/ (American Bar Association) and www.aipla.org (American Intellectual Property Association).

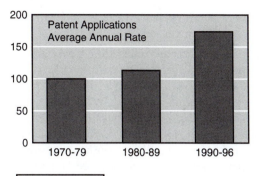

Figure 5-3

America's Patent Office Is Busier Than Ever

Source: *Business Week* (December 1, 1997), p. 28.

Data: U.S. Patent & Trademark Office

considered by economists to be leading indicators of productivity gains. The number of U.S. patent applications are 50 percent greater than in the 1980s.

Considerable applied research has been done using patents as an indictor of innovation. There is a great temptation to equate innovativeness as a concept with patent performance, but it would be wise not to give in to this oversimplification. Patents are merely the promise of potential, with no guarantee of commercial success. Further, many ideas cannot be patented, such as some engineering practices, and firms often patent inventions just to prevent other companies from claiming rights later.

Having said that patents are not a perfect indicator of innovative potential or realization, they can be used to make inferences about how organizations change. For example, one study used the overlap in patent citations between alliance partners to indicate changes in technological capabilities as a result of their association. The sample included 792 alliances from 1985 to 1986, of which 132 (16%) were equity joint ventures; 226 (29%) were unilateral contract-based alliances such as technology licenses and R&D contracts; and 434 (55%) were bilateral contract-based alliances such as cross-licenses, joint development, and technology-sharing agreements. In 280 (35%) of the alliances, both partners were U.S. firms. In 102 (13%) of the alliances, a U.S. and Japanese firm partnered. In the remaining 410 alliance cases, a U.S. firm partnered with a firm from another country, primarily in Europe. The study also used a control sample of 858 nonallied firms. Equity arrangements significantly promoted greater knowledge transfer, but there are limits to this method of enhancing capabilities. Further, alliance activity tends to promote increased specialization in time periods subsequent to initial alliance encounters as partner firms actually develop divergent capabilities.[9]

One noteworthy study using patents in manufacturing represents work-in-progress on the innovation process. Wesley Cohen, Richard Nelson, and John Walsh report the following results of a study of 1,164 cases (54% response rate) of U.S. R&D labs conducting manufacturing research:[10]

---

[9] D. C. Mowery, J. E. Oxley, and B. S. Silverman, "Strategic Alliances and Interfirm Knowledge Transfer," *Strategic Management Journal,* 17 (Winter Special Issue, 1996), pp. 77–91.

[10] W. M. Cohen, R. D. Nelson, and J. Walsh, "Appropriability Conditions and Why Firms Patent and Why They Do Not in the American Manufacturing Sector," presented at Science Policy & Technology Meeting, NBER (July 24, 1997), Cambridge, Massachusetts.

1. The effectiveness of patents relative to other mechanisms of protecting intellectual property has not increased since the 1980s.

2. Since that time, "Secrecy has ascended from being judged the least effective mechanism for protecting profits due to product innovation to a position of dominance," (p. 19).

These two parallel results are a puzzle because U.S. firms have doubled their rate of patent applications since 1980. One possible explanation is that, owing to increased technological competition, all appropriatability mechanisms may be valued more highly. Further, patents are used for more than just protection of intellectual property. They can be used for blocking other innovators, negotiation, and protection against infringement. A patent can now be used to signal potential litigation and prevent market or product group entry as a strategy. The authors also report that "large firm size was not particularly related to … measures of patent effectiveness," (p. 22) and was very industry-specific. The topic of patents is reintroduced in the chapter on public policy and innovation.

Four practical issues concerning patents and preventing others from using a firm's inventions are worth noting:[11]

▶ Be certain that the best way of making and using the claimed invention is fully discussed in the patent application.

▶ Make sure lab or R&D notebooks are witnessed frequently by other, noninvolved professionals in the organization (once a month minimum) to support a defendable record of the invention.

▶ Be careful and strategic in sharing secrets with customers, because seeking legal protection under the patent and intellectual property laws (trademarks, copyrights, etc.) at a later time may be difficult and complicated if business data to support the patent application depend on the customer's permission and cooperation.[12]

▶ Use *patent marking:* Products covered by patents or pending patent applications should have a marking that indicates the granted U.S. patent or "patent pending."

 ERVICE R&D

R&D in the service sector grew from 10 to 25 percent of all industrial research from 1988 to 1998. Consistent with these trends, the growth of service R&D is dominated by investment to improve information technologies.[13] Microsoft spends about 17 percent of sales on R&D, which is well above the traditional cutoff of 6 percent of sales spent on R&D by high-technology companies. Although manufacturing R&D still

---

[11] Many thanks to Luke A. Kilyk, patent attorney, for identifying these current issues in patent law, July 23, 1998.

[12] Joint ownership issues can also arise from such customer involvement without prior agreements addressing such issues, personal communication, L. Kilyk. See also Chapter 7, Case 7-1.

[13] J. E. Jankowski, "R&D: Foundation for Innovation," *Research-Technology Management,* 41, no. 2 (March–April 1998), pp. 14–20.

dominates the total research budget worldwide, in the United States, nonmanufacturing R&D accounted for about 25 percent of private research dollars in 1995.

In 1997, $206 billion was spent on R&D in the United States according to one estimate, making the R&D-GDP ratio about 2.6 percent. About 65 percent of this total is industry R&D, concentrated in a relatively small number of firms. Eight firms account for one fourth of all industrial R&D, 40 firms accounted for half of this amount, and 300 firms accounted for 80 percent of this total industrial total.[14]

Industry contracts about 2 percent of its R&D budget with university, not-for-profit, and government laboratories. Pursuant to the 1984 National Cooperative Research Act (NCRA), (see Chapter 10) 665 ventures had been registered under this law by 1996. Telecommunications accounts for one fifth of all research joint ventures, which have now reached nearly 20 million filings, including those under the NCRA.

Government contributes about 15 percent of the total R&D budget, and half of this is to firms building aircraft and missiles or with companies in scientific instruments and electrical equipment. Government laboratory participation in research joint ventures was made much easier by the 1986 Federal Technology Transfer Act, implemented under Cooperative Research and Development Agreements (CRADAs). CRADAs totaled more than 3,000 during 1992 to 1995, most by the Department of Energy (1,553), the Department of Defense (1,001), and the Department of Commerce (412). From 1986 to 1996, approximately 2,500 information technology alliances were formed, mostly among U.S. firms or between U.S. and European companies. Slightly more than 1,000 alliances have been formed in biotechnology worldwide.

National R&D spending has been growing at an inflation-adjusted rate of about 6 percent during the last 3 years, which has been matched only by Japan among the large global economies. The Group of Seven (G7, or United States, Great Britain, France, Italy, Germany, Japan, and Canada) has experienced a leveling off or decline in R&D expenditures into the 1990s.[15]

Nonmanufacturing firms accounted for only 8 percent of industrial R&D in 1985 but grew to about 25 percent of the total in just 10 years. Service-sector R&D rose to 26.5 percent of all R&D in 1998, passing manufacturing R&D, which was about 24 percent of company research in 1996.[16] Most of this growth was in computer software and biotechnology. Microsoft, Sun Microsystems, Amgen, Seagate Technology, and Genentech were not even in the top 100 R&D performers in 1986; in 1996, they were in the top 50. Computer programming, data processing, and other computer services accounted for $8.5 billion in 1995 nonfederal R&D. Wholesale and retail trade spent $7.5 billion, and communication services spent $4.8 billion on R&D. Finance and banking spent $700 million on R&D in 1995. These figures are similar to spending trends in Canada, where one third of business R&D is in services. Service R&D is 13 percent in Europe and 4 percent in Japan, but that percentage is growing.[17]

---

[14] Ibid.

[15] Ibid., pp. 14–15.

[16] P. Gwynne, "As R&D Penetrates the Service Sector, Researchers Must Fashion New Methods of Innovation Management," *Research-Technology Management,* 41, no. 5 (September–October 1998), pp. 2–4.

[17] J. E. Jankowski, "R&D: Foundation for Innovation," *Research-Technology Management,* 41, no, 2 (March–April 1998), pp. 14–20.

New approaches to R&D management are forced onto companies that support both manufacturing and service business, such as GE. GE now gets 40 percent of its profits from financial services. This is a tough challenge, because "they must invent their R&D institutions from scratch."[18] Anderson Consulting is another example. With limited resources for long-term projects, most research is done on solving problems rather quickly, since the jobs of manager-clients are changing so fast.

GE launched an internal services R&D strategy in 1988 to support NBC broadcasting and GE Capital Services, rather than contracting R&D outside the firm. Both GE and Anderson Consulting decided to begin R&D programs on services because of credibility and as a way to differentiate it from rivals. In addition, Anderson believes that the only way to get to the market fast with a new service is to do your own R&D. Then the question became, how do you do research in an area where the company has no experience?

GE tried an infiltration strategy: It sent a researcher, Prakash Rao, to apprentice in GE Capital's Corporate Credit operation. The goal was more than just learning the business; it was to find problems that can be solved by new technology. This eventually led to the automation of the system for authorization of auto leases. Financial modeling is a natural area to work in, and at any one time, 30 GE staff from the R&D center were working on projects for GE credit—often winning the work after bidding against outside suppliers.[19]

At Anderson Consulting, research has three purposes:

▶ Create new business for the company, such as a new Web-based offering.

▶ Find new ideas and "market offerings" and minimize technological risk.

▶ Serve a marketing function to convince clients that Anderson is working on the future … for them.

One of the major differences between R&D for product-based industries and service is the timing of technology transfer. Since clients are in a hurry to solve problems, and the life cycle of the service is typically short, especially in consulting, it is always at risk of becoming a commodity. The goal at Anderson is to be 3 to 5 years ahead of the market. At GE, timing is different for products and for services. For products, such as medical systems, timing is typically the same, one technology generation after another. For services, timing has to be negotiated every time with clients.

Timing and life-cycle pressures have prompted Anderson to establish new types of collaborations with academic and industrial laboratories to adapt to the service sector. New services are often co-developed with hardware and software suppliers, as well. In one recent case, Anderson assembled information technologies from a dozen different companies, including Compaq, Hewlett-Packard, and Intel. GE has launched a program whereby all R&D staff work directly with company clients, regardless of business sector, manufacturing and services alike. The watchword for GE R&D: Be "vital."[20] R&D bench personnel have to be able to clearly articulate

---

[18] P. Gwynne, "As R&D Penetrates the Service Sector Researchers Must Fashion New Methods of Innovation Management," *Research-Technology Management,* 41, no. 5 (September–October 1998), p. 2.

[19] Ibid., p. 3.

[20] L. S. Edleheit, "GE's R&D Strategy: Be Vital," *Research-Technology Management,* 41, no. 2 (March–April 1998), pp. 21–27.

the business benefits of their ideas. This is often the most difficult thing for new recruits to learn when they join the GE laboratory.

R&D INTENSITY

The single most common indicator of degree of innovative potential of a firm is its **R&D intensity,** or the annual ratio of R&D expenditures divided by sales. High-tech firms typically spend more than 6 percent of sales each year on R&D, and much of that goes for salaries and overhead of scientists and engineers—technical employees. Another ratio, the number of patented inventions to real R&D expenditures (patent-R&D ratio) or, alternatively, the number of scientists and engineers has declined in the United States and other economies since the 1960s. Three explanations have been offered for this decline:

- ▶ Technological opportunities have been exhausted.
- ▶ Expanding of markets has raised the value of patents and competition in research has resulted in greater R&D expenditures per patent.
- ▶ Rising costs of dealing with the patent system has led researchers to patent fewer inventions.

One study using industry data found that the last explanation was most plausible—a decline in the propensity to patent has decreased the patent/R&D ratio.[21] An alternative to R&D intensity, **R&D stock,** is emerging as a measure of technological capability, but is not yet widely used.[22]

SCIENTISTS IN ORGANIZATIONS

 ### Ethical Considerations

Technological assessment seeks to avoid the unintended, negative consequences of innovating: introducing products and services commercialized for the first time. Anything unprecedented always has some associated risk. Beginning with the

---

[21] S. Kortum, "Equilibrium R&D and the Patent-R&D Ratio: U.S. Evidence," *American Economic Review,* 83, no. 2 (May 1993), pp. 450–457.

[22] Personal communication, Pierre Monahan, May 1999: Is R&D well-correlated with other innovation indicators such as patents, publications, references, and innovation data? Quite a bit of research has been done on R&D and patents. The best survey is probably the one by Z. Griliches, "Patent Statistics as Economic Indicators," *Journal of Economic Literature,* 28, no. 4 (1990), pp. 1661–1707. There is also his "Productivity, R&D and the Data Constraint," article, in *American Economic Review,* 84, no. 1 (1994), pp. 1–23. Recently innovation data have been collected. Some effort is under way to compare them with R&D. Crepon, Duguet, and Mairesse, *NBER* 1998, working paper 6696, "Research Investment, Innovation and Productivity" looks at the French firm data for a relationship between R&D, innovation data, and patents.

choice of which research project to pursue or fund, the ethics of technology applies.[23]

The U.S. Congress used to have a technical branch called the Office of Technology Assessment, charged with the responsibility of evaluating technologies and providing policy advice. This office was closed in 1995. The Frankenstein hypothesis (technology will eventually turn on its master), introduced in Chapter 1, is still a motivator in the field of science ethics as well as technology assessment. Other branches of government, of course, are still charged with health (e.g., the Food and Drug Administration), safety, and environmental issues (e.g., the Environmental Protection Agency), but these are primarily regulatory and review tasks, not guidelines about what is right and wrong in developing new technology.

One of the most important ethical issues in science today is the debate over biotechnology's ability to alter human genetics. The U.S. Supreme Court has ruled that it is legal to issue patents on knowledge of codes contained in human and animal cells, and the U.S. Patent Office has issued thousands of patents on parts of the human genome. Only France has refused to issue such patents. Value ethicists insist that we take responsibility for our actions, yet doctors are committed to treat illness even when there is always a probabilistic outcome of care. A person is more than what can be mapped and examined under a microscope. What happens when biotechnology migrates out of disease cures and into other areas?[24] Cloning of animals has already begun,[25] but many scientists and lawmakers are opposed to human cloning.

In the fall of 1996, and for the first time, ethics questions were included on the fundamentals in engineering, which encourages engineers who want to earn the P.E. (Professional Engineer) license to get prior ethics training.[26] Software engineering now has a code of ethics. The code contains eight keyword principles related to decisions and behavior of professional software engineers, including *product, public, client, management, colleagues* and *self.* An example is the code for product: "Software engineers shall, insofar as possible, assure that the software on which they work is useful and of acceptable quality to the public, employer, the client, and the user, completed on time and at reasonable cost, and free of error."[27]

If business ethics is any indicator, what makes decisions with ethical implications so problematical is that the choice is seldom between what is *right* and what is *wrong*. Typically, the choice is between the lesser of two evils. For example, laying off an employee will clearly have a negative impact on the person and his or

---

[23] D. Remenyi and B. Williams, "Some Aspect of Ethics and Research Into the Silicon Brain," *International Journal of Information Management,* 16, no. 6 (December 1996), pp. 4011–411.

[24] E. B. Flowers, "The Ethics and Economics of Patenting the Human Genome," *Journal of Business Ethics* 17, no. 15 (November 1998), pp. 1737–1745. Also see, "Clones and Clones: Fact and Fantasies About Human Cloning," *Economist,* 349, no. 8094 (November 14, 1998), p. S11.

[25] J. Hamilton and J. Flynn, "Commentary: When Science Fiction Becomes Social Reality," *Business Week,* no. 3517 (March 10, 1997), pp. 84–85.

[26] M. Lowery, M. Rabins, and L. Holtzapple, "Why Care About Ethics," *Chemical Engineering,* 104, no. 8 (August 1997), pp. 125–127.

[27] D. Gotterbarn, K. Miller, and S. Rogerson, "Software Engineering Code of Ethics," *Communications of the ACM,* 40, no. 11 (November 1997), pp. 110–118. Also see J. Adam, "The Privacy Problem," *IEEE Spectrum,* 32, no. 12 (December 1995), pp. 46–52.

her family. But if staff reductions determine the survival of a company, which outcome is worse? It is even more complicated as more and more companies go global, where values differ. According to the experts, "Companies can navigate these ethical storm waters by implementing a true ethics program with teeth, not by merely trotting out a piece of paper. And by recognizing that, despite cultural differences, certain core ethical values are held by all people around the globe."[28]

In engineering, the conflict is often between cost and quality. "If engineers reduce their ethical guidelines to the minimum of 'do no harm,' standards of quality may fall proportionately."[29] There are also ethical blind spots to contend with in all fields. In engineering, safety is always an issue, but ecological safety is typically not a consideration.[30] Dozens of firms have taken active leadership in the "new" natural environmental movement, often called "beyond compliance," which should change this.[31] In addition, academic research on the natural environment is in resurgence.[32] Yet, *green wars* are by no means over. Not only have some companies not "received" the message of environmental stewardship,[33] many developing countries of the world think it is rather high minded of the West to assume that the developing countries have fewer pollution credits coming because they were last to modernize. Yet, environmental engineers, the world over, have had to deal with this conflict for many years.[34]

✕ Scientists as Managers

The landmark work on scientists and engineers in organizations was published in 1976 by Pelz and Andrews. Not only did the work set the standard and tone for hundreds of subsequent studies on human resources and R&D management, but many of their findings are still applied today and have modern relevance. For example, their results suggest that there is an optimal project assignment profile for a successful (productive) engineer. Some variety and, therefore, at least two projects actually stimulate creativity among successful engineers. Obviously, too many projects also hamper creativity and performance.[35]

Numerous other studies have followed. It would be impossible to review them all here, but one of the most interesting and useful is by Robert Keller. Keller

---

[28] M. Davids, "Global Standards, Local Problems," *Journal of Business Strategy,* 20, no. 1 (January/February 1999), pp. 38–43.

[29] J. Enyart, "Can a Symbol Make You a Better Engineer?" *Civil Engineering,* 68, no. 5 (May 1998), p. 6.

[30] S. Hole, "The Ethics of Remediation," *Civil Engineering,* 67, no. 4 (April 1997), p. 6.

[31] S. Lerner, "The New Environmentalists," *Futurist,* 32, no. 4 (May 1998), pp. 35–39. Also see "Industrial Ecology: Doing Business in a Sustainable World," *Environmental Manager,* 9, no. 11 (June 1998), pp. 1–4.

[32] S. L. Hart, "Beyond Greening: Strategies for a Sustainable World," *Harvard Business Review,* 75, no. 1 (January/February 1997), pp. 66–76.

[33] P. M. Morse, "Sustainable Development," *Chemical & Engineering News,* 76, no. 31 (August 3, 1998), pp. 13–16.

[34] S. Sebasco, "Best Professional Judgment: A Synthesis of Environmental Law, Waste Discharge, Effluent Limitations and Engineering Ethics," *Water Engineering & Management,* 143, no. 10 (October 1996), pp. 18–21.

[35] D. Pelz, and F. Andrews, *Scientists in Organizations* (Ann Arbor, Mich.: University of Michigan, Survey Research Institute, 1976).

studied how research managers interact and evaluate their technical subordinates. The key moderating variable was the self-esteem of the employee. The higher the self-esteem of the subordinate, the more subordinate and manager agree on performance evaluations. Technical employees with low self-esteem tend to overestimate or underestimate their performance compared with their boss's assessment. It makes sense, because engineers and scientists with high self-esteem often base their self-image on accurate assessments of all the feedback they get on the job. Technical employees with low self-esteem tend to filter out some types of information, which starts a cycle of underassessment or overassessment of personal performance.[36]

Not only is the motivation of engineers and technical employees a unique challenge,[37] and one that does not necessarily follow "common sense" rules (e.g., the only thing that matters is the work itself), but engineers and scientists often get promoted to management positions early in their careers. This might include not just technical management, but, in many cases, management in other parts of the organization such as operations or service. For most R&D professionals, it becomes obvious early in their careers that the money is in management.[38]

Project groups tend to perform best if their longevity is between 1 and 4 years. New project teams perform relatively poorly, as their inexperience would predict, and teams with a history of 5 or more years also experience degraded performance. It is not surprising that long-tenured groups within R&D require more direction. Control works better than more participation because the latter only affects satisfaction, not performance. Control affects both. The longer a technical group has been together, the more successful a "traditional" type manager will be.[39]

Perhaps one of the most interesting and useful research streams in this category is the work done on the dual ladder structural adaptation in R&D. This is typically installed to give outstanding technical performers an alternative to administration for promotion.

Dual Ladder

Ralph Katz and his colleagues have studied dual ladders in R&D organizations for many years.[40] Scientists and engineers are often quite skeptical about alternative ways of rewarding their achievements outside the traditional, immediate supervisor

---

[36] R. T. Keller and W. E. Holland "The Measurement of Performance Among Research and Development Professional Employees," *IEEE Transactions on Engineering Management,* EM-29, no. 2 (May 1982), pp. 54–59.

[37] M. K. Badawy, "One More Time: How to Motivate Your Engineers," *IEEE Transactions on Engineering Management,* EM-25, no. 2 (May 1978), pp. 37–42.

[38] T. Allen and R. Katz, "The Dual Ladder: Motivational Solution or Managerial Delusion?," *R&D Management,* 16, no. 2 (April 1986), pp. 185–197; and "Age, Education, and the Technical Ladder," *IEEE Transactions on Engineering Management* 39 (3) (1992), pp. 237–242.

[39] R. Katz, "Managing Creative Performance in R&D Teams," in R. Katz (ed.), *The Human Side of Managing Technological Innovation* (New York: Oxford University Press, 1997), pp. 177–186.

[40] R. Katz, M. Tushman, and T. Allen, "The Influence of Supervisory Promotion and Network Location in Subordinate Careers in a Dual Ladder RD&E Setting," *Management Science,* 41 (1995), pp. 848–863.

evaluation. This skepticism may be because technical managers are often promoted for *both* technical *and* human relation skills. Being promoted on the "alternative" **dual ladder** may be perceived as a consolation prize under these circumstances. Further, even in companies with successful dual ladders, the technical ladder often does not pay as well as the managerial ladder.

Many practitioners complain that the dual ladder does not solve the problems it addresses, but often the concept is not implemented correctly in firms. There is a critical stage in a technical person's career in which switching to the managerial ladder makes a difference. This should be taken into account in administration of this concept.

Personnel Mobility and New Technology

There is growing evidence to support the notion that movement of people across organizational boundaries—sometimes called **mobility** or **personnel flows**—can have an important impact on the innovation process. In one study of the semiconductor industry over an 18-year period, executive migration had a significant effect on strategic change, especially on subsequent product-market entry decisions by the executive's new firm. Smaller top management teams with shorter tenures precipitate more change.[41]

The same has also been found for the introduction of major process changes, both in manufacturing (e.g., durable goods and food processing) and service (e.g., transportation). In particular, changes at the vice presidential level and above have been found to be significantly correlated with the initiation of radical process technology introduction. Further, internal movement of engineers and engineering managers across departmental boundaries and within the hierarchy (lateral or promotional changes) has been found to be instrumental in the successful implementation of these radical process change initiatives. Incremental process changes, apparently, do not exhibit these patterns.[42]

INTEGRATING R&D AND THE ORGANIZATION

Capitalizing on R&D

Ultimately, the trick seems to be getting the most out of R&D investments and organizations. How do the successful firms do it? Does technology have the positive impact on company performance, as so many have argued? We explored this

---

[41] W. Boeker, "Executive Migration and Strategic Change: The Effect of Top Manager Movement on Product-Market Entry," *Administrative Science Quarterly,* 42 (1997), pp. 213–236.

[42] J. Ettlie, "Intrafirm Mobility and Manufacturing Modernization," *Journal of Engineering and Technology Management,* 6, nos. 3&4 (May 1990), pp. 281–302; J. Ettlie, "Manpower Flows and the Innovation Process," *Management Science,* 26, no. 11 (November 1980), pp. 1086–1095; J. Ettlie, "The Impact of Interorganizational Manpower Flows on the Innovation Process," *Management Science,* 31, no. 9 (September 1985), pp. 1055–1071.

question by compiling data from public sources on R&D investment and financial performance as proxies for new technology utilization and economic success. In these Fortune 1000 companies, 1997 sales growth and earnings growth were significantly correlated, $r = .191$ ($p < .01$, $n = 780$). The results of the regression analysis are used to explain the variance in sales growth. R&D has been shown to have a greater direct impact on market growth than financial indicators, and results are true to this precedent.[43] R&D intensity (R&D as a percentage of sales) is the only statistically significant predictor of sales growth for the complete data cases in the Fortune 1000, $\beta = .10$ ($p = .02$, $n = 558$). That is, *only R&D intensity*—not sales per employee (productivity), the number of employees (size), or return on equity (ROE)—*can account for a significant (albeit small) variance in percentage of sales growth* in the largest U.S. companies.[44] These findings are similar to those reported in other empirical studies.[45]

Some of the well-known labs have been around for many years, modeled on Edison's lab. Box 5-1 summarizes the vagaries of two of these household names in the R&D game: SRI and Sarnoff Labs. Successful capitalization and commercialization of R&D seem to rest on at least two critical factors: leadership and an effective and timely spinoff strategy. There have also been some efforts to apply accounting methods to R&D.[46] There is also evidence that the emergence of dominant designs during periods of ferment in a technological trajectory is an issue of timing and collateral assets. After the dominant design emerges, emphasis shifts to process development and scale production.[47]

R&D is effective only if it either supports or "stretches" organizational strategy. How to get this right is a continuing challenge. As mentioned in the previous chapter, ABB's business strategy and plans influence technology strategy development and are, in part, a result of current performance.

How does one integrate the technical function with the rest of the organization? Clearly, balance will be required between corporate and decentralized (e.g., divisions, projects, dispersed locations, product lines or plants) R&D funding. Most R&D today is decentralized, at least funding-wise. But how do divisions or programs stay in sync? Who is responsible for coordination and eliminating redundancy? How can senior managers avoid having two decentralized units invent the same new product?

Some of these technology coordination issues are covered under the rubric of technology sharing. Some companies (e.g., DaimlerChrysler) put teams of new idea thinkers together led by key corporate executives such as Robert Lutz (vice-chair-

---

[43] See, for example, J. E. Ettlie, "R&D and Global Manufacturing Performance," *Management Science,* 44, no. 1 (January 1998), pp. 1–11.

[44] Although the correlation matrix is not given with these regression results, the coefficient for R&D and sales per employee was $r = -.03$, n.s. (not significant), and for R&D with ROE, and number of employees, $r = .01$, n.s., and $r = .02$, n.s., respectively. In other words, no significant interaction effects were detected.

[45] R. Lau, "How Does Research & Development Intensity Affect Business Performance?" *South Dakota Business Review,* 57, no. 1 (September 1998), pp. 1–4ff.

[46] B. Nixon, "Research and Development Performance: A Case Study," *Management Accounting Research,* 9, no. 3 (September 1998), pp. 329–355.

[47] J. Utterback and F. Suarez, "Innovation, Competition and Industry Structure," *Research Policy,* 22 (1993), pp. 1–21.

BOX 5-1

Breaking Ground for Blockbusters

The strategic challenge of managing R&D is getting your money's worth. That is, R&D is an expensive and risky proposition, and some people still don't accept the idea that creativity can be programmed. There are two ways that invention can pay off. It can promote incremental improvements in existing products and services, or it can help create new products and services—breakthroughs that often open up whole new industries.

SRI International, in Menlo Park, California, and Sarnoff Corporation (formerly the David Sarnoff Research Center, in Princeton, New Jersey) are two premiere research labs that specialize in breakthroughs. Although SRI (formerly the Standford Research Institute) is the "soul" of Silicon Valley, it was there long before silicon chips and has a broad, multidisciplinary mission.

Sarnoff is even older. Contributing seminal work in TV, it continues groundbreaking work in semiconductors, electronics, and materials. In 1986, four years after being established by RCA, Sarnoff invented the color TV tube. Then came the liquid crystal display (LCD) and the charge-coupled device (CCD), at the heart of every video camera.

SRI has an equally impressive track record: magnetic inks for credit cards and checks, which spawned Paul M. Cork's Raydum Corporation; and in the 1960s, the modem, the mouse, on-screen windows, hypertext (for point and click surfing); during the 1970s, medicine for malaria and a blood-clot inhibitor.

In 1986 the two labs became one when we denoted Sarnoff to SRI for a tax write-off and $65 million cash. By the early 1990s, the two, now together, "slipped into the red," prompting Paul Cook to return as chairman and hire William P. Sommers as president (formerly with Booz, Allen & Hamilton, Inc.). By 1994, SRI was profitable, and Sarnoff returned a net profit in 1995. Since 1994, the two think tanks have founded twenty startup businesses to commercialize their research. These include DIVA Systems (1997), which markets a video on-demand system called Onset via cable TV, operating just like a VCR (for 24-hr. return periods).

The secret of this success for turnaround? Part of the answer is clever optimization on "troves of technology itching to be free," because of the new entrepreneurial freeway under the new spinoff strategy, which allows for both royalty and equity sharing. Another part of the answer goes back to the successful route of SRI and Sarnoff. According to Douglas Englebart (now 73), responsible for the mouse, on-screen windows, and many more inventions, "The market isn't the best or even a good guide to what's best for mankind." For Englebart, these innovations weren't an end in themselves but "steps along the way" to profoundly impact the way humans interact. This is the type of vision that breakthroughs are made of and can be spawned by well-managed labs like SRI and Sarnoff.

SOURCE: O. Port, "Tales From Spin-off City," *Business Week* (February 23, 1996), pp. 112–116.

man) to invent the future for the whole company. DaimlerChrysler is a platform-driven company. It uses "technology clubs" to keep up with developments, such as those in engine technology, that will affect more than one platform. This type of pan-technology thinking and idea integration may be a key to the company's future if the best concepts and technologies are to be found and implemented.

Before the merger, Chrysler also had a reputation as being among the best to work with among the first-tier supplier community. Doubtless, much of Chrysler technology is sourced in this way.

Fostering Entrepreneurs and Intrapreneurs

The professional venture capital industry is valued at $43.5 billion, and this does not even include the so-called financial "angel" that often backs startups that cannot get funding from other (even personal) sources. Not all **entrepreneurs** are high-technology (R&D intensity approximately greater than 6%) inventors or spinoffs from large companies, but many scientists and engineers or college professors have started their own technology-based businesses. A well-known example is Seymour R. Cray, who in 1972 announced he would leave Control Data Corporation (CDC) and form a new company, Cray Research, with the partial backing of CDC. Cray left partly because CDC would not fund his proposal to develop the 7600, a supercomputer, in-house. He went on to help invent the first supercomputer.

Most of these new product startups, estimated to be about 20 percent of entrepreneurs, involve some type of technology, and one of these stories is summarized in Box 5-2.

This is the case of *Un-du,* a product for removing adhesives, temporarily, for manipulation. It shows how launching a new product by entrepreneurs is difficult at every step. It is not just a matter of resources—that is a critical issue, to be sure—it is also an issue of infrastructure and public awareness. In a sea of new businesses, some are more worthy than others—but which ones? The issue extends to internal entrepreneurs, as well. So-called **intrapreneurs** often get their starts within large companies when a fund is created for such internal ventures. 3M does this, as do many other companies. In this way, the resources will be available, the inventor or innovator is allowed to capture the benefits along with the sponsoring company, and the risk of startup is covered. Often established marketing channels can be used and space may be created in-house so that the progenitor does not have to revert to the garage.

Gifford Pinchot calls intrapreneurs "dreamers who do." That is, in most organizations, people are often thought of as "dreamers," or "doers." Contrast the intrapreneur with the inventor: An inventor asks questions like "wouldn't it be wonderful if…" while intrapreneurs ask, "who can I get to help me with this…" Pinchot's recommendations on how to succeed at intrapreneurship are summarized in Box 5-3.

Managing intrapreneurs is another matter. Special rewards and "discretionary" time of about 15 percent are typically recommended. Further, special organizational structures such as unique teams will need to be created. Finally, intrapreneurs need to know that they don't have to wait for permission for action.

Funding R&D

Since innovation funding is risky by nature, it is not surprising that a great deal has been written about how to fund it and how not to fund it. To implement overall organizational objectives and a consistent technology strategy, R&D projects are

BOX 5-2

The Story of "Un-du"

What does it take to introduce a successful new consumer product? Better, what does it take to be successful the *first* time you try? Maybe a better mousetrap sells itself, but its not obvious in the twenty-first century. Consider the case of "un-du," of Doumar Products. This product is an "adhesive neutralizer." This is a better mousetrap: it can remove oil-based labels, stickers, price tags, bumper stickers, masking tape, and gum. But after two years of market tests, trade shows, and home shopping networks, Doumar is only "creeping" toward commercial success. There have been brushes with financial failure, fears of copycat products from larger competitors, and fears of legal battles from deep-pocket challengers.

Technical entrepreneurship is not easy. New, small businesses account for most of the employment gains in any given year, but introducing an innovative new product is the risky form of new startup business. With 600,000 to 700,000 new businesses created each year in the U.S., less than 20 percent have a new product or something distinctive. But these can add up. Harvard Business School recently surveyed its graduates, and half classified themselves as entrepreneurs.

Un-du seems typical. In November 1997, Reading China and Glass, a kitchen and dining room superstore, placed the first major retail order for Un-du, but Doumar ended the year with $38,000 in revenues and $400,000 in expenses. Gary Reiching, CEO, says, "We went through much more money than we thought we would." To meet orders, production capacity had to be expanded (in Texas), people had to be hired, computer and phone systems had to be installed. When production was moved from Chicago, thousands of poorly capped bottles of Un-du evaporated. Everybody pitched in and refilled the bottles by hand, and they have the blisters to show for it. Doumar's executives have twice taken pay cuts to stay afloat. Suppliers and employees are paid first. December 1997 was the first month everyone was paid on schedule.

The biggest, looming concern is Magic American Corporation, a Cleveland-based company that makes specialty cleaners, with $30 million in annual sales and a well-established distribution chain. Magic American recently announced that it was instigating an investigation by the Consumer Product Safety Commission (CPSC) of Doumar's labeling of the flammable product. Mr. Reiching said the CPSC concluded there was no problem, but the incident caused considerable stress on top of all the other problems of startup for the new company. Buyers have told Doumar that Magic American has leaked a rumor of the introduction of a cut-price version of Un-du under their popular GooGone brand. At a recent trade show, the Magic American booth featured a "Sticker Lifter" for the first time in a package similar to Un-du. Even though GooGone uses a slower-acting solvent, does not preserve the adhesive on the tape or label being removed, and does not leave oil surfaces stain-free, as Un-du does, it has a plastic lifting tool, not covered by the patent held by Doumar. This clearly puts pressure on Doumar to go national or international quickly to establish leadership and brand image.

Source: B. J. Feder, "Good Product. Sound Plans. No Sure Thing," *New York Times* (January 8, 1998). Bl.

BOX 5-3

Succeeding at Intrapraneurship

Every new idea will have more than its share of detractors. There is no doubt that being an intrapreneur is difficult, even in the most tolerant of companies. So how can people succeed at it?

1. *Do anything needed to move your idea forward.* If you're supposed to be in research but the problem is in a manufacturing process, sneak into the pilot plant and build a new process. If it is a marketing problem, do your own marketing research. If it means sweeping the floor, sweep the floor. Do whatever has to be done to move the idea forward. Needless to say, this isn't always appreciated, and so you have to remember the next steps:

2. *It is easier to ask for forgiveness than for permission.* If you go around asking, you are going to get answers you don't want, so just do the things that need to be done and ask later. Managers have to encourage their people to do this. It may be necessary to remove some layers of management that complicate and slow down the approval process.

3. *Come to work each day willing to be fired.* I began to understand this more from talking to an old sergeant who had seen a lot of battle duty. He said, "You know, there is a simple secret to surviving in battle; you have to go into battle each day knowing you're already dead. If you are already dead, then you can think clearly and you have a good chance of surviving the battle."

Intrapreneurs, like soldiers, have to have the courage to do what's right instead of doing what they know will please the myriad of people in the hierarchy who are trying to stop them. If they are too cautious, they are lost. If they are fearful, the smell of fear is a chemical signal to the corporate immune system, which will move in quickly to smother the "different" idea.

I find that necessary courage comes from a sure knowledge that intrapreneurs have—that if their employer were ever foolish enough to fire them, they could rapidly get a better job. There is no way to have innovation without courage, and no real courage without self-esteem.

4. *Work underground as long as you can.* Every organization has a corporate immune system. As soon as a new idea comes up the white blood cells come in to smother it. I'm not blaming the organization for this. If it did not have an immune system it would die. But we have to find ways to hide the right new ideas in order to keep them alive. It is part of every manager's job to recognize which new ideas should be hidden and which new ideas should be exposed to the corporate immune system and allowed to die a natural death. Too often it is the best ideas that are prematurely exposed.

SOURCE: G. Pinchot III, "Innovation Through Intrapreneuring," *Research-Technology Management,* 30 (March–April, 1987), reprinted in R. Katz (ed.), *The Human Side of Managing Technological Innovation* (New York: Oxford 1997), pp. 288–295.

typically thought of as a portfolio. This set of projects is usually considered within a broader context of a management system for the technical function. This linking of strategic planning and R&D projects in a portfolio is illustrated in Figure 5-4.[48] Risk, which is an essential feature of the technical projects of any organization, is estimated in these portfolios by plotting the degree of uncertainty against time in the state of the art of a given field.

Projects investigating beyond what is currently known are highly risky and involve basic or fundamental R&D. Projects "below" the line of current state-of-the-art typically have a technical success probability of 70 or 80 percent. In the early stages of a program, only an estimate of technical feasibility may be sought. The more radical the technology, the longer it typically takes to develop an idea into something that can actually be tested with potential customers. Periodic review of the portfolio might shelve or unshelve projects, depending on strategic or even tactical priorities and ongoing projects' successes and failures.

When one realizes that most technical knowledge is actually outside of any given organization, external events must be factored, periodically and as events unfold, into the mix of portfolio review. Portfolio analysis was one of the first methods to be formalized in the R&D management literature. (One of the others was project management using Program Evaluation Review Technique [PERT] and other project management tools.) One approach to this formal portfolio analysis is presented in Box 5-4. All of this work is designed to formulate technical and R&D policy, but it is highly dependent on how probabilities of success and utilities of outcomes are estimated. Therefore, the formalization is only as good as the best educated guesses of team members or managers at the time of the analysis.

A recent survey of 205 businesses[49] found that although the criteria vary that are used by successful R&D portfolios, the two top criteria were *strategic fit and leverage of core competencies* (90.4% of responding firms) and *payoff* (86.8% of responding firms). Risk and probability of success was third (76%) and timing was fourth (66%). Even then, some overriding, external set of events may be a bigger influence on policy than these portfolio results. Clearly, it is often the case that managers and engineers do not even follow their own best advice and seek outside advice on portfolio management. When risk is escalating but policy dictates that growth be encouraged, there are often conflicts in meetings and among actors in the typical company that has formalized the R&D and technical function. This situation also is likely to put a strain on the relationship between corporate offices and divisions that often see little practical significance in the change of central policies.

Portfolio analysis is a tool. How this tool is used, as with any tool and any decision-making process, depends on the organization. The results of these analyses depend on the inputs more often than the model selected. There are many good models to select from, many of them conveniently packaged in software. Any professional can produce data to support a case—most of the time in good faith. People do have honest disagreements about the facts and their mean-

[48] P. A. Rousell, K. N. Saad, and R. J. Erickson, *Third Generation R&D* (Boston: Harvard Business School Press, 1991), Figure 8-2, p. 154.

[49] R. G. Cooper, S. J. Edgett, and E. J. Kleinschmidt, "Best Practices for Managing R&D Portfolios," *Research-Technology Management,* 41, no. 1 (July–August 1998), pp. 20–47.

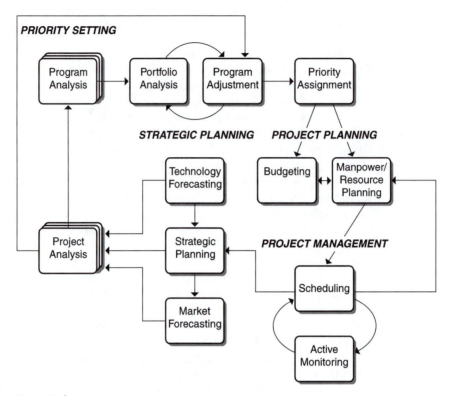

Figure 5-4   Linking Strategic Planning to Project Planning and Execution

SOURCE: P. A. Rousell, K. N. Saad, and R. J. Erickson, *Third Generation R&D* (Boston: Harvard Business School Press, 1991), Figure 8-2, p. 154. © 1991 IEEE.

ing. What does a company really *know?* Firm representatives will often claim, for example, that they "know" what competitors are doing, but are probably more likely to be good predictors of a competitors' reactions to technology moves than their "proactive" initiatives, which are likely in progress. One recent survey of 205 businesses found that no single approach to R&D portfolio management is in use among high-performing firms. Rather, a number of different performance metrics were used, including alignment of objectives and strategy, cycle time, and portfolio balance.[50]

During the early 1990s, one of the U.S. automobile companies in serious financial condition dropped active funding of any project in manufacturing R&D that could not be shown to have a return within 18 months. The red ink had just become too great, for too long a time, to allow anything riskier in the portfolio for manufacturing. This did not affect new product R&D directly, but this R&D funding crunch did affect vehicle programs. In some cases, teams were being asked to develop new models with half the funds previously allocated to a new program.

---

[50] Ibid., pp. 20-33.

BOX 5-4

Formalizing the R&D Portfolio Analysis

Inevitably, there are more projects to be researched than there are funds available. This is a normal and a healthy situation. A model derived from the work of Kenney and Raiffa [1976], which takes into account multiple objectives, preferences, and value tradeoffs, is suggested for deciding which projects to select among competing requirements. The main problem in using such an approach is the tendency by technical users to quantify items that do not lend themselves to quantification.

In developing a policy (at higher levels) or in making specific project choices among competing demands (at lower levels), the decision maker can assign utility values to consequences associated with each path instead of using explicit quantifications. The payoffs are captured conceptually by associating to each path of the three a consequence that completely describes the implications of the path. It must be emphasized that not all payoffs are in common units, and many are incommensurate. This can be described mathematically as follows [Kenney and Raiffa 1976, p. 6]:

$$a' \text{ is preferred to } a'' \Leftrightarrow \sum_{i=1} P'_i U'_i > \sum_{i=1} P''_i U''_i$$

where a' and a'' represent choices, P probabilities, and U utilities; the symbol < = > reads "such that."

Utility numbers are assigned to consequences, even though some aspects of a choice are either not in common units or are subjective in nature. This, then, becomes a multiattribute value problem. Assignment can be done informally or explicitly by mathematically formalizing the preference structure, which can be stated mathematically [Kenney and Raiffa, 1976, p. 68] as:

$$v(x_1, x_2, \ldots, x_n) \geq v(x'_1, x'_2, \ldots, x'_n)$$

$$\Leftrightarrow (x_1, x_2, \ldots, x_n) \geq v(x'_1, x'_2, \ldots, x'_n)$$

where v is the value function that may be the objective of the decision maker, x_i is a point in the consequence space, and the symbol reads "preferred or indifferent to."

After the decision-maker structures the problem and assigns probabilities and utilities, an optimal strategy that maximizes expected utility can be determined. When a comparison involves unquantifiable elements, or elements in different units, a value tradeoff approach can be used either informally, that is, based on the decision-maker's judgment, or explicitly, using mathematical formulation.

After the decision-maker has completed the individual analysis and has ranked various policy alternatives or projects, then a group analysis can further prioritize the policy alternatives or specific projects.

After research project selection and prioritization, an overall analysis of the research portfolio should be made. The research project portfolio should contain both basic and applied research. The mix would depend on the organizations:

▶ Organization
▶ Size
▶ Research staff capabilities

▶ Research facilities

▶ Access to different funding sources.

SOURCE: R. K. Jain, and H. C. Triardis, *Management of R&D Organization* (New York; John Wiley & Sons, 1990), pp. 15–51; R. L. Kenney, and H. Raiffa, *Decisions with Multiple Objectives: Preferences and Value Tradeoffs* (New York: John Wiley & Sons, 1976), pp. 6, 68; reprinted by Cambridge University Press, 1993.

To return to the example of ABB, **business technology evaluation (BTE)** is at the heart of both control and planning of the technical and business units of the firm (Figure 5-5). A small, corporate evaluation team is responsible for BTE at ABB. This team:

▶ Ranks ABB business units with regard to need to conduct audits and works with local managers to establish benchmarks and measurement standards

▶ Provides audit leadership and represents the chief-technical officer (CTO) to ensure timeliness and quality of audits

▶ Identifies external resources for BTE (e.g., consultants)

▶ Advises to top managers on programs to fill technical gaps

The BTE is a three-stage process (Figure 5-5). Each stage takes 1 to 2 months to complete, but the stages can overlap. Each audit starts with a question, such as whether the unit has the right technology to compete effectively. Some audits start with a routine financial summary and interviews with various members of the unit, which generates a focus and suggestions for improvement. Stage I structured data collection includes history, status and strategy, technical strengths and weaknesses, nontechnical capabilities, market requirements, and financial evaluations.

	Business Technology Evaluation		
	Stage 1	Stage 2	Stage 3
Focus (What)	Structured Information Collection	Analysis of Current Situation	Gap Analysis and Identification of Options

Methods (How)	• Consensus with respect to key issues
	• Interviews
	• Reviews of existing documents
	• Internal view on competencies
		• Workshop, e.g.
		  - market needs and/or opportunities
		  - technology position assessment
		  - competitive position
		• Capabilities assessment
		• Proposals for focused subsidiary projects
			• Subsidiary projects
			• Definition of key gaps
			• Identification of options to fill gaps
			• Integrated technology and business evaluation
			• Improvement recommendations

Figure 5-5   ABB's Approach to Conducting Business Technology Evaluations

SOURCE: H. M. Stillman, "How ABB Decides on the Right Technology Investments," *Research-Technology Management* (November–December 1977), Figure 5, p. 17.

Stage II of the BTE is analysis of these data and leads to collaborative market, technology, and competitive assessments. Capability assessment evaluates infrastructure capabilities relative to competitors.

Stage III of the audits focuses on scenarios or alternatives for improvement of overall performance. It seems essential to this process that action planning be conducted with local leadership so that the changes will actually be effectively implemented. Examples have included reallocation of R&D funds to a specific technology, adopting a new concurrent engineering process, or developing business in a specific country.[51]

Again, with all this emphasis on "logical" and "systematic" audits and evaluations, it is easy to forget how external events can often nullify this careful, thoughtful work. Take the example of IBM's recent R&D restructuring.

CEO Louis V. Gerstner, Jr. has redirected IBM R&D[50] so as to change the philosophy of this patent derby winner—perhaps forever. A cut of $1 billion in the R&D budget, a move to team the labs with marketing in the divisions and "get its research into its own products first," was the mandate. It appears to be paying off. Not only does IBM have the first viable voice entry system for PCs, its computer beat the world's champ at chess (see Chapter 1). Basic, globalized R&D are hardly dead, but the mix and philosophy and culture of R&D are quite different from the "country club" days of old (see Case 5-1).

 REAL OPTION VALUES IN R&D

In some R&D projects, managerial flexibility has value because information continues to be gathered about project technical performance and market outcome potential. The value of this flexibility has become known as the *real option value*. Huchzermeier and Loch[52] added to this concept the idea that beyond actual abandonment, there is also the option of corrective action. Options pricing theory suggests that higher uncertainty in project payoffs increases real option value of managerial decision-making flexibility. But uncertainty can result not just from market payoffs but from budgets, technical performance, market requirements, and project schedules. In their model (Figure 5-6), the real option value is diminished by market requirement varability, and this, in turn, destroys the value of flexibility responding to this information. At some extreme value, there is no option benefit that may keep the project alive.

The implications of this model are that for R&D projects, the result of increasing variability may diminish the value of flexibility beyond the point at which flexibility will ever be exercised, which reduces its value. This runs counter to established option pricing theory intuition and incorporates better risk management in R&D.

---

[51] H. M. Stillman, "How ABB Decides on the Right Technology Investments," *Research-Technology Management,* (November–December 1997), pp. 14–34.

[52] A. Huchzermeier and C. H. Loch, "Project Management Under Risk: Using the Real Options Approach to Evaluate Flexibility in R&D," Working paper, WHU Koblenz and INSEAD, February, 1999.

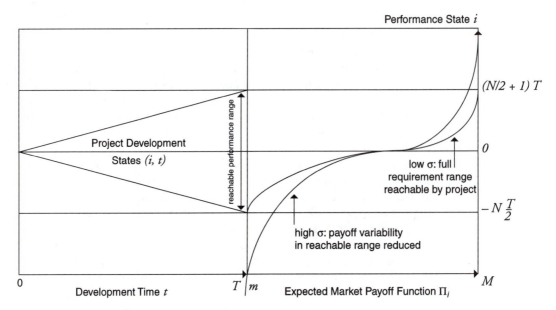

Figure 5-6   The Effect of Increased Requirements Variability

The model suggests when it is not worthwhile to delay commitments—for example, in postponing a design freeze—thus maintaining flexibility in R&D projects.

✺ Idea Generation and Communication Patterns in R&D

Although it may seem obvious, the source of ideas for successful innovations is typically outside the firm, and it comes through someone responsible for the marketing function. Several studies of this issue are listed in Table 5-1. How this information is coordinated with the technical and operations function is less obvious.

Perhaps one of the most significant series of empirical studies ever published on the R&D management process was done at Northwestern University by A. H. Rubenstein and his associates,[53] and at MIT by Tom Allen and his associates.[54] Chakrabarti and O'Keefe studied the role of the "key communicator" in the R&D laboratory and found that frequency and importance of communications were often *inversely* related. Allen and his associates, on the other hand, extended this notion of a "two-stage" communication process—to and from the key communicator or technical gatekeeper—in the R&D lab setting. The MIT group found that the most effective communication pattern depended on the stage of the R&D project.

---

[53] A. K. Chakrabarti and A. H. Rubenstein, "Interorganizational Transfer of Technology—A Study of Adoption of NASA Innovations," *IEEE Transactions on Engineering Management,* 23, no. 1. (February 1976), p. 20. A. K. Chakrabarti and R. D. O'Keefe, "A Study of Key Communicators in Research and Development Laboratories," *Group and Organizational Studies,* 2, no. 3 (Sept 1977), pp. 336–346.

[54] T. J. Allen, M. L. Tushman, and D. M. S. Lee, "Technology Transfer as a Function of Position in the Spectrum from Research Through Development to Technical Services," *Academy of Management Journal,* 22, no. 4 (1979), pp. 694–708.

$\mathcal{T}_{ABLE}$ 5-1   Sources of Ideas for Innovations Developed Within the Firm

Author	Study	N	% from Outside the Firm
Langrish et al.	Queen's Awards	51	65
Mueller	Du Pont	25	56
Myers/Marquis	Five industries	157	62
Utterback	Instruments	32	66

SOURCE: From data contained in J. M. Utterback, "Innovation in Industry and the Diffusion of Technology," *Science,* 183 (February 15, 1974).

1. "Research projects perform best when project members maintain high levels of communication with colleagues outside their organization."

2. "Product and process development projects … show higher performance when external communications" are done by technical "gatekeepers," who are very often research managers or informal leaders in the lab.

3. Technical service R&D does not follow either pattern and might best be coordinated and communicated by other managers available to follow-up on projects.[55]

These results are illustrated graphically in Figure 5-7, which plots a skew coefficient for communication and project performance. Note that there is almost no skew for research projects (either high or modestly high in success) and a great deal of skew for very successful development projects (skew coefficient is about 1.75).

Structuring R&D for Success

The matrix management idea of crossing functional organizations with projects never seems to die. Managers still talk about this idea as if it was the latest fad in restructuring companies. The likely origin of this idea was in some R&D organiza-

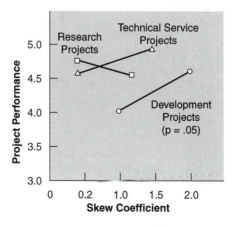

Figure 5-7

Relationship Between Project Performance and the Degree to Which the Distribution of External Technical Communication Is Skewed Across Project Members

SOURCE: Allen, et al., 1979 (p. 703, Figure 2).

---

[55] Ibid., pp. 694, 702.

tion—*when* is not certain (many companies like TRW used it in the 1950s and called it *matrix*). But the idea of each project progressing through stages and drawing on the technical resources of various units of the firm—the sciences at first and engineering and development groups later—until the project is released to operations was widespread in R&D management circles at least a generation ago, and likely longer.

Marketing might have a large say in the funding early in the cycle, but if decentralized units shared in funding, line managers might also decide the fate of many projects in formal reviews or informal directives. This is why it is difficult hard to find an organization that actually practices the "matrix" approach to either R&D or the firm as a whole. Most firms that use it resort to a modified project-based structure that is not too concerned with "missing cells" in the matrix structure, as long as the work is getting done.

Regardless of whether a true matrix actually exists in the firm, what is really at stake is whether a balance can be struck between the decentralized needs of product and service groups and the corporate knowledge-trust and knowledge-generating machine.

What makes an effective R&D organization? Evidence from the mainframe computer industry shows that establishing aggressive targets at each stage of the R&D process in resource-rich firms results in larger market share.[56] Although this provides clear support for the "first-mover" strategy as translated into R&D goals and also reinforces the resource-based view of the firm, which stresses building capability above all other strategies, it is not very specific about the intermediate steps in this R&D value-adding process.

Ford Motor Company's decision to integrate global operations in 1994 under the Ford 2000 program is essentially a matrixing of the old organizations at Ford. The goal was to eliminate duplication of effort, standardize components, reduce the number of suppliers, and save $3 billion by the year 2000. R&D consolidation was crucial to this strategy since it was estimated that by 2000, 50 percent of the content of a vehicle would be electronic, which has not traditionally been a core strength among the car makers. Ford's version of the matrix organization links manufacturing, marketing, sales, and purchasing. Managers have two bosses: one in the Vehicle Program Centers (VPCs) like FWD (large front-wheel drive), and the other in a functional structure. Individuals need **T-skills**, or deep expertise in a disciplined integrated structure organization. The Ford 2000 matrix (circa 1997) is depicted in Figure 5-8.[57]

It is interesting to note that the Ford 2000 plan has recently given way to new president Jacques Nasser's aggressive cost-cutting onslaught at Ford. In just 14 months on the job, he has saved billions of dollars, primarily by shifting production from low-volume, low-profit vehicles to high-flying, hot-selling sport utilities. This approach appears to be working.[58] It is not clear how Ford 2000 will evolve under

---

[56] T. Khanna and M. Iansiti, "Firm Asymmetries and Sequential R&D: Theory and Evidence from the Mainframe Industry," *Management Science,* 43, no. 4 (April 1997), pp. 405–421.

[57] "Practice Case: Ford Motor Company and Ford 2000" in A. Afuah, *Innovation Management: Strategies, Implementation, and Profits* (New York: Oxford, 1998), pp. 283–293.

[58] R. Simison "Ford's Heir-Apparent Is a Maverick Outsider," *Wall Street Journal* (February 13, 1998). Also see the *Wall Street Journal* (January 13, 1999). Ford's purchase of Volvo continues the trend of filling out the product line, covered in R. Simison, "Ford to Acquire Volvo's Auto Operations," *Wall Street Journal* (January 28, 1999), p. A3.

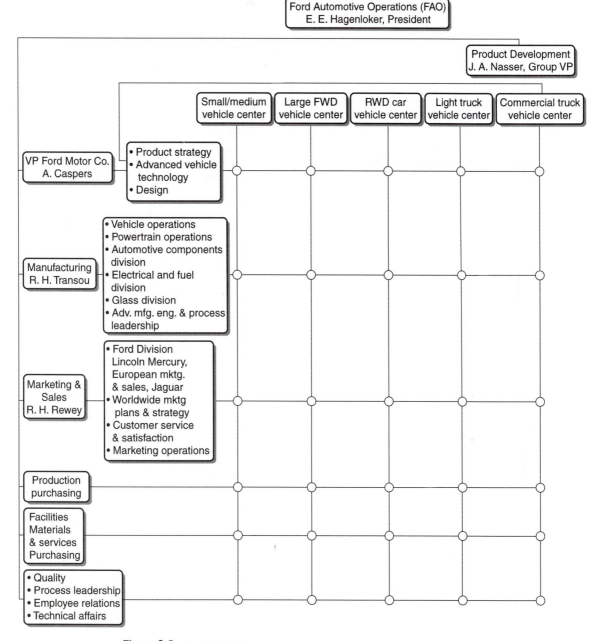

Figure 5-8 Ford 2000 Matrix

A. Afuah, *Innovation Management:* Strategies, *Implementation, and Profits* (New York: Oxford, 1998), p. 290, Figure 13.7. (*Note:* This structure is circa 1997.)

these new conditions, but the process deserves watching, Most matrix organizations do not work well without significant modification to the "project" form; many cells are better off empty.

Michale Menke recently published the results of a benchmarking survey of 79 highly regarded R&D organizations, which resulted in the complication of 10 practices for making good decisions and 10 additional practices for enhancing competitiveness.[59]

Table 5-2 summarizes the best practices for excellent decision making in R&D. Hiring the best people and focusing on end-customer needs are the top two practices. However, note that end-customer need focus is the least well actualized (effective usage). Only understanding the drivers of industry change is less well actualized (number 4 on the list).

These ten best practices can be implemented by adopting internal practices that enhance competitiveness, such as learning from post-audits and portfolio analysis, which are both discussed in this chapter. From an internal perspective, insisting on alternatives was the most difficult practice to implement. This suggests that even well-managed technical organizations struggle to maintain openness to new ideas.

The way to use this best practice benchmarking information is quite simple. Rate your unit (0–7 scale) on these practices. Focus on the most important (top four on the list) where there are significant gaps between your unit and the benchmark. Don't make the same mistake common in new product development exercises (e.g., quality function deployment, or QFD) where an endless list of customer wants and needs is used to determine product or service features.

TABLE 5-2   The Ten Essential Practices for Excellent R&D Decision Quality

Decision Quality Best Practice	Potential Contribution to Decision Quality (0–7)		Actualization* (0–100%)	
	Mean	Benchmark	Mean	Benchmark
Hire the best and maintain expertise	6.4	7.0	60	94
Focus on end-customer needs	6.2	6.7	48	83
Determine, measure, and understand end-customer needs	6.1	7.0	46	88
Understand drivers of industry change	6.1	7.0	41	79
Use cross-functional teams	6.1	6.7	55	98
Use a formal development process	6.0	6.8	60	96
Coordinate development with commercialization	6.0	6.8	49	92
Agree on clear, measurable goals	6.0	6.7	50	91
Coordinate long-range business and R&D plans	6.0	6.3	39	82
Refine projects with regular customer feedback	5.9	6.8	45	90

* Actualization = frequency of use × quality of execution (i.e., effective usage).

From Menke, 1997 (p. 49, Table 1).

---

[59] M. M. Menke, "Managing R&D for Competitive Advantage," *Research-Technology Management* (November–December 1997), pp. 40–42. For R&D and technology audit methodologies see Richard Goodman, *Technology and Strategy: Conceptual Models and Diagnostics* (New York: Oxford University Press, 1994). For audit of technology strategy with products see R. Burgelman, M. Maidique, and S. Wheelwright, *Strategic Management of Technology and Innovation* (2nd ed.) (Chicago: Irwin, 1996), and especially, Chapter 4 of P. Dussauge, S. Hart, and B. Ramanantsoa, *Strategic Technology Management* (New York: John Wiley & Sons, 1992).

Overall, the evidence suggests that there continue to be increased pressures on R&D resources and this, in part, leads us to the discussion of one strategy for meeting this challenge: collaborative R&D.

COLLABORATIVE R&D _____

There are two irreversible trends in global business: Companies continue to form more alliances,[60] and companies continue to reduce the number of suppliers they deal with directly.[61] The literature on collaborative R&D is quite extensive and includes models and investigations on a variety of forms such as virtual collaboration.[62] This collaboration can range from the "simple" cooperation between two firms for the purposes of joint R&D,[63] to R&D consortia between competitors, federal laboratory–industry R&D collaboration, and university laboratory collaboration.[64] In 1992, $1.14 billion of the $16.4 billion in university R&D came from industry.[65] In particular, Bozeman and his colleagues studied 229 industry–federal laboratory collaborative projects and found a commercialization rate of 22 percent, with an additional 38 percent having new products under development.[66]

Global comparisons of these relationships have become popular.[67] For university–industry technical consortia, cooperative R&D centers located at universities tend to "continually change, adapt, and search for an appropriate mode of operation," according to Geisler and colleagues.[68] Success factors vary by stage of evolution, but tend to be common across many universities and technical areas. For example, maintaining a high reputation and technology transfer with multiple funding sources are important for the continued success of a mature center. However, companies often narrowly define technology transfer success in terms of the

---

[60] R. Osborn and J. Hagedoorn, Special Issue on Organizational Alliances, *Academy of Management Journal,* 40, no. 2 (April 1997); E. Whittaker and D. Jane Bower, "The Shift to External Alliances for Product Development in the Pharmaceutical Industry," *R&D Management,* 24, no. 3 (July), pp. 249–260; A. M. Thayer, "Combinatorial Chemistry Becoming Core Technology at Drug Discovery Companies," *Chemical & Engineering News,* 74, no. 7 (February 12, 1996), pp. 57–64.

[61] H. Feron, Personal communication, Center for Advanced Purchasing Studies, Arizona State University, Tempe, AZ, 1995.

[62] R. C. Harris, "The Virtual R&D Laboratory," *Research-Technology Management,* 39, no. 2 (1996), pp. 32–36.

[63] J. S. Katz and B. R. Martin, "What Is Research Collaboration?" *Research Policy,* 26 (1997), pp. 1–18.

[64] B. Bozeman and M. Crow, "Technology Transfer from U.S. Government and University R&D Laboratories," *Technovation,* 11, no. 4 (1991), pp. 231–246.

[65] A. M. Thayer, "Biotechnology Industry Looks to More Creative Financing Options," *Chemical & Engineering News,* 71, no. 34 (August 23, 1993), pp. 10–13.

[66] B. Bozeman, M. Papadakis, and K. Coker, "Industry Perspectives on Commercial Interactions with Federal R&D Laboratories: Does the Cooperative Technology Paradigm Really Work?" Georgia Institute of Technology, Final Report to the National Science Foundation, Contract No. 9220125, 1995.

[67] J. Liker, J. Ettlie, and J. Campbell (eds.), *Engineered in Japan* (New York: Oxford, 1995).

[68] E. Geisler, A. Furino, and T. J. Kiersuk, "Toward a Conceptual Model of Cooperative Research: Patterns of Development and Success in University-Industry Alliances," *IEEE Transactions on Engineering Management,* 38, no. 2 (May 1991), pp. 136–145, esp. p. 142.

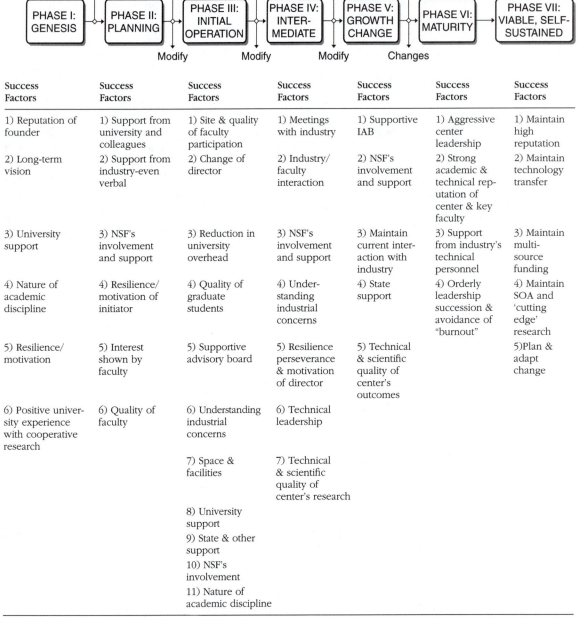

Success Factors	Success Factors	Success Factors	Success Factors	Success Factors	Success Factors	Success Factors
1) Reputation of founder	1) Support from university and colleagues	1) Site & quality of faculty participation	1) Meetings with industry	1) Supportive IAB	1) Aggressive center leadership	1) Maintain high reputation
2) Long-term vision	2) Support from industry-even verbal	2) Change of director	2) Industry/ faculty interaction	2) NSF's involvement and support	2) Strong academic & technical reputation of center & key faculty	2) Maintain technology transfer
3) University support	3) NSF's involvement and support	3) Reduction in university overhead	3) NSF's involvement and support	3) Maintain current interaction with industry	3) Support from industry's technical personnel	3) Maintain multi-source funding
4) Nature of academic discipline	4) Resilience/ motivation of initiator	4) Quality of graduate students	4) Understanding industrial concerns	4) State support	4) Orderly leadership succession & avoidance of "burnout"	4) Maintain SOA and 'cutting edge' research
5) Resilience/ motivation	5) Interest shown by faculty	5) Supportive advisory board	5) Resilience perseverance & motivation of director	5) Technical & scientific quality of center's outcomes		5) Plan & adapt change
6) Positive university experience with cooperative research	6) Quality of faculty	6) Understanding industrial concerns	6) Technical leadership			
		7) Space & facilities	7) Technical & scientific quality of center's research			
		8) University support				
		9) State & other support				
		10) NSF's involvement				
		11) Nature of academic discipline				

SOURCE: E. Geisler, A. Furino, and T. Kiresuk, "Toward a Conceptual Model of Cooperative Research: Patterns of Development and Success in University-Industry Alliances," *IEEE Transactions on Engineering Management* 28, no. 2 (May 1991), pp. 136–145.
NSF = National Science Foundation; SOA = state-of-the-art.

Figure 5-9   Generalized Phase-Model of Generation, Development, and Growth of University–Industry Cooperative Research Center (IUCRC)

number of quality students that can eventually be hired. Geisler and colleagues outlined these stage dependencies (Figure 5-9).

In this treatment of collaborative R&D relationships, two initial distinctions are made with regard to type: those with and those without direct government involvement. These two types are taken up in greater detail later. It should be noted, however, that formalization of a technical alliance may not be sufficient to differentiate its importance. Bench scientists and engineers do engage frequently in informal collaboration.[69] The examples of the Low Emissions Paint Consortium (LEPC) and SEMATECH are presented later to illustrate implications for a theory of collaborative innovation.

✶ Industrial R&D Collaboration

R&D collaboration without direct involvement of government may be harder to examine than one might think on the surface. There are obviously numerous examples of R&D associations that have no formal government involvement. But even the case of the LEPC discussed later, which had no official government role, did, in fact, take inspiration from government action. First, it was influenced by the 1984 Cooperative R&D Act, and second, it was motivated in part by federal Environmental Protection Agency (EPA) actions and forecasts of EPA actions following amendments to the Clean Air Act.

A starting point in the discussion of technical collaboration is to apply the notion of vertical integration to knowledge generation. When is it prudent to buy versus make new technology? Rubenstein (Chapters 6 and 8) argues that the only sustainable technology strategy is one in which external sources of technology augment or combine with internal sources.

> There should be a significant contribution by internal technical people to assure their motivation, continued interest, "handles" for continued improvement and innovation, a residual of imbedded technology capabilities related to the particular field of technology … and the competitive advantage that goes with having the capability to innovate continuously in a particular technology or set of technologies.[70]

Wheelright and Clark warn that many companies "often separate the management of partnerships from the rest of the development organization," which jeopardizes the success of new product development (NPD) projects. "Even when the partner company takes full responsibility for a project, the acquiring company must devote in-house resources to monitor the project, capture the new knowledge being created, and prepare for the manufacturing and sales of a new product."[71]

---

[69] K. Kreiner, and M. Schultz, "Informal Collaboration in R&D. The Formation of Networks Across Organizations," *Organization Studies,* 14, no. 2 (1993), pp. 189–209.

[70] A. H. Rubenstein, *Managing Technology in the Decentralized Firm* (New York: John Wiley & Sons, 1989), pp. 218–219.

[71] S. C. Wheelright and K. B. Clark, "Creating Project Plans to Focus Product Development," reprinted from the March-April, 1992 issue of *Harvard Business Review* in R. A. Burgelman, M. A. Madique, and S. C. Wheelright (eds.), *Strategic Management of Technology and Innovation* (2nd ed.) (Chicago: Irwin), pp. 838–849, esp. p. 842.

The authors argue that the long-term goal of all of this is to build critical capabilities, including personnel development and infrastructure (e.g., computer-aided design systems).

Although little is known about the overall success rate of collaborative R&D and technical alliances, joint venture (JV) survival after 6 years in the original governance form varies from 35 percent with Japanese partners to 46 percent with domestic partners only in the United States. After 75 years, JV of U.S. multinationals survive intact at a rate of only 31 percent, and owned subsidiaries are even less

BOX 5-5

Litespec, Inc.

Litespec, Inc. was formed as a 51-49 joint venture (JV) between AT&T and SEI (Sumitomo Electric, Inc.) of Japan with an initial capitalization of $10.9 million in 1989 to make optical fiber cable. SEI had established U.S. manufacturing operations but had to cease operations when the company lost a patent infringement suit to the original inventors of optical fiber, Dow-Corning. AT&T had established an alternative technology base with patents, and SEI sought out AT&T as a partner. By 1993, capacity of the JV had expanded tenfold, with 155 full-time employees in place. This "factory-of-the-future" contracts purchasing, shipping and receiving, accounting and human resources (primarily to AT&T).

Litespec fiber quality is nearly the best in its class on key technical measures and is especially outstanding in attenuation measures (loss of signal over distance). In addition, the JV has achieved excellent performance in splicing optical fibers and cable. Not only is Litespec financially successful, but it has begun an export program, has entered the Japanese market, and has introduced new optical fiber products (e.g., specialty fiber). From the AT&T perspective, the JV is successful because the technology is already being transferred to Atlanta operations. From the SEI perspective, the JV is successful because top management believes that the Japanese market will not be protected forever, so all Japanese corporations will eventually be forced to globalize or they won't survive.

What are the keys to success for a high-technology JV with a competitor? Several are listed: First, clear protection of intellectual property in the founding agreement; second, extremely cautious selection policy for employees on both sides of the Pacific Ocean. Employees, technical staff, and managers have extended training and development periods before assignment. The organizational structure is well integrated, especially in management, with representatives from both AT&T and SEI (e.g., the president's position is rotated among AT&T and SEI managers). There is an aggressive Kaizen (continuous improvement program), which is atypical for a high-technology firm. Seven "Model Shop Teams" are in place. They are self-managing in safety, housekeeping, product location, maintenance, etc. at Litespec, and 12-hour shifts are now in operation. Litespec appears to have been successful in capturing the best of American and Japanese business practices in its JV formation and institutionalization.

---

* This case summary is based on a presentation by Dr. Basant K. Tariyal, president of Litespec, Inc., at the University of Michigan College of Engineering, Ann Arbor, Michigan, summer 1993.

likely to be sustained, at a rate of 16 percent. All international JVs survive under that governance form at a rate of 45 to 50 percent.[72]

An example of a U.S.–Japanese joint venture in high-tech manufacturing is presented in Box 5-5. Note the key features of the Litespec organization: protection of technology rights, autonomy from the parents, and creative organizational solutions to the challenges of JVs between two cultures.

✕ Theoretical Perspectives on Joint R&D

A number of game-theoretic[73] and other economic perspectives[74] have appeared that attempt to model R&D collaboration. But most of these treatments seem to underestimate the role of R&D cost and scarce resources[75] or are inconsistent with empirical documentation and the reality of true spillovers in R&D.

The simple case of duopoly is depicted in a figure from Motta.[76] Two firms play a multistage game where they (1) decide to enter an industry, (2) make decisions on the levels of R&D spending, and (3) choose outputs and quality levels. These two competitors choose levels of investment in R&D at the second stage (see Figure 5-10) with and without cooperation. "The amount of R&D performance at equilibrium decreases when the information leakage rate, ϕ, increases."[77] $\overline{\phi}$ is the spillover among cooperating firms. R_c and R_{nc} refer to R&D levels with and without cooperation. As spillovers increase, the need for cooperative R&D (R_{nc}) decreases.

At some point, cooperation pays off and results in higher quality levels. All this depends on the technological spillover between the two firms with and without cooperation. If there is little spillover, cooperation benefits both firms and society, because the firm can now redirect R&D or resources elsewhere, assuming efficient allocations. In this example, it is assumed that R&D is directed toward improving product or service quality. The issue for implementation becomes this: Who will share information first?[78] For the LEPC, Case 5-2, the final question might be, Who will implement the new production technology first?

---

[72] J. E. Ettlie and P. Swan, "U.S.–Japanese Manufacturing Joint Ventures and Equity Relationships," in J. Liker, J. Ettlie, and J. Campbell (eds.), *Engineered in Japan* (New York: Oxford University Press, 1995), pp. 278–308.

[73] M. Motta, "Cooperative R&D and Vertical Product Differentiation," *International Journal of Industrial Organization,* 10 (1992), pp. 643–661.

[74] M. T. Kamien, E. Muller, and I. Zang "Research Joint Ventures and R&D Cartels," *American Economic Review,* 82, no. 5 (December 1992), pp. 1293–1306; M. L. Katz, "Joint Ventures as a Means of Assembling Complementary Inputs," *Group Decision and Negotiation,* 4, (1995), pp. 383–400; and M. K. Perry, "Vertical Integration: Determinants and Effects," in R. Schmalensee and R. D. Willig (eds.), *Handbook of Industrial Organization* (Amsterdam: North-Holland, 1989), pp. 183–255.

[75] L.-H. Roller and B. Sinclair-Desgagne, "Heterogeneity in Duopoly," Working Paper, CIRANO, Montreal, Quebec, Canada, October 1996.

[76] M. Motta, "Cooperative R&D and Vertical Product Differentiation," *Journal of Industrial Organization,* 10, no. 4 (1992), pp. 643–662.

[77] Ibid., p. 650.

[78] Motta, 1997, personal communication.

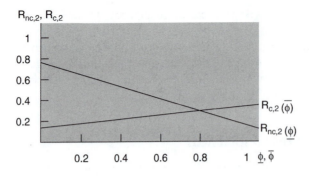

Figure 5-10
Cooperative and Non-Cooperative Levels of R&D in the Duopoly Case

SOURCE: M. Motta "Cooperative R&D and Vertical Product Differentiation," *International Journal of Industrial Organization,* 10 (1992), pp. 643–661, Figure 1.

The strategic management perspective has emphasized issues such as individual and network alliances, governance structures, and the public policy impact on alliances.[79] However, these perspectives have failed to capture the richness of the actual technical issues embedded in these alliances and their outcomes. In particular, the way in which partners protect technology is critical. "Many firms have found that the benefits of interorganizational cooperation may be outweighed by costs arising from unintended leaks in product or process technology, market insight, and other knowledge-based assets to the alliance partner. Successful alliance management involves a process of designing, staffing, and monitoring the collaborative interface to balance the requirements for learning and information sharing with protection of intellectual capital."[80] Two case histories are presented next to illustrate the complexities of collaborative R&D.

Lessons from Sematech

Peter Grindley and colleagues[81] have published an in-depth case study of SEMATECH to derive lessons for the design and management of other consortia that are funded from public and private sources. SEMATECH (Semiconductor Manufacturing Technology Consortium), established in 1987, is just one of many such technology consortia in the United States, Japan, and Europe. The details of U.S.,

---

[79] Y. Miyata, "An Analysis of Cooperative R&D in the United States," *Technovation,* 16, no. 3 (March 1996), pp. 123–131; J. P. Choi, "Cooperative R&D with Product Market Competition," *International Journal of Industrial Organization,* 11, no. 4 (1993), pp. 553–571, found that if you assume that total industry profit decreases as the spillover rate increases due to intensified post-innovation competition, the private incentive for cooperative R&D is less than the social incentive; S. Folster, "Do Subsidies to Cooperative R&D Actually Stimulate R&D Investment and Cooperation?" *Research Policy* 24, no. 3 (May 1995), pp. 403–417, found that subsidies that require cooperation in the form of result-sharing agreements significantly increase the likelihood of cooperation, but they decrease the incentives to conduct R&D which corroborates the work by Bozeman and Crow.

[80] C. C. Baughn, J. H. Stevens, J. G. Denekamp, and R. N. Osborn, "Protecting Intellectual Capital in International Alliances," *Journal of World Business,* 32, no. 2 (Summer 1997), pp. 103–117.

[81] P. Grindley, D. C. Mowery, and B. Silverman, "SEMATECH and Collaborative Research: Lessons in the Design of High Technology Consortia," *Journal of Public Analysis and Management,* 13, no. 4 (1994), pp. 723–758.

European, and Japanese technical consortium are quite different in their structure and operating procedures.[82]

First and perhaps foremost, SEMATECH, and most likely other consortia, evolved rather substantially after their founding. In this case, SEMATECH shifted from "horizontal" research cooperation to "vertical" collaboration among members—major users of semiconductor process equipment and materials. "In many respects, SEMATECH now resembles an industry association, diffusing information and best-practice techniques, setting standards, and coordinating generic research ... (and) now is concerned as much with technology diffusion as with the advancement of the technological frontier,"[83]

Grindley and his colleagues drew the following conclusions:

1. SEMATECH emphasizes near-term results, like many other industry-led U.S. consortia.

2. The change from a "horizontal" to a "vertical" collaborative strategy evidently contributed to the decision of several of the original members of SEMATECH to leave the consortium.

3. SEMATECH's efforts have been insufficient to prevent several equipment firms from exiting the industry.

In spite of these overall results, many believe that SEMATECH alone accounted for the significant turnaround in the semiconductor industry, now dominated by U.S. firms rather than Japanese firms.[84] Indeed, U.S. companies passed the Japanese in market share of semiconductor manufacturing equipment in 1992. U.S. companies reached parity with the Japanese, with Intel leading the way in semiconductors in 1992 as well.[85]

In 1992, SEMATECH employed 722 personnel, of which 225 were assignees from member firms, funded at a level of $100 million from the Advanced Research Projects Agency of the federal government, with matching funds from members and a small annual contribution from the state of Texas (the facility is located in Austin). SEMATECH was originally founded to provide a research facility for member firms to improve manufacturing processes for semiconductors, but now focuses on strengthening the semiconductor manufacturing equipment (SME) industry. The revised research strategy is illustrated by the official announcement in January 1993 that "it has achieved its goal of manufacturing 0.35 micron line-width integrated circuits,"[86] This was a generic result rather than being applied to a specific product or outcome.

---

[82] H. E. Aldrich and T. Sasaki, "Governance Structure and Technology Transfer Management in R&D Consortia in the United States and Japan," in J. Liker, J. Ettlie, and J. Campbell (eds.), *Engineered in Japan* (New York: Oxford University Press, 1995), pp. 70–92; J. Peterson, "Assessing the Performance of European Collaborative R&D Policy: The Case of Eureka," *Research Policy*, 22 (1993), pp. 243–264.

[83] Grindley et al., 1994, p. 724.

[84] *New York Times* (October 6, 1994).

[85] Grindley et al., 1994, p. 739.

[86] Ibid., pp. 730–731.

The shift in strategy, which came about in large part as a result of the difficulty of developing a research agenda and the reluctance of member firms to share information, was associated with a change in SEMATECH's intellectual property policies. Originally, member firms had an exclusive, two-year license on results. Now members have priority in ordering and receiving equipment, which nonmembers can eventually have access to once member demand is satisfied. Not surprisingly, there has also been an evolution in the project portfolio: The 1988 budget devoted 20 percent to supplier contracts; in 1991, this figure was roughly 50 percent and was expected to rise. An area of great activity is the Equipment Improvement Projects (EIP), which was instituted in response to the criticism of low reliability of U.S. semiconductor manufacturing equipment.

Challenges remain. The experience of the U.S. lithographic stepper industry indicates that support for collaborative technology development and improvement is not sufficient to save smaller, undercapitalized companies, with limited technical and managerial resources, up against larger competitors. Further, the changed emphasis on infrastructure has shifted appropriatability challenges upstream in the value-added chain. At least one case of sharing of proprietary data has surfaced. Foreign firms have also increased their acquisition of U.S. SMEs since SEMATECH changed its collaborative strategy. Because nonmember proposals are occasionally funded, membership benefits have been questioned. Finally, equipment testing at SEMATECH does not take the place of beta site installation, so the efficiency of the development process has been challenged.[87]

In summary, the lessons of SEMATECH are these:

1. Refocusing on short-term technology development rather than long-term R&D helped SEMATECH, but this still leaves the longer-term basic research issues unresolved by such consortia.

2. SEMATECH alone cannot resolve the competitive issues of the SME industry, but the "generic" technology development approach works for most members.

3. SEMATECH's centralized structure appears to have "enhanced" its flexibility and responsiveness of its research agenda, especially compared with Western European consortia.

4. Horizontal collaboration may be difficult in industries where product innovation depends on process innovation.

Although there may be clear differences among industries that require different models of collaborative R&D, it seems clear that the direct and persistent involvement of member companies is critical to the success of any such alliance. When small firm members are strained in this regard, they have the additional problem of collaboration. However, in the case of SEMATECH, the focus on a particular industry weakness, rather than a broad remaking of an industry, appears to have worked.

---

[87] Ibid., pp. 745–746.

[88] J.E. Ettlie, "Low Emissions Paint Consortium," University of Michigan Business School, 1995 (reprinted as Case 5-2).

✖ The Low Emission Paint Consortium

An example of collaborative R&D in manufacturing is the LEPC in the U.S. automobile industry.[88] This consortium was developed using the enabling legislation of the 1984 Cooperative R&D Act to help Ford, GM, and Chrysler (before merger to Diamler-Benz) comply with increasingly stringent air quality standards and EPA (Environmental Protection Agency) regulation.

In 1985, surface coatings and coating operations accounted for 27 percent of all industrial emissions of volatile organic compounds (VOCs, pronounced "v-o-sees"). Exposed to sunlight, these VOCs contribute to the formation of lower atmosphere (tropospheric) ozone. Amendments to the Clean Air Act, passed in 1990s were designed to significantly reduce VOC emissions. As Case 5-2 illustrates, GM, Ford, and Chrysler determined that it was in all their interests to cooperate to develop a new painting method that would reduce VOC emissions.

The key to understanding the persistence of this consortium is embedded in the case itself: "The pre-consortium committee had tentatively agreed on one important principle: If the big three did not stick together, the supplier community could not be persuaded to invest in the development costs needed to implement the pilot production facility. The supply community would ultimately benefit, but the payoff had to be large enough to "make a leap 10 times greater than anything we have done before in paint," as Ernie McLaughlin, the Chrysler representative said."[89]

From more or less the beginning of the collaboration among Ford, GM, and Chrysler, it was assumed that some government funding would be available for the powder coating project. But as Case 5-2 explains, government funding did not materialize. Some consortium members thought that was better in the long run any way, since government money meant government interference. The options for resolving the funding crisis were difficult to implement.

Crucial learning in the case appeared to boil down to two issues:

1. Is it necessary for competitors to stick together to get the full participation in R&D collaboration among suppliers?

2. Are environmental issues truly noncompetitive and exempt from the normal concerns about "spillovers" and "appropriation" of benefits of investments in new technology?

A preproduction R&D facility was eventually located at the Ford Wixom Assembly plant in Michigan, which is why it was selected for the collaborative R&D example. The case is both leading-edge practice and accessible. Although this collaboration is touted as a model of cooperation among competitors under the umbrella of the U.S. car organization, the final results of this experiment may not be known until the 12-year contractual period is expired. Clear-coat paint was being applied to cars in the pilot facility (as early as 1996), but the goal of elimination of all VOCs from the painting process is still far off. Design of experiments continues to seek an optimal proven process. The partners continue to ask: Who will be the first to commercialize the process? Further, is the exclusion of the other world players in the auto industry (i.e., Japan and Europe) a critical issue in the persistence of this R&D consortium?

---

[89] Ibid., p. 4.

Other Cases

The trend in both of these cases (SEMATECH and the LEPC) and much of the literature on technological collaboration suggests that the evolution of the partnership relationships seems essential to their persistence. Swan and Ettlie[90] found that there has been a trend toward more sophistication and complexity in governance structures for managing partnerships in landed Japanese manufacturing transplant alliances in the United States. In particular, firms have gone beyond just joint ventures and wholly owned subsidiaries, exploiting partial equity relationships more recently in Japanese direct investment cases. Partial ownership by Japanese parents was significantly more likely in high-tech manufacturing partnerships with U.S. companies. Joint ventures were more typical in politically sensitive industries (e.g., steel and automobile) and when the Japanese firm had experience with the product at home.

Later we report in depth (Chapter 12) on four case studies of U.S.–Japanese manufacturing alliances. Some consistent threads can be noted coursing throughout these four cases, which illustrate and expand on the results of the secondary analysis of the large database of direct investments.

1. All four cases seem to follow an established stereotypical pattern in U.S.–Japanese manufacturing joint ventures: The Japanese partner brings production know-how to the partnership and the U.S. company brings marketing and/or product technology to the partnership. All four alliances had excellent operating performance (e.g., quality levels).
2. Achieving profitability in the venture was more challenging, but the Japanese partner also tends to stick with the venture much longer than a U.S. company would in the same circumstances. Joint ventures (as opposed to total or partial ownership) are more likely in politically sensitive industries such as automobiles and steel.
3. There seem to be clear differences between high-tech and low-tech manufacturing alliances: High-tech collaborations seem more difficult to manage, the motives for formation of the venture are usually quite different, and the outcomes are more difficult to predict. High-tech companies are more likely to use partial ownership.
4. A very integrated organization structure seems to be the successful way to structure these alliances—with no "shadow" Japanese organization structure in place. Litespec, Inc. (Box 5-5) is a good example, with alternative levels of the firm occupied by American and Japanese managers that rotate in these key positions from the home organization and within the hierarchy. For example, the vice president of R&D (American) replaced a Japanese president after 5 years, and a Japanese manager took his vacant spot.

Emergent Models of Persistent R&D Collaboration

Two important theoretical arguments with regard to the persistence of R&D and other technical collaborations across organizational boundaries emerge from this discussion:

[90] P. Swan and J. E. Ettlie, "U.S.-Japanese Manufacturing Equity Relationships," *Academy of Management Journal,* 40, no. 2 (April 1997), pp. 462–479.

1. Founding conditions (e.g., the industry, state of technology development, and competitive context) all appear to set up strong boundary conditions within which these collaborations operate.[91] That is, a strong cohort effect is hypothesized as operating in these technology alliances.

2. All technical alliances, including formal R&D collaborations that meet the requirements of the Cooperative R&D Act of 1984, evolve within these founding boundary conditions in order to survive. This is not a case of volatile environment so much as a process of learning objectives and strategies in uncharted waters.

The recent case of the Channel Tunnel tends to support this theoretical approach. Centralized decision making created cohort difficulties and an absence of flexibility that inhibited evolution of this project.[92] Further, Bolton found that the decision to join an R&D consortium was different for firms during the start-up phase of the alliance (i.e., firms were stimulated to join early on by substandard performance), as opposed to the late adopters, "who were no longer stimulated solely by substandard performance."[93]

SUMMARY

The purpose of research and development is to foster new knowledge creation, support new product and service development, and enhance operations process technology as appropriate. Most R&D funding is applied (problem solving), and most of this is spent on new products or services. The R&D ratio or a measure of R&D intensity is the first rough approximation of how much an organization emphasizes research, and it is calculated by dividing the R&D budget by sales per year. Firms that spend more than 6 percent of sales on R&D are typically called high tech, but there is no hard and fast rule. Other measures used to gauge R&D capability are R&D stock, patenting rate, and number of R&D employees. R&D performance measures vary by the stage of the research process being audited. A good track record for applied research will engender higher budgets as supported by decentralized operations, such as divisions or business groups.

Investment in service-sector R&D in the United States has grown to nearly 25 percent of the total R&D expenditures, which were $206 billion in 1997. This percentage is lower in other countries, but growing. One significant change in the R&D funding profile of the United States is the growing proportion of R&D contracted to universities, which is currently about 2 percent of the total, but increased about 5 percent per year. The overall R&D investment rate is growing about 6 percent per year, although R&D ratios are in decline, like the number of patented inventions to R&D investment and number of R&D employees. There is no agreement on the extent to which this trend is problematical.

---

[91] G. P. Pisano, "The R&D Boundaries of the Firm: An Empirical Analysis," *Administrative Science Quarterly,* 35 (1990), pp. 153–176.

[92] A. Genus, "Managing Large-Scale Technology and Inter-organizational Relations: The Case of the Channel Tunnel," *Research Policy,* 26 (1997), pp. 169–189.

[93] M. K. Bolton, "Organizational Innovation and Substandard Performance: When Is Necessity the Mother of Innovation?" *Organization Science,* 4, no. 1 (1993), pp. 57–75, esp. p. 57.

There is a growing interest in science and engineering ethics, partially fueled by new biotechnology abilities. Dual ladder can help with some human resource issues that are unique to R&D organizations, and mobility of technical and managerial people within and between organizations has been shown to be a significant factor in initiating (managers) and implementing (engineers) process innovations. R&D investment promotes firm success primarily by increasing sales and market share. Many companies have successfully implemented technical strategies by promoting "intrapreneurship," and matrix structures. Collaborative R&D and alliances for innovation are on the rise.

DISCUSSION QUESTIONS

1. Read and analyze Case 5-1. What changes have been made in R&D funding, strategy, and structure at IBM? Why were these actions taken?

2. What has been the impact of these changes so far?

3. What are the long-range implications of these changes (pros and cons)? Defend your positions.

4. Read and analyze Case 5-2. Assume the role of Ernie McLaughlin (the LEPC representative from Chrysler) and make a recommendation to your management on which option (if any) to pursue.

5. What is your justification for selecting this option?

6. Assume you are Richard Pearson, the Ford rep to LEPC. What option did you recommend, and why?

7. Assume you are Tom Meschievitz, the LEPC rep from GM. Which option are you going to support, and why?

8. What do you think are the next critical steps in managing this technology consortium?

ADDITIONAL CASE SUGGESTIONS

1. There are a number of good cases on R&D management. One of the many that involves new product technology is Intel Systems Group, HBS 9-691–040.

2. Many "beyond compliance" cases are available. One is Chrysler Corporation (A): The Jefferson North Assembly Plant, The Amos Tuck School, Dartmouth College, 1995, 13 pages. A video is available.

✗ CASE 5-1

Gerstner Slashed R&D by $1 Billion; for IBM, It May Be a Good Thing

IBM's latest research breakthrough—that it can boost the power of computer chips 40% by implanting them with microscopic circuits made of copper instead of

SOURCE: "Lab Experiment: Gerstner Slashed R&D by $1 Billion," *The Wall Street Journal* (October 6, 1997), pp. A1, A5. Bart Ziegler, reprinted by permission of *The Wall Street Journal* © 1997 Dow Jones and Company, Inc. All rights reserved worldwide.

less-conductive aluminum—rocked the industry. But the discovery, announced two weeks ago, was also sweet vindication for the company's combative chairman, Louis V. Gerstner Jr.

When Mr. Gerstner swept into International Business Machines Corp. $4\frac{1}{2}$ years ago as the first outsider to run the computer giant, the Armonk, N. Y., company was hemorrhaging money and losing market share. Mr. Gerstner shuttered plants and laid off thousands. But one move was especially shocking: He ordered a $1 billion cut in IBM's once-sacred research-and-development budget.

Some said that Mr. Gerstner, who previously ran companies selling credit cards and cookies, had no business tinkering with a technological treasure. They warned of a threat to U.S. competitiveness and feared the Nobel Prize-winning IBM Research Division, which invented such seminal computing devices as the hard-disk drive and memory chips, would be irreparably harmed. "If IBM is getting out [of basic research], who's going to do it?" an alarmed official of the National Science Foundation asked at the time.

But now it appears the cost-cutting and refocusing at IBM Research wasn't such a bad thing after all. Instead of resulting in a demoralized, damaged operation, the changes have energized many at IBM's three major research labs, in Silicon Valley, New York State and Switzerland.

Gone is the heavy emphasis on research for its own sake. Today what matters is getting the fruits of that research to market—and fast.

The changes are helping solve an age-old problem for IBM: Though its labs turned out groundbreaking technology for decades, too often those advances showed up first in the products of competitors. For example, IBM invented a breakthrough computer design called RISC, for reduced instruction-set computing. Unable to protect it with patents, IBM sat back for years while Sun Microsystems Inc. and others turned it into commercial fortunes. IBM missed other industry-altering inventions entirely. Rivals developed the microprocessor and the "graphical user interface"—read Windows—that drove the PC industry and led to huge profits.

This sorry history frustrated Mr. Gerstner. He fumed as Microsoft Corp. and Intel Corp. won much of the industry's adulation and market share, even though they did little basic research and in many instances built their businesses largely on inventions made elsewhere.

Customer Service

And so the new chief executive ordered his company to get its research into its own products. First.

That fiat forced an attic-cleaning. IBM Research abandoned unpromising areas of inquiry, emphasized projects with greater potential and got rid of lower-ranked staff. Scientists were directed to spend much more time with product developers and even customers, something unheard of in the IBM of old.

"This used to be a country-club atmosphere," says Hans Coufal, who works at IBM's Almaden Research Center in San Jose, Calif., where he is trying to perfect a device that one day might replace computer hard drives by storing data in holograms. Under the new regime, Mr. Coufal says, "I really enjoy solving real-world

problems, having the feeling that I'm really needed and appreciated."

The big unknown, however, is whether IBM has lost the serendipity factor. "Eureka!" moments in the lab can't be scheduled into business plans like the launch of a new line of PCs. Instead, they require years of patient, long-term research.

Goodbye Blue Sky

Hundreds of scientists left IBM as it cut research-and-development spending to $5 billion a year from about $6 billion and imposed an even steeper cut of 37% in just the Research Division's $650 million annual budget alone. Many who stayed turned their focus from blue-sky efforts to more mundane product matters. Gone was IBM's quest to be the first to measure the mass of the smallest subatomic particle, the neutrino, in hopes of furthering Einstein's theories. In its place were efforts to develop a foldable keyboard and to improve the little "eraser-head" used to control the cursor in IBM laptop computers. "The long-term outlook went very sour," says Richard Webb, a respected physicist who departed in frustration amid the downsizing in 1993. "Almost everything became short-term directed: solutions and applications."

Mr. Webb, who had been exploring the physical behavior of atoms in very small devices, laments that by cutting his team from a dozen to just two, IBM lost "some brilliant young people ... All the infrastructure I had built up over 15 years was basically destroyed." Now running a research program at the University of Maryland in College Park, he argues that the cutbacks could come back to haunt IBM and other corporate labs. "How long is this going to go on before the technological superiority of this nation is in danger?"

But a close look at IBM's global research effort shows it has hardly abandoned basic science or long-term projects, at least not in the areas it regards as most important to its business. Instead of spreading itself too thin, IBM now tries to target areas where it has both extensive background and the best minds. The Research Division's budget has slowly grown back to about $600 million this year, and its staff is up to 2,785 from fewer than 2,500 three years ago. IBM estimates that 10% to 15% of its researchers are engaged in long-term work.

Paul Horn, IBM's research director, says the overhaul was about more than just cost-cutting. Fifteen years ago, IBM had an iron grip on the mainframe-computer business and controlled the speed with which new technology entered the market. "Now, winning is taking ideas that are very far out and being the fastest in converting them into significant technological advantage," he says.

Any concern about speed-to-market was unheard of in 1945, when Thomas J. Watson Sr., IBM's founder, started the company's first formal science operation by opening a lab at Columbia University in New York. Wallace Eckert, the lab's first director, said at the time that the center's mission was to carry out "scientific research where the problem is dictated by the interest in the problem and not by external considerations."

That ethos continued for many years. In 1961, IBM opened the Thomas J. Watson Research Center in Yorktown Heights, N.Y., an imposing, semicircular building with sweeping glass-and-stone walls. The Research Division became best-known for its basic science involving such esoteric but fascinating areas as fractal geometry and superconducting materials.

Generous research funding continued until the early 1990s, when the mainframe market soured and IBM faced financial crisis. The first cuts began even before Mr. Gerstner arrived, as IBM brass ordered James McGroddy, then its research director, to slash $50 million from the division's spending in late 1992.

"We had been a very rich and happy corporation," says Mr. McGroddy, now retired. "And we were consuming capital like crazy. A lot of things could easily be done much better." He pushed to have 20% of the Research Division personnel working on projects that could directly lead to products and customer services, up from just 2% in 1990. He held meetings to explain why the overhaul was needed, telling scientists "we're going to make a big turn. This change is real." Some were outraged. "They didn't buy the story we were telling," Mr. McGroddy says now.

The pressure intensified after Mr. Gerstner's arrival on April 1, 1993. By 1995, the Research Division budget had plunged to $475 million from $650 million in 1991. Employment at the labs fell to fewer than 2,500 by 1994, down about 1,000 jobs from 1990, with most of the cuts coming from the research ranks rather than the support staff. The division vacated rented buildings and consolidated at IBM-owned sites, shrinking its operation in upstate New York to two buildings from a half dozen. The cuts in the number of buildings and in support staff (to 300 from 600) produced annual operating savings of about $30 million.

Consolidating Brains

IBM also combined research efforts that had been spread out among various labs, in an effort to end overlap. All its work on disk drives, for instance, was moved to its Almaden center in Silicon Valley. Mr. McGroddy killed projects that no longer looked fruitful because of changes in technology, or were ones in which IBM didn't have the best skills, among them "magnetic bubble" memories, astrophysics and chips made from an exotic substance called gallium arsenide. Some researchers in these areas moved to surviving projects inside IBM's labs, while others left to pursue their projects at universities.

At the same time, IBM expanded promising programs that could help customers sooner. These included voice-recognition systems, Internet-security software, data-storage technology and biometrics, which is the use of biological signatures to identify people.

"The difference that the Gerstner regime introduced was, it wasn't enough anymore to just move ideas into the product world. What was important for us in Research was to understand what the market wanted" and then work from there, says Inder Gopal, who left IBM Research last year to join Prodigy Inc.

One way IBM Research responded to Mr. Gerstner's call is a program called First of a Kind, which pairs research projects nearing completion with an IBM customer to help solve a real-world problem. The intent is to come up with a solution that can be replicated for many customers.

Taking Dictation

In one such pairing, researchers developed a voice-response system for radiologists by working with Memorial Sloan-Kettering Cancer Center in New York and Massachusetts General Hospital in Boston. Previously, doctors examined patients' X-rays and dictated their findings into tape recorders for later transcription, causing a delay. Now they can dictate to a PC, which automatically turns the diagnosis into text. The resulting IBM product is now sold to hospitals across the nation.

The research arm's closer interaction with IBM product developers also is paying off. This year alone, work at IBM's labs has found its way into the processing chips inside IBM's popular new mainframes; a wireless modem that links PCs through the airwaves; and a tiny disk drive for laptop computers that can store five billion bytes of information. The Research Division's most-hyped success this year had little to do with business computing: It was Deep Blue, the supercomputer that whipped chess-master Garry Kasparov.

IBM's copper-chip breakthrough, another collaboration between researchers and product people, is likely to have the most long-term impact. The goal was especially elusive: how to form the microscopic circuits on the silicon base of computer chips using copper instead of the traditional aluminum. Copper is a much better conductor of electricity, which means more electrons can move across even tinier circuits, allowing more circuits to be etched into each chip. Added circuitry, in turn, means a more-powerful chip.

Atoms Askew

But copper atoms are unruly. Rather than stay put, they tend to seep into the silicon, contaminating it. "I was starting to think the problems were insurmountable," recalls Randall Isaac, the IBM Research vice president who heads the scientific part of the team. Coating the copper with a barrier to keep the atoms in place was one potential solution, but that required making the copper lines so thin that their advantage over thicker aluminum circuits was negated.

"In the early '90s, one of the break-throughs was to discover a barrier that was thin enough and sticky enough," Mr. Isaac says, declining to discuss the material, which IBM regards as a trade secret. "The ability to find that was one of the outgrowths of our strength in materials science. The resulting technique changes one of the fundamentals of chip making," says John Kelley, a vice president at IBM Microelectronics, the chip division.

Despite the emphasis on pushing research into products, some IBM scientists still do work that is years away from leaving the lab or may never see the light of day. One such scientist is Don Eigler, who gained fame as the first to manipulate individual atoms with a special microscope, spelling out the letters I-B-M with the tiny particles.

Like a Video Game

In his lab at IBM's Almaden center, a mountainside complex surrounded by a 690-acre wildlife preserve, Mr. Eigler moves the mouse attached to a PC. His commands are carried out in tandem in an adjacent room by a needle-like mechanism on a machine the size of a refrigerator. As the microscope's tip passes over a thin layer of copper and manganese, a representation of the manganese atoms appears on the computer's screen as a series of gray blobs. By applying a tiny electric current to the tip, Mr. Eigler can pick up an atom and then set it down nearby. It is an amazing achievement, but one that his exotic setup handles as easily as if this were a video game.

His research into the movement of atoms on surfaces might one day be important in making hard drives and chips. Or it might never help out with products.

Yet even Mr. Eigler, working on some of the "purest" research at IBM, worries about the bottom line. The scientist, who favors black T-shirts and jeans, proudly gives tours to delegations of customers. "It's always a crack-up to me to let them move atoms around. Everybody loves it," he says. His purpose is more than mere show-and-tell, he says; he hopes it "helps build a relationship." Why bother? "I'm an IBM stockholder."

CASE 5-2

The Low Emission Paint Consortium (LEPC)*

It was September 1991. The 1990 Clean Air Act Amendments were just beginning to have an impact on U.S. manufacturing. Plans for a 15 percent reduction in VOCs (volatile organic compounds) by 1996 in ozone nonattainment areas for stationary sources were to be submitted by state air regulators to the Environmental Protection Agency (EPA) by November 15, 1993.[94]

Dick Acosta, vice president of manufacturing, Chrysler Corporation, had convened a meeting to discuss future paint developments. Ernie McLaughlin, manager of paint

* This case was prepared as a basis for class discussion rather than to illustrate either effective or ineffective handling of an administrative situation. Copyright 1995 John E. Ettlie, all rights reserved. This case is not to be reproduced by any means—electronic, mechanical, photocopying, recording or otherwise—without the permission of the author. The cooperation of representatives of the Low Emission Paint Consortium (LEPC) and its suppliers is gratefully acknowledged during the preparation of this case.

systems, was summarizing a proposal to build a $20 million pilot facility to test a new painting technology: powdered clear coat. "None of our current paint facilities can be used to test powdered clear coat. An existing paint booth cannot be modified for test runs. This is a leap ten times greater than anything we have tried before in paint."

"That's an awful lot of money, Ernie—especially for an unproved process," Dick said. "Isn't there some way we could get our suppliers to share the cost of development for powdered clear coat? Or ... do you think ... maybe Ford or GM might be interested?" Maybe there was a way to reduce the risk of going ahead with new automotive painting technology. Then fate intervened.

Two weeks after the Chrysler meeting, John Young, manager of paint systems for Ford Motor Company, called Ernie McLaughlin (a former Ford employee in paint systems) on the telephone. "Ernie, my boss is asking us how to reduce the investment to tackle an unproved coating technology. Is powdered paint really worth it? And how can we get somebody to share the cost?" The seeds for the Low Emission Paint Consortium (LEPC) had been planted.

Background

In 1985, surface coatings and coating operations accounted for 27 percent of all industrial emissions of VOCs. Exposed to sunlight, these VOCs contribute to the formation to lower atmosphere (tropospheric) ozone. Amendments to the Clean Air Act passed in 1990 were designed to significantly reduce VOC emissions of both stationary (point) and mobile (e.g., transportation) sources. Methods for abatement were suggested in the legislation, and the 1991 annual EPA survey of VOC emissions indicated that 1.86 million metric tons of VOC were emitted by industrial surface coating operations— a 15% reduction from 1986 when 2.2 million metric tons were emitted. Other sources of VOC emissions increased by 5% during that same period. The U.S. position in world trade in paints remained strong even though only a few European countries regulated VOCs and no regulations existed in Japan.[95] The EPA was encouraged by these results and appeared to be determined to push even harder with VOC regulation.

Approximately 90 percent of all pollution resulting from automobile manufacturing occurs during final assembly, and 90 percent of these waste streams result from painting and coating processes. The majority of paint facilities in North America at the time (circa 1991) involved a four-step process of (1) wash (phosphate) and ELPO (an electro-deposition dip process for rust-proofing); (2) primer application; (3) base (color) coat application; and (4) clear or finish coat application.

It seemed clear that the original equipment manufacturers could anticipate being regulated into either costly or unprofitable operations in the near future. Abatement was viewed as a non-value-added operation and inconsistent with the EPA's other initiatives in the areas of pollution prevention and development of new environmental technologies for manufacturing.

A second legislative development set the stage for cooperation among domestic organizations. In 1984, the U.S. Congress passed the National Cooperative Research and Development Act, which was designed to allow companies to work together in precompetitive technical collaboration. This legislation was followed in 1989 by the National Competitiveness Technology Transfer Act, which encouraged federal agencies to establish cooperative agreements with industry. This was later followed by the 1993 National Cooperative Research and Production Act designed to further facilitate industrial collaboration

and minimize the legal risks when companies elect to work together to solve technical problems.[96]

Representatives from Ford, Chrysler, and GM began meeting in March 1992 under the umbrella of the MVMA (Motor Vehicle Manufacturers Association), which later became the AAMA (American Automotive Manufacturers Association).[97] All parties agreed initially that it was just a matter of time before VOCs would have to be eliminated from the painting process. Further, there was tentative agreement on one essential enabling condition for cooperation: the Big Three were not in the paint business. Any particular competitive advantage derived from a technical advance in paint would likely be short-lived because the OEMs (original equipment manufacturers) did not make paint or paint systems— these were supplied from outside. Therefore, pooling resources made sense in this highly regulated part of the business. No proprietary product information need be exchanged to make cooperation possible. Most of the competitive advantage in the industry was based on new product introductions.

After the first 6 months of meetings, the committee of Ford, GM, and Chrysler representatives agreed that it might be feasible to substitute powder primer (currently being used by GM and Chrysler) and powder clear coat for those two stages of the painting process. Coupled with the substitution of "water" base coat (greatly reduced VOC borne pigment application), nearly 90 percent of VOC emissions could be eliminated. This held out the promise of the elimination of most of the EPA regulatory burden for future auto painting and coating operations in stationary sources for the industry at much lower development cost. The collaborative goal was not only desirable, it would eliminate the need to try to overcome the traditional adversarial relationship between the EPA and the auto industry, because most of the problem would be prevented at the source.

During the first 6 months of meetings, the committee representatives also agreed to build a new powder clear coat prove-out facility that could duplicate production car application at high line speeds. The site had to be

---

95 B. Bonifant, "Competitive Implications of Environmental Regulation in the Paint and Coatings Industry," *Management Institute for Environment and Business* (MEB), Washington, D.C., 1994.

96 T. Meschievitz, Y. Rahangdale, and R. Pearson, "USCAR Low Emission Paint Consortium: A Unique Approach to Powder Painting Technology Development," *Proceedings, SURCAR,* Cannes, France, June 15–16, 1995.

97 The AAMA (and its predecessor, the MVMA which included the transplant firms) was primarily a lobbying organization and political consortium, not a technical cooperation forum. The advent of USCAR, a neutral, not-for-profit technical venture started by Ford, Chrysler, and GM, in June 1992, provided an alternative auspicious organization which the paint committee eventually sought out. By June of 1995, USCAR hosted 13 active consortia for the Big Three.

near the technical centers of the three car companies (southeast Michigan), had to have complete car painting capability (insisted upon by Ford and Chrysler), but did *not* necessarily have to be convertible to a full production facility after termination of the pilot project.

Since the "high" option (full car body application) for a pilot production facility was selected by the committee, there were two important implications. First, the project was now quite expensive, even when shared by the three companies: $20 million. Second, ready access to car bodies would be a real advantage, so an assembly plant host would likely be the winner in the site decision. It was. The Ford Wixom assembly plant was tentatively selected during these preliminary meetings as the location for the pilot production facility for the first powder electrostatic clear coat application in the auto industry.

The decision to build the facility at the Ford Wixom assembly plant was a compromise. Chrysler had agreed to fund its initial portion of the project with an equal balance of cash and in-kind contribution, and Ford had agreed to fund its initial portion of the project with cash contributions: the value of making its production facility available to the project. GM, on the other hand, already had a small powder lab at its tech center and believed itself to be ahead in powder prime application, and would have little to gain by locating the powder clear coat facility at a Ford assembly plant. GM also considered emission standard timetables to be quite uncertain, validation in production type facility a possibly unnecessary step beyond a more limited, technical center paint system for "clips" (fender and hoods mounted on clip fixtures for test purposes). "Why couldn't the suppliers' facilities be used?" asked one GM representative.

However, there were advantages to a consortium, too. GM would have to pay only one third of the cost of a full-blown production prove-out facility, zero emission standards appeared to be approaching—more rapidly than had been expected, and paint is ultimately supplied anyway, eroding any sustainable advantage. Many at GM and on the consortium believed emissions issues to be a noncompetitive issue—and several other environmental cooperative projects were underway. Integration issues in a normal production facility were unknown. No existing facility could be used to test full production powder clear coat.

Eventually, the committee agreed to accept GM's offer of powder primer technology, equipment, and know-how as an in-kind contribution that would totally fund its initial obligation. No new cash would be initially required of GM for full and equal partnership in the consortium.

The pre-consortium committee had tentatively agreed on one important principle: if the Big Three did not work together, the supplier community would not see the benefit of participating in the development costs needed to implement the pilot production facility. The supply community would ultimately benefit, but the payoff had to be large enough to "make a leap 10 times greater than anything we have done before in paint," as Ernie McLaughlin, the Chrysler representative, said.

The LEPC

Ford (Edison, New Jersey) and GM (Framingham, Massachusetts) had separately experimented with powdered paint in the 1970s, but had dropped the development work due to technical problems. Powder primer was being used by GM and powdered chip-preventive coating was being used by Chrysler when the three companies first met to discuss cooperation on paint systems. A series of three monthly meetings, starting in December 1992, led to the establishment of the LEPC in February 1993, under the auspices of USCAR. The proposal presented at the January 1993 meeting established the founding principles:

- Partners would share equally in all aspects of the consortium.
- All Partners had to agree on every decision taken—no 2-1 votes could pass an issue.

At the February 1993 meeting of USCAR, the charter was ratified to establish the LEPC, with a mission statement that read, in part, "To conduct joint research and development programs on paint-related technologies to reduce or eliminate solvent emissions from automotive painting systems."

The consortium was now able to concentrate on the design details for the facility and supplier selection.

Paint System Supplier Selection

The next critical decision to be tackled by the consortium was the paint system supplier. Paint itself could wait, since much of the work was already underway in parallel at the major (and some new, e.g., Kodak Coatings) paint suppliers. Eventually the choice of systems supplier was narrowed to two: ABB and other.

The selection criteria included not only technical competence issues such as powder booth design (magnitude 3 in the weighting), but also political concerns. If a foreign-based supplier such as ABB were selected, government funding to make up the difference in the funding needed to reach the $20 million level might be jeopardized.

Eventually ABB was selected as the paint systems supplier and with other suppliers, agreed to cost share $4 million in kind for the project. That left a total of $4.2 million outstanding shortfall that had to be funded. This $4.2 million funding requirement was an unexpected roadblock for the consortium. Some consortium members believed that the LEPC might not survive another year until new government fiscal year appropriations became available. And even if new federal funds were available, the old fears of EPA interference in auto industry operations died hard.

The Funding Crisis: Survival of the LEPC

From more or less the beginning of the collaboration between Ford, GM, and Chrysler, it was assumed that some government funding would be available for the powder coating project. Proposals were submitted to NIST (National Institute of Science and Technology, U.S. Department of Commerce), which failed to be funded, and then EPA, and copied other federal agencies. The Environmental Technology Initiative (ETI) proposal at EPA was outstanding until December 1994, when it became obvious, after several feedback deadlines were passed by the EPA, that Congress was not going to fund the ETI. Many members of the consortium were against EPA funding, thinking it would harm the effort in the long-run, because of the past adversarial relationship between the auto industry and the EPA.

The LEPC reported to the management committee at USCAR during their regular monthly meeting in December 1994 that there would be a shortfall of $4.2 million and waited for the reaction. The management committee recommended the representatives of the big three go back to their companies and get the rest of the money ($1.4 million a piece). GM representatives were skeptical that their firm would approve any new funding. Even operating budgets had been very difficult to obtain, and the consortium was about to make a 10-year commitment to an R&D project. GM needed profits now, not in 10 years.

There was doubt about additional funding, even at Ford and Chrysler. These two firms had already allocated millions to the LEPC, but none of this money had actually been spent, just budgeted. The purpose and goals of the LEPC were reopened at all three firms, and suddenly

there were grave doubts about going forward. Maybe it was time to cut losses and take chances alone. Several new options emerged after this critical December 1994 USCAR meeting.

Option 1: Split the $4.2 million and limit the consortium to just Ford, Chrysler, and ABB. Ford and Chrysler had initiated the LEPC, and GM had been a reluctant partner from the beginning. The project had already been sited at Ford Wixom. The USCAR charter allowed for drop-outs in consortia under its articles of incorporation.

Option 2: Press for agreement, and petition top management in all three companies, as was the original intention and purpose of LEPC, for equal cost sharing. Keep the consortium going as planned with full participation of GM, Ford, and Chrysler to focus the supplier community on the problem. Reconsider the site selection at Wixom and possibly move the pilot to a GM plant to secure GM participation.

Option 3: Opt for a less aggressive technical solution to prove-out powder clear coat. For example, a scaled-down pilot facility could be installed adjacent to an existing plant, with little greenfield building required. Limit technology to primarily off-the-shelf powder application to initiate research on the project. Get something going, but install a pilot facility that did not require the additional $4.2 million.

Option 4. Cut losses for all partners. Go back to the individual projects that preceded the consortium, and chalk it up to learning. Limited test facilities in R&D laboratories could be used until the EPA mandated changes and funding from the government and other sources (e.g., suppliers) could be obtained. Dissolve the LEPC, at least for the time being.

As options emerged, it became clear that the existence of the LEPC hung in the balance. The partners considered the options and their derivates as 1995 dawned cold and clear in southeast Michigan. Would the consortium survive? Would it survive in a form that would focus the supplier community? The next LEPC meeting, scheduled for late January 1995, was approaching. Some consortium representatives, especially from GM, doubted the meeting would even take place. Many of the original arguments, pro and con, for a paint consortium resurfaced. Other members felt that the consortium had progressed too far to give up now—in any form. Ernie pondered which option to back.

Chapter 6

Economic Justification and Innovation

> To introduce the concept of economic justification for innovation and to present several alternative approaches to this issue—both philosophically and practically. This chapter expands on these concepts and approaches by presenting several cases of economic planning for new technology projects, including the adoption of computer-aided design (CAD) technology by Simmonds Precision Products.

When organizations make or buy new technology products or services, it is usually considered an investment in the future. Therefore, the finance department of the organization is typically involved in the early stages of planning for a new technology project. These projects come up in even the most placid settings. For example, companies seldom replace broken or worn out equipment with the same model when the older model cannot be repaired. Usually, they buy a new, more advanced model.

But are the traditional finance-based methods of evaluating proposed investments (e.g., discounted cash flow [DCF] analysis) adequate for making important decisions about new technology? That is the essential issue before us here.

Once a proposal has been reduced to a net present value (NPV) or a return on investment (ROI) percentage, other important strategic issues may be overlooked. Contributing to this problem is the contention that the training and experience of general managers will influence the extent to which the product of these traditional methods will go untempered. Consider the factors not captured in the financial analysis, or assumptions that may not be warranted, for example. Proposals to incorporate risk are appealing, but largely untested.[1] A related, but separate, issue is how we account for new technology once it is in place, including post-audits of new technology investments.

Two seminal articles will be used as points of departure in the discussion of these challenges. Robert Hayes and William Abernathy argued in "Managing Our Way to Economic Decline"[2] that a sharp increase in corporate presidents' professional origins toward "financial and legal areas" in the 1960s and 1970s led to decisions based on financial criteria alone, causing vulnerability to competition that took a broader view of the future. It is easy to extrapolate from this observation that this led to shorter-range thinking and underinvestment in new technology.

The problem is far more complex, of course, and some applied research has investigated this issue. (See Box 4-2, "General Managers and Manufacturing Innovation"). Even as the profile of managers changed in the 1980s (CEOs from production and operations increased from 33% to 39% from 1984 to 1987),[3] the issue of whether the traditional methods of capital investment are suited to new technology decisions still remains.

General managers with manufacturing experience are more likely to mount aggressive technology strategies, but are also more likely to emphasize direct labor savings from new technology investments in operations. By contrast divisional managers deemphasize direct-labor savings, and concentrate on investments in training and making organizational changes needed to capture the benefits of new processing technologies. *When divisional managers have manufacturing experience, the new system that is installed achieves significantly higher utilization (80%) than when the divisional manager does not have manufacturing experience (61% utilization).*

The second seminal article, "Must CIM Be Justified by Faith Alone?",[4] was written by Robert Kaplan. In this article, Kaplan addresses the problems of using DCF to justify a particular type of new technology, computer integrated manufacturing (CIM), which involves both the move to programmability of the units of production and the integration of these islands of flexible automation with computers. Kaplan contended that traditional DCF analysis can be used to justify this technology if the method is properly applied. In particular, he believes that the real cost of capital (about 8%) is rarely used in these analyses; typically, double-digit rates are used, perhaps to hedge against the risk of using new processing technology for the first time. This and the way decisions are made in companies (small investments can be approved by plant managers; others must be approved by the board) lead to incremental decisions rather than revolutionary projects. Plant managers tend to propose projects they can approve at the plant level, which might not be sufficient to include new technology.

Companies also underinvest in technologies such as CIM because they fail to evaluate relevant alternatives. For example, most companies fail to take into account that once a new technology becomes available, one or more of the firm's competitors will adopt it. Can current technology sustain cash flows, market share, and profit margins?

---

[1] See for example, P. Liang and F. Song, "Computer-Aided Risk Evaluation for Capital Investment," *Omega, International Journal of Management Science,* 22, no. 4 (1994), pp. 391–400.

[2] *Harvard Business Review* (July–August, 1980), pp. 67–77.

[3] *Wall Street Journal* (October, 18, 1988).

[4] *Harvard Business Review* (March–April, 1986), pp. 87–95.

Another problem is that only easily quantified savings such as labor, materials, or energy are typically incorporated into traditional investment analyses. Often neglected are inventory savings, longer useful life of more flexible and, therefore, more adaptable technology, reduced floor space requirements, higher quality, and even the less tangible increases in flexibility, shorter throughput time, and increased learning. On the other hand, some companies expense software and training for new technology, when they are really part of the investment—a significant part in most cases—which often takes place after new systems are installed (see Box 6-1). Companies installing new software for modern manufacturing systems typically delay development into the software maintenance phase of the project. All these practices render the products of DCF and other traditional methods of justification misleading.

The importance of Kaplan's argument stems, in part, from the dichotomy introduced in Chapter 2. Most R&D in Western firms is spent on new products. Therefore, it becomes much easier to think of investment in new-product-related technologies as "options" on the future of the company, because competitors also face this uncertain future. Manufacturing R&D is often not considered to be a core capability, because manufacturing equipment that embodies this technology is typically purchased from suppliers. R&D managers are more experienced with budgeting for technological risk. But when other units of the organization are involved, an alternative, more traditional investment analysis is applied. Perhaps worse, when new operations technology is involved, representatives of finance must often accept the information provided by the other functions or suppliers as accurate, with little or no alternative methodology or information to challenge these views. The opposite extreme is also dangerous: sophisticated economic analyses techniques are out of reach of decision makers in many companies. The survey evidence actually supports this latter conclusion (discussed later).

R&D managers submit budgets for internal projects and are eventually faced with similar challenges. Who knows exactly what the probability of successful completion of a new technology project might be? These are educated guesses, at best, and often are based on previous project histories that don't apply to the current situation. Rubenstein[5] points out that the time horizons for planning must fit the firm's situation. Projected R&D project returns must be timed to fit with other strategic company moves, such as stock offerings and long-term debt incurrence.

By its very nature, new technology projects are difficult to fit into the "normal" flow of events in the life of an organization. It is not surprising that budgets for radical departures from the past in new product–process system installation, such as the new dishwasher line in GE's Appliance Park, Kentucky, had a budget "buffer" built in to the program equivalent to 10 percent of the original budget on a project projected to have a 25 percent internal rate of return (IRR).[6] What is the current state of practice for economic justification of new technology projects? This issue is taken up next. First, the issue of R&D investment is presented, and then the topic of economic justification for operations process technology is addressed.

---

[5] A. H. Rubenstein, *Managing Technology in the Decentralized Firm* (New York: John Wiley & Sons, 1989), p. 184.

[6] J. Carey, 1997, "Getting to 'Eureka!'" *Business Week* (November 10, 1997), p. 139

BOX 6-1

Manufacturing Software Maintenance

Manufacturing software development and maintenance (like all software maintenance) has emerged as one of the critical problems delaying the timely deployment and effective application of new manufacturing and operations processing technology. After an in-depth investigation of manufacturing plants undergoing modernization of productive systems, it was found that plant users were *more satisfied* with the maintenance process when *some software development was delayed until after the first release of the new system*. The underlying problem of effective new system deployment is often the lack of understanding of general requirements and methods for assisting in the conversion of performance objectives into requirements. For learning to take place, experience with new systems (not just plans or prototypes) is required. *It is extremely difficult to do economic planning and evaluation in this complex environment.*

The challenge of getting new operations and manufacturing software right and getting it delivered on time has become a preoccupation with many managers. Consider the following:

▶ Programmer productivity increases at only 4 percent per year.

▶ A Government Accounting Office (GAO) report on software contracts found that 47 percent of projects delivered were never used.

▶ Maintenance is often 60 percent of software budgets, not including major software enhancements.

These statistics seem rather frightening in and of themselves, but they are even more significant in the face of the more than 200 software tools that are currently available specifically to enhance the productivity of development and maintenance. Computer-aided software engineering (CASE) tools, which promised so much, have really failed to solve the problem of timely, effective delivery of manufacturing systems. CASE technology takes much too narrow a view of the software development process for manufacturing systems and does not address requirements generation in a way that recognizes the true nature of most modernization projects. A balance between customized software and getting moving with something that works, even if it is not perfect, is the approach that is usually recommended.

Users delegate much of software development and maintenance to suppliers and have great difficulty learning their requirements quickly enough to have an appropriate influence on total system design. Professionals differ greatly on their perceptions of whether software or other factors are most important. Information professionals are generally pessimistic about the potential of current state-of-the art tools to solve maintenance problems. We concentrated primarily on the users' perceptions and experience during the software development process and, especially, the software maintenance cycle for advanced manufacturing systems in thirty nine North American plants currently modernizing operations (e.g., installing flexible automation). We measured user's satisfaction with manufacturing software maintenance from answered questions. "How satisfied are you with the software maintenance function?" (Users also report higher satisfaction if they influence the design phase of the overall system equally with suppliers.)

Of eight possible software maintenance activities listed, such as debugging and optimization, only two are significantly correlated with overall satisfaction with software maintenance: *adjustments for new hardware and software,* and *modifications due to requirements, specification, or standards changes.* Our preliminary interpretation of this result is that users tend to prolong the development cycle into maintenance to compensate for lack of understanding of requirements. Users reporting greater satisfaction also report lower system personnel turnover. Cycle time achieved was significantly correlated with inclusion of adjustments for new hardware and software in the definition of maintenance, functional extensions, modifications due to specification changes, and optimization. In summary, we found significant relationships between overall satisfaction with manufacturing software maintenance and trends for inclusion of some, but not all, software development activities in maintenance (post-release project stages).

These results suggest that one of the problems that precipitates the frequent reports of software problems in manufacturing technology modernization is the difficulty users and suppliers have learning requirements in user production plants. Since satisfied users are more likely to include changes due to new requirements and new specifications in software maintenance, to the exclusion of other activities, they appear to be prolonging the development cycle. Learning requirements and developing tools to promote this specification ought to be the key focus of both users and technology suppliers.

One of the implications of these results is that it is very difficult to economically plan and evaluate new technology projects that involve development of new operations software.

SOURCE: John E. Ettlie and Christopher E. Getner, "Manufacturing Software Maintenance," *Manufacturing Review,* 2, no. 2 (June, 1989), pp. 129–133.

$\mathcal{R}$&D INVESTMENT

Two characteristics of the R&D process make application of investment analysis to innovation creation unique: risk and time. First, because R&D seeks to create at least some new knowledge, even if in application, uncertainty is involved. Second, R&D does not pay off immediately. Therefore, a lengthy time horizon usually enters into the investment equation.

Investments in U.S. R&D were expected to reach $192 billion in 1997, an increase of 4.2 percent over $184 billion spent in 1996. According to *Business Week*,[7] most of this money comes from the private sector. This increase is mostly due to growth in R&D spending in the industrial sector and the assumed connection between focused investments in new products and market growth.

R&D investments are now generally thought of as "portfolios" of projects in low, medium, and high-risk ventures. Further, R&D projects, like the creative process,

---

[7] T. Studt and J. Duga, "Increased R&D Is Tied to Long-term Economic Growth", *R&D Management*, 39, no. 1 (1997), p. 35–40.

evolve over time, so R&D investments must also be considered over what most would consider to be multiple budget periods, often at odds with the traditional annual budgeting cycle of the rest of the organization. Figure 6-1 illustrates one approach to balancing high- and low-risk investments over this time period and these investment streams.

According to James Matheson and Michael Menke[8] (Figure 6-1) the cornerstone of developing an effective R&D portfolio strategy is to focus on decision quality. This starts with evaluating the quantifiable characteristics of the company's products: defect rates, useful life, and overall customer satisfaction.

Note that in Figure 6-1, the model information is schematically coded: rectangles are decisions, ovals are uncertainties, squares are results, and arrows are influences. For example, the model starts with the R&D funding level (the box in the lower left). This, in turn, influences decisions about commercialization options and R&D results, which, in turn, influence market values and R&D project values. The authors recommend a six-step process using spider diagrams (six-pointed star map of value) to help value projects in the R&D portfolio:

1. Identify the appropriate frame—the unique context and decision elements— for the project.

2. Generate creative, achievable alternatives.

3. Develop meaningful, reliable information.

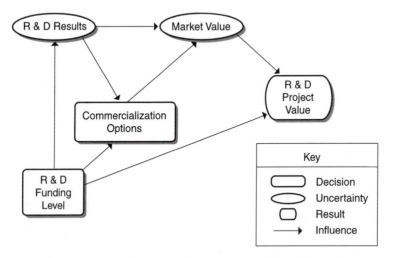

Figure 6-1   An Influence Diagram Identifies Key Decisions and Uncertainties that Help Determine an R&D Project's Potential Value

SOURCE: J. E. Matheson and M. M. Menke, "Using Decision Quality Principles to Balance Your R&D Portfolio," *Research-Technology Management* (May–June, 1994), p. 39, Figure 1.

[8] J. E. Matheson and M. M. Menke, "Using Decision Quality Principles to Balance Your R&D Portfolio," *Research-Technology Management* (May–June, 1994), p. 39.

4. Establish clear values and tradeoffs.

5. Apply logically correct reasoning.

6. Build a commitment to action.

Ultimately, R&D projects are classified according to some scheme. For Matheson and Menke, this method is summarized in Figure 6-2. Projects ultimately are classified as **bread and butter** (high technical success, but relatively low commercial success), **oysters** (long shots, but with potentially big payoff), **pearls** (a few projects with both high technical and commercial success probability), and **white elephants** (projects that should be shelved for later or discontinued). Other types of projects require different management approaches. Pearls, for example, probably need an entrepreneurial approach. Bread-and-butter projects just need to be kept on budget and on schedule, because it is normally just a matter of time before they pay off. Oysters need special care because they are longer term, and it might take many oysters to get a pearl. Try to take on the tough technical challenges first in these projects—you want to find out as soon as possible if there is a pearl in there.

JUSTIFYING NEW OPERATIONS TECHNOLOGY

The state of the art for justifying new technology projects varies by the situation and type of technology being considered. New technology is embodied in new products and embedded in materials and hardware–software operations systems that often combine new technology with the technology of an earlier day.

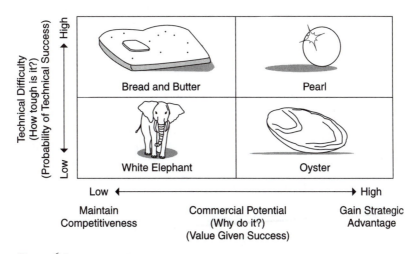

Figure 6-2 The Portfolio Grid Distributes R&D Projects According to Their Probability of Technical Success and Potential Commercial Value Given Success

SOURCE: J. E. Matheson and M. M. Menke, "Using Decision Quality Principles to Balance Your R&D Portfolio," *Research-Technology Management* (May–June, 1994), pp. 38–43, Figure 4.

In the case of advanced manufacturing technology, we have some evidence on the state of the art from a recent study done by Michael Small and Injazz Chen.[9] The authors surveyed 125 durable goods manufacturing plants in the United States with sales of more than $5 million. Respondents were asked to describe the justification techniques used for the evaluation of advanced manufacturing technology (AMT) projects for at least 1 of 16 types such as computer-aided design (CAD), flexible manufacturing systems (FMS), automated materials handling, or inspection equipment and information technologies such as JIT (just-in-time).

Manufacturing plants use a mixture of justification techniques. One plant reported using six of the seven techniques listed as options in the survey. The results are reproduced in Table 6-1. Small and Chen found, like others before them, that there are typical patterns in these justifications data for AMT:

1. Payback and ROI (return on investment) are the most popular techniques (about 53% and 40% of these plants, respectively).

2. Net present value (NPV, 27%) and internal rate of return (IRR, 16%), ranked next in popularity.

3. The use of more sophisticated techniques like risk analysis (5.2%) and weighted scoring models (2.6%) is quite rare.

Further, they found that plants using a combination of economic and strategic justification to determine whether new technology will further its objectives were significantly more likely to be successful with these new technologies than plants that

TABLE 6-1   Usage of Justification Approaches by Plant Size

Plant Size	% of Small	Small	% of Med.	Med.	% of Large	Large	Plant Size Not Reported	Total Plants Using Approach	% of All Reporting Plants
Justification approach									
Strategic alone	6	7.7	0	—	0	—	0	6	5.5
Economic alone	17	21.8	5	26.3	1	12.5	0	23	21.1
Strategic and economic	48	61.5	14	73.7	7	87.5	4	73	67.0
Economic and other	1	1.3	0	—	—	—	0	1	0.9
None	5	6.4	0	—	—	—	0	5	4.6
Other	1	1.3	0	—	—	—	0	1	0.9
Total	78	100.0	19	8	8	100.0	4	109	100.0

Small: $5 million < annual sales < $50 million

Medium: $50 million < annual sales < $200 million

Large: $200 million < annual sales

N = 116 (number of respondents providing information on annual sales = 105).

Source: M. H. Small and I. J. Chen, 1997.

[9] M. H. Small and I. J. Chen, "Economic and Strategic Justification of ATM—Inferences from Industrial Practices," *International Journal of Production Economics,* 49 (1997), pp. 65–75.

used just one method of evaluation. They concluded that "developing easily accessible and understandable means to incorporate strategic criteria into the decision-making process will be the major change to AMT investment in the future."[10] They used factor scores of twelve measures of success, including the amount of time to complete projects, production changeover times, overhead costs, revenues, quality, and variety of products manufactured at the plant, based on self-report methods.

Boyer and colleagues used cluster analysis to group 202 durable goods manufacturing plants by type of approach to investing in AMT.[11] *Traditionalists* do not invest heavily in AMT. *Generalists* make moderate investments in design, manufacturing, and administrative (e.g., MRP, JIT, activity-based accounting) *AMT; high investors* use all three types of AMT extensively; and *designers* emphasize design AMT, such as CAD, engineering, and process planning. Not surprisingly, the greatest increases in technology usage between 1994 and 1996 were for electronic mail.

Initial results showed no relationship between type of investment approach to AMT and success at one point in time (1994). But Boyer[12] later reported that when follow-up data from a subsample (141 plants) two years later (1996) were evaluated, generalists had significantly higher profit and to a lesser extent, growth; high investors were next. Designers had the lowest self-reported performance scores of the four investment approaches.

The implication of these findings, which build on the portfolio approach to funding R&D projects, is that the managers who understand that technology is a system—a relationship between various types of technologies (new, old, low-risk, high-risk, made versus purchased, and so on)—are the most successful.

These results are in general agreement with field studies that used objective measures of performance with new processing technology. Table 6-2 summarizes four sources, all of different types, but all using objective data of performance outcomes with new operations technology. The first entry in Table 6-2 is an academic benchmarking study on the application of flexible automation (manufacturing and assembly) in U.S. durable goods plants.[13] These plants averaged 40 percent ROI and 32.6 percent reduction in scrap and rework using new flexible automation systems. Swamidass[14] found that firms in the same industry groups averaged nearly $60,000 greater productivity (sales per employee) with modern manufacturing technologies ($141,000 sales per employee without new technology versus $200,000 with new technology).

The third entry in Table 6-2 concerns the use of the German software package SAP R/3 for enterprise integration. Results have been mixed for the 7,000 cases in the installed base, as would be predicted by the academic applied research studies. Dell Computer has dropped R/3, but Chevron saved $30 million per year, Compaq Computer cut inventory in half, Microsoft saved $18 million per year, and Owens-Corning has made significant gains using this software. Owens-Corning will

---

[10] Ibid., p. 74.

[11] K. Boyer et al., *Journal of Operations Management,* 15, no. 4 (1997) p. 331. They measured this by indications of worker empowerment, quality leadership, and coordination through nontechnical means. Unlocking the potential of advanced manufacturing technologies.

[12] Ibid.

[13] J. Ettlie and J. Penner Hahn, "High Technology Manufacturing in Low Technology Plants," *Interfaces* 23, no. 6 (November–December, 1993), pp. 25–37.

[14] P. Swamidass, "Technology, People and Management," *IEEE Spectrum* (September 1993), pp. 68–69.

$\mathcal{T}$ABLE 6-2   Summary of New Operations Technology Payoffs

• Durable goods plant modernization programs averaged 40% ROI, 32.6% reduction in scrap and rework (from 4.3% to 2.9%), and 54% through-put time reduction (Ettlie and Penner-Hahn, 1993, p. 31).

• Swamidass (1993) found that these same industry groups (SIC 34–39) averaged $141,000 in sales per employee, while those firms using certain modern technologies averaged $200,000 per employee.

• White, Clark and Ascarelli (1997) in a *Wall Street Journal* article, report on the usage of a German software package, SAP's R/3, for integrating enterprise operations (see Case 9-1). Nearly 7,000 firms are reportedly using the software. Some firms have failed in implementation (e.g., Dell Computer has dropped it). Others are reporting great savings. For example, Chevron says their $100 million investment will save $30 million per year. Compaq Computer says R/3 slashes inventory from $2.2 million per year to $1.2 million per year. Microsoft saves $18 million per year using R/3. Owens-Corning will save $15 this year and $50 million next year, including the elimination of 400 jobs. Sounds like process reengineering–type savings.

• Majumdar (1995) evaluated the impact of switching technology on 40 key U.S. telecommunications firms and found that the immediate effects were significantly higher efficiency and over time this greatly enhanced firm performance (e.g., market share).

• McGuckin, Streitwieser, and Doms (1995) analyzed data collected by the Department of Commerce and found that technology use increased average relative labor productivity by 37% (difference between no technology use and highest technology use) in 1988 and 40% in 1992.

Sources: J. Ettlie and J. Penner-Hahn, "High Technology Manufacturing in Low Technology Plants," *Interfaces* 23, no. 6 (November–December, 1993), pp. 25–37; P. Swamidass, "Technology, People and Management," *IEEE Spectrum* (September 1993), pp. 68–69; J.B. White, D. Clark, and S. Ascarelli, "This German Software Is Complex, Expensive—and Wildly Popular," *Wall Street Journal* (March 14, 1997), pp. A1, A8; S. K. Majumdar, "Does New Technology Adoption Pay? Electronic Switching Patterns and Firm-Level Performance in US Telecommunications," *Research Policy*, 24 (1995), pp. 803–822; R.H. McGuckin, M.L. Streitwieser, and M. Doms, "The Effect of Technology Use on Productivity Growth," Center for Economic Studies, U.S. Census Bureau, Washington, DC (May 1-2, 1995).

eliminate 400 jobs with R/3. These are the type of improvements often reported with successful business process reengineering (BPR)—even though the reported failure rate of BPR is about 75 percent.[15]

Majumdar[16] studied 40 major firms in the U.S. telecommunications industry to see if adoption of electronic switching technology affected performance. It did. In the short run, new switching technology significantly enhanced efficiency by improving scale economies, allowing housekeeping tasks to be routinized, and in other ways. In the long run, these efficiencies substantially affected organizational performance such as market share and adding more business lines.

The last entry in Table 6-2 is a study of more than 36,000 firms on the application of 17 advanced manufacturing technologies from 1988 to 1992. Labor productivity gains averaged 37 percent and 40 percent, respectively, in those two years.

Those are the overall results. What accounts for the difference or variance in gains? This is covered in-depth by Chapter 9. However, a preview is given by

---

[15] White J.B., Clark, D., and Ascarelli, S., 1997, "Program of Pain: This Gerwan Software Is Complex and Widly Popular," *Wall Street Journal* (March 14, 1997), p. A-1, A-8.

[16] S. K. Majumdar, " Does New Technology Adoption Pay? Electronic Switching Patterns and Firm-Level Performance in US Telecommunications," *Research Policy*, 24(1995), pp. 803–822.

results reported by Boyer, Leong, Ward, and Krajewski: *When investment in new AMT is coupled with investment in manufacturing infrastructure, the greatest benefits from these new operations technology adoptions are realized.*[17] This issue is discussed in the next section when post-audits of new technology projects are presented.

JUSTIFICATION IN PRACTICE

The formal models, methodologies, and equations of new technology economic justification can be quite helpful in allowing people to stay focused on top-priority issues: costs, benefits, timing, and scenarios for outcomes. There is little argument about this. But it might be worth pausing for a moment and discussing how this process—whether back of the envelope or rigorous to the point of documenting every possible vantage point and contingency—actually unfolds in practice.

Before delving too deeply into this topic, it should be made clear that one of the great ironies of this process of economic justification—the ultimate equation of "garbage in, garbage out,"—doesn't let you off the hook if you are wrong. In fact, there is a tendency *not* to document all the potential benefits (e.g., anything new presents opportunities for learning) of these projects, because these unaccounted for benefits will be eroded by unforeseen costs. Therefore, any help you can get from formalization of the justification process is usually good. Discipline will ultimately set you free to explore those issues that you can't formalize. Until you formalize the proposal—say, in a NPV equation—you are not free to consider the subtle aspects of the challenges of new technology.

Some analysts and professionals will continue with even more sophisticated modeling after the basics are finished, or will conduct a sensitivity analysis or test assumptions for the robustness of the analysis after the projected net return is calculated. This is done to reveal hidden assumptions, potential potholes, or "gotchas" and weaknesses in the analysis; the goal is to really push for objectivity. An innovation champion, or even a group of people working on a proposal, can easily drift from objectivity into advocacy during the course of a major project planning exercise. When there is time, talent, and rigor, this can be desirable; but for new technology, you can rarely capture everything. Short-term payoffs and *low-hanging fruit* (easy, obvious changes with big payoffs) are emphasized to manage risk (see Case 6-1).

On one particular consulting project, the author encountered a team using a software package that actually assisted the analyst in justifying new technology by letting "outcomes" back up or explode backward into the elements of an economic capital budgeting exercise so that the ends (outcomes of the new technology project like purchase of a robotic system) could be used to justify the means (inputs such as costs for training options and cash stream projections). It is not clear whether this approach stimulates creativity in really understanding the dynamics of process of managing technological innovation or just helps people find information that supports their view of the world, especially a future world.

---

[17] Boyer et al., (1997)

Some aspects of justification are subjects of great debate. One such aspect is choosing a technology supplier or partner. There are many formal models for this decision, including weighing criteria for selection and probabilities of technical success. An example of this process was mentioned in Case 5-2 on LEPC (Low Emissions Paint Consortium). In the LEPC case, consideration was given to several criteria for selection not formally included in the analysis that is documented in the case. For example, when more than one supplier was involved, which is very typical, the planning team tried to decide how the suppliers would work together. Since this technology of powdered clear-coat is not off the shelf, long hours of working together could turn into pure torture if the partners did not have common learning and working styles. It's a hedge against uncertainty.

Many of us have heard or have first-hand experience of cases where planners have "fudged" the numbers or included some information and not other information to make a certain case—positive or negative—for a decision position or alternative. Far too much is made of this practice to dwell on it here. Experience often teaches that it is *what we are unaware of* in this process that is most revealing about its unfolding, rather than what we consciously include or exclude. Most formal treatments of capital budgeting, especially for new technology, urge people to include all the "hidden" costs and benefits in the analysis to keep objectivity alive: Let logic and cool heads prevail. The problem is that unless we have some idea of the difference between the probability distributions of confidence on information, such as competitor responses to our moves, this exercise can be quite frustrating, and some groups cannot deal with it. Good projections, that is, those that are valid for the information available, have at least five common characteristics:

1. They are the product of a sincere attempt to capture many aspects of a problem—and this comes from including the inputs of all relevant disciplines (e.g., marketing, R&D, operations, finance and suppliers).

2. They are documented with the best information available, often from consultants who have no ax to grind, and include contingencies and option purchasing values (staying in a game in case it becomes important tomorrow—as in the early days of biotechnology in the drug industry).

3. They use a time horizon consistent with the culture of the organization. That is, the firm has to be agile enough to meet the timing of the project plan and the projections cannot be so far into the future to be impossible to evaluate.

4. They are simple enough to be understood by everyone.

5. They consider more than one scenario for the future, but do not underestimate competitors.

This last point is worth considering for a moment before moving on. The author was recently involved in planning for a new global product by a major durable goods manufacturer. In the early deliberations of framing a marketing and manufacturing strategy—really a business plan—for the launch of this product, one of the company representatives said that none of the firm's competitors was working on this product category. He was both excited and apprehensive about the project, because his firm has a reputation and track record of being a fast follower rather than a leader or first mover.

During the course of the conversations, it was easy to dwell on the need to keep the project secret, given its early stages and this contention that competitors had not gotten wind of the planned move. Interestingly, other members of the group eventually argued that although confidentiality was important, it would be much more prudent to assume that competitors were working on a similar product idea or could move quickly to imitate it when the news finally got out, as it always does. The reason was simple. A fast moving and therefore lower-cost launch, which got the company on the learning curve sooner, was a much more sustainable strategy. This attitude is a healthy way to approach the uncertainty of innovation projects, even though this product was going to use off-the-shelf, proven technology, because hidden costs and benefits are more quickly revealed using this method. This is learning more quickly by actually *doing,* rather than *deciding to do.* Target costing can help, but only good information can inform good decisions and projections.[18]

 POST-AUDITING INVESTMENTS IN NEW TECHNOLOGY

It will come as no surprise to readers that organizations audit the results of investments in new technology against planned projections of net benefits or against new technology budgets and project goals. But at this point, a little game of Jeopardy might be in order. What percentage of new technology projects in manufacturing operations are post-audited? Is it (a) 25 percent, (b) 33 percent, (c) 50 percent, (d) 75 percent, or (e) 95 percent? The answer may surprise you. About a third or 33 percent, of all major new technology projects in manufacturing technology are formally post-audited.

Robert Howell and Stephen Soucy[19] summarized the results of a survey for the National Association of Accountants and found that more than 65 percent of respondents said they did not perform post-investment audits or audited only on selected investments in advanced manufacturing technology. This 35 percent post-audit rate is in virtual agreement with results reported by Ettlie and Stoll.[20] They reported that in only 14 of 39 cases (35.9%) of U.S. flexible automation installations studied with on-site visits to the durable goods manufacturing plant was a post-audit conducted sufficient to calculate an achieved ROI. At first glance this may seem an alarmingly low percentage, but many quality experts argue that the results of technology investment projects are captured in other, objective production measures already in place. To post-audit projects is to add an unnecessary cost of quality (non-value added) to overhead or burden for that unit.

---

[18]G. Boer and J. Ettlie, "Target Costing Can Boost your Bottom Line," *Strategic Finance,* 111, no. 10 (July 1999), pp. 49–52.

[19] "Capital Investment in the New Manufacturing Environment," *Management Accounting* (November, 1987).

[20] J.E. Ettlie and Stoll, *Managing the Design Manufacturing Process* (New York: McGraw-Hill, 1990), p. 63.

The results from Ettlie and Stoll are presented in Table 6-3, arrayed against the type of restructuring used in design and manufacturing departments to accommodate the adoption of the new manufacturing technology system. Note first that the range of ROI outcomes was quite large: from 1 percent to 119 percent (average was 40% as reported earlier for the same study in Tables 6-1 and 6-2).

More important, when the degree of restructuring is taken into account (from 0, or none, to 5, or the use of cross-functional teams), greater organizational changes (e.g., cross-functional teams) are associated with higher ROI on the project. All but one of these 14 cases that had 20 percent or less ROI (4 cases) used no restructuring. Four of these cases that achieved 40% or more ROI, used either dotted-line relationships for coordination between design and manufacturing or cross-functional teams. The key point here is that administrative (e.g., new organizational structures) changes and technological innovation in operations need to be deployed together to ensure successful outcomes that typically show up on a post-audit review. (See Chapter 9.)

$\mathcal{T}$HE BALANCED SCORECARD

The balanced scorecard was originally introduced by Robert Kaplan and David Norton, in now well-known articles,[21] primarily as a means of trying to capture intangible measures in the corporate performance appraisal process. In the first

$\mathcal{T}$ABLE 6-3   Cross-Tabulation of Special Structures to Manage Simultaneous Engineering and ROI of Projects

Special Structures	ROI												
	1%	5%	11%	15%	20%	24%	30%	36%	40%	45%	50%	100%	119%
None	1	1		1	1					1			
Advertising													
Manufacture Engineering							1	1					
Formalize approval						1							1
Dotted line for new position											1	1	
Cross-functional team				1					1		1		

ROI = return on investment; n = 14 cases.

SOURCE: Ettlie & Stoll, *Managing the Design-Manufacturing Process* (New York: McGraw-Hill, 1998), p. 63.

---

[21] R. S. Kaplan and D. P. Norton, "The Balanced Scorecard—Measures That Drive Performance," *Harvard Business Review*, 70, no. 1 (January/February 1992), pp. 71–79; R. S. Kaplan and D. P. Norton, "Using the Balanced Scorecard as a Strategic Management System," *Harvard Business Review*, 74, no. 1 (January/February 1996), pp. 75–85.

article, the authors summarized their work with 12 companies and describe ways that complement the financial measures with operational measures on customer satisfaction, internal processes, and the organization's innovation and improvement activities. They used what they called a **balanced scorecard** to measure four "balanced" perspectives: customers' views, imperatives for excellence, prospects for improvement and value creation, and how companies look to shareholders. In the second article, Kaplan and Norton extended the balanced scorecard to measure strategic management and the learning organization aspects: translating vision, communicating, business planning, and feedback.

The authors' first contribution is, perhaps, most relevant here. Undervaluing the innovation capacity of an organization will lead to misplaced investments and a relentless commitment to incremental change. Most of the time this is just fine. That's why large, sluggish companies can continue to survive and why some small, aggressive, innovative firms fail. But eventually, balance is required in a grand fashion: the balance between incremental and discontinuous change.

A number of companies have incorporated balanced scorecards into their technology justification process,[22] as well as other, creative ways of improving innovation justification.[23] Multiple case studies and surveys are also available on information technologies and flexible manufacturing, all with the intention of going beyond the traditional discounted cash flow models for capital budgeting.[24]

A rather detailed case study of Chrysler (now DaimlerChrysler) Corporation's justification of rapid prototyping technology adoption includes a step-by-step outline on preparing a proposal and developing information for an innovation justification.[25] This Chrysler case includes information on benchmarking and comparative data for other companies preparing justifications for this technology. Methodologies have also appeared for evaluating the option value of participating in a technology to hedge against future contingencies.[26]

In all these treatments of the justification process, the single most important thing to remember is that any methodology will have to be adapted to the organizational context and conditions under which economic justification will be undertaken. In the equation for change, data and supplied information from sellers of technology will all have to be weighed against the opportunities for learning that will be thrust upon any company facing the future. Risky, yes, but challenging and exciting, too.

---

[22] W. Leavitt, "Technology and Profit: Crunching More than the Numbers," *Fleet Owner,* 93 (October 1998), pp. 51–55.

[23] W. Webb, "Case Study No. 2: Goodyear Shows How Technology Provides Strategic Advantage," *Presentations,* 10, no. 12 (December 1996), p. 38; B. Anderson, J. Wiedenbeck, and R. Ross, "Nondestructive Evaluation for Detection of Honeycomb in the Sawmill: An Economic Analysis," *Forest Products Journal,* 7, no. 6 (June 1997), pp. 53–59.

[24] R. Slagmulder and L. Werner van Wassenhove, "An Empirical Study of Capital Budgeting Practices for Strategic Investments in CIM Technologies," *International Journal of Production Economics,* 40, no. 2, 3 (August 1995), pp. 121–152; B. Lee, "The Justification and Monitoring of Advanced Manufacturing Technology: An Empirical Study of 21 Installations of Flexible Manufacturing Systems," *Management Accounting Research,* 7, no. 1 (March 1996), pp. 95–118.

[25] T. Sorovetz, "Justifying Rapid Prototyping," *Manufacturing Engineering,* 115, no. 6 (December 1995), pp. 25–29.

[26] R. Kumar, "A Note on Project Risk and Option Values of Investments in Information Technologies," *Journal of Management Information Systems,* 13, no. 1 (Summer), pp. 187–193. Also see footnote 52, Chapter 5.

*S*UMMARY

One of the most difficult challenges in the management of technological innovation is to accurately predict what outcomes will result from an unprecedented project or program. Some organizations don't even try to make these predictions, arguing that capital budgeting has no place in the innovation game. Most companies at least go through the motions of documenting an estimate of return on investment or simple payback period, but these estimates usually just replicate the current hurdle rate for going forward, and they are really for bookkeeping purposes. Other companies have attempted more sophisticated approaches to justification of new technology, in some cases based on rigorous models of investment alternatives. Only about a third of companies investing in major new projects in manufacturing and operations audit their results after the fact, and some quality experts say this is an avoidable cost when the results will be obvious by other metrics. Parallel projects offset some of the risk in R&D, but this is usually a costly alternative.

Alternatives to the traditional justification methodologies such as net present value calculations have been suggested. These include calculating the option value of continuing to participate in a new technology, contingent on competitor behavior. One approach suggests that software and training be expensed rather than included in investment calculations. Some members of innovation-proposing groups resist documentation during capital budgeting to capture hidden benefits and offset hidden costs as the technology is understood better and unfolds. Few people take into account the value of learning and the potential increases in capacity to innovate as one of the major benefits adopting a new technology. Technology is a system and "generalists" eventually prevail.

Regardless of the method used, good projections can be obtained by following five simple rules: (1) include inputs from all the disciplines and functions affected by the new technology investment, (2) document and include contingencies, (3) use a time horizon consistent with the culture and context of the firm, (4) use a simple method understood by everyone (e.g., payback is typical), and (5) include more than one scenario of the future. Benchmarking, like that used in the balanced scorecard, can be useful.

*D*ISCUSSION QUESTIONS

1. Summarize a case history from your own experience about economic justification of a new technology investment. How accurate was the original estimate of return? Explain any variances.

2. Read Case 6-1 on Simmonds Precision Products: Does CAD Work?

a. Do you think a 24-month pay-back period is reasonable for new technology investments? Defend your answer.

b. Why are companies conservative in estimating benefits from new ventures?

c. Is it really impossible to estimate the "intangible" benefits of a new technology system? Take an example (e.g., creativity enhancement) and discuss.

d. How can the strategic benefits of such new technology investments be captured?

3. Review Case 6-2 to understand the various traditional approaches to capital budgeting.

ADDITIONAL CASE SUGGESTIONS _____

1. One of the best cases ever written on economic justification for new technology is in the transportation (service) sector: Burlington Northern: The ARES Decision (A): HBS 9-191-122.

✂ CASE 6-1

Simmonds Precision Products: Does CAD Work?

Simmonds Precision Products designs and manufactures measurement, control, and display systems for industrial and aerospace customers. This is a summary of the Simmonds Instrument Systems Division program of justification and implementation of computer-aided design (CAD) and computer-aided manufacturing (CAM) technology. The division is a $100 million annual sales unit of Simmonds located in Vergennes, Vermont.

Like many other companies, Simmonds debated whether to use traditional economic justification and planning models to assess CAD/CAM technology. Capital equipment justification at Simmonds, as at other companies, was dominated by conservative rules such as using direct labor savings and a requirement that payback be obtained in two years or less. Available and budgeted dollars were compared before projects were approved. Capital purchases were reviewed quarterly.

In reviewing source material for CAD/CAM adoption, glowing reports of productivity gains of 10, 20, and 40 to 1 were typical. The detailed information needed to support a payback justification of two years was difficult to find. When details were available, such costs as service were often left out of calculations.

Printed circuit (PC) design at Simmonds presented the greatest potential opportunity to make comparisons, because historical design data were available and the area had adopted computer-aided drafting several years earlier. Mechanical design also had potential, but comparisons were more difficult and experienced users were hard to

find. A third area, manufacturing and graphics, was considered. It was found that a 40-month payback was likely instead of a 24-month payback required by current policy.

Intangibles were then considered, based on the reports of other users. These included promotion of standardization and enhancement of creativity. However, the company elected not to include these benefits in its analysis, because it concluded that hidden costs, such as "psychological factors," would offset these benefits. This is typical of the way people address risk and unanticipated consequences in these cases. These risks are real and should not be diminished. It is difficult to quantify them and fit them into these decisions, but it can be done.

Simmonds' top management continued to support study of the technology and reinforced the strategy that was moving toward integration. Some new technology was going to be needed to facilitate this strategy implementation. A consultant was called in and helped with the capital proposal but was conservative in projecting benefits from adoption.

A CAD/CAM system was adopted. The implementation plan included training, a full-time, centralized design group, and diversion of high-pressure tasks out of the project. The system achieved nearly 100 percent reliability.

Post-audit information is available for PC design. On average, 67 hours and $75 in vendor fees were saved on every standard design made during the first year. PC design time was reduced on average from 119 to 50 labor hours. This data was collected from a computerized project management information system. In the time it used to take to do a feasibility layout, the company could now do four or five layouts. Excluding intangibles, PC design savings were $154,000 during the first year. By the end of 20 months, a total saving of $498,000 had accrued along with a 100 percent reduction in cycle time for production of designs.

In mechanical design, results were not documented since the design process was not automated. A savings

SOURCE: This case was prepared by J. E Ettlie. Drawn in part from R.C. Van Nostrand, "CAD/CAM Justification and Follow-Up: Simmonds Precision Products Case Study," *CAD/CAM Management Studies* (New York, NY, Auerbach Publishers, Inc., 1987). Other material of interest is: Forslin, et al., "Computer-Aided Design: A Case Strategy in Implementing a New Technology," *IEEE Transactions on Engineering Management*, 36, no. 3 (August 1989), pp. 191–201.

of $18,600 was projected in manufacturing as a result of reduction in numerical control programming (NC), but a loss resulted when compared with training costs. Graphics, however, were greatly enhanced.

Production time for graphics was reduced from 2 to 6 hours to 15 to 60 minutes. CAD/CAM had a significant impact on error reduction at Simmonds. A 24 percent reduction in *errors per drawing* (.26 to .20 errors on average) was documented. The cost to correct errors had been running about $14 per error and was reduced to $9.50 per error.

Direct labor reduction in engineering was reduced by 27 percent, permitting an equivalent increase in workload. Overall, after-tax savings for the first 20 months ran about 20 percent ahead of two-year payback expectations.

The centralized design staff experienced lower than average absenteeism, but had to work 10-hour shifts due to staffing limitations. Further, spread of the user base

has been a problem at Simmonds, in spite of this positive initial experience.

Compared with experiences in other settings, such as construction, engineering consulting, and architecture,[27] the Simmonds experience seems typical. Simmonds chose the area easiest to automate (PC) and found it was difficult to spread the application of this technology across the firm. The short-term payoff was high, but the long-term application of this and other technologies of integration is in doubt. However, they have a success to build on, and there is hope that it can be done.

---

[27] J. E. Ettlie, "Innovation in Manufacturing," in D. O. Gray, et al. (eds.), *Technological Innovation: Strategies for a New Partnership* (North-Holland, Amsterdam, 1986), pp. 135–144, has documented the case of failure of a CAD system in an architectural firm.

✳ CASE 6-2

Capital Costs and Investment Criteria

Capital costs affect decision problems in production/operations management whenever a physical asset or an expenditure that provides a continuing benefit or return is involved. From an accounting point of view, the original capital expenditure must be recovered through the mechanism of depreciation and must be deducted from income as an expense of doing business. The number of years over which the asset is depreciated and the allocation of the total amount to each of these years (i.e., whether depreciation is straight-line or at some accelerated rate) represent alternative strategies that are directed toward tax policy. We must remember that all of these depreciation terms and allocations are arbitrary and have not been designed from the point of view of cost data for decision making.

Opportunity Costs

Suppose that we are discussing an asset that is used for general purpose, such as an over-the-road semitrailer truck. Assume that we own such a truck and that the question is. "How much will it cost us to *own* this truck for one more year?" These costs of owning, or capital costs, cannot be derived from the organization's ordinary accounting records. The cost of owning the truck for one more year depends on its current value. If the truck can

be sold on the secondhand market for $5000, this is a measure of its economic value. Because it has value, we have two basic alternatives: we can sell it for $5000 or we can keep it. If we sell, the $5000 can earn interest or a return on an alternate investment. If we keep the truck, we forego the return, which then becomes an *opportunity cost* of holding the truck one more year. Also, if we keep the truck, it will be worth less a year from now, so there is a second opportunity cost, measured by the decrease in salvage value during the year.

The loss of opportunity to earn a return and the loss of salvage value during the year are the costs of continued ownership. They are opportunity costs rather than costs paid out. Nevertheless, they can be quite significant in comparing alternatives that require different amounts of investment. There is one more possible component of capital cost for the next year if the truck is retained, the cost of possible renewals or "capital additions." We are not thinking of ordinary maintenance, here, but of major overhauls, such as a new engine or an engine overhaul, that extend the physical life of the truck for some time. In summary, the capital costs, or the costs of owning the truck, for one more year are as follows:

1. Opportunity costs:
   a. Interest on salvage value at beginning of year
   b. Loss in salvage value during the year
2. Capital additions or renewals required to keep the truck running for at least an additional year

---

SOURCE: E. S. Buffa and R. K. Sarin, *Modern Production/Operations Management* (New York: John Wiley & Sons, 1987).

TABLE 6-4 Year-By-Year Capital Costs for a Semitrailer Truck, Given a Salvage Schedule (Interest at 10%)

Year	End Salvage Value Year-	Fall in Salvage Value During Year	Interest on Opening Salvage Value	Capital Cost. Sum of Fall in Value and Interest
New	$10,000	—	—	—
1	8,300	$1,700	$1,000	$2,700
2	6,900	1,400	830	2,230
3	5,700	1,200	690	1,890
4	4,700	1,000	570	1,570
5	3,900	800	470	1,270
6	3,200	700	390	1,090
7	2,700	500	320	820
8	2,300	400	270	670
9	1,950	350	230	580
10	1,650	300	195	495

By assuming a schedule of salvage values, we can compute the year-by-year capital costs for an asset. This is done in Table 6-4 for a truck that costs $10,000 initially and for which the salvage schedule is as indicated. The final result is the projected capital cost that is incurred for each year. If we determine the way in which operating and maintenance costs increase as the truck ages, we can plot a set of curves of yearly costs. The combined capital, operating, and maintenance costs curve will have a minimum point. This minimum defines the best cost performance year in the life of the equipment. Beyond that year, the effect of rising maintenance costs more than counterbalances the declining capital costs.

Obsolescence and Economic Life

By definition, when a machine is obsolete, an alternative machine or system exists that is more economical to own and operate. The existence of the new machine does not cause an increase in the cost of operating and maintaining the present machine. Those costs are already determined by the design installation, and condition of the present machine. However, the existence of the new machine causes the salvage value of the present machine to fall, inducing an increased capital cost. For assets in technologically dynamic classifications, the salvage value schedule falls rapidly in anticipation of typical obsolescence rates. Economic lives are very short. On the other hand, when the rate of innovation is relatively slow, salvage values hold up fairly well.

Table 6-5 compares year-by-year capital costs for two machines that initially cost $10,000 but have different salvage schedules. The value of machine 1 holds better; machine 2 has more severe obsolescence in its salvage schedule. The result is that capital costs in the initial years are greater for machine 2 than for machine 1. The average capital costs for the first five years are

TABLE 6-5 Comparison of Capital Costs for Two Machines Costing $10,000 Initially but with Different Salvage Schedules (Interest at 10%)

	Machine 1				Machine 2		
Year-End Salvage Value	Fall in Value During Year	Interest at 10% on Opening Value	Capital Cost	Year-End Salvage Value	Fall in Value During Year	Interest at 10% on Opening Value	Capital Cost
$10,000	—	—	—	$10,000	—	—	—
8,330	$1,670	$1,000	$2,670	7,150	$2,350	$1,000	$3,850
6,940	1,390	833	2,223	5,100	2,050	715	2,765
5,780	1,160	694	1,854	3,640	1,460	510	1,970
4,320	960	578	1,538	2,600	1,040	364	1,404
4,020	800	482	1,282	1,360	740	260	1,000
3,350	670	402	1,072	1,330	530	186	716
2,790	560	335	895	950	380	133	513
2,320	470	279	749	680	270	95	365
1,930	390	232	622	485	195	68	263
1,610	320	193	513	345	140	49	189

Machine 1 $1,913

Machine 2 $2,198

Therefore, if the schedules of operating expenses for the two machines were identical, machine 1 would seem more desirable. However, because the timing of the capital costs is different for the two machines, we adjust all figures to their equivalent present values.

Present Values

Because money has a time value, future expenditures will have different present values. Because money can earn interest, $1,000 in hand now is equivalent to $1,100 a year from now if the present sum can earn interest at 10 percent. Similarly, if we must wait a year to receive $1,000 that is due now, we should expect not $1,000 a year from now, but $1,100. When the time spans involved are extended, the appropriate interest is compounded, and its effect becomes much larger. The timing of payments and receipts can make an important difference in the value of various alternatives.

Future Single Payments

We know that if a principal amount P is invested at interest rate i it will yield a future total single payment S in n years hence if all the earnings are retained and com-

pounded. Therefore, P in the present is entirely equivalent to S in the future by virtue of the compound amount factor. That is:

$$S = P(1 - t)^n$$

where $(1 - n)^n$ = the compound amount factor for interest rate i and n years.

We can solve for P to determine the present worth of a single payment to be paid years hence:

$$P = \frac{S}{(1 + i)^n} \times S \times PV_p$$

where $PV_{1p} = 1/(1 + i)$,^{n} the present value of a single payment of $1 to be made n years hence with interest rate i. Therefore, if we were to receive a payment of $10,000 in 10 years, we should be willing to accept a smaller but equivalent amount now. If interest at 10 percent were considered fair and adequate, that smaller but equivalent amount would be:

$$P = 10,000 \times 0.3855 = \$3,855$$

because

$$\frac{1}{(1 + 0.10)^{10}} = PV_{1p} = 0.3855$$

Section Three

New Products, New Processes

Chapter 7

New Products

*C*HAPTER OBJECTIVES

To introduce the concept of new product development from various functional perspectives. This chapter reviews the issues, models, and methods of the new product development (NPD) process. Idea generation is taken up in an exercise at the end of the chapter. To test the model of predicting the probability of success of a new product commercialization, the case of Acuson and the company's new product, the Sequoia, is included at the end of the chapter. The launch of the Sequoia presents the challenge of making predictions about the likely success of a new product. Finally, the issue of continuous improvement of a product in the field is introduced with a case from 3M Health Care, also at the end of the chapter.

It was a gray day in late November 1995 at the Boston meeting of the Decision Sciences Institute. The city site of this professional association moves every year, but the purpose is the same. This is the meeting where many of the faculty in business schools from around the country gather once a year to compare notes on research, teaching, and academic life in general. An important session, titled "Global Empirical Research on Operations Management," is about to begin. In a hotel conference room with a capacity of 50, more than 70 people are trying to fit in. People are sitting on the floor, in the doorway, straining to see in from the hall. Global manufacturing is a hot issue.

Six ongoing global manufacturing projects were updated by my colleagues for this eager group. The details of these projects are far too numerous to recount here, but some interesting, even startling, convergences in the results of these projects are worth noting. (Manufacturing strategy was formally introduced in Chapter 8.)

First, it seems clear, especially among multinational manufacturing companies, that what firms focus on and emphasize in manufacturing strategy and practices is similar all over the world. For example, my colleague, Jay Kim from Boston University, reported from the Manufacturing Futures Survey that *the current, top manufacturing priority in Japan, the United States, and Europe is* **new product development.** Period.

Second, and most important for practitioners, there appears to be some early but solid indications that successful practices are also similar around the world, regardless of economic region. For example, Peter Ward, from The Ohio State University, reports that successful manufacturing strategies are similar in Singapore and the United States. Confronted with the same business environments, successful manufacturers choose similar strategies, regardless of location. For example, the more dynamic the business environment, the more successful companies emphasize delivery performance, flexibility, and quality competitive strategies. Poor performers emphasize cost to a fault, while often pursuing these same initiatives ineffectively. These results held up even across industries sampled in the study and can be taken as very robust.[1]

Another example of this type of convergence was given by my colleague, Clay Whybark from the University of North Carolina, Chapel Hill, representing the Global Manufacturing Research Group. He reported that North American and Western European non–fashion-textile and small-machine tool companies differ very little in manufacturing practices such as sales forecasting and materials management methods.[2]

In our own work, which is part of the International Manufacturing Strategy Survey, funded in part by the London Business School and Chalmers University in Sweden, we also observe convergence. For example, we have found that R&D intensity (R&D expenditures as a percentage of annual sales) is significantly related to existing and improved market share, across twenty countries and among all the durable goods manufacturing industries. Market share improvement is also significantly enhanced by the following:

▶ Positive changes in the speed of new product development (note the agreement with Jay Kim's findings)
▶ On-time deliveries
▶ Customer service

These factors are driven by computerization of manufacturing.

Bottom line: New product development is the hot button and is likely to be more than just a passing fancy. Recall the R&D investment profile data in Chapter 1: Current data indicate that the majority of R&D dollars are now being spent on the new product development (NPD) process.

WHAT IS A NEW PRODUCT?

New products are consumer or industrial offerings for the first time, but how many of these offerings are really new? Table 7-1 provides one summary:

---

[1] The details of the first part of this work are found in P. T. Ward, R. Duray, G. K. Leong, and C.-C. Sum, "Business Environment, Operations Strategy, and Performance: An Empirical Study of Singapore Manufacturers," *Journal of Operations Management,* 13 (1995), pp. 99–115.

[2] A full account of these results is given in G. Vastag and D. C. Whybark, "American and European Manufacturing Practices: An Analytical Framework and Comparisons," *Journal of Operations Management,* 12 (1994), pp. 1–11.

TABLE 7-1   New Product Development

Year	New Products Introduced	% New
1997	25,261	6%
1996	24,496	7%
1986	NA	19%

SOURCE: *Marketing News,* March 30, 1998

That is, according to Table 7-1, most new products are really not **new to the world,** but just copies or *one-off* imitators of existing products, with only slight changes from existing products. This is important to keep in mind when evaluating the literature on new product development. It is important to always ask, "Is this (or are these) new product(s) really new to the world?" The *newness rate* is in decline, from 19 percent in 1986 to 7 percent in 1996 and 6 percent in 1997, apparently because more new products are being introduced that are *not* new to the world.

NEW PRODUCT DEVELOPMENT

Ford Motor Company announced in the summer of 1996 that it was "overhauling" the firm's product development system. Instead of 36 months, it will take only 24 months to develop a new car, which will reduce cost by $1 billion annually.[3] Not to be outdone, Toyota and Mazda have both since announced that they will develop a car in 18 months, most likely because Nissan had said they would launch a car in 19 months.[4] Car companies are not alone. As indicated earlier, most companies in Europe, the United States, and Japan now report that new product development is their number one strategic manufacturing priority, according to the Boston University Manufacturing Futures Survey. But is there really anything new here? Let's take a closer look.

Not mentioned in the article about Ford's revamping of the NPD process are product performance and quality. Many people believe there is a tradeoff between speed to market, quality, and product performance. A recent applied research article on this subject is a good starting point in finding out what is new about new product development. The article was authored by Morris A. Cohen and Jehoshua Eliashberg of the Wharton School, University of Pennsylvania, and Teck-Hua Ho, formerly of the Anderson Graduate School of Management, University of California at Los Angeles, and now part of the Wharton School in the Marketing Department.[5] Cohen and his colleagues have developed a model that has much to

---

[3] M. Connelly, "Ford to Revamp Development," *Automotive News,* 70, p. 1.

[4] *Automotive News,* January 27, 1997, p. 24, and *Automotive News,* March 17, 1997, p. 3, respectively.

[5] M. A. Cohen, J. Eliashberg, and T.-H. Ho, "New Product Development: The Performance and Time-to-Market Tradeoff," *Management Science* 42, no. 2 (February, 1996), pp. 173–186.

say about the additive multistage model of the NPD process, but some of their most interesting conclusions are these:

▶ Concentrate efforts on the most productive stages of the new product development process—this may vary by firm—and outsource non-core strengths. Don't allocate efforts evenly across all the stages of the NPD process.

▶ There is little point in developing an *ambitious* new product if the competitive performance is either very low or very high.

▶ Concentrating on time to market alone and minimizing this time period tend to lead to incremental product improvement and do not maximize profits. Product performance must also be taken into account.

▶ New products with superior performance effectively act as an entry barrier— both time-wise and performance-wise—for competitors.

▶ Replacing existing products always delays the time to market and performance target for the new product vis-a-vis introducing the first generation of new products.

▶ The optimal strategy is to use faster speed of improvement to develop a better product rather than to develop a product faster.

This last result, in particular, contradicts much common wisdom that it is better to use incremental product improvement than significant product improvement as a competitive weapon.

Do these conclusions hold up in practice? The early indications are that they do. For example, in our recent survey of the new products and the development process efforts for U.S. durable goods manufacturing, we asked representatives of 126 new product development teams if they had a program in place to upgrade the new product development process. In nearly 90 percent of these cases, managers answered yes to this question.

What was the focus of these programs to improve the new product development process? We expected **time to market** to be the most important issue and to dominate these survey reports, given the popular and professional publications of the day. This was *not* the case: In 47 (39%) of the valid response cases of new product development, **quality** was the most important focus of the program development effort for NPD. True, time to market was second, with 44 (36%) of the cases, but it was not first, and it did not dominate responses. Quality and time to market accounted for 91 (75%) of the valid responses. (Recall that this includes 13 or 11%, of the respondents who said they had no new program to upgrade the NPD process. Five respondents did not answer this question.)

We concluded that a balanced strategy of NPD effort improvement was the key to success in durable goods manufacturing. Further, an integrated approach to new product development, well beyond the minimal notion of simultaneous engineering teams, is required and significantly supports product market and customer knowledge development efforts. These NPD process improvement efforts can significantly enhance the odds of new product success. For example, **balanced sourcing of ideas** (i.e., giving equal weight to R&D and marketing in new product idea generation and refinement) can improve the odds of a new product's commercial success by 30 percent.[6] Further, the well-established literature on technological gatekeepers shows that the success of the development process in R&D depends on the two-step flow of communication: First to or from a technological gatekeeper—a formal or informal team leader in the lab—and then to or from team members in the R&D groups. Research and service use a different, one-step, communication pattern (scientists and managers, respectively).

$\mathscr{T}$HE NEW PRODUCT DEVELOPMENT PROCESS

As an alternative to the flavor of the month, we generally do get a flavor of the year, or flavor that lasts about a half-decade, from time to time. For example, the *Wall Street Journal* published an article on the "Next Big Thing," which essentially discussed how the process reengineering gurus are trying to "remodel" their approach to changing organizations by taking people into account.[7] If this sounds as ridiculous to you as it does to me, we are on the same wavelength.

We have endured time management, knowledge creation, the Lopez factory of the future in Brazil (see Chapter 12), and endless management gurus, and all the attendant hype that goes with these big splash mavens and buzzwords. We have become conditioned to expect another outrageous fad, but it seems unlikely that product development by fad is the best way to approach this challenge.

It is argued here that *the* continuing challenge is the **new product (or service) development process (NPD).** It is so important (perhaps the single most important issue) that it would be difficult to spend too much time pondering this issue.

It is not merely the cost to develop new products that is at stake. The actual quality of new products and supporting services continues to be a nagging issue. Lexus and BMW not only have good products, they are getting better at the NPD process as they introduce new products. They are hard to catch because they have learned how to improve products in ways that please customers with sustainable internal quality efforts. They have learned how to learn. They are building capability every time they experiment with new initiatives, new products and features, and new engineering and manufacturing processes. Not only are products difficult to imitate in timely fashion, but also the culture that enables new product and new service introduction is difficult to imitate.

Fortunately, help is on the way. Numerous, high-quality and big-impact applied research projects are underway on this challenging subject of managing the NPD process. We present just a few here.

Robert G. Cooper, and Elko Kleinschmidt at McMaster University in Hamilton, Ontario, Canada, have recently published an article that is an example of the cur-

---

[6] See J. E. Ettlie, "Integrated Design and New Product Success," *Journal of Operations Management,* 15, no. 1 (February 1997), pp. 33–55.

[7] J. B. White, "Next Big Thing," *Wall Street Journal* (November 26, 1996), pp. A1, A13.

rent best information becoming available on this challenging subject of the NPD process.[8] Cooper and his colleague did a benchmarking study of 161 business units and found that there were four critical drivers of several important performance measures (e.g., profitability and success rate of new products). There is space here only to summarize the findings of this important study, so do not take this as a substitute for the original article if NPD is on your mind:

▶ When it comes to profitability, the strongest driver is the *existence of a high-quality, rigorous new product process*—you need to emphasize upfront homework, "tough Go/Kill decision points," very sharp early product definition, and flexibility. Merely having a formal new product development process does not distinguish high from low performers. It is how the NPD is structured that matters.

▶ The role of a new product strategy in the business unit has a significant impact on performance. This strategy must be clearly communicated and must contain new product goals for the business unit. The areas of focus need to be clearly delineated, and the role of new products in the long-term plan should be well understood by all.

▶ Resources are important. Adequate resources of money and people and focused R&D funding are critical to success. Just having cross-functional teams is not enough—it is the quality of these teams that matters.

▶ R&D intensity is also very critical. R&D intensity is the percentage of sales spent on R&D. (Other research has found that only about half the R&D intensity of a firm or business unit can be accounted for by the industry in which the firm competes. The auto industry typically spends 3 to 4 percent of sales on R&D—which is not a high-technology level. This would have to nearly double before autos would be considered high technology.) Further, R&D intensity does not predict profitability, per se, but usually predicts market share or market share increases.[9]

✺ The R&D–Marketing Interface

Essential to the understanding of the success of NPD and new service development is an understanding of the relationship between R&D and marketing. But there is more to this issue than meets the eye. There are subtle constraints on incorporating the "voice of the customer" in any organization—it is so obvious, it is often overlooked. Everyone in a company "agrees" with the idea that customers are important, but strategy tends to carry the day; companies don't want to stray too far from their core competence. Herein lies the tension. Can customers be satisfied in a dynamic world by the core capabilities of the firm?

Setting aside, for the time being, the idea that no organization can generate all the technology needed to "surround" a new product or new service development program, there are few instances where a customer has actually invented the new

---

[8] R. G. Cooper and E. Kleinschmidt, "Winning Businesses in Product Development: The Critical Success Factors," *Research-Technology Management* (July–August, 1996), pp. 18–29.

[9] J. E. Ettlie, "R&D and Global Manufacturing Performance," *Management Science,* 44, no. 1 (January 1998), pp. 1–11. Also review Chapter 5 on this issue.

product for you. Enlisting the aid of lead users helps convert VOC (voice of the customer) into product ideas,[10] but this conversion process is difficult and takes time (Case 7-1).

Essential to getting new products and new services in timely fashion with the right attributes to satisfy customers' unspoken needs is the management of the interface between R&D and marketing. But the functions remain distinct in this process. There are just a few key areas where intense interaction and information sharing are paramount. These include *understanding customer needs, monitoring market developments, and monitoring multiple R&D projects.*[11]

Time Compression in the New Product Development Process

As mentioned in the next section, perhaps the single biggest mistake that managers make in understanding the NPD process is adopting some new approach or method such as cross-functional teams for the first time and thinking that it will speed up the development process for new products or new services. While it is true that most of the methods used to improve NPD do eventually speed things up, it also takes time to learn how to use these new methods. That slows things down. The payoff in speed comes later, with the second or third application of the new methods.

Having said that, several general guidelines have been proven to work when it comes to taking unnecessary time out of the development process. The first is to simplify. Next, eliminate noncritical steps.[12] Reconsider all the milestones, all the features, all the tests, and focus on just the value-added steps from the *customer's* viewpoint. In the Hewlett-Packard (H-P) case (see Case 3-2), a critical point was reached in the development of the first ink-jet printer just before launch. Engineers wanted to get the technical details right on the product, and market research showed that the first adopters didn't care about technical elegance. H-P improved the product after the first introduction and continues to improve it.

If you want to speed things up *don't add more people* and *don't ask for more hours.* More people will slow the process down (as they try to catch up and learn what is going on) and "turning up the heat" will disrupt the creative thinkers on the team. Most new product teams are already self-motivated and are working at

---

[10] E. von Hippel, "New Product Ideas from "Lead Users," *Research-Technology Management,* 32, no. 3 (May/June, 1989), pp. 24–27. C. Wagner and A. Hayashi, "A New Way to Create Winning Product Ideas," *Journal of Product Innovation Management,* 11, no. 2 (March 1994), pp. 146–155.

[11] A. Gupta and D. Wilemon, "Changing Patterns in Industrial R&D Management," *Journal of Product Development Management,* 13, no. 6 (November 1996), pp. 497–511. Also see R. K. Moenaert and W. E. Souder, "Context and Antecedents of Information Utility at the R&D/Marketing Interface," *Management Science,* 42, no. 11 (November 1996), pp. 1592–1610; T. Haggblom, R. J. Calantone, and C. A. Di Benedetto, "Do New Product Development Managers in Large or High-Market-Share Firms Perceive Marketing–R&D Interface Principles Differently?" *Journal of Product Innovation Management,* 12, no. 4 (September 1995), pp. 323–333; A. K. Gupta and D. Wilemon, "Improving R&D/Marketing Relations: R&D's Perspective," *R&D Management,* 20, no. 4 (October 1990), pp. 277–290 with respect to offensive R&D strategies and the effectiveness of the R&D-marketing interface see A. N. Link and R. W. Zmud, "Additional Evidence on the R&D/Marketing Interface," *IEEE Transactions on Engineering Management,* 33, no. 1 (February 1986), pp. 43–44.

[12] M. Millson, S. Raj, and D. Wilemon, "A Survey of Major Approaches for Accelerating New Product Development," *Journal of Product Development Management,* 9 (1992), pp. 53–69.

physical capacity, anyway. Asking for more will only hurt. This is the time to work smarter, not harder. Pressure and learning do not go together. It is speed-up of learning that is at the heart of accelerating the NPD process. Look what happened when the heat was turned up on the Apple Newton development project (*New York Time*, December 12, 1993). The results were more than painful on the Newton project—they were tragic.

Finally, the two biggest strategic barriers to speeding up a development project are the *wrong technology* and *meddling general managers*. Use only incremental technology when you are trying to meet a project deadline—don't try anything new when you have to make time (keeping in mind that a mix of incremental and breakthrough projects ensure long-term success). And if general managers leave a team alone, the group will usually capitalize on the window of opportunity. How many times is it absolutely necessary to speed things up as opposed to reducing the cost of NPD, long-term? These are two different goals. If a general manager intervenes once a project is started, not only will things slow down, but morale will be adversely affected because trust will be eroded.

THE SEVEN MYTHS OF THE NEW PRODUCT DEVELOPMENT PROCESS

Numerous articles and books have been published on NPD, and they all basically say the same thing: Know your customer. Few go much beyond that. Here, we will attempt to do that. First, the myths of NPD must be confronted.

1. *The customer is number one.* Although it seems obvious on the surface, it is simply not true in the successful NPD. Your organization is number one. Put your people first, and they will figure out what the customer wants. The Southwest Airlines case can be used to illustrate this.[13] Reviews of applied research findings, presented later, also support this notion.

2. *The marketing department dominates the successful new product launches.* Again, not true, or true only for short periods of time during the early stages of the NPD. Successful new product or new service development requires a *balanced* integrated approach. If one function in the organization gets the upper hand, eventually, if not sooner, something will go wrong. The key functions are R&D, marketing, and operations. Both the sharing of technology among multiple projects and the speed of technology leveraging are important to sales growth.[14]

3. *Shortening the time to market is the issue.* False. Timing in the marketplace is everything. Companies have been so slow in the past and have had such

---

[13] See K. and J. Freiberg, *Nuts: Southwest Airlines Crazy Recipe for Business and Personal Success* (Austin, TX: Bard Press, 1996).

[14] K. Nobeoka and M. A. Cusumano, "Multiproject Strategy and Sales Growth: The Benefits of Rapid Design Transfer in New Product Development," *Strategic Management Journal,* 18, no. 3 (1997), pp. 169–186.

bloated NPD budgets and costs that any reduction in the time to market looked good. Unfortunately, this axiom became a substitute for thinking and strategy review. Shorter product introduction times tend to shorten product lifecycles, as well, which is not a socially responsible or sustainable policy or philosophy for the natural environment of the planet.

4. *Adopting new software packages—as well as new team management principles, new suppliers, customers, and wallpaper for the copy room—will shorten the NPD.* Not true. Especially the first time you change your NPD process, for every day that you take out of the schedule by using these valuable methods and techniques, you will have to add back at least one day to learn how to use them. Boeing's development history of the new 777 aircraft, launched in June 1995, is a prime example. Boeing was smart enough to actually add additional months into the development cycle so employees could learn Boeing's new approach to NPD. (See Chapter 11.)

5. *The thing that makes NPD projects late is your customer changing specifications.* It only seems so. Rather, it is the absence of a robust NPD that causes late delivery of new products and services. The use of the term *robust* here is derived from statistics. A robust inferential statistic, like the Student's *t*-distribution test of the difference in population means, is robust against the assumption of the shape (normal or gaussian distribution) of the populations being compared and from which you are sampling randomly. Don't use unproven technology or further R&D, and don't let general managers interfere with the NPD if you want to be on time.

6. *Competitive benchmarking will guarantee success in new product or new service development effort.* Michael Johnson and I have done research on the use of quality function deployment in new product and service development that qualifies this axiom. Although both voice of the customer and internal operations process improvement promote success, competitive benchmarking used to improve operations actually has a negative effect on keeping the voice of the customer "deployed" across the various stages of the development process. Only companies that are able to resolve the internal conflict that is often set up by competitive benchmarking and market research designed to capture the customer's voice are actually successful at developing new products or processes.[15]

7. *Most new products fail once they are introduced into the marketplace—just a few are big winners.* Not really. About 60 percent of new products succeed after introduced (return some multiple of the investment to develop and launch them).[16] New product ideas do fail along the way, sometime after they are born and before they are approved for launch. Estimates vary, but of all new ideas, perhaps one in seven is realized.[17] But once they are out there, most succeed. This does not mean you cannot increase the odds by as much as 30 percent (footnote 6).

---

[15] See J. Ettlie and M. Johnson, "Product Development Benchmarking versus Customer Focus in Applications of Quality Function Deployment," *Marketing Letters,* 5, no. 2 (1994), pp. 107–116.

[16] A. Griffin, "PDMA Research on New Product Development Practices, Updating Trends and Benchmarking Best Practices," *Journal of Product Innovation Management,* 14 (1997), pp. 429–458.

[17] *Wall Street Journal* (May 1, 1997), p. A1—survey of 400 product development professionals.

PREDICTING NEW PRODUCT SUCCESS

Mitzi Montoya-Weiss and Roger Calantone have published a meta-analysis (systematic statistical review of the literature) on new product performance.[18] For statistically inclined readers, their table, summarizing the statistical results of the meta-analysis is reproduced as Table 7-2.

For discussion purposes of this chapter, the Montoya-Weiss and Calantone results have been truncated, and the definition of the variables for the top four sig-

TABLE 7-2   Correlations of Strategic, Process, Market, and Organizational Factors with New Product Success

Factor	Number of Studies	Percent of Total[a]	Number of Measures	Average Measures/ Study	r	$\lvert r \rvert$	Range	
Strategic factors:								
Technological synergy	6	50	18	3.0	.218	.273	−.332	.446
Product advantage	5	42	22	4.4	.311	.363	−.426	.518
Marketing synergy	5	42	24	4.8	.137	.303	−.312	.479
Company resources	3	25	4	1.3	.297	.297	.191	.446
Strategy	1	8	9	9.0	.324	.324	.190	.510
Development process factors:								
Protocol	7	58	27	3.9	.293	.341	−.471	.599
Prof. technical activities	7	58	27	3.9	.256	.282	−.352	.415
Prof. marketing activities	5	42	20	4.0	.308	.337	−.297	.517
Prof. pre-develop. activities	5	42	14	2.8	.240	.288	−.331	.370
Top management support/skill	2	17	12	6.0	.232	.260	−.169	.380
Financial/business analysis	1	8	4	4.0	.182	.267	−.170	.330
Speed to market	1	8	1	1.0	.177	.177	.177	
Costs	0	0	0	0	0	0	N/A	
Market environment factors:								
Market potential	4	33	18	4.5	.179	.244	−.260	.453
Environment	2	17	4	2.0	.293	.293	.180	.380
Market competitiveness	0	0	0	0	0	0	N/A	
Organizational factors:								
Internal/external relations	3	25	15	5.0	.305	.305	.145	.604
Organizational factors	3	25	16	5.3	.304	.304	.080	.500

[a] Twelve studies were included in this analysis.

SOURCE: M. Montoya-Weiss and R. Calantone, "Determinants of New Product Performance: A Review and Meta Analysis," *Journal of Product Innovation Management* 11 (1994), pp. 397–417.

[18] M. Montoya-Weiss and R. Calantone, "Determinants of New Product Performance: A Review and Meta-Analysis," *Journal of Product Innovation Management,* 11 (1994), pp. 397–417.

nificant correlations of new product success are compiled in Box 7-1. We focus on
Box 7-1 now for the discussion of predicting new product success.

What the authors found, essentially, is that to ensure the success of your next
new product, you need to cover these four bases:

1. *Customer perception of product advantage.* The new product must be clearly
   better than the competition on quality, cost/benefit ratio, and function.

2. *Protocol (product and marketing).* Your organization must have a first-rate
   marketing and technical department that gets it all right—concepts that are
   feasible to make to satisfy customer needs.

3. *Proficiency in marketing activities.* Market research must be excellent; prototypes must represent final needs, sales, service, and so on.

4. *Strategy for the project.* The corporate strategy and new product goals must
   be consistent.

These are not the only factors associated with new product success, but they are
the most important. Study Table 7-2 for a comparison of these factors with the others evaluated. Note that speed to market was not very important. Montoya-Weiss
and Calantone believe this could be because not many studies have rigorously

---

BOX 7-1

Significant Correlates of New Product Success

1. Customer perception of product advantage (.363)

   Product Advantage. Product advantage refers to the customer's perception of
   product superiority with respect to quality, cost/benefit ratio, or function relative to
   competitors.

2. Protocol (product and marketing requirements) (.341)

   Protocol. Protocol refers to the firm's knowledge and understanding of specific
   marketing and technical aspects prior to product development; for example, (1) the
   target market; (2) customer needs, wants, and preferences; (3) the product concept;
   and (4) product specification and requirements. This factor includes "origin of idea"
   measures as well.

3. Proficiency in marketing activities (.337)

   Proficiency of Market-related Activities. This factor specifies proficiency of marketing
   research, customer tests of prototypes or samples, test markets/trial selling, service,
   advertising, distribution, and market launch.

4. Strategy for the project (.324)

   Strategy. This factor indicates the strategic impetus for the development of a project
   (e.g., defensive, reactive, proactive, imitative). Measures of product positioning
   strategy are included, as are measures of "fit" between the new product and
   corporate strategy.

SOURCE: Montoya-Weiss and Calantone, 1994.

investigated speed. Materials presented earlier suggest that speed is the *only* important factor under relatively *rare* circumstances. In some industries, such as high-technology-products markets where product lifecycles are short, speed is essential. Occasionally a firm encounters unusual circumstances, for example, when a competitor is about to enter your product or geographic space. Timing is the issue.

$\mathcal{U}$SING MODELS OF NPD FOR COMMERCIAL SUCCESS

What are the causes of successful new product introduction? We studied 126 new durable goods products[19] introduced between 1990 and 1992. One of the first questions we asked was whether these firms had a program to revamp and upgrade the NPD process. The vast majority (90%) said they did. What areas did the program cover? The frequency distribution in order of importance (no program and missing cases are excluded, percentages are rounded) is presented in Table 7-3. These results indicate that quality and time to market (cycle time of the NPD) are the two key drivers of these NPD upgrading efforts, as mentioned earlier.

The results of the causal model analysis are summarized in Figure 7-1. Not only do these results verify and replicate earlier findings on commercial success of new products, including the success/failure rate of 60/40 of new products, once they are introduced,[20] the empirically supported model expands our knowledge considerably about what works to promote a successful NPD. The implications of the results are as follows:

1. Commercial success of new durable goods products depends directly on the degree to which the launch firm or business unit *understands market (and customer) needs*. No shock here.

$\mathcal{T}$ABLE 7-3   Frequency Distribution of NPD Programs

Area of NPD Revamp	f(%)
Quality	47 (37%)
Time to market	44 (35%)
Plant modernization	4 (3%)
Suppliers	3 (2%)
Other	11 (9%)

---

[19] J. E. Ettlie, "Integrated Design and New Product Success," *Journal of Operations Management,* 15, no. 1 (February 1997), pp. 33–55.

[20] Abbie Griffin, "PDMA Research on New Product Development Practices, Updating Trends and Benchmarking Best Practices," *Journal of Product Innovation Management,* 14 (1997), pp. 429–458.

2. Market-need understanding, in turn, is promoted significantly by an *integrated approach to design*. This is more than just teams of representatives of the various departments in the firm; this is a disciplined approach to design, with skills sets integrated to synergize the development process. Job rotation (including cost accountants), permanent transfer across disciplines such as design and manufacturing engineering, compatible CAD (computer-aided design) systems, common databases, and new policies such as salary equity in the engineering disciplines are part of this new approach to NPD.

3. Integrated-design approaches are promoted significantly by three other factors. First, an *early mover strategy*—the attacker's advantage. That is, it is not necessary to be first; an early or fast follower can enjoy some or all of the advantages of being first in moving in a new product area.[21] Second, *adopting or developing CAD-CAM systems* is proprietary to the firm. These systems fit the unique requirements of the company. Third, *NPD method benchmarking* promotes integrated design. That is, determine not only which firm has a

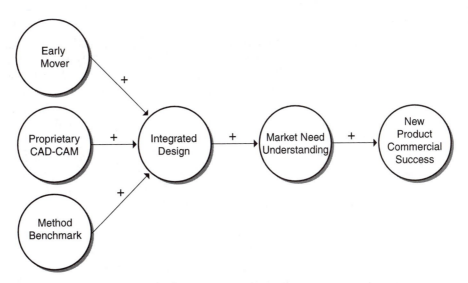

Figure 7-1 Commercial Success of New Durable Goods Products in the United States

SOURCE: J. E. Ettlie, "Integrated Design and New Product Success," *Journal of Operations Management*, 15, no. 1 (February 1997), pp. 33–55.

---

[21] Two recent publications reinforce these findings. The first and early mover advantage is a much more complex issue than most strategists have acknowledged. For example, in a comprehensive review of the literature on first mover advantages, it was found that "Entry order effects exist, especially with respect to market share, but they are better specified as interactions than as direct effects," p. 1116 in M. B. Lieberman and D. B. Montgomery, "First-Mover (Dis) Advantages: Retrospective and Link with the Resource-Based View," *Strategic Management Journal,* 19 (1998), pp. 1111–1125. In addition, another empirical study found that "first-movers and early-movers enjoy both a highly sustainable pricing advantage and a moderately sustainable market share advantage," p. 683 in R. Makadok, "Can First-Mover and Early-Mover Advantages Be Sustained in an Industry with Low Barriers to Entry/Imitation?" *Strategic Management Journal,* 19 (1998), pp. 683–696.

practice in NPD that is best, but understand what that means for your firm. If it is a unique practice, it will be hard to imitate, by definition.[22] So the key is to understand how your firm can uniquely capitalize on the knowledge of others.

Yes, benchmarking is popular and is *required* by the Malcomb Baldrige National Quality Award guidelines, but it is poorly understood. Common sense is often wrong. For example, the Hawthorne experiments, which spawned the Hawthorne effect and the Human Relations School of Management, did not really prove that productivity will improve simply by paying more attention to the worker. Alternative explanations and a closer, objective look at these famous data suggest that people were afraid of losing their jobs, and they would have done nearly anything to keep them, including working under experimental conditions.[23] In other words, the entire Human Relations movement in management was started using only partially correct assumptions, at best.

✕ The Platform Approach to Product Development

Perhaps the most important theme to emerge in product development over the last two decades is the **platform approach** (Figure 7-2). It has been used successfully by many companies (e.g., Sony for portable cassette players, and Hewlett-Packard for inkjet printers) to launch a variety of products, improve others with derivatives, and renew some faded ideas with intergenerational technologies. Many believe Boeing's series of commercial aircraft (up until the Boeing 777) were all derivatives of the first jetliner, the 707.

The product family is the unit of analysis, and it is used to guide decisions in R&D, such as when a firm should renew its underlying technologies and designs of new products. "Streams of new products generated by firms may be thought of as evolving product families. A product family is defined as a set of products that share common technology and address a related set of market applications."[24]

The diagram of product families and their platforms suggests an evolutionary model of how a single product family undergoes successive platform extensions and new platform development, with respective follow-on product developments on each platform version. The commercial success of one product family not only sustains itself, but also makes possible new platforms. Both incremental and potentially radical innovations are sustained by this process.

If this platform approach sounds too tidy, it may actually be more difficult to pull off than it looks on paper. One case in the auto industry will serve as an example of this problem. When a company divides its business into platforms,

---

[22] See J. Barney's, "Organizational Culture: Can It Be a Source of Sustained Competitive Advantage?" *Academy Management Review,* 11, no. 3 (1986), pp. 656–665.

[23] R. H. Frank and J. D. Kaul, "The Hawthorne Experiments: First Statistical Interpretation," *American Sociological Review,* 43, no. 5 (October 1978), pp. 623–643; S. R. G. Jones, "Was There a Hawthorne Effect?" *American Journal of Sociology,* 98, no. 3 (November 1992), pp. 451–468.

[24] M. H. Meyer, and J. M. Utterback, "Product Development Cycle Time and Commercial Success," *IEEE Transactions on Engineering Management,* 42, No. 4 (November 1995), p. 297.

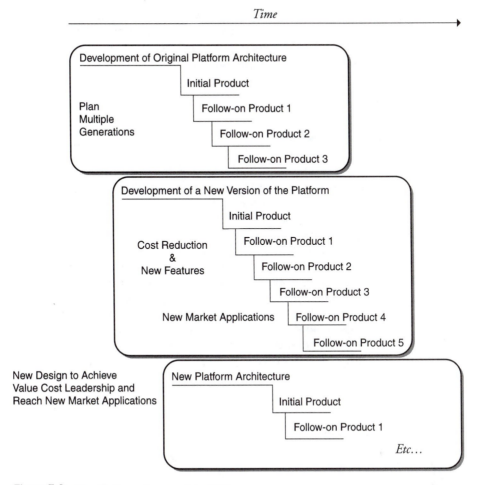

Figure 7-2   The Platform Approach to NPD

SOURCE: M. H. Meyer and J. M. Utterback, "Product Development Cycle Time and Commercial Success," *IEEE Transactions on Engineering Management,* 42, No. 4 (November 1995), p. 297.

such as car models, the relationship between the platforms becomes critical to sustaining technological leadership to sustain the effort. If most of the resources of the company are devoted to the platforms themselves, little will be left, unless it is outsourced to suppliers, for technological convergence and sharing. Since all the platforms run in parallel—much more so in practice than is shown in Figure 7-2—then the platforms compete for scarce resources and run the risk of not having the new technology when renewal is mandated. Toyota has used a strong chief engineer model to resolve these disputes.

One advantage of the platform approach is that it helps promote customization of the product to subgroups of customers. As long as specifications are met for a wider group of market niches, the company is bound to be successful.[25] On the

---

[25] R. B. Lieber, "Now Are You Satisfied? The 1998 American Customer Satisfaction Index," *Fortune,* (February 16, 1998), pp. 161–163; J. Martin, "Your Customers Are Telling the Truth," *Fortune* (February 16, 1998), pp. 164–168.

other hand, product proliferation can erode the cost advantage of the platform method. The point: Increased customization promotes customer satisfaction, but variety is costly. Some type of balance must be struck between these two criteria. A good operations organization can reduce the delivered cost of any product or service. But if it is the wrong product or service, who cares?

$\mathcal{S}$ ET-BASED DESIGN

Ward and Seering coined the term **set-based design** in 1987[26] to refer to a process of specification development that gradually narrows options by eliminating inferior alternatives until a final solution is reached. Ward refers to the old or more traditional type of concurrent engineering approach to design as *point-based,* depicted graphically in Figure 7-3.

Ward and colleagues[27] used Toyota's product development process as an example of set-based design to illustrate how this new approach violates all the "rules" of the point-based approach. For example, Toyota uses many prototypes and tests them early in the process. In the United States and Europe, only one or two prototypes are used, and they generally don't appear until the end of the process. This approach doesn't slow down Toyota; quite the contrary, those known parts of the specifications are released early in the process; especially to suppliers. Figure 7-4 illustrates this approach. Set-based design advantages are summarized in Box 7-2.

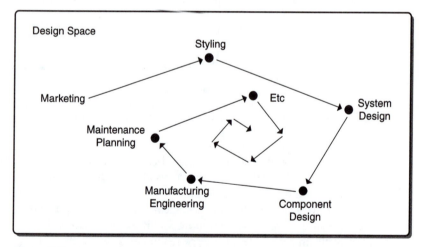

Figure 7-3   Point-Based Design
SOURCE: A. Ward et al.,[27] Figure 8-4.

[26] A. Ward and W. Seering, "Quantitative Inference in a Mechanical Design Compiler," *Proceedings of the First International ASME Conference on Design Theory and Methodology,* Montreal, Quebec, Canada, 1989, pp. 89–98.

[27] A. Ward, D. K. Sobek, J. J. Cristiano, and J. K. Liker, "Toyota, Concurrent Engineering, and Set-Based Design," in J. Liker, J. Ettlie, and J. Campbell (eds.), *Engineered in Japan* (New York: Oxford, 1995), pp. 192–216.

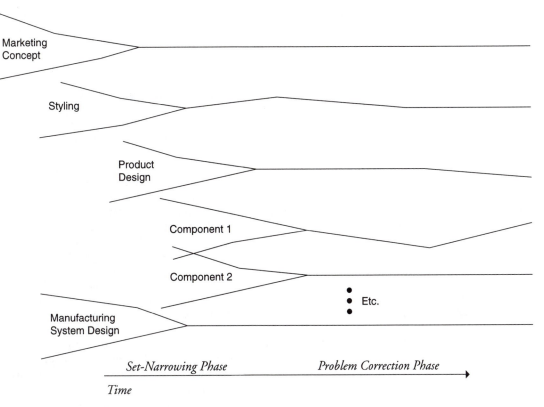

Figure 7-4 Toyota's Set-Based Design Process
SOURCE: A. Ward et al., 1995, Figure 8-5.

BOX 7-2

The Advantages of Set-Based Design

1. Set-Based Design Enables Reliable, Efficient Communications

In conventional, point-to-point search, every change made by part of the organization may invalidate all previous communications and decisions. Because designs are highly interconnected in ways that may not be obvious, it is generally impossible to know whether a particular change will invalidate previous decisions or facts. Often, teams simply run out of time to make more changes and so hastily patch together something that fits.

Most of us have experienced this phenomenon in the simplest of all concurrent engineering problems—selecting a meeting time. With a group of any significant size, agreement on a meeting time satisfactory to all parties requires a long period of time and intense communication. This is the dilemma of a point-to-point search.

Conversely, in a set-based approach, all communications describe the whole set of possible solutions. As the set narrows, the surviving solutions remain true (a fact that can be demonstrated using formal logic.)

BOX 7-2 (continued)

A set-based approach to planning a meeting would be for all the participants to submit the times that they would be available to meet within the desired time frame. Each person agrees not to schedule any additional commitments until an agreement on the meeting has been reached.

This difference between point-based and set-based communications has a number of consequences. Most obviously, it eliminates work wasted on solutions that later must be changed (e.g., scheduling and rescheduling meetings). Second, it reduces the number and length of the meetings required for communication. In the conventional approach, every change requires a new meeting. Furthermore, because the consequences of the decisions are unclear, several decisions must be made collectively, which can result in relatively prolonged meetings. Conversely, Toyota's engineers and suppliers can work mostly independently, because each meeting communicates information about an entire space of designs including suppliers.

A third consequence of set-based design regards the reliability of information. With a point-based approach, members of the team have strong incentives to delay getting started if the information on which they must rely is subject to change. This incentive is much reduced if people can count on their information's being correct. As long as the participants in our meeting example agree not to schedule any other commitments until this time is set, we can be sure that they will be available during the set of possible meeting times they submitted. This may be a major reason that Toyota can allow the parts of the team to get started when they think they need to, rather than having to force them to follow a rigid schedule, and it promotes trust.

2. Set-Based Design Allows Much Greater Parallelism in the Process, with Much More Effective Use of Subteams Early in the Process

It makes little sense, in terms of the conventional paradigm, to start planning the manufacturing process before the product is defined. If the design is still in the iteration loop, it will be subject to further modifications that are neither bounded nor predictable and that could nullify significant portions of process planning, thereby discouraging early process design. Conversely, in the set-based paradigm, it makes perfect sense to think about, early in the design, the set of manufacturing processes that might apply to a set of possible products. Thus, innovation in the manufacturing may drive innovation in the product design, as described in Whitney's discussion of Nippondenso's jikigata designs. That is, the manufacturing team is free to focus on a new part of the product design space, to assume that the product will be designed just as much to fit the new manufacturing system, as they will have to fit the manufacturing system to the new product.

Development Strategy Framework

It is important to compare the set-based approach to other approaches to design that have been advocated in order to see how different it really is. There appear to be clear similarities between set-based approaches and those advocated by Wheelright and Clark. Their **development strategy framework** is reproduced in Figure 7-5. In particular, there is the same *funnel* compression, but also note the absence of a *parallelism* and early prototyping outlined by Toyota and the set-based design methodology. This paralleled approach to development is well known in R&D management circles. To meet an aggressive deadline when technical uncertainty is operating, options are kept open until they are mutually resolved. This approach is gen-

3. Set-Based Design Allows the Most Critical, Early Decisions to Be Based on Data

It is widely (and, we think, correctly) believed that the earliest decisions about designs have the largest impact on the ultimate quality and cost but that such decisions also are made with the smallest amount of data. Powerful engineering analysis tools, such as finite element analysis, are difficult to apply until the design has been detailed. In consequence, major changes often must be made late in the design process. Engineering change orders are expensive, and many organizations try to reduce them by "doing it right the first time." But this solution is equivalent to telling members of the organization to try harder and be more careful, usually not particularly useful advice. Toyota has a specific mechanism for "doing it right": Explore the space of possible designs before making the important decisions.

That is, before Toyota's managers establish specifications for subsystems, they already have seen a variety of subsystems being designed and tested. They therefore can optimize their specification decisions in order to determine the best fit between subsystems and the best overall system.

4. The Set-Based Process Promotes Institutional Learning

Designers are notoriously resistant to documenting their work. One reason may be the sense that documentation is generally useless. Describing the process of changes by which a design arrived at its final configuration is equivalent to providing a set of directions to where you are now—but the next design will use the current one as a starting point, and the directions will be useful only if the team is tempted to backtrack.

Conversely, the Toyota process helps the members of the team form mental "maps of the design space," because a larger fraction of the space is systematically explored. As an example, Toyota's suppliers usually give Toyota their test data, analysis results, and trade-offs between different factors on several design alternatives—valuable information on which sound decisions can be made for the current vehicle. This knowledge is useful in the future, too; for example, the cooling-fan design that was too large for the current car may be perfectly suited to the next one. Hence, members of the Toyota team start with a far better picture of what they want than other designers do, and then they refine that picture more deeply by further exploring of the design space.

Only about 5 percent of Toyota's first-tier suppliers reported problems created by the lack of knowledge on Toyota's part, compared with 22 percent for other Japanese companies and over 50 percent for U.S. OEMs.

SOURCE: A. Ward et al., 1995.

erally more costly, but can pay off in the long run by delaying final tradeoffs until technical viability or feasibility is fully understood. How does Toyota afford this more expensive, time-consuming process and still meet deadlines? Not only does it benchmark other companies such as Honda and DamlierChrysler Corporation, but it assigns more engineers working more hours to projects (during and *after* work).

The Four-Phase Approach

As a final contrast, compare these two approaches (Figures 7-4 and 7-5) with the General Motors Corporation four-phase approach, summarized in Figure 7-6.

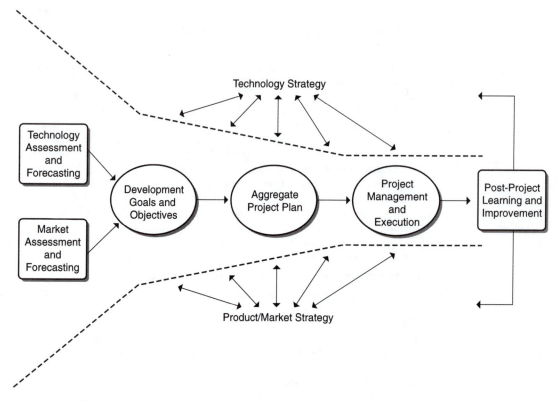

Figure 7-5   Development Strategy Framework

Using this proposed framework for development strategy, the technology and product/market strategies play a key role in focusing development efforts on those projects that collectively will accomplish a clear set of development goals and objectives. In addition, individual projects are undertaken as part of a stream of projects that not only accomplish strategic goals and objectives, but lead to systematic learning and improvement.

SOURCE: S. Wheelwright and K. Clark, *Revolutionizing Product Development* (New York: Free Press, 1992). Reprinted with permission of the Free Press, a Division of Simon & Schuster, Inc. Copyright © 1992 by Steven Wheelwright and Kim B. Clark.

The **four-phase approach** is designed to accomplish two things: delegate design to the people closest to the development process and use nonreversible (except for safety) "gates" to proceed through the design process. In this way, things are done right the first time. There are also at least two barriers to successfully implementing any "gate" procedure in the NPD. First, once the general specifications have been approved by general management, the process will be destroyed if top managers reverse themselves later in the development cycle. Second, if information is withheld or missing from the development groups and their NPD process, it will eventually erode any trust and performance increments achieved along the way.

Note the differences between the four-phase and set-design approaches. There is no "funnel" and no "parallelism" in the GM approach. Further, it takes GM nearly twice as long as Toyota to go through the four phases. By then, markets, customers, and technologies might have moved on.

GM Vehicle Development Process

NAO Vehicle Launch			
Phase 0	**Phase 1**	**Phase 2**	**Phase 3**
1. Bubble-up initiation	1. Approval to build	1. Approval to start	1. Performance
2. Concept initiation			
3. Concept requirement			
4. Concept alternate selection			
5. Concept direction	2. Final approval	2. Production	
6. Divisional design approval			
7. Concept approval			

Figure 7-6   GM's Four-Phase Approach

SOURCE: A. Fleming, "Think Bank: Launch Center's Goal Is To Get Our Designers On The Road Sooner," *Automotive News* (February 22, 1993), p. 3, ff.

Benchmarking and Experimentation in the NPD Process

Many of the methods already outlined involve rapid iteration of ideas at various stages of the development process. Empirical evidence from research studies on the design process is beginning to systematically document the effects of this approach, and they are positive.

For example, Stefan Thomke found that experimentation, which is really a form of problem solving, can account for 43 percent of the difference in project outcomes during new product development of integrated circuits.[28] In particular, "a given experiment can be conducted in different "modes" (e.g., computer simulation and rapid prototyping) and ... users will find it economical to optimize the switching between these modes as to reduce total product development cost and time." Prototype iterations work better in this industry. This approach is also being documented in combinatorial chemistry and is having an impact on the economics of the drug-discovery process.[29]

The task of forecasting in the marketing arena is making flexibility in development more important. Experimentation methodologies promise to help with this problem, but this is not the only solution.[30] An entire array of methods and techniques will have to be brought into the NPD if success probabilities are to be increased. Benchmarking has the potential to be one of the best.

In our study of 126 new products[31] we asked people to nominate the best design and new product development companies. The results are summarized in Table 7-4. Which companies are the best benchmarks? Clear winners are Hewlett-Packard (by far, with 10 mentions and in different industry groups),

---

[28] Stefan H. Thomke, "Managing Experimentation in the Design of New Products," *Management Science,* 44, no. 6 (June 1998), pp. 743–762.

[29] S. Thomke, E. von Hippel, and R. Franke, "Modes of Experimentation: An Innovation Process—and Competitive—Variable," *Research Policy,* 27, no. 3 (July 1998), pp. 315–332.

[30] S. Thomke and D. Reinertsen, "Agile Product Development: Managing Development Flexibility in Uncertain Environments," *California Management Review,* 41, no. 1 (Fall 1998), pp. 8–30.

[31] See footnotes 19.

𝒯ABLE 7-4   Which Organizations Are Good NPD Process Benchmarks?

Company Named	Frequency
Hewlett-Packard	10
Motorola	4
Honda	3
Toyota	2
IBM	2
Sun, GM, Ford, Milliken, Martin Marietta, Ingersoll Rand, Cannon, General Dynamics, Boeing, Chrysler, Xerox, Compaq	1 each

SOURCE: Adopted from J. Ettlie, "Integrated Design and New Product Success," *Journal of Operations Management,* 15, no. 1 (February 1997), pp. 33–35.

Toyota, Motorola, Honda, and IBM. Since H-P is mentioned so often, it is not surprising that others have documented its approach to design (Box 7-3).

Note that customer and user needs, along with strategic alignment, are the first two criteria on the H-P list. That is, the key implied issue is the resolution of *things*

BOX 7-3

Successful Product Criteria

Wilson's Criteria

Edith Wilson of Hewlett-Packard identifies ten crucial success points that seem to distinguish the successful projects from the unsuccessful. Her conclusions are based on her Stanford University thesis, when for a year she probed seventeen projects in such diverse areas as microwave and communications, electronic instruments, analytical instruments, medical products, and work stations. The ten success points are as follows:

1. **Customer and user needs.** The entire team must understand the needs and the problems of the potential user or customer and identify how the product will satisfy those needs or resolve those problems.

    Difficulties in this area are typically caused by the team:

     Not allotting sufficient time or resources to studying customer needs, perhaps because of insufficient funding

    ▶ Segmenting the market improperly, or grouping several markets together

    ▶ Not calling on the right customers

    ▶ Not being properly trained in customer research methods, or using them improperly (this might occur if the team is top-heavy with technical people and lacks adequate representation of marketing)

    ▶ Not calling on users of competitive products

2. **Strategic alignment.** The product must fit into the long-term strategy of the business unit. Otherwise, it may not get the support it needs from senior management, marketing, technical, or other groups.

Strategic alignment problems often occur because senior management has not planned a long-range strategy. Or if a corporate strategy has been selected, the goals of the various groups in the organization may not be aligned with it. Indeed, without clear and consistent strategic goals, various groups might be unwilling to commit their resources in any particular direction, fearing that a later shift in strategy will undermine their efforts.

3. **Competitor analysis.** The team must understand not just the products that competitors develop but how the competitors are satisfying the needs of the customer and solving the customer's problems. The team's product must do those things better than the competition is expected to do at the time of product release.

Problems might arise here if the team looks primarily at a competitor's product but misses the competitor's distribution channels, marketing strategy, or product support.

4. **Product positioning.** The product must be properly positioned in the market relative to other products. In the market segment, the product must provide a higher value to the customer than any competitor's product.

Major problems here are the failure to identify the right market segment and the failure to describe in sufficient detail why the customers in the segment will find that the product has more value than the competitor's product.

5. **Technical risk level.** The level of technical risk must be appropriate for the strategic purpose of the product. Risk analysis should be done for all facets of the product, including piece parts, processes, and marketing plans. High levels of risk should be addressed early in the development process.

Frequent problems here include

▶ Poor assessment of the limitations of the technology or the skill base of the team

▶ Too much risk for the purpose of the product

▶ Too much risk for the time and budget allotted

▶ Failure to understand that a key component obtained from a supplier might soon be superseded by the supplier bringing out a new generation of that component

6. **Priority decision criteria list.** The team should establish a list of priority goals and performance standards. A typical list would include

▶ Time to market

▶ The product's key features

▶ Quality, reliability, and design for manufacturability goals

▶ Technology strategy

▶ Strategy for flexibility and modularity (platforms)

Without a clear list of priorities, a team lacks direction and tends to drift, change, and revise its decisions. Failure to specify priorities often occurs because the team has an inadequate understanding of what is required to make the product successful. That often results from

▶ Insufficient understanding of the customer

▶ Insufficient understanding of the competition and why the competitor's product sells

▶ Failure to project what the market or competitor will be doing at the time of product release

▶ Lack of understanding of what can be achieved technically within the time and budget provided

---

BOX 7-3 (continued)

7. **Regulation and government compliance.** The company should know and comply with government requirements on patent infringements, health and environmental regulations, UL standards, and global standards.

8. **Product channel issues.** The right distribution channel must be selected or developed.

9. **Endorsement by upper management.** Senior management must approve the project and support it with staffing and financing and when difficulties arise in its development. Problems here might occur if senior management does not understand how the project helps the firm reach its strategic goals.

10. **Project planning.** The team should develop detailed staffing and funding requirements based upon accurate schedules and financial projections. Problems here might include

    ▶ Erroneous budgeting

    ▶ The shifting of staff or budget to complete another late project

---

Source: Adopted from W. I. Zangwil, *Lightning Strategies for Innovation: How the World's Best Firms Create New Products* (New York: Lexington Books, 1993). Reprinted with permission of The Free Press, a division of Simon & Schuster, Inc. Copyright © 1993 by Willard I. Zangwill.

---

gone right, or the voice of the customer, which promotes customer satisfaction, loyalty, and repurchase, balanced against *things gone wrong,* or the conformance to internally set standards. It is rather easy to make the leap to the more traditional views of quality, such as those of Juran (fitness for use) and Feiganbaum (what the buyer says it is) when analyzing the best approach to design.[32]

ADVICE FOR ENTREPRENEURS WITH NEW PRODUCT IDEAS

All that has been said about the NPD applies double to the company startup because a new product or new service failure means a company failure. A quick review of the main dos and don'ts follows:[33]

1. *Avoid "me-too" products.* For example, at one time there were 150 companies offering wine cooler products. Why enter such a market?

---

[32] J. R. Evans and J. W. Dean, *TOTAL Quality* (Minneapolis: West Publishing, 1999.)

[33] This material is summarized in L. Tiffany, "Hot Tips: Got a Lemon?" *Business Start-ups* (May 1999), pp. 80–81.

2. *Don't assume you are first with a new idea.* Homework usually reveals that competitors have already tried the new product or service, long ago, and failed.

3. *Know your margins.* Underestimating margins is a typical mistake made by start-up companies. In retail, 50 percent margins are typical; will the price support this profit? And don't forget trademarks, samples, and testing.

 ## SUMMARY

New products and services have emerged at the end of the decade of the 1990s as the preferred strategy for competition. The shift in R&D funding had already occurred a decade earlier. Not surprisingly, most companies are revamping the new product development (NPD) process in their organizations. The focus of these efforts is primarily on quality and cycle time reduction.

Most new products are not "new to the world," but are modifications of existing product and service offerings. Truly new products, especially for consumers, may now represent only about 6 percent of all U.S. offerings every year. However, on average, 60 percent of these new products are successful (returning a multiple of the investment) once they are introduced, and these new products have some distinctive feature that customers find attractive; they are rarely just copies of an existing offering. If one tracks a product from the time it is just a concept, this percentage declines considerably—perhaps only 1 in 60 new ideas ever sees the light of day, and this varies by industry. New products that combine understanding of customer and market needs as well as leverage the best technical capability of the organization are significantly more likely to be commercially successful. This matching process between a firm's technical capabilities and market needs is facilitated by an integrated approach to the new product and service process, as well as an aggressive, early mover strategy, design software tailored to firm needs, and benchmarking competitive NPD process characteristics, not just rival product ideas.

Although the platform approach to sustained new product development is very popular because of it success, there are drawbacks to this strategy. One apparent weakness is that redundancy in technology development erodes investment in leading-edge features that can be reliably incorporated into new products, especially for consumers. Reliance on suppliers does not completely solve this problem. Although customers view customization as the primary ingredient in satisfaction, it is still up to the producer to find features that "surprise and delight" the end user. Ultimately, it is the internal operations and satisfaction of new product teams that determine success.

Four key criteria must be satisfied to maximize the probability of new product success: (1) product advantage must be clearly seen by customers, sometimes called the "value equation," or benefit/cost or net benefit of new product use; (2) the firm needs to have significant marketing and technical capability to understand customers and deliver new technical solutions to problems; (3) the firm needs to sustain proficiency in market-related activities like market research and prototype testing with customers; and, finally, (4) the new product should "fit" the strategy of the company (e.g., leading edge products should be introduced by "first mover" companies). Hewlett-Packard, often mentioned benchmark example of outstanding NPD uses a ten-point checklist that incorporates many of these and additional criteria.

One emerging approach to the new product development process that is showing great promise is called set-based design. This approach is designed to consider many more ideas for new products very early in the development cycle and then narrow these ideas down to a feasible set for testing, in order to avoid design rework. Toyota's new product development process incorporates set-based design and traditional plan–do–check–act quality cycles (see Chapter 12 for a summary). However, the key to all of these approaches is *balancing the inputs* of various parts of the organization, with special attention to achieving parity in *technical and marketing* contributions into the discussions of NPD.

DISCUSSION QUESTIONS

1. Apply what you have learned in this chapter and previous chapters about successful new product and service introduction to the following "idea source" exercise. Below is a listing of potential sources of ideas for new products. First, indicate which are the most common sources—that is, the parts of the organization or environment that usually generate new product ideas. Second, indicate which of these sources (name at least two) are associated with new product success. Third, indicate which of these sources (name at least two) are associated with new product failure.

Potential Sources of New Ideas for Products or Services

Inside the firm

- R&D staff ☐
- R&D first-level supervision ☐
- R&D middle management ☐
- VP of R&D ☐
- General management ☐
- Marketing/distribution/sales ☐
- Production ☐
- Engineering ☐
- Finance ☐
- Technical services ☐
- Other ☐

Outside the firm

- Customer ☐
- Government representative ☐
- Vendor/supplier ☐
- University consultant(s) ☐
- Private consultant ☐
- Technical/professional colleague, but not a paid consultant ☐
- Other _____ ☐

Answer here:

a. Most common sources_____

b. Sources associated with new product success _____
_____

c. Sources associated with new product failure _____
_____

2. Read and answer the following discussion questions for Case 7-1.

   a. What is a "friendly" customer, and is it different from a "lead user?"

   b. What does this case illustrate about the new product development process, beyond what 3M documented and reported for the "Midas" project itself?

   c. What do you conclude from the numbers such as the learning curve costs on retrofitting, which are included in this case? Defend your position.

3. Read Case 7-2 on Acuson and use the materials from this chapter to predict whether this new product (the Sequoia) will be a success (return a multiple of the investment). Actually give a percentage of success prediction. Defend your percentage.

ADDITIONAL CASE SUGGESTIONS

1. There are numerous excellent cases on new product introduction. Just to name a few: Chaparral Steel: Rapid Product and Process Development, HBS 9-692-018; an older case, which is still excellent on meeting new product deadlines, is Sun Microsystems (A), 9-686-133.

2. Other good cases are Ritz-Carlton: Using Information Systems to Better Serve the Customer (also good for a quality course): HBS 9-395-064.

3. As mentioned in Chapter 5, a great case on strategy R&D and new products is Intel Systems Group, HBS 9-691-040.

✳ CASE 7-1

3M Health Care: The "Midas" Touch[34]

By far one of the best-known companies for new product development is 3M Corporation. 3M has been the source of many an inspirational story about the development of new ideas and the creation of whole new lines of business from a single new product introduction.[35] A recent case study of new product development from 3M Health Care is a case in point of how the company attacks new product problems.[36]

The case begins with problem reports in 1996 from hospital customers of 3M's open-heart surgery systems for life support during cardiac surgery. The second-generation 3M Health Care product for blood circulation and oxygen replenishment had a significant new feature—prevention of blood back flow—but it depended on a key component. This component was a 3M invention: an ultrasonic sensor that bounces very weak signals off of red blood cells and is noninvasive—it doesn't touch the blood itself. However, customer feedback led to the discovery that the ultrasonic sensor was being interrupted by electric noise in the operating room. There were 500 units in the field potentially affected by this problem. The key drivers in the response: patient safety and customer satisfaction.

The 3M team, code name "Midas," went to work immediately trying to determine the cause of the electric interference that was causing the problems with the ultrasonic signal and sensor. This required that team members have access to the operating room during surgery—not an easy request to get approved. But eventually, the team secured permission from a "friendly" customer to monitor surgery with the 3M flow rate sensor activated. Data showed that the interference was coming from electric cauterizing and, in some cases, the operating room lights.

Then the team went to work, led by Mr. Paco Varela, using a 3M-designated five-step product development and improvement process on a new concept for the sensor. At the same time, the group had to field a continuing and growing number of complaints from customers and offer alternative technologies (e.g., previous generation sensors) and solutions as a stop-gap until the problem could be solved. The crucial step in the redesign process came with the second stage: feasibility studies. "People have to have a goal or a direction in order to focus their energy," says Mr. Varela. The 3M team had to be sure of the alternative concepts that made the cut to feasibility testing before entering phase 3, "development," where most of the project expense and time was incurred.

After several concepts emerged, parallel development could begin. Once the final design had been tested, sources of supply, which had been a problem, were resolved, prototypes were validated, and customers' inputs resulted in several product modifications: One major change was that the sensor would be housed in an aluminum case, not plastic, as originally envisioned

---

[34] Copyright John E. Ettlie, 1998, all rights reserved. This case was written for classroom use and discussion purposes only and is not intended to illustrate either effective or ineffective management.

[35] See A. H. Van de Ven, et al., "Processes of New Business Creation in Different Organizational Settings," in A. Van de Ven, et al., (eds.) *Research on the Management of Innovation,* (New York: Harper and Row, Publishers, 1989), pp. 221–297, which documents the case of 3M's cochlear implants in the hearing health industry.

[36] This case is based, in part, on a presentation made by Paco Varela, "Reinventing Products Through a Process of Discovery Onsite with Customers," presented at the New Product Development Forum of the Product Development Management Association (PDMA) Meeting held at 3M Health Care, Ann Arbor, Michigan, July 14, 1998.

by the team. Finally, the product was submitted for 510(k)[38] approval. The final concept used a new idea of the "time of flight" of an ultrasonic signal, which provides both the rate and direction of blood flow.

Once the product was submitted for 501(k) approved, pre-production was validated and the product was sent to CAEs.[39] For market introduction, the product positioning was critical for achieving customer satisfaction since this re-development was an upgrade as well as an opportunity to respond to customer feedback. Customers who had the most problems were first to get replacements, free of charge. Customers without problems but interested in an upgrade were next, at a partial charge, and so on down the list of purchasers until all customers, including those who had been the most recent sales, were serviced.

Unique to 3M is the one-year, post-product launch audit of the project. This audit includes customer surveys, which are relatively easy, since 90 percent of these customers are in the United States (the system uses a disposable head in the centrifugal pump, which is not popular overseas due to cost). Feedback from direct salespeople and other sources by telephone is also

---

[38] A 510 (k) notifies the FDA that a medical device manufacturer intends to place a new device on the market. The FDA much then acknowledge the notification and provide clearance or market release.

[39] CAE stands for customer acceptance evaluation and is a term used internally by 3M Cardiovascular Systems.

included. Current complaint levels are down to two per time period, which is far below the industry standard, and are not related to the sensor.

Results from the audit included the following:

- Unit costs and development costs were within acceptable ranges (+ or – 10% on development cost).
- Retrofitting costs were about 12 percent lower than expected because it was primarily a labor cost and there was a significant learning curve on installation.
- Production and sales forecasts, as well as capacity, were updated.
- Supplier performance was significantly improved.

Lessons Learned

- A timely response (short and long term) to customer complaints and requests is critical.
- The problem must be fully understood before it can be truly solved.
- The "midas touch would never happen without "friendly" customer cooperation in this setting.
- Evaluate all the feasible options before going ahead.
- Results of the effort were communicated upward to 3M to aid the corporate new product development process.
- With this type of response, 10 to 12 percent growth rate can be sustained in the division.

CASE 7-2

New Ultrasound Machine Is Acuson's Bet for Breakthrough

Acuson Corp. technicians were in the midst of demonstrating their new Sequoia ultrasound machine in October when strange fire-red images flared on the device's screen.

As they struggled to fix what they thought was an embarrassing computer glitch, several cardiologists in the room suddenly realized what they were witnessing: blood, coursing through the tiny arteries at the tip of the heart. Never before had any noninvasive imaging technology been able to detect such detail.

"These guys started gasping and squealing like kids on Christmas Day," said William Varley, an Acuson vice president, who recorded the name of everyone present for posterity. "You were seeing things you thought you might not ever see."

The innovative instrument's rollout a few weeks ago came none too soon for Acuson, a pioneer in ultrasound,

which shoots sound waves into the body and converts their echoes into visible images. Founded in 1979, the company grew explosively on the strength of its groundbreaking first ultrasound product, the 128.

But since 1991, the company's growth has stalled, reflecting market saturation, still competition and health care cost containment. Last year, its net income plunged 61% to $7.1 million, or 25 cents per share, on sales of $329 million. After spending nine years and much of its cumulative research outlays of $350 million since 1987 on the Sequoia, Acuson thinks it has produced the breakthrough technological encore it sorely needs.

Machine "Exquisitely Sensitive"

Some prominent outsiders agree. Beryl Benacerraf, a radiology professor at Harvard Medical School, is one of

38 doctors who have placed orders. "This is the platform for a new era of ultrasound systems." Dr. Benacerraf said. "It's so exquisitely sensitive, it opens up whole new avenues of possibilities." She and some others who have tested the machines believe it can provide information that currently requires more expensive and painful invasive procedures, such as cardiac catheterization, which can cost $5,000 or more, compared with less than $500 for an ultrasound scan. Clear, detailed and readily available pictures of those critical heart arteries, say, or of barely formed human fetuses, will simplify diagnoses and permit earlier therapeutic intervention, Dr. Benacerraf said. "When it arrives, you're not gonna get me out of that room," she added.

Other medical imaging experts are less enthusiastic, noting that the last thing budget-constrained hospitals need is another pricey piece of diagnostic equipment. And they say they have yet to be convinced that the Sequoia, at a cost of up to $350,000 per unit, is sufficiently superior to make existing state-of-the-art ultrasound devices costing about half that obsolete. In addition, a competitor, Advanced Technology Laboratories Inc. of Bothell, Washington, said it has used similar technology in its ultrasound machines since 1991.

Meanwhile, on Wall Street, several analysts said they won't even attempt to make sales projections for at least another six months. "The key question is, how will it improve patient care," said Harvey Klein of Klein Biomedical Consultants, a market research firm in New York. "I don't think (Acuson), or anyone, really knows."

Company's Stock Has Risen 15%

However, since the Sequoia's unveiling, Acuson's stock has risen 15%—including a rise of 3.1% or 62.5 cents, to $20.625 in early trading Monday at the New York Stock Exchange.

Moreover, there is evidence that the machine is already saving lives.

Take the case of Shannon Buckmaster, a 25-year-old who underwent heart surgery when she was four. Several months ago, Ms. Buckmaster suddenly lost sight in her left eye. Her doctors at the Cleveland Clinic suspected a blood clot, but found no signs of trouble in her heart using conventional ultrasound equipment.

But a Sequoia prototype happened to be on hand and clearly revealed a foreign object. In open-heart surgery a few days later, doctors removed a piece of catheter inadvertently left behind from her previous operation. Caked with clots, one of which had broken off and lodged in her eye, it was a ticking time bomb that could eventually have caused a stroke, said James Thomas, director of cardiovascular imaging at the Cleveland Clinic. Today, Ms.

Buckmaster has regained most of her eyesight and is back at work.

"We got some very gorgeous images on her with the Sequoia," Dr. Thomas says. "It was really critical in making the right diagnosis."

The Soul of the New Machine

Behind those images lies the application of complex physics. Ultrasound echoes return in waves with two components of information: amplitude, or the height of the waves; and phase, or the distance between each wave. Many commercially available ultrasound devices measure just amplitude. But the Sequoia's powerful computer circuitry processes both sets of data simultaneously, generating sharper images far more rapidly.

The Sequoia, like the 128 before it, is largely the brainchild of Samuel Maslak, Acuson's 47-year-old chairman and chief executive. Dr. Maslak became interested in ultrasound while studying electrical engineering at the Massachusetts Institute of Technology. He had taken his pregnant wife in for an ultrasound exam using the comparatively crude systems of the early 1970s. "It looked like a bad weather map," Dr. Maslak recalls. "The resolution was poor and it wasn't very accurate." That was a good thing for Dr Maslak: The images—falsely, it turned out—indicated problems with the fetus.

Dr. Maslak developed his first ultrasound products as an inventor and project manager for Hewlett Packard Co. His work led to patents, held by H.P. on some of the most important early ultrasound advances. But he became frustrated by H.P's lack of interest in pushing ultrasound further ahead. With two colleagues, he hatched the 128 from a spare bedroom in his house, which he remortgaged to fund the project and found Acuson. That instrument helped make ultrasound diagnosis the second most common form of medical imaging after chest X-ray machines. Today, Dr. Maslak's Acuson stock is worth about $40 million.

In a recent interview at company headquarters here, Dr. Maslak said he considers the Sequoia "even more revolutionary" than the 128. While that may not assure its success in the market, Acuson has already agreed to a request from the curator of the Smithsonian Institution's medical collection to donate one of each of the instruments.

Ralph T. King, Jr. *The Wall Street Journal* Europe, Tuesday, May 11, 1996. Reprinted with permission of Wall Street Journal © 1996 Dow Jones and Company, Inc. All rights reserved worldwide.

Chapter **8**

Operations Strategy & Innovation

$\mathscr{C}$HAPTER OBJECTIVES

To introduce the concepts of operations strategy, joint production, and economies of scope. This chapter reviews the importance of manufacturing strategy, focus, and economies of scope versus economies of scale. The Case 8-1 is The Gleason Works.

$\mathscr{O}$PERATIONS STRATEGY

An organization's operations strategy starts with a statement about "how it proposes to create for itself that chosen form of competitive advantage," or how it will differentiate itself for survival, growth, and profitability (if a for-profit firm), according to Robert Hayes and his colleagues at the Harvard Business School.[1] This turns out to be a rather significant challenge, given the complexity and typically dispersed operations facilities of most firms and organizations. Such terms as *strategic fit* (i.e., congruence between corporate, business, and operations strategy—in design, organization, and management), *strategic consistency* (i.e., coordination of functional strategies such as marketing and R&D), and *continuous improvement* (i.e., raising the bar ever higher) have been central themes in the treatments of corporate strategy. However, these simple ideas are often static and of little help when organizations pursue the "one best way," and they fail to affect performance. Operations strategy is more than a set of goals, actions, and tasks designed to service

---

[1] R. H. Hayes, G. P. Pisano, and D. M. Upton, *Strategic Operations* (New York: The Free Press, 1996).

customers and deliver products better than competitors. Hayes and his colleagues say that it is the systematic building of operations capabilities that makes all the difference in the world of global competition.

Schmenner[2] divides operations choices into three broad categories:

▶ *Technology and facilities* (e.g, vertical integration, equipment, plant size)

▶ *Operating policies* (e.g, forecasting, purchasing, pacing, and quality)

▶ *Operations organization* (e.g., control, measurement, talent)

For the purposes of this book, it is the *technology* issues that dominate. *Without the application of the computer to the design and manufacturing of goods, there would be little to say about a "revolution" in scope.* Technology and operations are closely liked.

✳ Manufacturing Strategy

Often defined simply as the way a firm fills orders better than competitors, the strategy of the manufacturing function has alluded formal study until relatively recently. A German company in the printing press business has the following manufacturing strategy: Produce all large parts and components in the home plant with flexible manufacturing systems and buy all small parts from qualified suppliers. So, it does not have to be difficult. The question is: Which strategy is most successful?

The rapidly growing interest in manufacturing strategy has begun to produce a wealth of literature on the subject,[3] and manufacturing structure was originally borne by the discussions of strategy. The historical development of the subject is presented first.

Perhaps the most significant modern contribution to the literature and practice of manufacturing strategy was made by Wickham Skinner. In 1974, Skinner published an article called "The Focused Factory." The world of manufacturing strategy has not been the same since. Skinner said that in order to apply the concept of focus in manufacturing, four things are required (see Box 8-1). The bold contention in Box 8-1 is worth repeating: "A factory that focuses on a narrow product mix for a particular market niche will outperform the conventional plant, which attempts a broader mission."[4]

Skinner later observed a simple fact about the way manufacturing was conducted in the 1960s and 1970s, primarily in American industrial sectors: "In spite of common technology, a common set of competitors, and a common industry structure, and common market practices, different companies often would have devel-

---

[2] R. W. Schmenner, *Production/Operations Management: From the Inside Out* (5th ed.) (New York: Macmillan, 1993), R. W. Schmenner, *Plant and Service Tours in Operations Management* (Upper Saddle River, N.J.: Prentice-Hall, 1998). Also see: R. W. Schmenner, "International Factory Productivity Gains," *Journal of Operations Management,* 10, no. 2 (April 1991), pp. 229–254

[3] J. E., Ettlie, M. Burstein, and A. Feigenbaum, (eds.), *Manufacturing Strategy: The Research Agenda for the Next Decade* (Boston, Mass.: Kluwer Academic Publishers); J. G. Miller and A. V. Roth, "A Taxonomy of Manufacturing Strategies," *Management Science,* 40, no. 3 (March 1994), pp. 285–304.

[4] W. Skinner, "The Focused Factory," *Harvard Business Review,* 52, no. 3 (May/June 1974), pp. 113–121.

BOX 8-1

Focus in Manufacturing

What are the basic changes required to apply the concept of focus in manufacturing? I can identify four:

1. Seeing the problem not as "How can we increase productivity?" but as "How can we compete?"

2. Seeing the problem as encompassing the efficiency of the *entire* manufacturing organization, not only the efficiency of the direct labor and the work force. (In most plants, direct labor and the work force represent only a small percentage of total costs.)

3. Learning to focus each plant on a limited, concise, manageable set of products, technologies, volumes, and markets.

4. Learning to structure basic manufacturing policies and supporting services so that they focus on one explicit manufacturing task instead of on many inconsistent, conflicting, implicit tasks.

A factory that focuses on a narrow product mix for a particular market niche will outperform the conventional plant, which attempts a broader mission.

SOURCE: W. Skinner, "The Focused Factory," *Harvard Business Review,* 52, no. 3 (May–June 1974), p. 114. Reprinted by permission of *Harvard Business Review.* Copyright ©1974 by the President and Fellows of Harvard College; all rights reserved.

---

oped quite different manufacturing policies."[5] He was one of the first to observe that if a firm had a manufacturing philosophy—a consistent set of manufacturing policies focused in one direction—it was more likely to be successful. Out of these notions, he developed his now famous idea of **the focused factory.**

The idea of focus in manufacturing is deceptively simple, and has been embellished many times subsequent to Skinner's original notion. "Focused manufacturing is based on the concept that simplicity, repetition, experience, and homogeneity of tasks breed competence."[6] If one focuses operations on customer needs, manufacturing becomes a superior competitive weapon. Skinner listed five key characteristics of the focused factory:

1. Process technologies (e.g., no more than one unproved technology per factory)

2. Market demands (e.g., one or two market demands per plant)

3. Product volumes (e.g., segregate large and small volume production)

---

[5] W. Skinner, *Manufacturing in the Corporate Strategy* (New York: John Wiley & Sons, 1974, p. 6).

[6] Ibid., p. 70.

4. Quality levels (e.g., a common approach of a variety of tasks, involving equipment, tooling, etc.)

5. Manufacturing tasks (e.g., only one or two tasks, clear success criteria)[7]

However, empirical tests of the focused factory concept have met with limited success in showing the superiority of this approach.[8] Focus alone, it would seem, is not sufficient to secure success in operations. We argue here that at least one other consideration in the form of management of technology would have to be added to this paradigm. Often, accounting systems also have to be changed to make focus work.[9]

Hayes and Wheelwright[10] did much to build on these basic ideas. They introduced a framework of manufacturing strategy that included eight decision categories. The first four decision categories—capacity, facilities, technology, and vertical integration—they called *structural categories*. They conceived of these first four elements as foundation characteristics, changing infrequently, difficult to reverse, and with long-term impact on the firm. Their second four decision categories—work force, quality, production planning/materials control, and organization—were referred to as *infrastructural*. "It is this pattern of structural and infrastructural decisions that constitutes the 'manufacturing strategy' of a business unit."[11]

A number of more recent conceptual contributions to the manufacturing strategy literature also illustrate the evolution of the topic. For example, Hill has developed a framework for connecting manufacturing strategy to corporate decisions. His framework starts with corporate objectives and the proceeds to marketing strategy, order winning products, and then manufacturing strategy. Under manufacturing strategy, he includes process choice (technology, capacity, and inventory) and infrastructure (support, planning and control, quality, and organization).[12]

Anderson, Schroeder and Cleveland[13] argue in their review of progress to date in the manufacturing strategy literature that the field boils down to two common themes: Formulating and implementing a manufacturing strategy is central to guiding manufacturing; and the content of a manufacturing strategy includes cost, quality, flexibility, and technology. Ward, Bickford, and Leong[14] and, earlier, Ettlie,

---

[7] Ibid., p. 71.

[8] S. Wathen, "Manufacturing Strategy in Business Units: An Analysis of Production Process Focus and Performance," *International Journal of Operations & Production Management,* 15, no. 8 (1995), pp. 4–13.

[9] S. H. Hanks and G. N. Chandler, "Patterns of Functional Specialization in Emerging High-tech Firms *Journal of Small Business Management,* 2, no. 2 (April 1994), pp. 23–36.

[10] R. H. Hayes and S. C. Wheelwright, *Restoring Our Competitive Edge: Competing Through Manufacturing* (New York: John Wiley & Sons, 1984).

[11] Ibid., p. 32.

[12] T. Hill, *Manufacturing Strategy: The Strategic Management of the Manufacturing Function* (London: Macmillan, 1985).

[13] J. C. Anderson, R. G. Schroeder, and G. Cleveland, "The Process of Manufacturing Strategy: Some Empirical Observations and Conclusions," *International Journal of Operations & Production Management,* 11, no. 3 (1991), pp. 86–101.

[14] P. T. Ward, D. J. Bickford, and G. K. Leong, "Configurations of Manufacturing Strategy, Business Strategy, Environment and Structure," *Journal of Management* 22, no. 4 (1996), pp. 597–626.

Burstein, and Feigenbaum[15] conclude that the field has suffered from a lack of theoretical development and, especially, rigorous empirical validation. Ward and his colleagues argue for four basic strategic configurations:

▶ Niche differentiation

▶ Broad differentiation

▶ Cost leadership

▶ Lean competition

Many authors have responded to this challenge. Ward and his colleagues developed scales to measure cost importance, quality importance, delivery-time importance, and flexibility importance.[16] Chand and colleagues[17] developed a model of the optimal path for process improvement activities that have a positive effect on reducing quality costs. These conclusions are similar to those of Dean and Snell[18]—showing the relationship between a broad range of techniques such as just-in-time manufacturing, and the importance of quality (i.e., the quality assurance function) in the manufacturing strategy to overall performance. Empirical evidence from the "lean" manufacturing study of the auto industry at MIT[19] showed that technological innovation applied "upstream" in the value-added chain had the greatest impact on the best car companies. These results were replicated by Dan Luria and Sean MacLinden.[20] A comparative study of 561 U.S.–Canadian, Korean, and European plants found that status as a process (versus discrete part) factory and location had no impact on productivity.[21]

Jeff Miller and Aledia Roth[22] found that firms differ in two important dimensions, regardless of industry, in their manufacturing strategies:

▶ The ability to differentiate from competitors in products and services

▶ The scope of their product lines and markets

Perhaps one of the most interesting hybrid strategies to emerge during the last decade is the use of modular manufacturing to produce using a "mass customization" strategy. By using fixed options at each stage of the production process,

---

[15] Ibid.

[16] P. T. Ward, J. K. McCreery, L. P. Ritzman, and D. Sharma, "Competitive Priorities in Operations Management," *Decision Sciences,* 29, no. 4 (Fall 1998), pp. 1035–1046.

[17] S. Chand, H. Moskowitz, A. Novak, I. Rekhi, and G. Sorger, "Capacity Allocation for Dynamic Process Improvement with Quality and Demand Considerations," *Operations Research,* 44, no. 6 (November/December 1996), pp. 964–975.

[18] J. W. Dean Jr. and S. A. Snell, The Strategic Use of Integrated Manufacturing: An Empirical Examination, *Strategic Management Journal,* 17, no. 6 (June 1996), pp. 459–480.

[19] J. Womak, D. Jones, and D. Roos, *The Machine That Changed the World* (New York: Harper, 1990).

[20] The Industrial Technology Institute and Office for the Study of Automotive Transportation at the University of Michigan.

[21] R. Schmenner, "International Factory Productivity Gains," *Journal of Operations Management,* 10, no. 2 (April 1991), pp. 229–254.

[22] J. G. Miller and A. V. Roth, "A Taxonomy of Manufacturing Strategies," *Management Science,* 40, no. 3 (March 1994), pp. 285–304.

many alternative product or service configurations can be achieved. However, this approach appears to be best suited to low-technology industries with large volume requirements, such as newspapers, college textbooks, and jeans.[23] This approach was pioneered by Panasonic's National Bicycle Co., Ltd. in Japan.[24]

Molhotra, Steele, and Grover[25] concluded after a Delphi study of U.S. manufacturing managers in seventy-five companies that quality management, manufacturing strategy, and process technology were the top three strategic issues. It seems relatively safe to conclude that it is an element from the structure decision category—*technology*—and an element from the infrastructural category—*quality*—that are the two paramount issues in manufacturing strategy to resolve in the global competitive race.

JOINT PRODUCTION AND ECONOMIES OF SCOPE

Having coined the phrase **economies of scope** several years earlier, Panzar and Willig,[26] in their seminal follow-up article, proposed a fundamental model of multi-product firms and sharable inputs. Multiproduct firms exploit excess capacity and, therefore, create cost savings. In other words, "when there are economies of scope, there exists some input (if only a factory building), which is shared by two or more product lines without complete congestion."[27] They go on to show the conditions that promote the formation of multiproduct firms, even if this does not conform perfectly to the classic definition of joint production.

This model is expanded in Baumol, Panzer, and Willing to show when it may be efficient to combine two or more multiproduct firms or plants. The **theory of contestable markets**[28] says that when there is free entry into a market, exploitation of a natural monopoly is limited by the costs of exit, not entry. Therefore, the magnitude of sunk costs is crucial in determining the need for regulatory protection.[29] When applied to a single production line or cell, the concept of scope generally falls under the rubric of flexible manufacturing.[30] Cells allow considerable latitude

---

[23] R. S. M. Lau, "Mass Customization: The Next Industrial Revolution," *Industrial Management,* 37, no. 5 (September/October 1995), pp. 18–19; also see: S. Kotha, "Mass Customization: Implementing the Emerging Paradigm for Competitive Advantage," *Strategic Management Journal,* 16 (Special Issue) (Summer 1995), pp. 21–42.

[24] T. E. Bell, "Bicycles on a Personalized Basis, *IEEE Spectrum* (September 1993), pp. 32–35.

[25] M. K. Malhotra, D. C. Steele, and V. Grover, "Important Strategic and Tactical Manufacturing Issues in the 1990s," *Decision Sciences*, 25, no. 2 (March/April 1994), pp. 189–214.

[26] J. C. Panzar, and R. D. Willig, "Economies of Scope," *American Economic Review,* 71, no. 2 (May 1981), pp. 268–272.

[27] Ibid., p. 268.

[28] W. J. Baumol, "Contestable Markets: An Uprising in the Theory of Industry Structure," *American Economic Review,* 72, no. 1 (March 1982), pp. 1–15. Baumol, et al. (1982).

[29] M. E. Beesley, "Commitment, Sunk Costs, and Entry to the Airline Industry," *Journal of Transport Economics & Policy,* 20, no. 2 (May 1986), pp. 173–190.

[30] K. E. Stecke, "Formulation and Solution of Nonlinear Integer Production Planning Problems for Flexible Manufacturing Systems," *Management Science,* 29, no. 3 (March 1983), pp. 273–288.

in application of empowered work force and increased worker satisfaction, as well as additional flexibility gains.[31]

Alchian and Demsetz[32] defined team or joint production as "production in which (1) several types of resources are used and (2) the product is not a sum of separable outputs of each cooperating resource. An additional factor creates a team organization problem—(3) not all resources used in team production belong to one person." That is, regardless of who owns what, it is impossible to determine the exact contribution of each team member to the output. Further, Alchian and Demsetz say, "Team productive activity is that in which a union, or joint use, of input yields a larger output than the sum of the products of the separately used inputs."[33] This forms the fundamental motivation for joint production. Only the organization, contracts, and informational and payment procedures used among owners of teamed inputs are of interest to the authors, not the motivation for multiple ownership of these resources.

The importance of scope in manufacturing cannot be minimized. It significantly enhances the idea of focus that Skinner originated in the following way. Even with a focused facility, it is implicitly assumed that once volumes are determined, all the other important decisions for that facility will follow in lockstep. That is, for example, if volumes are going to be large—hundreds of thousands of units a year—then the size of the plant, the vertical integration, the inventory, logistics, and technology decisions all follow this volume determination.

The idea of scope is quite different. Now it is argued that a few smaller plants alternating production between several "jointly" produced parts or products can outperform larger factories dedicated to one production product (not necessarily one customer). The ideal scope varies by situation, of course, but in the ideal, there is no penalty for changing from one product to another—no lost production time.[34] This contrast is depicted in Figure 8-1. More realistically, the premium paid for additional flexibility is compensated for by the ease of switching between products that are truly demanded by customers (not by inventory policies), or between new products. The second assumption of most manufacturing strategy thinking until now has been that once a capital investment in plant and/or equipment has been made, it is irreversible. A plant is good for 30 or 40 years, and you can only close it; you can't afford to change it. But scope and its enabling technologies allow for the possibility that a production facility can be changed to allow not only for many existing products, but for new products not even known yet. *This is a powerful concept: it reduces changeover costs to near zero, and reduces changeover time to near zero, all enabled by the computer applied to manufacturing design and operations.*

---

[31] R. Magjuka and R. Schmenner, "Cellular Manufacturing, Group Technology, and Human Resource Management. An International Study," *International Journal of Management,* 10, no. 4 (December 1993), pp. 405–412.

[32] A. A. Alchian and H. Demsetz, "Production, Information Costs, and Economic Organization," *American Economic Review,* 62 (1972), pp. 777–795.

[33] Ibid., p. 794.

[34] J. D. Goldhar and M. Jelinek, "Plan for Economies of Scope, "*Harvard Business Review,* 61, no. 6 (November/December 1983), pp. 141–148.

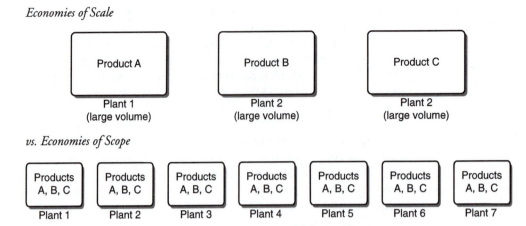

Figure 8-1   Economies of Scale versus Scope in Manufacturing
SOURCE: Adapted from Goldhar and Jelinek, 1983.

The Second Industrial Divide

In *1984*, George Orwell wrote a fictional account of political mind control. In the *year* 1984, Michael Piore and Charles Sabel published *The Second Industrial Divide*. The thesis of this book was simple: The limits of the mass production model (economies of scale) have essentially been reached in modern industrial economies. This is due primarily to the limits of special purpose machinery and increasing capital versus labor intensity of industrialized countries of the world. "The brief moments when the path of technological development itself is an issue we call *industrial divides* [emphasis added].[35]

The first industrial divide was the emergence of mass-production technologies in the nineteenth century. The second industrial divide, which is the topic of the book and the period we're going through now, is the modern-day application of the craft methods of production coupled with general-purpose equipment, which affords considerably more flexibility and avoids dehumanization of work. New regulatory and public policies will be needed to allow this to happen, but there are many examples around the world to cite as models of how this transformation and *divide* can happen. Piore and Sabel cite social-security expenditures (Table 8-1) around the world as evidence of disparity (e.g., the United States spends less on social security and social programs and lags behind countries such as Austria.)

One primary example that Piore and Sabel document as illustrative of the second industrial divide is northern Italy. The flexible networks of small, cooperating companies co-producing industrial goods is today known the world over as one of the unique success stories of small firms. "Flexible specialization," as they call it, is the "strategy of permanent innovation: Accommodation to ceaseless change, rather than an effort to control it … based on flexible, multi-purpose equipment, skilled workers, and the criterion through politics, of an industrial community that restricts the forms of competition to those favoring innovation."[36]

[35] Michael Piore and Charles Sabel, *The Second Industrial Divide* (New York: Basic Books, 1984), p. 5.
[36] Ibid., p. 17.

TABLE 8-1   Social-Security Expenditures and Gross Domestic Product per Capita in Selected Industrial Economies in the 1970s

	Total Expenditures of Social Security Schemes* as Percentage of GDP (1977)	Growth of Social Expenditures: Percentages of GDP (1973–1979)	Average Annual Percentage Rate of Growth of Per-Capita GDP (1975–1979)
Austria	21.1	2.7	3.8
France	25.6	4.7	3.4
West Germany	23.4	4.9	4.0
Italy	22.8	0.3	3.0
Japan	9.7	5.8	4.3
United Kingdom	17.3	2.5	2.4
United States	13.7	1.6	3.7

* Social security schemes include medical-care benefits, cash benefits, and benefits in kind other than for medical care (social-welfare schemes for the aged, disabled, children and housewives, etc.).

SOURCES: Piore and Sabel (1984, p. 12). International Labor Office, "The Cost of Social Security: Tenth International Inquiry, 1975–77" (Geneva: ILO, 1981); *United Nations Yearbook of National Accounts Statistics,* 1980, vol. 2, International Tables (New York: UN, 1982); M. G. Schmidt, "The Welfare State and the Economy in Periods of Economic Crisis: A Comparative Study of Twenty-three OECD Nations," *European Journal of Political Research,* 11 (1983), pp. 1–26.

The Italian version of flexible specialization is summarized in excerpts from Piore and Sabel in Box 8-2. This tradition, documented until 1983 in the second industrial divide, continues today with an interesting twist: Italian firms continue to import and adopt new manufacturing concepts from abroad, as well as to innovate in flexible networks of cooperation. This new production paradigm, which relies on technological (new generations of flexible automation) and organizational innovation (inventory conservation techniques like just-in-time purchasing and manufacturing), was documented most recently by Spina and colleagues.[37] Recall the manufacturing strategy practiced by a German firm, mentioned earlier: *The company manufactured the larger, heavy parts in-house with flexible manufacturing systems and outsourced the smaller parts.* This simple strategy is one that worked for this small firm and illustrates the essence of flexible specialization. That is, make–buy decisions shape the configuration of the supply chain, and production flexibility choices shape the configuration of manufacturing systems in ways that have important impacts on the emergent strategy of a firm.

Our research has shown that facilities are becoming more focused (scheduling fewer part or product types) in their plants, and their agility (number of part families per unit of change over time) is significantly higher when production systems are being used to satisfy flexible customer demands.[38] For twenty plants randomly selected in durable goods manufacturing, this number of different part families

[37] G. Spina, E. Bartezzaghi, R. Cagliano, D. Draaijer, and H. Boer, "Strategically Flexible Production: The Multifocused Manufacturing Paradigm?" *International Journal of Operations & Production Management,* 16, no. 11 (1996), pp. 75–95.

[38] J. Ettlie and J. Penner-Hahn, "Flexibility Ratios and Manufacturing Strategy," *Management Science,* 40, no. 11 (November 1994), pp. 1444–1454.

(parts grouped by type–usually shape) that could be produced in any hour of production averaged 6.7. The median was 7.8 per hour. The more flexible the plant, as measured by these ratios of part family production capability per hour, the better it was able to meet multiple customer needs—now and in the future. Future product flexibility is the way these plants reduce direct labor costs.

This second conclusion—that future product flexibility was related to the way plants implemented the concept of scope—is based on additional results presented in Table 8-2. In this table, the measure of product flexibility—products changed (12 of 14 added parts) during the initial implementation period of modernizing flexible manufacturing systems—was significantly correlated with both initial total direct labor costs (which averaged about $20 in the U.S. plants we studied from 1988 to 1989) and the percentage of labor savings realized after the installation of the new flexible manufacturing system (which averaged about 24%). That is, plants with higher labor costs adopted more future product flexibility and also realized significantly greater direct labor savings after modernization.

BOX 8-2

Examples of "Flexible Specialization": Italy

Italian developments reversed in crucial ways the Japanese pattern. Yet these developments produced a surprisingly similar result: a flexible network of small- and medium-sized firms, using more and more numerical control (NC) technology to adapt to rapidly shifting markets. Japanese suppliers had been encouraged to exercise their autonomy by the mass producers they served, but the Italian small producers turned to forced-draft innovation largely to escape the domination of mass producers that wanted the dependence of the small firms.

Italian employers responded to the strike waves of the 1960s with a strategy of radical decentralization of production. There is no indication in the early commentary that this response was conceived as anything but a short-term expedient for regaining control of production and bidding time; once the worker militancy had passed, operations were to be regrouped in the large factories. The new shops used rudimentary technologies; evaded taxes and payments to the social-security system; ignored health-and-safety regulations; and, when the market demanded it, insisted on brutally long working hours.

What happened next caught managers, trade unions, workers, and government officials by surprise, although it had been foreshadowed in Prato and elsewhere: Dependent subcontractors began to federate. They used their collective capacities to devise innovative products and processes that gave them increasingly independent access to markets. The Brescian mini-mills, for example, moved at least as fast as their American counterparts in continuous casting; the farm- and construction-equipment industry in Emilia-Romagna got into production of sophisticated hydraulic-control devices; the Sassuolo ceramic makers devised new clay mixtures, tunnel ovens, and microprocessor-based devices for sorting output by subtle differences in the hues of each tile.

From the mid-1970s on, these changes were caught in the wide-meshed net of Italian statistics. Wage levels in areas such as Emilia-Romagna (where there were virtually

$\mathcal{T}$ABLE 8-2 Correlation of Total Hourly Costs and Percent Labor Savings to Product Flexibility

	Total Hourly Costs ($r = .41$)	Percent Labor Savings After New System Installation ($r = .48$)
Product Flexibility*	0.41 ($n = 20, p = .036$)	0.48 ($n = 13, p = .047$)
Mean	$19.65	23.8% (median = 10%)
Standard deviation	$ 5.37	27.9%
n	34	21

* Product flexibility is measured by whether the original planned parts and part families were changed during the course of the modernization project, including the first 2 years of production. Of the 14 that changed, 12 *added* or *planned to add* new parts (sig. Binomial test, $p = .0065$).

SOURCE: J. Ettlie and J. Penner-Hahn, 1994, p. 1451, Table 4.

---

no large firms and a proliferation of small shops) drew even with the levels in Piedmont, the most industrialized Italian region. Similarly, unemployment rates fell: In 1966 the rate was 4 percent for Italy, 4.3 percent for Emilia-Romagna, and 2.5 percent for Piedmont; in 1976 the rates in both Emilia-Romagna and Piedmont were 2.8 percent, three-quarters of the national average. Statistics on regional trade suggest that firms in decentralized industries were increasingly selling their output directly to foreign customers, rather than to large Italian firms for subsequent export.

This transformation of the supplier sector was also reflected in changes in the Italian machine-tool industry. As in Japan, the growing demand for flexible equipment led to a boom in production of NC equipment for (and often by) small shops: At the end of the 1970s, Italy ranked behind West Germany but well ahead of France and Great Britain as West Europe's second largest producer of NC equipment. Turin became a center of small industrial-automation and robotics firms, often serving the needs of the small-shop sector. Dozens of consultancies sprang up around Bologna to adapt large-firm technology to the needs of small shops, and to help automate artisanal processes (such as firing ceramics and annealing metals) to allow for subsequent modification of product and process. Leading American equipment makers began to market Italian shoe machinery because of its flexibility; and Italian ceramic-production machinery appeared on world markets.

Four coincident factors were crucial to this innovative turn: the Italian extended family; the view of artisan work as a distinct type of economic activity; the existence of merchant traditions connecting the Italian provinces to world markets; and the willingness of municipal and regional governments (often allied to the labor movement) to help create the infrastructure that the firms required but could not themselves provide. In the context of technological advance and market reorientation suggested by the earlier survey of industrial successes, these four conditions turned what might have been a regression in the industrial division of labor into an advance in the new direction.

SOURCE: Adopted from Piore and Sabel, 1984, pp. 226–224. Copyright © 1984 by Basic Books, Inc. Reprinted by permission of Basic Books, a member of Perseus Books, L.L.C.

Note that this finding is nearly identical to the results reported in the 1960s by economists who studied the diffusion of the first generation of this technology—numerical control (NC) machine tools—discussed in the first chapter and reported by Nabseth and Ray. This consistency across the decades using this technology indicates the persistent effects of scope in the economics of manufacturing. But it should not be forgotten that *the key to creating scope and making this a viable option to scale is the flexible technology afforded by computer technology applied to the factory floor.*

Implementing Manufacturing Strategy

Perhaps the most significant finding in case studies of flexible, focused factories is that in spite of well-articulated, published, and well-thought-out manufacturing strategies, they were not known at the plant level. For example, Ford Motor Company's manufacturing strategy (1990), is presented in Box 8-3. How well was this strategy implemented at the plant level? No one really knows. But that is the fundamental question in all policy deployment. If one looks closely at the elements of this manufacturing strategy, there are important similarities between the four major challenges outlined in this Ford statement and the Toyota production system, which was and continues to be the benchmark to achieve in automotive manufacturing design and manufacturing practice. Further evidence of this conclusion and the subsequent outcomes of this hot pursuit of Toyota appear in Mary Walton's book describing how Ford developed and launched the 1996 Taurus.[39] The Taurus design team tried to match the existing engineering and features achievement of the Toyota Camry, but by the time the new Taurus specifications were complete, Toyota was already pursing another strategy, taking cost out of future models.

This calls attention to one of the four basic features outlined in Phase I of successful transition strategies for manufacturing modernization introduced in the next chapter: *New technology adoption must be integrated with the overall business plan for the unit and company.* What does it take to implement strategy? At least two issues need to be resolved before one can answer this question. First, who formulates policy and strategy? And second, how general does corporate strategy have to be to be applied consistently across the entire organization?

Economies of Scope Become "Agility"

For many, the challenge has become not whether scale is better than scope, but how to implement scope. Many of these people and companies have joined the Agile Manufacturing Enterprise Forum (AMEF) at Lehigh University. Forum companies "struggle to implement lean-flexible production concepts." The vision was somewhat unclear when the AMEF got started, and there may still be confusion about its purpose, since agility implies "breaking out of the mass production mold with highly customized products."[40] Mass customization is only one version of agility, so the definitions of this new "paradigm" are, apparently, evolving.

---

[39] M. Walton, *Car: A Drama of the American Workplace* (New York: Norton, 1997), reviewed in *Business Week* by K. Kerwin (July 21, 1997), p. 14. The Toyota Production System (TPS) is summarized in *The Machine that Changed the World* and detailed in John Shook's training manual on the TPS.

[40] J. Sheridan, "Agile Manufacturing: Stepping Beyond Lean Production," *Industry Week* 242, no. 8 (April 19, 1993), pp. 30–46.

BOX 8-3

Ford's Manufacturing Strategy (circa 1990)

For many of us, the decade of the 1980s was a fight to survive—in a contest staged on a worldwide playing field. This contest required us to return to the basics of improving the QUALITY—and COST COMPETITIVENESS—of our products, and improving the relationships with our people. Those of us here today have survived these turbulent eighties.

The 1990s will increasingly change the manufacturing business—as worldwide competition becomes stronger, the business environments change. This we will witness and experience with the full enactment of the European Economic Community in 1992, the opportunities in the Eastern bloc, and the continued opening of markets in the Third World. This period will bring dynamic changes to the global business environment, and manufacturing must be prepared to address the technologies, processes and techniques that will emerge.

Manufacturing Strategy

Today, I would like to focus on the actions and strategies within Ford that are necessary to successfully meet these new technical and business challenges. Our future successes in integrating technical opportunities depend on how well we can forecast and plan for these changes. We believe the four major challenges in this process will be:

First, create a *Technology Strategy* that complements our business plan, and does not encourage technology for technology sake.

Second, integrate our *Global Resources* to identify, develop, and implement optimum worldwide technical and business solutions.

Third, establish *Cross-functional Teams* that utilize the principles of simultaneous engineering to develop technical ideas into products and processes to provide the best customer value.

Fourth, pursue *Continuous Development and Improvement of Our Skills* to effectively operate in a changing technical environment.

These are the key strategic initiatives we will use at Ford in pursuit of our vision of being a low-cost producer of the highest-quality products and services that provide the best customer value. It is clear that we cannot continue as a world-class manufacturer without the correct balance of product, business and manufacturing strategies.

SOURCE: J. E. Ettlie, "Ford Motor Company: Saline Plastics Plant," University of Michigan Business School (1990), p. 9 of the Case Appendix.

Until recently, however, there was little or no systematic evidence that agility was worth it. It was clear that companies were paying a premium to purchase (rarely develop) the flexible manufacturing systems needed to implement scope—25 percent higher and sometimes more than conventional technologies. Then the evidence began to trickle in to document what agility really was and how it fits into the overall global manufacturing picture. In theory, the value of scope grows as the rate of change in the business environment accelerates.[41] In one recent study of 600 durable goods companies in twenty countries, agility was shown to contribute significantly and uniquely to increasing market share in addition to R&D investments (see Figure 8-2).[42]

In a path-analytic model, R&D intensity was significantly associated with improvements in market share ($r^2 = 34\%$), controlling for firm size, previous market share, and regardless of industry or region of the world. Market share increases were also significantly correlated with improvements in manufacturing agility ($r^2 = 4\%$). Agility improvement was significantly correlated with R&D intensity, as well as with computerization in manufacturing and controlling for firm size and region. Also, agility exhibited industry effects, with electronic equipment firms elevated on this measure. Computerization exhibited regional (not industry) differences, with South American firms depressed on this measure.

Agility in manufacturing was measured by the average of improvements (percentage) in five areas: speed of product development, on-time deliveries, customer service, manufacturing lead time, and delivery time. The Cronbach alpha (standard-

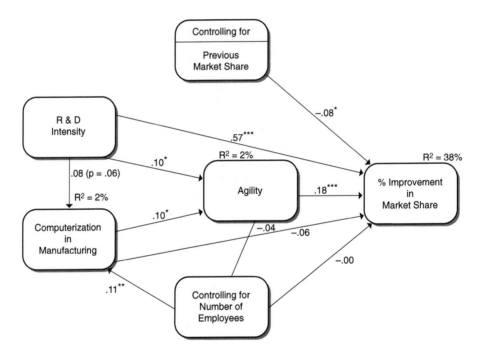

***p<.01; **p<.05; *p<.10.

Figure 8-2   What Causes Global Improvement in Durable Goods Market Share?

Reprinted by permission, Ettlie, "R&D and Global Manufacturing Performance," Vol. 44, no. 1, January 1998. Copyright 1998, The Institute of Management Sciences (currently INFORMS).

---

[41] D. Lei, M. Hitt, and J. Goldhar, "Advanced Manufacturing Technology: Organizational Design and Strategic Flexibility, *Organization Studies,* 17, no. 3 (1996), pp. 501–523.

[42] J. Ettlie, "R&D and Global Manufacturing Performance," *Management Science,* 44, no. 1 (January 1988), pp. 1–11.

ized item alpha) of this scale was 0.75 (a more appropriate measure, since these are percentages). The measure used was the average of these percentage improvements (mean = 24%, SD = 27% in Figure 8-2). The percentage of improvement in product variety would seem a natural for this scale, based on the more traditional measures of flexibility. However, when it is included, it lowers the standardized item alpha to 0.71, and the corrected item-total correlation for this question is only 0.21, whereas the other items have item-total correlations ranging from 0.41 to 0.56. This reinforces the results reported in Ettlie and Penner-Hahn reviewed earlier: *Product changeover speed and part family variety appear to be the more valid measures of flexibility, not part count or variety, per se.*

Mass Customization

Mass customization extends the concept of joint production to capture the best of both worlds in manufacturing—better customer response and satisfaction by tailoring products and economies of scale savings.[43] "Interactive Custom Clothes, for example, allows you to type in your exact measurements, your choice of 35 denims, and such variables as fit, style, and leg silhouette to produce a novel concept—jeans that fit. You can also customize items such as swimsuits, cars, and greeting cards.[44] Other examples include Dell computers assembled to your exact specifications, Levis cut to fit your body, and pills with the exact blend of vitamins, minerals, and herbs that you like. BMW, Mattel, McGraw-Hill, Wells Fargo, and many leading Internet businesses are adopting mass customization, including the logistics and marketing capability needed for implementation.[45] Custom Foot makes shoes that meet individual tastes and size requirements with mass customization with six retail locations, including a flagship store in Westport, Connecticut.[46]

When they decided to reconfigure a new highly modifiable engine, the New 1000 Series, Perkins engineers figured that there are one trillion possible variants in seven engines, each of which can be modified to fit customer requirements. A big factor in accomplishing the mass customization capability was that the designs were a paperless, or fully CAD-developed, engine.[47] Infinite Technology Group Ltd., a leader in mass customization of commodity products, expected to generate more than $40 million in revenue at the end of 1998, handling assembly and test for Sun Microsystems Inc., Digital Equipment Corp, Alpha, IBM Corp. AS/400 and RISC 6000 systems, and others.[48]

JIT (just-in-time) can be applied to low-tech industries and can be used with a traditional MRP (material requirements planning) system to accommodate mass

---

[43] B. J. Pine, *Mass Customization: The New Frontier in Business Competition* (Boston, Mass.: Harvard Business School Press, 1993).

[44] L. Falkenberg, "Virtually Made to Order," *Money,* 1, no. 12, (money.com Supplement). Fall 1998, pp. 60–61.

[45] E. Schonfeld, "The Customized, Digitized, Have-It-Your-Way Economy," *Fortune* 138 no. 6 (September 28, 1998), pp. 114–124.

[46] J. Martin, "Give 'em Exactly What They Want," *Fortune,* 136, no. 9 (November 10, 1997) pp. 283–286.

[47] G. Vasilash, "Mass Customization at Perkins: An Engine with One-Trillion Possibilities," *Automotive Manufacturing & Production,* 109, no. 2 (February 1997), pp. 42–44.

[48] W. S. Hersch, "Systems Integrator ITG Banks on Customization," *Computer Reseller News,* 792 (June 8, 1998), pp. 133–134.

customization. One carpet manufacturer met standard orders within 24 hours by tailoring its JIT manufacturing techniques,[49] which often mirror changes needed in the supply chain.[50] Intelligent Manufacturing Workstation (IMW) concepts facilitate mass customization implementation in manufacturing, primarily in metal bending.[51]

Hewlett-Packard has become a classic example of implementing mass-customization, postponing the task or differentiating of a product for a specific customer until the latest possible moment. But to accomplish this, products and manufacturing systems must be designed with independent modules, and the supply network must be dedicated to the facilities performing the customizing facility to be cost-effective.[52]

Industrial Bicycle Co. of Japan (NIBC) has mastered the dynamics of mass customization in a firm that encourages knowledge creation.[53] Many products or services formerly available only through a mass production environment are now customized, including newspapers, college textbooks,[54] and even power generation.[55]

✳ Economies of Scope Go Beyond Manufacturing

Perhaps, one of the most interesting developments since the agile manufacturing forum started is the spread of economies of scope outside manufacturing. A sampling of the publications in this area from 1994 to 1998 reveals considerable spread of the concept to industries such as health care, where scope reduces cost.[56] For example, combining gynecology and pediatrics is among the best examples of maximizing scope economies.[57] Economies of scope in pharmaceutical R&D pay off because diverse portfolios capture internal and external knowledge spillovers;

---

[49] Z. K. Weng, "Tailored Just-in-Time and MRP Systems in Carpet Manufacturing," *Production & Inventory Management Journal,* 39, no. 1 (First Quarter 1998), pp. 46–50.

[50] J. D. Oleson, "Developing Custom Manufacturing Supply Chain Capabilities," *National Productivity Review,* 17, no 2 (Spring 1998), pp. 73–80.

[51] D. A. Bourne, "IMW: The Key to Mass Customization," *Robotics World,* 16 no. 1 (Spring 1998), pp. 51–52.

[52] E. Feitzinger, and H. Lee, "Mass Customization at Hewlett-Packard: The Power of Postponement," *Harvard Business Review,* 75, no. 1 (January/February 1997), pp. 116–121.

[53] S. Kotha, "From Mass Production to Mass Customization: The Case of the National Industrial Bicycle Company of Japan," *European Management Journal,* 14, no. 5 (October 1996), pp. 442–450; S. Kotha, "Mass Customization: Implementing the Emerging Paradigm for Competitive Advantage," *Strategic Management Journal,* 16 (Special Issue) (Summer 1995), pp. 21–42.

[54] R. S. M. Lau, "Mass Customization: The Next Industrial Revolution," *Industrial Management* 37, no. 5 (September/October 1995), p. 18.

[55] K. C. Choi and T. B. Jarboe, "Mass Customization in Power Plant Design and Construction," *Power Engineering,* 100, no. 1 (January 1996), pp. 33–36.

[56] T. Gonzales, "An Empirical Study of Economies of Scope in Home Healthcare," *Health Services Research,* 32, no. 3 (August 1997), pp. 313–324; D. Dunn, S. Sacher, W. Choen, and W. Hsiao, "Economies of Scope in Physicians' Work: The Performance of Multiple Surgery," *Inquiry,* 32, no. 1 (Spring 1995), pp. 87–101.

[57] D. Prior, "Technical Efficiency and Scope Economies in Hospitals," *Applied Economics,* 28, no. 10 (October 1996), pp. 1295–1301.

that is, there is more potential for synergy.[58] Scope experiments are underway in commercial airlines,[59] banking,[60] and financial services.[61]

 Occasions for New Process Technology Incorporation

Although major technology-driven change is rare in any organization, larger firms, in particular, are almost continuously purchasing new hardware and software systems that typically "embed" incremental technology. Therefore, a near continuous review of operations strategy with respect to technology issues is becoming necessary in companies with more than fifty employees. Furthermore, with the rate of new product and new service introduction escalating (see Chapter 7) with precipitation of new process and new information technology adoption, the occasion for new technology consideration in the transformation core is becoming an ongoing business.

$\mathscr{S}$UMMARY

Thousands of books and articles have been written about the innovation process from the perspective of marketing and R&D. Rarely, and only rather recently, has attention turned to the operations function as it relates to innovation. Yet, it may be that the ultimate challenge of implementing innovative ideas will depend on how well the operations group can incorporate technology, especially purchased technology, needed to deliver new products and services.

In this chapter, functional strategies for operations were introduced. Essential to any operations strategy are the technology choices that are made, consistent with the business plan and other functional strategies of the firm (see Chapter 4). Focus and generic strategic types (e.g., niche differentiation) are typical of the choices that need to be made. Regardless of choice, all operations strategies need to help the organization differentiate itself from competitors and adopt an appropriate scope in product lines and facilities. The most important theoretical distinction that needs to be made here is the difference between joint production (multiple products on one line or in one network) and co-production (co-ownership of the means of production). The latter topic is taken up in Chapter 11. Variants on the theme of joint production are flexible manufacturing, flexible networks (e.g., those in northern Italy), agility, and mass customization.

---

[58] R. Henderson and I. Cockburn, "Scale, Scope, and Spillovers: The Determinants of Research Productivity in Drug Discovery," *Rand Journal of Economics,* 21, no. 1 (Spring 1996), pp. 32–59.

[59] S. Kindel, "Economies of Scope," *Financial World,* 162, no. 18 (September 14, 1993), pp. 42–43.

[60] A. Zardkoohi and J. Kolari, "Branch Office Economies of Scale and Scope," *Journal of Banking & Finance,* 18, no. 3 (1994), pp. 421–433.

[61] W. Barnett and G. Zhou, "Financial Firms' Production and Supply-side Monetary Aggregation Under Dynamic Uncertainty," *Federal Reserve Bank of St. Louis Review,* 76, no. 2 (Mar/Apr 1994), p. 133.

DISCUSSION QUESTIONS

Read "Meeting the Future Head-On", which is a recent history of The Gleason Works, and answer the following questions (Case 8-1).

1. Why did Gleason's adoption of cellular manufacturing fail to deliver the expected results at revitalizing the plant?

2. What was the strategy that resulted from the re-evaluation of plant programs after cells didn't deliver needed performance improvements?

3. What will determine the success of this strategy?

4. What is likely to be the next challenge for Gleason?

CASE SUGGESTIONS

1. Perhaps the best service operations management case available is: Shouldice Hospital, HBS 9-683-068, and there is a video called "A Stitch In Time."

2. A great case on packaging innovation (not a product, not a process, a hybrid technology): Campbell Soup Company, HBS 9-690-051.

3. A terrific case on multiple plants and multiple technologies in need of modernization with other concerns: "ITT Automotive: Global Manufacturing Strategy (1994)" HBS: 9-695-002.

✳ CASE 8-1

Meeting the Future Head On
By Gary S. Vasilash

The story, related by David J. Burns, vice president, Machine Products, The Gleason Works (Rochester, New York), is a familiar one. During the mid-1980s action was taken on the factory floor of the venerable (as in nearly 130 years old) precision gear production machinery manufacturer. More than 400 machines were rearranged to form functional cells. And while that was thought to be a good thing to do—and cells are a good arrangement for machinery—Burns admitted the consequences weren't what they were thought—or anticipated them—to be: "We didn't see all of the benefits we were hoping to get. "

By 1989 costs were rising. Lead times for Gleason products were stretching out further and further.

James S. Gleason, chairman and president of the company, asked one of those questions that people ask only after swallowing deeply—especially people who have their name on the door of the firm that, at that time, was in the town in question for nearly a century-and-a-quarter: "Do we want to keep manufacturing machines in Rochester?"

Realize that about two-thirds of the company's sales are outside the U.S., so a move abroad could be more readily justified for The Gleason Works than for other domestic companies that sell here but which have transferred production Over There.

And The Gleason Works has manufacturing facilities abroad: in Baudour, Belgium (which the company is selling in 1993, not because it is abandoning a continental presence, but, Jim Gleason explained, because the plant, at about 200,000 square ft, is just too big) and in Plymouth, England. What's more, in 1991, Gleason entered into what is described as a "strategic alliance" with a Japanese machine tool manufacturer, Okamoto. Okamoto Machine Tool Works, which is based in Yokohama, produces, among other products, spur and helical gear grinding machines. Presumably, there was a possibility that Okamoto could have become a primary source of products for Gleason, that Gleason could have employed a strategy used by several U.S. consumer goods manufacturers, which is to totally source products from another company and simply relabel the equipment.

Could have, but didn't. (The alliance that was formed does involve some relabeling. Gleason is customizing some Okamoto-built gear grinding machines for U.S. and European markets and is selling them under the Gleason name. Okamoto is finishing the assembly of some Gleason machines for the Asian market. In addition the two companies are collaborating on the development of gear-making equipment.)

Staying There

Jim Gleason asked the question about whether to continue in New York. And he answered it.

Yes, the company would continue manufacturing machine tools in Rochester. There was—and is—a strong infrastructure in place. There were experienced people. And while there are places that might seem to be less expensive, Jim Gleason told me that all things considered, staying in Rochester made more sense. But he also stressed that it wouldn't be, that it couldn't be, business as usual. Things had to change. Jim Gleason said that while the company once started expanding its product offerings, this expansion wasn't one that permitted the people working for the company to manufacture these products such that they would truly be the best in the world. Or, at the very least, competitive with the best in the world.

"In today's market," Gleason stated with no uncertainty, "you've got to be among the best producers."

So he said that the company had to get to its core. Get to the fundamentals. Get to a point where its resources would be both concentrated and leveraged. Get back to building gearmaking machinery.

Yes, they would continue to build machines in Rochester. But they would not build them in a manner which had been the status quo, a status quo that, while undergoing some modifications—such as the cellular manufacturing—had, in effect, grown through the ages. That approach couldn't cut it. But what would?

A New Approach

One of the first things that was decided was that the approach would be a focused one, one of a manageable size. This wouldn't be a case of taking on more than could be reasonably expected to be successful. That is, the company consists of three business groups: Standard Products, Special Products, and Tooling Products. Rather than trying to reorganize, or reengineer, the entire organization, people at Gleason determined that the Standard Products Group would be the initial area where change would occur.

Standard Products Group, as its name implies, manufactures machines that are, in effect, catalog items, such as the PHOENIX line of computer-controlled gear cut-ters, grinders and hobbers. PHOENIX, which was launched into the market in 1988, which implements, to a great extent, electronics in place of mechanics, has proven to be successful for the company. It represents the direction that Gleason machinery will take today and in the years to come.

So while there were people looking at how to manufacture products in the 1990s and beyond, there were also engineers at Gleason, during this same period, that were focused on what products would be manufactured in the 1990s and beyond. During the period that Standard Products manufacturing was undergoing a change, seven new machines were introduced for the production of both parallel and bevel/hypoid gears. Which is more machines than Gleason had ever before introduced in such a concentrated period.

Not Standing Still

All of this underlines the fact that while a company may be venerable, while a company may have highly respected technology, while a company may have its products in leading manufacturing firms literally around the world, there is no lock on success—nor even survival. What Jim Gleason and his staff acknowledged—and what they have come to grips with in a way that is certainly uncharacteristic of old-line capital equipment builders and even advanced in relation to what are typically considered to be "enlightened" manufacturers of durable goods—was that all of the rules have changed and will keep on changing. Realize that a company founded in 1865 that is continuing to produce equipment in 1993 is doing some things right. But history is not necessarily the best guide to the future. A new compass is required. And while it may be more comfortable to hew to the tried-and-true, to move ahead one cannot simultaneously stay behind.

So The Gleason Works moved. And invested, during a two-year period, some $40-million in new precision gear-making development and manufacturing capability. Realize what this number represents: in 1990, the company had sales of $176-million. In 1991 sales were $177-million. In 1992, sales fell to $147-million. $40-million is not an insignificant sum at The Gleason Works.

In January, 1991, the Gleason board gave the go-ahead. Ground was broken in March of that year. The goal was to have a fully operating factory and new products being put through it by September, 1992. The target was hit by June, 1992.

Around the World

Richard Johnstone joined the Gleason team as vice president, Machine Technology, at the period of the crux, when the manufacturing and product strategy was being redefined. Johnstone, a manufacturing veteran, joined up with David Burns in an investigation that would lead to the shape of things to come.

The two travelled the world, visiting more than 30 manufacturing firms—those producing consumer electronics, automobiles, automotive products, machine tools.

They spent lots of time on planes. Lots of time in hotel restaurants and bars. Lots of time talking, arguing, thinking, reconsidering. They tried to determine how what they were seeing could be applied to manufacturing standard products at Gleason. What they were seeking was efficiency in low-volume (one complete machine per day, or 250 per year), high-variety (as many as a dozen different models) production. Whereas the true system leadtime had been nine to 10 months, they were looking to create a situation where 30 days would be the measure. (Or, another way to look at it is that 24 hours is the unit of measure, as that is how often a machine is to be built.)

Burns said that he came to the realization that the traditional scenario meant that there were as much as 50 percent of the operational assets tied up in inventory, and that by eliminating inventory, they would be freeing up the money. Assets could be put to productive use, not simply sit in storage areas. Burns admitted that it was something he had a somewhat difficult time coming to grips with, something that is more easily said than understood. "But it's such a powerful tool," he commented.

The Success Factors

Burns said that there are six success factors.

One is an environmentally controlled facility that's equipped with highly precise manufacturing equipment. Although Standard Products operates in a new factory, it is not a greenfield site. Rather, they are operating in two areas that had been foundries: One built in the first decade of this century, the other in the fifth decade. The total space involved is 150,000-square feet—and all of it is temperature controlled. (In the clean room area, not only is the temperature controlled to ±1 degree F, but the humidity is controlled, as well.)

Not only did the machinery in the plant have to be precise, but another success factor calls for flexibility that allows rapid changeover flexibility.

The biggest investment in equipment was placed through Toyoda Machinery USA (Arlington Heights, Illinois). Within 14 months, two double-column machining centers (both BN-25A machines, which are big—as in a table measuring 98 × 157 in.—and powerful—as in a 35-hp spindle drive) and two horizontal five-axis machining centers (both FH100 machines, which have 31.5 × 31.5-

in. pallets and a 30-hp spindle drive motor). Through design for manufacturing techniques implemented at Gleason, including the standardization of bearing sizes used in the gear-making machines produced by the company, the number of tools stored on the machining centers was standardized at 120. In the not-so-distant past, it was possible to require more than 1,600 preset tools to machine the castings for one unit. (Another success factor: new products specifically designed for efficient manufacture.)

Burns explained that one of the primary reasons why Toyoda was picked as a supplier was the company's personnel's willingness to work with Gleason. For example, Burns said that they needed a rotary index accuracy on the tables of the horizontal machining centers that was one-third that normally supplied by Toyoda and that it was necessary that the machines be built to one half the normal build tolerances. There was the issue of time. Apparently, Toyoda sent in three work teams that worked 24 hours per day for nearly eight weeks, installing the bridge mills. "They wanted 13 weeks to do the job," Burns recalled. "We wanted them to do it in six." (Note: a third horizontal machining center was added in the first quarter of 1993.)

Authority—and Responsibility

Another success factor: People. In the traditional arrangement, the number of indirect personnel was, all things considered, not insignificant. But with a rearranged Standard Products, there would be a great minimization of what Burns described as "interventionists": people who tended to interrupt the flow. That is, there is no purchasing department. There are no expeditors. Two material planners work in the factory. The plan calls for the Standard Products factory to have a staff of 150 people; of that number, 125 will be direct. That, compared to the status quo, is a change on the order of 80 to 90 percent.

But making the change from a conventional organization to a new one hasn't been easy. Historically, the people who make the most are the people who have the greatest individual skills, as in a machinist that is able to make the perfect part when others tend to scrap them. But in the new scenario, people work in teams and the machinery itself is capable. People have been given authority. For example, there are no time clocks in the Standard Products area and the teams are able to set their own hours. But they have also been given responsibility.

First-line managers are gone. Which means that the various teams must not only help keep their work areas clean, but they must also schedule the next day's production so that they will meet the overall requirements of the main schedule. Some people have found this to be a bit too demanding and have left.

Training has been a big part of preparing the people for this new arrangement; and it continues to be important, with the people spending 10 percent of their time in some training program.

Information Power

Another factor is an information network that permits paperless manufacturing. One of the things that Richard Johnstone emphasized in the development of the new factory was the implementation of a comprehensive information system. This is a network that ties together the engineering department, the sales department, the service department, the suppliers, and the plant floor personnel. Working from an IBM AS/400 at the top, it goes through to the intermediate level where there is computer-aided design, and bills-of-materials and such-like, then to workstations both on the factory floor and at suppliers. "This affects, almost instantaneously, the way we do business," Burns said, explaining that whereas the people involved in a project can now access the same information at the same time—such as an industrial engineer, a design engineer, and an operator all looking at a part drawing on individual terminals—in the past, it took days for information to make its way through the various departments. Johnstone described the arrangement as "a cooperative spirit achieved through communications." He noted that one of the pitfalls of downsizing in organizations is that there tends to be a limitation of what people know. But in the Gleason system, there are complete instructions and procedures available on the workstations located throughout the plant-illustrated with video images—so that there's not a problem should the person who normally does the job be out of the loop for whatever reason. The comprehensive information management system in place in the plant allows the people involved in the process to boost their capabilities, be they on the factory floor or in an engineering office.

Tight Tolerances

Although there are steps being taken to be a low-cost producer, there is no possibility of cutting any corners in the production of the machines. "A profile error of five to 10 millionths of an inch on the surface of a bevel gear makes the difference between whether a transmission will sing or be silent," Johnstone said. He explained that this means that the gear-cutting equipment must be highly accurate in its manufacture, such that all of its components are combined and related so that errors are not created in the end products. These process demands have led to the development at Gleason of test consoles that are able to perform comprehensive testing and measuring of the subassemblies. Given the broad capabilities of these units, which are housed in a clean room where subassemblies are produced, Johnstone called them "virtual instrumentation" which helps the people at Gleason to build what Johnstone claimed are "the most accurate machine tools in the world."

Success Through Suppliers

Suppliers are key success factor. This become visibly evident when Burns stood in an area where there had been inventory and there are kitted goods ready for movement to point of use. There are no conventional inventory racks in the entire plant. Burns explained that there are 16 core suppliers, one for each type of commodity. For example, Torrington supplies the bearings; GE Fanuc supplies control packages. Burns said that it was necessary to have the chief executives of each of the supplier companies commit to meeting the Gleason requirements.

Burns admitted that Gleason isn't a huge manufacturer with lots of clout with suppliers. He admitted that one major bearing company simply wasn't interested in meeting the Gleason requirements. "To serve manufacturers around the world, we need the assistance of our suppliers," he said, adding, in no uncertain terms, "And we couldn't do what we're doing here without our suppliers.

Today, suppliers, which have computer access to the bills-of-materials, know what they must deliver for the machines being built at Gleason and when it must be delivered. When their supplies are delivered, they are kitted and put in a preassigned location. The person making the delivery goes to a workstation terminal and inputs the information related to the delivery. This input, now part of the network, is used by, among other interested parties, accounting. If the supplier has 30-day net terms with Gleason, then a check is automatically generated.

Jim Gleason said,"There are two things that are vitally important. One is empowering people. The second is reducing cycle time between order and delivery." He adds that The Gleason Works will continue to work on those two things. "We've really just started," he said, modestly. "We still have a long way to go."

But they're getting there.

SOURCE: G. S. Vasilash, "Meeting the Future Head-On," *Production*, 105, no. 7 (July 1993), pp. 50–55. Copyright Gardner Publications, Inc. Reprinted with permission.

Chapter 9

Process Innovation

𝒞HAPTER OBJECTIVES

To review the issues, models, and methods of the new process development. To take stock of the performance of process innovation. A model of successful implementation of process technological innovation is presented, with new empirical results from a survey of enterprise resource planning (ERP) systems in 60 U.S. companies. The chapter ends with a "cookbook" summary of how to implement process innovation. A case study of SAP's R/3 German software installations promotes discussion of these issues.

Let's review the case introduced in Chapter 2. It was 1983. Gillette had just finished market testing a prototype of the Sensor razor with 500 men, and the results were promising. The problem: how to mass-produce the high-technology blade and cartridge system of the future. Seven years later, and after incorporating a new resin called Noryl for blade cartridges and investing millions of dollars to co-develop a new laser spot-welding technology with a supplier, the razor was ready for launch. All of these manufacturing innovations were unanticipated. Manufacturing technology is different from new product technology.

Most of the R&D resources in the United States are spent on developing new products.[1] In fact, companies *expect* to spend R&D money on new product development. However, when companies launch new products or upgrade operations, they tend to *purchase* new processing (e.g., manufacturing or computer) equipment from outside the organization, even though this equipment is usually avail-

---

[1] M. Wolff, "Meet Your Competition," *Research-Technology Management* (January–February 1995), pp. 18–24.

able to competitors. This new equipment often embodies new technology, but companies prefer to buy the best equipment available rather than develop this technology or design systems in-house.

There continue to be outstanding exceptions to this rule. Quad Graphics, Inc. and Honda North America, Inc. are two.[2] These companies develop outstanding new processing technology systems to produce their products. But even Quad Graphics and Honda—and other very outstanding manufacturers such as Toyota, Merck, GE, Johnson & Johnson, Motorola, and Hewlett-Packard—purchase a small fortune in new equipment every year. Manufacturing firms are not alone. Banks and insurance companies purchase billions of dollars worth of computer systems. This is one of the things that makes operations process technology different: Few companies that actually depend on this technology instigate all or part of these changes themselves. These innovations in operations are not linked to manufacturing systems or information systems. Even the mature railroad industry, which has not changed significantly since the 1950s when diesel replaced steam power, is innovating with AC power units and advanced scheduling technology.

The second thing that makes operations process technology different is that operations management has been relegated to the backroom for the last three decades, and we are just now beginning to upgrade our operations talent in engineering and management again and to pay these people equitably. People can say that manufacturing matters, but most companies have still not stepped up to embrace this principle of corporate balance and integration between the functions. Until manufacturing truly matters, process technology will *not* have the same status or receive the same attention as product technology in a company. Outstanding companies pay attention to both. The history of the Malcolm Baldrige National Quality Award selection process suggests that just a handful of U.S. companies are truly outstanding.

The third thing that makes operations processing technology different is the development challenge of software in hardware–software systems. With typical software maintenance costs exceeding 50 percent of information department budgets, one gets an idea of how important and difficult manufacturing and operations

BOX 9-1

Case Summary of Auto Electronics Plant

Overall yield for the "A" (disguised) line was 98.5 percent (1.5 percent defects—mostly in floating parts, e.g., bad clinch). The "B" (disguised) line has 3 percent defects and others 2.5 percent. With the Kaizen (continuous improvement) project, in 6 months with teams meeting daily, defects were reduced by 50 percent from 2.9 percent to 1.5 percent and then down to 1.39 percent most recently. Two months earlier, an X-ray inspection machine had also been installed in the auto-insertion department.

---

[2] R. Ynostroza, "Quotes from the Quintessential Printer," *Graphic Arts Monthly,* 66, no. 7 (July 1994), p. 10.

software can be. Software is not like mechanical-, or hydraulic- or electronic-based hardware systems. Software follows its own set of operational rules. In worst-case scenarios, such as General Motors Corporation in the 1980s, billions of dollars are spent with little payback to show for the effort. Perhaps even worse is that a large percentage of new operations technology installations don't fail outright, they just limp along, often for years, unable to contribute significantly to the strategic mission of the firm but with no viable alternative.

New manufacturing systems are the focus of the remainder of this chapter, but many of the trends summarized here apply to hardware–software systems in other economic sectors, as well. What successful process-focused companies have in common, whether they develop their own manufacturing technology or adapt this technology from outside the firm, is that they are serious about manufacturing R&D. These companies have also learned that changes in administrative policy and practice are critical to making manufacturing process innovations work. Manufacturing technology is different.

Take, for example, the case of a Japanese transplant auto electronics company that we visited in 1994 (Box 9-1). *This case illustrates how technological innovation and organizational innovation can work together to keep leading-edge firms at the front of the pack.* It is an extension of the cultural lag hypothesis from anthropology—that societal adjustments to new technology follow (lag) their introduction or successful use. This was the extended model of organizational lag by Evans and eventually by Damanpour (1984), who showed how this theory applies to companies. Here, it is a matter of matching changes simultaneously and avoiding this lag.

For the last decade, my colleagues, students, and I have studied hundreds of durable goods companies in the United States and around the world with an eye toward understanding why some of these firms are better process technology innovators and adapters than others.[3] We have developed a simple model that describes the differences that separate an unchanging, vulnerable manufacturing firm typical of the 1970s and 1980s, and the successful new process technology integrator of the 1990s. The summary of this work is presented next.

$\mathscr{I}$MPLEMENTING NEW PROCESS TECHNOLOGY

New processing technologies do not implement themselves. New systems are usually purchased outside and their development is episodic, especially for major modernization or new product and service launch. Therefore, appropriation or capture of benefits from these investments is problematic, primarily because the technology is theoretically available to anyone who can pay for it, including com-

---

[3] J. E. Ettlie, W. P. Bridges, and R. D. O'Keefe, "Organizational Strategy and Structural Differences for Radical versus Incremental Innovation," *Management Science,* 30, no. 6 (June 1984), pp. 682–695; J. E. Ettlie and E. Reza, "Organizational Integration and Process Innovation," *Academy of Management Journal* 34, no. 4 (October 1992), pp. 795–827; J. E. Ettlie and J. Penner-Hahn, "Flexibility Ratios and Manufacturing Strategy," *Management Science,* 40, no. 11 (November 1994), pp. 1444–1454.

petitors.[4] The extant literature reviewed below on appropriation of manufacturing technology rents suggests two important conclusions.

1. *Successful modernization hinges on the specific mosaic of technologies adopted.*
2. *Performance of manufacturing technology depends on which (if any) organizational innovations are adopted in conjunction with deployment.*

These two generalizations are quite far-reaching and complex, so they are taken up separately. To the extent that a firm's resources determine how outcomes will be pursued, the role of government becomes more important.[5]

The Adoption of Manufacturing Technologies

During the last decade, the relative absence of rigorous applied research on the adoption of manufacturing technology has been replaced by a number of important contributions in both the academic and applied literature. Much of this literature has been reviewed elsewhere.[6] We focus here on just a few of the studies most relevant to the central questions of this inquiry. For the time being, we will set aside the limitations of this work and return to future research needs as an ancillary issue later.

Perhaps the most comprehensive data available on the investment in manufacturing technology, primarily in the durable goods and assembled products industries, resulted from collection in two panels by the U.S. Department of Commerce (DC) in 1988 and 1993. Fortunately, comparative data were also collected in Canada at approximately the same time (1989). These data have been analyzed by several research teams, but we focus here on just a few for brevity. Efforts to duplicate this effort in Europe are also relevant, but, again, will be mentioned only in passing to maintain the focus of this report.

Seventeen specific manufacturing technologies used in durable goods manufacturing (SIC 34–38) were included in the DC survey. These data have subsequently been augmented with statistics from the Census of Manufacturing and data from other sources to develop a comprehensive picture of technology impact for 7,000 plants.[7] Earlier results from nearly identical data showed that the more technologies plants adopted *(technology intensity),* the higher the rates of employment growth and lower closure rates, controlling for other explanatory factors. Plants adopting six or

---

[4] See, for example, D. Echevarria, "Capital Investment and Profitability of Fortune 500 Industrial: 1971–1990," *Studies in Economics and Finance,* 18, no. 1 (Fall 1997), pp. 3–35, who reports that "only 25% of the Fortune 500 … were able to obtain significantly increased profitability," p. 35.

[5] It is important to control for industry effects in these generalizations: experience varies widely by economic sector. See R. S. M. Lau, "Operational Characteristics of Highly Competitive Firms," *Production and Inventory Management Journal,* 38, no. 4 (Fourth Quarter 1997), pp. 17–21.

[6] J. E. Ettlie and E. Reza, "Organizational Integration and Process Innovation," *Academy of Management Journal,* 34, no. 4 (October 1992), pp. 795–827; J. E. Ettlie and J. Penner-Hahn, "Flexibility Ratios and Manufacturing Strategy," *Management Science,* 40, no. 11 (November 1994), pp. 1444–1454.

[7] Much of this section is based on D. N. Beede, and K. H. Young, "Patterns of Advanced Technology Adoption and Manufacturing Performance," *Business Economics,* 33, no. 2 (April 1998), pp. 43–48.

more of these 17 possible choices (e.g., numerically controlled machine tools) were found to pay premiums of 16 percent for production workers and 8 percent for non-production workers. As much as 60 percent of the variance in wage premium paid by large plants can be explained by adoption of these manufacturing technologies. Between 1998 and 1993, increases in computer-aided design (CAD) and local area networks (LANs) were most prominent. Labor productivity, generally, is significantly enhanced by adoption of these technologies, which is typical of patterns established in earlier generations of research on this subject.

Analysis of the comparable Canadian (1989) data has yielded similar results, with the added findings that manufacturing technology adoption is coincident with R&D spending by larger plants, and with variance across industries. Adoption of inspection and programmable control technology appears to promote growth faster than other technologies, but it is not clear if controlling for other factors would sustain this result. Most important, there is an indication in the Canadian data that the mosaic of technologies adopted does matter, not just the number of technologies purchased. A comparable result for information technology has also emerged in one applied study introduced later (adoption of EDI, or electronic data interchange).

There is considerable variance in the adoption mix of technologies in these data. In the United States, the most frequently used technologies, adopted stand-alone or in combinations, are CAD and numerical control (NC), even though this pattern is found in only 2 to 4 percent of cases. About 18 percent of these plants adopt unique combinations of technologies (e.g., common to only one or two plants), and adoption patterns generally do not follow industry groups.

The highest rate of job growth is associated with adoption of 11 of the 17 technologies studied in the United States. In particular, LAN technologies, either combined with CAD or used exclusively for the factory, was associated with a 25 percent faster employment growth rate than plants that did not adopt any of the surveyed technologies from 1982 to 1987. CAD and NC were associated with a 15 percent higher job growth rate during the same period. Programmable logic controllers (PLCs) and NC yielded a 10 percent higher employment growth rate. On the other hand, CAD and digital representation of CAD for procurement experienced a 20 percent slower job growth rate, but very fast productivity growth.

Productivity levels were 50 percent higher (than nonadopters) among companies that used the following technologies: CAD, CAD output for procurement, LANs, inter-company networks, PLCs, and shop-floor control computers. Earnings for production workers versus nonproduction workers were more directly associated with adoption of these technologies. For example, production worker employment growth was 35 percent higher in plants that adopted LANs and shop-floor control. But in 60 to 80 percent of the technology categories, there were higher earnings levels for both job categories.

Two general conclusions can be drawn from these results in addition to the primary finding that the pattern of adoption determines performance, rather than simply the number of technologies used. First, outcomes vary according to which technologies are adopted and which *type of performance is measured*. This was called the organizational effectiveness *paradox* in earlier research.[8] Second, the

---

[8] R. E. Quinn and K. S. Cameron, "Organizational Effectiveness Life Cycles and Shifting Criteria of Effectiveness," *Management Science* (1983), pp. 33–51.

combination of stand-alone technology such as CAD and integrating technologies such as LANs has the greatest impact on performance, regardless of outcome measure. Linking fabrication with assembly in successful plants suggests that *functional coordination* is essential to appropriation of adopted technology benefits. This integrating aspect of manufacturing technology is taken up in the next section.

Anecdotal reports indicate considerable variance in success with enterprise integration programs, as well,[9] so this appears to be a fertile context in which to investigate a perennial research question: how to capture benefit from purchased technology. The one report that did make an attempt to document reported differences in information technology investments found that EDI was where payoffs occurred, similar to the integrating technologies in manufacturing.[10]

In summary, the literature and empirical findings on manufacturing technology adoption indicates the following:

1. Technology matters generally—especially new design and operations technology that promotes coordination, but it depends on which performance measure is tracked.

2. The *mosaic* of manufacturing technologies matters—not just the extent or number of technologies adopted (e.g., local area networks adopted with or without CAD account for 25% faster employment growth in adopters versus nonadopters).

✖ Assimilation of New Manufacturing Process Technology

Assuming that new investment in processing equipment is warranted,[11] how do successful firms assimilate new operations technology? First of all, successful manufacturing firms tend to purchase technology that can be exploited for all its benefits—whether they are using it for a new product or experimenting with a new technology for a future product. Second, the so-called *phased approach*, in which companies or plants progress from a more rudimentary practice level to a more sophisticated level, does have some merit to describe what happens, but it is far from perfect. At the risk of describing what sounds like a phased approach, model "transition" *states* (not stages or phases) are presented in Figure 9-1. The principle of equifinality from general systems theory is the underpinning of this approach—there are any number of equally good ways of achieving an outstanding end.

Therefore, Figure 9-1 is not meant as a summary of a prescriptive migration path, but is a method of highlighting the differences between successful and unsuccessful practice. It is only for clarity and convenience that the states are presented in this manner. There is enough uncertainty and randomness in any change

---

[9] J. B. White, D. Clark, and S. Ascarelli, "Program of Pain, This German Software Is Complex, Expensive and Wildly Popular," *The Wall Street Journal* (March 14, 1997), pp. A1, A8.

[10] Deloitte & Touche, LLP, "Leading Trends in Information Services," Ninth Annual Survey of North American Chief Information Officers," Deloitte & Touche Consulting Group, 1997.

[11] R. S. Kaplan and A. A. Atkinson, "Justifying Investments in New Technology," *Advanced Management Accounting* (Englewood Cliffs, N.J.: Prentice-Hall, 1989), pp. 473–519.

process, especially one involving new processing technology, to make generalizing risky. Most firms do not pass through these stages as if marching up a mountain, giving the impression that everything can be planned in advance and according to some milestone chart. On the other hand, successful firms we encounter do all of these things well and are exemplary assimilators of new processing technology.

The Starting State and First Transition

When companies or plants begin to modernize, they usually start the journey toward a well-integrated production unit with a traditional hierarchy. A "pyramid" structure is usually the first to go, as indicated in the schematic of Figure 9-1. Layers are often removed. But if you look at what the successful companies do (listed next to State 2), they don't necessarily downsize (although equality of sacrifice in a downturn is one key characteristic of these companies). Successful manufacturers do integrate business plans and technology strategies, use technology agreements with their union, if they have a union, and share business data freely inside the firm. In short, the communication–empowerment issues are initially (and only tentatively) resolved in this state.

As a consequence of these administrative changes, significantly higher throughput is achieved when new processing technology has been adopted. The productive unit can claim State 2 status, which is a significant improvement. A successful installation of a flexible, integrated manufacturing or assembly system should improve throughput an average of 50 percent, with exceptional cases doing even better in steady-state. *In general, the principle operating throughout these states and cases is that the greater the leap in technology, the more new policies, practices, organization structures and vision are needed, consistent with the culture of the firm. Depending on which state the productive unit is in and which dimension is chosen for integration, different performance measures will be affected with different results* (see Figure 1-1).

An illustration of one of the key differences between successful and unsuccessful process innovation adopters in manufacturing will be used here: If there is a union, there is a technology agreement with the union that enables value capture and collaboration for modernization (see Figure 9-1 under hierarchical integration, the four bullets). The case that comes to mind immediately is General Motors Corporation, introduced in Chapter 1, and the summer 1998 strike in Flint, Michigan.

They used to say that what was good for GM was good for the country. They also used to say that the more union workers you had on your payroll, the more employees could afford to buy your cars. The world has changed. The new order of the global economy has three principles for manufacturing:

1. Markets are global.
2. Competition is global.
3. Standards for performance are global.

Having said that, let's set aside the global issues and just stick with our own backyard. Why are Ford's costs and Chrysler's costs (before the merger with Daimler-Benz) less than GM's? And why don't Ford and Chrysler have strikes? The answers to these questions are related.

GM's cost structure has always been higher, but when you have a market share of 50 percent you actually need a cost structure that includes high investment in R&D and new equipment to stay ahead. With a market share hovering at 30 percent, and with overcapacity in the industry, a bloated cost structure won't work. GM has been slow to address this problem. Ford has aggressively cut costs. Chrysler was the most outsourced of the Big Three, so suppliers are taking up their slack. Toyota can make a profit at 80 yen to the dollar.

But what about strikes? Ford does more than just work with its UAW department. Nearly 20 years ago, Ford joined the University of Michigan in one of the most innovative in-plant education programs ever undertaken. Eventually installed in more than 60 Ford sites, the Employment Transition Program, funded with a nickel set-aside from a contract negotiation, was originally designed to address what some estimated at that time to be a 20 percent illiteracy rate in assembly plants. Our late colleague, Professor Jean Gordus, documented one Ford case after another of how this program transformed the company.

Quietly, this program grew to many course offerings after work and after shifts to include every subject needed and requested by the work force. In the summer, some plants had courses on astronomy that the whole family attended. Employees on the line would work quietly in their team areas on course assignments before and after their shifts. And they discussed shift coordination issues as a result. The amazing outcome? The "second shift" got better and didn't blame the first or third shift for poor quality, and vice versa.

Do people matter at Ford? Yes. Although Chrysler (before the merger) was late in adopting this program, the company had its own brand of caring about people and the community. DaimlerChrysler still manufactures cars in Detroit. What can we say about the others?

For instance, at General Motors, look at the issues that were being contested in the 1998 summer strike. GM failed to make good on a plan to invest all of a planned $300 million in the plant to upgrade production systems. The company balked at this investment when efficiency did not improve in the plant as forecasted. The union contended that the strike was set off by GM when it removed dies for a new product and shipped them to an Ohio plant, continuing their strategy to pit one local union against another. Blaming the strike on a few dies is posturing. And GM used the strike as an excuse to cancel some unprofitable car programs, which Ford has already done.

We have done extensive work on plant modernization. Years of research reveal three important findings relevant to this strike:

1. There is no significant correlation between having a union and modernization success.

2. Firms successfully adopting new processing technology in their plants have *local technology agreements with their unions.*

3. Contract language, always a bone of contention, doesn't matter.

Do GM plant managers or local union presidents know what the national UAW contract says about new technology? If you are met with puzzled faces when you ask this question, don't be surprised. It turns out that it hardly matters. The national contract is not relevant. Only the local agreement really matters. Update the national agreement, by all means, but don't be fooled by what it really means.

Concentrate on the local agreements when it comes to successful production technology adoption.

Recall the basic issue here: GM's cost structure is the highest among major automakers. GM argued that the cost structure in Flint at the stamping plant on strike was also higher than the rest of its system: average wage was $69,000 a year including overtime, while Ford assembly workers averaged $55,000. Ford produced 33 vehicles per worker hour, while GM averaged 27. Ford has continued to report record profits and with high demand and lower costs, who is surprised.

GM and its union have plenty of good examples within the corporation to emulate as models of the future. Its Oklahoma City plant had a difficult but successful launch of the Chevrolet Malibu. Both the union and the plant did not keep their contract promises, but traditional agreements and contracts cannot cover what is required to launch a new car. Technology agreements are needed for that. More important, both the company and the union were able to overcome the "old way" of doing business. This was a low-cost (in some areas half the cost of an older model), successful, new GM vehicle launch, and the company and the world have much to learn from it. There is much to learn at New United Motor Manufacturing Inc. (NUMMI) too. The GM–Toyota joint venture in Fremont, California, recently launched a new vehicle, but there were legitimate problems with the new assembly technology cited by California's state version of OSHA.

Our third finding from studies of nearly 100 manufacturing plant modernization programs was that the answer to union-management technology issues is not obvious: Although having a local technology agreement is significantly correlated with successful plant modernization, *contract language, per se, does not predict success.* If you know why this was the case—that contract language becomes obsolete quickly in a rapidly changing world of new technology in products and plants— then you also know what the next step should be for GM and the UAW. History will judge if any of these machinations amount to any good for either side.

State Three: The R&D–Manufacturing Interface

Although there is considerable experience in outstanding companies to show that concurrent engineering—designing products and production processes at the same time—pays off in the long run, only recently has this wisdom been documented in broad-based, systematic, in-depth studies of manufacturing firms.[12] Many companies, such as GE, have been doing concurrent or simultaneous engineering for at least 10 years, but most companies do not share successful strategies, except under rare circumstances and behind the closed doors of benchmarking alliances or corporate sharing exercises.

This closer coordination or integration of design and manufacturing is indicated in State 3 (Figure 9-1). Teams are important and are used most often to achieve integration in this state. Nearly 17 percent of the variance in return on investment (ROI) for these projects can be accounted for by structural changes of this type, with successful teams being the most extreme structural mechanism. However,

---

[12] J. E. Ettlie, and H. W. Stoll, *Managing the Design-Manufacturing Process* (New York: McGraw-Hill, 1990); J. E. Ettlie, "Product-Process Development Integration in Manufacturing," *Management Science,* 41, no. 7 (July 1995), pp. 1224–1237.

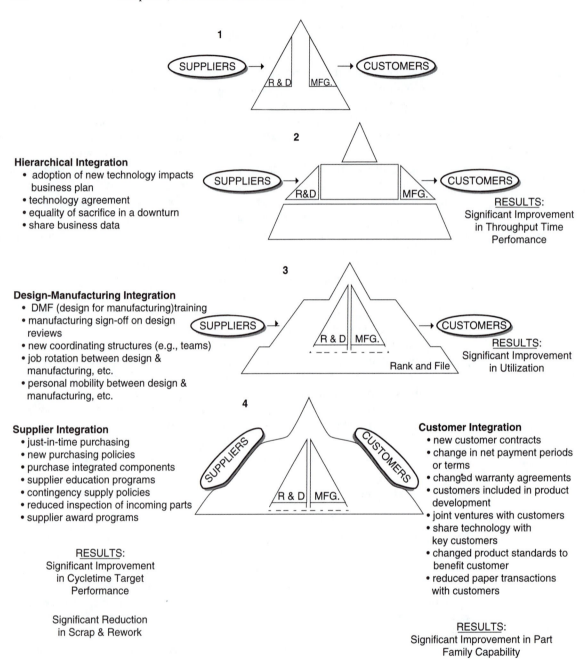

Hierarchical Integration
- adoption of new technology impacts business plan
- technology agreement
- equality of sacrifice in a downturn
- share business data

RESULTS:
Significant Improvement
in Throughput Time
Perfomance

Design-Manufacturing Integration
- DMF (design for manufacturing)training
- manufacturing sign-off on design reviews
- new coordinating structures (e.g., teams)
- job rotation between design & manufacturing, etc.
- personal mobility between design & manufacturing, etc.

RESULTS:
Significant Improvement
in Utilization

Supplier Integration
- just-in-time purchasing
- new purchasing policies
- purchase integrated components
- supplier education programs
- contingency supply policies
- reduced inspection of incoming parts
- supplier award programs

RESULTS:
Significant Improvement
in Cycletime Target
Performance

Significant Reduction
in Scrap & Rework

Customer Integration
- new customer contracts
- change in net payment periods or terms
- changed warranty agreements
- customers included in product development
- joint ventures with customers
- share technology with key customers
- changed product standards to benefit customer
- reduced paper transactions with customers

RESULTS:
Significant Improvement in Part
Family Capability

Figure 9-1   Summary of the Transition States for Manufacturing Process Technology Assimilation

other structural changes, including changes in job responsibility, new titles, dotted-line reporting relationships, and even job-sharing arrangements are among the other novel adaptations being used.

Systematic survey work, including hundreds of in-plant case studies, indicates that there is more to this practice than just forming a team of design and manufacturing engineers. As would be expected, considerable training in such techniques as design-for-manufacturing is also required, along with manufacturing sign-off of design reviews (called the *gate process* at GE and Northern Telecom).

More rare is the use of job rotation between functions and mobility across functions (personnel transfers)—including the core group of design and manufacturing, but also accounting, industrial engineering, quality, marketing, and other nontraditional areas such as external suppliers, customers. Before the merger with Daimler-Benz, Chrysler Corporation included their advertisers on the NEON project teams and used QFD (Quality Function Deployment) to structure the simultaneous engineering process. It is this and other more rare practices that distinguish the best in class from the also-rans. Notice in Figure 9-1 that there are dotted lines below the triangles in State 3. This is to indicate one of these rare, successful practices—the removal of status barriers between engineers and technicians. But this could apply to breaking down any status barrier during modernization—office employees, staff support personnel, anyone who can help capture more value from a new technology application. Saturn Corporation, GM's newest division, was one of the rare examples of this practice.

In short, it takes more than teams. When integration between R&D and manufacturing is successful, the bounty is realized in significantly higher new processing technology system utilization. Single shift utilization averages about 72 percent (with 87 percent uptime) in U.S. durable goods plants after modernization. Some companies (e.g., Rockwell) have flexible manufacturing systems running unattended, multiple shifts well in excess of 70 percent utilization, including all the "normal" interruptions in the process.[13] This represents a steady improvement in utilization since 1971 of about 1 percent per year on average in durable goods manufacturing. These trends are summarized in Figure 9-2. Other, very successful companies have documented utilization rates in excess of 90 percent.

The last two decades have seen considerable change in the NPD (new product development) process among successful durable goods manufacturers (see Figure 9-3). In the 1970s, products were developed in serial fashion—a linear progression from R&D to production and distribution or service. In the 1980s, simultaneous engineering was introduced for overlapping design and manufacturing. In the 1990s a core team of key change agents and champions followed the project from inception to delivery and continuous improvement, with a support "shell" of related disciplines coming and going as needed on the project.

What about the next decade? One likely scenario is the global product development cycle and introduction. First, the 24-hour day will be adopted for product development. Engineering teams in Europe will work on a project, then electronically pass it to North American teams, who, 8 hours later, will transfer work to Japan or Asia. Theoretically, projects could be completed in a third of the time it now takes.

Later, when the project is ready to launch, it would be possible to introduce the new product simultaneously in all three economic regions of the world.

Can it work? Probably not as well as the theory. First, some translation due to cultural differences will slow the 24-hour development day to more like 12 hours—at least that has been the precedent in basic R&D according to Phil Birnbaum-More's work at USC. Second, many engineering teams already work more than 8-hour days, especially as the project nears completion. Third, some products may

---

[13] G. Vasilash, "Automating NC," *Production,* 105, no. 12 (1993), p. 80.

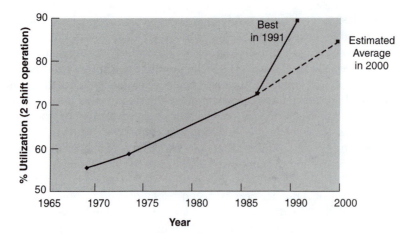

Figure 9-2   Average Utilization Rates for Flexible Automation

Sources: J. Ettlie "Technology Transfer in the Machine Tool Industry: The Utilization of NC Machine Tools in Captive Shops," unpublished Masters Thesis Northwestern University, August 1971; J. Ettlie: "A Longitudinal Study of Social Learning and the Technology Transfer Process" unpublished Ph.D. dissertation Northwestern University, June 1975.

1987 data in Ettlie (1988), Avg. = 72%.

1991 "best" data from G. Vasilask, "Rockwell Graphics Systems Cedar Rapids," *Production* (January 1992), pp. 50–55. 72% utilization of FMS on a three-shift basis = $^{14.4}/_{16}$ (allowing 4 hours for maintenance and setup) = 90% on a two-shift basis.

share common core elements, but will have to be localized for regional conditions. Global operations technology is taken up in Chapter 11.[14]

The Ultimate State: Supplier and Customer Integration

Perhaps the most critical state to achieve is that which integrates suppliers and customers into the process of manufacturing effectively with new technology. This is indicated by State 4 in Figure 9-1. Supplier integration, which involves JIT (just-in-time) purchasing for modernization, as well as other progressive purchasing practices (e.g., supplier education programs and reduction of the cost of inspection), could be the most critical challenge, because it best illustrates what separates the successful from the truly brilliant new process technology assimilator. The key hurdle to clear is the establishment of cohesive integration of quality strategies and technology strategies for all product units of the firm. Without this integration, neither new technology nor quality initiatives will work well. This is why the Baldrige prize is so difficult to drive to the bottom line and why so many new processing systems fail. Box 9-2 summarizes one of the most important innovations in supplier coupling: JIT II.

---

[14] See G. M. Chryssochoidis and V. Wong, "Rolling Out New Products Across Country Markets: An Empirical Study of Causes and Delays," *Journal of Product Innovation Management,* 15 (1998), pp. 16–41. The authors found that 15 of 22 sequential product roll-outs experienced delays, while 8 simultaneous launches were timely, suggesting that simultaneous launch can be less risky.

1970's Serial Fashion

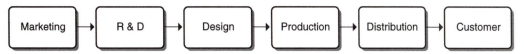

1980's Simultaneous Engineering

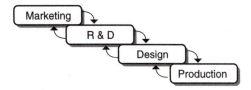

1990's The Core Team Approach

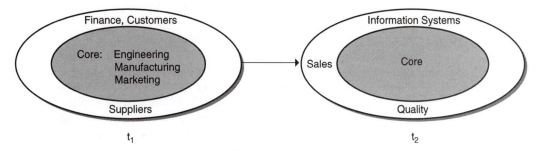

2000: Global Product Development—24-hour Work Days

Figure 9-3 How the NPD Process Has Changed in the Context of Process Innovation.

BOX 9-2

JIT II

Bose Corporation introduced the concept of JIT II (just-in-time II) in the late 1980s by eliminating purchasing agents and supplier's sales personnel (and the cost associated with these positions). Bose replaced these jobs with "in plants"—representers from suppliers who have complete access to functional managers, forecasts, and scheduling systems. In plants represent the interests of both companies under ideal circumstances and for the benefit of both supplier and customer. Apple Computer has saved $10 million a year in inventory costs at its Fountain, Colorado, warehouse using third-party management.

SOURCE: F. R. Bleakley, "Strange Bed Fellows," *The Wall Street Journal,* January 13, 1995, pp. A1, A6.

When suppliers are integrated into the process, new processing systems significantly reduce scrap and rework and meet or exceed cycle-time targets. Successful companies typically get 110 to 115 percent of projected cycle time targets on new systems and exceed 30 percent reduction in scrap and rework with new manufacturing technology systems. Before modernization, U.S. durable goods plants average about 4.2 percent in scrap and rework in a typical year. After modernization, they average about 2.8 percent. About a third of these very successful cases reduce scrap and work to 1 percent or less of manufacturing cost.

Finally, and most obviously, customer integration (e.g., new contracts for delivery, warranty agreements, joint ventures, and so on) promotes greater realized flexibility (e.g., more part numbers) of new manufacturing systems. Successful modernized plants can offer a wide range of product to customers at no additional cost. At Steelcase, a former 28-day cycletime has become 5 to 7 days. Rework is down 50 percent. With ISO 9000, real cost is down 30 percent, and a focused factory program has produced 2,000 days of consistent schedule completion. A powder paint line has reduced emissions 50 percent, with the use of an environmentally friendly water-based adhesive for the desk-top line. All this was achieved with a sevenfold increase in production efficiency.[15]

It seems clear that supply chain management from supplier to customer (including internal suppliers and customers) is one of the key features of combining technological and administrative innovation. This ultimate state in the model (State 4 in Figure 9-1) represents the epitome of integration of internal and external resource leverage. EDI and CAD technology have become an essential way of doing business for many manufacturing firms, and this is just the beginning of what is possible. AT&T, which has won the Malcolm Baldrige National Quality Award three times, says that more than 17,000 new customers sign up for cellular service each day (1994 Annual Report, AT&T). The impact of telecommunications technology on manufacturing can only be imagined. But the need to assimilate these technologies with administrative innovations can be anticipated.

$\mathcal{S}$ERVICE INNOVATIONS

Service innovation was introduced in Chapter 1 and service R&D was reviewed in Chapter 5. What about implementing service innovations and capturing value from the purchase of important services such as information technology?

As indicated earlier, it is likely that the growth in modern economies will come from intellectually based services. Intellectual services, such as software, will be at the heart of service innovation in the foreseeable future.[16] Examples include Enterprise Resource Planning (ERP) systems. Companies worldwide are investing more than $10 billion every year in ERP systems alone. ERP is described in more detail later in the chapter (see Box 9-4).

Small manufacturing firms benefit significantly from purchased, innovative services that they would not otherwise be able to develop without outside

---

[15] F.R. Bleakley, "Strange Bed Fellows," *Wall Street Journal* (January 13, 1995), pp. A1, A4

[16] J. B. Quinn has defined (see footnote 21).

help.[17] Programmable switching technology, alone, has had tremendous impact on the telecommunications industry.[18] Even larger manufacturing firms are tending to buy, rather than develop, their own services—especially software.[19] The outsourced-information services sector of the economy is now estimated to be $32 billion worldwide.[20] Yet, to capture the benefits of, especially, information services (IS), companies often report the need to transform themselves.

Companies need internal service capability, no matter what business they are in. In addition to all the people employed in services business in the United States (almost 79% of all jobs in 1996), it has been estimated that another 12 percent of the work force in manufacturing perform activities in information services. These are the knowledge-based assets of the organization: people, databases, and systems.[21] Perhaps only customer service is more important, and this quality function can also be significantly enhanced with information systems.[22]

An example of changing information services within a manufacturing firm is Bose Corporation. Bose is probably best known as the manufacturer of speakers for car and home sound systems. The company recently undertook a major reorganization of the information services function, which has had dramatic impact on performance (see Box 9-2).

Changing from a functional-based to a process-based organization is the challenge. Using business process reengineering[23] and local experimentation with total quality initiatives,[24] Bose took the long view toward understanding organizational change. Sustained process improvement was the goal, and IS performance at Bose was gradually but dramatically improved from 1992 to 1994. Late schedule performance improved from 20 percent to 8 percent tardy project completions; percentage projects over budget fell from 60 percent to 15 percent.[25]

Public sector management and innovation policy are introduced in Chapter 10, but a special category of service, state, and local government, which accounts for a substantial portion of the GDP, is far too important to go unmentioned until then. More than 20 years ago, landmark research on state and local government innova-

---

[17] A. MacPherson, "The Contribution of External Service Inputs to the Product Development Efforts of Small Manufacturing Firms," *R&D Management,* 27, no. 2 (April 1997), pp. 127–144.

[18] K. Mazovec, "Service Innovation for the 90's," *Telephony,* 235, no. 11 (September 14, 1998), pp. 78–82.

[19] J. E. Ettlie, "ERP: Corporate Root Canal?" presented at Rochester Institute of Technology, Rochester, NY (January 25, 1999).

[20] R.-D Kempis, and J. Ringbeck, "Manufacturing's Use and Abuse of IT," *McKinsey Quarterly,* no. 1 (1998), pp. 138–150.

[21] J. B. Quinn, "Leveraging Intellect," *Executive Excellence,* 10, no. 10 (October 7–8, 1993).

[22] This includes data mining and call center automation, see B. Violino, "Defining IT Innovation," *Information Week,* 700 (September 14, 1998), pp. 58–70, which summarizes the 10th annual survey of 500 top information companies. Top priorities among respondents were year 2000 fixes, e-commerce, and customer service.

[23] M. Hammer and J. Champy, *Re-engineering the Corporation* (New York: HarperCollins, 1993).

[24] T. H. Davenport, "Need Radical and Continuous Improvement? Integrate Process Reengineering and TQM," *Planning Review,* 23, no. 3 (May-June 1993), pp. 6–12.

[25] W. Harkness, W. Kettinger, and A. H. Segars, "Sustaining Process Improvement and Innovation in the Information Services Function: Lessons Learned at the Bose Corporation," *MIS Quarterly,* 20, no. 3 (September 1996), pp. 349–368.

tion revealed significant findings. Two researchers, in particular—Robert Yin and Irwin Feller—warrant special mention because of their seminal contributions. Much of this research was motivated by the idea that local government's slow rate of productivity improvement was caused by the reluctance or inability to adopt technological innovations that could enhance government performance.

Feller extends the hypothesis that state and local governments have a strong tendency to adopt service-augmenting rather than cost-reducing innovations by concentrating on government decision making.[26] Unless major new activities are being proposed in a local jurisdiction, such as the introduction of a mass transit system, most innovation decision making is centered about senior-level agency officials. Elected offices (governors, mayors, state legislators, city council representatives, etc.), are rarely directly or centrally involved in adoption decisions involving new technology. For example, Feller and his colleagues studied the diffusion of highway and air pollution technologies in state agencies. The researchers found that adoption decisions were made primarily by senior career officials and technical specialists.[27] These officials and experts are paid to achieve organizational goals, which do not emphasize cost reduction. Rather, most state and local agencies are in place to solve regional problems and provide services. Hence, service-augmenting innovations tend to win out over cost-reducing options, unless they overlap and can accomplish both at the same time. Rarely will a cost-reducing innovation even be considered for adoption unless it also has some service-enhancing potential.

Robert Yin studied the life histories of six types of local public sector innovations, including computer-assisted instruction in local education, police computer systems, mobile intensive care units, closed-circuit educational television, breath testing for driver safety by the police, and jet-axe adoption by local fire departments.[28] Yin found that the conditions for the routinization of new technologies varied by internal conditions at the local agency involved in the adoption. Regardless of agency, however, in the early stages of its life history, an innovation must gain increased support by agency practitioners to survive. An innovation is fully routinized in an agency when it "disappears," or is no longer recognized as new. To be accepted, a new technology must survive a higher proportion of "passages" in local government, such as changes in governance and management. Passages are organized into three broader stages of gradual incorporation of technological innovation by local agencies: *improvisation, expansion, and disappearance.*

The findings of Robert Yin also suggest that the time required to implement an innovation varies with depth and breadth strategies. The depth approach takes longer in the improvisation stage; it takes less time in expansion and disappearance stages. A breadth approach may require less time in improvisation and expansion stages but more time in the disappearance stage. If an innovation is

---

[26] I. Feller, "Managerial Response to Technological Innovation in Public Sector Organizations," *Management Science,* 26, no. 10 (October 1980), pp. 1021–1030.

[27] I. Feller and D. Menzel, "Diffusion Milieus as a Focus of Research on Innovation in the Public Sector," *Public Sciences* (March 1977), pp. 49–68.

[28] R. K. Yin, "Life Histories of Innovations: How New Practices Become Routinized," *Public Administration Review,* 41, no. 1 (January/February 1981), pp. 21–28.

early in its life cycle, a broadly implemented strategy is less likely to lead to institutionalization.[29]

The challenge of making government more responsive and productive and the inability to integrate quality programs, information technology, and innovation management remain significant hurdles for the next decade in the service sector. Perhaps because so much can be done just with service quality improvement interventions, technological innovation may be in the distant future or out of reach of many service firms or public agencies. With cost reductions of 30 percent or more in the typical service industry after quality and business process reengineering, and corresponding absence of administrative innovation adoption in some parts of the service sector,[30] the additional benefits of information and new technology and sustainable development[31] are far from being realized.

REALIZATION OF INTEGRATED SYSTEMS IN MANUFACTURING

The convergence of these empirical trends in successful manufacturing firms indicates the potential leverage of joint product and process innovation. The implications are far reaching. First, it is no longer good enough to be satisfied with mastering single "distinctive competencies" to survive and prosper in today's competitive world. It is the merging of multiple strengths and technologies that matters.

As the popularity of benchmarking in manufacturing grows, it becomes more obvious that standards of excellence are relatively easy to identify and measure. How to achieve and exceed these standards emerges rather early in the benchmarking exercise as the real challenge. Business process reengineering (BPR) case histories have taught this lesson well. Only about 30 percent of BPR cases are unqualified successes. Corporate cultures are difficult or impossible to duplicate. How can success be uniquely achieved?

The lessons from our empirical work suggest that technology matters in manufacturing, and technological innovation is far more important and more complex than has been generally realized. In particular, one has to acknowledge that as new prod-

---

[29] K. Lindquist and J. Mauriel, "Depth and Breadth in Innovation Implementation: The Case of School-Based Management," Chapter 17 in A. Van de Ven, H. Angle, and M. Scott Poole (eds.), *Research on the Management of Innovation* (New York: Harper & Row, 1989), pp. 561–582.

[30] K. Newman, "Re-engineering for Service Quality: The Case of the Leicester Royal Infirmary," *Total Quality Management,* 8, no. 5 (October 1997), pp. 255–264; also see G. Gianakis and C. P. McCue, "Administrative Innovation Among Ohio Local Government Finance Officers," *American Review of Public Administration,* 27, no. 3 (September 1997), pp. 20–286, in which survey results indicated that in local government, less than 4% of respondents had adopted tools such as strategic planning, total quality management, and financial trend monitoring.

[31] D. F. Ball, "Management of Technology, Sustainable Development and Eco-Efficiency: The Seventh International Conference on Management of Technology," *R&D Management,* 28, no. 4 (1998), pp. 311–313.

ucts and new product technology become even more central to successful competitive strategies, it will be more difficult to balance other innovations in the corporate system. This applies to both internal and external management challenges. For example, joint ventures, joint production, alliance management, and supplier contracts are all examples of this complexity, and their use is growing. Seldom are these arrangements free of new technology concerns. More typically, new technology is at the heart of these alliances and their management.

Since process reengineering is so difficult to imitate, it is not surprising that it fails more often than not, and that benchmarking often conflicts with voice-of-the-customer information during new product development.[32] Therefore, the *paradigm shift* popularly used to describe the transition of organizations from an outdated structure to a new form has little meaning. No model can be taken as this template, and, therefore, no paradigm shift is really possible—at least not yet. Only a representational form is possible. Although the representational states in Figure 9-1 have empirical grounding (e.g., supplier integration using JIT purchasing to implement loose coupling), it is not the practices that are important but the ideal state that matters in a dynamic world. Practices come and go, as do their measures. Best practices are fleeting. Mercedes benchmarked Ford Motor Company in building its Tuscaloosa, Alabama, plant. "Now Detroit is the benchmark," and Ford is the best in labor productivity. But Ford still benchmarks Toyota.[33] When will the benchmark move on to another standard?

The tension between innovation types in firms (e.g., product versus process innovation, or administrative versus technological innovation) becomes the emerging issue in most companies today. Success depends on this tension.

Evidence of this tension emerges in the case histories from well-recognized leading manufacturing companies that struggle with product-versus-process innovation: Hewlett-Packard, Motorola, Boeing, Ford Motor Company, and 3M are all examples. Taken in the context of the growing uneasiness with *buzzword management*, or TLAs (three-letter acronyms), and the inability of current movements such as "lean" or "agile" manufacturing to capture the vision of the future for manufacturing, it becomes clear why so many of us have become restless and impatient with current philosophies of change.

An interesting case in point is the "green" movement in manufacturing. The current corporate trend toward conservation of the natural environment is the first modern, serious attempt to take costs that are normally external to the company (e.g., disposal of products) and internalize them through waste-minimization programs and recycling. Although many companies are aggressively responding to the need to reexamine decisions and programs in this area, there is clear reluctance to be a leader in green manufacturing, with the rare exception of companies in industries that have traditionally had environmental problems (e.g, chemicals and paper).

A survey by Grant Thorton reported by the National Center for Manufacturing Sciences[34] indicated that only 21 percent of mid-sized manufacturers have a full-time environmental manager, while 41 percent have part-time environmental managers.

---

[32] J. E. Ettlie and M. D. Johnson, "Product Development Benchmarking versus Customer Focus in Applications of Quality Function Deployment," *Marketing Letters,* 5, no. 2 (1994), pp. 107–116.

[33] *New York Times,* March 4, 1995, p. 17.

[34] National Center for Manufacturing Sciences (NCMS), *Focus* (January 1995), pp. 1–3.

DOES NEW PROCESS TECHNOLOGY PAY?

Case studies can be selected to prove a point. First, they can be compared with general trends for benchmarking purposes. Does it pay to invest in new process technology? Studies of operations technology adoption outcomes were summarized (see Table 4-2). A brief review of this table shows that durable goods plant modernization programs averaged 40 percent ROI, 32.6 percent reduction in scrap and rework (from 4.3% to 2.9%), and 54 percent through-put time reduction. These same industry groups (SIC 34-39) averaged $141,000 in sales per employee, while those firms using certain modern technologies averaged $200,000 per employee. Nearly 7,000 firms are reportedly using SAP's R/3, for integrating enterprise operations. Some firms have failed in implementation (e.g., Dell Computer has dropped it). Others are reporting great savings. For example, Chevron says its $100 million investment will save $30 million per year. Compaq Computer says R/3 slashes inventory from $2.2 million per year to $1.2 million per year. Microsoft saves $18 million per year using R/3. Owens-Corning saved $15 million in 1997 and $50 million by 1999 including the elimination of 400 jobs. Sounds like process reengineering-type savings (Case 9-4).

For 40 major firms in the U.S. telecommunications industry, new switching technology significantly enhanced efficiency by improving scale economies, allowing housekeeping tasks to be routinized, and in other ways. In the long run, these efficiencies substantially affect organizational performance such as market share and adding more business lines.

U.S. Department of Commerce data indicated that process technology adoption has increased average relative labor productivity by 37 percent (difference between no technology use and highest technology use) in 1988 and 40 percent in 1992.

Ettlie and Penner-Hahn support these results. Table 9-1, reproduces their benchmarking results, which compare a case study of the installation of a flexible assembly system for automotive components and a larger, in-plant study of similar types of flexible production automation. Sample firms average 24 percent labor productivity gains, and the flexible automation case study achieved 75 percent labor productivity improvement. The other results, not reported in Table 9-1, are equally impressive. For example, 94 percent of target cycle time was achieved, on average; there was a 39 percent reduction in cost per part, median payback was 3 years, and absenteeism was an average of 1 percent among new system personnel. This same approach can be used in any plant.

MANUFACTURING CREDOS

Even the hard-core manufacturing companies are saying goodbye to the old ways of doing things. New ways of acquiring technology are appearing everywhere. New ways of bridging the gap between former "enemies" are being found. For example, marketing and manufacturing actually talk to one another now.[35] In one

---

[35] See *Production Economics*, 37, no. 1 (November 1994), which is devoted to this problem.

$\mathscr{T}$ABLE 9-1   Summary of Benchmarking Results for AMT Performance

Measure	Automotive Plant Flexible Assembly System	Domestic Plant Study + (1987)
Initial cost	$12 million	$3.5 million (estimated average or median if skewed)
Time to install	11 months	11.71 months ($n = 28$)
Cycle time (% of target achieved)	73%	94% ($n = 32$)
Uptime	82.4%	58% ($n = 35$)
Throughput reduction	50%	54% ($n = 24$)
Scrap and rework as a percentage of total cost	N.A.	2.8% ($n = 27$)
Reduction in cost per part number	55%	39% ($n = 11$)
Labor savings	75%	24% ($n = 21$)
Reduction in operations per part number	16.5	2.0 ($n = 15$)
Number of parts	18	55 ($n = 24$)
Part families	4	3.5 ($n = 20$)
Changeover time	0.33 hours	0.45 hours ($n = 19$)
Part families/changeover time	12 (4 ÷ 0.33 hr) per hour	7.8 (3.5 ÷ 0.45) per hour
Personnel turnover	6%	7% ($n = 20$)
Payback (years)	6	Avg. = 5.85, median = 3.0 ($n = 10$)
Absenteeism	NA	1% ($n = 18$)
ROI	NA	40% ($n = 14$)
Percent utilization	65%	48% ($n = 34$)
Inventory turns in system	188 turns	24 ($n = 14$) plant median = 6.5 ($n = 20$)

In performance comparisons between case study systems and survey results (1) up-time was normalized per three-shift basis, actually 87 percent per two-shift basis; (2) the outlier was deleted for personnel turnover; (3) utilization was normalized per three-shift basis, actually 72 percent per two-shift basis; and (4) comparable numbers for scrap and rework were not available although plant first-run quality was at 87 percent. New system first-run quality was the same at the last data collection in March 1990, 87 percent.

Source: Ettlie and Penner-Hahn, "High Technology Manufacturing in Low Technology Plants", *Interaces,* 23, no. 6, p. 25.

small U.S. durable goods company, the two functions have been combined. Box 9-3 describes another new high-water mark in breakthrough thinking for manufacturing. Steel plants will take on a whole new look with these new philosophies. Consider the case of Gallatin Steel Company in Ghent, Kentucky. "Forty percent of its 200 workers have college degrees, mostly in mechanical engineering or metallurgy. Another 20 percent have 2-year degrees. The president of this automated facility owned by two Canadian steel companies remarked that 'with 200 people we will produce as much steel as it used to take 5,000 people to make.'"[36]

Novel employee empowerment programs are springing up in many industries— not just to foster goodwill, and not just to promote productivity, but to make employees more mobile, both within and without the company. Kaizen teams are spreading from applications like those in Japan at Daihatsu[37] to Clarion Manufac-

---

[36] R. F. Celeste, "Strategic Alliances for Innovation: Emerging Models of Technology-based, Twenty-first Century Economic Development," *Economic Development Review* 14, no. 1 (Winter 1996), pp. 4–8.

[37] *Japan Management Review* 2, no. 2 (1994).

BOX 9-3

Innovation in the Steel Industry

In 1994, LTV announced that it will be the first U.S. integrated steelmaker to build a minimill. They will team with British Steel PLC and Sumitomo Metal Industries to construct a $450 plant with new technology developed through this joint venture called Trico Steel Co. They will use the opportunity of a new launch to engender a new "culture" in steelmaking at this new site Yet the field of minimills is crowded, and the industry will soon learn how many is too many.

SOURCE: *Wall Street Journal,* (December 20, 1994), p. A2; *Business Week* (March 13, 1995).

turing in Kentucky. Clarion is the perennial winner of the J. D. Power award for auto stereos in its class.

Aside from technology and work force issues, the credo of the 2000s in manufacturing is going to be knowledge-building through new learning regimens. Higher education programs, such as those at MIT, Stanford, Northwestern, and Michigan, are well underway in creating a new breed of engineering-manufacturing manager. A manufacturing-experienced manager will be able to aspire to the CEO position once again. Women will be plant managers in not just a few isolated industries and instances, but broadly in manufacturing. Plant managers will have a voice in the strategy of the corporation, and in some cases, such as at Toshiba,[38] "knowledge works" factories actually lead corporate strategy experiments.

Significant human resource issues loom during the next decade that will challenge even the "new breed" of manufacturing manager. Temporary employment continues to rise at an alarming rate,[39] and overtime in factories is at record highs.[40] Even in successful companies, more and more employees at all levels are asking, "Where do I fit into a new breed of company?" For example, at Steelcase, management seems continually distracted by "human resource shadow-boxing. One minute you think you have the quixotic people conundrum cornered and figured out, the next the shadow leaps up an adjacent wall." Team accomplishments have made technological achievement possible at Steelcase, but this same process that empowers the work force and where everything happens in real time, brings about a struggle to avoid disenchantment and distrust. What comes next after empowerment?[41]

---

[38] M. Furman, "Knowledge Factories at Toshiba," in J. Liker, J. Ettlie, and J. Campbell (eds.) *Engineered in Japan* (New York: Oxford University Press, 1995), pp. 217–233

[39] *Wall Street Journal* (February 1, 1994).

[40] *Wall Street Journal* (May 10, 1994).

[41] R. Bergstrom, "Probling the Softer Side of Steelcase; A Reflection, "*Production,* 106, no. 11(November 1994), p. 54.

Companies with overall high job satisfaction also have customers who are satisfied. The proudest service advisers in the automobile industry are at Lexus, Infiniti, Saturn, and Toyota—also the industry leaders in quality.[42] Manufacturers that have products with high customer satisfaction can now accurately predict positive changes in market share.[43]

Gone are the days of consistency in functional strategies as the touchstone of evaluating plans. Some strategies have to lead the way. The credo for manufacturing in the next century will be to assume this leadership position by managing inconsistencies. These firms will have mastered at least one principle: Match technological change with changes in policies, practices, and structures for integration in order to achieve and maintain functional balance. Enterprise integration software and information systems are just one example of this challenge.[44] The rest will either not survive or will survive painfully.

ENTERPRISE RESOURCE PLANNING SYSTEMS

As mentioned earlier, nowhere is the issue of value capture from purchased technology illustrated better than in the adoption of **enterprise resource planning (ERP) systems.** ERP is best defined as hardware-software systems for integrated major business systems except R&D and suppliers/customers.

Successive waves of manufacturing and operations planning technologies have washed over companies since the 1960s. Early material requirements planning (MRP) systems were mainframe based and home grown. Gradually, over the years, more functions were added (MRP II) and eventually, distributed processing systems became the basis for ERP systems such as SAP AG's R/3.[45]

The popular press has not been kind to ERP implementation, implying that the difficulty of implementing these new systems is more than most companies expect, and in some cases, they give up all together (see Box 9-4). The media use headlines like "Program of Pain," and "Software that Can Make a Grown Company Cry"; the latter story refers to ERP as "corporate root canal" and "oral surgery."[46] A lot is at stake here. U.S. companies spend about $250 billion annually on computer technology, yet one survey found that 42 percent of corporate information technology projects are termi-

---

[42] *Automotive News* (March 5, 1995), p. 20.

[43] M. L. DeLean, "AT&T's Quality Journey: An Insider's View on Bottom Line Improvement," presented at the University of Michigan Business School (December 14, 1994).

[44] See, for example, T. Davenport, "Putting the Enterprise into the Enterprise System," *Harvard Business Review* (July-August, 1998), pp. 121–131; C. Deutsch, "Software that Can Make a Grown Company Cry," *New York Times* (November 8, 1998), p. B1, ff.

[45] R. Chase, N. Aquilano, and F.R. Jacobs, *Production and Operations Management* (New York: Irwin Mc-Graw-Hill, 1998), pp. 668–677. Relevant Web sites given by the authors are http://www.sap.com and the APICS Software Buyers Guide http://lionhrtpub.com.

[46] J. B. White, D. Clark, and S. Ascarelli, "Program of Pain: This German Software Is Complex, Expensive—and Wildly Popular," *Wall Street Journal* (March 14, 1997), pp. A1, A8; C. Deutsch, "Software that Can Make a Grown Company Cry," *The New York Times* (November 8, 1998), p. B1, ff.

BOX 9-4

The Enterprise Resource Planning (ERP) Challenge

The late Carl Sagan, planetary scientist at Cornell University, was famous for saying "…billions and billions and billions … of stars." Now I will say it too, in a slightly different way: *billions and billions of dollars.* That is how much is going to be spent every year in the foreseeable future on ERP (Enterprise Resource Planning) systems—often just called enterprise integration systems. The bad news: My best estimate is that about 25 percent of that money will be wasted because of lack of understanding of how to manage major change in a company.

Problems with Y2K, the situation in which computers read "2000" as "00" and translate the date as 1900, revealed to many companies that most of their current information resources are badly out of date and incompatible.

Most big companies have upgraded, or are in the process of revamping, their information systems. General Motors Corporation, for example, wants SAP, the German software supplier of ERP systems, to establish an office just to support its needs. Suffice it to say that GM and many, many other large and small companies have had a checkered history in installing new technologies during the last decade. Dell Computer canceled its software contract in January 1997 after spending $150 million, up from the originally estimated $115 million. Dell finally determined the system it was installing couldn't handle the sales volume it was anticipating. Furthermore, as more companies adopt SAP systems, as opposed to Baan or suppliers, help becomes a scarce resource.

So a lot can be learned from the companies undergoing major upheaval and installing ERP systems and from managers who are willing to talk about it. Mike Radcliff, vice president and chief information officer of Owens-Corning, is one of these people. Based on Radcliff's experience at Owens-Corning, my estimate of 25 percent wasted effort in installing these new systems is not far off. In fact, others have reported similar experiences. Just as they approach the final selection decision on which hardware and software systems to buy, they run out of money.

The consultants, or "rent-a-bodies," as Mike refers to them, are just part of the unanticipated expense. They can help you get down the learning curve fast, but very quickly, most companies know just as much as consultants about how to change their culture. At Owens-Corning (OC), they originally budgeted 7 percent for training. In reality, training cost about 13 percent—so they were off by half. Further, since Owens was in the process of growing through acquisitions at the time they launched their SAP installation, adding seventeen new businesses before they were through, they went off their 2-year installation timetable almost immediately. Now they estimate that it will take twice that long to do it right.

Key learnings from OC? There are many. The most fundamental decision you have to make is *not whether to reengineer, but which business processes to reengineer, and in what order.* In the OC case, it was finance first. Get finance on board, and the rest, which will have a common accounting system, will come along. Filling customer orders was next, and so on.

SOURCES· Personal communications with Mike Radcliff, Owens Corning; also, J. B. White, D. Clark, and S. Ascarelli, "Program of Pain: This German Software Is Complex, Expensive—And Wildly Popular," *Wall Street Journal* (March 14, 1997), p. A1,A8; T. A. Stewart, "Owens Corning: Back from the Dead," *Fortune,* reprint, 1997; L. K. Romei, "New Technology Strengthens New Commitment," *Managing Office Technology,* 41, no. 7 (July 1996), p. 18.

BOX 9-4 (continued)

You are betting a lot to save a lot. OC had estimated that it was spending $30 to $35 million a year maintaining antiquated information systems. Now it estimates savings of $50 million a year.

OC started by redefining its markets. Growth at home was difficult because of OC's dominant position in the United States. Further, OC went to delivery of building systems, going from an average $1,000 per house in 1992 to $6,000 per house today. It took many acquisitions to do that and "reinventing" the supply chain to implement this new strategy, but the company has doubled in size as a result.

After OC redefined its market, it realized that its current information systems would not even come close to being able to implement this new strategy. Further, it realized that a "technology Band-aid" would not solve the problem. So OC decided on a total enterprise integration solution to its problem, throwing out nearly 200 legacy systems and commonizing the entire corporation for the first time in its history.

The key to success—you've heard this before—was organizational culture change. OC's version of culture change focused on very specific business outcomes, such as order fill rates of 99 percent, determined by benchmarking best practices to target action. Each member of the staff had training to get an "operator's license" to use the new systems. Those that couldn't or wouldn't get this "license" could no longer continue in their job, and as many as 20 percent of OC employees were affected in this way. This is major organizational change, not "nibbling at the margins," as my colleague C. K. Prahalad used to say.

nated before completion.[47] Many of these massive investments in computer technology are coincident with business process reengineering,[48] but these projects fail to meet their objectives in 50 percent to 70 percent of the cases documented.[49] It appears that the more radical the change being attempted, the higher the failure rate.

In spite of the risks involved, the quest for better performance using computer technology continues. In the auto industry alone, it is estimated that more extensive use of EDI[50] between suppliers and original equipment companies could save

---

[47] B. Wysocki, "Some Firms, Let Down by Costly Computers, Opt to 'De-Engineer," *Wall Street Journal* (April 30, 1998), p. A-1, A-8. To put this statistic in perspective, more than a dozen studies have reported the nearly identical failure rate, about 40 percent, for new products after they have been introduced (see Chapter 7 on new products) and a recent review in A. Griffin, "PDMA Research on New Product Development Practices, Updating Trends and Benchmarking Best Practices," *Journal of Product Innovation Management,* 14 (1997), pp. 429–458.

[48] "Throughout our discussion, the terms *business process redesign* and *business process reengineering* (BPR) are used interchangeably, referring to the critical analysis and radical redesign of existing business process to achieve breakthrough improvements in performance measures." J. T. C. Teng, V. Grover, and K. D. Fielder, " Business Process Reengineering: Charting A Strategic Path For the Information Age," *California Management Review,* 36, no. 3, p. 12.

[49] T. H. Stewart, "Reengineering: the Hot New Managing Tool," *Fortune,* 128, no. 4 (August 23, 1993), pp. 41–48.

[50] "In the 1970s and 1980s, businesses extended their computing power beyond the company's walls, sending and receiving purchase orders, invoices, and shipping notifications electronically via EDI (Electronic Data Interchange). EDI is a standard for compiling and transmitting information between computers, often over private communications networks called value added networks (VANs)," U.S. Department of Commerce, "The Emerging Digital Economy" (April 1998), p. 12,

$1.1 billion, or about $71 per car. Although EDI is a popular way to establish electronic integration within and between firms, one of the important emerging technological interventions used to guide investments in new computer system is enterprise integration. Enterprise resource planning systems attempt to standardize their information systems in the modern world of primarily distributed processing, among other reasons, to avoid the high cost of hardware–software system maintenance. The way this works is through the adoption of "enterprise software, programs that can manage all of a corporation's internal operations in a single powerful network."[51]

For example, Owens-Corning (see Box 9-4), expected to avoid an annual expense of $35 million in information system maintenance by installing an SAP, Inc. enterprise-wide information system.[52] Owens-Corning started by redefining its markets to be global and broader than just insulation in an attempt to increase the proportion of materials it supplied in a typical building (e.g., a residential home). The company reengineered the finance process first and then went on to reengineer other business processes, replacing all but a few legacy systems that were inherited through recent acquisitions. Another example is GM, which estimates that it is saving $400 million a year after information systems were integrated. Finance alone at GM had 1,800 systems, of which 70 percent are scheduled to disappear.[53]

We argue here that the challenge of enterprise integration, which is a technological intervention designed to achieve better coordination, is an example of what economists call the **appropriation of rents** problem. That is, since the bulk of enterprise technology systems, like other process technology, is now supplied, rather than developed internally by organizations, it is challenging to capture the benefits of these investments. Organizations tend to invest R&D in new products and services, not new process technology. Any purchased technology is theoretically available to all organizations—including competitors. Further, because of the popularity of these new hardware–software systems,[54] all customers are now competing for scare resources of supplier attention, since only a handful of companies can provide this technology. Consulting companies do take up some of the shortfall by providing the temporary labor and advice needed to plan and implement these systems. However, consultants learn from their hosts and sell their accumulated knowledge to the next client, further eroding the innovator's proposed advantage. Therefore, the appropriation or capture of benefits from innovating in this way becomes an even more difficult challenge than value capture from proprietary product or service technology. Anecdotal reports indicate considerable variance in success with enterprise integration programs. This appears to be a fertile context in which to investigate the more general research question: *How do we account for the differences in outcomes of adoption of new process technology designed to intervene and promote coordination (e.g., enterprise integration*

---

[51] S. Baker, "SAP's Expanding Universe," *Business Week* (September 14, 1998), pp. 168, 170. The market for enterprise software is now dominated by SAP and is estimated to be about $12 billion per year, and if installation is included, this rises to about $30 billion.

[52] J. B. White, D. Clark, and S. Ascarelli, "Program of Pain, This German Software Is Complex, Expensive, and Wildly Popular," *The Wall Street Journal* (March 14, 1997), pp. A1, A8.

[53] K. Jackson, "Exec Has Everyone at GM Talking," *Automotive News,* 73, no. 5786 (September 28, 1998).

[54] Ibid., SAP grew at a rate of 66% in the first half of 1998.

computer systems)?[55] This is precisely what we did, and the preliminary results of this ongoing study are presented next.

Successful Adoption of ERP Systems

A recent study of ERP by the Meta Group of Stanford, Connecticut, found the following:[56]

▶ Average time to implement ERP is 26 months.

▶ Cost of ownership after 2 years ranges from 0.4 to 1.1 percent of company revenues (SAP is 0.67 %).

▶ It takes 2.5 years to achieve quantifiable ROI.

▶ 90 percent of quantified benefits are the result of cost reduction.

▶ Recommendations: consolidate all under ERP.

We surveyed 60 Fortune 1000 companies currently installing or having recently completed EPR installations.[57] Companies in the survey were spending an average of $40 million on their new ERP system. We found, significantly, that three factors accounted for interim progress (firms ahead of competitors in their industry) with ERP:

1. As expected, developing your own ERP system significantly slows companies in progressing toward ERP installation. Making as opposed to buying an ERP system was significantly and inversely related to ERP interim success. *Don't make—buy or buy tailored—ERP systems is the implication.* (The average company purchased 80 percent of its new ERP system.)

2. Goal structure of ERP projects is very important. Presented with a list of six possible goals such as cost reduction, global data integration, and Y2K, the significant predictor of progress with ERP installation was *customer response*. The clear message: The way to bring order to a chaotic ERP planning and implementation project is to focus on your customer.

3. Third and finally, *leadership* is very important. But it is important in a way that might make many general managers very uncomfortable. It is not just a matter of having a vision and then communicating this vision over and over and over that will produce ERP results. It is very much a social learning interpretation of leadership.[58] That is, *leaders must demonstrate the behaviors they want the rest of the organization to follow to get results.* Company senior managers who reported making the best progress toward implementing ERP

---

[55] The same question could be asked and investigated for EDI, CAD, and any number of other technological interventions designed to promote integration (e.g., tight coupling).

[56] Results can be found on the Internet at:
http://www.news.comNews/Item/0%2C4%2C34578%2C00.html?sas.mail.

[57] J. Ettlie, "Technology and Weak Appropriation Conditions," presented at the European Operations Management Association, Venice, Italy, June 7–8, 1999. Research assistants on this project were Glenn Gibson, Kelly Bernhardt, Madhur Kapoor, and Kamran Parekh.

[58] See, for example, J. Ettlie, and A. H. Rubenstein, "Social Learning Theory and the Implementation of Production Innovation," *Decision Sciences,* 11, no. 4 (October 1980), pp. 648–668.

answered yes to the following question: "Do all division general managers actually use the information system (hands on)?"

These three predictors—**make/buy/buy tailored, goal structure, and leadership**—accounted for 30 percent of variance in successful ERP adoption performance, controlling for industry (about 60% of the firms were manufacturing) and scale (sales or number of employees, it makes no difference), and other factors. Although these results are preliminary, the signals are clear: goals, leadership, and make/buy decisions figure very importantly in ERP deployment.

Cookbook Process Innovation Deployment— The "Implementation Question"

Although there is no easy answer to the question of "can you give the outline, the one liner, or the cookbook of change management for new technology in operations?" it is worth taking a stab at it, given all the accumulated evidence in this chapter. Having stated the disclaimers, I offer one humble attempt at answering the "how do you really do it" question.

1. *All significant change—whether technology-centered or not—begins and ends with leadership.* But as we have just seen in our results from EPR adoption, it is not as simple as having a vision and smooth communication style. It does matter if the senior managers involved are technology literate; they have to demonstrate technology participation, one way or another, from start to finish. And as several respondents in our ERP survey said, "ERP is never done," implying, like quality, that technology change is never finished.

2. *All significant process technology change has to be linked to the product or service strategy of the organization.* Operations changes cannot be separated from customer-sensitive responses—products and process generally change together.

3. *All successful process technology change involves the simultaneous adoption of new technology and new organizational strategies and structures.* What is new in technology changes, so what is new in organizational innovation also changes. For example, in modern, successful companies, people move more "optimally" than they did 10 years ago—they aren't held back from promotion and challenges and they aren't moved too quickly, either. This type of human resource strategy has to be orchestrated by a senior officer of the firm who has a clear, legitimate voice in all strategic decisions. Balance in functional influence of the innovation process is essential. There is no room generally, for a "square table" to launch technological change—only a "round table" will work.

4. *The simultaneous changes that involve organizational innovations have been documented in this chapter* (e.g., technology agreements in union contracts), *but they will be different tomorrow.* However, these organizational innovations are likely to continue to appear in the four categories summarized in Figure 9-1: *hierarchical integration, design-manufacturing integration, supplier integration, and customer integration.*

5. *There must also be balance between benchmarking and customer voice.* This is discussed at length in Chapter 7, but is worth mentioning here as well because of point 2.

UMMARY

The challenge of innovation and the operations core often to what economists call "appropriation of rents," problems. Most operations and information technology is purchased outside the organization, and is theoretically available to everybody, including competitors. The model introduced in this chapter, which has been supported in empirical studies in durable goods manufacturing, strongly suggests that the key capturing benefits from purchased technology is to simultaneously adopt organizational innovations that support integration of the organization. These organizational innovations unfold in four phases (see Figure 9-1). First, organization structure is modified, changing hierarchy (including work force and union issue resolution) and interfunctional relationships change (e.g., design-manufacturing integration). Then supplier and customer relationships are modified. This is how to appropriate rents: adopt new relationship-enhancing innovations that cannot be copied by rival firms.[59]

When this simultaneous and closely coupled adoption of technological and organizational innovation approach is used by firms, results are quite impressive. Even average levels of quality (30%) improvement and throughput reduction (50%) are significant. And the mosaic of technologies adopted does matter, not just the number of purchased technologies. For example, adoption of local area networks has had a dramatic impact on faster employment growth. Add to this the active promotion of co-evolution of firm and technology core, and the performance enhancement often doubles (e.g., 100% throughput reduction).

Service innovations in the operations core have followed a similar pattern. However, much of service sector adoption of new technology involves information system purchase. Major changes, such as ERP (enterprise resource planning) system adoption, which can cost as much as $50 million to over $1 billion, have emerged as a major challenge. Preliminary results from a survey of sixty U.S. companies indicate that **goals** (i.e., be customer focused), **leadership** (general managers must demonstrate implementation behaviors), and **make/buy decisions** (i.e., buy or buy tailored, but don't make ERP systems) figure prominently in adoption performance of large, new, complex information systems.

$\mathscr{D}$ISCUSSION QUESTIONS

1. Read Case 9-1. What is meant by "Program of Pain?"

2. Is there any way to reduce the stress of enterprise integration without sacrificing performance?

3. If you were a senior manager at Owens-Corning, how would you react if you learned that your best competitor was also installing SAP R/3?

---

[59] Many thanks to Paul Caproni for reinforcing this point in a personal communication, February 12, 1999.

ADDITIONAL CASE SUGGESTIONS

CASE 9-1

Program of Pain: This German Software Is Complex, Expensive, and Wildly Popular

Microsoft has it. Coca-Cola wants it. Building-materials maker Owens-Corning has been installing it for two years at a cost of about $100 million. General Motors is thinking about getting it and could spend 10 times that much.

It is R/3, a complex software system from the German company SAP AG that ties together and automates the basic processes of business: taking orders, checking credit, verifying payments, balancing the books. Never run into it? Odds are you will soon. Propelled by the same corporate herd instinct that drove re-engineering, empowerment, and downsizing, SAP's R/3 is becoming the new standard equipment of global big business.

This is all the more remarkable because installing R/3 is the corporate equivalent of a root canal. The software is fiendishly complex and expensive to configure. Companies must play host to armies of consultants who sometimes charge as much as five times what the software itself costs and can stay on the job for years. Software costs vary widely from company to company: Owens-Corning Fiberglas Corp. says software costs for its R/3 project came to about $15 million to $20 million. "It depends on the deal," says Bonnie Digrius of the Gartner Group, a technology consulting firm in Stamford, Conn. Some companies have seen their R/3 project budgets double.

Weeks of Upheaval

Then there is the human factor. Because R/3 is so complicated, it is usually cheaper for companies to change the way their people work than to change the way the system works. As a result, R/3 projects produce weeks of organizational upheaval, punctuated by high-stress days like the recent Monday morning at Owens-Corning when the Toledo, Ohio, company's $1 billion-a-year roofing-and-asphalt unit switched all its order-processing to the new R/3 network – and the system crashed for half an hour.

"The pain level is about a six or a seven" on a scale where 10 is a "hurricane," Owens-Corning Chief Executive Glen Hiner says. "We are spending $100 million, which is a lot of money for this company. We have no savings as of yet."

But Mr. Hiner expects to save a lot, starting later this year. And he says Owens-Corning had no choice, other than to keep spending $30 million a year to maintain an archaic collection of computers. "Our growth agenda forced us to go to this," he says.

Mr. Hiner has lots of company. Egged on by consultants, some of the biggest names in U.S. business are lining up to join the nearly 7,000 companies already using R/3. Among the heavyweights on SAP's customer list: International Business Machines Corp., oil giant Chevron Corp. (which estimates its $100 million R/3 investment will pay back $50 million a year in cost savings) and consumer-products giant Colgate-Palmolive Co.

Success Stories

Compaq Computer Corp. uses R/3 to monitor order backlogs on a daily basis, and John White, chief technology officer, says the system helped the personal-computer maker slash inventories last year to $1.2 billion from $2.2 billion, even as revenue rose 23%, to $18.1 billion.

Microsoft Corp. is delighted with the software system. The company spent 10 months and $25 million installing R/3 to replace a tangle of 33 financial-tracking systems in 26 subsidiaries. Microsoft puts annual savings at $18 million, and Chief Executive William Gates calls SAP "an incredible success story."

Riding these sorts of testimonials, SAP AG saw business in the unit that includes the U.S. surge 47% last year. The Walldorf, Germany, concern owns 26% of the total market for "enterprise software," compared with 8%

for No. 2 Oracle Corp. SAP rang up 38% overall revenue growth last year, and it has projected another 25% to 30% growth this year from 1996 revenue of $2.4 billion. SAP has mushroomed into the world's fourth-largest software company, behind Microsoft, Oracle and Computer Associates International Inc.

SAP's success has been an even bigger bonanza for the consulting industry. By the year 2000, total corporate spending on consulting related to R/3 and other enterprise systems is projected to grow to as much as $15 billion, from $5.5 billion in 1996, according to industry estimates. That doesn't count such big-ticket items as training. Much of this growth is driven by corporate angst about aging computers that aren't programmed to recognize the year 2000. Rather than recode antiquated mainframes, many companies are junking them in favor of PC-based networks running R/3, which has no problem with the 21st century.

SAP is spawning some megadeals, such as Coca-Cola Co.'s "Project Infinity," a $300 million campaign that includes a global R/3 installation led by the consulting arm of Big Six accounting firm Ernst & Young. Coke wants a manager in Atlanta to be able to look at a table on a PC or laptop and know up to the minute how sales of 20-ounce bottles of Coke Classic are doing in India.

General Motors Corp., meanwhile, has installed R/3 in 20 test locations, and is weighing a "billion dollar" decision on whether to go all the way—a move that could influence hundreds of suppliers to the world's largest auto maker. But GM's choice could depend on SAP's willingness to create a new unit solely to guarantee "total support," says Ralph Szygenda, GM's chief information officer. "A lot of companies buy these systems and they're worse off than they were," he says.

SAP's rivals second that. "This stuff is just too difficult to use," says Lawrence Ellison, Oracle's chief executive.

Most experts agree that R/3 is particularly unforgiving of corporate disorganization. Struggling Apple Computer Inc. turned to the system in 1994 to make sense of its incompatible order-management and financial systems. But Apple's free-wheeling corporate culture rebelled at R/3's push toward standardization.

Apple executives waffled over whether operating units or the central computer systems staff should run the project, then wrangled over how to change about 200 business operations. Estimates that the system might be installed within 18 months went by the boards. Now, Jody David, Apple's R/3 project manager, says the company plans to have all its order-management and financial operations running on R/3 by mid-1998. But the company has for now put on hold its plan to use the system for manufacturing. "The system consolidation will

provide tremendous benefits," Ms. David says. "But it is a costly and time-consuming process."

End of Genesys

In January, Dell Computer Inc. quietly canceled most of a two-year-old R/3 project, code named Genesys, after its budget swelled to $150 million from $115 million and tests showed that the software couldn't handle the sales volume Dell was expecting. Dell won't comment, but people familiar with the project expect the company to use home-grown software for many tasks R/3 was supposed to manage.

SAP executives defend their product. "People say it's typical German software, it's overengineered," says Vice Chairman Hasso Plattner, who lives part-time in Silicon Valley and livens up SAP jamborees by jamming on his electric guitar. But SAP, he says, simply has "thought about much more functionality than anybody else." SAP is also trying to expand the group of consulting firms qualified to install R/3 and is pushing a simplified installation technique called "Accelerated SAP." Some recent installations took three to five months, says Paul Wahl, chief executive of SAP's U.S. unit.

Those quickie conversions are rare. More typical are projects like the one at Owens-Corning, where executives congratulate themselves for sticking to a two-year timetable, while other companies are heading into their third or fourth year. At Owens-Corning, R/3 is much more than a software tool. It has become the engine for a broad company overhaul. "We made this a business initiative, not a systems initiative," Mr. Hiner, the CEO, says.

Mr. Hiner wanted Owens-Corning to grow to $5 billion a year in sales from $2.9 billion in 1992 through a combination of acquisitions, overseas expansion and more aggressive marketing of the company's traditional building products. Up until now, customers called an Owens-Corning shingle plant to get a load of shingles, placed a separate call to order siding, and another call to order the company's well-known pink insulation.

Mr. Hiner's vision: Owens-Corning should offer one-call shopping for all the exterior siding, insulation, pipes and roofing material that builders need. R/3 will give Owens-Corning the ability to make that happen, by allowing sales people to see what is available at any plant or warehouse and quickly assemble orders for customers.

Autonomous Fiefs

Sounds simple. But Owens-Corning traditionally had operated as a collection of autonomous fiefs. "Each plant had its own product lines," says Domenico Cecere, president of the roofing and asphalt unit. Each plant also had its own pricing schedules, built up over years of cutting unique deals with various customers. Trucking was parceled out to about 325 different carriers—picked by the individual factories. Technology? Forget it. Most Owens-Corning factories limped along with decade-old PCs.

R/3, however, effectively demanded that Mr. Cecere's staff come up with a single product list and a single price list. The staff initially fought ceding control over pricing and marketing to a computer-wielding central command. "My team would have killed it, if we'd let them," he says. "Our first meeting … they just threw up their hands."

Owens-Corning grossly underestimated the cost of training employees to use the new computers and software. Company planners expected to devote about 6% of the total project budget to training. In fact, that number will be closer to 13%. Training was so time consuming that one plant in Mr. Cecere's unit shut down briefly because people responsible for ordering raw materials were in class.

"We were just naive," says David L. Johns, director of global development for information services and a key player in the R/3 effort. "When you completely change the way people work, it's a big deal."

Internal Logic

One way in which it is a big deal is that factory-floor employees will be using R/3 to confirm shipments of insulation or roofing shingles as they leave the plant. In the same key strokes, they will also update the company's general ledger. But if they make a mistake and don't catch it right away, R/3's internal logic will force Owens-Corning's finance staff to hunt for that transaction to balance the books.

Overall, Owens-Corning is cutting about 400 jobs as it consolidates functions using R/3. That number could rise as the company looks to save $15 million this year and $50 million next year.

The War Room

For Mr. Cecere, D-Day came this past Monday, when his unit's old computers were shut down and the SAP-equipped order-intake center opened for business at Owens-Corning's new headquarters office on the Toledo waterfront. About 60 people worked most of Saturday and Sunday to transfer data from the old to the new systems. Monday morning, members of the R/3 installation team gather in a "war room" near the order center, hunching over laptops and fielding phone calls. Striding in around 10 a.m., Mr. Cecere grabs a cellular phone from a colleague and calls the plant manager in Medina, Ohio, to ask how it is going. "Better than expected," he reports with a grin.

Meanwhile, Andy Sundermeler, a new recruit, takes orders for shingles over a headset, and keys them into a R/3 table on his PC. To the average PC user, R/3 looks like any other database entry form. Blank cells are labeled "quantity," "price" or "product description." As Mr. Sundermeier taps in figures, the table calculates how much more material would fit onto a truck. He is trying to arrange the order so one truck can drop some shingles at the job site, and the rest at a warehouse.

"I didn't know how the old system worked," he says. "In my mind, that's probably an advantage."

The Wall Street Journal Friday, March 14, 1997. Reprinted by permission of Wall Street Journal © 1997 Dow Jones and Company, Inc. All rights reserved worldwide.

Section Four

Managing Future Technologies

Chapter 10

Public Policy

𝒞HAPTER OBJECTIVES

To introduce and debate the major issues of public policy and innovation. To review the empirical evidence concerning public policy and other governmental interventions such as patent law, cooperative research and development agreements (CRADAs), funding for innovation (e.g., incubators), and the R&D tax incentive. To stimulate thinking on this topic, the case involving Microsoft and antitrust actions is included at the end of the chapter along with discussion questions.

What is at issue concerning government and technology? The concern over public policy and innovation stems primarily from two sources. Does technology benefit the common good (society), or is it primarily a private benefit captured by the innovator? Markets often fail to balance innovation benefits between the innovator and society. Worse, the negative, unintended consequences of new technology (e.g., pollution) often are borne by society and not the private originator.

The second source of interest in public policy stems from the idea there is such a thing as a national system of technical innovation—a spirit called **technonationalism,** which is "a strong belief that the technological capabilities of a nation's firms are the key source of competitive prowess, with a belief that these capabilities are in a sense national and can be built by national action."[1] For example, when an innovation is too costly and risky to attract private investment, and the innovation has great potential social benefits, the government of a nation often gets involved, primarily based on the assumption of comparative advantage.

There is legitimate concern about the incompatibility between the innovation process and public policy. This is the debate over unnecessary (or excessively costly) intervention into the innovation process, which is not only harmful to free enterprise and creativity, but is ultimately harmful to society. The benefits from

---

[1] R. R. Nelson and N. Rosenberg, "Technical Innovation and National Systems," in R. R. Nelson (ed.), *National Innovation Systems: A Comparative Analysis* (New York: Oxford, 1993), p. 3.

innovation may not only be diluted, but the idea of public intervention here may be counter to the founding principles of a country. In the United States, for example, it could be argued that government does not understand the technology and science underlying innovations and is not capable of prudent policy and regulation. Microsoft is provided as an example in Case 10-1.

Managers of the innovation process and innovative companies usually want two things from government:

1. Predictability (no surprises)
2. Regulation of the outcomes (if absolutely necessary), not the process of innovation—part of the means to achieve ends.

From this standpoint, a candidate for "ideal" innovation regulation might be the Environmental Protection Agency's standards for emission content. But as can be seen from the case introduced in Chapter 5 on the Low Emission Paint Consortium (LEPC), even that is not simple. The auto industry would rather be out of the regulation business than have standards imposed of any type—arbitrary or otherwise. The same might be said for CAFE (Corporate Average Fleet Economy) standards for fuel efficiency of automobiles or emission standards for cars. If you make the average very high for miles per gallon or make emissions zero (as California tried to do), you may eliminate all but one technology. In the latter case, this would be electric vehicles using state-of-the-art engine technology.

A further extension of this debate concerns the controversy over "picking winners" in public policy. It is one thing for government to fund basic R&D, say, in universities, to foster progress on high-risk projects that no private sector entity can justify. It is quite another for the government to go "downstream" in the innovation process and fund specific technology projects, such as a given energy alternative to fossil fuels. Economists debate this issue much like managers argue the merits on both sides. Smaller countries are more focused in their research and they patent more abroad, which complicates matters even more.[2]

James A. Henderson, chairman and chief executive officer of Cummins Engine Company, Inc., recently said that just wanting to do the socially responsible thing is not enough. What is the corporately responsible thing to do in an era of emphasis on shareholder value? Even if employees are the number one concern of every corporation, it is not always obvious what should be done in the employees' best interest. Many times the needs of employees and society are the same, as in the area of education, training, and development. Sometimes, however, they conflict—mobile benefits send the signal to some employees that they should move on to their next station (e.g., job) in life. Without knowing it the company was sending a message to some employees to leave.[3]

The controversy over the U.S. trade deficit with key import partners often fuels the debate about public policy and technology. When the trade deficit soared 17 percent to $11.07 billion in September 1997, it was assumed to be caused by Asian

[2] D. G. Mcfetridge, "The Canadian System of Industrial Innovation," in R. Nelson (ed.), *National Innovation Systems* (New York: Oxford, 1995), p. 303.

[3] "Corporate Responsibility in an Era of Shareholder Value," the 1997–1998 William K. McInally Memorial Lecture, by James A. Henderson, Chairman and Chief Executive Officer of Cummins Engine Company, Inc., January 21, 1998, University of Michigan Business School, Ann Arbor, Michigan.

economic and currency turmoil.[4] And other reports of cost cutting by Asian car markers designed to redress yen-dollar exchange rate tensions may have reinforced these effects. Toyota is said to have designed current generation cars to make money at 80 yen to the dollar.

PATENTS

More than 5 million patents have been issued in the United States since the first patent law of 1790.[5] However, only about 2 percent of these patents have ever been commercialized. Firms vary in their propensity to seek patents for ideas that warrant protection.[6] The rate of patenting has been relatively stable for many years, even though research employment has risen steadily. This is likely the result of the trend for technological breakthroughs to generate patents, but discoveries become more difficult to achieve as a technological frontier advances (see Chapter 5).[7] Patent law continues to evolve and vary by country, and should probably be considered one of the major strategies governments use to foster innovation.[8] The Japanese, for example, recently announced that Japan was reforming its patent office to significantly speed up the application process.[9] At issue currently in the United States is the interface between patent law and antitrust law: On the one hand, patents grant owners the right to exclude others from using a product; on the other hand antitrust law seeks to control this power to exclude.[10] We already know that the value of patent protection varies greatly by technology field and country.[11] The U.S. drug industry, for example, is quite concerned about the erosion of patent protection by the growing effort internationally to make pharmaceuticals available in developing countries.[12]

---

[4] "U.S. trade deficit soars 17%," *The Globe and Mail* (Toronto, Canada) (November 21, 1997), p. B6.

[5] S. Forbes, "A Force for Freedom and Prosperity," *Forbes,* 160, no. 13 (December 15, 1997), p. 28.

[6] See the discussion in J. Ettlie, "The Commercialization of Federally Sponsored Technological Innovation," *Research Policy,* 11, no. 3 (June 1982), pp. 173–192. This is not the same as the propensity to seek patents, which is much higher. For example, in Europe's largest industrial firms, the propensity to patent ranged from 8.1 percent in textiles to 47 percent in instruments. See A. Arundel and I. Kabla, "What Percentage of Innovations Are Patented? Empirical Estimates for European Firms," *Research Policy,* 27 (1998), pp. 127–141.

[7] S. S. Kortum, "Research, Patenting, and Technological Change," *Econometrica,* 65, no. 6 (November 1997), pp. 1389–1419.

[8] See, for example, A. Jacobs and E. Hnellin (eds.), *Patents Throughout the World,* (Clarke Boardman and Callaghan Publishers, 1995).

[9] "Big Patent Reforms on the Way," *Focus Japan,* 25, no. 6 (June 1998), pp. 12–13.

[10] R. H. Marschall, "Patents, Antitrust, and the WTO/GATT: Using TRIPS as a Vehicle for Antitrust Harmonization," *Law & Policy International Business,* 28, no. 4 (Summer 1997), pp. 1165–1193.

[11] M. Schankerman, "How Voluble Is Patent Protection?" *Rand Journal of Economics,* 29, no. 1 (Spring 1998), pp. 77–107.

[12] "U.S. Drug Industry Wary of Efforts to Weaken Patents," *Chemical Market Reporter,* 253, no. 20 (May 18, 1998), p. 17; also see J. Sood, "An International Patent Protection System: A New Approach," *Thunderbird International Business Review,* 40, no. 2 (March/April 1998), pp. 165–179; and R. DeJule, "Global Trends in Patents Are Increasing Competition and Fostering Creativity," *Semiconductor International,* 20, no. 14 (December 1997), p. 15.

The Patent Cooperation Treaty of 1995 revised U.S. patent law. Patents filed before June 8, 1995, have a term of 20 years from the date on which they were filed, or 17 years from the date issued, whichever is longer. Patents filed after June 8, 1995, have a term of 20 years from the filing date, and if the U.S. Patent Office is slow in issuing a patent, it could shorten the term. Applicants can also file in 85 countries simultaneously when they pay an additional $3,000 fee. The European and U.S. Patent offices now both provide the full text of patents online free of charge.[13]

Intellectual property can be protected by a patent or by other means; the "best" way may vary by situation. According to one estimate, if a high-tech company gave another company all the information it had on one of its manufacturing processes, it would still cost the second company 75 percent more than the first company to start up the process. Tacit knowledge and craft details are learned by doing and are embedded in these complex technologies.[14] Given all the ways knowledge occurs, it is not surprising that any change in U.S. patent law would be controversial since the way to protect knowledge is still so variable. For example, proposed reform of the patent system currently pending as legislation would require publishing secrets 18 months after filing and make it easier to challenge existing patents, all with the intention of harmonizing patent laws in the United States with Japan and Europe.[15] But the ever-increasing globalization of trade will continue to put pressure on governments to coordinate their patenting and intellectual property laws and practices.[16]

GOVERNMENT-SANCTIONED COOPERATIVE AGREEMENTS

CRADAs

The LEPC, which was included as Case 5-2, was formed, in part, under the 1984 National Cooperative Research & Development Act (NCRA), which permits (but does not exempt antitrust action concerning) precompetitive technical collaboration in the United States. After this Act was passed, thousands of **CRADAs** (Cooperative Research & Development Agreements) formed between companies, government laboratories, and universities. Do they work? The answer is yes and no; that is, the empirical evidence and theoretical models show mixed results and are subject to interpretation.

Paul Olk and Katherine Xin compared U.S. collaboration with four other countries (France, Germany, United Kingdom, and Japan). They say that the "U.S. has been only marginally successful in mimicking the foreign organizational arrange-

[13] P. Blake, "The Arrival of Free Patent Information," *Information Today,* 15, no. 3 (March 1998), pp. 19–20.

[14] J. F. Coates, "Intellectual Property Concerns Overdone, Not Half-Baked," *Research-Technology Management,* 41, no. 2 (March/April 1998), pp. 7–8.

[15] S. Forbes, "Patently Wrong," *Forbes,* 161, no. 6 (March 23, 1998), p. 28; H. Schwartz," Patents—Whose Rights Do They Serve?" *Pharmaceutical Executive,* 17, no. 9 (September 1997), pp. 26–30.

[16] F. Ferne, "Patents, Innovation, and Globalization," *OECD Observer,* no. 210 (February/March 1998) pp. 23–27.

ment."[17] Bozeman and Pandey compared just the United States and Japan and focused primarily on government laboratories' collaboration with industry. Although the mission and motives of government laboratories in both countries are similar, there are also differences, including the fact that U.S. labs have twice as many cooperative agreements as the Japanese. Further, U.S. labs with agreements have more patents, and rate technology transfer efforts were more effective.[18] When Bozeman and Choi compared 134 government labs with 139 university labs in the United States, they found that cooperative R&D, as measured by number of interlaboratory agreements, is not a strong predictor of technology transfer to either firms or government.[19]

One economic model comparing cost and value of R&D investments by firms before and after the 1984 NCRA predicts that appropriability can be increased by both diversification and cooperation among firms, but the cooperative R&D will sacrifice competition that is present with diversification alone. Diversification in the absence of the NCRA may have been more socially desirable, and the effect of the law could be to decrease investment, moving firms away from the social optimum.[20]

Olk and Young studied 184 CRADA memberships in the United States and found that continuing membership was a function of how much discretion an organization had over resources used in the collaboration—making the party less dependent on the relationship. Rather, transaction cost theory was a significant predictor of continuity of the consortium. Poor performance increased the likelihood that members would leave, and good performance was associated with staying. Further, membership conditions did influence continuity, but only a few select conditions applied. Having "fewer alternatives to the consortium increased the likelihood of leaving rather than decreasing it," which led the authors to conclude that, "a joint venture represents a different kind of alternative than contracting or internal research."[21] Network ties and involvement based on knowledge-related issues were good predictors of continuity. Learning had a negative relationship. Involved members will continue to stay in a consortium that is performing poorly, consistent with the idea of "technical side-bets." Knowledge-related involvement was important when performance was poor, while ties were credited with more importance when performance was good (which is inconsistent with transactions cost theory in which ties represent hostage arrangements).[22]

Although these results may seem contradictory prima facia, Andrew Van de Ven and colleagues found similar patterns among intensive case studies of the innovation process done over time on such innovations as the cochlear implants to eliminate

---

17 P. Olk and K. Xin, "Changing the Policy on Government-Industry Cooperative R&D Arrangements: Lessons from the U.S. Effort," *International Journal of Technology Management*, 13, no. 7 (1997), pp. 710–728.

18 B. Bozeman and S. Pandey, "Cooperative R&D in Government Laboratories: Comparing the U.S. and Japan," *Technovation*, 14, no. 3 (April 1994), pp. 145–149.

19 B. Bozeman and M. Choi, "Technology Transfer from U.S. Government and University R&D Laboratories," *Technovation*, 11, no. 4 (May 1991), pp. 231–245.

20 J. T. Scott, "Diversification versus Cooperation in R&D Investment," *Managerial & Decision Economics*, 9, no. 3 (September 1988), pp. 173–186.

21 P. Olk and C. Young, "Why Members Stay or Leave an R&D Consortium: Performance and Conditions of Membership as Determinants of Continuity," *Strategic Management Journal*, 18 (1997), pp. 855–877, esp. p. 866.

22 Ibid.

hearing impairment. That is, researchers typically do not drop a line of inquiry in the face of failure, and they persist well beyond what outside observers would consider to be logical and prudent.[23] In particular, there are many instances in the innovation process at the bench level for individuals, in which "little rational learning appeared to occur," and further, "superstitious learning occurs when the subjective experience of learning is compelling but the connections between actions and outcomes are loose."[24] That is, evaluations can be formulated as to whether outcomes are positive or negative, and managers can act according in funding or not funding continued action. But this occurs whether learning is rational or superstitious. In good times, only "exceptionally appropriate courses of action will lead to judgments of innovation failure," while in bad times, no course of action will lead to "outcomes judged to be successful."[25] It is not surprising that the misspecification of causality in the innovation process is common, given the uncertainty of the endeavor. And this, in part, explains the story imparted earlier by the senior R&D manager at Canon, who said that bench researchers and project engineers are judged more on their persistence on a project than on the "objective" technical merits of progress.

This insight about how to manage bench research at Canon and the way the innovation process proceeds in many settings accounts for the counterintuitive notion that makes management in these uncertain settings the so-called "consistency" or "congruence" idea of goals and policies. Resource controllers and research managers often diverge in their thinking. Quinn and Cameron reinforce this notion generally when they suggest that it is incorrect to overemphasize one set of organizational effectiveness criteria rather than another and advocate balance or capacity to respond to multiple effectiveness criteria.[26]

It should also be remembered that departure and continuity are not the same as success and failure, just as in the discontinuance of a joint venture, where one party purchases the interests of one or more of the others, and the "entity" continues a successful life. AT&T has had a policy of eventually ending all joint ventures in this way.

Consistent with the anecdotal evidence in the LEPC, members in the Olk–Young sample may be considering the future benefits of collaboration somewhat independently of current returns. In the LEPC, a widely promulgated contention by the members of USCar was that this initial consortium was going to serve as a "model" for future collaboration among the Big Three auto producers. True, a dozen more consortia have been added under USCar, but there is no systematic evidence that these subsequent collaborations are using this "model." In fact, at least one anecdote suggests that learning within the USCar consortia actually makes it easier to form consortia outside this model, to work with noncompetitors on new technology projects. This calls into question the single explanation of "consortia as precursors to more embedded relationships," a notion, advanced in the literature and cited by Olk and Young.[27]

[23] A. H. Van de Ven, H. L. Angle, and M. S. Poole (eds.), *Research on the Management of Innovation* (New York: Harper & Row, 1989).

[24] Ibid., p. 204.

[25] Ibid., p. 205.

[26] R. E. Quinn and K. S. Cameron, "Organizational Life Cycles and Shifting Criteria of Effectiveness," *Management Science,* 29, no. 1 (1983), pp. 33–51.

[27] P. Olk and C. Young, "Why Members Stay or Leave an R&D Consortium: Performance and Conditions of Membership as Determinants of Continuity." *Strategic Management Journal,* 18 (1997), p. 873.

The largest U.S. collaborative R&D organization doing cross-industry consortia is the National Center for Manufacturing Sciences (NCMS), located in Ann Arbor, Michigan, with an office in Washington, D.C. Begun in 1987, NCMS has grown to be supported by more than 220 dues-paying members.

✖ NCMS

The NCMS is a not-for-profit industrial consortium of U.S., Canadian, and Mexican corporations. With more than 200 members, NCMS has accumulated R&D revenues from 1987 to 1996 of more than $400 million, of which 94 percent went to manufacturing projects. In 1996, the NCMS R&D program totaled $64 million, and the organization has managed $285 million spread among 100 DoD (Department of Defense) projects. It has been estimated that for every dollar spent on NCMS research, $5 has been returned to participating companies, which is similar to the returns estimated by other federal laboratory commercialization.

The management structure of NCMS focuses activities in strategic interest groups (SIGs), but the structure has evolved since NCMS was founded. The current structure relies heavily on active initiation of projects by NCMS corporate staff, although many of these technical staff personnel and managers came from member organizations.

GOVERNMENT-SUBSIDIZED RESEARCH AND DEVELOPMENT

At any one time in the recent history of U.S. R&D spending, the federal government has accounted for up to half, and typically no less than a third, of all R&D expenditures. The current rate is about 40 percent of all R&D.[28] Although other countries and regions of the world (e.g., Singapore) have had successful policies to promote innovation, the United States is still the world leader in number of patents awarded and percentage of GDP devoted to R&D. The rate of innovation appears to be accelerating in the United States, and the federal government, at least according to one report, can take some of the credit for this trend.[29]

Barry Bozeman and his colleagues have reported on a study of 229 industry–federal laboratory collaborative projects involving 27 labs and 219 firms.[30] Their findings are summarized as follows:

---

[28] In 1996, the proposed federal budget for all R&D was $7.3 billion, or about 40% of all U.S. R&D, estimated to be about $18.25 billion (see Geisler and Clements[51]).

[29] D. Hanson, "Study Confirms the Importance of Federal Role in Technology Commercialization," *Chemical & Engineering News,* 73, no. 48 (November 27, 1995), p. 16.

[30] B. Bozeman, M. Papadakis, and K. Coker, "Industry Perspectives on Commercial Interactions with Federal Laboratories," Report to the National Science Foundation, Contract No. 9220125, January 1995.

▶ 22 percent of these interactions led to marketed products, with 38% having new products underway

▶ Monetary benefits of projects exceeded costs at a ratio of 3 to 1.[31]

▶ 90 percent of the projects *did not* result in a single new hire by the participating firm.[32]

In nearly all of the surveys responses, participants overwhelmingly say they had a good interaction with government. In the Bozeman work, it was 89 percent approval on the "smile" scale, or overall satisfaction ratings, but the author is quick to add that there are a few big winners in these federal laboratory–company interactions that returned in excess of $10 million to the company. In general, however, three general factors correlated with success: (1) the interaction was focused on a new product introduction, (2) the laboratory contacted the company, and (3) the company and the lab had previous experience working together.[33]

✳ Incubators

The purpose of a business incubator is to "accelerate the successful development of entrepreneurial companies through an array of business support resources and services." Incubators are typically subsidized by local, state, or federal government sources. The first business incubator appeared more than 30 years ago in Batavia, New York, in response to a plant closing, but incubators as a movement and industry did not really begin until the late 1970s and 1980s. Today, it is estimated that there are more than 530 incubators in operation throughout North America.

Regional studies suggest that incubators are an effective business development tool, requiring only modest investment and yielding excellent returns to the regional economy in diversified industry base and employment. One recent study[34] of 50 incubation programs and 126 firms in operation since at least 1991 and tracked to 1996 found that about 80 percent of these efforts receive some sort of operating subsidy, and they would suffer—especially the new technology incubators—without government assistance. Return on public investment in terms of tax revenues was calculated to be $4.96 for every dollar of estimated public operating subsidies. In 1996, when the study ended, the average incubator was servicing 15 clients with 13 employees. Incubators averaged 21 graduates from the incubators still in business, had created an average of 468 new jobs directly attributable to each incubator, and had affected substantial, local spinoff employment (using the multiplier of 1.5 typical of macroeconomics models, but this does not include job creation outside the region).

Technology firms (34% of the sample and 40% of the incubators) had the highest survival rate (90%) after graduation from incubators, followed by mixed-use

---

[31] Elsewhere (see Ashley, 1996 in footnote 46), Bozeman has said that if you don't control for firms that have not invested their own money, this ratio is 4 to 1, and if you do, the ratio drops to 3 to 1 (average benefit to a firm was $1.8 million and average cost was $544,000).

[32] Bozeman et al., 1995, p. vi–vii. "Job creation is the single criterion by which laboratory-industry interactions could not be said to have been particularly successful... This seems not to be a function of limited time for jobs to develop; the pre-1985 projects had a job creation rate inferior to the post-1990 ones."

[33] Ibid, p. viii.

[34] L. A. Molnar, et al., *Business Incubation Works,* (Athens, OH: National Business Incubation Association, August 1997).

incubator firms (86%) and empowerment incubator companies (87%). Companies in mixed-use incubators (49% of the sample) included service, distribution, light manufacturing, technology, and similar types of firms. Empowerment or *microenterprise* incubators (11% of the sample), as they were called in the study, "faced economic challenges" such as high unemployment or distressed, deteriorating neighborhoods. Their mission was often mixed use and targeted toward low-income-, minority- or female-owned businesses.

Typical of young companies, firms in incubators were financed primarily by private savings (87%) and personal or family loans (56%). But technology incubators seem to be different from other startups; they benefit more from incubators and the co-location with other startup, technology-based enterprises.

Most technology incubators seek to commercialize a new product or service, are sponsored by a university, and are located in an urban or suburban environment. Technology incubators do better on a number of other dimensions, as well. Technology incubators have fewer tenants than empowerment incubators, according to incubator managers, but technology incubators had significantly higher average revenues in 1996 ($21.9 million versus $3 million for empowerment and $5.9 million for mixed used incubators). Technology incubators also had much higher average employment (257 people versus 90 for empowerment and 80 for mixed-use incubators). In spite of the rigor of this University of Michigan project, the study tried but failed to produce a comparable control group to validate the results, even though a mixed sample of respondent types and presurvey focus groups was included in the investigation.[35]

Evaluation of these incubators (or any government intervention) continues to be a topic of debate. The central issue is how incubators ought to be compared with the higher or lower investment options—especially startups with alternative forms of assistance or no assistance at all. Various, alternative control groups have been suggested, including inventor societies, patent holders, near participants, and program referrals. The latter group was used in one evaluation of the Department of Energy (DOE) Energy-Related Inventions Program (ERIP). By monitoring both types of cases (i.e., program participants, and nonparticipants referred to the program), Brown, Curlee, and Elliot demonstrated the relative commercial success of the government-supported intervention.[36]

Not surprisingly, technology incubators are plentiful in Silicon (formerly Santa Clara) Valley, where 3,000 new businesses start up every year. Typical of these models of planned innovation is the incubator just off Interstate 280 across from a strip mall in San Jose, created by the National Aeronautics and Space Agency (NASA) in 1993[37] Originally, the NASA incubator was set up to be a home to spin-

---

[35] Ibid., pp. B-1, ff. Three methodologies were used systematically: (1) the survey of 126 firms in 50 incubators; (2) a total economic impact study of a subsample of 4 business incubators and 23 firms; and (3) a survey of 35 business incubator program managers and 72 stakeholders from 50 incubators programs. Stakeholders were 38 board members and 34 community leaders. However, the proposed methodology also called for a validation, control sample of comparable firms not receiving incubator assistance. According to a personal communication with the senior author (1998), a sufficient sample of these matching firms could simply not be found from comparable business categories in each region.

[36] M. A. Brown, T. R. Curlee, and S. R. Elliot, "Evaluating Technology Innovation Programs: The Use of Comparison Groups to Identify Impacts," *Research Policy,* 24, no. 5 (September 1995), pp. 669–684.

[37] M. Lewis, "The Little Creepy Crawlers Who Will Eat You in the Night," *The New York Times Magazine* (March 1, 1998), Section 6, pp. 40–46, 48, 58, 62, 79–81.

off technology from the space agency, but no companies stepped up until Netscape was incorporated in April 1994. The NASA incubator includes a software company based on an idea designed to speed access to corporate databases. It started with $190,000 in credit card debt. Other startups are efforts to exploit the Internet, enhance factory productivity, and enhance vision using software technology. The goal of the latter company, called Sightech, is to be worth $600 million.

Silicon Valley has a unique culture and entrepreneurs and incubator affiliates are often members of what could be considered a "closed society" of aspiring technologists and very successful businessmen (primarily—few are women) who created the old technologies of the valley.[38] For example, one group of business owners, called the "Band of Angels," hears aspirants' (often incubator tenants') presentations periodically (usually once a month) at the Los Altos Golf and Country Club in Silicon Valley. It is estimated that venture capital investment in the valley has quintupled, from $0.5 billion in 1990 to $2.5 billion in 1997. The average target of this investment has also increased, from a $50 million growth potential to about $250 million today, which leaves a need for funding smaller potential growth companies in the $50 million to $100 million range. This is where the angels come in—they are looking to recreate the thrill they once knew in starting their own companies. The Small Business Administration estimates that a total of 250,000 angels invest $20 each year.[39] One venture capitalist, John Doerr, estimates that 5 times out of 10 startup companies make his money vanish quickly, 4 out of 10 return it without much interest, and 1 in 10 do extraordinary things. In 1997, the Kleiner Perkins portfolio of technology companies employed 162,000 people, had revenues of $61 billion, and stock market value of $125 billion.[40]

This "closed" valley culture may not be limited just to venture capitalists, angels, aspiring technological entrepreneurs, and fat cats. There seems to be an ethnic connection in Silicon Valley, as well.[41] There are at least four "culture clubs" operating Silicon Valley ethnic networks, including India, Pakistan, Bangladesh (The Indus Entrepreneurs and the Silicon Valley Indian Professional Association), Korea (Korean American Society of Entrepreneurs), and Taiwan (Monte Jade Science and Technology Association). Since 23 percent of those working in the valley are immigrants, it is not surprising that they join a local association of kinship to "bypass the local power structure." Going through channels could take 2 weeks to get an appointment in the valley. Indians, Israelis, and various Europeans dot the landscape, but the Chinese-Americans are the most concentrated, accounting for 60,000 to 70,000 foreign-born engineers. Yet Monte Jade (Taiwan) has a relatively small membership at 460 individuals and 180 companies—including Applied Materials, Inc, and Hewlett-Packard. Glass ceilings and language barriers are very much a part of this story.

Mainstream venture capitalists (e.g., Sequoia Capital LLP) are already including partners from successful immigrant-owned companies and setting up funds that

---

[38] E. M. Rogers and J. K. Larsen, *Silicon Valley Fever: Growth of High-Technology Culture* (New York: Basic Books, 1984).

[39] P. DeCeglie, "Pennies from Heaven," *Business Start-ups,* 11, no. 2 (February 1999), p. 23.

[40] M. Lewis, "The Little Creepy Crawlers Who Will Eat You in the Night," *The New York Times Magazine* (March 1, 1998), Section 6, pp. 40–46, 48, 58, 62, 79–81.

[41] D. Takahashi, "Ethnic Networks Help Immigrants Rise in Silicon Valley," *Wall Street Journal* (March 18, 1998).

appeal to them. Foreign investment is growing, but the ethnic networks are also opening up membership as resistance to foreign-born engineers decreases. It goes both ways. Monte Jade now has a 20 percent membership level born outside of China. These American chapter members see themselves as bridges to the mainstream.

Peter Allen, owner of the First & Miller Technology Center, attracts 20 active tenants in his incubator, and has a waiting list. "They co-locate with other software companies, at $18 per square foot, in small spaces and short-term leases. We aren't subsidized and charge the market rate." But Peter can't find the one biotechnology floating around Ann Arbor spinning off from the University of Michigan and looking for space. "I have 20,000 square feet of wet lab and can't find a buyer," says Peter.[42] This may explain why high-technology incubators work: It's the synergy with other company startups with similar endowments and owner motivations.

Maybe high-technology firms need cheap-space incubation and synergy. And maybe other startups don't. Diane Rossi, who started "Have Dogie, We'll Do," in Chicago in 1990 now has a thriving clean-up business and is looking into recycling opportunities. At $10 a visit to your backyard to clean up after your dog, she now has about 200 regular customers. But even if it's a job nobody else wants like dog-do or garbage pickup, a business does not start itself, and it has continuing problems. Diane is always looking for good part-time help.[43] The same thing is now happening in Europe. Research on 500 small companies there recently revealed an increase in 183,000 jobs combating an 11 percent unemployment rate in Europe.[44]

There is more irony in the Silicon Valley incubator story. In nearby Sunnyvale, California, dubbed "Vacuum Tube Valley" by reactionaries holding periodic swap meets, a revival of the industry replaced by the silicon wafer thrives. Pushed primarily by audiophiles, in relentless pursuit of a "rich sound" only heard from tubes, it is claimed, they tread the ground as inventor Lee DeForest, who hooked up the first vacuum tube to phone equipment and a loudspeaker in 1911 in Palo Alto at the Federal Telegraph Company. Vacuum tubes propelled the radio, broadcasting, hi-fi, television, and recording industries for years. Invention of the transistor in 1947 nearly ended all that, but tubes, hot running and all, survived to maintain a current niche market of $100 million a year. About 80 percent of these sales are to professional musicians and recording studios; the rest is the high-end consumer audio equipment market, including a share from some U.S. companies that have restarted production such as Westrex Corporation in Atlanta. *Vacuum Tube Valley* is actually a publication for the industry. Writers and readers for the publication claim they aren't Luddites, just lovers of the unique sound they say tubes provide. But they also wear T-shirts that say things like "Analog Retentive."[45]

---

[42] Personal communication with Peter Allen, March 19, 1998.

[43] P. Thomas, "Diane Rossi Changes Her Unlucky Life Via Unlikely Business," *Wall Street Journal* (March 20, 1998), p. B1.

[44] J. Flynn, H. Dawley, S. Baker, and G. Edmondson, "Startup to the Rescue," *Business Week* (March 23, 1998), pp. 50–52

[45] J. O'C. Hamilton, "Where the 'Tube Guys' Hunt for Sweet Sound," *Business Week* (March 30, 1998), pp. 16E2–4.

Advanced Technology Program

A comparable government effort, producing cases similar to Bozeman's studies, was started by the National Institute of Science and Technology (NIST). The advanced technology program (ATP) was established in 1990 to offer cost-sharing awards to industry for high-risk enabling technologies with broad-based economic benefit. Early reports indicated that 70 percent of the 125 companies and nonprofits participating in the program said they would not have gone ahead without the funding.[46] In a more recent evaluation of ATP projects,[47] the following positive results were reported:

1. There were 38 ATP completed projects (1991–1997), with a total NIST contribution of $64.5 million.
2. Most (34) were single-company projects, and most were small-company (28 with 20–400 employees) projects in seven technology areas (e.g., chemical, energy, biotech, computers, and electronics).
3. Two thirds of projects reported they would not have proceeded without ATP support.
4. Seven projects received awards for technology.
5. 63 percent introduced a new product/service.
6. 60 percent of the 27 small, single-applicant companies more than doubled in size since funding.
7. Twelve projects failed or were discontinued, but just three projects have paid back the investment.
8. Projects vary widely in returns: one (process monitoring and control for auto bodies) is a consortium with Chrysler and GM and is expected to return $65 to $160 million by 2000 after being installed in about half their plants.

Energy-Related Inventions Program

Another federal program that has received a great deal of evaluation attention is the DOE's Energy-Related Inventions Program (ERIP), started in 1974. It is among the longest-running such programs designed to assist in commercialization of new technology so the technology will survive. The results here are even more impressive using similar indicators. For a population of 609 ERIP technologies, results are as follows:[48]

- 24 percent (144 of 609) of these energy-related technologies have entered the marketplace and generated sales.

---

[46] S. Ashley, "Federal Labs and Industry Come Together," *Mechanical Engineering,* 118, no. 10 (October 1996), pp. 80–84.

[47] W. F. Long, *Advanced Technology Program: Performance of Completed Projects,* NIST Special Publication 950-1 (Gaithersburg, MD: U.S. Department of Commerce, Economic Assessment Office, March 1999).

[48] M. A. Brown and C. G. Rizy, "Evaluating the Economic, Energy, and Environmental Impacts of a Technology Commercialization Program," *Proceedings of the 1997 Energy Evaluation Conference* (Chicago: DOE, pp. 255–260).

▶ ERIP has generated a 20-to-1 return of sales to grants ($47.5 million in grants generated $961 million in sales) and an 8-to-1 return of sales to total program appropriations ($124 million).

▶ Five energy-saving technologies in 1994 alone saved enough power to meet the energy needs of the entire United States for 12 hours.

These ERIP results compared favorably with much larger federal assistance programs—perhaps, in part, because only 2 percent of all energy inventions pass through the DOE screening process to become candidates for commercialization. Since about 2 percent of all inventions are commercialized, this rate seems comparable. The Gas Research Institute (GRI) has operated a similar program since 1978, and the European Commission (EC) has conducted an exploitation program since 1968; the results are comparable. The GRI had a budget of $1.41 billion in 1991. The EC had 50 inventions on the market by 1990 as a result of several billions of R&D dollars in funding.

These results from the ERIP also compare favorably to the Small Business Innovation Research (SBIR) program, which spends considerably more money. "Between 1983 and 1993, eleven federal agencies gave nearly 25,000 SBIR awards worth more than $3.2 billion to more than 50,000 firms ... in 1992, SBIR firms had received only $471 million in sales." Further, the New York Manufacturing Extension Program invested $12.9 million between April 1993 and December 1994, resulting in an added-value impact of $29 million to $108.7 million. ERIP invested $12.4 million during this same period and generated $133 million in sales, which is nearly identical.[49] These indicators of the ERIP program impact are summarized in Table 10-1.

The similarity between success rates in incubators, ATP projects, and the ERIP program outcomes is hard to ignore: about 25 percent succeed at commercialization, with a payback of three to eight times the amount invested. These ratios have

TABLE 10-1   Indicators of Program Impacts

Benefit Category	Indicator of Program Impact
Market entries	At least 144 ERIP technologies commercialized, representing a 24 percent commercialization rate
Sales	$961 million (in 1994) dollars) of sales generated by these 144 technologies through 1994
Spinoffs	An additional $98 million (in 1994 dollars in sales generated by 52 spin-off technologies
Employment	757 job-years supported in 1994 and 6,646 supported in 10-year period, 1985–1994.
Taxes	$4.4 million in ERIP-related tax revenues returned to the U.S. Treasury in 1994

SOURCE: M. A. Brown, "Performance Metrics for a Technology Commercialization Program," *International Journal of Technology Management,* 13, no. 3 (1997), p. 243, Table 3.

[49] Ibid., p. 258.

remained relatively constant since the beginning of these programs, or at least when systematic evaluation began. Granted, the commercialization success rate of a new product once it is introduced in the United States is about 60 percent, but the program evaluations start tracking technology before it is introduced into the marketplace. One study found that even after exploration, screening, and business analysis, it takes seven new product ideas to get one to market, or a commercialization rate of about 14 percent.[50] Further, one or two blockbuster products can often offset many new product failures, as indicated by Bozeman's findings.

The explanation of patterns of success is enriched by another large study of commercialization of federal laboratory technology. Eli Geisler and Christine Clements studied 428 scientist and engineers in 43 laboratories[51] and found that commercialization of federal laboratory technology depends on the combined efforts of lab management and companies involved:

- Commercialization is enhanced if senior lab management actively supports cooperation with industry and provides incentives for collaboration.
- Scientific personal with intrapreneurial attributes and positive attitudes toward commercialization will be more successful *(the best predictor of success)*.
- Commercialization is enhanced if company personnel perceive federal laboratory colleagues as being willing to take risks and deal with ambiguity.
- Prior collaboration between the laboratory and company improves commercial success.

The research found that average investments in cooperation with federal labs was about $450,000 and a reported average of perceived benefits was about $1 million, leading to a reported average cost–benefit ratio of about 2-to-1.[52] However, these benefits will not be realized unless labs promote and foster intrapreneurial behavior among technical staff. This research is generally consistent with other research on the culture of successful R&D laboratories.[53]

R&D Tax Credits

When introduced in the mid 1980s by the Reagan administration to simulate U.S. innovation, the 25 percent tax credit on all new R&D was a very effective means of promoting overall success and productivity of firms reported its use.[54] However,

---

[50] Ibid., p. 257. Also see M. A. Brown, "Performance Metrics for a Technology Commercialization Program," *International Journal of Technology Management,* 13, no. 3 (1997), pp. 229–243.

[51] E. Geisler and C. Clements, "Commercialization of Technology from Federal Laboratories: The Effects of Barriers, Incentives and Role of Internal Entrepreneurship," Final report to the National Science Foundation, Grant no. 94-01432, August 1995.

[52] Ibid., p. xi.

[53] For example, J. McGourty, L. Tarshis, and P. Dominick, "Managing Innovation: Lessons from World Class Organizations," *International Journal of Technology Management,* 11, no. 3, 4 (1996), pp. 354–368.

[54] M. N. Baily and A. K. Chakrabarti, "Innovation and U.S. Competitiveness," *Brookings Review,* 4. no. 1 (Fall 1985), pp. 14–21.

there were, and continue to be, several problems with this incentive. First, it applies only to new R&D, so firms already making the "right" decision cannot benefit directly from this incentive. Second, what qualifies as R&D is often subject to interpretation, based on National Science Foundation guidelines. Does engineering application work qualify? Does purchased R&D or contracted technical work or collaborative R&D qualify? What about indirect benefits from tax credits for location?[55]

More recently, a review of R&D tax credits in the United States and twenty-two other industrial countries raised questions about today's usefulness of this government intervention. The R&D tax credit has not been successful in the long run in stimulating R&D spending.[56] First, tax incentives do not distinguish between total R&D spending levels and the portion that is successful. Second, not all R&D spending that qualifies for a tax credit has an equal impact on productivity growth. Finally, R&D tax credits ignore the increasing role that external sources of technology have on the firm. Such sources as universities, technology centers with public subsidies, cooperative R&D programs, joint ventures and consortia, and federal laboratories, are providing an increasing share of the technology sourcing pie. One study estimates that 73 percent of the papers cited by U.S. industry patents are public science: from academic, governmental, or other public institutions.[57] The question may be how firms effectively blend and manage internal and external sources of technology, rather than how to fund R&D.[58]

The knowledge that ultimately impacts firm performance originates outside companies from universities, state and federal laboratories or centers, joint ventures, consortia, and so on. Firms that combine effective use of internal and externally sourced technology appear to be the winners, and the tax credit for R&D, as it is currently applied, does not seem appropriate for the current era of innovation process management.

Another concern with the R&D tax credit is the differences in firms and economic sectors and industries that might apply it. In manufacturing alone, there are considerable differences in technological opportunity, market size, and ability to capture benefits (appropriability). R&D-intensive industries, such as the high-tech sectors of the economy, are more able to capture the benefits of innovation, which raises the private value of R&D investments. The evidence on R&D, productivity, and new products suggests that R&D-intensive industries have fewer new products per dollar of R&D and average total factor productivity growth relative to research intensity. R&D tax credits may not make sense for high-tech industries.[59]

Separately, but in related, recent developments, Representative Christopher Cox (R-California) has backed a plan to tax Internet transactions, which have been mostly tax-free thus far. Although states would set their own rates, each could be

---

[55] See for example, L. Chappell, "Economist Finds Kentucky's Toyota Incentives Pay off," *Automotive News* (November 9, 1998), p. 66.

[56] D. Leyden and A. Link, "Tax Policies Affecting R&D: An International Comparison," *Technovation*, 13, no. 1 (January 1993), pp. 17–25.

[57] F. Narin, K. S. Hamilton, and D. Olivastro, "The Increasing Linkage Between U.S. Technology and Public Science," *Research Policy*, 26, no. 3 (1997), pp. 317–330.

[58] D. P. Leyden and A. W. Link, "Tax Policies Affecting R&D: An International Comparison," *Technovation*, 13, no. 1 (January 1993), pp. 17–25.

[59] P. Klenow, "Industry Innovation: Where and Why," *Carnegie-Rochester Conference Series on Public Policy*, 44, (June 1996), pp. 125–150.

taxed only once under this proposal, and states would accept a 3-year freeze on new taxes. For 30 years the Supreme Court has maintained that a physical presence in a state is required for taxation, and with mail order there were no problems with this definition. This does not apply to e-commerce, of course,[60] or using Web based marketing and research capability.

Despite its checkered history, the R&D investment tax credit continues to have interest in both the public and private sectors as a policy to stimulate innovation in the United States.[61] The credit was created in 1981 for only *new* R&D, but in its current form it allows a 20 percent tax credit on corporate research spending over a historical base level. So it is not surprising that the way in which R&D is measured is at issue in assigning tax credits and deciding on tax credit policies for R&D.[62] About $2 billion in R&D tax credits were taken by U.S. companies in 1997. Its effectiveness has been studied, debated, and argued; but a Coopers and Lybrand study recently concluded that companies would spend $41 billion more on R&D from 1998 to 2010 if the credit is permanently extended. A coalition of 1,000 major U.S. companies and 36 professional and trade associations back and actively lobby for the credit. High-tech states such as Texas and California are big backers, and support comes from both parties. But making the credit permanent would remove from lawmakers the opportunity to vote for the popular tax break on a more frequent basis. Politics may dictate whether this will become a temporary or permanent measure.

$\mathcal{L}$OW-IMPACT MANUFACTURING AND TECHNOLOGICAL INNOVATION

Low-impact manufacturing has become a popular term to refer to all environmentally friendly industrial practices for preservation of the natural ecology of the planet. There are several important policy experiments in progress in the United States involving the adoption of pollution-prevention technology directly sponsored and sanctioned by the U.S. Environmental Protection Agency (EPA). The LEPC Case mentioned earlier (see Chapter 5) has had only indirect EPA involvement, but will have important policy implications because the new technology practices developed by this consortium will likely be adopted by the EPA as standards.

The EPA is sponsoring the Metal Finishing 2000 project, which also has important technological implications in manufacturing.[63] This project has several "model

---

[60] H. Gleckman, "The Tax Man Eyes the Net," *Business Week* (April 6, 1998), pp. 131–132.

[61] G. Hitt, "What Has 9 Deaths and Always, to Date, A New Lease on Life?" *Wall Street Journal* (October 23, 1998).

[62] F. R. Lichtenberg, "Issues in Measuring Industrial R&D," *Research Policy,* 19, no. 2 (1992), pp. 157–163.

[63] U.S. Environmental Protection Agency, "Metal Finishing 2000: Lessons Learned and New Project Guidance," Common Sense Initiative, Metal Finishing Sector, Strategic Goals Program, Washington, D.C., July 1998.

companies, including Marsh Plating Corporation in Ypsilanti, Michigan. The metal finishing was one economic sector selected for the "fast track" experiment with industry participation, whereby firms can renegotiate environmental regulatory mandates if technological changes can be shown to improve overall natural environmental performance. This process involves the granting of "operational flexibility and incentives to achieve ambitious environmental goals," in order to motivate other companies to follow this model.[64]

Lessons learned to date on the program include, but are not limited to, the following:

1. Establish an equal and early partnership between regulators and stakeholders.
2. Plan to resolve any interagency regulatory issues before engaging stakeholders.
3. Link with existing programs.
4. Use the "championship" model (one or more strong, persistent supports of new projects) of change to foster leadership and broker consensus.

All of these lessons are based on the assumption that agencies can go "beyond compliance." Some of the early returns and technology experiments are well documented by the EPA, but the "indirect" benefits of incorporating the natural environment into business planning and "first mover" advantage this gives companies are difficult to evaluate. This is an active research stream, with many contributions yet to be made.[65]

$\mathcal{T}$HE MANUFACTURING EXTENSION PROGRAM

Perhaps the most daunting public policy challenge in manufacturing, as illustrated by the EPA's Metal Finishing 2000 project, is the coordination of various initiatives, all designed to "help" any sector of the economy. This has become especially important recently with the trend toward more tailored regional development policies for the promotion of technology leadership in the United States and throughout the world.[66] One example of these many initiatives is the Manufacturing Extension Partnership (MEP). The MEP was begun by the NIST in 1989 with three centers. Often, it is just called the manufacturing extension program. This program has grown to include centers in 42 states and Puerto Rico.[67]

---

[64] Ibid., p. i.

[65] S. L. Hart, "Beyond Greening: Strategies for a Sustainable World," *Harvard Business Review,* 75, no. 1 (January/February 1997), pp. 66–76; S. L. Hart, "A Natural-Resource-Based View of the Firm," *Academy of Management Review,* 20, no. 4 (October 1995), pp. 986–1014.

[66] M. Storper, "Regional Technology Coalitions: An Essential Dimension of National Technology Policy," *Research Policy,* 24, no. 6 (November 1995), pp., 895–911.

[67] E. S. Oldsman, "Manufacturing Extension Centers and Private Consultants: Collaboration or Competition," *Technovation,* 17, no. 5 (May 1997), pp. 237–243.

One systematic evaluation of the MEP program matched eight centers in two states with comparable company samples from the Annual Surveys of Manufacturers and Census of Manufacturers. *MEP clients had 3.4 to 16 percent higher labor productivity than matched nonclients.* These findings are quite important, given that the MEP program was originally begun to reach U.S. small- and medium-sized firms (SMEs) that traditionally have been less productive than larger plants.[68] There are 370,000 SMEs in the United States.

The hypothesis driving these types of programs is that SMEs are slower to adopt modern manufacturing techniques and equipment. The study also found that clients grew faster than nonclients, single-unit clients were more likely to use the MEP, and there was no relationship between plant age and technology usage. Small plants were much less likely to become clients than larger plants. Plants with high sales growth during this same period (1987–1992) but with lower productivity were more likely to become clients. There were also clear and significant industry differences, as in the earlier U.S. Department of Commerce study (including the Canadian companion study) on technology adoption, which need to be taken into account for any policy action.[69] Therefore, MEP services focused on improving productivity, such as the adoption of new technology, are more likely to be more effective than those offering services such as ISO 9000 information. The latter is more useful to gain and keep clients, not improve effectiveness of a process.

Summarizing, MEP clients had the following profile: larger, single-unit plants experiencing greater sales growth and lower productivity (industry differences notwithstanding), located near an MEP center. The methodology used in the study also has implications for federal agency evaluation, given The Government Performance and Results Act of 1993, which requires annual reports on outcomes.

What do these data on the effectiveness of the manufacturing extension program really mean? How should we interpret them? Dan Luria has done extensive, comparable research on the state of Michigan's extension service. He reports that how SMEs are defined makes a great deal of difference in targeting extension services.[70] Of the 380,000 manufacturing establishments in the United States, 375,000 have fewer than 500 employees that add $783 billion to the economy. But this figure is misleading, because many of these smaller establishments are actually plants of larger companies. Luria believes the extension program should be focused on single-plant establishments with more than 20 and less than five hundred employees, or about 75,000 target plants, to maximize the added value

---

[68] R. S. Jamin, "Evaluating the Impact of Manufacturing Extension on Productivity Growth," forthcoming, *Journal of Policy Analysis and Management,* 16, no. 1 (1999). There are 370,000 small and medium sized manufacturers in the U.S. This study also contends that The Government Performance and Results Act of 1993, which requires all federal agencies to submit annual performance reviews is likely to promote more adoption of systematic matching methodologies like the one used in this study as their standard.

[69] Ibid., p. 18. "The estimates for the 2-digit SIC dummies suggest that plants in SIC major groups 30 and 33 through 38 are all more likely to become clients relative to other industries."

[70] D. Luria, "Toward Lean or Rich? What Performance Benchmarking Tells Us about SME Performance, and Some Implications for Extension Services and Mission," Industrial Technology Institute, Ann Arbor, Michigan, Presented at Manufacturing Modernization: Learning from Evaluation Practices and Results, Atlanta, GA, September 11-12, 1996.

of extension services, which average about 20 hours of consultation. Luria estimates that one guideline could double the effect of extension services using this approach.

Dziczek, Luria, and Wiarda[71] reported mixed results for the impact of manufacturing extension services in Michigan. When client versus nonclient improvement were compared, clients did better on employment and sales growth, had quicker startups, more CAD (computer-aided design) usage, more inventory turns, greater training expenditures, and more training on statistical quality concepts. However, with respect to growth in payroll per employee and labor productivity, clients did *not* outperform nonclients.

GOVERNMENT REGULATION

Government is probably best known for regulation—promoting the common good in ways the Constitution writers could not have predicted. But the extent to which regulation, as opposed to direct and indirect support of R&D spending, for example, plays a role in the innovation process is much more controversial. Market regulation, in particular, might have an important direct effect on innovation propensity, especially by creating a surrogate market—in particular, for developing countries. Four types of regulations have obvious relevance:[72]

- ▶ Regulation aimed at avoidance of danger to life and health
- ▶ Regulation safeguarding the noninterference of the use of technology with other users
- ▶ Regulation to ensure minimum standards of comfort in the working and living environment
- ▶ Regulations to safeguard the natural environment

The latter category has received considerable recent attention, and figures significantly in the LEPC case presented in Chapter 5. Although gasoline has been taxed and retaxed endlessly, U.S. gas prices are still very low. Now Vermont, Minnesota, and Maine are debating replacing property taxes with fossil fuel taxes. It is likely that it will be a long time before such legislation is accepted, but in the Netherlands, about $900 million is raised annually from gas and electricity taxes, which return premiums to social security. Consumption is not down, so Holland is likely to increase the tax to raise $1.7 billion in the coming year. Tax shifts are now on the books in Denmark, Finland, and Sweden. U.S. transportation industries are understandably not thrilled about such a trend, which would cost them millions.[73]

---

[71] K. Dziczek, D. Luria, and E. Wiarda, "Assessing the Impact of a Manufacturing Extension Center," *Journal of Technology Transfer,* 23, no. 1 (1998), pp. 29–35.

[72] E. Braun and D. Wield, "Regulation as a Means of Social Control of Technology," *Technology Analysis & Strategic Management,* 6, no. 3 (1994), pp. 259–272.

[73] J. Carey, "Commentary: Give Green Taxes a Green Light," *Business Week* (April 13, 1998), p. 31.

Threats by the EPA to invoke superfund status for manufacturing sites, such as GE's Pittsfield, Massachusetts, where PCBs (polychlorinated biphenyls, an alleged cancer-causing agent) were used to make transformers when the chemical was legal, do not seem to have had any impact on new technology use.[74]

Although the EPA may not have a great track record with industry, there are many outstanding exceptions at the agency where initiatives have led to considerable change in the government–industry relation for the natural environment. As mentioned earlier, one is the National Strategic Goals Program in the Metal Finishing sector. In particular, the flexible track segment under this "common sense" umbrella shows great promise to reinvent the relationship between manufacturing and regulators. It is not clear how much new technology, however, will be utilized in this effort.[75]

Trade regulation, such as the controversial proposal to ban export of "dual-use" technology (high-technology military items with commercial applications) to potential foreign adversaries is likely to continue to increase in importance, especially with recent revelations about China's unauthorized use of U.S. technology. There are several sides to this debate, including the argument that since the United States is not the only source of high technology for military use (the backbone of U.S. strategies), it would only hurt the United States to unilaterally ban export.[76]

U.S. government oversight of the Internet has created considerable work for people in Washington. Three primary concerns have emerged for lawmakers.[77] First, U.S. governors have moved aggressively to tax Internet commerce, and a bill has already been passed in the House to stop this movement. Second, parents are concerned about pedophiles stalking children on the Internet, and the House has passed legislation to help prosecutors track these offenders. Third, Hollywood and publishers are concerned about how to protect movies, software, and copyrights, and this is under study. In addition to these issues, encryption of data is also under discussion, which is part of a larger privacy issue. Gambling and junk e-mail are also problematic. A recent report from a study chaired by Vice President Al Gore said that "…we must redouble our efforts to remove barriers that can stifle the growth of the Internet and of electronic commerce."[78] Overseas competitive issues, such as IBM's use of *e-business,* will also likely continue to crop up as issues needing government resolution.[79]

---

[74] W. M. Carley, "GE Plant, River Face Superfund Status," *Wall Street Journal* (April 7, 1998), p. A-2. Also see, William Carley, "Battle of the Housatonic Pits GE Against EPA," *Wall Street Journal* (July 27, 1998), p. B1.

[75] Readers are urged to visit the Web site for this program: www.strategicgoals.org.

[76] L. D. Tyson, "Washington Can't Keep High Tech to Itself, so Why Try?" *Business Week* (July 6, 1998), p. 18.

[77] L. Alvarez, "Internet Is New Pet Issue in Congress," *New York Times* (June 28, 1998), p. 14.

[78] U.S. Department of Commerce, *U.S. Government Working Group on Electronic Commerce,* First Annual Report, November 1998, National Technical Information Service, Springfield, VA., PB99-105496.

[79] R. Narisetti, "IBM Battles Start-Up Over `e-business'," *Wall Street Journal* (July 2, 1998), p. B10.

GOVERNMENT AND THE
SERVICE ECONOMY

For economic reporting purposes, all government activity is counted as part of the very large service economy.[80] Growing interest in the management and business implications of the service economy has not escaped the government.[81] One study, in particular, found that adoption of administrative innovations was positively related to fund balances in Ohio local government in subsequent years.[82] There are a number of case studies of government reform, including studies of the Forest Service and the Department of Commerce's Trade Information Center.[83] However, the postal service is probably among the best illustrations of how government services and technological innovation interact.

The U.S. Post Office Department became a semi-independent governmental agency called the U.S. Postal Service 25 years ago, and changes in the agency have not stopped since. Ironically, most of these changes are invisible to a typical post office customer. E-mail services and backroom operations innovations are among these changes. The U.S. Post Office is discussed more thoroughly in the next section (Box 10-2).[84]

✳ Government Procurement of
New Technology

Time was, in the days of large defense budgets, that the federal government would have broad impact on innovating in the private sector just by tendencies to pur-

---

[80] Except for the U.S. Postal service covered in Box 10.2 which has been assigned SIC code 4311 in the Standard Industrial Classification Manual (Office of Management and Budget), 1992, Washington, D.C.), all other governmental activity falls with in SIC codes 9111 (Executive Offices) to 9721 (International Affairs).

[81] Business cases on the service sector can be found in W. E. Sasser, C. W. L. Hart, and J. Heskett, *The Service Management Course* (New York: The Free Press, 1991); also see innovation in service generally is introduced in F. Galouj and O. Weinstein, "Innovation in Services," *Research Policy,* 26, no. 4, 5 (December 1997), pp. 537–556; an overview of innovation in government appears in R. Lewis and W. Delaney, "Promoting Innovation and Creativity," *Research-Technology Management,* 34, no. 3 (May/June 1991), pp. 21–15.

[82] G. Gianakis and C. P. McCue, "Administrative Innovation Among Ohio Local Government Finance Officers," *American Review of Public Administration,* 27, no. 3 (September 1997), pp. 270–286.

[83] K. H. Mettke, "Reinventing Government: A Case in Point," *Tapping the Network Journal,* 3, no. 3 (Fall 1992), pp. 14–16; M. Zaineddin, and M. B. Morgan, "A New Look: The Commerce Department's Trade Information Center Continues Its Tradition of Excellence with Expanded Services," *Business America,* 119, no. 5 (May 1998), pp. 16–17.

[84] Literature on the technology investments at the post office include: B. Bot, J. H. Ivo, P. A. Girardin, and C. S. Neumann, "Is There a Future for the Postman?" *McKinsey Quarterly,* no. 4 (1997), pp. 92–105; G. H. Anthes, "Postal Service Technology Budget Misdelivers," *Computerworld,* 31, no. 23 (June 9, 1997), p. 33; D. A. Andelman, "Pushing the Envelope," *Management Review,* 86, no. 6 (June 1998), pp. 33–35; S. Rosen, "More Than Postage Stamps Sends Messages at the Postal Service," *Communication World,* 15, no. 5 (April/May 1998), p. 43; T. Minahan, "Strategy Shift Pushes More Business to Parcel Carriers," *Purchasing,* 124, no. 4 (March 26, 1998), pp. 87–89; T. T. Duffy, "Signed, Sealed and Delivered," *Communication Week,* no. 604 (April 3, 1996), p. 43; "Neither Rain, Nor Sleet, Nor Shrinking Bandwidth," *CIO* 9, no. 15 (May 15, 1996) p. 22; N. Wice, "Snail Mail Meets e-mail," *Working Woman,* 22, no. 11 (November 1997), p. 22.

chase some goods, such as high-tech weapons system and other related products and services, such as software.[85] This is no longer the case. Nelson says that the three broad technology policy issues of the day are now these:[86]

1. Government support of applied research
2. The decline in private-sector funding of basic research
3. Intellectual property rights

Procurement, per se, does appear on this list. But, the federal, state, and local governments continue to be a force in technology developments through purchases. Also, demonstration projects, like the current effort in photovoltaics, often create standards for procurement.[87]

Procurement policies are problematical because they are designed to serve two, often divergent, goals simultaneously. First, procurement has to satisfy government needs, and the product purchased has to be evaluated based on an assessment of future performance. Second, procurement is also called on to meet various economic, social, and often political ends. Sometimes these additional objectives are not fully stated or published.[88] Governments in industrialized countries buy about 10 percent to 15 percent of all production in those nations, and it appears that their purchasing influence on innovation falls into one of three categories:

1. The technological capacity of the public sector
2. The value of orders that allows the supplier to reduce the risk associated with innovation
3. The relationship between needs and requirements

Coordination among government and initiatives continues to be one of the foremost challenges to achieving technology policies goals. Should governments intervene on the supply side or demand side of innovation? Case studies suggest that supply-side procurement has been more effective. Higher concentration of orders promotes innovation among suppliers, but often conflicts with political objectives of distribution of benefits across regions. Civilian procurement has promoted higher R&D productivity than military procurement. Two new trends in procurement—freer trade agreements and privatization of public services (see the following post office example)—have yet to be systematically evaluated.[89]

---

[85] D. C. Mowery and R. N. Langlois, "Spinning Off and Spinning On (?): The Federal Government Role in the Development of the U.S. Government Software Industry," *Research Policy,* 25, no. 6 (September 1996), pp. 947–966. Also see K. M. Peters, "Technology Outpaces Procurement Process," *Government Executive* (August 1998), pp. 85–59, which indicates that technology like the Intel processor and avionics for the F-15 and F-16 change before the orders can actually be filled. Electronic technology is changing with generational turnover every 18 months or 2 years, driving procurement costs up.

[86] Richard R. Nelson, "Why Should Managers Be Thinking about Technology Policy?" *Strategic Management Journal,* 16, no. 8 (November 1995), pp. 581–588.

[87] B. K. Farmer, "Moving Photovoltaics from the Lab to Utility Application," *Electricity Journal,* 8, no. 2 (March 1995), pp. 50–55.

[88] R. Dalpe, "Effects of Government Procurement on Industrial Innovation," *Technology and Society,* 16, no. 1 (1994), pp. 65–83.

[89] Ibid., pp. 78–80.

Infrastructure renewal, alone, accounts for billions of dollars in government-sponsored investments each year, some done specifically to upgrade obsolete technologies. The U.S. government acquires considerable technology through various sources, but outside of military procurement, the history has been checkered. One such case is in air-traffic control technology (see Box 10-1).[90]

The FAA is currently involved in an air-traffic control technology "mess." A $500 million budget to upgrade air traffic control will have to be at least tripled, it is estimated, to actually make even the incremental changes needed for safety and avoidance of costly airplane delays. Latest reports indicate that a scaled-down version of this modernization will be pursued, but this is still part of a $34 billion upgrading program, dating back to 1981 and extending beyond 2000.[91] This is not a model on how to modernize and encourage technology.

It is the rule rather than the exception for government agencies to "require" more money. The 1999 $217 million highway bill is an example. It included pork items such as $14 billion to buy barges for a company that transports new cars to dealers in Brooklyn and Manhattan, and $2.75 million for an access road to the Dayton baseball stadium.[92] These items were part of a bill that is intended to rebuild the U.S. infrastructure.

The situation at the U.S. post office (see Box 10-2) may not be much better, and may be even more controversial, given the anticompetitive issues raised by investments there. New legislative proposals to segment postal services into competitive and noncompetitive services accompany these continuing investments in new technology, which are projected to be $3.6 billion through 2001. There is some discussion about segmenting postal service into regulated, overnight first-class delivery and de-regulated package delivery, following examples in Europe.

High-speed bar code readers are rarely seen by the public, but are a staple of mail-processing technology. Trends toward paperless payment systems and communication through e-mail have cut into the post offices' core business—first-class mail at a common, low price. Even the government continues to make life difficult for its postal service, encouraging paperless payment and electronic tax filing. Post office competitors in overnight package delivery, such as Federal Express, create even more pressure for reform and innovation in postal services.

Projections for procurement of information technology by all state governments in the United States forecast a near-linear, steady upward slope through the year 2001 to near $30 billion, from about $20 billion in 1996. Examples of this trend include the proposed expenditures to outsource Connecticut's state information technology systems to a private company—some sixty-five agencies—in a 7-year program at a cost of $1 billion. Connecticut expects to save $50 million per year with this program. The total market for U.S. information services was about $150 billion in 1998, but software glitches abound.[93]

[90] The FAA case is covered in J. Cole, "Near Miss: How Major Overhaul of Air-Traffic Control Lost Its Momentum," *Wall Street Journal* (March 2, 1998), pp. A-1, A10.

[91] J. Ott, "New ATC Techniques Keep Air Traffic Flowing," *Aviation Week & Space Technology* 148, no. 5 (February 2, 1998), pp. 51–53.

[92] D. Harbrecht, "Will Tons of Highway Pork Flatten the Balanced Budget?" *Business Week* (April 13, 1998), p. 41.

[93] Wendy Zeller, "The Promised Land for Outsourcing?" *Business Week,* (July 6, 1998), p. 39. Also see N. Gross, M. Stepaner, and O. Dort, "Software Hell," Business Week, (December 6, 1999), pp. 104–118.

BOX 10-1

The FAA Modernization Program:
When Radical Technology Fails, It's "Quick-Fix Time"

It all started when President Ronald Reagan fired striking air controllers who were employees of the FAA and devised a plan for an Advanced Automation System to replace the antiquated system. Software problems killed that version of modernization in 1993.

Flight delays now cost airlines millions of dollars each year, and in 1997 there were 225 near misses, up 22% from 1996, comparing just the first 11 months of each year.

Then FAA director, David Hinson, had an alternative plan ready. He proposed a "revolutionary" solution that would save money and reduce the risks of air travel. He was calling for a network of 30 ground-based stations to augment a Department of Defense satellite-based navigation system. It would cost an estimated $400 million to $500 million. Four years later, the plan is just getting implemented, and costs are now estimated to be many multiples of the original budget. Unforeseen technical problems, escalating complexity of the system, and dismay over the prospects of installing expensive, as-yet untested equipment on board—especially on 180,000 small general aviation aircraft—have all but killed the original proposal, which is now estimated to cost $14 billion, if it could be carried out.

In place of the long-term plan, and offered as a quick-fix, is an alternative, simpler set of initiatives that include software upgrades and new procedures being tested at an en-route center near Seattle. Dallas is testing two systems to improve sequencing and spacing of inbound commercial jets. In Indiana and Tennessee, and at certain times of day, a prototype "conflict probe" system is being tested that warns controllers if flight paths converge and threaten an intersection up to 30 minutes before a collision would occur. Mike McNally, president of the 17,000-member air-traffic-controllers union, says conversion to the new system will take time, but at this point, controllers would even welcome a "new transistor."

More recent news on the system was not encouraging. On May 5, 1999, four major airports (Chicago, New York, Newark, and Philadelphia) all experienced delays, in some cases for hours, and cancellations, due primarily to new air-traffic-control software.

SOURCES: J. Cole, "Near Miss: How Major Overhaul of Air-Traffic Control Lost its Momentum," *Wall Street Journal* (March 2, 1998), p. A-1, A10; S. Carey, "Airports Have Delays, Cancellations Due to Problems in Air-Traffic Control," *Wall Street Journal* (May 7, 1999), p. A20.

Technology and the Trust Busters

Section 2 of the Sherman Antitrust Act prohibits monopolistic behavior. The Justice Department sued to block Lockheed Martin's purchase of Northrop Grumman, saying that the merger of the two military contractors "could hurt innovation and undermine national security." Microsoft continues to wrestle with the Justice Department over the department's allegations of aggressive monopolistic practices.

BOX 10-2

Technology and the U.S. Post Office

The U.S. Post Office is often the brunt of jokes—from incompetence to "snail mail" to workplace violence. If you have visited the post office lately, you might not notice much difference from your very first visit. But back-room operations have changed gradually since 1970 and radically in the last 10 years. Today, the post office is in an intense, competitive battle with the likes of Federal Express and other small-package delivery services. Part of this dispute is over what constitutes fairness under the Post Office public charter for universal service at a low, uniform rate, the price of stamps not with standing.

The Post Office began its push for increased operating efficiency during a time of continuing increases in demand for mail services. The U.S. postal service delivers 43 percent of the world's mail, which breaks down to 603 million pieces of mail every day (in 1996). The good news is that bar coding, letter-sorting technology, zip codes, and other changes have resulted in 91 percent of local first-class mail being delivered overnight, nationwide. And, there hasn't been a taxpayer subsidy in 15 years. The bad news is that not all the technology experiments at the post office were successful (e.g., E-com in the early 1980s and Postal Buddy, electronic kiosk was dropped in 1993 after one year). Further, the Post Office lost $6 billion in revenues to competitors like FedEx from 1988 to 1994. Reducing the cost of operations continues to be the greatest technology opportunity. In 1996, expenses rose 4.7 percent and revenue gained only 3.9 percent. Labor costs were expected to rise 6 percent in 1997.

Not surprisingly, the Postal Service intends to invest billions in labor-saving technology, primarily in high-speed sorting and bar-coding equipment—proven innovations. But it is the Post Office move to work with partners such as Xerox that has competitors most worried. In a recent promotion of a new product, Xerox entered a single copy of a mailing into a computer in Anaheim, California, and seconds later it emerged at a Global ePost printer in Germany, which was then delivered by German Post Office. The U.S. Post Office now has a mailbox in cyberspace. Electronic postmarks, hand delivery of e-mail to customers without computer access, and Internet access to governmental agencies are also coming.

Other carriers in the private sector have also been busy investing in new technologies. FedEx and UPS are spending $1 billion per year on Web-based tracing and tracking information technology. UPS, for example, saved $15 million in 2 years (1994–1996) by establishing sixty-five technical support centers, cutting travel and managing telephone calls.

More than 25 years ago, the Post Office Department became the quasi-independent U.S. Postal Service. Now the issue is what constitutes fair competition between this $56 billion semi-private governmental agency and FedEx, UPS, and Mail Boxes, etc. One proposal is to divide the Post Office into two product offerings: noncompetitive mail like first-class letters, which would have a fixed, capped rate, and competitive mail, where rates would be set according to market conditions. Congress is also considering allowing private companies to deliver the mail, and electronic mail is under study. Congress has already mandated that all federal payments be made electronically by 1999, which will further cut into post office volume losses by another $100 million a year.

(continues)

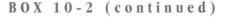

BOX 10-2 (continued)

In the last 5 years, the Post Office has experienced a 33 percent drop in business-to-business mail as a result of faxes, e-mail, and electronic data interchange (EDI). Forecasts indicated that PC (personal computer) households will pay discretionary bills electronically at a rate of 30 percent within 10 years in the United States (15% to 25% in Europe). Sweden and Finland have abolished their postal monopolies, and the European Union limits postal service letters to 350g (Denmark's limit is 250g and Germany's is 200g). The Netherlands now seats half of its post service board, including the CEO, from outside the industry. All of these trends suggest that the post office around the world will continue to change, both as a direct and as an indirect result of new technology.

SOURCE: This case is based in part on the following sources: B. Bot, J. H. Ivo, P. A. Girardin, and C. S. Neumann, "Is There a Future for the Postman?" *McKinsey Quarterly,* no. 4 (1997), pp. 92–105; G. H. Anthes, "Postal Service Technology Budget Misdelivers," *Computerworld,* 31, no. 23 (June 9, 1997), p. 33; D. A. Andelman, "Pushing the Envelope," *Management Review,* 86, no. 6 (June 1998), pp. 33–35; S. Rosen, "More Than Postage Stamps Sends Messages at the Postal Service," *Communication World,* 15, no. 5 (April/May 1998), p. 43; T. Minahan, "Strategy Shift Pushes More Business to Parcel Carriers," *Purchasing,* 124, no. 4 (March 26, 1998), pp. 87–89; T. Duffy, "Signed, Sealed and Delivered," *Communication Week,* no. 604 (April 3, 1996), p. 43; "Neither Rain, Nor Sleet, Nor Shrinking Bandwidth," *CIO,* 9, no. 15 (May 15, 1996), p. 22; N. Wice, "Snail Mail Meets e-mail," *Working Woman,* 22, no. 11 (November 1997), p. 22.

Deregulation in the rail industry, which has caused a rash of recent mergers, has shipping customers in an uproar over poor service and gouging pricing practices.[94] Previous deregulation of commercial air traffic helped create the hub-and-spoke system in the United States, which may have complicated this problem because of local monopoly effects.[95] It seems that the honeymoon is over for companies that took advantage of merger fever, closely followed by alliance fever and high-tech immunity.[96]

The Microsoft case, still unresolved at this writing, has caused a great stir, and attention has now been refocused on the practices of high-technology firms generally and the emerging technologies of cyberspace or the World Wide Web and networks. It was originally reported that the Justice Department believes it has "enough new evidence to move quickly against Microsoft Corporation, in alleging "'illegal maintenance and extension" of a monopoly on personal-computer operating software. But Microsoft released Windows 98 on time, and the case still hadn't been settled. Microsoft spokespersons said that the "central issue of this case is

---

[94] "U.S. Sues Lockheed," *New York Times* Business Section (March 29, 1998); D. Bank and J. R. Wilke, "Browser Bruiser: Microsoft and Justice End a Skirmish, Yet War Could Escalate," *Wall Street Journal* (January 23, 1998), p. A1; B. Ingersoll, "Deregulation Aids Rails Too Much, Shippers Say," *Wall Street Journal* (April 2, 1998), pp. A-2, A-4.

[95] B. Ingersoll, "U.S. Curbs Big Airlines from Deterring Start-Ups," *Wall Street Journal* (April 7, 1998), p. B-2; D. Field, "Airline Lifts off on Sense of Fare Play," *USA Today* (July 23, 1998), p. B1.

[96] S. Garland, "The FTC's Eager Sheriff," *Business Week* (July 6, 1998), pp. 65–66.

protecting the ability of Microsoft and every other company to innovate and improve their products.[97] The strong lobby of competitors such as Sun Microsystems, Novell, and Netscape Communications have influenced congressional and Department of Justice initiatives.[98] Several states are preparing to take their own actions against Microsoft for antitrust behavior, with or without Department of Justice action, as well as unrelated actions of antitrust abuses in the credit-card industry.[99] As of this writing, the Microsoft defense appeared to be faltering.[100] Intel was also a target of Justice Department investigations into abuse of monopoly power but settled out of court.[101]

INTERNATIONAL COMPARISONS

Perhaps the most comprehensive international study of government and innovation involving 15 countries is summarized in Richard Nelson's book, *National Innovation Systems*.[102] It is difficult to generalize across all these countries, even when they are divided into groups such as the three used here: large, high-income countries; small, high-income countries; and low-income countries.[103] There does seem to be a general trend toward a positive impact across the board on innovation from government support of education and training systems and a university system responsive to industrial needs, as well as fostering effective collaboration generally.[104] An example is CERN, the particle physics laboratory in Geneva, which was acknowledged to be the world's foremost accelerator facility especially after U.S. plans for a similar project were discontinued.[105]

Fiscal, monetary, and trade policies also make a difference, especially when they make exporting attractive. There is a trend toward cooperative R&D in gov-

[97] J. R. Wilke, "U.S. Closes in on New Microsoft Case," *Wall Street Journal* (April 6, 1998), pp. A-3, A-6.

[98] P. C. Roberts, "Microsoft Is the Victim of a Legal Mugging," *Business Week* (April 13, 1998), p. 16.

[99] J. R. Wilke, "States Ready Antitrust Move Over Microsoft," *Wall Street Journal* (April 9, 1998), pp. A-3, A-10.

[100] M. France and S. Garland, "Microsoft: How Vulnerable?" *Business Week* (February 22, 1999), pp. 60, 80; J. Wilke, "Browser-Beaten: As Microsoft Struggles with Antitrust Case, Tactical Errors Emerge," *Wall Street Journal* (February 18, 1999), pp. A1, A10; J. Wilke and K. Perine, "Microsoft Targeted in Two More Lawsuits," *Wall Street Journal* (February 22, 1999), p. B15.

[101] S. Garland, A. Reinhardt, and P. Burrows, "Now It's Intel in the Dock," *Business Week* (March 1, 1999), pp. 28–29. D. Hamilton and D. Takahashi, "FTC, Readying its Intel-Monopoly Case, Lists Witnesses From 8 More Companies," *Wall Street Journal* (February 22, 1999), p. B15.

[102] R. R. Nelson, *National Innovation Systems* (New York, Oxford University Press, 1993).

[103] For example, "Funds Boost for Research," *Professional Engineering*, 11, no. 22 (December 9, 1998), p. 13, the European Commission has set a L10.5 billion budget to support scientific research over the next four years.

[104] J. Blau, "Jenoptik Sparks Jena Tech/Innovation Park," *Research-Technology Management,* 43, no.1 (January/Febuary 1999), pp. 3–5; E. Grande and A. Peschke, "Transnational Cooperation and Policy Networks in European Science Policy-Making," *Research Policy* 28, no. 1 (January 1999), pp. 43–61.

[105] W. Sweet, "Bold Ambitions, Mixed Performance," *IEEE Spectrum,* 35, no. 10 (October 1998), p. 57.

ernment innovation policies, but government support of university research and laboratories varies by industry in its impact. In biology, chemistry, and pharmaceuticals, there has been a positive effect. Government support doesn't cost much, relatively speaking, and does spark innovation.

Among well-established economies, there is a remarkable institutional continuity. Little has changed in 100 years in the traditional institutions. Great Britain and the United States are quite "restrained" in their innovation policies outside of defense, while newer governments are quite active in promoting change, especially in low-income nations. But in the end, innovation performance depends on the firms themselves. Government can help, or fail to impede, company innovation, but government cannot make up for a weak private-sector innovation capability.

A demanding home market helps promote strong firms. And large firms, globally, do not necessarily have the advantage, since small firms, like those in cooperating networks in Italy, can make up for resource deficiencies quite well. Smaller markets are making headway in covering the ground between them and the larger markets.[106]

Military procurement that promotes generic technology production does spill over to the private sector, but general benefits from this type of investment and those in space and nuclear power have been limited. There is no strong support for one high-tech policy over another; that is, promoting high technology positions a country favorably in the world community to become sufficient in "upstream" technologies, such as in Singapore. Exceptions such as Canada and Austria show that there are alternatives. A complication in reaching a conclusion here is that small firms are often involved in high-technology industries and may underreport R&D spending. In general, countries that fund breakthroughs (high risk research) and promote taking advantage of existing technology have been most successful in their innovation policies. But the future trends suggest that since sectors differ in their response to government policies and globalization of R&D and global business alliances are increasing, the role of an individual country's innovation policy is likely to diminish over time. One exception is in the area of establishing fair standards for protecting and transferring technology.

 UMMARY

Government attends to the common good, and given the importance of technological innovation to the wealth of any nation, there is a role for public technology policy in any country. At issue is the balance of public and private costs and benefits of technological innovation.

From the manager's perspective, government ought to be predictable and concerned with outcomes, not the process of delivering results. To the extent that these two conditions are not met, there is often a perceived conflict between the public and private sector on these matters.

---

[106] J. Eaton, E. Gutierrez, and S. Kortum, "European Technology Policy," *Economic Policy* no, 27 (October 1998), pp. 403–438.

Most governments have a long history of intervention into technological innovation in their countries. Historically, patent laws have been used to stimulate innovation by protecting originators of new ideas from the loss of benefit capture from new ideas. Governments have funded, with a fair amount of success, those risky research projects that the private sector will not attempt. More recently, laws and programs have allowed more collaboration between various institutions such as government laboratories, universities, and private companies. But public and private versions of all of these initiatives exist, such as incubators, which seem to work best for new technology startups. Many of these programs appear to generate multiples of returns on investments, but rarely create any new jobs. European technology appears to have been quite successful at fostering cross-national boundary collaboration in R&D and technology development.

R&D tax credits and government procurement appear to have, at best, a mixed record of performance in stimulating innovation that works. Experiments to stimulate technological solutions to preserve the natural environment are just beginning, with encouraging results, but it is really too soon to evaluate the total impact of these programs. Antitrust concerns in the computer software industry are also pending. *Overall, government does a much better job on the supply side (e.g., funding risky, public interest R&D) of technological innovation than on the demand side (e.g., procurement).*

DISCUSSION QUESTIONS

1. Read Case 10-1 on Microsoft. On what grounds is the government pursuing its case against Microsoft?
2. What is Microsoft's argument in retort to this action?
3. Does monopoly encourage or discourage innovation?
4. What was the outcome of this Case?

ADDITIONAL CASE SUGGESTIONS

1. As mentioned in Chapter 1, there is an excellent case on the Denver Airport and local government's attempt to stimulate technology development: BAE Automated Systems (A), HBS 9-396-311 (15 pages).

CASE 10-1

Microsoft and Justice End a Skirmish, Yet War Could Escalate

Microsoft Corp. settled a legal skirmish with the U.S. Department of Justice, but its hardball tactics have set the stage for what may be a wider and costly war.

The software giant yesterday accepted terms to avoid a contempt-of-court citation sought by the Justice Department for allegedly violating a federal court order.

It will do what the agency has sought, and a federal judge has wanted, for weeks: give the nation's personal-computer makers the right to ship the current version of its best-selling Windows 95 operating system on their machines without also being forced to display Microsoft's software for browsing the Internet.

But the company, by its effort to defer compliance and its aggressive—some say arrogant—posturing in the case, has committed what is widely seen as a colossal public-relations blunder, angering both presiding Judge Thomas Penfield Jackson and the antitrust regulators. Now, Justice Department investigators are building a new antitrust case against the software giant that could reach far beyond the narrow issue before the court yesterday, and could affect Microsoft's planned introduction of Windows 98 later this year, lawyers and officials familiar with these efforts say. The case—if it goes forward—would attack the heart of Microsoft's strategy of using Windows to muscle into new markets.

"Bill Gates finally understood he made a huge strategic and public-relations blunder in the way the company tried to respond to the judge's order," says Sam Miller, a San Francisco attorney who was part of the Justice Department team that pursued an initial antitrust case that led to a 1995 consent decree. "It finally sank in that their arrogance backfired."

Federal prosecutors wouldn't comment on the prospects of a new case and say they have made no final decision. "We have an active and continuing investigation into several Microsoft business practices," says Justice's antitrust chief, Joel Klein. Practices under investigation include Microsoft's investments in new video technology, its stake in former rival Apple Computer Inc. and, more broadly, its effort to extend its dominance of desktop software into new markets.

But the looming introduction of Windows 98—and the threat that it would crush competition in the Internet-browser market—is what most worries antitrust enforcers.

This dust-up is but the latest in a series of skirmishes that go back to 1994. Justice sued originally on the grounds that Microsoft was using its licensing practices with PC makers to smother competition. Mr. Gates cagily settled that case with a consent decree in 1995, agreeing to make minor changes and preserving Microsoft's right to develop "integrated" products. It was considered a major victory for Microsoft, which continued its startling growth. The browser case is actually a reprise of the 1994 litigation; browsers, which connect PC users to the ever-expanding Internet, are already a huge business.

Microsoft may yet wriggle out of harm's way, in part by adopting a more conciliatory attitude. Yesterday's settlement began to jell when Mr. Gates's top attorney called Mr. Klein last Thursday to propose the settlement, after he briefed Microsoft's CEO on the company's progress in court. In two days of hearings, Judge Jackson signaled increasing impatience at Microsoft's stance.

The settlement won't diminish Microsoft's immense marketing power much. The PC makers say they will continue to voluntarily bundle the company's browser because it is free and a powerful product. "We aren't making any changes," said a spokeswoman for Compaq Computer Corp., the world's biggest PC maker.

Microsoft could settle the Justice Department's suit, and perhaps any future suit, on the same terms without losing much clout. That's because its Windows operating systems have already become the standard for the computer industry and it has so much scale and momentum that a huge army of software developers will still continue to build programs, including ones for Internet commerce and interactive television, for Microsoft and Microsoft alone.

On the other hand, Microsoft's hard-line attitude so far seems only to have emboldened, not discouraged, regulators. According to antitrust lawyers familiar with the government's investigation, one approach under consideration is that the Justice Department demand that Microsoft provide a version of Windows 98 without Internet access to computer makers who want it. That would give Netscape Communications Corp., Microsoft's chief browser rival, a fighting chance and ensure that Microsoft wouldn't be able to capture a lock on consumer access to the Internet, some of those close to the investigation believe.

These people say the government also is reviewing Microsoft's contracts with Internet-service providers, the companies that connect consumers to the Internet and distribute browsers. These contracts could be challenged in court if they give preferential treatment to Microsoft's Internet Explorer, they say. Justice Department lawyers are also asking questions across the computer industry and are poring over hundreds of contracts Microsoft struck in the past two years with major providers of information or entertainment on the Internet.

Justice Department officials remain wary of stopping Windows 98 outright, and Microsoft said yesterday that it expects no delays in the product's launch. But the government's success so far in court—which surprised even Justice Department officials—and negative public reaction to Microsoft's hard-nosed legal tactics have heartened the government.

Still, the decision of whether to file a broader antitrust case against Microsoft under Section 2 of the Sherman Antitrust Act, which outlaws monopolistic behavior, depends in part on whether the Justice Department prevails in a pending appeal sought by Microsoft that will be heard in Washington on April 21. Microsoft has said that Judge Jackson overstepped his bounds last month when he ordered Microsoft to stop forcing computer makers to preinstall its Internet software as a condition for getting access to Windows 95.

On the courthouse steps yesterday, Mr. Klein hailed Microsoft's sudden decision to settle. "Competitors and innovators should know that their products can compete on their own merits and not be snuffed out by Microsoft's use of monopoly power."

Microsoft's lead counsel, Richard Urowsky, said the agreement leaves other issues in the larger case unresolved, including Microsoft's claim that it has the right to integrate its Internet software with its Windows system. "Microsoft will continue to defend the software industry's right to update and enhance products without unnecessary government interference," said William Neukom, Microsoft senior vice-president and general counsel.

Mr. Neukom declined to speculate on whether the Justice Department would file a broader antitrust case. "We're a company that has allocated a responsible amount of resources to understanding the laws that bear on our business," he said. In antitrust law, "the fundamental notion is, `What's good for the consumer?'" he said. "As long as the answer is, they're getting better goods and services and lower and lower prices, then there can't be a violation of antitrust law."

The settlement came as Microsoft took other steps to soften the harsh image it has projected in the case. Microsoft just hired Haley Barbour, former head of the Republican National Committee, the GOP's fundraising arm. The company also has hired Mark Fabiani, the former White House lawyer who fielded questions about Whitewater and other Clinton administration scandals, to work on its Internet-product strategy.

Separately, Netscape said it would give away its Navigator browser free in an effort to add millions of new users. Microsoft already gives its browser away and has gained market share rapidly at Netscape's expense.

Certainly the settlement announced yesterday will do little to stanch the losses at Netscape. Once in command of more than 90% of the browser market, Netscape's share has steadily dwindled, and it is now spilling red ink and planning layoffs in the face of Microsoft's marketing blitz. "This is one small step in a very long march," says James Barksdale, Netscape's chief executive officer, who is hoping for additional action by the Justice Department.

Gary Reback, an attorney who has represented Microsoft's competitors, says the Justice Department has to do more than launch "surgical" strikes against specific practices of the company, which Mr. Klein, the agency's antitrust chief, has previously indicated would be the department's strategy. "These are markets where if you

step in early, you can do arthroscopic surgery," Mr. Reback said. "The free market will then take over and the better products will win. The longer you delay stepping in, the more drastic the remedy has to be to restore competition."

According to yesterday's agreement, Microsoft will let computer makers install Windows 95 but delete the Internet Explorer icons—the pictures that launch a program with a click of a computer mouse, from the computer's "desktop" or opening screen.

The agreement came after it began to look more likely that Microsoft was headed for a defeat before Judge Jackson. The company has challenged the judge at every turn in the case, which was filed in October and alleged that Microsoft violated the 1995 agreement with the Justice Department. That agreement, among other things, prohibited Microsoft from tying computer makers' use of other Microsoft products to the use of Windows. The government said the link between Explorer and Windows was a violation; Microsoft called it a permissible and natural integration of the products.

After the judge's initial ruling last month restricting the way Microsoft markets the products, Mr. Gates chose to comply by offering computer makers a commercially worthless version of Windows 95. Next, when the judge named a Harvard law professor to advise the court on technical matters, Microsoft accused the expert, Lawrence Lessig, of bias. Mr. Gates's lawyers even scolded the judge in court, declaring that his order was "senseless," and filed immediate appeals of each of his rulings.

Those tactics damaged Microsoft in the court of public opinion. Steve Ballmer, the company's executive vice president and Mr. Gates's top lieutenant, recently admitted that the number of people who are enthusiastic about the company and its products had clearly taken a dip. He also admitted that the company's morale had suffered.

People inside the company say Microsoft lost sight of how the perception of common sense and courtesy could profoundly shape its prospects. "You have some of the most serious negative attitudes and perceptions that the company has ever experienced, and it's beginning to seep into other sectors," says one former Microsoft executive who remains in contact with its inner circle.

While a Fortune magazine poll concluded this week that 73% of business executives consider Microsoft one of America's great businesses, a more recent Merrill Lynch survey indicated that the company's standing among technology opinion-leaders has suffered. In a survey of 50 corporate chief information officers, 59% said they believe that Microsoft abuses its power, though 62% believe Microsoft should be allowed to integrate its Internet browser and operating systems.

Major Microsoft customers say they currently have no plans to stop supporting the Microsoft standard. And PR strategists say Microsoft can still restore its public image, just as Intel Corp. did after suffering a PR disaster by insisting the company, rather than customers, would decide whether to replace a defective microprocessor, creating the famous "Pentium flap." But Microsoft will have to change tactics, fast, they say.

"I'm astonished at the way Microsoft is presenting its case to the public," says Gershon Kekst, a PR veteran of many merger wars between big companies. "If they don't frame the issue persuasively, then if they haven't already suffered irreparable damage, they will."

Antitrust lawyers say Microsoft clearly underestimated Judge Jackson. Known to friends as "Pen Jackson," he has spent 16 years on the bench, winning a reputation as visceral and blunt, dealing harshly with defendants who dare to defy the court.

"He's not sympathetic to cute or clever arguments," says Steve Newborn, a former federal antitrust enforcer who successfully argued for the Federal Trade Commission in one of the judge's few prior antitrust cases. "If you try to put one over on him, you're going to be in deep trouble."

Federal auto-safety regulators felt the judge's wrath when he found that they had rigged brake tests as evidence in a 1980s case alleging that a line of General Motors Corp. cars was unsafe. In a sharp rebuke, he threw out the charges. In another celebrated case, the judge gave the maximum prison term allowed under sentencing guidelines to Washington Mayor Marion Barry, who had been videotaped smoking crack cocaine.

Lawyers who have practiced before Judge Jackson say the former litigator is more impressed with a tough cross-examination than a scholarly legal brief. In four days of contentious hearings on the government's charge that Microsoft hadn't complied with his order, he grew visibly frustrated with Microsoft's highly technical arguments.

Microsoft's defense rested on its belief that it knew more about the black art of software development than the government—and the judge—and it repeatedly stressed that point. It couldn't comply with the order as written, the company said, because removing Internet software from Windows would disable the operating system. But the government's attorney responded to the judge's questions with simple answers, and used Microsoft's own "add/remove" tool that comes with Windows to do what the judge had asked Microsoft to do.

Microsoft's tactic raised this question, though: If it knew so much about programming, why couldn't it just do what Judge Jackson asked? Harvey Goldschmid, a Columbia University antitrust expert, said the company's strategy seemed more focused on tripping up Judge Jackson than on complying with his order. "They tried to make the judge look foolish" in the hope that an appeals court might later reverse him, Mr. Goldschmid said.

Judge Jackson's frustration with Microsoft finally exploded when he responded last week to the company's efforts to remove Mr. Lessig, calling them "trivial ... defamatory ... and not made in good faith."

The court strategy, authorized by Mr. Gates personally, speaks reams about the company's self-image and psychology, which is synonymous with the personality of Mr. Gates. Its managers have learned to aggressively attack detractors and competitors inside, and outside, its high-tech world.

"Bill Gates is Microsoft," says Alan Brew, a partner in the San Francisco corporate branding consultancy Addison Seefeld and Brew. "The character of the whole company is cloned in the form of this combative, young, arrogant leader."

Don Clark and Michael Schroeder contributed to this article. David Bank and John R. Wilke. *Wall Street Journal,* January 23, 1998, A1. Reprinted by permission of Wall Street Journal © 1998 Dow Jones and Company, Inc. All rights reserved worldwide.

Chapter 11

Globalizing Change

𝒞HAPTER OBJECTIVES

> To review the notion of global operations and innovation. To introduce the concepts of the co-production imperative and reverse technology transfer. To examine the global, co-production issues introduced in the chapter by presenting the joint venture case of I/N Tek and I/N Kote for analysis and the case of the Boeing 777.

In her book on global operations management, Therese Flaherty defined global operations in two important ways. **Globalization** is, of course, the internationalization of operations—doing business overseas. But it is more. "Almost every business is now global in the sense that its managers must think, plan, and/or act with reference to current potential international customers, suppliers, competitors, partners, and models."[1] Further, with respect to technological innovation, she added, "In globalizing companies, headquarters managers no longer dictate product development and technology choice … subsidiary professionals often lead technology development."[2]

Indeed, one of the most important emergent trends of the 1990s is the globalization of R&D. In a study of globalization of Japanese pharmaceutical firms investing in biotechnology research, Joan Penner-Hahn[3] found that complementary fermentation skills and market presence in an off-shore region predicted moves abroad. Nontraditional (no prior drug history) Japanese firms were more dependent on market presence. Drug firms with fermentation skills—that is, skills that signifi-

---

[1] Therese Flaherty, *Global Operations* (New York: McGraw-Hill, 1996), p. 2.

[2] Ibid., p. 53.

[3] The Internationalization of R&D: A Firm-Level Study, unpublished Ph.D. dissertation, University of Michigan, Ann Arbor, Mich., 1995.

cantly support biotechnology R&D—were more likely to globalize because they were more able to capitalize on opportunities abroad.

Phil Birnbaum-More (1994)[4] has reported that he could not find a single successful case of global cooperation in research within companies attempting 24-hour research (not development) in his recent study in Japan. Many R&D managers, including those at Ericsson, the electronics firm in Sweden, have made global R&D cooperation their number one priority. The issue in simplified form is one of technological integration in the face of localized market and technology implementation issues. Case 11-1 discusses I/N Tek and I/N Kote, a joint venture between Inland Steel Corporation and Nippon Steel Corporation, to illustrate these issues. Current globalization in the steel industry and other manufacturing sectors is actively underway, especially among "mini mills" such as Nucor.

In a study of U.S.–Japanese manufacturing joint ventures, Swan and Ettlie[5] found that there has been a trend toward more sophistication and complexity of governance structures for managing partnerships in landed transplants alliances in the United States. In particular, firms have gone beyond just joint ventures and wholly owned subsidiaries, exploiting partial equity relationships more recently in Japanese direct investment cases. Partial ownership by Japanese parents was significantly more likely in high-tech manufacturing partnerships with U.S. companies. Joint ventures were more typical in politically sensitive industries (e.g., steel and autos) and when the Japanese firm had experience with the product at home.

In a study of global sourcing among 600 durable goods manufacturing firms in 20 countries, Ettlie and Sethuraman[6] found that firms relying on off-shore sources of supply were significantly more likely to spend more on R&D and have greater revenue from new products. This was especially true of U.S. firms in the sample. *That is, the more innovative the firm, the more global the sourcing strategy.*

Mountains of words have been written on sourcing strategy; however, many economic treatments have focused on transactional economies and market imperfections.[7] But sourcing decisions cannot be neatly wrapped up in one theory. For example, the merits of transaction cost theory are still heavily debated.[8] And some have argued that just-in-time (JIT) purchasing, touted as a cost-reducing, quality-enhancing inventory management philosophy, merely shifts costs upstream in the supply chain.[9]

To establish the boundaries of global innovation issues in operations, this chapter looks at co-production. Alliances and globalization are two of the most important, seemingly unrelentless trends in business today. Co-production incorporates these two trends. This chapter proposes a general model of co-production and suggests the circumstances under which co-production is the preferred choice of governance.

---

[4] 2nd International Product Development Conference, April 1994, Gothenberg, Sweden.

[5] P. Swan and J. E. Ettlie, "U.S.-Japanese Manufacturing Equity Relationships," *Academy of Management Journal,* 40, no. 2 (April 1997), pp. 462–479.

[6] J. E. Ettlie and R. Sethuraman, "Locus of Supply and Global Manufacturing," University of Michigan Business School Working Paper, 1999.

[7] M. K. Perry, "Vertical Integration: Determinants and Effects," in R. Schmalensee and R. D. Willig (eds.), *Handbook of Industrial Organization* (Amsterdam, North-Holland, 1989), pp. 183–255.

[8] S. Ghoshal and P. Moran, "Bad for Practice: A Critique of the Transaction Cost Theory," *Academy of Management Review,* 21, no. 1 (Jan 1996), pp. 13–47.

[9] C. Whybark, personal communication, 1995.

JOINT PRODUCTION VERSUS CO-PRODUCTION

Having coined the phrase *economies of scope* several years earlier, Panzar and Willig's seminal, follow-up article proposed a fundamental model of multiproduct firms and sharable inputs. Multiproduct firms exploit excess capacity, and, therefore, create cost savings. In other words, "when there are economies of scope, there exists some input (if only a factory building) which is shared by two or more product lines without complete congestion."[10] They go on to show the conditions that promote the formation of multiproduct firms, even if this does not conform perfectly to the classic definition of **joint production.** Further, the magnitude of sunk costs is crucial in determining the need for regulatory protection.[11] When applied to a single production line or cell, the concept of scope generally falls under the rubric of flexible manufacturing.[12]

As mentioned in Chapter 8, joint production is production in which several types of resources are used, and the product is not a sum of separable outputs of each cooperating resource. An additional factor creates a team organization problem—not all resources used in team production belong to one person. That is, regardless of who owns what, it is impossible to determine the exact contribution of each team member to the output. This forms the fundamental motivation for joint production. Here we are interested in only the organization, contracts, informational and payment procedures used among owners of teamed inputs, not the motivation for multiple ownership of these resources.

The motivation for multiple ownership is central to the concept of co-production, when two or more contributors to the production process share ownership and physical space (i.e., facilities) to coordinate for a final output. Other inputs may or may not be shared in this configuration, and, generally they are unique. Co-production is but one method of managing the supply chain or external architecture and networks.[13]

Unfortunately, *co-production* has been used variously to refer to simultaneous production, as a condition of foreign direct investment, or for R&D alliances.[14] The term has even been applied to coordination between two functions in a firm. Finally, co-production appears to have been used as a synonym for joint produc-

---

[10] J. C. Panzar, and R. D. Willig, "Economies of Scope," *AEA Papers and Proceedings,* 17, no. 2 (May 1981), pp. 268–272, esp. p. 268.

[11] M. E. Beesley, "Commitment, Sunk Costs, and Entry to the Airline Industry: Reflections on Experience," *Journal of Transportation Economics & Policy,* 20, no. 2 (May 1986), pp. 173–190.

[12] K. E. Stecke and J. Browne, "Variations in Flexible Manufacturing Systems According to the Relevant Types of Automated Materials Handling," *Material Flow* 2 (1985), pp. 179–185; A. K. Sethi and S. P. Sethi, "Flexibility in Manufacturing: A Survey," *International Journal of Flexible Manufacturing Systems,* 2, no. 4 (July 1990), pp. 289–328.

[13] J. Kay, *Why Firms Succeed* (New York: Oxford Press, 1995).

[14] T. R. Adler, R. F. Scherer, S. L. Barton, and R. Katerberg, "An Empirical Test of Transaction Cost Theory: Validating Contract Typology," *Journal of Applied Management Studies,* 7, no. 2 (December 1998), pp. 185–200; and D. I. Deeds and C. W. L. Hill, "An Examination of Opportunistic Action Within Research Alliances: Evidence from the Biotechnology Industry," *Journal of Business Venturing,* 14, no. 2 (March 1999), pp. 141–163.

tion (e.g., chips can be substituted in more than one product.[15] To confound matters even more, the term *joint production* has been used recently to refer to contract manufacturing and cooperative production agreements, generally.[16]

Co-production is defined here as *coordination of uniquely owned operational resources at one or more site*. Co-location is essential to this definition. Actual co-producing of products by representatives of two or more legal entities can be seen as just one type of collaboration or coupling between unique owners of resources. In one extreme, for example, parts could just be delivered by a supplier under contract to a production facility; co-production is at the other extreme. In between are JIT purchasing deliveries, JIT II partnerships, which eliminate buyers and sales at the interface,[17] and contract manufacturing, which has been forecast to grow worldwide from $42 billion in 1995 to $95 billion in 1999—a 22 percent increase.[18] Contract manufacturers often run different customers products on the same manufacturing line, so this could be considered a form of joint production, assuming the raw materials and information needed for manufacture are owned by these different customers, and co-location, even if temporary, is required to co-design products and processes.

*T*HE CO-PRODUCTION IMPERATIVE

Lengnick-Hall argues that co-production (i.e, customers and producers providing resources to enhance competitive quality) is more likely when customization rather than conformance is needed to satisfy the demand.[19] Co-production is more costly with today's technology, so why push it? Co-production can be made more effective by understanding three key factors: the *clarity of the task*, the *ability to do the work*, and the *motivation to do the work*. Although health care systems were the primary example used, concepts such as the resulting reciprocal relationships that develop in co-productive relationships should involve concepts that are difficult to imitate, and are therefore sought after, regardless of context.

This general model can be stated simply as the *co-production imperative:* When technological economies dominate a value-added chain or system, co-production is the preferred form of governance.[20] The stages and examples of the co-production imperative are presented in Figure 11-1.

---

[15] G. R. Bitran, and S. M. Gilbert, "Co-production Processes with Random Yields in the Semiconductor Industry," *Operations Research,* 42, no. 3 (May/June 1994), pp. 476–491.

[16] J. Papanikolaw, "Contract Oligonucleotide Manufacturing," *Chemical Market Reporter,* 255, no. 3 (January 18, 1999), pp. FR16.

[17] F. R. Bleakley, "Strange Bedfellows: Some Companies Let Suppliers Work on Site and Even Place Orders," *The Wall Street Journal* (January 13, 1995), pp. A1, A6.

[18] J. Carbone, "Buyers Want More from Contract Manufacturers," *Purchasing,* 120, no. 10 (June 20, 1996), pp. 47–48.

[19] C. A. Lengnick-Hall, "Customer Contributions to Quality: A Different View of the Customer-oriented Firm," *Academy of Management Review,* 21, 3 (July 1996), pp. 791–824.

[20] For an example, see S. Hansell, "Is this the Factory of the Future?" *Business Week* (July 26, 1998), Section 3, pp. 1, 12.

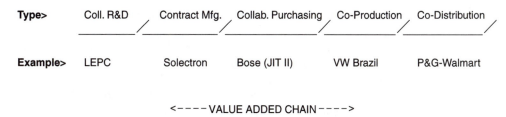

Figure 11-1   The Co-Production Imperative

The model in Figure 11-1 illustrates five types of co-production arrayed across the value-added chain. These stages include but are not limited to (1) collaborative R&D; (2) contract manufacturing; (3) collaborative purchasing; (4) co-production; and (5) co-distribution. There are obviously many other stages and examples that could be included on this continuum, but only these are shown to illustrate the range of the concept.

✻ Collaborative R&D as a Form of Co-production

The literature on collaborative R&D is quite extensive and includes models and investigations in a variety of forms. This collaboration can include "simple" cooperation between two firms for the purposes of joint R&D, or collaboration between R&D consortia on the supply chain, between competitors,[21] and between government and industry.[22] Research joint ventures are perhaps the most complex.[23] Global comparisons of these relationships have become popular.[24]

In the experience of multinational corporations, coordination of global technical resources had evolved gradually from simple decentralized accounting to true global integration. For example, Dow Chemical started rotating technical managers from around the world through its Midland, Michigan, headquarters, more than 30 years ago. But serious global coordination and synergy building did not occur until Dow began concentrating technical resources into technology centers in 1965.[25] The latest addition to these centers is a focused group on the natural environment.

Competitive pressure and scarce technical resources have forced global companies to seek out technology and leverage the best at each location it supports. Competitive position in one country usually affects its position in another country or region. Just

---

[21] R. Osborn and C. C. Baughn, "Governing U.S.-Japan High Technology Alliances," in Liker et al. *Engineering in Japan,* (New York: Oxford University Press, 1995), pp. 93–114.

[22] For example, M. A. Brown, "Performance Metrics for Technology Commercialization Program," *International Journal of Technology Management,* 13, no. 3 (1997), pp. 229–249.

[23] A. N. Link, "Research Joint Ventures," University N. Carolina Greensboro, working paper EC0951101, November 1995; E. Gerslov, "When Whales Are Cast Ashore," *IEEE Transactions* on *Engineering Management,* 42, no. 1 (February 1995), pp. 3–8.

[24] H. E. Aldrich and T. Sasaki, "Governance Structure and Technology Transfer Management in R&D Consortium in the United States," in Liker, et al., *Engineered in Japan* (New York: Oxford University Press, 1995), pp. 20–92.

[25] See an article related to this topic: V. Chiesa, "Globalizing R&D Around Centers of Excellence," *Long Range Planning,* 28, no. 6 (December 1995), pp. 19–28.

reproducing resources in each country is not the best use of technical resources. Most companies seek some balance between global integration and local response.[26] For Dow Chemical, and in the agricultural chemical business, the competition in a less developed country might be a machete. Not surprisingly, new terms such as *transnational* have been invented to describe this process of balancing global and local needs. Localizing R&D speeds the learning process of local requirements and exploits unique technical capabilities of the region. Technology typically does not follow the same economic block and geographical boundaries that are convenient for financial analysts.[27] For example, the search for expertise in net-shape technology (forming parts to near final shape to avoid the expense of material removal to meet final specifications) led Ohio State researchers to Monterey, Mexico, and a local research institute there. The Monterey expertise in net shape was built up gradually over hundreds of years. Why? Monterey was where the Mexican beer industry started, and the glass industry flourished, as a result. Shaping and forming glass for the beverage industry led to developing expertise in forming technology. Another case is that of telecommunications, where the United States has assumed world technology leadership.[28]

Mapping a firm's technology, product, and service base globally is the final step in this strategy implementation process. With rare exception, technical support and technical center liaison with suppliers follow the manufacturing function overseas. Occasionally, R&D will precede manufacturing and follow marketing.[29] But a hot growth market is a clear signal about where firms will typically establish lead technical capabilities. The primary goal of the foreign laboratory is to make local innovations.[30] Hewlett-Packard did this in Singapore for inkjet printers with an eye on the Japanese market and competition.

Ericsson, the Swedish company that makes cellular phones, is another unique example of how to manage global technical resources. The company has several laboratories focused on technical disciplines and product lines, and these facilities are well networked.[31] Most likely precipitated by Ericsson's drive to decentralize R&D, the company's leadership continues to try to maintain the balance between product and technology focus and fights the tendency to be "too content with the status quo."[32] This boils down to tension between group managers and technology

[26] V. Chiesa, "Strategies for Global R&D," *Research-Technology Management,* 39, no. 5 (September/October 1996), pp. 19–25. On R&D networks for multinationals, see R. Pearce and M. Papanastassiou, "R&D Networks and Innovation: Decentralized Product Development in Multinational Enterprises," *R&D Management,* 26, no. 4 (October 1996), pp. 315–333.

[27] For example, in the banking industry, imaging systems, credit scoring, advanced ATM (automated teller machines), and other technologies appear around the globe: C. Lobue and E. Berliner, "A Look at Banking's Best Practices around the Globe," *World of Banking,* 15, no. 4 (Winter 1996–7), pp. 5–8. Also, information technology tends to be regional rather than global in its development: G. Duysters and J. Hagedoorn, "Internationalization of Corporate Technology Through Strategic Partnering: An Empirical Investigation," *Research Policy,* 25, no. 1 (January 1996), pp. 1–12.

[28] A. Kellerman, "Fusion of Information Types, Media and Operators, and Continued American Leadership in Telecommunications," *Telecommunications Policy* 21, no. 6 (July 1997), pp. 553–564.

[29] J. Penner-Hahn, "Firm and Environmental Influences on the Mode and Sequence of Foreign Research and Development Activities," *Strategic Management Journal,* 19 (1998), pp. 149–168.

[30] V. Chiesa, "Strategies for Global R&D," *Research-Technology Management,* 39, no. 5 (September/October 1996), p. 23.

[31] Ibid., p. 24.

[32] J. Blau, "Ericsson Decentralizes for Quicker Research Payoff," *Research-Technology Management,* no. 2 (March/April 1998), pp. 4–6.

managers. The company is organized into 20 major businesses, which all have their own R&D focused primarily on development. Central coordination of this network encourages expertise-sharing.

Ericsson has 20,000 people in 40 R&D centers in 20 countries. Ericsson spends about 20 percent of sales on R&D (in 1997, that was $2.9 billion). Companies in small countries such as Sweden have looked internationally for markets sooner than their counterparts in larger countries. Technology is quick to follow. Ericsson recently established a new center in Japan to work on applied wireless research and multimedia systems, 50 kilometers from Japan.

To support and leverage this growth and high rate of R&D investment, Ericsson also partners with other companies such as Texas Instruments in the area of micro-electronics and universities such as MIT and Stanford. All this is in a quest to stay 10 years ahead of production. Third generation will enter the market in about 2002, and fourth-generation technology is in R&D. In some areas of the world, analog technology is being replaced by second-generation digital technology. A continuing, number-one challenge has been to coordinate global technology generation and development. Little academic research has informed practice on this issue to date.

GE has its own approach to this problem in its quest to maintain the legacy of Thomas Edison.[33] Divisions have most (80–90%) of the total R&D budget, and a business is not obligated to go to corporate R&D for technical help. A unit can turn to any source, including a university. But divisions are not allowed to cut support of the corporate group by more than 20 percent a year. High-risk projects account for 25 percent of the corporate budget and come from other sources, including the U.S. government. Only 50 percent of corporate R&D support comes from GE businesses; the rest is on contract (25%). Corporate R&D teamed with the aircraft engine group to produce the GE 90 jet engine, now considered the world's most powerful, efficient, and quietest engine (in spite of early problems). GE uses the "one coffee pot" team approach in GE Power Systems, because the people working in the H-class advanced future gas turbine sit at the same table—research, engineering, marketing, manufacturing, and service representatives. GE business units source technology globally, and the corporate R&D center supports this activity by sponsoring research at universities and national laboratories around the world, including Japan, India, Russia, Ukraine, and China.

The echo in this message should be clear. An individual firm cannot generate all the new technology it needs alone. It must go outside for some of the technical resources needed to solve problems. Small- and medium-sized enterprises have always faced this dilemma, and many have prospered.[34] Unique approaches to this problem have continued to surface. For example, the Primus Venture Partners fund, capitalized at $100 million and characterized as providing "patient" capital to fund new companies and revitalize old or mature ones, is a partnership between public and private funds. Initiated by CEOs of major Cleveland-area companies and banks, the partnership matches contributions of private funds with public-sector

[33] L. S. Edelheit, "GE's R&D Strategy: Be Vital," *Research-Technology Management*, 41, no. 2 (March/April 1998), pp. 21–27.

[34] G. Delmestri, "Convergent Organizational Responses to Globalization in the Italian and German Machine-building Industries," *International Studies of Management & Organization*, 27, no. 3 (Fall 1997), pp. 86–108.

organizations such as the State Teachers Retirement Board of Ohio and the Public Employees' Retirement System of Ohio.[35]

The example used in Figure 11-1 for collaborative R&D is that of the Low Emissions Paint Consortium (LEPC) in the U.S. automobile industry, and this case is included in Chapter 5 for analysis.[36] This consortium was developed using the enabling legislation of the 1984 Cooperative R&D Act to help Ford, GM, and Chrysler comply with increasingly stringent air quality standards and EPA regulation. A pre-production R&D facility was located at the Ford Wixom Assembly plant in Michigan, and that is why it was selected for the co-production imperative example.[37]

Contract Manufacturing

One of the limitations of the core competence,[38] resource-based theory,[39] and competence-building approaches to operations strategy is that these theories tend to exclude all the important helpmates most organizations use to accomplish things. Toyota, by many accounts, is the best manufacturing company in the world, but this company outsources as much as 70 percent of the work to make cars.[40] U.S. durable goods manufacturers outsource an average of 54 percent of their production,[41] and this hasn't changed much in the last decade.[42] In electronics manufacturing alone, the average manufacturer contracts for $5.24 million every year in printed circuit boards, and so on. Electronics manufacturers can save as much as 24 percent by outsourcing.[43] In biopharmaceutical manufacturing, the 1996 contract manufacturing market was estimated to be $360 million in 1996, and is likely to grow at a rate of about 29 percent to about $1 billion by 2000.[44]

The worldwide market for contract manufacturing services was forecast to grow from $42 billion in 1995 to $95 billion in 1999 (22% increase). About half of this market is based in the United States and Canada. There is a "growing demand for turnkey manufacturing in which the OEM not only outsources the manufacture of a

---

[35] R. F. Celeste, "Strategic Alliances for Innovation: Emerging Models of Technology-based, Twenty-first Century Economic Development," *Economic Development Review,* 14, no. 1 (Winter 1996), pp. 4–8.

[36] J. E. Ettlie, "The Low Emission Paint Consortium (LEPC)," University of Michigan Business School, Ann Arbor, Michigan, 1995.

[37] Also see J. Peters and W. Becker, "Vertical Corporate Networks in the German Automotive Industry," *International Studies of Management & Organization,* 27, no. 4 (Winter 1997–98), pp. 158–185.

[38] C. K. Prahalad and G. Hamel "The Core Competence of the Corporation," *Harvard Business Review* (May–June, 1991), pp. 79–91.

[39] B. Wernerfelt, "A Resource-based View of the Firm," *Strategic Management Journal,* 8, no. 2 (1984), pp. 187–194.

[40] K. Langfield-Smith and M. R. Greenwood, "Developing Co-operative Buyer-Supplier Relationships: The Case Study of Toyota," *Journal of Management Studies,* 35, no. 3 (1998), pp. 331–354.

[41] J. Carbone, "Cost Is the Bottom Line," *Purchasing,* 124, no. 8 (May 21, 1998), pp. 38–41.

[42] J. E. Ettlie, *Taking Charge of Manufacturing* (San Francisco: Jossey-Bass, 1988).

[43] J. Carbone, "Outsourcing Boards Is Just the Beginning," *Purchasing,* 124, no. 4 (March 26, 1998), pp. 52–56.

[44] Chemical Market Reporter, "Biopharmaceutical Manufacturing Moves to The Custom Arena," *Custom Manufacturing/Outsourcing 98 Supplement* (January 19, 1998), pp. FR20-FR22.

board, subsystem, or entire system, but buys the parts as well," which results in focusing on just their core strengths.[45]

Firms that do contract manufacturing typically share their productive systems through co-location among many customers, even when their designs are proprietary. Often the cost of technology, such as surface mount, forces companies to contract out, including assembly.[46] Dow Chemical recently established a contract manufacturing service to take advantage of this growth market[47] and IBM has been in this business for many years.[48] Even the food industry has examples of contract manufacturing.[49] Before the merger with Damlier-Benz, smaller, start-up companies that are not vertically integrated often get their start with a new product idea that can be manufactured by someone else. High-growth, small companies can also capitalize on the outsourcing trend among their larger customers.[50]

Global sources of supply in contract manufacturing can save even more money than local contractors.[51] However, if the contracted manufacturer is a "controlled foreign corporation" or CFC, there may be recent changes in the tax code and tax implications for the contractor. The current tax codes should be consulted, depending on who is assumed to carry the risk for raw materials and other inventories.[52]

Perhaps among the best known and benchmarked cases of contract manufacturing is the Solectron Corporation.[53] Solectron has won many awards and contracts with Apple Computer and many other firms. Although Solectron controlled only 6.4 percent of the $23 billion electronic contract manufacturing business, it has grown tenfold since it was started, to $513 million in sales (1994), of which 35 percent comes from outside the United States.

✴ Collaborative Purchasing

Partly stimulated by Japanese models of supplier partnerships in manufacturing with long-term associations, companies such as GE, Ball Corporation, Honeywell, and IBM allow suppliers on site for better coordination of activities. Originated by

---

[45] J. Carbone, "Buyers Want More from CMs," *Purchasing,* 120, no. 10 (June 20, 1996), pp. 47–48.

[46] Anonymous, "Contract Manufacturing: Make It Up," *Economist,* 338, no. 7950 (January 27, 1996), pp. 58–59; UK 66–67.

[47] A. Thayer, "Dow Enters Contract Chemical Business," *Chemical & Engineering News,* 73, no. 50 (December 11, 1995), p. 7.

[48] L. Marion, "Radius Reaches for "Leaning Edge," *Electronic Business Today,* 21, no. 11 (November 1995), pp. 50–51.

[49] S. Tiffany, "Continuous Technology Speeds Production at Jo El," *Candy Industry,* 160, no. 4 (April 1995), pp. 24–29.

[50] L. Armstong, "Hot Growth Companies," *Business Week* (May 26, 1997), pp. 90–102.

[51] G. Frazier, "Enhance Your Supply Chain," *Electronic Business,* 24, no. 2 (February 1998), pp. 21, 85.

[52] See, for example: A. Granwell and S. Dirk, "U.S. Ruling Signals Sharp Turn," *International Tax Review,* 9, no. 1 (December 1997/January 1998), pp. 13–16; D. K. Dolan, C. M. DuPuy, and P. A. Jackman, "Contract Manufacturing: The Next Round," *Tax Management International Journal,* 27, no. 2 (February 13, 1998), pp. 59–66.

[53] F. Cap, "The Continuing Quest for Excellence," *Quality Progress,* 28, no. 12 (December 1995), pp. 67–70.

Bose Corporation, the term *JIT II*[54] has come to be known as a way of eliminating sales agents on the supply side and buyers from the purchasing department on the customer side to reduce the clutter of antiquated supply chain management.

Bose now has 14 "in plants" working on commodity supply issues, actually coordinated by the first "in-plant" representative from G&F industries, a small commodity plastics supplier. In-plants have to sign confidentiality agreements, but most suppliers have to sign these, anyway. Since these JIT II suppliers typically become sole sources of the product or service rendered, they can afford to lower prices, and two jobs are "saved" in the process. Apple will not allow suppliers in house; it built a warehouse nearby instead to reduce inventories.[55]

An alternative to JIT II is networked suppliers, similar to the northern Italian experiment in flexible networks of collaboration (see Chapter 8 on flexible specialization). The Topsy Tail Company, with sales of $80 million, makes a hair-care gadget. It uses a network of 20, coordinated suppliers to save hiring nearly 50 employees. Startup companies often don't have the capital to invest in manufacturing operations—ergo the alternative, which is flexible, focused supplier network. At Topsy Tail, this started with tooling and injection molding of this plastic hair product, saving $5 million in capital costs. These and other production partners have been added. They are now collaborating in the rollout of three new products and they manage these relationships with performance clauses in most contracts.[56]

Much of the new outsourcing partnership trends involve global purchases, motivated by factors beyond the traditional cost pressure and market access, including technology and supplier networks.[57] Since the trend is toward more outsourcing, organizations generally spend more time considering sources of supply beyond traditional local suppliers.[58] Strategic, global partnerships are part of a new trend in globalization of markets and management practices. Although it is true that wages of less skilled U.S. workers have fallen steadily, the contribution of global trade to this trend continues to be debated.[59] Balance of payments issues persist, but organizational trends continue toward more outsourcing and more global sources of supply. Management of the supply base continues to grow in strategic importance as a source of added value and opportunity for improvement in operations and profitability.[60] For example, automotive seating was outsourced at a level of 1

---

[54] R. Shapiro and B. Isaacson, "Bose Corporation: The JIT II Program (A)," "President and Fellows of Harvard College, Harvard Business School, Boston, 1994.

[55] F. Bleakley, "Strange Bed Fellows: Some Companies Let Suppliers Work On Site and Even Place Orders," *Wall Street Journal* (Jan 13, 1995), p. 41.

[56] E. M. Montgomery, "Innovation+Outsourcing=Big Success," *Management Review,* 83, no. 9 (September 1994), pp. 17–20. Also see B. Prida and G. Gutierrez, "Supply Management: From Purchasing to External Factory Management," *Production & Inventory Management Journal,* 37, no. 4 (Fourth Quarter 1996), pp. 38–43.

[57] J. M. Murray, M. Kotabe, and A. R., Wildt, "Strategic and Financial Performance Implications of Global Sourcing Strategy: A Contingency Analysis," *Journal of International Business,* 26, no. 1 (First Quarter 1995), pp. 181–202.

[58] S. Fawcett and J. Scully, "Worldwide Sourcing: Facilitating Continued Success," *Production and Inventory Management Journal,* 39, no. 1 (First Quarter 1998), pp. 1–9.

[59] R. C. Feenstra and G. H. Hanson, "Globalization, Outsourcing, and Wage Inequity," *American Economic Review,* 86, no. 2 (May 1996), pp. 240–245.

[60] *Purchasing,* "Strong Supply Relationships Reduce Cost, Spark Innovation," 124, no. 1 (January 15, 1998), pp. 45–46.

percent in 1984 and had increased to 81 percent in 1995.[61] Although target costing has done much to bring engineering and procurement together in companies, there is still a large gap between these two functions.[62]

The pharmaceutical industry has done much to modernize supply-chain management through simplification and consolidation. In this industry, the pressure to eliminate outdated product has been growing steadily for the last 5 years. For example, Abbot Laboratories is experimenting with one novel way of eliminating old products by not accepting outdated merchandise for exchange product, and gives all direct-buying customers an allowance of 1 percent of gross purchases.[63] Merck also has new packaging alternatives and supply chain innovations underway to increase fresh fill rates.

✖ Co-Production

Many examples of co-production, or actually sharing of productive facilities, have been implemented by manufacturing companies and their suppliers over the years without much fanfare. The Buick Reatta was produced by the Cadillac Division of General Motors Corporation in Lansing, Michigan, during the late 1980s and early 1990s. Most do not know that PPG, the car's paint supplier, owned the paint facility in this plant and operated the paint application with complete autonomy. UAW workers were not covered by their contract provisions when they crossed over into the paint booth. The original PPG proposal called for their purchasing body-in-white cars, painting them, and selling them back to GM.

One recent celebrated example of co-production is the VW truck plant in Brazil. Lopez's Plant B, for VW Brazil, is now being self-touted as "the third industrial revolution."[64] Although history will be the ultimate judge of that assertion, some preliminary thoughts on this "revolutionary" concept of "fractal" or "Plateau 6" manufacturing, as Lopez calls it, are worth pursuing.

First, let's review the concept for the VW Greenfield truck plant in Resende, Brazil, which is scheduled for startup in November and eventually will produce about 40,000 vehicles:

- ▶ VW workers (only 400 are going to staff the plant) will do no assembly—assembly will be done by first-tier suppliers. VW personnel will be responsible for engineering, quality, and distribution.
- ▶ Suppliers will complete total subsystems, including drive train—and will pay plant overhead costs.
- ▶ The plant will build to order, not to forecast or inventory.

---

[61] D. Smock, "This Lear's the King of Interiors," *Plastics World,* 54, no. 10 (October 1996), pp. 32–37.

[62] T. Laseter, "Supply Chain Management: the Ins and Outs of Target Costing," *Purchasing,* 124, no. 3 (March 12, 1998), pp. 22–25.

[63] H. Fleming, "1% Credit: Abbot Innovation Concerns Some Pharmacists," *Drug Topics,* 142, no. 9 (May 4, 1998), p. 66.

[64] *Automotive News* (February 26, 1996). Also note the trend in outsourcing information services documented in Q. Hu, C. Saunders, and M. Gebelt, "Research Report: Diffusion of Information Systems Outsourcing: A Reevaluation of Influence Sources," *Information Systems Research,* 8, no. 3 (September 1997), pp. 288–301.

- The T-shaped plant will pay suppliers only after a vehicle passes final inspection.

There are a number of new co-production facilities in Europe, including IBM and several auto company plants: the Mercedes-Benz and Swiss watchmaker, SMH, are producing the SMART car in Hambach, France, using *modular* production—which is another name for co-production. Suppliers investing in the assembly facility included Magna, Eisenmann, VDO, Krupp Hoesch, Bosch, and others. Suppliers work onsite, full time in a DaimlerChrysler transmission plant in Kokomo, Indiana.[65]

As with other co-production examples, not everyone is impressed. Woodruf, Katz, and Naughton[66] suggest that coordination is even more challenging when there is such a close-linked, sub-assembly plant design. D. J. Schemo argues that most of the cost savings of this modular design come from suppliers having to invest in plant and equipment, and the low wages in Brazil.[67] This case is included for analysis and discussion in Chapter 12.

Navistar International Corporation is opening a new plant in Escobedo, Mexico, near Monterrey as a test bed for new truck assembly methods, but they call the Lopez concept "a step too far."[68] They have opted not to have suppliers in-plant; modules will be delivered to the plant, instead. The $167 million, 700,000-square-foot plant will use modular assembly, building 20 trucks per shift, initially, although capacity is 65 Class 6 to 8 trucks per shift and 195 per day. Eventually buses will also be added to production.

The Mexican plant is a Y-shape configuration, and results of the experiment will be used in the Navistar "next generation" truck and bus program promised for mid-2001. At the base of the "Y" is the body shop and paint facility. Medium-1 and heavy-duty trucks are diverted onto separate assembly lines and mated with chassis and cabs at the end of the line, which have been proceeding in the opposite direction down the line. Trucks will be supplied with Navistar diesels built in Melrose Park, Illinois, and body stampings from Navistar's Springfield, Ohio, plant, where trucks are also assembled. Although the Mexican market is small compared with the U.S. market, it has doubled between 1996 and 1997 to about 13,000 trucks. Navistar forecasted total U.S. and Canadian market sales at 220,000 in 1998.

Co-Distribution

Where P&G once ruled the supply chain, the locus of control has shifted to companies such as Wal-Mart, which buy in such large quantities that they have turned the tables on such giant manufactures. Prices, deliveries, and even product choices are "co-distributed" by these large retail and commodity softgoods producers. Instead of a regional distribution policy, P&G has been forced to reorganize distribution in

---

[65] *Automotive News,* January 20, 1997, p 19.

[66] D. Woodruff, I. Katz, and K. Naughton, "V.W's Factory of the Future," *Business Week* (October 7, 1996) pp. 55–56.

[67] D. J. Schemo, "Is VW's New Plant Lean or Just Mean?" *New York Times* (November 19, 1996), pp. C1, C5.

[68] J. Couretas, "Navistar Has a New Plant and New Plan for Mexican Market," *Automotive News* (April 27, 1998), p. 28.

a hierarchy. In one part of distribution, outbound logistics are now focused on just a few large customers. For the rest, the older system prevails. Electronic data interchange has revolutionized the potential of these distribution networks to the point that they are co-managed by supplier and customers.

At the core of Wal-Mart's success in changing distribution practices is an evolving information system.[69] Wal-Mart has 2,800 U.S. locations and may face as many as 20,000 queries from just one location on a holiday weekend (see Box 11-1). In 1995, Wal-Mart profit growth had stalled, and Randy Mott, vice president and chief information officer, went to work to reverse the trend. Perhaps the most controversial aspect of the Wal-Mart approach to co-distribution is that Mr. Mott believes strongly in developing applications in-house, rather than purchasing them and integrating systems as a third-party customer, which is contrary to the general outsourcing trend (see Chapter 9). But Wal-Mart is in contention for the global standard in leveraging technology for co-distribution.

Wal-Mart is not an isolated example, although leading-edge practice is always rare. Others include Wainwright Industries, past winner of the Baldrige award, Kraft Foods, and Michelin tires. Wainwright, for example, is an extension of GM's nearby van-assembly plant. It receives and stores parts from other GM suppliers, kits them to save 25 production operations at GM, then ships every 20 minutes, all with electronic orders from the GM assembly plant. Wainwright also reengineered the way housings are made, reducing cost by 35 percent for motor housings and many other components.[70] Michelin has pioneered in the e-commerce arena[71] and Kraft improved processing of invoices to the point that $3 million will be saved in three years by reducing the per-invoice cost from $7 to $4. Productivity is up 30 percent by changing workflow, elimination of paper and steps in the processing and automating tax calculations online. Application of this learning has improved customer service: calls are answered in 3 minutes instead of 5.[72]

GLOBAL NEW PRODUCT LAUNCH

The difficulty of global, simultaneous R&D and surprising success of simultaneous new product launches was introduced earlier (Chapters 5 and 7). The R&D function, traditionally, has been the last to be globalized by a firm. Yet,

[69] C. Wilder, "Chief of the Year: Wal-Mart CIO Randy Mott Innovates for his Company's and Customer's Good," *Information Week*, 662 (December 22, 1997), pp. 42–48.

[70] M. A. Verespej, "Wainwright Industries," *Industry Week*, 245, no. 19 (October 21, 1996). Profit sharing of 25% of all net income for all team associates except the three owners, "un-suggestion" systems, which reward only implemented solutions, and education (not training) for basic skills (7% of payroll vs. 2% U.S. average) is part of the secret to the success at Wainwright Also see: A. D. Wainwright, "People-first Strategies Get Implemented," *Strategy & Leadership*, 25, no. 1 (January/February 1997), pp. 12–17; J. H. Sheridan, "Culture-Change Lessons," *Industry Week*, 246, no. 4 (February 17, 1997), pp. 20–34.

[71] R. Garner, "Driving Forces," *Computerworld*, 31, no. 39 (September 29, 1997), pp. 90–91.

[72] B. Cole-Gomolski, "Oh, I Wish I Had a Better Invoice System," *Compterworld*, 32, no. 20 (May 18, 1998), pp. 53–54.

BOX 11-1

*Information Technology Enables Co-Distribution at Wal-Mart**

Wal-Mart sales had grown to $93.6 billion in 1995, but profit growth was flat. Up steps Randy Mott, chief information officer, to the rescue. He not only convinces management to increase information staff by 40 percent, he was able to leverage their efforts to develop new applications at reducing store inventories and increasing the responsiveness of the supply chain. The result: During the first nine months of 1997, profits were up 14 percent, on sales increases of 12 percent. Third-quarter inventory levels were much lower.

Wal-Mart used to receive just one shipment of seasonal items at Christmas, and now stores get three or five. Testimonials abound: Bill Eisenman, senior vice president of NCR, says that Wal-Mart controls inventory losses better than any other retailer. Randy Mott has been with Wal-Mart for his entire career of 20 years, and his approach reflects this experience. The secret is simple. Technology is a tool. Wal-Mart is not in the technology business. It is a retailer, first and foremost. The rule is to understand a process before you automate it. The net result is that Wal-Mart is always on the leading edge of technology. Mr. Mott pioneered quick-response merchandise replenishment, use of massively parallel processing, and supply-chain management.

Wal-Mart uses its RetailLink private network to share inventory and sales data directly with suppliers so the vendor can manage inventory. Next will be the Net which will involve 4000 suppliers. Next to be added to the Net will be Wal-Mart's CarrierLink for freight haulers that supply distribution centers. All this will be linked to the corporate intranet.

The current innovation preoccupation is with "data mining" and "data warehousing." What items sell and who buys them? How can Wal-Mart stores be tailored to local customers? These questions can be answered from this IT (information technology) resource. Mr. Mott believes in using applications developed in-house (which is counter to the trend—see Chapter 9). With few exceptions such as human resources systems supplied by PeopleSoft, Mott believes the software should fit the system, not the system modified to fit the software. He also believes the job is never done: he practices continuous improvement in technology, whether or not people think it has "arrived." It is one thing to warehouse data and quite another to "create" knowledge and embed this knowledge in organizational routines that add value to products and services. But interfirm, learning networks are clearly one of the most important sources of potential knowledge building.

---

* This case is based in part on C. Wilder, "Chief of the Year: Wal-Mart CIO Randy Mott Innovates for His Company's and Customer's Good," *Information Week* 662 (December 22, 1997), pp. 42–48; R. E. Cole, "Introduction: Special Issue on Knowledge and the Firm," *California Management Review,* 40, no. 3 (Spring 1998), pp. 15–21; and J. Lincoln, C. Ahmadjian, and E. Mason, "Organizational Learning and Purchase-Supply Relations in Japan," *California Management Review,* 40, no. 3 (Spring 1998), pp. 241–264.

ironically, technology does not obey traditional economic boundaries and can be as unique as the markets serviced. Operations lies somewhere in between, depending on how important and costly the inbound and outbound logistics of a product might be.

One study found that 15 of 22 sequential products were late, but, surprisingly, all simultaneous launches were on time. These cases are summarized in Table

$\mathscr{T}_{ABLE}$ 11-1   Focal Cases of Global New Product Launch

Product Area	Number of Cases	Nature of New Product
Telecommunication products	2	PBX systems
	1	GSM mobile telephone
	1	Modem (ISDN)
	2	Modems (analog)
	1	PC-telephony integration platform
Electronics and computer products	2	TV sets
	1	PC monitor
	1	Sound mixing system
	2	Laser black and white medium/high-speed printers
	1	Solid ink color printer
	1	Matrix black and white bar-code printer
	2	Ethernet print servers
	1	Ethernet 10/100 adapter card
	1	Ethernet port switch
	1	Ethernet multiplexer
	1	RS232 adapter (signal converter)
Photographic equipment	1	High- and ultra-high-speed camera
	1	Medium-speed industrial camera
	1	Medium-speed professional camera
	2	Handstand still 35 mm cameras
Measuring instruments	1	Security identification and lamination system
	1	Climatic data recording instrument
	1	Dynamometer
	1	Electric data recording/testing instrument

SOURCE: G. M. Chryssochoidis and V. Wong, "Rolling Out New Products Across Countries," *Journal of Product Innovation Management,* 15 (1998), p. 26.

11-1. It seems clear that our notions of globalization and new technology need to be reviewed. As mentioned earlier, technical management at Ericsson considers global, coordinated new product development (NPD) the top strategic challenge in the cellular phone business. Ericsson management has determined that no one company is doing this so well as to be considered a benchmark of practice on global, around-the-clock development. In addition, the study on sequential NPD found the following:

1. Global roll-out of new products is relatively unaffected by the toughness of the local regulatory and legal environment.
2. Critical to timeliness is a company's capacity to "leverage company resources and to ensure sufficiency in both marketing and technology." Internal project organization is critical to this process.
3. Timely product launch is essential to new product success.

Relationships between marketing and R&D are often strained,[73] and there is very little interaction between marketing and operations in most firms.[74] Yet, greater collaboration between marketing and other functions promotes success (see Chapter 7). Globalization puts even greater pressure on coordination skills and policies, since different markets are being entered. It is ironic that marketing, perhaps the most obvious of all functions since an organization cannot exist without a customer, is so difficult to implement. Enterprise Resource Planning systems have at least allowed for the *promise* of assisting collaboration electronically, but this promise has yet to be realized (see Chapter 9).[75]

The trend to outsource technical help has blossomed into a movement. And now the trend is global. In 1997, ASME International surveyed 600 executives in U.S. manufacturing, utilities, service, and trade companies, and found that outsourced engineering ranged from 48 percent to 65 percent. In 1983, manufacturers were the primary employer of engineers, but by 1993 that had changed, with professional service contractors leading the way. Manpower, Inc., in Milwaukee, reports that demand for information service skills is growing by 40 percent per year, and demand for designers and engineers is growing at a rate of 25 to 30 percent. The United States produces only about 12 percent of the first technical degrees worldwide, so international competition in technical talent is keen. As engineers prepare for foreign assignments and engage in 24-hour development projects, and as companies globalize, the hunt is on for the best technical talent at the lowest cost.[76]

✶ Reverse Technology Transfer

Sometimes, unwanted "spillovers" of technology between nations become a concern of national technology policy. This is often referred to as **reverse technology transfer.** An example is Hughes Space & Communications Co., which recently defended its security procedures designed to guard its satellites 24 hours a day when they are in China. Hughes maintains that the safeguards are adequate to protect against technology transfer, especially in the absence of Defense Department monitors. This is to be distinguished from legal and legitimate or sanctioned transfer between countries, such as in the machine tool industry.[77]

The exponential growth of information technology, in particular, has increased the need for new security procedures, and considerable R&D is underway in this arena.[78] In aerospace, this is a chronic problem because of the volumes of data

---

[73] K. B. Kahn and J. T. Mentzer, "Marketing's Integration with Other Departments," *Journal of Business Research,* 42, no. 1 (May 1998), pp. 53–62.

[74] D. Clay Whybark, "Marketing's Influence on Manufacturing Practices," *International Journal of Production Economics,* 37 (1994), pp. 41–50.

[75] A. Brackin, "Collaboration Evolution," *Manufacturing Systems,* 16, no. 2 (February 1998), p. 156.

[76] A. J. Rothstein, "Outsourcing: An Accelerating Global Trend in Engineering," *Engineering Management Journal,* 10, no. 1 (March 1998), pp. 7–14.

[77] H. Davies, "Some Differences Between Licensed and Internalized Transfers of Machine Tool Technology: An Empirical Note," *Managerial & Decision Economics,* 13, no. 6 (November/December 1992), pp. 539–541.

[78] W. Rhodes, "Each New Technology Sets Security Back," *AS/400 System Management,* 26, no. 8 (August 1998), pp. 57–58.

that must be shared to implement designs. Boeing has had to strengthen controls on the transfer of technical data to its Ukrainian and Russian partners in the Sea Launch venture so that the U.S. government would lift a suspension that has halted most work on the project.[79]

 The Twenty-first Century Jet

At its peak, the Boeing 777 development organization was 10,000 people strong. Therefore, it is not surprising that Boeing guarded the management techniques used to launch this new 350-passenger commercial aircraft as closely as wing shape, production rate, or avionics. The backbone of these NPD methods was the design-build teams composed of representatives from tooling, planning, manufacturing, engineering, finance, and material, or occasionally a customer (e.g., United Airlines) or a supplier (in some cases, a Japanese partner). First versions of the 777 were due to be delivered in May 1995, and United flew the first fare-paying passengers on June 7, 1995, but this new jet began as computerized images in 1991. Years of effort and billions of dollars in resources went into the project, all in response to the airline customers' need for a new fuel-efficient airplane, and development efforts by McDonnell Douglas (the MD-11/12) and Airbus (the A-330-340) at the time.[80]

In the process of launching the 777, Boeing not only introduced a new airplane, but also reinvented its development process for commercial aircraft. Case 11-2 introduces this new airplane and development philosophy.

$\mathscr{S}$UMMARY

Two inescapable trends in our generation are globalization and alliance making. Related to this, and by no means a new topic, what to make and what to buy and, most importantly, *where* to buy it or collaborate, continues to perplex academicians and practitioners. Why? Probably because no one theory or successful practice has isolated the "gene" of organizations in their context. Knowledge has been added to land, labor, and capital as an essential input to the firm, but knowledge is an intangible asset and is difficult to imitate.[81] In this chapter a new perspective is offered, which attempts to identify the key constructs needed to structure this debate. Technological innovation and the process that leads to the development of new products and services are at the heart of these new constructs. Cycles of changes in core technologies can be used to explain not only the patterns of effective buying and making, but also to inform practice. This is not just a matter of the circumstances under which one ought to make or buy, as in transaction cost theory, but also is a matter of how to change circumstances.

---

[79] J. Anselmo, "U.S. Reviews Plan to Lift Sea Launch Suspension," *Aviation Week & Space Technology,* 149, no. 7 (August 17, 1998), pp. 31–32.

[80] K. Sabbagh, *Twenty-First-Century Jet* (New York: Scribner, 1996).

[81] M. Nakamura and J. Xie," Nonverifiability, Noncontractibility and Ownership Determination in Foreign Direct Investment, with an Application to Foreign Operations in Japan," *International Journal, of Industrial Organization,* 16, no. 5 (September 1998), pp. 571–599.

Whether or not a firm has business overseas, managers cannot afford to assume that the best competitor in the world will not eventually be a home turf challenger. An organization cannot make everything it sells and cannot generate all the technology it needs. Therefore, the co-production imperative has emerged as one of the persistent challenges of our epoch.

Co-production (sharing the ownership of the means of production) is distinguished from joint production (one production line used for two or more products or services). Multiple ownership of operations capability has the advantage of spreading risk and adding flexibility to scheduling. Co-production has the disadvantage of being difficult to coordinate and hard to reverse without severe consequences. Joint ownership is also vulnerable to any single partner weakness or the combined weakness of both contributors. Five types of co-production are identified, organized by the life-cycle stage and the value-added chain. Co-production is codified beginning with *collaborative R&D* and *contract manufacturing*, followed by *collaborative purchasing, co-production*, and *co-distribution*.

R&D has been the last function to globalize, traditionally practiced exclusively in the firm's home country. Now companies often maintain more than one foreign R&D operation. Ericsson of Sweden, for example, has 40 R&D centers in 20 countries, which is typical of firms with corporate offices in small countries. A company cannot generate all the technology it needs, and a firm can partly make up for this by looking for technology wherever it occurs—often coincident, but not necessarily co-located, with global markets.

Contract manufacturing is growing at a rate of 20 per year in the United States, and companies typically collaborate on designs and share the means to create these product plans. Compatible design software has been one of the consequences of joint product planning, whether or not there is contract manufacturing. Collaborative purchasing is practiced by dozens of firms that share space with suppliers who have access to production scheduling and planning. The sales and purchasing functions of the two firms, respectively, are eliminated for any particular product category covered by this arrangement, often called JIT (just-in-time) II. Co-production has been tried by many companies, and the auto industry is currently beginning extensive experimentation with modular, shared manufacturing, including truck production in Brazil (see Chapter 12). Co-distribution, including joint control of distribution, sharing packaging, and dedicated logistics suppliers or contract warehousing, is growing in importance as companies become more specialized. All five forms of co-production are important because they set the standard for practice around the world.

Among the most challenging of the current global technology issues is simultaneous, multiple-country, new-product launch. Although systematic research results on this topic are limited, what findings do exist indicate that global coordination is desirable and can actually decrease the proportion of late project launches, formally done in serial fashion, if done correctly. Coordination of 24-hour, global, basic research has not been as successful to date, but the early returns suggest that applied research and global new product launch are feasible.

DISCUSSION QUESTIONS

1. Read Case 11-1. What is the competitive strategy of I/N Tek and I/N Kote (discuss separately as needed)? Has it been successful?

2. How do the operations of joint ventures affect the parent companies?

3. What is the most significant challenge for the future of these two joint venture companies (I/N Tek and I/N Kote)?

4. Read Case 11-2. What is Boeing's strategy?

5. How successful has Boeing's strategy been? How successful is this strategy likely to be in the next 5 years?

6. What should Boeing do next?

ADDITIONAL CASE SUGGESTIONS

1. Hewlett-Packard: Singapore (A), HBS 9-694-035 is a nice "part 2" to the inkjet printer case in Chapter 3.

2. Schiff der Zukunft (Ship of the Future): HBS 9-692-082.

CASE 11-1

I/N Tek and I/N Kote*

"We are different than the other joint ventures in the steel industry. The Inland Steel people who came to I/N Tek knew that the Nippon Steel Corporation technology was the best in the world, and they knew it was the key to their success in the future. They were eager to learn and work with us to create a successful enterprise. The other companies in this industry have not been so lucky."—Kazuhiko Fudaba, Vice President of Operations, I/N Tek, New Carlisle, IN

Inland Steel Corporation and Nippon Steel Corporation: Background

Not only was Inland Steel one of the first suppliers to the Automotive Industry, going back to the days of Henry Ford Senior, the company prided itself on being a high-end supplier of quality steel products. Pressures to operate efficiently in a cleaner natural environment drove Inland and its major competitors to convert from open hearth technology and ingots to the basic oxygen furnace and continuous casting during the 1960s and 1970s. By the early 1980s domestic integrated steel companies were faced with declining margins on steel products, competition from other materials, especially aluminum and plastic, and an unfavorable balance of supply and demand for sheet steels.

To take a pro-active position in the industry, several studies were commissioned aimed at addressing the long-term strategic decision to serve the domestic consumer durables manufacturers. The conclusion: Inland's future was in its own hands—steel could retain its major supplier position if products could be offered that satisfied the increasingly demanding needs of customers. The result was a commitment to create a first-class, cold-rolled sheet finishing operation that was customer focused.

Frank W. Luerssen, then the president of Inland, traveled to Japan to investigate the best technology available for finishing operations. Nippon Steel Corporation (NSC) was identified as the leader in finished products, and a $4 million detailed feasibility and engineering study was approved by Inland's board in April 1984. However, by 1985, losses had eroded Inland's balance sheet to the point that Inland had insufficient funds and leverage to undertake the major investment.

---

* This case was prepared for classroom discussion only and does not necessarily represent either good or poor administrative practice. Copyright © John E. Ettlie, 1993, and revised © 1994, all rights reserved. Information for this case was developed with the assistance of Mr. Peter Swan. The author wishes to thank the employees of I/N Tek and I/N Kote for their cooperation in the preparation of this case.

Coincidentally, NSC was faced with the challenge of serving it traditional customers that were expanding into the U.S. Eventually a 60 percent (Inland)-40 percent (NSC) joint venture called I/N Tek was born in March 1987, with a memo of understanding to create a cold-roll mill in the United States after Nippon Steel was able to arrange for major financing from Japanese lenders.

Construction began in August 1987, and first commercial product was run in New Carlisle, Indiana, in March 1990. During construction of I/N Tek, a second joint venture between the same two parents began to be discussed. This led to the formation of I/N Kote, a 50-50 joint venture for production of zinc and zinc alloy coated steels for the automotive industry.

I/N Tek features an essential and unique stage of finishing operations in the tandem rolling process that produce coiled sheet to high tolerance thickness and uniform specifications. Designs of tandem mills, this one supplied by Hitachi in Japan, are based on original sketches made by Leonardo DiVinci.

After early startup problems, I/N Tek was able to achieve an operating ratio of 90 percent. This working ratio was 59 percent when Shinichi Yokoi, Equipment Technology consultant, arrived in New Carlisle in 1990 during the early stages of the learning curve and equipment debugging. His challenge was to increase operating efficiency. Root cause analysis found that operating ratios were low because of equipment, people and operating procedures. Although the rolling mill has the same design as the model plant in NSC's Japanese operations, the detailed design of the system was left to equipment suppliers and local engineers. As a result, the technology transfer from Japan to the U.S. was not in perfect fidelity to the original.

"One of the Japanese engineers that was originally assigned to I/N Tek told us to run our tandem mill at higher strip tensions—he said, 'you'll eventually figure out why higher tension is better'—and we did figure it out. Our problems allowed us to learn more about this technology," said Tom Cayia, process technology manager. In some U.S.-Japanese joint ventures where the Japanese partner supplies the processing technology, it is sufficient that Americans just follow instructions. That was not the case here. A hybrid culture resulted—with Japanese employees becoming Americanized and American employees becoming Japanized.

When I/N Tek opened, competitor facilities generally had islands of processing for finishing coils—roll a coil off, process, and re-roll. I/N Tek is an integrated facility. As a result, if any stage of the I/N Tek process goes down it slows or stops other parts of the operation. The more integrated the design of any production facility, the greater the potential for increased capacity utilization

and productivity enhancement (e.g., through inventory avoidance, product uniformity and throughput maximization) but also, the greater the consequences of the failure of just one part of the system. In a cold-rolled operation, this happens when there is a coil failure (coils are welded together to form a continuous operation), which results in starving a furnace during annealing operations. The "furnace is king" expression describes the efforts to avoid this type of failure in an integrated operation. Fuzzy logic software is currently under experimentation to monitor pyrometer readouts in order to predict weld failure and reduce downtime.

Shape control technology had recently been installed at the end of the I/N Tek line and was presented in the first technology transfer exercise back to NSC in the fall of 1993 by a team led by Tom Cayia, Process Technology Manager: "At first we just visited Japan to find out what they were doing. Now we have something to show them and I think we sold some of their plants on adopting this new shape control equipment."

I/N Kote, being the more recently opened facility, is slightly behind I/N Tek in its learning curve relative to operating efficiency and quality. Two types of galvanizing lines, using technology supplied from NSC, as well as French and Austrian equipment makers, were installed at the end of the I/N Tek line and supplied by an ASRS (Automatic Storage and Retrieval) system unique to the steel industry and similar to that currently used in the paper industry for rolled product. "But the ultimate performance of both facilities is very much dependent on incoming rolled product from the basic supply source: Inland Steel," according to Mr. Fudaba. "Our challenge is to stay ahead of our competitors—anyone can install this equipment. Where will we be in ten years? In Japan, a vice president, has broad responsibility for planning and operations. In the United States, a vice president has more limited authority."

Japanese-U.S. Steel Joint Ventures

"Japanese steel makers have poured billions of dollars into American joint ventures. NKK's experience (with National Steel) has been so bad that it must decide whether to pull out," says Susumu Awanohara, in an article in the *Far Eastern Economic Review* (November 11, 1993, p. 56). So William Detrich's fears expressed in a recent book, *In the Shadow of the Rising Sun,* that the U.S. steel industry is becoming a Japanese "colonial outpost," do not wash with reality. (See Exhibit 11-1.)

National steel—71% owned by Japan's NKK, the world's fifth largest steel maker, and after $2 billion invested over 10 years of modernization—is one case in point. National recently reported its nine-month net loss "ballooned to US$103.6 million from the year earlier US $25.7 million; it largely blamed bad management-labour relations for the deteriorating performance," (*Far Eastern Economic Review*, November 11, 1993, p. 56). "Moreover, NKK's refusal to recruit top-level outsiders to restructure the company is prolonging the illness..." (*Far Eastern Economic Review*, *November*, 1993, p. 57).

Exhibit 1 reproduces a summary of Japanese investment in U.S. steel making from this same article (*Far Eastern Economic Review*, November 11, 1993, p. 58). Note that Nippon Steel has joint investments in both of Inland's integrated facilities and that Nippon Steel owns 13% of ISI stock and finishing operations (I/n Tek and I/N Kote). "In steel, value-added tends to increase 'downstream,' so Inland is shifting the product mix to favour cold-rolled and coated steel. Moreover, the U.S. government has provided protection from foreign competition more at downstream than at upstream. Last summer, the government upheld most dumping complaints filed against imported coated products, some complaints against cold-rolled imports and none against hot-rolled imports," (*Far Eastern Economic Review*, November 11, 1993, p. 59).

MillI/Nium®

I/N Tek has recently introduced a new product called MillI/Nium®, which finally exploits the unique capability of the state-of-the-art finishing operations in the North American steel industry. The product has tolerances achieved only in Japan for rolled coils, and it is being offered only to original equipment manufacturers, not steel service centers and distributors at a premium price negotiated in each case. This negotiation proceeds based on the customer's assessment of the added value that they obtain using the new product.

"This product can be introduced now because I/N Tek has stabilized its operations and can consistently meet this high quality of dimensional control better than any of our competitors," declares John Mountsier, Product Technology Manager. "This facility is positioned to move up-scale, and Inland was formally preoccupied with increasing overall market share in the normal lines of business. Now is the time to move on a quality product because demand in the industry is generally picking up."

Finish Processing Challenges for the Next Decade

Shinichi (Shin) Yokoi outlined the challenges for I/N Tek for the next 20 years by going to the white board and drawing a graph of the processing failure rate on the *y*-axis and years on the *x*-axis. The curve looks like a bathtub with the failures declining and stabilizing in a flat trough. After a few years, due to aging and deterioration, the curve (frequency of failures) begins to rise. "Our challenge is to improve continuously so that the curve never goes up again after it stabilizes at this low failure rate level where we are now. Other companies are acquiring comparable technology, and if we stand still, they will leapfrog us eventually."

Decision making processes were different at Nippon Steel Corporation for Shin than they are at I/N Tek. "In Japan, if a manager wanted a roller replaced in order to fix a quality problem, he would tell the maintenance manager and the maintenance manager would tell a technician to change it. Here, we have a group meeting and it takes a long time to decide what to do, because everyone needs to understand what the problem is, while it takes a long time, our team member's ability has been improved."

Shin reports to an American manager, F. Howard, who is in charge of equipment technology, and meets with him every Wednesday. On Thursdays, all the Japanese employees (six in I/N Tek) meet, regardless of their reporting relationship. "This gives us a chance to see the whole operation and not just our small part of the process," says Shin.

Premium flat-rolled product introduced

Customers at last week's Customer Forum in Chicago were treated to more than they expected — the debut of Inland's newest and most sophisticated product.

In a futuristic 25-minute presentation to about 80 customer representatives, Sales & Marketing's Scharlene Hurston and Tim Treacy took the wraps off the cold-rolled product produced at I/N Tek.

Introduction of the product, called MillI/Nium, will be backed by an eight-month print advertising campaign in four nationally recognized trade magazines:

Appliance, Ward's Automotive World, Metal Forming, and *Purchasing*.

The ads were created by Juhl Marketing Communications of Mishawaka, Ind., the advertising agency for I/N Tek and I/N Kote.

The double-page ads will run on a variety of schedules in the magazines. *Purchasing* magazine has the most ambitious schedule, with six insertions.

"These magazines were deemed most effective in reaching the markets and audiences that we feel have the greatest opportunity of benefiting from the MillI/Nium product," said Hurston, communications & training manager in Investor & Commercial Relations.

The ad campaign marks the end of a drought for Inland trade advertising and the company's first introduction of a totally new product in several years.

"Our time has come," said Steve Bowsher, vice president of Sales & Marketing, in a letter to sales representatives throughout the company.

"While it may have taken us a while to get here, we have a product that truly is the best of its kind.

"MillI/Nium represents a break-through for Inland in supplying OEM (original-equipment manufacturers) customers with a cold-rolled product that meets their application-specific needs."

MillI/Nium initially is being marketed only to OEMs that can derive the greatest benefit from its superior product features. Hurston explained.

Initial target audiences include the appliance; automotive; heating, ventilation and air conditioning; and office-furniture industries, as well as a limited number of strip applications where tight gauge tolerances are critical.

"MillI/Nium will offer cost advantages and product enhancements to these industries versus other cold-rolled sheet supplied by our competitors," Hurston said.

"As a result, we expect to get paid more for MillI/Nium than for other cold-rolled sheet products."

MillI/Nium also will come with a no-questions-asked guarantee on its suitability for use, Hurston said.

Steel industry practice dictates that customers absorb the first 2 percent of any steel rejection.

That practice will be waived for MillI/Nium customers, she said.

"In the case of MillI/Nium, we're saying we'll pick up the cost of the whole rejection.

"The confidence level of the product is so high, and the confidence level in our ability to research and analyze the needs of the customer is so high, that if we haven't done our homework well enough, we'll eat it."

This 100-percent fitness-for-use guarantee is the reason Inland is pricing MillI/Nium on a "value" basis, rather than the traditional published "book-price" basis.

"MillI/Nium is a very untraditional steel," she said.

"Before we sell it to a customer, there will be a complete analysis of what the customer is currently using and the cost-advantages provided by using MillI/Nium.

"That analysis will determine the price of the MillI/Nium product to that customer."

Inland product managers already are considering applications where the corrosion-resistant surface of MillI/Nium would benefit customers.

"One of the reasons that we came up with the name 'MillI/Nium' is that we might want to expand it beyond cold-rolled and create a whole family of new mill products," Hurston said.

MillI/Nium supplants another I/N Tek product.

"There are a number of differences between MillI/Nium and the I/N Spec product," Hurston said.

"We really haven't sold or promoted I/N Spec in some time, and this is a vastly different product on a number of levels.

"That's why we chose to introduce MillI/Nium at this time, largely because of higher levels of confidence, in the product and the market."

Exhibit 11-1. Japanese Steelmaking in the United States

	Joint venture (founded)	Shareholder (share %)
Integrated facility	National Steel (1984)	NKK (71) National Intergroup (18) Publicly held (11)
	Armco Steel (1989)	Kawasaki Steel (50) Armco (50)
	USS/Kobe Steel (1989)	Kobe Steel (50) USX (50)
	Inland Steel Industries (1989)	Nippon Steel (13)
	I/N Tek (1987)	Nippon Steel (40) Inland Steel (60)
	I/N Kote (1989)	Nippon Steel (50) Inland Steel Ind. (50)
	California Steel Industries (1984)	Kawasaki Steel (50) CVRD (Brazil) (50)
	L-S Electro Galvanising (1985 & 1989) *Two ventures*	Sumitomo Metal (40 & 50) LTV Steel (60 & 50)
	Wheeling-Nisshin (1984) *Two ventures*	Nisshin Steel (80) Wheeling-Pittsburgh (20)
	Protec Costing (1990)	Kobe Steel (50) USX (50)
	Nucor-Yamato (1987)	Yamato Kogyo (49) Nucor (51)

Source: Japan Steel Information Center, *Far Eastern Economic Review* (November 11, 1993), p. 50.

MillI/Nium represents the highest premium-quality sheet available from the I/N Tek line, she said.

"The (I/N Tek) facility clearly has gone through a learning curve and is producing a product that is demonstrably superior to anything else that's available in the market at this time.

"And that's not us saying that. It's what customers are saying.

"MillI/Nium truly is the dawning of a new era of quality and service for customers."

✖ CASE 11-2

BETTING on the 21st Century Jet

Boeing is gambling billions on the 777 and notching up the risk with a radical computer-aided design and an untested notion about worker participation. Here's why.

Traveling by commercial jet is about as thrilling as riding a rush-hour bus. Creating that jet, on the other hand, rings of grand adventure. It is today's equivalent of building the Panama Canal or the transcontinental rail-road—a glamorous and romantic task that is so costly, so risky, so technically demanding, that only a handful of companies in the world dare to do it.

The corporation that tries to make a genuinely new model of a large commercial aircraft can expect to spend about $5 billion over five years or so before getting anything back. If the project is a success, the company will have created a marvelous, beautiful machine that will circle the earth ceaselessly, safely, and profitably for decades to come. But if the effort fails, the company will be crippled, if not broken.

In its bid to build a plane for the 21st century. Boeing Co. has taken on all these perils and then added an extra level of risk by designing it in a radically new way. The Boeing 777, a twin-engine, medium-to long-range widebody scheduled to go into service in May 1995, will be the company's first plane designed entirely on computers. Boeing's three-dimensional digital design system comes with its own computer-generated human model who crawls into the images on the screen to show how difficult it would be for a real person to reach the problem area and make a repair.

The system enables Boeing to skip the usual paper drawings and full-scale mock up, going straight from computer images to building the real thing. In the past, planes sprang straight from the brains of Boeing renowned design engineers. This time the design process reflects the views of the airlines that will fly the plane, the mechanics who will maintain it, and the many others who will help build it, price it, and market it. Some 235 "design/build" teams, whose members are drawn from all these groups, are creating the detailed plans for the plane

More than ever before, Boeing is relying on Japanese partners to help manufacture the plane. The company has also made a controversial bid to get early approval from the Federal Aviation Administration to fly a twin jet on long over-water routes. Despite the extraordinary reliability of modern jet engines, aviators prefer four engines when they are a long way from an airport.

"The 777 causes me to sit bolt upright in bed periodically," admits Dean Thornton, president of Boeing's Commercial Airplane Group. He looks like a relaxed, self-confident man who normally doesn't lose much sleep. "It's a hell of a gamble," he continues. "There's a big risk in doing things totally differently. It's not going to fail, but the degree of success is uncertain. It depends on the market."

The market isn't promising right now. Eastern, Midway, and Pan American folded last year: America West, Continental, and TWA are in Chapter 11. But Boeing's economists foresee passenger miles more than doubling worldwide by 2005. They estimate that between replacing old planes and adding new ones, the world's airlines will need about 8,500 new jets in the next 14 years.

Even so, why should Boeing have taken such a jumbo risk? It's not as if it were in trouble and had to resort to desperate gambles. On a scale virtually unmatched by any other U.S. corporation, it dominates its world market and is the nation's largest exporter. Although Boeing is losing military business, the commercial backlog stands at 1,605 aircraft, and the four current models—the 737, 747, 757, and 767—all sell profitably. The 777 will fill the niche between the 218-passenger 767 and the 419-passenger 747.

What Boeing hopes to secure with the 777 is the future. "This is an offensive, not a defensive, strategy," says Phil Condit, the executive vice president who runs the 777 program. Japan patiently strengthens its aerospace capability by supplying more and more parts to foreign manufacturers, getting ready for the day when it could become a major competitor. Airbus Industrie, the four-nation European consortium, keeps building market share with advanced new aircraft. The remaining participant in the big jet stakes, McDonnell Douglas, could soon have entree to the rich Pacific market through an alliance with Taiwan Aerospace Corp.

When it faces these rivals as a designer, Boeing is preeminent, but as a manufacturer it is just average. With each succeeding jet, more of the actual building gets farmed out. "Is this the beginning of the hollowing out of Boeing?" asks John Ettlie, director of manufacturing management research at the University of Michigan's business school. "I have great respect for them. but they have a long way to go in manufacturing." Therefore, to stay on top, Boeing must find ways of building planes better.

If Boeing's new approach to design works—and so far, as engineers complete the designs and turn to preparations for manufacturing, it is doing well—the 777 will be an efficient, economic plane with a lot fewer bugs than new planes usually have. As a result, Boeing could save the millions it usually spends in fixing design problems during production and after the plane has been delivered to the airlines.

To be fair, as risks go, the 777 isn't quite in the same class as the 747 or the 767. Boeing bet the company on both those planes, but this time around, it has a healthy $3 billion in cash. Still, should the 777 flop, business historians a generation from now might point to it as the beginning of the end for the company.

Perhaps what makes the people of Boeing take these risks is the sheer size of the challenge. The 777 spills superlatives. Its digital design uses the largest cluster of mainframe computers in the world, eight IBM 3090-600Js. The finished plane will roll out through doors almost as big as football fields. The plant itself, at Everett, Washington, which builds the 747 and the 767, already covers as much land as 45 football fields, and will swell to the size of 76 to accommodate the 777 assembly line.

The plane will be Boeing's first fly-by-wire aircraft, which means that the pilot's commands will be transmitted electrically rather than mechanically to the rudder and flaps. Its twin engines will be the largest and most powerful ever built, with the girth of a 737's fuselage and a thrust, or propulsive power, of between 71,000 and 85,000 pounds, compared with about 57,000 pounds of the latest 747 engine. The cockpit will be crammed with new electronics and also liquid-crystal displays that will lead the pilot through his checklists and carry written messages to and from the airport con-

trollers when the voice channels get too crowded around rush hour.

Aircraft makers say it is time to stop designing and to start building when the weight of the paper exceeds the weight of the plane. That rule of thumb won't work for the 777 because all the designs are inside the memory of the project's eight IBM mainframes. Paper drawings are run off for the use of senior executives who don't have terminals in their offices, but 100% of the design will be created digitally.

Boeing has used computer-aided design before but has never relied so totally on the computer, skipping not only the paperwork but also the full-size metal-and-wood mock-up that designers have always built to test their drawings. Being three-dimensional and capable of displaying solid objects, the digital system shows how all the pieces fit together. If two parts clash—say a tube can't get around a spar—the problem shows up on the screen.

The digital system—called Catia (for computer-aided, three-dimensional, interactive application)—came from Dassault Aviation in France, where it was used to help build French fighter planes. IBM and Boeing enhanced the software to detect clashes, Boeing's term for parts that either do not fit or cannot work with each other the way they are supposed to. In the process, they created Catia-man, a computer-simulated human who can climb inside the three-dimensional images and play the role of the mechanic. Catia-man recently discovered that a human mechanic would not be able to reach the red navigation light on the roof of the plane to change the bulb. Without the limber model, says Condit, "we might not have found out about the bulb until we built a mock-up, or until final assembly, or even until some airline called to say we've got a plane grounded in Chicago because we can't change a light bulb."

The design teams and the computers are not meant to speed delivery of the 777—the time from first contract to first arrival of the plane will be about 55 months, compared with 50 months for the 767. But they are meant to make a better plane from the outset. Typically, engineers are still designing when manufacturing begins, and they keep making changes as problems show up in the factories and on the flight lines. Tools and dies and maintenance manuals have to be reworked and unusable parts scrapped. When the 747-400 started flying passengers three years ago, Boeing had to assign an extra 300 engineers to the plane to get rid of bugs that hadn't been spotted earlier.

The 777 teams and computers are supposed to find these bugs before they show up at the plant, much less in the air. With all the engineers looking at the same up-to-date data on their screens, they can see and work out conflicts. They can call up the name and phone number of the engineer responsible for a particular piece and deal with him directly to solve clashes. By putting in effort and money up front, Boeing hopes to make a plane that is really ready for service when it's delivered.

Like other proud, successful engineering companies, Boeing used to figure it knew what was best for the customer. When in the mid-1980s it began thinking about producing a new plane, it tried at first to sell the airlines on a bigger, better 767. But, says Alan Mulally, vice president of engineering for the 777, "the airlines kept telling us, 'No, Boeing, you're not listening.'" Phil Condit outlines Boeing's response: "We did what I call aggressive listening. We really tried to understand what the customers were telling us." In the jargon of the day, the 777 is a consumer-driven product. Starting in 1986, dozens of Condit's people traveled extensively, visiting airports and airlines, talking to pilots, passengers, and mechanics, and soaking up ideas.

What they heard was that the gap between a 767–300 configured for 218 passengers and a 747–400 with seats for 419 is too big to fill by stretching the 767. Airlines need to fine-tune their fleets to fit their routes fairly closely. A route with too many passengers for a 767 might not provide enough for a 747 to operate profitably, but a plane with 300-plus seats could be just the right size. As it happens, that slot is partially filled now by old McDonnell Douglas DC-10s and Lockheed L-1011s that will begin retiring in the mid-1990s, just as the 777 comes into service.

The competition is aware of this gap in the market too. McDonnell Douglas got in the slot first with the three-engine MD-11, which has been flying passengers for a year. There are 136 firm orders and 157 options for the MD-11, a derivative of the DC-10. Airbus Industrie, which Boeing regards as its most serious competitor, has 258 orders for its two entries in this class, the twin-engine A330 and the four-engine A340. The A340 will go into service early in 1993, and the A330 will follow in about a year. Coming late to market hasn't hurt Boeing in the past because the company profited by the mistakes of others and arrived with advanced technology.

Boeing learned from its clients that they wanted not just one 777 but an eventual family of planes built around the basic model. Since all the members of the family can share maintenance, parts, training, and operating procedures, an airline can save money while serving different markets. The first 777 that appears in 1995 will be a basic version of the three-class, medium-range plane that can carry 328 passengers 5,000 nautical miles. The long-range version (6,400 nautical miles) will follow in 1996 and seat a maximum of 328 passengers in three classes as well. These two could lead to stretch versions carrying 20% more passengers.

By October 1990, Boeing had configured the basic plane, and United Airlines put the 777 program in business by placing the first order for 34 of the aircraft. It has an option to buy 34 more at a price between $106 million and $129 million apiece. Each will have Pratt & Whitney engines. Other customers can order engines from other manufacturers.

With United's order in hand, the Boeing board approved the 777, and the engineers at project headquarters in Renton, near Seattle, began fine-tuning their designs early in 1991. In the past United would have placed its order and then sat back for four years awaiting delivery. This time United is right in there with Boeing and its engineers, along with the representatives of the suppliers and other airlines.

"We have definitely influenced the design of the aircraft," says United's 777 program manager, Gordon McKinzie, who works out of a Boeing office in Renton. For example, Boeing usually installed one very long panel under the leading edge of the wing to allow access to the slat mechanisms. (Slats perform a similar function to flaps increasing lift on take-offs and landings). "It was a nightmare for our mechanics," says McKinzie. "They had to remove scores of screws just to check out one problem." The solution was easy: several small panels instead of one big one.

In the cabin, United and a potential customer, American Airlines, persuaded Boeing to redesign the cover plates for reading lamps. Now a flight attendant, informed by a central panel that a bulb has burned out, will simply stick in a new one. The repair doesn't have to wait for a mechanic.

Besides United's legions, many more people have become intimately involved in creating the 777: Representatives from other airline customers, engine manufacturers, pilots, mechanics, and scores of suppliers, from the Japanese manufacturers of fuselage parts to the British suppliers of flight computers—all found their way to Renton. So have Boeing people who would not normally have much say about design—manufacturing engineers, plant representatives, and finance and marketing experts. Many of them sit on the design/build teams.

For the first time, this Boeing project has a chief mechanic. Jack Hessburg, representing the people who will maintain the plane, forgotten players in the past. Hessburg has a mechanical engineering degree, but just to make clear whom he represents he has shown up at meetings in Renton with a big red mechanic's towel hanging out of his rear pants pocket. "The gate mechanic touches a plane more than anyone," he says, and the ones he brought in both from Boeing and from the airlines told the design engineers things they never knew.

For example, a Japanese mechanic politely expressed his frustration at working in the most congested part of previous Boeings, the electronics and electrical bay under the cockpit. The door to the panel he was working on would swing shut, and his head would block the light. You can't do your best, he said, while holding a flashlight between your teeth and bracing the panel door open with your backside. Solution: Put a latch on the door to prop it open and move the light.

The biggest group of outsiders at Renton come from Japan. They are the emissaries of a consortium made up of Fuji Heavy Industries, Kawasaki Heavy Industries, and Mitsubishi Heavy Industries that has worked with Boeing since the early days of the 747 and that plays a bigger role with each new wide-body model. The consortium builds 15% of the 767's fuselage and will be making 20% of the 777's. Shin-ichi Nakagawa of Mitsubishi, who heads the group of 250 Japanese engineers working in the U.S. on the 777, was among the first Japanese sent to Seattle 19 years ago for the 747. After working alongside Americans at their terminals in Renton a year or more, most of Nakagawa's engineers are heading back to Japan to shift to production design. They will be linked directly into the digital design system in Renton. The fuselage will be built in sections in Japan and shipped to that immense plant in Everett.

The Japanese are familiar with teams of design and production engineers, says Nakagawa, but they haven't experienced Boeing's all-embracing teams that include customers, suppliers, and support people. They are grouped into sections for each of the main pieces of the plane. Section 41, for instance, is responsible for the nose of the aircraft and is divided into ten teams of up to 50 people each, for the roof, the floor, the flight deck, and so forth. Each team determines its own mix of insiders and outsiders.

All this sharing-with-outsiders stuff doesn't come naturally to the straight arrows bred in the Boeing culture. A visit to headquarters leaves an impression of a top management made up mostly of men with British last names, mixed with a few teeth-crunching Germanic ones. They have a proud corporate history and the can-do, tight-lipped attitude of military elite. Says Neil Standal, who manages the 777 subcontractors: "At first, people were reluctant to ask questions in team meetings, but now you have to shut them up."

To let everyone know that the 777 project is different and that it is okay to step outside the box of Boeing tradition, the company issued team members teal golf shirts with white 777 logos and encouraged employees to wear them to work—but only on Fridays. This is *Boeing,* after all.

The man at the center of the new culture is Phil Condit, 50, who has the wide, mobile grin and the jug ears of a Dwight Eisenhower. He stands a good chance of becoming president of the commercial aircraft division, Boeing's largest, and eventually chairman of the whole company, if he can successfully guide all the complexities of the 777 program.

In any earlier project, he says, most of his time would have been spent solving technical and contracting problems. "Now," he adds, "I spend 70% to 80% of my time on people issues. It is phenomenally important to tell everyone what is going on, and I use every device I can get my hands on." These include orientation sessions, question-and-answer sessions, information sheets, and just a lot of meetings with everyone from customers to production workers. Condit has a tremendous advantage personally in that he can explain esoteric matters in clear, forceful language, and with some passion when he talks about the 777.

Boeing wants early permission from the FAA to fly long over-water routes, like California to Hawaii, from the day it delivers the first plane to United in three years. That flight takes planes more than two hours' flying time away from any airport, an exceptionally long distance. What makes the goal of early approval controversial is that the 777 has only two engines. Normally, the FAA would first certify a twin-engine plane for flights not more than one hour from an airport, then two hours, and finally, after a couple of years' service, a full three hours so the plane could fly anywhere in the world. What Boeing wants is three-hour certification—what aviators call Etops for extended-range twin-engine operations—immediately. And it has developed an elaborate test program to get it.

Condit argues that the reliability of jet engines has reached the point where the "engine count" is no longer a safety issue. In-flight jet engine failures have become so rare they don't even figure statistically. Kenneth Waldrip, a Northwest 747 captain who heads the new aircraft evaluation committee for the Air Line Pilots Association, thinks Boeing should get high marks for the new plane but has reservations about early Etops. Says he: "Every time we get a new engine, we always get a surprise." He sees two engines as the wave of the future because they are more fuel efficient and cost less to maintain, but for extra security he prefers four. Says Waldrip: "If you've got four engines and one quits, its no big deal, but if one quits on a twin-engine plane, things get dicey."

The FAA won't certify the 777 for any service unless it is convinced that the plane can take off and fly on one engine. Says Anthony Broderick, associate FAA administrator for regulation and certification: "This will be the most thoroughly tested and proven plane ever on the day the first passenger steps aboard, but we have not guaranteed early Etops." That is one more risk Boeing must take.

Despite the pressures on him, Condit retains his man's-gotta-do-what-a-man's-gotta-do attitude. "My strong feeling is that you retain your competitive position by continuously improving what you do," he says. "Our job is to make sure we keep turning out the best planes in the world." The 777 will be the best test so far of Boeing's ability to do that.

J. Main, " Betting on the 21st Century Jet," *Fortune Magazine*, 125 (April 20, 1992), p. 102.

Chapter 12

Managing
Future
Technologies

CHAPTER OBJECTIVES

To summarize what we know about technology management and to introduce guidelines for applying this knowledge in practice. In the end, it is leadership that matters in the innovation process. Examples and exercises include Thomas Edison's Menlo Park laboratory, Silicon Valley, the food industry's transition from rigid to flexible packaging and current new product struggles, management of Technology and BPR (business process reengineering), new financial service products and the banking industry, Toyota's approach to new product introduction and continuous improvement, SEMATECH, and the history of radar. Innovation in food packaging during the last two decades is the first case example. The second case, at the end of the chapter, is the VW truck plant in Brazil.

How far have we come since Thomas A. Edison set up his shop of invention and pioneered the concept of organized innovation? This social invention of the industrial R&D laboratory resulted in the patents for the phonograph (1877), the motion picture projector (1891), and talking motion pictures (1913). Perhaps symbolically most telling was the sight on New Year's Eve, 1880, when Edison hung 50 lightbulbs in and about his Menlo Park laboratory and invited the public to take a look. Edison went on to invest in electric power generation—*backward vertical integration,* in modern terms—of the Pearl Street district of lower Manhattan, which first sent electric current to customers on September 5, 1882. This is also how the General Electric Company got its start, and many other enterprises were initiated in complementary as well as competitive fashion, with technological innovation as the driving force.

PRODUCT OR
PROCESS INNOVATION

At first glance, it seems obvious that products (outputs) and processes (throughputs and inputs) are different, and this distinction was taken up in the first two sections of this book. But it is worth summarizing why it is so important to make the distinction, and then review how blurring the boundaries between these two types is necessary to manage the innovation process. This is one of those subtle points about the innovation process that can be confusing. It is like saying, "new products are developed and new operations processes are purchased," but then saying in the same breath, "I lied; they go hand-in-hand and have to be managed as one."

First the distinction. The original, separate works by Abernathy and Utterback did not include the evolutionary metaphor, which shows an interesting evolution in their work. Most people easily grasp the nature of "maturing" products or industries (slow growing, low margins and low tech are typical of maturity), but the curves are much more complex than those in Chapter 3. When process technology and non assembled products are at issue, product innovation is less important.[1]

One critical difference between a new product and a new process is the "try-out" phase in the innovation process. Individuals can experience a new product, but it is the *system* that is at stake when the process changes. The experience that people have had with business process reengineering (BPR) is very instructive on this point.[2] BPR represents significant organizational upheaval, and, according to several sources, nearly 75 percent of BPR cases do not meet their objectives, which is a polite way of saying that radical change is risky.

A summary case study of BPR at Hewlett-Packard appears in Figure 12-1. Notice that the percentages given in this case of reengineering the sales process are somewhat lower than is typical of a reengineering case. Hammer and others advocate making changes that result in triple-digit performance changes, and usually of more than 50 percent, which is not the case in this example.

The cases on manufacturing software development also show that the goals for new system development evolve over time, often "leaking" into the launch period or even the maintenance phase of new hardware–software system adoptions (see

▶ 135 sales reps trained to use laptop computers (inventory information + e-mail/peers/managers)

▶ Time spent in meetings down by 43%

▶ Travel time down by 13%

▶ Time spent with customers up by 27%

▶ Sales rose by 10%

Figure 12-1   Business Process Reengineering Case Summary: HP Sales Process
SOURCE: Teng, Grover and Fiedler *California Management Review* (1994), p. 17.

---

[1] J. M. Utterback, *Mastering the Dynamics of Innovation,* (Boston: HBS Press, 1994, p. 130).

[2] M. Hammer, "Reengineering Work: Don't Automate, Obliterate," *Harvard Business Review* (July-August 1990), pp. 104–112; D. H. Davenport, "Need Radical Innovation and Continuous Improvement? Integrate Process Reengineering and TQM," *Planning Review,* 21, no. 3 (May-June 1993), pp. 6–12.

Chapter 5). The point is, the try-out phase of new process technology differs from that for new products and, to some extent, new services. New products can be used and most customers know immediately what the attributes of the product are relative to their needs.

This difference in the try-out or "warm-up" phase of innovation also have much to do with the advantages that can accrue from process changes. Yes, most organizations put a higher priority on new products and services than new processes, but companies that do both well have a distinct advantage over their competitors. Toyota Motor Company is a premier example. Know widely for excellence in manufacturing (and appropriate use of manufacturing technology), Toyota is just as good at product development. One only has to hear the story of Toyota's entry into the U.S. luxury car market with its Lexus line once to appreciate the significance of their approach to product quality. And, of course, Toyota employees and managers do not see these two pieces of the innovation process separately—interlocking Deming cycles of Plan-Do-Check-Act are used in product development as well as continuous improvement of manufacturing processes. This process of new product development at Toyota is presented in Figure 12-2.

Personnel are transferred to the new product release during the midstages of continuous improvement (Figure 12-2), so that the continuity of design and technology decisions is maintained. This system is used not just for the Lexus but for all of Toyota's products, so people can also be transferred from one platform to another within the company and will understand the general game plan before they even arrive at a new assignment.

The relationship between quality and new technology is intimate at Toyota, and illustrated well by the summary of observations of Chakravarty and Chase.[3] In their

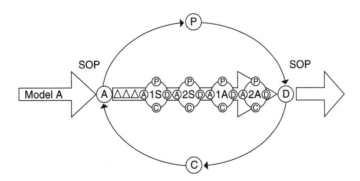

Key: SOP = Start of production

Ⓐ Ⓟ Ⓓ Ⓒ = Act, Plan, Do, Check

Figure 12-2   Toyota Product Development

Source: Prepared remarks Kunihiko Masaki, President—Toyota Technical Center, U.S.A. at the U-M Management Briefing Seminar on Integrated Product Process Development, Traverse City, Mich., August 8, 1995.

[3] A. Chakravarty and A. Chase, "Tracking Product-Process Interactions: A Research Paradigm," *Production and Operations Management,* 2, no. 2 (Spring 1993), pp. 72–93.

summary paradigm, innovations impact manufacturing, process, and product technology equally, and all three indirectly but eventually impact engineered quality. Marketing affects commercialization directly. Unfortunately, this highlights one of the limitations of this "ideal case": More money is spent on innovations for new products than for new services. To balance the two, therefore, takes considerable effort.

Gary Vasilash recently reported on a survey that was done by SAE International (formerly the Society of Automotive Engineers) on bridging the gap between design and manufacturing engineering. During a panel discussion of the survey, Frank Ewasyshyn, then vice president of advanced manufacturing engineering for Chrysler Corporation, said that "It's easier to get vehicle engineers to go into manufacturing and to come out than it is to get manufacturing engineers to go into vehicle engineering and to come out," (p. 8).[4] There are probably many explanations of why there are occupational or discipline differences on this mobility tendency, but since design and manufacturing engineers are typically very different when hired into companies (design engineers have more status and higher salaries, typically) and companies spend more on new products, who is surprised at differences downstream? It is all part of the challenge of integration.

SEVEN SAWS OF THE INNOVATION PROCESS

Much of what we know today about the innovation process and its management is a systematic extrapolation of these well-known historical examples such as Edison's Menlo Park laboratory. Table 12-1 summarizes some of the relevant state-of-the art conclusions and the implications of this knowledge about the innovation process.

These **seven saws** on the innovation processes are explored in greater detail next.

The Life-cycle Metaphor

A consistent thread throughout the introductory chapters of this book suggests that the life-cycle concept is still among the best metaphors for the innovation process. Even with the caveats associated with the use of any metaphor, understanding the innovation process as one unfolding over time is a good starting point for all the other conversations one might have about this process and the stories one could tell that are relevant to its management.

Jelinek and Shoonhoven (1993)[5] described the early phases of the technology life cycle in great and rich detail in their book about Silicon Valley. This concept or idea-generation phase of the innovation process is hidden from the view of outsiders, and less is known about it than the stages of the process that are downstream. Jelinek and Schoonhoven summarized five in-depth case histories from Sili-

---

[4] G. Vasilash, "Building Bridges," *Automotive Manufacturing and Production* (July 1997), pp. 8–9.

[5] M. Jelinek and C. B. Schoonhoven, *The Innovation Marathon* (San Francisco: Jossey-Bass Publishing, 1993).

TABLE 12-1   Implications of the Innovation Process

What We Know	Implications
The life-cycle metaphor is useful to explain the innovation process	How we manage depends on where we are in the life-cycle, including government policy (Chapters 2, 3, and 10).
The first distinction is radical versus incremental technology	Successful companies manage radical technology and incremental technology differently (R&D intensity varies by industry); for example, radically new products need lead users for testing, and radical process adoption often may require new hires in senior management (Chapters 4, 5, 7, and 9).
New products are different than new operations processes.	New products tend to be developed in-house and new operations technology tends to be purchased. Both significantly enhance performance (Chapters 1, 4–7).
Economic justification of new technology projects is challenging but not impossible.	Simpler methods (e.g., return on investment) are most often used in practice, but managers who understand that technology is a system of relationships among technologies are the most successful (Chapters 4–6).
The new product development (NPD) process requires balance in functional orientation.	One way to effectively manage the NPD process is to use the platform approach (Chapter 7), but there is danger of technological obsolescence. Successful new product criteria are well known (e.g., "the value equation").
The cultural lag hypothesis can be applied to organizations.	Effective capture of value from new products and new processes requires the matching of technological innovations with administrative innovations (Chapters 7–9).
Globalization and alliance formation are two important contextual trends for innovating.	Emerging markets, scarce resources, and technology trajectories require global strategies and co-production acumen (Chapters 5 and 11).

con Valley: Hewlett-Packard, Intel, Motorola, National Semiconductor, and Texas Instruments. The electronics industry is high tech by most measures; it has spent nearly 10 percent of sales on R&D for decades. The all-industry average is 3 percent or less in the United States. So the pressure to innovate in this industry is real and persistent. Their overall point, as called out by the book's title, *The Innovation Marathon,* is that most competitors have access to similar technology in this industry, and developments can be matched quickly. What is required is "constant improvement, and constant balance" between the various functions of the firm and balanced excellence to fuel the innovation engine to compete in this arena.

The author's findings about the "roots" of the innovation process can be summarized in three key themes:

▶ Innovative ideas come from nearly everywhere.

▶ Generating ideas is *not* the issue—choosing from among many ideas and harnessing this creative energy *is* the challenge.

▶ Innovation cannot be "walled off" as the unique responsibility of one group—it must be managed as a pervasive process.

Jelinek and Schoonhoven further describe the innovation process by using the metaphor of successive stages of a filtering process. Ideas are selected first by individual innovators themselves, regardless of their level in the firm—scientists, engineers, managers, it doesn't matter. Often the term *110 percent busy* is used to describe how people are "bootlegging" preliminary activities into their crowded schedules. And it goes both ways—people are seeking new projects, and new projects are seeking people. But the first screen is a self-screen. It is purposefully informal in most cases, but culture will often dictate which ideas are shared. The literature on creativity (see Chapter 3) predicts that the more creative the person, regardless of occupation, the more the individual will "blurt" out ideas, before carefully thinking them through. That is, creative individuals "think outloud" and have many failed ideas for every successful one. It often goes against the grain of most companies—going around "blurting" all the time. But the culture that allows this, and allows innovators to stand apart from the background noise of a company, will enjoy a greater sustained innovative run at the competition. Time is the scarce resource, so the more excited about the idea the innovator is, the more it will be worked on.

The next stage in the process for Jelinek and Schoonhoven is the application of the second critical screen: buy-in by others. Again, time is the critical resource. The idea has to be good or potentially high-payoff to warrant signing on, since personal credibility is at stake. The project must be worthy. When the innovator "goes public," the stakes go up. It may take "a half a million dollars to even find out the feasibility" of a project, according to Paul Stoft at Hewelett-Packard.[6] Ultimately, it is the balancing of risk and cost that has to be determined, both to the individual and the firm. Failed ideas have a large role to play in this process, not only do they inform learning, but ideas can be shelved and then called upon later to be reconfigured. All ideas, new and old, are eventually changed. "Old ideas or failed ideas from the past that hung on are part of every decent engineer's repertoire."[7]

Formal hurdles and approvals are often next; the economic justification process was covered earlier in Chapter 5. Most companies have a very formal project life cycle with phases and checkpoints, but operating in the background are the informal choices and criteria. Links between functions and even suppliers are often part of this informal process—even in the early "laboratory" stage of the process. The idea must have an ultimate customer and competitive promise to be pursued. It is not surprising that many successful ideas are born with a customer or marketing read of a customer situation. At Intel, a critical early stage in the screening process is the Technical Review Group of the corporation. But the review is more than R&D technical; it will also involve marketing, finance, and manufacturing. It has to be convincing: "Seduce me with your ideas," is the challenge.[8]

It is not surprising that persistence is often a key requirement that individuals demonstrate in cases of successful innovation. The following case is illustrative. During the course of a project comparing different approaches to product development in Japan, the United States, and Europe, I had the privilege to interview the deputy director of R&D for a large, well-known Japanese corporation that makes business machines such as printers and copiers, cameras, and video equipment.[9]

The interview took place in Tokyo after regular business hours, and it was an opportunity to talk about how R&D management differed in Japan and the United

---

[6] Ibid., p. 179.

[7] Ibid., p. 184.

[8] Ibid., p. 204.

[9] J. Ettlie, C. Dreher, G. Kovacs, and L. Trygg, "Cross-National Comparisons of Product Development in Manufacturing," *Journal of High Technology Management Research*, 4, no. 2 (1993), pp. 139–155.

States. My respondent made it quite clear that their way was one that relied heavily on demonstration of persistence. Once a technical person is promoted into management in this, or any other company, two things happen. First, the manager can no longer keep up with the technical field he left as well as he did before (the manager is hardly ever a she). Second, the manager now has to supervise technical people trained in other areas of discipline, such as mechanical engineering versus electrical engineering. The manager can no longer rely on pure technical judgment to make decisions about projects and people. An alternative method has to be adopted, according to my senior R&D respondent from Japan.

The method used in this Japanese firm, which is adopted to ensure that the people spend their time on the projects with the best chance of technical and commercial payoff, is to have technical managers constantly challenge subordinates to see if they are truly committed to their ideas. After work and after many rounds of drinks, only the persistent younger engineers will be trusted. These junior, often bench, scientists and engineers must continue to press their ideas and point of view, under the most disadvantageous circumstances, day in and day out, night in and night out. Over and over they will be challenged by their managers—the pros and cons will be discussed openly in these working/drinking groups, composed almost always exclusively of men. Sometimes the discussions last well into the night. Only the hearty, robust people and ideas survive.

Radical versus Incremental Technology

We know that types of innovations make a difference. The second and third entries in Table 12-1 concern the most critical innovation categories for managing change. The first key that unlocks understanding across a complex array of situations and time frames is whether the technology involved is a radical or an incremental departure from the past. The second is the product–process dimension, discussed at the beginning of this chapter. The radical–incremental attribute applies for industry comparisons, the total organization, a unit within a firm, a group or team, and for individuals. It doesn't matter how coarse or fine the level of aggregation, the degree of departure from the past is the key to getting started on the right managerial foot.

This important radical–incremental distinguishing feature of the innovation process became very apparent to us when we began our study of the U.S. food industry, which began undergoing a shift from rigid to flexible packing in the early 1980s.[10] Cans were being replaced—or so it seemed at the time—by new packaging such as the retortable pouch—essentially a flexible can. The *retort* part of the name refers to the cooker that sterilizes food within the container once it is closed. During the actual canning process, the racks of cans are actually dragged through cold water to reverse the cooking process and maintain the taste of the food (such as canned corn). One of the technical problems encountered with the retortable pouch was that food would splash on the sealing edge during filling.

There was also a significant shift occurring in the demographics of the country at that time, and the microwave oven was becoming much more popular. With

---

[10] J. E. Ettlie, W. P. Bridges, and R. D. O'Keefe, "Organizational Strategy and Structural Differences for Radical Versus Incremental Innovation," *Management Science*, 30, no. 6 (June 1984), pp. 682–695

more women in the work force and more convenience in food preparation sought, flexible and alternative packaging concepts took off.

The retort pouch was adopted by the U.S. military for field rations because it was safer in combat (a general observed that a soldier can hurt himself falling on a can of food, but a pouch is soft and flexible). They didn't anticipate that vermin would "attack" pouches in warehouse storage, or that the pouch (which is a poly-laminate of plastic and aluminum) leaves a metal ash when incinerated and is diffi-cult to recycle. The point of all this is that there is a new science, a new playing field at hand, when a radical shift in technology occurs. Sails are radically different than steam engines. Saws cut with a different "science" than lasers. Piston engines for airplanes are substantially different from jet engines—radically different to the point that a whole new knowledge set and skill base had to be invented.

In the food study, we tracked adoption of radical packaging technologies in a mature industry—rather like water being poured on the hot stones of a sauna. We wanted to know if innovation was really possible in a slow-growth, regulated, large, U.S. industry. We found that, eventually, the successful companies installed new strategies and organizational structures both to adopt and capture value from these radically new packaging concepts. These mature companies changed their R&D project funding criteria to "take more chances by allowing more projects to fail," or became more decentralized in decision making or added new job titles like director of technology or chief technology officer. The struggle continues in this industry to be innovative (see Box 12-1).

In the paper-making industry, Lauvila found that increases in material (financial) resources and competitive pressures encouraged management to adopt advanced instead of conventional production technology.[11] This suggests that the concentration of firms in an industry, as well as merger activity that creates or dilutes resources, could have an impact on how radical the technological departures will be in decision making.

In the machine tool industry, Ehrnberg and Jacobson[12] studied two historical discontinuities: the transition from conventional to computer-numerical control (CNC) and the transition from stand-alone CNC to flexible manufacturing systems (FMS). They found that of five possible warning signals of technological disconti-nuities (patents, scientific publications, number of new entrants into an industry, performance of innovations, and relative price changes of substitutes), CNC and FMS exhibited differences in their warning patterns. For CNC, relative prices of substitutes changed first, followed by a sharp rise in entrants, substitution of tech-nology, and then the simultaneous appearance of patenting and publications. Therefore, for CNC, patents and scientific publications did not act as a warning for discontinuity. For FMS, "increases in entry preceded the rise in publications, which, in turn, preceded the increase in diffusion."[13] Ehrnberg and Jacobson argued that the reason patents do not precede diffusion is that the control technology that comes from the computer technology and enables CNC machines to be built is out-

---

[11] J. Laurila, "The Thin Line Between Advanced and Conventional New Technology: A Case Study On Paper Industry Management, *The Journal of Management Studies*, 34, no. 2 (1997), pp. 219–239.

[12] Ehrnberg and Jacobson, "Indicators of Discontinuous Technological Change: An Exploratory Study of Two Discontinuities In the Machine Tool Industry", *R&D Management*, 27, no. 2 (1997), p. 107.

[13] Ibid., p. 119.

BOX 12-1

Innovation in the Food Industry

The food industry struggled with the transition from rigid to flexible packaging during the 1980s and 1990s. Launches of new products fell 20 percent in 1996, the sharpest decline in two decades, and at a time when new product development and introduction has become the primary way of competing in most manufacturing industries (see Chapter 4). U.S. companies have mastered mass production of off-the-shelf commodities, but shoppers have switched preferences to specialty foods. European imports such as Swiss butter, which is 30 percent easier to spread, and modified packaging that keeps lettuce and baked goods longer, are capitalizing on this consumer trend. U.S. food companies have become like the U.S. car companies of the 1980s—they have lost touch with their customers.

What to do? Current responses seem to be modest tweaking of older products. The "healthy choice" varieties of existing products take fat out and substitute sugar. Real breakthroughs that can be patented take years to develop and are risky. Evidence Procter & Gamble's introduction of snack chips containing olestra, which prevents fat metabolism, but also causes diarrhea among some consumers. It is not surprising that people are more willing to experiment with electronic gismos but are cautious about what they eat.

The food industry spends less than 1 percent of sales on R&D, so breakthroughs in new products are less likely. When a patentable product does come along, such as rice cakes or soft-and-chewy cookies, they are immediately imitated by "me too" products.

Unless a long-shot project can be assured to generate at least a $100 million brand, it is likely to get killed, and with downsizing, fewer technical staff are available to generate and evaluate such ideas. Universities are getting into the act (e.g., the Research Alliance at the University of Massachusetts in Amherst has a food-science pilot facility that industry can use), as they have in other industries.

Kellogg is planning to open a $75 million research center in Battle Creek, Michigan. Campbell is introducing a new line called Intelligent Cuisine to appeal to the aging ("graying") population—and has 40 healthier (reduces blood pressure and cholesterol in clinical trials) versions of existing items such as French toast, sausage, and grilled chicken Dijon. This effort cost Campbell $20 million and a 5-year development cycle, but company representatives say this is what is required today to reinvent itself and to compete. Radical product shifts require corporate technology strategies.

Sources: J. Ettlie, W. P. Bridges, and R. D. O'Keefe, "Organizational Strategy and Structural Differences for Radical Versus Incremental Innovation,"*Management Science* 30, no. 6 (June 1984), pp. 682–695; J. Ettlie, "Organizational Policy and Innovation Among Suppliers to the Food Processing Sector," *Academy of Management Journal* 26 (March 1983), pp. 27–44; M. J. McCarthy, "Slim Pickings: Food Companies Hunt for the `Next Big Thing' But Few Can Find One," *Wall Street Journal* (May 6, 1997), pp. A1, A6.

---

side the machine tool industry. In addition, if the technological change is not science-based, publications will not signal or warn that a discontinuity is coming.

Radical shifts in the banking industry were taking place about the same time. Not only do commercial banks invest billions of dollars in financial systems every year ($30 billion from 1981 to 1985, according to Hunter and Timme,[14]) financial institutions have become quite innovative in introducing new service products.

Nord and Tucker[15] conducted an in-depth study of a variety of financial institutions and the introduction of NOW accounts (interest-bearing checking accounts, which became legal outside New England on January 1, 1981) during this period. Their results are quite consistent with the notion of understanding technology as either radical or incremental (which they call *routine*). No one outside New England had to design the product from scratch, so the innovation presented some interesting opportunities for a "controlled" comparison. Every firm adopting NOW accounts essentially started at the same time—when they became legal at the beginning of 1981. Banks and savings and loans offered the product, but their histories were significantly different. The result of their analyses of NOW accounts appears in Table 12-2.

The authors divide financial institution cases into four categories of degree of success in implementing NOW accounts. At the top are the very successful cases, such as First Commercial Bank. Next are the moderately successful cases, such as Second City Bank; then come the moderately unsuccessful cases, such as First Regional Bank, and finally come the unsuccessful cases, such as Second National S&L.

$\mathcal{T}$ABLE 12-2   Classification of Firms on the Basis of Success in Implementation of NOW Accounts

---

Very Successful
First Commercial Bank
Second Commercial Bank
Third Commercial Bank
Second Capital S&L
First City Bank
Moderately successful
First National S&L (after consultants)
Second City Bank
First Neighborhood S&L
Second Neighborhood S&L
Moderately unsuccessful
First Regional Bank
First Capital S&L
Unsuccessful
First National S&L (before consultants)
Second National S&L

NOTE: The ordering *within* classes is not intended to reflect a ranking of success.

SOURCE: W. R. Nord and S. Tucker, *Implementing Routine and Radical Innovations* (Lexington, Mass.: D.C. Heath Company, 1987), p. 307, Table 12-1.

---

[14] W. C. Hunter and S. G. Timme, "Technological Change in Large U.S. Commercial Banks," *Journal of Business,* 64, no. 3 (1991), pp. 339–362.

[15] W. G. Nord and S. Tucker, *Implementing Routine and Radical Innovations* (Lexington, Mass: D.C. Heath & Company, 1987).

This is a limited number of cases, but do you see the pattern in these success/failure categories? Look carefully at the designations for each institution and count the frequencies of S&Ls versus banks in each category. Now do you see the pattern?

NOW accounts were a "radical departure from past practices for S&Ls, but a rather routine one for banks" (p. xi).[15] Given this context, it is not surprising to see the patterns of success and failure in Table 12-2. Banks with checking experience—a high-transaction business—generally did much better with NOW accounts than S&Ls.

Hunter and Timme tested the Galbraith–Schumpter hypothesis of scale bias: larger firms with larger R&D budgets innovate at a faster rate than smaller firms that are resource constrained.[16] The hypothesis assumes that product mix is constant and that technological advancement affects all factors equally. Hunter and Timme used a sample from the Federal Reserve end-of-year reports and report of income and dividends for the 7 years 1980 to 1986. This is nearly identical to the period studied by Nord and Tucker. Technological change was defined as the unexplained residual in the estimating equations for a sample of 219 banks. As a result of innovation, real costs were reduced by approximately 1 percent per year, holding other factors constant. However, larger banks did not innovate faster than smaller banks, and the Galbraith–Schumpter hypothesis, therefore, is not supported by these results. It is worth noting that larger banks did enjoy a larger percentage of cost savings than smaller banks. A subgroup of the largest banks averaged cost reductions of about 1.5 percent, and a subgroup of the smallest banks in the sample averaged a cost savings of about 0.25 percent, suggesting scale economies of these effects. Apparently, there is a need to expand the scale of output to become more cost efficient.

Finally, if there was ever any doubt that high tech and low tech are different, Silicon Valley firms are working hard to institutionalize these differences. A dozen Silicon Valley companies and venture capitalists have formed a bipartisan political action committee called the Technology Network.[17] Spawned from a campaign to defeat Proposition 211 in California during the fall of 1996, the network first supported a bill in Congress (Reps. Ann Eshoo, D. Calif., and Rick White, R. Wash.) to establish uniform state rules for shareholder lawsuits against sometimes volatile high-tech companies.

Overall, it seems clear that the role of degree of departure from past practice—the radical–incremental dimension of technological innovation—applies in many different industry settings and is an important decision parameter in managing change. The more radical the technological innovation involved, the more changes in policy and organizational structure will be required for success.

New Products and Competitive Response

With notable exceptions (e.g., Dan Schendel, Tushman and Anderson) the R&D management and new product development literature does not attend to competitive response. The marketing literature, on the other hand, has taken up this challenge, and a summary of this literature appears next.

---

[16] W. C. Hunter and S. G. Timme, "Some Evidence of the Impact of Quasi-Fixed Inputs on Bank Scale Economy Estimates", *Economic Review* (Federal Reserve Bank of Atlanta), 76, no. 3 (May/June 1991), p. 12.

[17] D. Bank, "Silicon Valley Businessmen Form Bipartisan PAC," *Wall Street Journal* (July 8, 1997), p. B8.

1. Organizations usually compete based on strengths and tend not to change if new capabilities are required, even in the face of significant competitive challenge. Some companies have to nearly fail before they change or must sustain a significant "jolt" before they mount significant response to competitive threat. Epson's reaction to Hewlett-Packard's entry into the printer market with inkjet is typical. Epson continued to push its own technology as the initial competitive response, but simply positioned and sold it differently.

2. The more significant a company's move, the more likely that significant response will be delayed.[18] It took years for the established airlines to imitate Southwest Airlines' challenge in U.S. air travel.

3. New entrants typically challenge with new technology in their products and services, but are usually ignored by incumbents.

4. When a new product is announced or introduced by an *incumbent,* there is a 50–50 chance that competitors will respond with a new product.[19] It breaks down like this: competitors are likely to respond 42 percent of the time by introducing a new product, 33 percent will take another market action such as reducing price on an existing product, and 22 percent will issue a new product announcement. About 75 percent will take some competitive reaction position.

5. In industries with high patent protection (usually high-tech industries, which are more concentrated), firms are likely to react to competitive new product introductions with a marketing mixed response rather than with a new product; patents erect barriers against product initiatives.[20]

6. About 60 percent of firms will have some type of reaction to any new product introduction, whether from a new entrant or incumbent, but there is a tendency to take incumbents more seriously because they are established firms.[21]

Overall, it seems clear that new products are very much a part of the competitive moves of all companies, and the greater the perceived threat, the greater the response. However, companies do not always see moves by new entrants as big threats, or they believe that patent protection will serve as a substantial buffer to protect them from competitive moves.

✳ Justify My Technology

Madonna sang, "Justify my Love." But we know some people are in love with novelty and new technology. Robert Kaplan[22] said (to paraphrase): "Justify my technology—but not on faith alone." The evidence continues to mount, however, that most decision makers rely on rather simple capital investment analyses techniques

---

[18] W. T. Robinson, "Marketing Mix Reactions to Entry," *Marketing Science,* 7, no. 4 (Fall, 1988), pp. 368–385.

[19] T. S. Robertson, J. Eliashberg, and T. Rymon, "New Product Announcement Signals and Incumbent Reactions, *Journal of Marketing,* 59 (July 1995), pp. 1–15, especially pp. 9–10.

[20] Ibid., pp. 9–10.

[21] D. Bowman and H. Gatignon, "Determinants of Competitor Response Time to New Product Introduction, *Journal of Marketing Research,* 32 (February 1995), pp. 42–53.

[22] R. Kaplan, "Must CIM Be Justified on Faith Alone," *Harvard Business Review,* 64, no. 2 (March/April 1986), pp. 87–96.

(e.g, return on investment) to make new technology decisions. So, we have to explore what "beyond faith" or "beyond love" is to understand how technological choices are made. Even when no new technology is chosen, this is a choice. The default option is then in force, driving many, many other decisions.

It has been argued in Chapter 6 that the context (e.g., history, mix of decision makers) can have a strong influence on the nature of the challenge and the process that unfolds for technology choice. For example, senior managers with manufacturing experience tend to mount more aggressive technology policies and adopt more advanced production technology in durable goods manufacturing. On the other hand, these same managers tend to favor more traditional investment criteria (e.g., labor savings) in innovation decision making. It was also shown how justification of new technology such as software, where little precedent exists in a firm or industry, tends to force the company to delay development of new systems well into the period after which the initial release of the technology is made. This greatly complicates both the justification and the evaluation of new technology ventures.

Understanding the context of the justification process is important. This is amply illustrated in a study by Stimpert and Duhaime.[23] The results of their study of a sample of Fortune 500 firms are summarized in Figure 12-3.

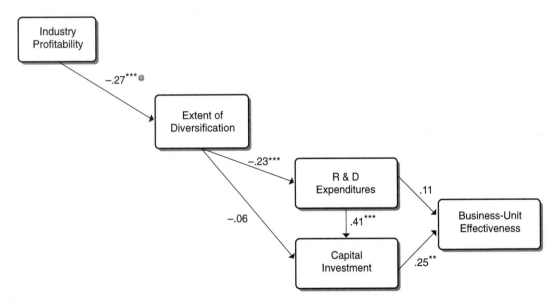

Figure 12-3 The Influence of Industrial Profitability, Diversification, R&D, and Capital on Business-unit Effectiveness

[a]Standardized estimates of the path coefficients are shown.

* $p < .05$

** $p < .01$

*** $p < .001$

Source: Stimpert and Duhaime, 1997, p. 573.

---

[23] J. L. Stimpert and I. M. Duhaime, "Seeing the Big Picture: The Influence of Industry, Diversification and Business Strategy on Performance," *Academy of Management Journal,* 40, no. 3 (June 1997), pp. 560–583.

The point of all of this is to see the justification process within its more typical context, rather than something that is an isolated decision-making event in the history of an organization. First, find capital investment near the bottom of the path diagram in Figure 12-3. Next, note that capital investment had a significant and direct path (empirical evidence of a possible causal impact) on business-unit effectiveness (path coefficient = .25). Not shocking, but something we would expect, so it increases our confidence in the other results of the analysis.

Next, look at the two path arrows coming into capital investment: R&D expenditures and extent of diversification. Of the two, only R&D expenditures were found to be significantly and directly related (path coefficient = .41). That is, as more is spent on R&D, more capital investment occurs in Fortune 500 firms. It makes sense. Most R&D is spent on new products, but to bring them to market often requires capital investment in new plant and equipment (see Chapters 4–6). However, note that R&D does not affect performance directly, which replicates Al Bean's work introduced in Chapter 2. The authors also found that industry context does make a difference. In Figure 12-3 this is shown by a negative path coefficient (–.27) between industry profitability and extent of diversification. In other words, as industry profitability wanes, it encourages diversification, which diminishes investment in R&D (path coefficient = –.23), most probably because it puts a strain on resources. It is not surprising, as observed earlier, that many companies create a "buffer" fund of cash held in reserve for radical new technology projects such as GE's launch of a new dishwasher in the 1980s.

What does this imply for the justification process? It is highly unlikely that a typical Fortune 500 firm will increase capital investment without upstream R&D commitments. These are all strategic decisions and are usually part of a technology strategy, which was covered in Chapter 4. But what about mature manufacturing, where R&D investments are difficult to justify? See the case of Shamrock Fastener Technologies in Box 12-2. Would you have taken this risk?

✳ Balance, Balance, Balance

Near the end of Chapter 7, the findings of a study by Montoya-Weiss and Calantone were introduced and summarized. To review, the authors were reported the results of a meta-analysis of the literature on new product success. They found that the most important predictor of commercialization performance was "customer perception of product advantage." The other factors, reordered by importance in predicting new product success, are reproduced in Table 12-3. It is not until well down this list that we come to a technical (R&D or engineering) predictor of success. After customer perception, protocol, proficiency in marketing, strategy, communications, etc., we come to the tenth predictor: proficiency in pretechnical activities. One might be tempted to conclude that marketing factors are more important than technical factors in predicting new product success from these meta-analysis findings. This would be a great mistake.

This article by Montoya-Weiss and Calatone was first brought to my attention by my colleague, Merle Crawford.[24] He had some interesting observations on this

---

[24] C. M. Crawford, "The Hidden Costs of Accelerated Product Development," *Journal of Product Innovation Management,* 9 (1992), pp. 188–199.

BOX 12-2

Shamrock's "Learning Factory"

Why would anyone want to invest in a high-technology plant for a commodity business? Ask Paul Morath, President of Shamrock Fastener Technologies, and he will tell you. First the results, answer: 1 ppm. That is, one-part-per-million quality failure levels—or virtually zero defects in supplied bolts and fasteners to the auto industry. Toyota's best supplier at the time was operating at 23 ppm. But can you make money doing this when you have to supply billions of fasteners a year?

On March 17, 1995, Shamrock opened its new $12 million plant in Sterling Heights, Michigan, jointly developed with Ring Screw Works, and several suppliers. This effort included National Machinery, which installed its first FX 64XL former, the first machine in its Formax line for fastener manufacturing at Shamrock's "Learning" factory, which they call a "research and production facility." Can-Eng also developed a new roller hearth mesh belt hardening furnace for the new plant to reduce damage to bolts during processing. It was quite a St. Patrick's Day.

The goal was simple, according to Morath. "We want to see why fasteners fail and why they work. Let's see why cylinder bolts used in aluminum blocks tend to bend in heat treating. Let's be able to reliably predict the results." Paul is often quoted as saying that this is literally the "nuts and bolts of the automobile industry," and he has made good on his promise to share what he has learned. He has opened his doors to everyone who is interested. The pay-off is that Shamrock now has to turn down business from its biggest boosters, Ford, GM, and DaimlerChrysler. However, Shamrock will supply the new Chrysler V-8 engine plant on Mack Avenue in Detroit, also rumored to be the "best in class." Birds of a feather…

Who visits the new plant? Dozens of Japanese and German firms come, but you can count on one hand the number of North American firms that have visited. More Koreans have seen the plant than Americans.

But why high technology in this business? Paul Morath says he always had a dream to build the perfect plant, and when National Machinery came to him and said the only way they could survive their foreign competition was to "leap-frog" the industry with a new, computer-controlled technology with a trial customer (beta site), he said yes. "Why shouldn't the North American auto producers have the best suppliers in the world? Why should equipment industries have to move offshore to survive or perish in the process?" That was the stake in the ground with the Shamrock flag on it, and the Big Three rallied around this plant.

What's next? Paul says: "We are out of capacity."

---

* SOURCES: *Fastener Industry News* (April 17, 1995); A. Wrigley, "Critical Times for Fastener Firms," *American Metal Market* (April 3, 1995), R. Sherefkin, "Fastener Company Opens New Plant," *Crain's Detroit Business* (March 13, 1998), "Shamrock Fastener Technologies Opens State-of-the-art Facility," *American Fastener Journal* (May/June 1995); P. Bielik and K. Van Sickle, "Tailor-made Quenchant Delivers," *Metal Heat Treating,* 3, no. 6 (November/December 1996), pp. 38–39; and personal communication with Paul Morath, President, Shamrock Fastener Technologies, April 1998.

$\mathcal{T}$ABLE 12-3   Significant Correlations of New Product Success

1. Customer perception of product advantage (.363)
2. Protocol (product and marketing requirements) (.341)
3. Proficiency in marketing activities (.337)
4. Strategy for the project (.324)
5. Communications (.305)
6. Organization groupings (.304)
7. Marketing synergy (.303)
8. Company resources (.297)
9. General operating environment (.293)
10. Proficiency in pretechnical activities (.288)
11. Proficiency in technical activities (.282)
12. Technical synergy (.272)
13. Financial/business analysis (.267)
14. Top management support (.260)
15. Market potential (.244)
16. Speed—cycle time (.177)

Absolute value of correlations averaged from M. Montoya-Weiss and R. Cantalone, "Determinants of New Product Performance: A Review and Meta-Analysis," *Journal of Product Innovation Management,* 11 (November 1994), pp. 397–417.

summary. First, when one does a meta-analysis of the new product commercialization literature, it will be dominated by marketing titles and journals—not engineering journals. Second, it may be that marketing factors are more important than engineering or technical factors because they *have* to be to balance the overwhelming importance of technical success, which must be achieved before it is feasible to go ahead with any type of serious new product launch. That is, there is a temporal order to causality in predicting new product success.

In fact, when one attempts to control for these issues in predicting new product success, as in the work of another colleague and friend, Bill Souder,[25] it turns out that the balance between "market pull" factors and "technology push" factors is the best single predictor of new product or new service success across a vast array of industries, economic regions of world, and throughout various epochs and stages of the product life cycle. In fact, it may be the single most robust predictor of new product success.

It takes three things to be successful with new products or services: balance, balance, and balance. When any one function or perspective dominates the new product development process over too long a time, it tends to lower new product success probability. This is simply too complex a process to be left up to the knowledge and philosophical view of one discipline. The core disciplines of

---

[25] W. E. Souder and J. D. Sherman, *Managing New Technology Development* (New York: McGraw-Hill, 1994).

R&D (including engineering), marketing, and operations are going to track with successful new product development throughout the life cycle, as illustrated in Toyota's approach to new product development summarized earlier in Figure 12-2. The other disciplines, such as accounting, purchasing, and information, all have critical roles to play in the process, but they come and go over the course of the life cycle rather than remaining fixed with the core group.

The term *disciplines* rather than *functions,* as in *cross-functional teams,* has been adopted here for a simple reason. Often the "function" of accounting is performed by people outside the accounting function, such as industrial engineering. Marketing work has to be done, but it can be done by a consultant.

Balance in the innovation process also allows for an important opportunity to be captured—capitalizing on everyone's creative potential in the organization and not just a few "designated" disciplines. This was mentioned earlier under the summary findings from the *Innovation Marathon:* You can't "wall off" the innovation process and expect it to be successful.

This applies outside of Silicon Valley, too. In our study of "nontraditional" innovation—that is, creativity on the job regardless of occupational category—Bob O'Keefe and I found that nearly every job category has something to offer to the innovation process, and it can be predicted, as well.[26] The scale we developed to measure innovation intentions has been reproduced many times in many textbooks, and we included it in Chapter 3 because it has become such a popular tool in predicting individual innovating success, regardless of occupation. How would you answer the question: Do you openly discuss how to get ahead with your boss?

Cultural Lag

William F. Ogburn originally proposed a theory of **cultural lag** in society: Technological and technical advances always precede the adaptations needed to adjust to them or use them effectively without harm.[27] This idea was applied to organizations by William M. Evan as the **organizational lag hypothesis**[28] and was expanded to two alternative models tested by Damanpour and Evan.[29] The two alternative models of organizational lag predict either technical system impact on the social system or mutual impacts. Administrative innovations were defined as those that affect the organization's social system.

The authors studied 85 public libraries, 40 technical innovations, and 27 administrative innovations and found the following:

1. Libraries adopt technical innovations (e.g., automated acquisition control systems) at a rate faster than administrative innovations (e.g., new structures).

[26] J. Ettlie and R. O'Keefe, "Innovative Attitudes, Intentions and Behaviors in Organizations," *Journal of Management Studies,* 19, no. 2 (April 1982), pp. 153–162.

[27] W. F. Ogburn, *Social Change* (New York: Viking, 1922).

[28] W. M. Evan, "Organizational Lag," *Human Organization,* 25 (1966), pp. 51–53.

[29] F. Damanpour and W. Evan, "Organizational Innovation and Performance: The Problem of Organizational Lag," *Administrative Science Quarterly,* 29 (1984), pp. 382–409.

2. Administrative and technical innovations have a higher correlation in high-performance organizations.

3. The greater the organizational lag in adoption of administrative innovations after technical innovations are in place, the lower the performance.

4. Adoption of administrative innovations tends to trigger the adoption of technical innovations more readily than the reverse.

These results are in clear agreement and are extended by applied research findings in manufacturing reported in-depth in Chapter 9 (e.g., Ettlie and Reza, 1994): Adoption of certain types of administrative innovations, coincident with new manufacturing process technologies, enhances loose coupling and integration in organizations. In particular, the integrating mechanisms of both the vertical hierarchy (general management linked with middle management linked with the rank and file), and internal disciplines and functions (R&D, engineering, design, and manufacturing) as well as context (i.e., suppliers and customers) significantly promote successful modernization of facilities (e.g, greater throughput, better utilization and cycle times, higher quality, and greater flexibility).

What is challenging about these results is that there is both theory and evidence to suggest that organizational cultures that can be leveraged for higher performance are *valuable* (enhance capabilities and learning), *rare,* and *difficult to imitate.*[30] There is evidence on the diffusion of organizational forms, practices, and structures. For example, in states in which civil service was not mandated during an initial period (1885–1904), larger cities with more immigrants, and more white- versus blue-collar workers, were more likely to adopt civil service.[31] But these institutional reforms, which had a built-in standard of conformity to practice, might be quite far removed from organizational or administrative innovations needed to change the culture of a company to capture value from a new technological innovation.

Reza studied the adoption of 29 resource recovery systems (RRSs, e.g., mass burn systems with heat recovery) implemented by local community governments (city, township, or regional boards) in the early 1980s. The sample covered Akron, two sites in Chicago, Duluth, Milwaukee, Nashville, Tacoma, and Wilmington, Deleware.[32] A summary of Reza's results follows:

1. Larger cities are more likely to have more knowledge about resource recovery systems (RRSs) and the alternative technologies to achieve recovery goals.

2. The participation of nonelected internal actors (e.g., appointed civil servants with a longer range view) at the early stages of the innovation process had a positive impact on the ultimate reliability, financial viability, and overall success of the RRS project (using expert panels of engineers to judge each case).

3. At the design stage of the project, the participation of external actors (e.g., private firms, federal government) promoted ultimate success.

---

[30] J. Barney, "Organizational Culture: Can It Be a Source of Sustained Competitive Advantage?" *Academy of Management Review* 11, no. 3 (1986), pp. 656–665.

[31] W. R. Scott, *Institutions and Organizations* (Thousand Oaks, Calif: Sage, 1995), p. 118.

[32] E. M. Reza, "Actors and Roles in Organizational Innovating Processes: Issues for the Recovery of Valuable Resources from Trash," unpublished Ph.D. dissertation, University of Michigan, Psychology, 1993.

4. Overall reliability of the RRS system is enhanced by greater local government control of the project during the development stage and if relatively simple and unsophisticated technologies are adopted.

These results in the public sector are consistent with both the anecdotal, case, and survey results in the private sector. Through benchmarking and other means, representatives of organizations are able to find inspiration both inside and outside their own context for change. This is not to say that technological change comes easily, nor to imply that every organization finds a way to meet the most challenging goals of global standards. Duplication of a successful culture seems quite unlikely, and, for most, undesirable to attempt, since circumstances vary. However, learning does take place, and technology can be transferred from one locale to another, even if it is essentially "reinvented" at the new site.

Globalization and Alliances

Of all the trends that seem established, globalization and alliance formation seem to be the most entrenched. Even if a firm does not do business overseas, the impact of business practices abroad will have increasingly more influence on the home front. In an open market environment, not only will competitive pressure be felt directly through market entry and global purchasing by customers, there is an indirect pressure on all participants within and, especially between, industries (e.g., suppliers to their customers and their suppliers, in turn) to upgrade procedures and meet global standards.

Findings from two, related streams of applied research on technology and alliances converge on one important saw: Relationships between partners evolve over time. What works at the beginning of a technology alliance will not be sufficient to make it work later in the life cycle. Two examples illustrate this point.

U.S.–Japanese Manufacturing Joint Ventures.

Chapter 5 on R&D management described the study by Ettlie and Swan that analyzed more than 1,200 cases from the Japan Economic Institute of direct investment by the Japanese in U.S. manufacturing. There has been a trend toward more sophistication and complexity in governance structures for managing partnerships in landed transplants alliances in the United States. In particular, firms have gone beyond just joint ventures and wholly owned subsidiaries, exploiting partial equity relationships more recently in Japanese direct investment cases. Partial ownership by Japanese parents was significantly more likely in high-tech manufacturing partnerships with U.S. companies. Joint ventures were more typical in politically sensitive industries (such as steel and autos), and when the Japanese firm had experience with the product at home.

Earlier, we also reported on four in-depth case studies of U.S.–Japanese manufacturing alliances.[33] These four case studies are summarized in Table 12-4. Some

---

[33] J. Ettlie and P. Swan, "U.S.–Japanese Manufacturing Joint Ventures and Equity Relationships," in J. Liker, J. Ettlie, and J. Campbell (eds.), *Engineered in Japan* (New York: Oxford, 1995), pp. 278–308.

*T*ABLE 12-4   Summary of Joint-Venture Case Studies

	Company L	Company W	Company D	Company C
Industry	Telecommunications	Auto supply	Auto supply	TV tube glass
Technology	High-tech (4%)	Low-tech (2.4%)	Low-tech (0.5%)	High-tech (4%)
Ownership	51–49%	50–50%	60–40%	50–50%
Structure	Hybrid	Segregated	Segregated	Segregated
Management	U.S. partner	U.S. partner	U.S. partner	U.S. partner
Contributions	U.S. product	U.S. marketing	U.S. process	Shared technology
Motive	Market/patent	Market/alliance partnership	License	Market/technology
Technology performance	Best in class	Good	Good, but…	OK
Technology transfer	Excellent	Little	None	Good
Production performance	Good	Good (CpK > 1.5)	OK, downsized	OK, downsized
Culture	Port in a storm; accommodation	Japanese persistence	Japan versus U.S. customer: expectation, trust	Rapid change
Lesson learned	Hybrid structure works	Technological specifications/ overdesign	U.S. negotiators weak	Technology not an end
Survival of joint venture	?	?	In jeopardy	OK

Industry R&D intensity (R&D expenses as a percentage of sales) and other factors.

<small>SOURCE: J. Ettlie and P. Swan, "U.S.-Japanese Manufacturing Joint Ventures and Equity Relationships," in J. Liker, J. Ettlie, and J. Campbell (eds.), *Engineered in Japan* (New York: Oxford, 1995), pp. 278–308.</small>

consistent trends can be noted in these four cases, which illustrate and expand on the results of the secondary analysis of the large database of direct investments. All four cases seem to follow an established stereotype pattern in U.S.–Japanese manufacturing joint ventures: the Japanese partner successfully brings production know-how to the partnership, and the U.S. company brings marketing and/or product technology to the partnership.

Achieving profitability in the venture was more challenging, but the Japanese partner also tends to stick with the venture much longer than a U.S. company would in the same circumstances. There seem to be clear differences between high-tech and low-tech manufacturing alliances: Low-tech companies seem more difficult to manage, and the motives for formation of the venture are usually quite different.

Finally, an integrated organization structure seems to be the successful way to structure these alliances—with no "shadow" Japanese organization structure in place. Company L (Table 12-4) is a good example. Alternative levels of the firm are occupied by American and Japanese managers, which rotate in these key positions from the home organization and within the hierarchy. For example, the vice president of R&D (American) replaced a Japanese president after 5 years, and a Japanese manager took his vacant spot.

SEMATECH

The case of SEMATECH was also introduced earlier to illustrate and collaborate R&D. SEMATECH is short for the Semiconductor Manufacturing Technology Consortium, established in 1987, and is just one of many such technology consortia in the United States, Japan, and Europe.[34] SEMATECH has been declared very successful.[35]

First and perhaps foremost, it can be concluded that SEMATECH and most likely other consortia evolve rather substantially after their founding. In this case, SEMATECH shifted from "horizontal" research cooperation to "vertical" collaboration between members—major users of semiconductor process equipment and materials,[36] very much like an industry association. working on generic technology. Second, learning to focus on short-term technology development leading to this sustaining of the "generic" approach works for the majority of members. Third, maintaining a centralized structure (similar to NCMS), which seems to keep the research agenda more responsive, is advised. Fourth, horizontal collaboration may be difficult in industries where product innovation depends on process innovation.

There may be clear differences between industries that require different models of collaborative R&D, but that the direct and persistent involvement of member companies is critical to the success of any such alliance. When small firm members are strained in this regard, they have the additional problem of collaboration to deal with. However, in the case of SEMATECH, the focus on a particular industry weakness, rather than a broad remaking of an industry, appears to have worked.

CORPORATE TECHNOLOGY SHARING

People are nearly always amazed when they find out that large company personnel learn more from the newspapers about their own corporate moves than from internal sources. And outsiders often know more about overall operations of large companies than middle managers and technical staff. Applying this axiom to the current topic, the problem of rationalization of and capitalization upon large, decentralized corporate technology resources is an issue.

Take the following case of Hewlett Packard.[37] The company had used its strength of entrepreneurial divisions to develop unique technological solutions, not limited by corporate standards. But in the 1970s, this eventually led to the overlap of product lines: "One division was developing a 'sweeping synthesizer,' while another was pushing to release a 'synthesized sweeper,'" even though the instruments were virtually identical. Further difficulty arose because the marketplace began to demand integrated systems."[38]

Al Rubenstein has compiled a comprehensive list of mechanisms that have been used for coordinating divisional R&D work, and this summary is reproduced in

---

[34] P. Grindley, D. C. Mowery, and B. Silverman, "SEMATECH and Collaborative Research: Lessons in the Design of High Technology Consortia," *Journal of Public Analysis and Management,* 13, no. 4 (1994), pp. 723–758.

[35] *New York Times,* Thursday, October 6, 1994.

[36] Grindley, et al., p. 724.

[37] K. E. Miller and D. A. Garvin, "Hewlett-Packard: Corporate, Group and Divisional Manufacturing (A)," President and Fellows of Harvard College, 1991.

[38] Ibid., p. 2.

Table 12-5.[39] There are at least 19 coordinating mechanisms—such as regular meetings of divisional R&D managers (number 3 in Table 12-5)—I add at least one more popular choice to this list: the use of *corporate technology centers* available to all and funded in great part by the divisions. Dow Chemical, IBM, Motorola, and many other companies use this approach to integrate and synergize the technical resources of the decentralized firm.

General Motors Corporation uses centralized teams of experts in technical areas such as electrical systems to accomplish this task of corporate technology integration. These teams provide "best practices and parts to new vehicles," since they do more car programs than any other automotive manufacturer.[40] Multiple models are emerging from common platforms using this strategy. But unlike the 1980s, these models are significantly different, often targeted for different markets (U.S. and Europe).

Rockwell International attempts to integrate technology with technical advisory councils, overseen by a technical advisory board. The structure of this approach in the early 1990s is reproduced in Figure 12-4. One unique aspect of this approach is

$\mathcal{T}$ABLE 12-5   Technology Networking Mechanisms

1. Technical gatekeepers or key communicators
2. Technical committees on specific topics or fields
3. Regular meetings of divisional R&D managers
4. R&D or technical advisory, coordinating, or steering committees
5. Formal/informal liaison/linkage agents between labs
6. Technical seminars
7. Exchange of "skill inventory" data
8. Cross-divisional project teams
9. Open across-division transfers and promotion opportunities for R&D people
10. Strong corporate R&D coordination staff to act as liaison agents
11. Systematic and effective (accessible, legible, timely, usable report exchange program)
12. Temporary cross-divisional transfers (for projects, training, renewal, communication)
13. Corporate R&D staff reviews and audits of divisional projects, programs, outputs, and personnel
14. Joint funding of projects and programs by two or more divisions
15. Strong incentives (positive and negative) for division managers to cooperate in R&D innovation area
16. Cross-divisional design reviews—"do unto others"
17. Joint idea generation efforts
18. Coordination of R&D technology segments of divisional long-range or strategic plans
19. Mutual program reviews
20. Technology centers—(e.g., Dow Chemical, IBM)—added by Ettlie (1998).

Adapted from A. Rubenstein, *Managing Technology in the Decentralized Firm* (New York: John Wiley & Sons, 1989), p. 142.

---

[39] A. H. Rubenstein, *Managing Technology in the Decentralized Firm* (New York: John Wiley & Sons, 1989), p. 142.

[40] C. Child, "GM to Cut Development Time by a Year," *Automotive News* (March 4, 1996), p. 24N.

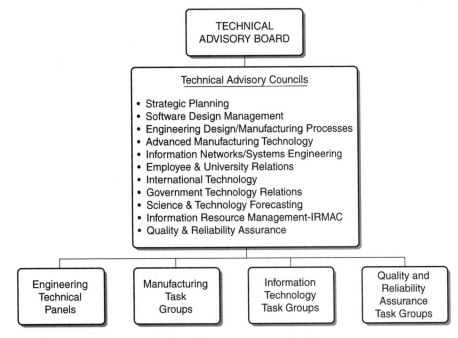

Figure 12-4 Rockwell International Technology Integration (circa: 1990)
SOURCE: Yankee Group Presentation, circa 1990, Wheeling, Illinois.

an effort in each important technology-sharing project or ongoing program to involve the divisional manager's office directly. This is one of the key issues that must be resolved in the tug-of-war between corporate integration aims and divisional goals for profitability.

Of all the technology sharing mechanisms, the potential for number 15 (incentives to divisional managers) is the greatest because senior managers control significant resources, and effective technology sharing relies on balancing short- and long-term resources. How can you tell which divisional managers are the best candidates to manage effective technology sharing? Ask the question: How does the manager manage direct technical resources (e.g., manufacturing engineering) versus indirect technical resources (e.g., advanced manufacturing engineers)? If they don't know the difference, they are not good candidates.[41]

THE INNOVATION THAT CHANGED THE WORLD

According to Womack, Jones, and Roos, *The Machine that Changed the World*[42] was the automobile. According to Robert Buderi, *The Invention that Changed the*

---

[41] A. H. Rubenstein, Personal Communication, 1990.

[42] New York, HarperCollins Publishers, 1991.

World[43] was radar, because this device was invented and perfected by the Western Allies and won World War II (see Box 12-3).

Others could argue, equally well, that the airplane is the innovation that changed the world. No, you say, it's not the airplane, it's the computer. No, the transistor came first, then the integrated circuit. My father might argue that it was the television that changed the world. And television is about to change again, this time to a high-definition format in the United States in 2006, making hundreds of millions of sets obsolete.[44]

The point is that innovations, especially major breakthroughs, have changed the world and will continue to change the world almost overnight and are rarely based on one person's actions. Moreover, gradual changes, which sometimes go unnoticed, are caused by incremental technological change. These gradual improve-

---

BOX 12-3

The History of Radar

In his new book, *The Invention that Changed the World,* Robert Buderi argues that the atom bomb ended the war but radar won it. One theme of the book: Necessity is the mother of invention. That is, confronted with problems that needed to be solved, scientists like Robert R. Everett invented solutions. The lesson: Invention may be for its own sake but innovations are not—they must have a payoff in an application.

The accelerating measure–countermeasure sequence of modern warfare led to practical radar, radar jamming and then radar jamming as an offensive weapon. Radar led to other breakthroughs—by accident. Attempting to detect a tower at six miles in 1944, scientists were foiled by high humidity, so they tuned the natural frequency of water vapor, which eventually led to the development of the microwave oven. This is why microwaves were originally called "radar" ranges when they appeared in lunch rooms in the 1960s.

Radar was not a single invention, but a system of devices that created an innovation that the military had to be convinced to use. Sound familiar? (see Gunfire at Sea in Chapter 1.) Many people have read or seen the story of how primitive radar on Hawaii detected approaching aircraft in the wee hours of December 7, 1941. Of course, the warning was never taken seriously or communicated effectively in time to make any difference before Pearl Harbor was bombed (see Gordon W. Prange, *At Dawn We Slept,* New York, McGraw-Hill Book Company, 1981).

The Opana Mobile Radar Station was located on the northern tip of Oahu at 230 feet above sea level near Kahuku Point. At 0400 on December 7, 1941, Privates Joseph L. Lockard and George E. Elliot went on duty, and just as they were about to shut down the unit as normally scheduled under then in force procedures, "the oscilloscope picked up an image so peculiar that Lockard thought something was wrong with the set, but a quick check proved otherwise" (*At Dawn We Slept,* p. 500). Elliot estimated the flight to be more than fifty planes. During the eight minutes it took to report the sighting to the information center, the blip moved 20 to 25 miles nearer Oahu.

---

[43] New York, Simon and Schuster, 1997.

[44] J. Brinkely, "Should You Roll Out the Welcome Mat for HDTV?" *The New York Times* (April 27, 1997), p. F9.

ments often add up to be more significant over time than the original break-through.

The approach in this book to this dilemma has been simply: "If you can't beat 'em, join 'em." A seminal study relevant to this point appeared more than 30 years ago.[45] Most people, including professionals in the field of technology management, are not aware of it, however. The authors' conclusions about attitudes toward automation and occupational group can be summarized as follows:

1. Engineers and designers reported favorable attitudes toward automation.

2. Workers reported unfavorable attitudes toward automation.

3. Managers were neutral as a group in their attitude toward automation.

The pursuit officer on duty, Lieutenant Kermit Tyler, had been assigned to the post only four days earlier "to assist the Controller in ordering planes to intercept enemy planes…" (p. 500). Neither the controller nor the aircraft identification officer was on hand. Tyler thought the blip was B-17s flying in from the mainland—and in fact a flight was headed in from California—because Hawaiian music was being played all night, which was typically done when a friendly bomber flight was due. This same music was a beacon for the Japanese carrier pilots.

Elliot and Lockard kept on observing until 0739 when distortion from a back wave from the mountains caused the blips to be lost 20 miles out. Lockard had forgotten to tell Tyler that the flight probably contained more than fifty planes. The sighting wasn't even reported later in the day, which would have helped track the Japanese aircraft carriers. In any event, Tyler never telephoned Major Kenneth P. Bergquist, operations officer of the Fourteenth Pursuit Wing, and it is not clear at that late moment if it would have made any practical difference (*At Dawn We Slept,* p. 501).

The investigation following the destruction of the U.S. fleet found that General Short operated coastal air watch and radar installations (5 mobile and 3 permanent sites were planned, but not completed in December 1941) only periodically for "training" purposes, and never took the threat of air attack seriously. It is difficult for radar to work, in any stage of technological development, when it is not turned on. A radar expert testified that "At no time before December 7, 1941, did this Command furnish either the authority or impetus badly needed to get the work or organization properly started" (*At Dawn We Slept,* p. 730).

The British, on the other hand, were able to develop a system to use RDF (radio direction finding), as Radar was known in the early days there. Radar stations were know as CH, since they were the first stations in the "Chain, Home" (see Colin Latham, and Anne Stobbs, *Radar: A Wartime Miracle,* Alan Sutton, London, Publishing Limited, 1995, p. 9).

SOURCE: R. Buderi, *The Invention that Changed the World: How a Small Group of Radar Pioneers Won the Second World War and Launched a Technological Revolution* (New York: Simon & Schuster, 1997), reviewed by M. L. Wald, "Jam Sessions: Forget Oppenheimer and Teller; Radar Researchers at M.I.T., the author says, won World War II," *New York Times Book Review* (June 22, 1997), p. 31. Thanks to Barbara Bryant.

---

[45] R. A. Hoppe and E. J. Berv, "Measurement of Attitudes Towards Automation," *Personnel Psychology,* 20, no. 1 (Spring 1967), pp. 65–70.

Hoppe and Berv interpreted this last finding by explaining that automation may be perceived as both rewarding and threatening to management. One could also argue that the closer one is, occupationally or organizationally, to the development of new technology or products and services that embody new technology, the more one's livelihood depends on its success, and, therefore, the more favorable the attitude. But even this explanation is too simple because innovations are not always successful. And when innovations are in their nascent stage, their failure rate is even higher.

Part of the answer lies in the nature of things. For some people, new technology, and novelty generally, is intrinsically valuable, and the learning process associated with it doesn't always follow predictable patterns—or at least not what common sense would dictate. Andy Van De Ven,[46] in a presentation at a professional conference, reported the results of what could be one of the most intensive microstudies of the innovation process leading up to the development of the cochlear implant used to enhance hearing in deaf or partially deaf people. When Andy tracked the development process, microevent by event for individuals working on the project, he found an amazing thing. When people encountered failure, they continued trying the same approach, over and over and over again. Further, they were not always encouraged in a *Eureka* sense by an "I've done it" success at this microevent level. It reminds one of the stories about Thomas Edison, who was said to have stayed in his workshop, sometimes going for long periods without eating or sleeping, or sleeping on the bench. The actual creation process is what drives people beyond common sense. The innovation process is a bona fide phenomenon. But Edison didn't do it alone—it was his leadership, primarily by example, that made the difference.

*L*EADERSHIP AND THE INNOVATION PROCESS

In the end, leadership makes the crucial difference in the innovation process, because the process is not a preprogrammed activity. Even when you have technology "on the shelf" you can't just pull it down and use it. As indicated in Chapter 4, there is a fair amount of accumulated evidence to confirm the idea that management attitudes toward innovation and change are significantly correlated with policies and outcomes.[47] Pro-change managers are likely to launch innova-

---

[46] A. Van De Ven, H. L. Angle, and M. S. Poole (eds.), *Research on the Management of Innovation* (New York: Harper & Row, 1989).

[47] J. Hage and R. Dewar, "Elite Values versus Organizational Structure in Predicting Innovation," *Administrative Science Quarterly,* 18 (1973), pp. 279–290; D. Miller, M.F.R. Kets de Vries and J. Toulouse, "Top Executive Locus of Control and its Relationship to Strategy-making Structure and Environment," *Academy of Management Journal,* 25, no. 2 (1982), pp. 237–253; and S. G. Scott, and R. A. Bruce, "Determinants of Innovative Behavior: A Path Model of Individual Innovation in the Workplace," *Academy of Management Journal,* 37, no. 3 (June 1994), pp. 580–607 found that leadership, managerial role expectations, career state, and problem-solving style are significantly related to individual innovative behavior, which, in turn, has a positive impact on the supervisor-subordinate relationship.

tive strategies and follow through on their implementation. Strategic and financial support of R&D is part of the necessary action required to make this happen, even in mature industries.[48] Most innovation is incremental, and even high-technology firms make small changes with their breakthroughs. When firms diversify into less mature industries, managerial attitudes toward change become more important in predicting new product introduction and the adoption of radical processing technology.[49]

Movement of senior managers across organizational boundaries is a trigger for change and is significantly correlated with the adoption of radical process technology.[50] Although these transitions are usually at the vice president level or higher in a company and usually come as a result of hiring an outsider, there are exceptions to the common wisdom that only outsiders can incite radical change in a firm. The case of Leonard Hadley, CEO of Maytag, which was summarized in Chapter 4, illustrates this point very well. Known for conservative management positions, he started his regeneration of the company by making European operations profitable and selling them. Then he pinned his hopes on the Maytag Neptune, an expensive front-loader, and the gamble paid off. The pattern established at Maytag, although on the surface quite surprising, is typical of other leadership stories in the innovation literature. Even the railroad industry is finally experimenting with navigation and control systems linked to satellites to eliminate accidents and increase efficiency. In this case, the conservative, merger-prone railroad industry pooled resources to spread the risks of adopting this new control system for operations.[51] Strategic alliances for innovation require general management leadership[52] in most cases because they commit the organization on a long-term basis and expose the core technology, at least in some instances, to outside influence and tampering, as well as potential leaks.

Many other firms and industries that once were noted for change and lost it, came back with new change strategies as the result of leadership. Bank of America is another case covered in Chapter 4. Only leadership can explain these kind of changes. Leaders initiate with vision and follow-up with policies and structures and practices to sustain change.[53] Even McDonald's Corporation is changing its time-

---

[48] N. Myhrvold, "What's the Return on Research?" *Fortune,* 136, no. 11 (December 8, 1997), p. 88.

[49] J. E. Ettlie, "A Note on the Relationship Between Managerial Change Values, Innovative Intentions, and Innovative Technology Outcomes in Food Sector Firms," *R&D Management,* 13, no. 4 (1983), pp. 231–244. At the very minimum, support for innovation moderates the relationship between leadership style and unit performance: J. M. Howell, and B. J. Avolio, "Transformational Leadership, Transactional Leadership, Locus of Control, and Support for Innovation: Key Predictors of Consolidated-Business-Unit Performance," *Journal of Applied Psychology,* 78, no. 6 (December 1993), pp. 891–902.

[50] J.E. Ettlie, "Manpower Flows and the Innovation Process," *Management Science,* 26, no. 11 (November 1980), pp. 1086–1095; J.E. Ettlie, "The Impact of Interorganizational Manpower Flows on the Innovation Process," *Management Science,* 31, no. 9 (September 1985), pp. 1055–1071.

[51] W. M. Carley, "Trainspotting: To Avoid Collisions, Some Railroads Test Satellite Positioning," *Wall Street Journal* (June 29, 1998), pp. A1, A6.

[52] Richard F. Celeste, "Strategic Alliances of Innovation: Emerging Models of Technology-based Twenty-first Century Economic Development," *Economic Development Review,* 14, no. 1 (Winter 1996), pp. 4–8.

[53] R. Quinn, *Beyond Rational Management,* 1988. Also: M. Verespej, "Lead, Don't Manage," *Industry Week,* 245, no. 5 (March 4, 1996), pp. 55–60.

honored and proven system of food production. The new "Made for You," kitchen set-up promises to be a significant change in McDonald's philosophy.[54]

Divestiture is also part of the strategic mosaic in technology leadership. For example, The Minnesota Mining and Manufacturing Company (3M) recently spun off its data storage and imaging businesses to operate at the pace of the digital storage industry.[55] 3M is known for its product innovation (see Chapter 7 and the case of the ultrasound sensor redesign). But 3M is divesting a unit competing in a fast paced industry and attempting to allow the company to compete with the autonomy it needs to be agile.

Leadership has been and will continue to be the single most important factor in strategy and innovation management. It is this nature of the innovation process that makes it so fascinating and challenges any leader, including future leaders. It often draws on the laws of nature, but has a life and logic of its own. Pursue it and you, too, will find out how this process defies the same laws of nature it emulates. Change leads to more change, and it is very difficult to predict the ultimate outcome. This technological safari can be frightening, at times, but if you go well equipped, you will find the journey rewarding in the most unexpected ways.

HE FUTURE

Those who are familiar with forecasting, and especially technological forecasting (see Chapter 4), know that most predictions are based on established trends. Revisiting a few of these "curves" is appropriate at this time, but first a few framing comments are in order. Technology tends to be specific to a discipline, industry, or economic sector. Few technologies, such as information systems, transcend these boundaries. Trends interact, and one may lead to another. And sometimes, reasonable predictions can be made based on a good understanding of what the real needs of a society are or will be (e.g., preservation of the natural environment).

For example, the Delphi forecasts done by the Office for the Study of Automotive Transportation (OSAT)[56] may or may not apply to all of durable goods manufacturing, manufacturing in general, and the private sector as a whole. Members of OSAT have made at least two predictions for the auto industry based on well-established trends. First, much of the technological innovation in the car and truck industry has recently been, and will continue to be, in electronics, computer, and telecommunications technology. In some cases, developments in these three areas are in the process of fusion[57] into single technological innovations, such as navigation and safety systems, that will begin to appear in cars.

---

[54] Richard Gibson, "McDonald's to Take Record Charge to Cover Office, Kitchen Changes," *Wall Street Journal* (July 15, 1998), B4.

[55] M. Ferelli, "3M Data Storage Spin-Off: Something Old, Something New," *Computer Technology Review,* 15, no. 12 (December 1995), p. 38. For more information on 3M and innovation see R. A. Mitsch, "R&D at 3M; Continuing to Play a Big Role," *Research-Technology Management,* 35 (September/October 1992), pp. 22–26.

[56] OSAT is part of the University of Michigan Transportation Research Institute (UMTRI) in Ann Arbor, Michigan, and specializes in contract research, primarily on and for the first tier suppliers to the auto industry.

[57] F. Kodama, "Technology Fusion and the New R&D," *Harvard Business Review,* 70, no. 4 (July/August 1992), pp. 70–78. Also see V. Chiesa and R. Manzini, "Profiting from the Virtual Organization of Technological Innovation: Suggestions from an Empirical Study," *International Journal of Technology Management,* 15, no. 1,2 (1998), pp. 109–123.

The second established trend in the auto industry is a consequence of the aging work force. Baby boomers are retiring, and they are not being replaced in manufacturing plants. Therefore, manufacturing technology is likely to get a demand boost from this industry during the next decade. There is a shortage generally of information science and system technologists, as well as engineers and PhDs in the computer-related disciplines. Business and engineering schools cannot graduate enough people with information system baccalaureate degrees.[58] At one point, SAP was advertising (and may still be) for 5,000 openings in its organization worldwide, in part to meet the demand for ERP (enterprise resource planning) systems (see Chapter 9). More MOT (management of technology) and EM (engineering management) programs are coming on line, but demand still exceeds supply.[59] We continue to find out more about what makes engineering and technical management unique, and not for everyone.[60]

These trends suggest that across many industries, *there is likely to be a growing tension between the various technology cores of organizations.* This tension results from the needed resource allocations to certain core technologies, such as new product and service technologies; operations technologies, such as those in manufacturing, and information technologies. It is not clear how managers of the future will resolve this tension, but it appears to be a real challenge, already being faced by many organizations. Will the technology trajectories of these various cores be mutually reinforcing, or will coordination and resource allocation be difficult? At this point, it is not clear.

Increasing use of *alliances* and *globalization* are two established trends that have been discussed several times throughout this text. Both trends have important implications for technology managers because the diversity of relationships is increasing rapidly. There will be continuing challenges to capture benefits and avoid the cost—or "reverse technology transfer penalties"—from working with representatives of other companies, universities,[61] and government or not-for-profit organizations. For example, in the area of pollution prevention, companies and environmental groups have already started to work together. Most companies do not have experience in managing these relationships, but this know-how is difficult to imitate and is therefore a competitive advantage.

Language and cultural barriers still prevent convergence to one, homogeneous, institutional form of technology management. Therefore, there is a need for technically trained people to acquire the language and understanding of other cultures. It will not be long before language requirements, including technical language fluency and experience, will not be optional, but a requirement for everyone. At the Tauber Manufacturing Institute (TMI) at the University of Michi-

---

[58] "The Student Population Boom," *Computerworld,* 32, no. 42 (October 19, 1998), pp. 104–105; M. K. Badawy, "Technology Management Education: Alternative Models," *California Management Review,* 40, no. 4 (Summer 1998), pp. 94–116.

[59] L. Richards, "President's Corner," *Engineering Management Journal,* 10, no. 4 (December 1998), pp. 3–4.

[60] D. Johnson and A. Sargeant, "Motives for Transition: An Exploratory Study of Engineering Managers," *Human Resource Management Journal,* 8, no. 3 (1998), pp. 41–53.

[61] For example: D. Roessner, C. P. Ailes, I. Feller, and L. Parker, "How Industry Benefits from NSF's Engineering Research Centers," *Research-Technology Management,* 41, no. 5 (September/October 1998), pp. 40–44.

gan, for example, one combined-degree program includes language and global internship requirements.

In some industries, the technological limits of current systems are in sight, and the economic limits of these technology curves are rapidly approaching. To build a fabrication facility in this industry now costs well over $1 billion. The computer chip industry finds itself in this situation, rapidly approaching the physical limits of miniaturization, and so a technological discontinuity is predicted. Biological computer chips are one alternative avenue. Energy is another area in which the "need" predicts a breakthrough possibility. But when and how this will come is only a guess.

Many chronic, unresolved problems in society could be assisted by technology. The question is whether this will happen, and when. Cures for cancer, AIDS, mental illness, and so on appear as topics in the newspaper almost daily. But the more mundane issues that afflict "normal" people do not get this type of attention. For example, most manufacturing facilities are located in remote, sparsely populated areas.[62] For people who crave the excitement and culture of the city, this is banishment to the hinterlands. But it doesn't have to be so. With new telecommunications—especially distance education, computer, and transportation technologies—this isolation can be removed. There are also shift work issues, quality of work life challenges, work-life conflicts, and a new Generation X in the work force.[63]

Regardless of which technology management arena you find yourself in, the key to the future is understanding that not all forecasts are going to be accurate and that some events will not be forecasted at all. Being able to capitalize on the unexpected with a learning organization requires technological and organizational innovations. When Lance Dixon tried bringing suppliers directly into Bose, Corp., for the first time to promote integration with a new organizational relationship, this was breakthrough thinking of the kind that will be essential to future survival.[64] Co-production, generalized up and down stream in the innovation life cycle is coming.[65] R&D is gradually globalizing, so new strategies and structures will be needed.[66] Companies already have active "beyond compliance" programs to protect the natural environment.[67] Organizational issues still loom as significant challenges in new product development teams.[68] Embedded in all of these examples is the persistent issue of how to simultaneously manage multiple innovation streams.

---

[62] For example, in the recent announcement of plant closings, Levi Strauss said the plants that would be in the next round of suspension were located in Harlingen and Wichita Falls, Texas; Mountain City, Tenn.; Valdosta, Ga.; Morrilton, Ark.; Warsaw, Va; Murphy, N.C.; and Cornwall, Ontario. See R.Quick, "Levi Strauss to Close Half of Its Plants in North America, Slashing 5,900 Jobs," *Wall Street Journal* (February 23, 1999), p. A6.

[63] C. Manolis, A. Levin, and R. Dahlsrtrom, "A Generation X Scale: Creation and Validation" *Educational & Psychological Measurement,* 57, No. 4 (1997), pp. 666–684.

[64] See one of Mr. Dixon's latest applications of this concept in L. Dixon, "JIT II: Ultimate Customer—Supplier Partnership," *Hospital Materiel Management Quarterly,* 20, no. 3. (February 1999), pp. 14–20.

[65] N. A. Assimakopoulos, "Systemic Industrial Management of HW/SW Codesign," *Journal of High Technology Management Research,* 9, no. 2 (Fall 1998), pp. 271–284.

[66] R. Pearce and M. Papanastassiou, "Overseas R&D and the Strategic Evolution of MNEs: Evidence from Laboratories in the UK," *Research Policy,* 28, no. 1 (January 1999), pp. 23–41.

[67] N. Chase, "Beyond Compliance," *Quality,* 37, no. 12 (December 1998), pp. 62–66.

[68] E. Miller, "Resolving Organizational Conflicts," *Computer-aided Engineering,* 17, no. 9 (September 1998), p. 94.

UMMARY _____

What we know about the innovation process is summarized in this chapter under seven headings. First, the persistent organizing mechanism for knowledge in this field is the life-cycle metaphor. How we effectively manage the innovation process very much depends on how far the product-service-process system has progressed in its life cycle.

Second, technologies vary in the degree to which they depart from existing practice and method. Only a small fraction of all new products introduced every year are actually the first of their kind, never seen by the world before. Again, the way we effectively manage a radical new technology, as opposed to an incremental change in technology, are different. For example, lead users or customers are often required for a truly novel product or service launch, and change in general management is often required before an organization will entertain adoption of a new process technology, like a new information system.

Third, new products or services and the operations required to delivered them should be distinguished for their differences. Companies typically invest most of their R&D on the former, and purchase the latter. More challenging is the idea that although they are different, product and process innovation are typically "joined at the hip." That is, innovation is a system, and it is nearly impossible to change one part of a system and not affect the other.

Fourth, economic justification for new technology is more than just a necessary evil, it is required to understand the innovation process in any given setting. Organizations have historically favored simple as opposed to complex justification schemes, and only rarely audit results directly, favoring overall performance enhancement measures instead.

Fifth, the favored competitive strategy of our era, new product development, requires functional balance throughout the technology life cycle. Initially, R&D and marketing are the key functions needed to balance technical capability with customer needs. Later, but not much after the initial stage of a project, operations involvement is essential. Other functions (e.g., finance, human resources and external partners) are also important, but not as critical as the first three disciplines.

Sixth, understanding the concept of cultural lag helps frame the approach to managing transitions with matching of technological and organizational innovations in organizations. Often, the creativity required for launching a new technology with the appropriate strategy and structure is just as important as the original invention. When technology and organization work together, remarkable performance enhancement is within reach.

Seventh, the two inexorable trends of our times are alliances and globalization. These trends are part of the contingent context of innovating today. Emerging markets, scarce resources, and technology trajectories require global strategies and partnerships. No organization can create all of the technology it needs to survive and prosper.

The common theme binding all of these general conclusions is that *leadership* is the key to managing technological change. Without vision, understanding, empathy, and demonstration of new behaviors needed to assimilate innovation, success will be elusive. The fact that so few, often otherwise well-managed, firms struggle with corporate technology-sharing issues aptly illustrates this point. *The spark of inventive genius is not enough. To bring a technology to fruition requires a delivery system that can only be designed with purpose, managed with care, and led with wisdom.*

DISCUSSION QUESTIONS

Reread Box 12-1: Innovation in the Food Industry, and the section on radical versus incremental innovation.

1. How does the innovation process differ in a mature versus a new industry? What are the implications of these differences for managing the innovation process?
2. As an executive of Kellogg, how would you proceed with guiding the new technical center in Battle Creek, Michigan?
3. As an executive at Campbell Soup, what might your contingency plan be in a comprehensive technology strategy, should the "gray cuisine" approach fail or be successful for just a few years?

Read Case 12-1, "Is VW's New Plant Lean or Just Mean?"

4. How does Mr. Lopez's plan for a new assembly plant in Brazil differ from current car or truck assembly plants? Is this a radical ("third Industrial resolution") proposal?
5. What are the pros and cons of this type of plant?
6. What is your prediction of the outcome of this experiment? (Support your prediction.)

What's next? The third case for consideration and discussion is a case *you* write. This could be one of two types.

1. The first alternative is to conjure up an "ideal" organization that you would like to work for in the *future*. Do some stretch thinking. What is it about the current workplace in your country that ought to change? What innovations are needed to make this happen? Are there any organizations that currently approach this ideal?
2. The second part of this exercise is to consider becoming more directly involved in the activities of the professional associations that have groups devoted to the advancement of the state of the art of technology management. See the Academy of Management (TIM, the Technology and Innovation Management college http://www.aom.pace.edu/ email the Academy: AOM@academy.pace.edu), INFORMS (Institute for Operations Research and the Management Sciences), http://www.informs.org/) and the International Association for the Management of Technology (IAMOT: http://www.iamot.org/mot-conferences.html).

CASE 12-1

Is VW's New Plant Lean, or Just Mean?

RESENDE, Brazil—At first glance, the work force at Volkswagen's truck and bus factory here seems like any other, clad in unremarkable gray uniforms. But look at the pockets, and you will see the key to what Volkswagen executives call the factory of the future. The names stitched there are Rockwell, Cummins, Remon and MWM. What are conspicuously scarce are Volkswagen workers.

In this new factory some 100 miles northwest of Rio de Janeiro. Volkswagen employs a mere 200 of the 1,000 workers, those responsible only for overall quality control, marketing, and research and design. The assembly work—from counting spark plugs to bolting down engines—is left to suppliers.

This is the "dream factory" that José Ignacio López de Arriortua has long promised would revolutionize auto manufacturing Mr. López, Volkswagen's charismatic, controversial head of purchasing, quit General Motors in 1993 because that auto maker, he said, would never build it. General Motors, for its part, accused Mr. López of stealing its plans for "Plant X," and building it here.

Whatever its origins, the plant, inaugurated this month, transforms Volkswagen from a manufacturer into a contractor, overseeing the work of other companies. Some eight major subcontractors have their own shops along the assembly line, where their workers assemble components, including parts from 400 suppliers, before dropping them onto chassis.

Source: D. J. Schemo, "Is VW's New Plant Lean, or Just Mean?" *New York Times* (Sunday, January 19, 1998), pp. D1, D6.

Volkswagen is betting that the system will reduce the number of defective parts, improve efficiency and cut costs. If it does, it could become a manufacturing model for the developing world, where almost all growth in the auto Industry is expected to take place. According to Mr. López, it could apply to other types of manufacturing as well.

But industry analysts ask whether Volkswagen's factory for the future is lean, or merely mean: whether it achieves true gains in productivity, or furthers a trend toward squeezing subcontractors and employees. Volkswagen's subcontractors shoulder more direct costs and risks, and the assembly-line workers are paid roughly a third as much as auto workers in São Paulo.

While Volkswagen calls this new way of putting together trucks and buses a "modular consortium," it can look like a Russian doll of auto making The subcontractors include Brazilian companies like Delga Automotiva Industria e: Comercio Ltda: local subsidiaries of transnational corporations, like Rockwell International and Cummins Engine of America and Motorenwerk of Mannheim Eisenmann of Germany, as well as consortiums like Remon created for the venture.

This blurring of distinctions between suppliers and auto maker, as between electrical components and mechanical ones, is also a sign of change in auto manufacturing, said Sean McAlinden, manager of economic studies at the Office for the Study of Automotive Transportation at the University of Michigan. "Who's the customer and who's the supplier?" he said. "In the future, those boundaries may not make sense."

While truck makers and Japanese auto makers have long relied heavily on pre-assembled components, "We haven't heard of a completely supplier-run plant before," Mr. McAlinden said.

With South America's largest economy and population, and with more than 90 percent of its goods transported by truck, Brazil is an important testing ground for Volkswagen.

"How things work in a country like Brazil matter very much indeed," Mr. McAlinden said. "It doesn't even matter if the product isn't meant for outside Brazil. The most important prototype plants today are prototype plants for the third world."

For the moment, the factory is producing only one truck a day, because of delays in installing some equipment, such as an electronic overhead monorail. The cab factory and the paint shop are not finished, and so for now, every truck produced here is white. Suppliers are using the time to train workers, who were hired without experience.

Instead of a traditional assembly line, on which a single piece of metal grows part by part into a truck or bus as it moves from worker to worker, Resende runs subassembly lines parallel to the main line. The process begins with a chassis delivered to a loading dock; as the chassis moves along the main line, each supplier simultaneously assembles its components.

As the first stop for a chassis, workers from Iochpe-Maxion mount the gas tank, transmission lines and steering box.

At it moves down the line, Rockwell-Braselxos workers mount the axles and brakes. At the next stop, workers from Remon put on wheels and adjust tire pressure.

MWM/Cummins prepares and installs the engine and transmission. The cabs—supplied by the Ford Motor Company now, but eventually to be produced by Delga—are outfitted by VDO do Brasil, a unit of Adolf Schindling A.G. of Germany. Painting will be done by Elsenmann.

When the plant reaches capacity next year, its two shifts are expected to produce 100 trucks a day, using only 800 assembly workers, compared with 2,500 in traditionally designed plants in Brazil. And Volkswagen is betting that with suppliers on hand to inspect each component before it becomes part of a vehicle, quality will be high. Volkswagen pays suppliers only when trucks are completed and pass inspection. If a component is not up to quality, the supplier is not paid.

That, some analysts said, could solve a major drawback of developing countries: quality control.

In Japan, for example, Toyota does not need such a system, said James P. Womack, an efficiency expert and co-author of "Lean Thinking: Banish Waste and Create Wealth in Your Corporation," because only 5 parts in a million are defective; in much of the developing world, defective parts can run 15,000 to 20,000 per million.

The plant also saves on wages, which the suppliers have all set at $374 a month, which Volkswagen says is in line with factory work in the Resende area. And, any down time on the assembly line—say, because parts are missing—is charged to the workers, who must make it up without overtime.

The plant's manager, Luiz Antõnio Pinteado de Luca, said salaries usually accounted for about half the cost of producing trucks in Brazil. Nevertheless, he said he expected the biggest savings to come from logistics, even though one part of the strategy, just-in-time delivery, could be vulnerable to hitches like poor roads or strikes at supplier bases in São Paulo.

But industry analysts wonder how much of Volkswagen's lowered production costs depend upon simply paying workers and suppliers less.

"It's not clear how much is a fundamental efficiency game, and how much of it is a way to get people to work for less money." Mr. Womack said. Mr. López's calls for a third industrial revolution, familiar to industry insiders, never mentioned lowering salaries, he said.

"Merely cutting wages does not constitute a revolution," Mr. Womack said. "It constitutes a counter-revolution. In some ways."

Volkswagen calls its suppliers in Resende "partners," and it required them to put up $50 million of the factory's $300 million cost. Despite their capital investment, they are not, like true partners, sharing profits.

Given the reputation Mr. López has developed for muscling suppliers to lower prices, those at Resende said they designed their contracts with Volkswagen very carefully, building into prices, for example, allowances for Volkswagen's withholding payment until trucks are completed.

"Basically, we recognize that Mr. López is a tough negotiator and tough with suppliers," said Sergio Carvalho, director of sales and service at Rockwell do Brasil. "But we foresee the chance to grow our market share with Volkswagen."

Ricardo Chuahy, director of operations at Cummins do Brasil, concurred. "The concept is very aggressive," he said. "If it works, other manufacturers will copy Volks-wagen."

Similarly, Volkswagen maintains that the lower wages at Resende merely reflect the labor market. But while the plant's work force is expected to unionize eventually, local union leaders admit they are perplexed by its web of employers.

Much of the plant's success will depend on Volkswagen's ability to break into the domestic truck market dominated by Mercedes-Benz, a unit of Germany's Daimler-Benz, said José Roberto Ferro, an economics professor at the Getulio Vargas Foundation and local coordinator of the Massachusetts Institute of Technology's International Motor Vehicle Program.

Volkswagen is counting on the Resende plant to be an important source of exports to Europe and South America, but it does not have a corresponding international distribution network, he said.

"It's a nice solution, and the primary reason it sounds so neat is because labor is so cheap, and it gives Volkswagen a massive two-by-four to wield against its unions in São Paulo," Mr. Womack said.

If so, the message was not lost: last week, workers at General Motors and Volkswagen plants in São Paulo accepted management's first offer on a new contract.

Index